Lecture Notes in Computer Science 6419

Commenced Publication in 1973
Founding and Former Series Editors:
Gerhard Goos, Juris Hartmanis, and Jan van Leeuwen

Isabelle Bloch   Roberto M. Cesar, Jr. (Eds.)

Progress in Pattern Recognition, Image Analysis, Computer Vision, and Applications

15th Iberoamerican Congress
on Pattern Recognition, CIARP 2010
São Paulo, Brazil, November 8-11, 2010
Proceedings

 Springer

Volume Editors

Isabelle Bloch
Télécom ParisTech, Département Traitement du Signal et des Images, CNRS LTCI
46 rue Barrault, 75634 Paris Cedex 13, France
E-mail: isabelle.bloch@telecom-paristech.fr

Roberto M. Cesar, Jr.
University of São Paulo - USP, Institute of Mathematics and Statistics - IME
Department of Computer Science
Rua do Matão 1010, São Paulo, SP, CEP 05508-090, Brazil
E-mail: cesar@vision.ime.usp.br

Library of Congress Control Number: 2010937233

CR Subject Classification (1998): I.5, I.4, I.2.10, I.2.7, F.2.2

LNCS Sublibrary: SL 6 – Image Processing, Computer Vision, Pattern Recognition,
and Graphics

ISSN   0302-9743
ISBN-10   3-642-16686-5 Springer Berlin Heidelberg New York
ISBN-13   978-3-642-16686-0 Springer Berlin Heidelberg New York

springer.com

© Springer-Verlag Berlin Heidelberg 2010
Printed in Germany

Typesetting: Camera-ready by author, data conversion by Scientific Publishing Services, Chennai, India
Printed on acid-free paper   06/3180

Preface

Pattern recognition is a central topic in contemporary computer sciences, with continuously evolving topics, challenges, and methods, including machine learning, content-based image retrieval, and model- and knowledge-based approaches, just to name a few. The Iberoamerican Congress on Pattern Recognition (CIARP) has become established as a high-quality conference, highlighting the recent evolution of the domain.

These proceedings include all papers presented during the 15th edition of this conference, held in Sao Paulo, Brazil, in November 2010.

As was the case for previous conferences, CIARP 2010 attracted participants from around the world with the aim of promoting and disseminating ongoing research on mathematical methods and computing techniques for pattern recognition, computer vision, image analysis, and speech recognition, as well as their applications in such diverse areas as robotics, health, entertainment, space exploration, telecommunications, data mining, document analysis, and natural language processing and recognition, to name only a few of them. Moreover, it provided a forum for scientific research, experience exchange, sharing new knowledge and increasing cooperation between research groups in pattern recognition and related areas.

It is important to underline that these conferences have contributed significantly to the growth of national associations for pattern recognition in the Iberoamerican region, all of them as members of the International Association for Pattern Recognition (IAPR).

The scientific program included a tutorial day, with three topics addressed: an introduction to kernel machines, by Stéphane Canu; multimodal human – computer interaction for mobile computing, by Matthew Turk; and soft computing, f-granulation and pattern recognition, by Sankar Pal. We warmly thank the three speakers for having agreed to give these tutorials.

The next three days were organized in a single-track conference, with invited talks, oral presentations, and posters. We were very pleased to welcome four distinguished invited speakers: Alexandre Falcão on design of pattern classifiers using optimum-path forest with applications in image analysis; Stéphane Canu on recent advances in kernel machines; Matthew Turk on computational illumination; and Seth Hutchinson speaking on vision-based control of robot motion. We are very grateful and would like to thank them. The oral and poster sessions included 70 papers selected from 145 submissions. All submissions were double-blind reviewed by at least two reviewers. We thank all reviewers, who provided high-quality reviews in a short time.

To enhance the visibility of the best submissions and to stimulate further good scientific papers, some authors will be invited to submit an enhanced version of their paper to a special issue of International Journal of Pattern Recognition and Artificial Intelligence, to be published in 2012.

In addition, an award, consisting of a cash prize, a trophy and a certificate, was given to the author(s) of the Best Paper registered and presented at CIARP 2010. The aim of this award is to acknowledge and encourage excellence and originality of new models, methods and techniques with an outstanding theoretical contribution and practical application to the field of pattern recognition and/or data mining. The selection of the winner was based on the wish of the author to be considered to the prize, the evaluation and recommendations from members of the Program Committee and the evaluation of the IAPR-CIARP Award Committee. This committee, carefully chosen to avoid conflicts of interest, evaluated each nominated paper in a second review process, which included the quality of the oral and/or poster presentation.

The conference was organized by the University of Sao Paulo. We would like to thank all participants of the organizing committee and auxiliary committee, at USP and UFABC, for their tremendous work, which made the conference a success.

Finally, we would like to thank all authors and participants, who contributed to the high quality of the conference and scientific exchanges.

November 2010   Isabelle Bloch
                                                      Roberto M. Cesar-Jr.

Organization

CIARP 2010 was organized by the Institute of Mathematics and Statistics—IME-USP, Brazil, and Telecom ParisTech, France; endorsed by the International Association for Pattern Recognition (IAPR); and sponsored by several scientific societies listed below.

Co-chairs

Isabelle Bloch	Telecom ParisTech · France
Roberto M. Cesar-Jr.	IME-USP - Brazil

Organizing Committee

João Eduardo Ferreira	USP - Brazil
Ronaldo Hashimoto	USP - Brazil
Nina Tomita Hirata	IME-USP - Brazil
Roberto Hirata Jr.	USP - Brazil
David Correa Martins Jr.	UFABC - Brazil
Carlos Hitoshi Morimoto	USP - Brazil
Yossi Zana	UFABC - Brazil

Auxiliary Committee

Frank Dennis J. Aguilar	USP - Brazil
Andrèa Britto	USP - Brazil
Ana Beatriz V. Graciano	USP - Brazil
Marcelo Hashimoto	USP - Brazil
Willian Honda	USP - Brazil
Edwin D. Huaynalaya	USP - Brazil
Charles Iury	USP - Brazil
Jorge J.G. Leandro	USP - Brazil
Rafael Lopes	USP - Brazil
Fabrício Martins Lopes	USP - Brazil
Vitor Hugo Louzada	USP - Brazil
Rosário Medina	USP - Brazil
Jesus Mena-Chalco	USP - Brazil
Evaldo Oliveira	USP - Brazil
Evaldo Oliveira	USP - Brazil
Sìlvia Cristina D. Pinto	USP - Brazil

Giseli Ramos	USP - Brazil
Thiago T. Santos	USP - Brazil
Jihan M. Zoghbi	USP - Brazil

CIARP Steering Committee

Helder Araujo	APRP - Portugal
Eduardo Bayro-Corrochano	MACVNR - Mexico
Cesar Beltran-Castanon	PAPR - Peru
Marta Mejail	SARP - Argentina
Alvaro Pardo	APRU - Uruguay
Hemerson Pistori	SIGPR-SBC - Brazil
José Ruiz-Shulcloper	ACRP - Cuba
Alberto Sanfeliu	AERFAI - Spain
César Enrique San Martín Salas	UFRO - Chile

Program Committee and Referees

Carlos A.R.-Garcia	Bernardino C.-Toledo	Mauricio Delbracio
Olivier Alata	Mario Campos	Gilson G. de Lima
Hector Allende	Sergio Cano	Patrice Delmas
Leopoldo Altamirano	Xianbin Cao	Andreas Dengel
Laurence Amaral	Daniel R.S. Caon	Anne M. de P. Canuto
Beatriz Andrade	Juan Cardelino	Marcilio de Souto
Bilza Araujo	A. Carrasco-Ochoa	Alair do Lago
Nancy Arana	Bruno Carvalho	Hans du Buf
Francisco Arruda	Joao Carvalho	Luciano V. Dutra
Akira Asano	Cesar B. Castanon	Jose E.R. Queiroz
Humberto S. Azuela	Mario Castelán	Boris Escalante-Ramírez
Andrew Bagdanov	Cristiano Castro	Guaraci Jose Erthal
Virginia Ballarin	Roberto Cesar	Francisco Escolano
José-Miguel Banedí	Yung-Kuan Chan	Silvia Esparrachiari
Guilherme Barreto	Ting Chen	Miguel Arias Estrada
Leonardo Batista	Da-Chuan Cheng	Jose F.M.-Trinidad
Olga Bellon	Gerard Chollet	Jacques Facon
Csaba Benedck	Thiago Christiano	Luis E. Falcon
Josef Bigun	Regina C. Coelho	Mauricio Falvo
Isabelle Bloch	Eduardo B. Corrochano	Daniel S. Ferreira
Gunilla Borgefors	Anna Costa	Susana Ferrero
Dibio Borges	Fabio G. Cozman	Francesc J. Ferri
Antônio Braga	Valdinei F. da Silva	Gutemberg Guerra Filho
Ulisses Braga-Neto	Teófilo de Campos	Gernot Fink
Luc Brun	Andre Ponce de Carvalho	Joao Florindo
Marcel Brun	Karmele L. de Ipiña	Alejandro C. Frery
Odemir Bruno	Luis Gerardo de la Fraga	Maria Frucci

André Gagalowicz
Juliana Gambini
Karina Gibert
Lev Goldfarb
Herman Gomes
Alvaro Gómez
Adilson Gonzaga
Jesus Gonzalez
Jordi Gonzàlez
Wesley N. Goncalves
Antoni Grau
Michal Haindl
Andras Hajdu
Allan Hanbury
Ronaldo F. Hashimoto
Fang-Chao He
Laurent Heutte
Roberto Hirata Jr.
Tin Kam Ho
Michelle Horta
Estevam Hruschka Jr.
Yin Hsien
Atsushi Imiya
Julio C.S. Jacques Jr.
Javier Hernando Jesus
Xiaoyi Jiang
Claudio R. Jung
Martin Kampel
Zoltan Kato
Houssemeddine Khemiri
Sang-Woon Kim
Nahum Kiryati
Reinhard Klette
Vitaly Kober
Alessandro Koerich
Illya Kokshenev
Andreas Koschan
Walter Kosters
Nicolau L. Werneck
Neucimar Leite
Rubisley Lemes
Alexandre Levada
Xuelong Li
Zhao Liang
Jingen Liu

Zongyi Liu
Josep Llados
Fabricio Lopes
Ismael López-Juárez
Aurelio Lopez-Lopez
Ana Carolina Lorena
Xiaoqiang Lu
Teresa Ludermir
Ana María M.-Enríquez
Alejandro M.-Valencia
Alexei Machado
Regis Marques
Miguel Bernal Marin
David C. Martins Jr.
Nelson Mascarenhas
Joceli Mayer
Geraldo Medeiros
Marta Mejail
Elmar Melcher
Angélica
  Muñoz-Meléndez
Jesús P. Mena-Chalco
David Menotti
Miguel Moctezuma
Pranab Mohanty
Manuel Montes-y-Gómez
Carlos Hitoshi Morimoto
Elsa Ester Moschetti
Vittorio Murino
Soraia Musse
Heinrich Niemann
Laszlo Nyul
Evaldo A. Oliveira
Jaime Ortegón
Aylton Pagamisse
Anselmo Paiva
Zhi-Bin Pan
Joao Paulo Papa
Alvaro Pardo
Juan Ignacio Pastore
Ialis Paula Jr.
Helio Pedrini
Witold Pedrycz
Arturo Diaz Pérez
Petra Perner

Maria Petrou
Luciano Pimenta
Pedro Pina
Armando Pinho
Hemerson Pistori
Ioannis Pitas
Filiberto Pla
Rodrigo Plotze
Volodymyr Ponomaryov
Aurora Pons-Porrata
Jorge R.-Rovelo
Petia Radeva
Gregory Randall
Joao H.B. Ribeiro
Anderson Rocha
Evandro L.L. Rodrigues
Roberto Rodriguez
Manuel Graña Romay
Arun Ross
Nicolas Rougon
Jose Ruiz-Shulcloper
Eduardo S.-Soto
Claudio C. Sánchez
Robert Sablatnig
Robert Sabourin
Cesar E.S.M. Salas
Denis Salvadeo
Joao M.R. Sanches
Jose Salvador Sanchez
Carlo Sansone
Edimilson Santos
Thiago Santos
Beatriz Sousa Santos
Tadamasa Sawada
Mykola Sazhok
Homero Schiabel
Mauricio P. Segundo
Antonio Selvatici
Pierre Sendorek
Jacob Sharcanski
Luciano Silva
Nubia Silva
Sergio Simoes
Fátima Sombra
Biqin Song

Peter Sturm	Luz A. Torres-Mendez	Michel Westenberg
Luis Enrique Sucar	Andrea Torsello	Pingkun Yan
Akihiro Sugimoto	Florence Tupin	Meijuan Yang
Youting Sun	Juan V.L.-Ginori	Jun Zhang
Yi Tang	Ventzeslav Valev	Liangpei Zhang
Carlos Thomaz	Eduardo Valle	Qieshi Zhang
Nina Tomita Hirata	Jose R. Vallejo	Huiyu Zhou
Karl Tombre	Mario Vento	Vasileios Zografos
Klaus Tönnies	Max A. Viergever	Amin Zollanvari
M. Ines Torres	Shengrui Wang	
Ricardo Torres	Xiumei Wang	

Organization, Support and Sponsors

Brazilian Bioethanol Science and Technology Laboratory (CTBE)
Brazilian Neural Networks Society (SBRN)
Coordenacao de Aperfeicoamento de Pessoal de Nivel Superior (CAPES)
Chilean Association for Pattern Recognition (ChAPR)
National Council for Technological and Scientific Development (CNPq)
Cuban Association for Pattern Recognition (ACRP)
Fundacao de Amparo a Pesquisa do Estado de Sao Paulo (FAPESP)
Federal University of ABC (UFABC)
International Association for Pattern Recognition (IAPR)
Institut Telecom/Telecom ParisTech
Mexican Association for Computer Vision, Neural Computing and Robotics
    (MACVNR)
Portuguese Association for Pattern Recognition (APRP)
Spanish Association for Pattern Recognition and Image Analysis (AERFAI)
Special Interest Group on Pattern Recognition of the Brazilian Computer Society
    (SIGPR-SBC)
University of Sao Paulo (IME and BIOINFO - USP)

Table of Contents

Invited Talks

Color, Shape and Texture

Graphs and Hypergraphs

Biomedical Imaging

Retrieval, Mining and Learning

Learning, Recognition and Clustering

Bayesian and Statistical Methods

Coding and Compression, Video, Tracking

Speech, Natural Language, Document

Image Filtering and Segmentation

Feature Extraction, Shape, Texture, Geometry and Morphology

Face Segmentation and Recognition, Biometry

Statistical Approaches, Learning, Classification, Mining

Recent Advances in Kernel Machines

Stéphane Canu

LITIS - INSA Rouen - France
stephane.canu@insa-rouen.fr
http://asi.insa-rouen.fr/enseignants/~scanu/

Abstract. This talk will review recent advances in the kernel methods focusing on support vector machines (SVM) for pattern recognition. Topics discussed include the kernel design issue through the multi kernel approach and the optimization issue with emphasis on scalability and non convex cost functions.

I. Bloch and R.M. Cesar, Jr. (Eds.): CIARP 2010, LNCS 6419, p. 1, 2010.

Design of Pattern Classifiers Using Optimum-Path Forest with Applications in Image Analysis

Alexandre X. Falcão

Institute of Computing (IC) - University of Campinas (UNICAMP), Brazil
afalcao@ic.unicamp.br
http://www.ic.unicamp.br/~afalcao/

Abstract. Current image acquisition and storage technologies have provided large data sets (with millions of samples) for analysis. Samples may be images from an image database, objects extracted from several images, or image pixels. This scenario is very challenging for traditional machine learning and pattern recognition techniques, which need to be more efficient and effective in large data sets. This lecture presents a recent and successful methodology, which links training samples in a given feature space and exploits optimum connectivity between them to the design of pattern classifiers. The methodology essentially extends the Image Foresting Transform, successfully used for filtering, segmentation and shape description, from the image domain to the feature space. Several supervised and unsupervised learning techniques may be created from the specification of two parameters: an adjacency relation and a connectivity function. The adjacency relation defines which samples form arcs of a graph in the feature space.

The connectivity function assigns a value to any path in the graph. The path value indicates the strength of connectedness of its terminal node with respect to its source node. A connectivity map is maximized by partitioning the graph into an optimum-path forest rooted at its maxima (i.e., representative samples of each class/group, called prototypes). The optimum-path forest is then a pattern classifier, which assigns to any new sample the class (or group label) of its most strongly connected root. The methods have been successfully applied to several applications and this lecture demonstrates two recent ones: content-based image retrieval (CBIR) and 3D segmentation of brain tissues in MR images. In CBIR, user interaction is considerably reduced to a few clicks on relevant/irrelevant images along 3 iterations of relevance feedback followed by supervised learning in order to achieve satisfactory query results. The 3D segmentation of brain tissues is automatically obtained in less than 2 minutes. It exploits voxel clustering, some prior knowledge and does not require a brain atlas for that purpose, while many other brain tissue segmentation methods do. The lecture concludes by discussing some open problems and perspectives for the optimum-path forest classifiers.

I. Bloch and R.M. Cesar, Jr. (Eds.): CIARP 2010, LNCS 6419, p. 2, 2010.

Vision-Based Control of Robot Motion

Seth Hutchinson

Dept. of Electrical and Computer Engineering - The Beckman Institute
University of Illinois, USA
seth@uiuc.edu
http://www-cvr.ai.uiuc.edu/~seth/

Abstract. Visual servo control is now a mature method for controlling robots using real-time vision feedback. It can be considered as the fusion of computer vision, robotics and control, and it has been a distinct field since the 1990's, though the earliest work dates back to the 1980's. Over this period several major, and well understood, approaches have evolved and have been demonstrated in many laboratories around the world. Many visual servo schemes can be classified as either position-based or image-based, depending on whether camera pose or image features are used in the control law. This lecture will review both position-based and image-based methods for visual servo control, presenting the basic derivations and concepts, and describing a few of the performance problems faced by each. Following this, a few recent and more advanced methods will be described. These approaches essentially partition the control system either along spatial or temporal dimensions. The former are commonly referred to as hybrid or partitioned control systems, while the latter are typically referred to as switched systems.

I. Bloch and R.M. Cesar, Jr. (Eds.): CIARP 2010, LNCS 6419, p. 3, 2010.
© Springer-Verlag Berlin Heidelberg 2010

Soft Computing, f-Granulation and Pattern Recognition

Sankar K. Pal

Indian Statistical Institute, Kolkata 700108, India
sankar@isical.ac.in
http://www.isical.ac.in/~sankar/

Abstract. Different components of soft computing (e.g., fuzzy logic, artificial neural networks, rough sets and genetic algorithms) and machine intelligence, and their relevance to pattern recognition and data mining are explained. Characteristic features of these tools are described conceptually. Various ways of integrating these tools for application specific merits are described. Tasks like case (prototype) generation, rule generation, knowledge encoding, classification and clustering are considered in general. Merits of some of these integrations in terms of performance, computation time, network size, uncertainty handling etc. are explained; thereby making them suitable for data mining and knowledge discovery.

Granular computing through rough sets and role of fuzzy granulation (f-granulation) is given emphasis. Different applications of rough granules and certain challenging issues in their implementations are stated. The significance of rough-fuzzy computing, as a stronger paradigm for uncertainty handling, and the role of granules used therein are explained with examples. These include tasks such as class-dependent rough-fuzzy granulation for classification, rough-fuzzy clustering, and defining generalized rough entropy for image ambiguity measures and analysis. Image ambiguity measures take into account the fuzziness in boundary regions, as well as the rough resemblance among nearby gray levels and nearby pixels.

Significance of rough granules and merits of some of the algorithms are described on various real life problems including multi-spectral image segmentation, determining bio-bases (c-medoids) in encoding protein sequence for analysis, and categorizing of web document pages (using vector space model) and web services (using tensor space model). The talk concludes with stating the possible future uses of the methodologies, relation with computational theory of perception (CTP), and the challenges in mining.

I. Bloch and R.M. Cesar, Jr. (Eds.): CIARP 2010, LNCS 6419, p. 4, 2010.

Computational Illumination

Matthew Turk

Computer Science Department,
University of California, Santa Barbara, USA
mturk@cs.ucsb.edu
http://www.cs.ucsb.edu/~mturk/

Abstract. The field of computational photography includes computational imaging techniques that enhance or extend the capabilities of digital photography, a combination of computer vision, computer graphics, and applied optics. Computational illumination is an aspect of computational photography that considers how to modify illumination in order to facilitate useful techniques in computer vision and imaging. This talk will present research using multiflash imaging, coded shadow photography, and parameterized structured light, three families of techniques in computational illumination, where the results help to produce reliable information in scenes that is often difficult to robustly compute otherwise.

I. Bloch and R.M. Cesar, Jr. (Eds.): CIARP 2010, LNCS 6419, p. 5, 2010.
© Springer-Verlag Berlin Heidelberg 2010

Color Texture Analysis and Classification: An Agent Approach Based on Partially Self-avoiding Deterministic Walks

André Ricardo Backes[1], Alexandre Souto Martinez[2],
and Odemir Martinez Bruno[3]

[1] Faculdade de Computação - Universidade Federal de Uberlândia
Uberlândia MG Brasil
backes@facom.ufu.br
[2] Faculdade de Filosofia, Ciências e Letras de Ribeirão Preto (FFCLRP)
Universidade de São Paulo (USP)
Av. Bandeirantes, 3900
14040-901 Ribeirão Preto, SP, Brazil
asmartinez@ffclrp.usp.br
[3] Instituto de Física de São Carlos (IFSC)
Universidade de São Paulo (USP)
Avenida do Trabalhador São-carlense, 400
13560-970 São Carlos SP Brazil
bruno@ifsc.usp.br

Abstract. Recently, we have proposed a novel approach of texture analysis that has overcome most of the state-of-art methods. This method considers independent walkers, with a given memory, leaving from each pixel of an image. Each walker moves to one of its neighboring pixels according to the difference of intensity between these pixels, avoiding returning to recent visited pixels. Each generated trajectory, after a transient time, ends in a cycle of pixels (attractor) from where the walker cannot escape. The transient time (t) and cycle period (p) form a joint probability distribution, which contains image pixel organization characteristics. Here, we have generalized the texture based on the deterministic partially self avoiding walk to analyze and classify colored textures. The proposed method is confronted with other methods, and we show that it overcomes them in color texture classification.

Keywords: partially self-avoiding deterministic walks, texture analysis, color images.

1   Introduction

Texture is one of the most important visual attribute in computer vision and image analysis. It is a visual pattern which, in digital images, consists of sub-patterns. The sub-patterns are related to the pixel distribution in an image region and its characteristics, such as size, brightness and color. Although, there is no exact definition for texture in the literature, it is an attribute naturally comprehended by

I. Bloch and R.M. Cesar, Jr. (Eds.): CIARP 2010, LNCS 6419, pp. 6–13, 2010.

humans and responsible to improve the human vision process. Texture importance is presented in Ref. [2] for both, natural and artificial vision. In computer vision, there is a huge number of texture applications that are found in various areas. These applications range from aiding diagnoses in medical images [3], analysis of geological structures in images [4], microscope images [5] etc.

Texture has been thoroughly studied and many methods have been proposed to solve and improve the analysis [2,6]. These methods can be grouped in: image pixels spectral analysis (e.g., Fourier descriptors [7] and Gabor filters [8]), pixels statistical analysis (e.g., co-occurrence matrices [9], Feature-based Interaction Map [10]) and complexity analysis (e.g., Fractal Dimension [11,12]).

Recently, we have proposed a novel approach of texture analysis that achieved better results than most of the state-of-art methods [1,13,14]. It considers independent walkers leaving from each pixel of an image. With a given memory, each walker moves to one of its neighboring pixels according to the difference of intensity between these pixels, avoiding returning to recent visited pixels. Each generated trajectory, after a transient time t, ends in an attractor, i.e., a cycle of p pixels from where the walker cannot escape. These transient times and attractors contain characteristics of the pixel organization in that image.

For instance, consider a partially self-avoiding deterministic walk, where a walker wishes to visit N sites randomly distributed in a map of d dimension. The walker can move from one to another site following the rule of, at each discreet time step, to go to the nearest site not visited in the previous μ steps. The agent performs a partially self-avoiding walk, where the self-avoidance is limited to the memory window $\tau = \mu - 1$. The walker's behavior depends strictly on the data set configuration and on the starting site [15,16]. The walker's movements are entirely performed based on a neighborhood table, so that the distances among the sites are simply a way of ranking their neighbors. This feature leads to an invariance in scale transformations [17]. Each trajectory has an initial transient part of length t and ends in a cycle with period p. Both the transient time and cycle period can be combined in the joint probability distribution $S_{\mu,d}^{(N)}(t,p)$. The simplest case to deal with the deterministic walker is to consider $\mu = 0$, where the walker remains forever at the initial site $S_{0,d}^{(N)}(t,p) = \delta_{t,0}\delta_{p,1}$, where $\delta_{i,j}$ is the Kronecker's delta. Despite its triviality, this becomes interesting because it is the simplest situation of a stochastic walk [18]. For a memoryless walker ($\mu = 1$), the walker, at each time step, the walker must leave the current site and go to the nearest one. After a very short transient time, the walker becomes trapped by a couple of mutually nearest neighbors. The transient time and period joint probability distribution, for $N \gg 1$, is [19]: $S_{1,d}^{(\infty)}(t,p) = [\Gamma(1 + I_d^{-1})(t + I_d^{-1})/\Gamma(t + p + I_d^{-1})]\delta_{p,2}$, where $\Gamma(z)$ is the gamma function and I_d is the normalized incomplete beta function $I_d = I_{1/4}[1/2, (d + 1)/2]$. In the limit $d \to \infty$, one is able to calculate it analytically [20]: $S_{2,\infty}^{(N)}(t,p) = e^{-[3N(t+p-2)(t+p-3)/2]}/[(3 - \delta_{t,0})N]$. Analytical calculations [21] were also performed for the stochastic walk. When greater values of μ are considered, the cycle distribution is no longer peaked at $p_{min} = \mu + 1$, but presents a whole spectrum of cycles with period $p \geq p_{min}$ [15,16,20].

The presentation is organized as follows. In Sec. 2, we review how this walk can be used to analyse and classify textures in images [1] and the (t, p)-joint distributions are used to generate a single signature vector for colored images. In Sec. 3, experiments are described and performed on standard colored texture images. These experiment show that the presented algorithm outperform traditional methods (Chromatic moments [22], Color differential [23] and to the gray-scale deterministic walker previous version [1]). We address our final remarks in Sec. 4.

2   Walks on Color Images and Texture Signature

In Ref. [1], the partially self-avoiding deterministic walk has been proposed as a tools to texture analysis and classification. This algorithm has been developed to analyze gray level texture. Here, we generalize the algorithm to be capable to deal with colored images. A colored image, of $N = M_x \times M_y$ pixels, is formed by three layers, each one representing a color (red, green and blue). In each layer the color intensity varies, in integer values, from 0 to 255. Basically, the algorithm is exact the same of the previous version, but now one has a walker for each layer. The partial information of each walker is then joined in a single signature. Two pixels, (x_i, y_i) and (x_j, y_j) are considered neighbors if the Hamming distance is $d(i, j) \leq 2$.

A walker can only move according to the following rule: move to the nearest or furthest neighbor (i.e., the one which differs in the minimum or maximum intensity value, respectively, from the current position) and that has not been visited in the last $\mu(\mu \in [1, N])$ previous steps. This rule produces partially self-avoiding walks[1].

For each initial condition (i.e., the starting pixel), the walker produces a different trajectory. Notice, however, that different initial conditions can lead to the same attractor. Considering all pixels in the image as starting points, we compute the joint probability distribution of transient time t and attractor period p, $S_{\mu,2}^{(N)}(t, p)$. From the study of these distributions, using statistical techniques, it is possible to achieve a signature able to discriminate the image texture [1,13,14,17].

Previous studies have shown the $S_{\mu,2}^{(N)}(t, p)$ potential application in the classification of gray-scale textures [1,13,14]. Any change on image context affects the walk and, as a consequence, its joint probability distribution, achieved for an specific memory μ and walking rule. It makes this distribution a useful tool for texture analysis.

Many approaches can be used to extract relevant information from the joint probability distribution. Good results have been reported by the use of the histogram $h_\tau(n)$ on gray-scale textures analysis. This histogram represents the frequency that a trajectory of length n, where $n = t + p \geq \tau + 2$, is performed by the walker, using a specific memory range τ. From this histogram, a texture signature is easily built by selecting a total of m descriptors. In the case of color textures, each channel is processed by the deterministic walk independently, thus resulting in a joint probability distribution and, as a consequence, a histogram specific for that channel.

$$\boldsymbol{v}_\tau^{(C)}(m) = [h_\tau^{(C)}(\tau+2), h_\mu^{(C)}(\tau+3), \ldots, h_\mu^{(C)}(\tau+1+m)], \tag{1}$$

where C represent the channel explored in the texture. A texture signature which explores all color channels (R, G and B) with memory μ is defined as:

$$\boldsymbol{\psi}_\tau(m) = [\boldsymbol{v}_\tau^{(R)}(m), \boldsymbol{v}_\tau^{(G)}(m), \boldsymbol{v}_\tau^{(B)}(m)]. \tag{2}$$

As the joint probability distribution is modified according to the μ value, it is also interesting to evaluate a texture pattern considering the signatures computed for different memories μ:

$$\boldsymbol{\varphi}_M(m) = [\boldsymbol{\psi}_0(m), \boldsymbol{\psi}_1(m), \ldots, \boldsymbol{\psi}_M(m)] . \tag{3}$$

3   Experiments and Results

Experiments have been performed to determine the configuration of the signature, in terms of memory and walk rule, that leads to the best color texture classification. Signatures were evaluated in a texture classification scheme. The VisTex [24] is a set of colored images widely used as benchmark for texture analysis (see Figure 1). This database has been used 640 samples of 40 classes. Each class contains 16 texture samples of 128×128 pixels.

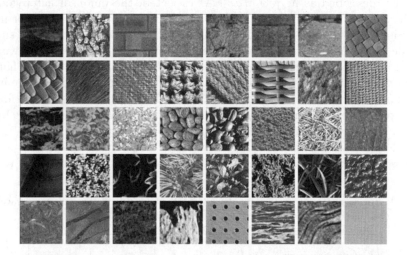

Fig. 1. One example of each of the 40 texture classes considered in the VisTex database

The evaluation of the signatures was performed using Linear Discriminant Analysis (LDA), a classification method based on supervisioned learning. LDA aims to find a linear combination of the descriptors (independent variables) that results in its class (dependent variable). This linear combination results in the data projection in a linear subspace where inter-classes variance is larger than intra-classes variance [25,26]. The *leave-one-out cross-validation* strategy was also used, where each sample from the database is used for validation while remaining samples are used for training. This is repeated until all samples were used for validation.

Previous experiments [13] conducted over $S_{\mu,2}^{(N)}(t,p)$ have shown that most image information is concentrated within few elements, where $0 \leq t \leq 4$ and $(\tau + 2) \leq p \leq (\tau + 5)$. From now on, we extract $m = 4$ descriptors from $h_\tau(n)$ to compose the feature vectors $\psi_\tau(m)$ (Eq. 2).

In Table 1, we show the success rate signatures (Eq. 2), evaluated according to different τ values, for both walking rules: agents guided to minimum and maximum intensity difference. The main difference between these walking rules concerns the regions where the attractors are found. The walk guided to the direction of the maximum pixel intensity difference locates attractors where modifications in image context are more abrupt, i.e., heterogeneous regions of the texture. Otherwise, walkers guided to the minimum intensity difference locate attractors, where the image present more homogeneous patterns. Heterogeneous regions are usually related to the presence of image contours or changes in texture patterns, both important visual attributes in the characterization of objects [27,28]. This explains the superior performance of the maximum difference in comparison to the minimum difference in the texture classification. As these walking rules produce signatures with different characteristics of the image, it would be interesting to evaluate the combination of these signatures into one (described as $Min \cup Max$). As expected, the union of heterogeneous and homogeneous texture information provides a more powerful tool for image analysis. We also note that, independent of the used walking rule, the success rate decreases as the memory increases. Each walker produces a self-avoiding trajectory, which depends on the memory used. This memory avoids that the walker visits some pixels of the image, so that, a better exploration of the image is performed. As the memory increases, more the agent has to walk to find an attractor. Higher memories endangers the local exploration of the texture by the walker, which reflects on the decreases of the success rate.

Table 2 shows the results obtained when multiple memories τ are used to compose the texture signature $\varphi_M(4)$ (Eq. 3). Note that this signature provides

Table 1. Success rate for $\psi_\tau(4)$ signature (Eq. 2) using different τ values and walking rules in the VisTex database

Texture signature	Memory(τ)					
	0	1	2	3	4	5
Min	56.87%	44.37%	33.91%	27.06%	20.47%	15.14%
Max	90.16%	65.78%	76.09%	59.84%	60.31%	30.16%
Min ∪ *Max*	94.37%	81.72%	81.41%	74.06%	70.31%	50.31%

Table 2. Success rate for the texture signature $\varphi_M(4)$ (Eq. 3) combining different τ values in the VisTex database

Texture signature	Multiple Memories (M)				
	1	2	3	4	5
Min	74.21%	77.65%	78.75%	79.06%	80.94%
Max	93.90%	94.53%	94.69%	94.53%	95.00%
$Min \cup Max$	96.25%	96.09%	97.03%	96.87%	96.72%

an increase in success rates in comparison to the results of Table 1, where each memory was independently evaluated. This approach enable us to characterize a texture using information collected from different scales, thus providing a more efficient image classification.

Finally, we compare our algorithm to other texture analysis methods, which are briefly described below. *Chromaticity Moments:* it is based on the concept of chromaticities as defined within the CIE XYZ color space, where each image pixel results in a pair of (x, y) chromaticity values. From the chromaticity values distribution, moments are computed to compose a feature vector that allows to characterize the image in terms of color and texture [22]. *Color Differential:* the method uses a fractal measure on the interaction between color bands of the image. It is based on the study of the intercolor volume enclosed between each two color surfaces. The method also considers the CIE-chromaticity value for material color information as an additional feature of the image [23]. This method is originally proposed for the segmentation of digital images, but it can be easily adapted to solve problems of texture classification.

Table 3. Comparison of the success rates for different color texture methods in the VisTex database

Method	Images correctly classified	Success rate(%)
Chromaticy Moments	534	83.44
Color Differential	599	93.59
Deterministic Walk (color)	621	97.03
Deterministic Walk (gray)	597	93.28

In Table 3 we show the success rate of our method to Chromaticity Moments and the Color Differential methods. In this comparison, the best result has been achieved by our method (using Eq. 3 with $M = 3$, for minimum and maximum walk rules). We also consider in this comparison the results of our method when disregarding the color information of the texture, i.e., walks performed only over the gray-scale version of the texture, where one clearly sees that a colored image has more information than a single gray-scale image.

We note that the deterministic walker's best result achieved better results from compared color texture methods. In fact, the use of ψ_μ signature computed for $\mu = 0$, and both minimum and maximum directions, as described in Table 1, provides a result better than Chromaticy Moments and Color Differential, thus evidencing the quality of the proposed approach in color texture analysis. Results also show that the use of color information provides a better identification of texture patterns, as the deterministic walker's performance over color texture is superior in comparison to gray-scale textures.

4   Conclusion

We have presented a generalized version of the texture feature extraction based on partially self-avoiding deterministic walks to deal with color textures. The proposed method uses walkers that explore the different color channels of an image on a given scale (memory). A simple signature vector is computed and numerical experiments have been conducted with a color texture database to evaluate the success rates. Our method has been confronted with the previous one and with other two state-of-art color texture algorithms. It has overcame all of them. The result demonstrates the great potential of the proposed method, combining color information of the texture and be capable of recognize it.

Ackowledgements

A.R.B. acknowledges support from FAPESP (2006/54367-9). A.S.M. acknowledges support from CNPq (303990/2007-4 and 476862/2007-8). O.M.B. acknowledges support from CNPq (306628/2007-4 and 484474/2007-3) and FAPESP (2006/54367-9).

References

1. Backes, A.R., Gonçalves, W.N., Martinez, A.S., Bruno, O.M.: Texture analysis and classification using deterministic tourist walk. Pattern Recognition 43, 685–694 (2009)
2. Tuceryan, M., Jain, A.K.: Texture analysis. In: Handbook of Pattern Recognition and Computer Vision, pp. 235–276 (1993)
3. Wu, C.M., Chen, Y.C., Hsieh, K.S.: Texture features for classification of ultrasonic liver images. IEEE Transactions on Medical Imaging 11, 141–152 (1992)
4. Heidelbach, F., Kunze, K., Wenk, H.R.: Texture analysis of a recrystallized quartzite using electron diffraction in the scanning electron microscope. Journal of Structural Geology, 91–104 (2000)
5. Anguiano, E., Oliva, A.I., Aguilar, M.: Surface texture parameters as a tool to measure image quality in scanning probe microscope. Ultramicroscopy 77(3), 195–205 (1999)
6. Zhang, J., Tan, T.: Brief review of invariant texture analysis methods. Pattern Recognition 35(3), 735–747 (2002), http://lear.inrialpes.fr/pubs/2002/ZT02
7. Azencott, R., Wang, J.-P., Younes, L.: Texture classification using windowed Fourier filters. IEEE Trans. Pattern Anal. Mach. Intell. 19(2), 148–153 (1997)
8. Jain, A.K., Farrokhnia, F.: Unsupervised texture segmentation using gabor filters. Pattern Recogn. 24(12), 1167–1186 (1991)

9. Haralick, R.M.: Statistical and structural approaches to texture. Proc. IEEE 67(5), 768–804 (1979)
10. Chetverikov, D.: Texture analysis using feature-based pairwise interaction maps. Pattern Recognition 32(3), 487–502 (1999)
11. Chaudhuri, B.B., Sarkar, N.: Texture segmentation using fractal dimension. IEEE Trans. Pattern Anal. Mach. Intell. 17(1), 72–77 (1995)
12. Backes, A.R., Bruno, O.M.: A new approach to estimate fractal dimension of texture images. In: Elmoataz, A., Lezoray, O., Nouboud, F., Mammass, D. (eds.) ICISP 2008. LNCS, vol. 5099, pp. 136–143. Springer, Heidelberg (2008)
13. Campiteli, M.G., Martinez, A.S., Bruno, O.M.: An image analysis methodology based on deterministic tourist walks. In: Sichman, J.S., Coelho, H., Rezende, S.O. (eds.) IBERAMIA 2006 and SBIA 2006. LNCS (LNAI), vol. 4140, pp. 159–167. Springer, Heidelberg (2006)
14. Backes, A.R., Bruno, O.M., Campiteli, M.G., Martinez, A.S.: Deterministic tourist walks as an image analysis methodology based. In: Martínez-Trinidad, J.F., Carrasco Ochoa, J.A., Kittler, J. (eds.) CIARP 2006. LNCS, vol. 4225, pp. 784–793. Springer, Heidelberg (2006)
15. Lima, G.F., Martinez, A.S., Kinouchi, O.: Deterministic walks in random media. Phys. Rev. Lett. 87(1), 010603 (2001)
16. Stanley, H.E., Buldyrev, S.V.: Statistical physics - the salesman and the tourist. Nature (London) 413(6854), 373–374 (2001)
17. Campiteli, M.G., Batista, P.D., Kinouchi, O., Martinez, A.S.: Deterministic walks as an algorithm of pattern recognition. Physical Review E (Statistical, Nonlinear, and Soft Matter Physics) 74(2), 026703 (2006)
18. Martinez, A.S., Kinouchi, O., Risau-Gusman, S.: Exploratory behavior, trap models, and glass transitions. Phys. Rev. E 69(1), 017101 (2004)
19. Terçariol, C.A., Martinez, A.S.: Analytical results for the statistical distribution related to a memoryless deterministic walk: dimensionality effect and mean-field models. Phys Rev. E 72
20. Tercariol, C.A.S., Martinez, A.S.: Influence of memory in deterministic walks in random media: Analytical calculation within a mean-field approximation. Phys. Rev. E 78(3), 031111 (2008)
21. Risau-Gusman, S., Martinez, A.S., Kinouchi, O.: Escaping from cycles through a glass transition. Phys. Rev. E 68, 016104 (2003)
22. Paschos, G.: Fast color texture recognition using chromaticity moments. Pattern Recognition Letters 21(9), 837–841 (2000)
23. She, A.C., Huang, T.S.: Segmentation of road scenes using color and fractal-based texture classification. In: ICIP, vol. (3), pp. 1026–1030 (1994)
24. Vision texture database (2009),
    http://vismod.media.mit.edu/vismod/imagery/VisionTexture/vistex.html
25. Everitt, B.S., Dunn, G.: Applied Multivariate Analysis, 2nd edn. Arnold, London (2001)
26. Fukunaga, K.: Introduction to Statistical Pattern Recognition, 2nd edn. Academic Press, London (1990)
27. Loncaric, S.: A survey of shape analysis techniques. Pattern Recognition 31(9), 983–1001 (1998)
28. da Fontoura Costa, L., Cesar Jr., R.M.: Shape Analysis and Classification: Theory and Practice. CRC Press, Boca Raton (2000)

Characterizing 3D Shapes Using Fractal Dimension

André Ricardo Backes[1], Danilo Medeiros Eler[2],
Rosane Minghim[2], and Odemir Martinez Bruno[3]

[1] Faculdade de Computação - Universidade Federal de Uberlândia
Uberlândia MG Brasil
backes@facom.ufu.br
[2] Instituto de Ciências Matemáticas e de Computação (ICMC)
Universidade de São Paulo (USP)
Avenida do Trabalhador São-carlense, 400
13560-970 São Carlos SP Brazil
danilome@gmail.com, rminghim@icmc.usp.br
[3] Instituto de Física de São Carlos (IFSC)
Universidade de São Paulo (USP)
Avenida do Trabalhador São-carlense, 400
13560-970 São Carlos SP Brazil
bruno@ifsc.usp.br

Abstract. Developments in techniques for modeling and digitizing have
made the use of 3D models popular to a large number of new applications. With the diffusion and spreading of 3D models employment, the
demand for efficient search and retrieval methods is high. Researchers
have dedicated effort to investigate and overcome the problem of 3D
shape retrieval. In this work, we propose a new way to employ shape
complexity analysis methods, such as the fractal dimension, to perform
the 3D shape characterization for those purposes. This approach is described and experimental results are performed on a 3D models data
set. We also compare the technique to two other known methods for 3D
model description, reported in literature, namely shape histograms and
shape distributions. The technique presented here has performed considerably better than any of the others in the experiments.

Keywords: Fractal dimension, complexity, 3D shape descriptor.

1 Introduction

The use of 3D models is growing on the Internet and in specific domains (e.g.,
Biology, Medicine and Archaeology). This fact is directly related to new acquisition technologies, such as 3D scanners, and to new 3D graphics rendering
technologies; these in turn are also related to the evolution of graphics hardware,
CPUs and modeling tools, that have eased the construction of 3D models [1,2].

This growth requires new efficient mechanisms to organize, search and retrieve these 3D models from large repositories. To solve that problem, efforts

I. Bloch and R.M. Cesar, Jr. (Eds.): CIARP 2010, LNCS 6419, pp. 14–21, 2010.

have been made to investigate the specific problem of 3D shape retrieval. Which has been solved by effective description methods. Generally, 3D shape retrieval approaches are based on feature methods, which calculate geometric and topological properties from 3D objects; graph methods, which extract a graph representing geometric meaning from shape components; and other methods (e.g., based on 3D appearance, shape deformation and view similarity) [3,2,4].

In this work, we propose to use shape complexity analysis methods, such as the fractal dimension, to perform 3D shape characterization. Fractal dimension is described in the literature as a non-integer value related to the complexity of a Fractal object (non-Euclidean geometry). In shape analysis, this property enables us to quantify the shape complexity in terms of space occupation and self-similarity [5,6,7,8]. We also compare this complexity analysis approach to other two known shape descriptors in the literature, based on shape histograms and shape distribution.

Thus, this paper starts describing how shape complexity analysis is performed in 3D models using a multi-scale approach (Section 2). In Section 3, we describe the experiments performed on the 3D model data base [9] (available at http://segeval.cs.princeton.edu) and the compared methods. Results are presented and discussed in Section 4, while Section 5 describes the conclusions drawn from this work.

2   Fractal Dimension Based Approach

Some of the literature on object descriptors define the fractal dimension as an interesting parameter to characterize roughness in an object [10]. Among the many approaches developed to estimate this parameter, Bouligand-Minkowski method [5,11,12] has emerged as the one that presents the most accurate results and has shown to be very sensitive to structural changes of the object. This method was originally developed for shape analysis. However, recent studies have described its use in texture analysis, an evidence that the method can also be effective in estimating the complexity of 3D models [6,13].

Let $S = [s_1, s_2, \ldots, s_N]$, be the set of vertices that compose the faces of a 3D model. Each vertex s_i is defined by the triple (x, y, z), where x, y and z are the coordinates of a vertex in R^3. Bouligand-Minkowski method is based on the study of the influence volume of an object computed from its dilation. Thus, let $V(r)$ be the dilation of S by a sphere of radius r:

$$V(r) = \left\{ s_j \in R^3 | \exists s_i \in S : |s_i - s_j| \le r \right\}, \qquad (1)$$

where $s_j = (x_j, y_j, z_j)$ is a point in R^3 whose distance from $s_i = (x_i, y_i, z_i)$ is smaller or equal to r. Figure 1 shows an example of this dilation process.

From the study of the influence volume, the fractal dimension D can be estimated as

$$D = 3 - \lim_{r \to 0} \frac{\log V(r)}{\log (r)}, \qquad (2)$$

where D is a number within $[0; 3]$ related to the roughness of the shape.

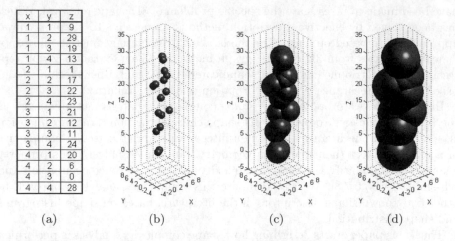

x	y	z
1	1	9
1	2	29
1	3	19
1	4	13
2	1	1
2	2	17
2	3	22
2	4	23
3	1	21
3	2	12
3	3	11
3	4	24
4	1	20
4	2	6
4	3	0
4	4	28

    (a)   (b)   (c)   (d)

Fig. 1. Example of the influence volume $V(r)$ computed for a set of points in (a); (b)-(d) Influence volume for different radius values ($r = \{1, 3, 5\}$). As the radius increases, more interaction among the spheres occurs, thus producing an influence volume characteristic for the set of points.

Regardless of the large sensitiveness of the method to structural changes, there are cases where a single non-integer value is not sufficient to describe all levels of detail present in the influence volume $V(r)$ for a specific object. A better description of the 3D model, in terms of its complexity, is achieved by using the concept of Multi-Scale Fractal Dimension [14,15,11]. Different from linear interpolation, which is commonly used to compute the angular coefficient of the log-log curve $r \times V(r)$, this approach exploits the infinitesimal limit of the linear interpolation by using the derivative of the log-log curve. As a result, a function that expresses the complexity of the object in terms of the spatial scale is yielded (Figure 2). This function enables us to perform a more effective discrimination of the object, and it is defined as:

$$D(r) = 3 - \frac{d \log V(r)}{dr},$$ (3)

where $D(r)$ represents the complexity of the object at scale r.

3 Evaluation of the Shape Descriptor

In order to evaluate the proposed approach, an experiment was performed using a set of artificial 3D models. This set comprises 380 3D models grouped into 19 different classes with 20 samples each. Each class is composed by different orientations as also variations (e.g., articulation) of a given shape structure. Figure 3 shows some examples of 3D models in the data set [9] (available at http://segeval.cs.princeton.edu).

Multi-scale fractal dimension curves were computed from each model. The technique was set up considering a dilation radius $r = 20$, and the derivative was

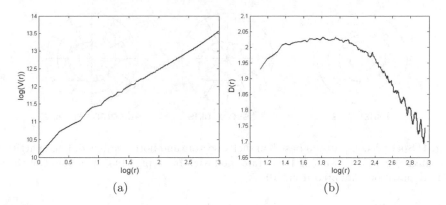

(a)   (b)

Fig. 2. (a) Log-log curve computed from shape dilation; (b) Multi-scale Fractal Dimension

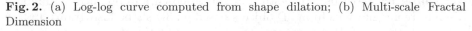

computed using the Finite Difference method [16]. Resulting curves were evaluated using Linear Discriminant Analysis (LDA), a supervised statistical classification method [17,18] which searches for a linear combination of the descriptors that results in its class. The main goal of the method is to find a linear combination that maximizes the intra-class variance while minimizes the inter-class variance. The *leave-one-out cross-validation* strategy was also used over the LDA.

3.1 Compared Approaches

This new formulation was implemented and compared to two known approaches, also implemented, for 3D shape description and matching. The compared approaches are: (i) 3D shape histograms and (ii) Shape distributions. These are statistical properties methods and they were selected as our approach resembles them, since it computes the distribution of influence volume for a specific dilatation radius. A brief description about those approaches is given below.

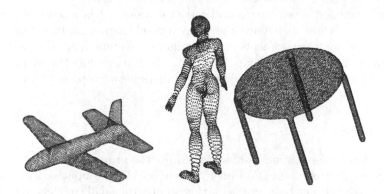

Fig. 3. Examples of 3D shapes used in the experiments

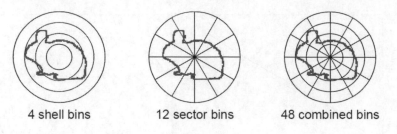

4 shell bins   12 sector bins   48 combined bins

Fig. 4. Space decomposition based on shells, sectors and both combined. Each partition is a single bin in the resulting histogram, and each bin represents the amount of shape in that partition. Adapted from [19].

3D shape histograms: Ankerst et al [19] proposed an approach to compute discrete representations from 3D objects based on 3D shape histograms. In this approach, the space is decomposed based on one of the three suggested techniques: shell model, sector model and the combination of the previous techniques, as shown in Figure 4. The histogram computation is performed with the chosen space decomposition technique, and each bin stores the amount of vertices positioned in each partition of the decomposed space.

To avoid translation and rotation problems, before the histogram computation a normalization step is applied over the 3D object. Firstly, the center of mass of the objects is placed onto the origin. Then, a 3×3 covariance matrix is computed over the coordinates of all points from which the eigenvectors, representing the principal axes of the original 3D object, and eigenvalues, indicate the variance of the points in the respective eigenvector direction, are achieved. Finally, the Principal Axes Transform [19] is performed over the 3D object.

Shape distributions: Osada et al. [20] proposed a method to describe 3D objects as a probability distribution sampled from the object as a shape function, which reflects geometric properties of the object. The method computes histograms, known as shape distributions, using a specific measure computed from randomly selected points on the surface of the 3D object.

To achieve good classification and retrieval results, it is essential to select a shape function whose distribution provides a good shape signature. Osada et al. [20] presented some experiments using distinct shape functions. The best results were achieved using the D2 shape function, which represents the shape of a 3D model by the distribution of Euclidean distances between pairs of points on its surface.

4   Results

Table 1 shows classification results yielded for the proposed and the compared approaches. Multi-scale fractal dimension curves were computed from each 3D object considered. The best results for this set of artificial 3D models were yielded considering dilation radius $r = 20$. Derivative was computed using the Finite

Table 1. Comparison of the success rates for different shape descriptors

Method	Objects correctly classified	Success rate(%)
3D shape histogram	165	43.42
Shape distribution	256	67.37
Shape complexity analysis (proposed approach)	320	84.21

Difference method [16], and the 130 first points of the curve were considered as descriptors of the 3D object.

For the 3D shape histogram, a histogram based on 10 shells and 8 sectors was considered instead of those proposed in the original paper (20 sectors and 6 or 12 shells). This configuration was preferred as it leads to a higher success rate (43.42%) than the one achieved for the other configurations (38.42%, for both 6 or 12 shells) for this set of artificial 3D models. For the dissimilarity of the shape distributions, it was measured based on L1 norm of the probability density function of the D2 shape function. A normalization step was performed by aligning the mean sample values of two compared probability density functions.

Results show that the proposed approach surpasses the effectiveness of the compared ones, as it is more robust in the classification of the 3D models evaluated. This is mostly due to the great sensitiveness and accuracy of the Bouligand-Minkowski method to detect small changes in the surface model. Moreover, the approach is invariant to rotation, i.e., no previous normalization step is necessary during its calculus, due to the use of the Euclidean distance. The main disadvantage of the method lies in the dilatation process, which is performed in a discrete space using the Euclidean Distance Transform (EDT) [21,22]. Since the original 3D model data was defined at interval $[0,1]$, it was necessary to normalize it to $[0,50]$ before the dilatation process took place.

Note that the shape distribution approach is also invariant to rotation. As this approach uses random sampling during calculations, it is also insensitive to small perturbations in the object (e.g., articulation). These characteristics of the method explain its performance.

The inefficient discrimination achieved by the 3D shape histogram is mostly due to the presence of articulation in some 3D models. Although, this method uses a normalization step to avoid rotation invariance and a quadratic form distance function as an adaptable similarity function, the presence of articulations and others small variations results in the same basic structure, for two different models, mapped in different bins of the histogram and, therefore, does not reflect the close similarity of the models.

5   Conclusions

This paper proposes a novel approach to discriminate 3D models based on shape's complexity analysis methods. Multi-scale fractal dimension curves are used to represent the 3D shape. These curves are computed based on the space occupation and self-similarity of the 3D shape.

The proposed approach was evaluated using a 3D model data set [9] and reported interesting results to discriminate different 3D models, significantly surpassing two other known methods: 3D Shape Histograms and Shape Distributions. The compared approaches are not sensible enough to make subtle distinctions. Whereas our approach improved the effectiveness and the results also demonstrated its robustness in dealing with different shape, rotation and articulation of 3D models. Furthermore, the parameterization of our approach is simpler than the compared.

In the future, we plan to perform new experiments in a larger data set (e.g., The Princeton Shape Benchmark [23]) and to compare our approach to other classes of shape discriminator methods.

Ackowledgements

A.R.B. acknowledges support from FAPESP (2006/54367-9). D.M.E. acknowledges support from FAPESP (2007/04241-1). R.M acknowledges support from CNPq (301295/2008-5). O.M.B. acknowledges support from CNPq (306628/2007-4).

References

1. Osada, R., Funkhouser, T., Chazelle, B., Dobkin, D.: Matching 3D models with shape distributions. In: SMI 2001: Proceedings of the International Conference on Shape Modeling & Applications, Washington, DC, USA, p. 154. IEEE Computer Society, Los Alamitos (2001)
2. Yang, Y., Lin, H., Zhang, Y.: Content-based 3-D model retrieval: A survey. IEEE Transactions on Systems, Man, and Cybernetics 37(6), 1081–1098 (2007)
3. Bimbo, A.D., Pala, P.: Content-based retrieval of 3d models. ACM Trans. Multimedia Comput. Commun. Appl. 2(1), 20–43 (2006)
4. Tangelder, J.W., Veltkamp, R.C.: A survey of content based 3d shape retrieval methods. Multimedia Tools Appl. 39(3), 441–471 (2008)
5. Tricot, C.: Curves and Fractal Dimension. Springer, Heidelberg (1995)
6. Backes, A.R., Casanova, D., Bruno, O.M.: Plant leaf identification based on volumetric fractal dimension. IJPRAI 23(6), 1145–1160 (2009)
7. da Costa, L.F., Cesar Jr., R.M.: Shape Analysis and Classification: Theory and Practice. CRC Press, Boca Raton (2000)
8. Carlin, M.: Measuring the complexity of non-fractal shapes by a fractal method. PRL: Pattern Recognition Letters 21(11), 1013–1017 (2000)
9. Chen, X., Golovinskiy, A., Funkhouser, T.: A benchmark for 3D mesh segmentation. ACM Transactions on Graphics (Proc. SIGGRAPH) 28(3) (2009)
10. Sarkar, N., Chaudhuri, B.B.: An efficient approach to estimate fractal dimension of textural images. Pattern Recognition 25(9), 1035–1041 (1992)
11. de Plotze, R.O., Falvo, M., Pádua, J.G., Bernacci, L.C., Vieira, M.L.C., Oliveira, G.C.X., Bruno, O.M.: Leaf shape analysis using the multiscale Minkowski fractal dimension, a new morphometric method: a study with passiflora (passifloraceae). Canadian Journal of Botany 83(3), 287–301 (2005)
12. Bruno, O.M., de Plotze, R.O., Falvo, M., de Castro, M.: Fractal dimension applied to plant identification. Information Sciences 178, 2722–2733 (2008)

13. Backes, A.R., de Sa Jr., J.J.M., Kolb, R.M., Bruno, O.M.: Plant species identification using multi-scale fractal dimension applied to images of adaxial surface epidermis. In: Jiang, X., Petkov, N. (eds.) CAIP 2009. LNCS, vol. 5702, pp. 680–688. Springer, Heidelberg (2009)
14. Emerson, C.W., Lam, N.N., Quattrochi, D.A.: Multi-scale fractal analysis of image texture and patterns. Photogrammetric Engineering and Remote Sensing 65(1), 51–62 (1999)
15. Gonzalez, R.C., Woods, R.E.: Digital Image Processing, 2nd edn. Prentic-Hall, New Jersey (2002)
16. Smith, G.D.: Numerical Solution of Partial Differential Equations: Finite Difference Methods, 3rd edn., Oxford (1986)
17. Everitt, B.S., Dunn, G.: Applied Multivariate Analysis, 2nd edn. Arnold, London (2001)
18. Fukunaga, K.: Introduction to Statistical Pattern Recognition, 2nd edn. Academic Press, London (1990)
19. Ankerst, M., Kastenmüller, G., Kriegel, H.P., Seidl, T.: 3D shape histograms for similarity search and classification in spatial databases. In: Güting, R.H., Papadias, D., Lochovsky, F.H. (eds.) SSD 1999. LNCS, vol. 1651, pp. 207–226. Springer, Heidelberg (1999)
20. Osada, R., Funkhouser, T., Chazelle, B., Dobkin, D.: Shape distributions. ACM Transactions on Graphics 21(4), 807–832 (2002)
21. Bruno, O.M., da Fontoura Costa, L.: A parallel implementation of exact Euclidean distance transform based on exact dilations. Microprocessors and Microsystems 28(3), 107–113 (2004)
22. Fabbri, R., da Fontoura Costa, L., Torelli, J.C., Bruno, O.M.: 2D Euclidean distance transform algorithms: A comparative survey. ACM Computing Surveys 40(1), 1–44 (2008)
23. Shilane, P., Min, P., Kazhdan, M., Funkhouser, T.: The Princeton shape benchmark. In: SMI 2004: Proceedings of the Shape Modeling International 2004, Washington, DC, USA, pp. 167–178. IEEE Computer Society, Los Alamitos (2004)

Multiresolution Histogram Analysis for Color Reduction

Giuliana Ramella and Gabriella Sanniti di Baja

Istituto di Cibernetica "E.Caianiello", CNR
Via Campi Flegrei 34, 80078 Pozzuoli, Naples, Italy
{g.ramella,g.sannitidibaja}@cib.na.cnr.it

Abstract. A new technique for color reduction is presented, based on the analysis of the histograms of an image at different resolutions. Given an input image, lower resolution images are generated by using a scaling down interpolation method. Then, peaks and pits that are present in the histograms at all resolutions and dominate in the histogram of the input image at full resolution are taken into account to simplify the structure of the histogram of the image at full resolution. The so modified histogram is used to define a reduced colormap. New colors possibly created by the process are changed into the original colors closer to them.

1 Introduction

The human visual system is able to distinguish a large number of colors. However, it generally groups colors with similar tonality, since even a few colors are often enough for image understanding. When considering a digital image, color reduction can be used analogously to generate a transformed image, where a smaller number of distinct representative colors are used, while the visual appearance of the original image and of the transformed image is as similar as possible. The increasing number of applications, e.g., [1-3], dealing with multimedia data where millions of distinct colors are present makes color reduction particularly useful, especially for storage and transmission purposes.

Color quantization can be seen as a clustering problem in the 3D space, where the coordinate axes are the color components and each point represents one of the colors in the image. By means of a clustering technique, points are grouped into an a priori fixed number of clusters, each of which is associated a representative color, generally obtained as the average of the points in the cluster [4-6]. The most known methods to build a colormap with an a priori fixed number of colors are the median cut algorithm [1], which is based on the popularity method suggested by Boyle and Lippman in 1978, and the octree color quantization algorithm [7]. Other quantization methods in the literature are based on histogram analysis [8-10], fuzzy logic [11,12], neural network [13,14] and multiresolution analysis [9,10,15].

In this paper, we present a color reduction algorithm, based on color distribution and on the use of multiresolution image representation. The method is a substantial modification and improvement of a method we have recently suggested, which is also in the framework of multiresolution histogram analysis [10]. With respect to our previous method, the main differences are: 1) a different strategy to obtain the

I. Bloch and R.M. Cesar, Jr. (Eds.): CIARP 2010, LNCS 6419, pp. 22–29, 2010.
© Springer-Verlag Berlin Heidelberg 2010

multiresolution image representation, 2) the process for simplifying the structure of the histogram, 3) the introduction of an updating of the colormap (both when building lower resolution representations of the input image and when computing the reduced colormap), and 4) the ability of the method to originate automatically a transformed image with a number of colors in the range established by the user.

One of the advantages of the suggested method is the possibility to obtain different transformed images, each characterized by a different number of colors. This makes our method useful for progressive transmission, where a transformed image quantized with a small/large number of colors can be initially transmitted, and versions with larger/smaller numbers of colors can be provided, if demanded by the receiver.

The paper is organized as follows. Some preliminary notions are given in Section 2; the method is described in Section 3 and experimental results are discussed in Section 4. Concluding remarks are finally given in Section 5.

2 Preliminaries

We work with RGB images and interpret colors as three-dimensional vectors, with each vector element having an 8-bit dynamic range.

Given a color image I, let H be the histogram of the values in any of the color components of I. We consider as peaks and pits of H the values that are relative local maxima and relative local minima, respectively. Formally, if $p-1$, p and $p+1$ are three consecutive values in H, and height(p) denotes the height of the bin associated to p in H, i.e., the number of pixels with value p, then:

- if (height($p-1$)$\leq$height(p) and height($p+1$)<height(p)) or (height($p-1$)<height(p) and height($p+1$)$\leq$height(p)), p is a peak;

- if (height(p)$\leq$ height($p-1$) and height(p)<height($p+1$)) or (height(p)<height($p-1$) and height(p) $\leq$ height($p+1$)), p is a pit.

Peaks and pits of H can be seen as vertices of a polygonal approximation of H. To simplify the structure of the histogram by retaining only the most significant vertices, we associate to each vertex v_i three parameters (see Fig. 1a):

- the area a_i of the region of the histogram dominated by v_i (i.e., the area of the triangle formed by the three successive vertices v_{i-1}, v_i and v_{i+1}),

- the cosine c_i of the angle formed by the two straight lines respectively joining v_i with v_{i-1} and with v_{i+1},

- the distance d_i of v_i from the straight line joining v_{i-1} and v_{i+1}.

The above parameters, introduced in [16] in the framework of 2D object's contour analysis to define the dominance of a vertex on the basis of criteria of perceptual significance, are here used in the context of multiresolution histogram analysis (see Section 3).

Lower resolution representations of a color image I can be obtained in different manners, e.g., by means of pyramids, and can be used to simplify the structure of the full resolution histogram. In this paper, we compute lower resolution representations

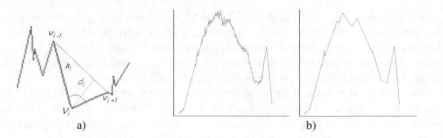

Fig. 1. a) The three parameters a_i, c_i, d_i associated to the vertex v_i, b) An histogram before, left, and after the simplification process, right

of I by means of a scaling down method based on nearest neighbor interpolation. The main advantage of this choice, with respect to using a Gaussian pyramid, is that any reduction factor f can be employed, instead of the reduction factor of 0.5 along each coordinate direction. Thus, lower resolution versions of I can be obtained, where resolution diminishes less abruptly along the levels. Another useful feature is that f can assume different values during the construction of the lower resolution images. In particular, a smaller f can be used to build the first lower resolution image, starting from the full resolution input image, and a larger f to build all successive lower resolution images, each of which is computed starting from the immediately previous one. The use of a larger value for f at the first scaling down step is motivated by the fact that even a rather strong compression does not dramatically alter the information contents, when done on the full resolution image. In turn, a smaller compression is advisable at the successive scaling down steps, i.e., when working with images that have already lost some information due to the resolution reduction.

3 The Algorithm

Our color reduction algorithm, based on the multiresolution analysis of color distribution in I, consists of two steps.

Step 1 is devoted to the following tasks: 1) construction of L lower resolution representations I_k of the input image I; new colors, possibly created in the images I_k, are changed to their closest colors present in I. 2) computation, for each color component of I, of the histogram H of I as well as the histograms H_k for the L lower resolution images I_k.

Step 2 is devoted to the multiresolution analysis of the histograms to identify values that can be grouped together and be replaced by a unique representative value in H. To this aim, the structure of H is simplified, by using information derived from H as well as from a subset of the L histograms H_k. The representative values found for the histogram H of the color components are combined, to generate the reduced colormap. New colors possibly created during histogram manipulation, are replaced by the color of the original colormap to which they result to be closer.

If the number of colors of the transformed image I' is in the range desired by the user the process terminates. Otherwise, Step 2 is repeated, after the number of lower resolution images taken into account is suitably increased/decreased, until the number of colors of I' is in the desired range. During Step 1, the original colormap is computed and is stored in a 3D array, where position (x,y,z) corresponds to the color with R=x, G=y, B=z. Then, standard OpenCV libraries are used to build the lower resolution images I_k via nearest neighbor interpolation. As pointed out in Section 2, different values for f can be used during scaling down. We have experimentally found, by analyzing images with different size and color distribution, that satisfactory results are obtained, in the average, by using a reduction factor f=0.5 for the first resolution reduction and f=0.8 for the successive ones. These values will be used as default values in this paper.

In general, a number of images I_k could be built by repeatedly applying the scaling down process, but images I_k with too small size do not adequately preserve the information contents of I. Thus, we consider only the L successive images I_k whose size, expressed in number of pixels, includes at least 32 pixels for row and column. As soon as a lower resolution image I_k is created, the corresponding color map is built. Colors that are present in I_k, but do not exist in I, are changed to their closest colors in the original colormap, before building the successive lower resolution image. The histogram H of I and the histograms H_k of the L images I_k are computed. Peaks and pits are detected on all histograms. Depending on the number of histograms H_k, out of the L computed, that will be used for multiresolution histogram analysis, the transformed image I' will be characterized by a different number of colors. A large number of resolution images will produce a transformed image with a small number of colors and vice versa.

Step 2 starts by examining N histograms, where it is $N= L/2 +1$ and is aimed at simplifying H. We look for a simplification of H, accounting for the permanence along the N histograms and the dominance in H (intended as perceptual relevance) of a vertex v_i. The permanence of v_i of H is checked by verifying if the value of v_i actually corresponds to a vertex in each H_k. The dominance of v_i is evaluated with respect to geometrical parameters of the triangles associated to all the vertices. The choice of these parameters is done to take into account factors influencing human perception such as the size of the region "viewed" by a vertex (the area a_i of the triangle associated to v_i) and the "cornerity" (roughly related to c_i) of the polygonal line including v_i. Moreover, the distance d_i is related to an often used measure of perceptual significance in the context of polygonal approximation. The dominance of a vertex is evaluated in the context of the overall shape, by referring to the average value of all areas of the triangles associated to all the vertices. The average value is a term of comparison for each area and guides the process of vertex selection by giving more evidence to the vertices having area larger than the average. The dominance of a vertex is also locally evaluated by comparing the geometrical parameters associated to each pair of consecutive vertices.

Let v_1, v_2..., v_n be the vertices of H and let A be the average of the areas a_i of the triangles associated to the vertices v_i, i=1,..,n. The following process is done to simplify H.

- Any v_i of H that is not present in all the H_k and is such that $a_i<A$ is not retained as a vertex. The values of the three parameters (a_i, c_i, d_i) for all surviving v_i of H, and the average area A are updated.

- Any pair of consecutive vertices (v_i, v_{i+1}) of H such that $(a_i<A$ and $a_{i+1}<A)$ and $(a_i=a_{i+1}, $ or $c_i=c_{i+1}, $ or $d_i=d_{i+1})$ is not retained as a vertex.

- Any v_i of H which is no longer a relative maximum or a relative minimum of H is not retained as a vertex.

In Fig. 1b, an histogram H is shown before and after the simplification process. Once the structure of H has been simplified, all values from a pit to the successive pit are replaced by a single representative value. Three cases are possible:

- If one single peak is in between two successive pits, the representative value is the value of the peak.

- If more than one peak is in between two successive pits, the representative value is the value of the leftmost peak.

- Otherwise, the representative value is the value of the leftmost pit.

After combining the representative values of the color components the representative colors are obtained. These may not be included in the original colormap. To limit the presence of false colors, each representative color that is not found in the original colormap is replaced by the closest color in the original colormap. Selecting $N=L/2 + 1$ histograms to identify the significant peaks and pits of H is in some cases already adequate to produce a transformed image I' with colors in the range desired by the user. Otherwise, Step 2 is automatically repeated by analyzing either $N+1$ or $N-1$ histograms. In fact, let $C1$ and $C2$ be the minimum and maximum number of colors desired by the user and let RC_1 be the number of resulting representative colors, as obtained when Step 2 is accomplished for the first time, i.e., by analyzing $L/2 + 1$ histograms. If it results $C1 \leq RC_1 \leq C2$, the obtained image I' is the final transformed image. If $RC_1<C1$ ($RC_1>C2$), $N'=N-1$ ($N'=N+1$) histograms are considered so originating a different simplification of H and, as a consequence, producing a new transformed image with a larger (smaller) number of colors. Step 2 is repeated as many times as necessary to obtain a transformed image I' with colors in the desired range.

Fig. 2. A set of test images

4   Experimental Results

We have applied the color reduction algorithm to a collection of images with different size and color distribution, taken from available databases, e.g., [17-19]. A small dataset including six 512×480 images, six 512×512 images, and six 768×512 images is given in Fig. 2. This dataset is used to show the performance of our method in terms of the obtained number of representative colors, accounting for the degree of color compression, and the compression ratio, computed as the ratio between the size of the output stream and the input stream expressed in bit per pixel [20].

Table 1 summarizes the quantitative measures for the images in the dataset, after one application of Step 2, where $L/2 + 1$ histograms are analyzed to simplify H. The number of colors in I and in I' are denoted by OC and RC_I, respectively. CR_I denotes the compression ratio of I'.

If the user desires a transformed image with a number of colors ranging, say, between $C1$ and $C2$ different colors, for some images in the dataset, the condition $C1 \leq RC_I \leq C2$ is not satisfied in one application of Step 2. These images are automatically processed again by using $N+1$ or $N-1$ histograms. In particular, $N+1$ histograms are considered if $RC_I > C2$, since by increasing the number of resolution levels taken into account the number of colors in the reduced colormap decreases. In turn, $N-1$ histograms are analyzed if $RC_I < C1$. If the condition $C1 \leq RC_2 \leq C2$ is still not satisfied after Step 2 is applied twice, multiresolution histogram analysis is repeated after furthermore increasing/decreasing the number of histograms. The process terminates as soon as with the current value N' of histograms, for the transformed image it is $C1 \leq RC_F \leq C2$.

Table 1 summarizes also the final results for the images in the data set, in correspondence with $C1=256$ and $C2=512$. The last column of the table denotes how many other histograms more (positive value) or how many histogram less (negative values) have to be used with respect to the starting $L/2 + 1$ histograms to satisfy the requirements of the user (and, hence, how many repetitions of Step 2 are necessary).

At most three repetitions of Step 2 have been necessary in order the number of colors of the transformed image is in the selected range. This has been necessary, for example, for the images "airplane" and "kodim22", for which the number of histograms leading to 263 and 265 colors respectively is diminished by 3 with respect to the initially selected number. The average compression ratio for the 18 images in the dataset is equal to 0.517, i.e., color information occupies after compression in the average 48,3% of its original size.

Fig. 3. Different resulting images, obtained with a different selection of the number of histograms

To show qualitatively the obtained results, refer to Fig. 3, where three different resulting images are shown for the input image "baboon", satisfying different requirements of the user as far as the final range of colors is concerned. The three

Table 1. Results after one application of Step 2 (columns 3,4) and final results for $C1=256$ and $C2=512$ (columns 5,6)

Image	OC	RC_1	CR_1	RC_F	CR_F	N'-N
cablecar	130416	1328	0,611	258	0,471	2
flower	111841	573	0,546	344	0,502	1
fruits	160476	1136	0,587	452	0,510	2
pens	121057	1036	0,593	364	0,504	2
soccer	139156	934	0,577	383	0,502	2
yacht	150053	648	0,543	381	0,499	1
lena	69904	87	0,400	304	0,513	-2
tiffany	79228	695	0,580	359	0,522	2
airplane	47819	65	0,387	263	0,517	-3
baboon	171045	640	0,536	460	0,509	2
housed	154605	148	0,418	329	0,485	-1
lake	168459	87	0,371	271	0,466	-1
kodim03	34871	474	0,589	474	0,589	0
kodim05	63558	956	0,621	512	0,564	1
kodim14	55117	487	0,567	487	0,567	0
kodim15	44576	446	0,570	446	0,570	0
kodim22	53351	62	0,379	265	0,513	-3
kodim23	72079	284	0,505	284	0,505	0

transformed images, from left to right, are characterized by 640, 460, and 224 different colors. The numbers of histograms that have been used to simplify H are respectively 6, 8, and 9.

5 Concluding Remarks

A color reduction algorithm has been introduced that generates a transformed image with a smaller number of colors but still maintaining the visual aspect of the input image satisfactorily. The algorithm is based on the analysis of the histograms at different resolutions of the input image, obtained by using a scaling down method based on nearest neighbor interpolation. Only peaks and pits present at all resolutions and dominating in the full resolution histogram are considered to identify the representative values defining the reduced colormap. Colors of the reduced colormap that are not present in the original colormap are changed into the closest colors in the original colormap.

The algorithm has a limited computational complexity and is not time consuming. It does not require pre-quantization and generates a transformed image with a number of colors in an *a priori* fixed range. It has been implemented on a Pentium 4 (3.39 GHz, 2 GB RAM) personal computer and has been applied to a large set of images, producing satisfactory results in terms of compression ratio.

Since different transformed images are obtained depending on the number of analyzed histograms, the method can be used for progressive transmission, where an image characterized by strong color reduction, i.e., quantized by using a large number of histograms, can be initially transmitted and better versions can be provided if demanded by the receiver.

References

1. Heckbert, P.S.: Color Image Quantization for Frame Buffer Display. In: Proc. ACM SIGGRAPH 1982, vol. 16(3), pp. 297–307 (1982)
2. Plataniotis, K.N., Venetsanopoulos, A.N.: Color Image Processing and Applications. Springer, Heidelberg (2000)
3. Rui, Y., Huang, T.S.: Image Retrieval: Current Techniques, Promising Directions, and Open Issues. Journal of Visual Communication and Image Representation 10, 39–62 (1999)
4. Braquelaire, J.P., Brun, L.: Comparison and Optimization of Methods of Color Image Quantization. IEEE Transactions on Image Processing 6(7), 1048–1052 (1997)
5. Bing, Z., Junyi, S., Qinke, P.: An adjustable algorithm for color quantization. Pattern Recognition Letters 25, 1787–1797 (2004)
6. Chen, T.W., Chen, Y.L., Chien, S.Y.: Fast Image Segmentation Based on K-Means Clustering with Histograms in HSV Color Space. In: Proc. of IEEE 10th Workshop on Multimedia Signal Processing, pp. 322–325 (2008)
7. Gervautz, M., Purgathofer, W.: A Simple Method for Color Quantization: Octree Quantization. In: Glassner, A.S. (ed.) Graphics Gems, pp. 287–293. Academic Press, London (1990)
8. Delon, J., Desolneux, A., Lisani, J.L., Petro, A.B.: A Nonparametric Approach for Histogram Segmentation. IEEE Transactions on Image Processing 16(1), 253–261 (2007)
9. Kim, N., Kehtarnavaz, N.: DWT-based scene-adaptive color quantization. Real-Time Imaging 11, 443–453 (2005)
10. Ramella, G., Sanniti di Baja, G.: Color quantization by multiresolution analysis. In: Jiang, X., Petkov, N. (eds.) CAIP 2009. LNCS, vol. 5702, pp. 525–532. Springer, Heidelberg (2009)
11. Ozdemir, D., Akarun, L.: A fuzzy algorithm for color quantization of images. Pattern Recognition 35, 1785–1791 (2002)
12. Shorter, N., Kasparis, T.: Fuzzy ART for Relatively Fast Unsupervised Image Color Quantization. In: Proc. of 19th Int. Conf. on Pattern Recognition. IEEE CS Press, Los Alamitos (2008) ISBN/ISSN: 978-1-4244-2175-6
13. Papamarkos, N., Atsalakis, A.E., Strouthopoulos, C.P.: Adaptive color reduction. IEEE Transactions Systems, Man, and Cybernetics 32(1), 44–56 (2002)
14. Atsalakis, A., Papamarkos, N.: Color reduction and estimation of the number of dominant colors by using a self-growing and self-organized neural gas. Engineering Applications of Artificial Intelligence 19, 769–786 (2006)
15. Robinson, J.A.: Adaptive Prediction Trees for Image Compression. IEEE Transactions on Image Processing 15(8), 2131–2145 (2006)
16. Arcelli, C., Ramella, G.: Finding contour-based abstractions of planar patterns. Pattern Recognition 26(10), 1563–1577 (1993)
17. http://sipi.usc.edu/database/
18. http://www.hlevkin.com/TestImages/
19. http://r0k.us/graphics/kodak/
20. Salomon, D.: Data Compression: The Complete Reference. Springer, London (2007)

Graph of Words Embedding for Molecular Structure-Activity Relationship Analysis

Jaume Gibert[1], Ernest Valveny[1], and Horst Bunke[2]

[1] Computer Vision Center, Universitat Autònoma de Barcelona
Edifici O Campus UAB, 08193 Bellaterra, Spain
{jgibert,ernest}@cvc.uab.es
[2] Institute for Computer Science and Applied Mathematics, University of Bern,
Neubrückstrasse 10, CH-3012 Bern, Switzerland
bunke@iam.unibe.ch

Abstract. Structure-Activity relationship analysis aims at discovering chemical activity of molecular compounds based on their structure. In this article we make use of a particular graph representation of molecules and propose a new graph embedding procedure to solve the problem of structure-activity relationship analysis. The embedding is essentially an arrangement of a molecule in the form of a vector by considering frequencies of appearing atoms and frequencies of covalent bonds between them. Results on two benchmark databases show the effectiveness of the proposed technique in terms of recognition accuracy while avoiding high operational costs in the transformation.

1 Introduction

Biological properties of molecules, such as chemical reactivity, mutagenicity or anti-cancer activity, are presumed to be correlated with the inherent molecular structure. Such assumption is what lies behind the Structure-Activity Relationship (SAR) analysis, where *activity* is any of the biological responses molecules might show off. Chemoinformatics has extensively dealt with this problem, usually by representing molecules in the form of labelled undirected graphs [8], describing the 2D structure of the chemical compounds. However, working with this molecular representation leads to the usual problem one encounters when dealing with graph-based representations, namely, the high computational complexity of the analysis and comparison of graphs, also known as graph matching [1].

Common sub- and super-graphs between pairs of graphs may be used to define graph similarity for the problem of graph matching [4,6]. Also graph edit distance is a powerful tool that defines similarity between graphs by the amount of distortion that is needed to transform one graph into another [5,2]. Even though there exist suboptimal solutions to these problems, they still suffer from high complexity.

In the last years, two new lines of research have been opened which allow the classical statistical machine learning methodology being applied to structural

I. Bloch and R.M. Cesar, Jr. (Eds.): CIARP 2010, LNCS 6419, pp. 30–37, 2010.

pattern recognition problems. Graph embedding, which associates a feature vector to each graph, and graph kernels, which define a kernel function between instances of graphs, are emerging and promising fields that aim at exploiting the benefits of both the representational power of graphs and the wealth of algorithmic tools of statistical machine learning.

The new method we present in this paper aims at performing the SAR analysis by embedding graph molecules into feature spaces. The next section sets out the details of the proposed procedure. Then, Section 3 presents a comparison of our methodology with different state-of-the art techniques using two different databases. Finally, Section 4 concludes the article.

2   Embedding of Molecular Graphs

The molecules embedding procedure we propose here associates a feature vector to each molecule, initially represented by a graph. It is originally based on a well-known approach to document and image classification [11], which is also called *bag of words* technique. The main idea behind it can be summarized as follows. By taking a glance at a document we can just describe its layout and the distribution of the paragraphs, but we can barely say to which class this document belongs. However, by taking a more careful look we may notice the existence of keywords that can give us some hints on the document topic. For instance, if we detect that in the document the words *brain, cell, disease, doctor*, etc. frequently appear, we can consider such a document as a *medical* one.

Technically, we need to provide a set of keywords, also known as *vocabulary*, and then just count the frequency of appearance of each keyword in the document. This results in a histogram of keywords appearing in the document that is used as the document representation. The histograms can be used as feature vectors to feed any machine capable to learn the document classes and perform the categorization task.

In this paper, we aim at defining a similar procedure with molecules. The nodes of a molecule graph are attributed with a chemical element. By letting the set of chemical elements be our *vocabulary* -in the sense it has been explained above- we can create a histogram of atoms appearing in each molecule. Yet, the fact that atoms in the molecule are linked by covalent bonds leads to an even richer description. To obtain such an enrichment, we need to transform the molecule graph into a new graph we shall call the *graph of words*. From this new graph, we will obtain the feature vector by taking into account node and edge attributes. The next sections formally define the embedding of molecules in vector spaces and two different ways of handling edge attributes.

2.1   Formal Definitions

The graph of words. Assume a set of molecules $M = \{g_1, \ldots, g_n\}$ is given. Each molecule is represented by a graph $g_i = (V_i, E_i, \mu_i, \nu_i)$, where V_i is the set of nodes, $E_i \subseteq V_i \times V_i$ the set of edges, μ_i is the function assigning atomic

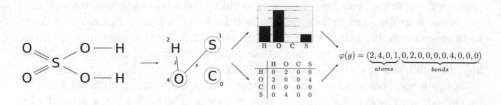

Fig. 1. Embedding of the Sulphuric Acid molecule using the ordered vocabulary $\mathcal{V} = \{H, O, C, S\}$. The first transition shows the graph of words construction for the molecule at the left. Following, the histogram of appearing atoms/words and the adjacency matrix of the graph of words are shown. Finally, the vector representation is the concatenation of both the histogram of atoms and the right upper diagonal part of the adjacency matrix.

elements to the nodes $v \in V_i$ and ν_i assigns to each edge $(u, v) \in E_i$ the kind of covalent bond that links the atoms.

Following the idea explained above, we define the vocabulary $\mathcal{V}$ by the set of existing atomic elements in any of the molecules of M. In the histogram representation we would just count the frequency of each node label in a graph, but since we want to use the bond information as well we transform each molecule $g = (V, E, \mu, \nu)$ into another graph $g' = (V', E', \mu', \nu')$ where

- $V' = \mathcal{V}$,
- E' is defined by: $(w, w') \in E' \Leftrightarrow$ there exists $(u, v) \in E$ such that $\mu(u) = w$ and $\mu(v) = w'$,
- μ' is the mapping $\mu'(w) = |\{v \in V \mid \mu(v) = w\}|$,
- and ν' is the edge labelling function defined by $\nu'(w, w') = |\{(u, v) \in E \mid \mu(u) = w, \mu(v) = w'\}|$.

In plain words, we represent a molecule graph by another graph whose nodes are the node vocabulary $\mathcal{V}$; note that each atom appears just once. We call this new graph the graph of words, in analogy to the bag of words representation. We label each node of the new graph by the frequency of occurrence of the corresponding atom. Note that this definition allows for an atom to be labelled with the zero attribute. Edges of the graph of words are those links between nodes that also occur in the molecule. For instance, if there is a bond between two atoms C and H in the molecule then we link the words C and H in the new representation. The label of such an edge will tell us how many times the corresponding edge occurs. Note that zero attributed edges are allowed and represent the fact that two atoms are not linked in the molecule.

By this procedure, we do not only have all information included in the histogram of words, but also how the words/atoms are structurally related in the molecule. The first transition step in Figure 1 depicts an example of this representation for a simple vocabulary of just four atoms.

Vector representation. Based on the graph of words representation it is straightforward to assign a feature vector to every molecule in M. Since we want to keep both the information about the atoms and the bonds, we *split* the graph of words into a histogram of atoms and the adjacency matrix (second transition in Figure 1). Let N be the number of atoms in the vocabulary. The histogram of atoms for all graphs in M can be formally written as a mapping $\phi_a : M \rightarrow \mathbb{R}^N$, where

$$\phi_a(g) = (\mu'(w_1), \dots, \mu'(w_N)). \tag{1}$$

The adjacency matrix of the graph of words is an $N \times N$ symmetric matrix $A = (a_{ij})$, where each entry a_{ij} describes the frequency of the relation between the ith and jth atoms, this is, $a_{ij} = \nu'(w_i, w_j)$. The fact that we control the vocabulary, makes this matrix easily sortable since, for every molecule, each entry (feature) of the matrix is describing the same information. Also, due to the symmetry of the matrix we can just consider the diagonal and the upper part of it. Therefore, we arrange the graph of words adjacency matrix as $\phi_b : M \rightarrow \mathbb{R}^p$, where

$$\phi_b(g) = (a_{11}, \dots, a_{ij}, \dots, a_{NN}), \ \forall \, i \leq j \tag{2}$$

and where $p = (N^2 + N)/2$. Finally, we can just concatenate both the atomic histogram information and the structural relations of atoms in a single vector as follows: $\varphi : M \rightarrow \mathbb{R}^{N+p}$, where

$$\varphi(g) = (\phi_a(g), \phi_b(g)). \tag{3}$$

The last transition of Figure 1 shows the final vector representation of the molecule on the left.

2.2   Edge Attributes Handling

The reader may have noticed that in the construction defined above the edge attributes of the molecules have been ignored. That is, there has been no attention paid on whether the atomic bond is either *single* or *double*. This representation is what we call R_1 or *all-in-one*, since the edges are all stored in one adjacency matrix. As an alternative, to consider the type of atomic bonds, we also define the R_2 or *separated* representation: based on the same construction, we may consider an adjacency matrix for each type of edge label separately and then concatenate all matrices in a single final vector.

For instance, in the example of Figure 1, the R_1 representation is the one depicted since edge attributes are neglected. For the second representation R_2 we should take the matrices

$$A_s = \begin{pmatrix} 0 & 2 & 0 & 0 \\ 2 & 0 & 0 & 2 \\ 0 & 0 & 0 & 0 \\ 0 & 2 & 0 & 0 \end{pmatrix} \quad A_d = \begin{pmatrix} 0 & 0 & 0 & 0 \\ 0 & 0 & 0 & 2 \\ 0 & 0 & 0 & 0 \\ 0 & 2 & 0 & 0 \end{pmatrix}$$

where A_s is representing the single bonds and A_d the double bonds. With this procedure, even though the final vector representation under R_2 will be larger and more sparse than under R_1, it will still keep information of the atomic bonds of the original molecule. In the experiments section, we will explore the two alternatives and discuss which one of our embedding procedures is more suitable.

2.3   Remarks

After the formal definition of our embedding has been given, we would like to point out its two strong points. On the one hand, the feature vector we assign to each molecule is storing both statistical and structural information. The first part of the vector ϕ_a is counting occurrences of atomic elements in the molecule, while the second part ϕ_b is describing the structure of these elements in the molecule. On the other hand, in contrast to most of the existing graph embedding techniques and feature extraction algorithms for graphs, our approach is very inexpensive in terms of algorithmic complexity. In fact, for a graph g with n nodes, only $\mathcal{O}(n^2)$ operations are required to transform g into $\varphi(g)$. This is in sharp contrast with other embedding procedures, for example [3], which are exponential in n.

3   Experiments

3.1   Databases

We applied our molecular embedding based on the graph of words representation to two different benchmark datasets of molecules. The Predictive Toxicology Challenge (PTC) database [7] is the result of a pharmaceutical experiment in which several molecular compounds are tested in four types of animals: Male Mouse (MM), Female Mouse (FM), Male Rat (MR) and Female Rat (FR). Each compound is assigned to either the positive or the negative class according to its carcinogenicity activity. This results in four two-class supervised classification problems in which the activity of the compounds for a specific animal should be discovered. The second set, the MUTAG database [13], is a set of molecular compounds tested for mutagenicity activity on *Salmonella typhimurium*. Again, the problem is a binary supervised classification task consisting of the determination of the activity of the molecules.

In Table 1 we show some statistics for each molecular database. In particular, we give the total number of molecules in every dataset (#TOTAL); how many of them are positive for carcinogenicity/mutagenicity (#POSITIVE); how many are negative (#NEGATIVE); the maximum order (number of nodes) in each dataset (MAX $|G|$) and the average order (AVG $|G|$); the number of different node attributes in the dataset ($|\Sigma|_v$), which is the number of atoms/words in the vocabularies we use for the proposed embedding; and the number of different types of atomic bonds in the molecules ($|\Sigma|_e$), which would be the number of adjacency matrices to consider in the R_2 representation of the graph of words embedding.

Table 1. PTC and MUTAG Datasets Statistics

	MM	FM	MR	FR	MUTAG
#TOTAL	336	349	344	351	188
#POSITIVE	129	143	152	121	125
#NEGATIVE	207	206	192	230	63
MAX $\|G\|$	109	109	109	109	28
AVG $\|G\|$	25.0	25.2	25.6	26.1	18.0
$\|\Sigma\|_v$	21	19	19	20	8
$\|\Sigma\|_e$	4	4	4	4	4

3.2   Reference Systems

In order to compare our results, we have selected two articles that report about molecular classification on the same datasets. In [9], a marginalized graph kernel between labelled graphs is proposed and compared to the Pattern Discovery algorithm [10]. The marginalized graph kernel is defined as the expectation of the joint kernel between labelled paths, where such paths are defined under a first-order Markov random model. The Pattern Discovery algorithm assigns each molecule to a feature vector where each attribute is counting the number of occurrences of a certain label path in the molecule. On the other hand, in [14], the authors exploit the fact that molecules can either be represented by 1D structures (SMILE strings), 2D structures (graphs), or 3D representations where spatial coordinates of the atoms are taken into account. Based on these facts, several kernels are defined for each representation. We will report here just the best ones for each case.

Even though there exist optimal and fast computational procedures for these approaches, they all suffer from higher complexity than ours since they are based on searching substructures in the graphs.

3.3   Results

Leave-one-out validation consists in testing every element in the dataset with the learnt model from the rest of existing available patterns. The accuracy rate of the whole system is the number of correctly classified patterns out of the total number in the dataset. In this section we detail the classification rate for the databases using leave-one-out validation and Support Vector Machines [12] as the learning machine.

In Figure 2 we see how the R_1 representation outperforms in all cases the R_2 representation, which takes into account the molecular bond types. This situation seems to be due to the sparsity of the R_2 representation. In Table 1 we can see that there are four different types of molecular bonds in the datasets. However, two of these four types barely appear as an edge attribute and so the proportion between these types and the other two is really low. Such circumstance creates adjacency matrices of the graph of words with almost all entries being zero; thus, the resulting vector representation consists of many zero values and just a few

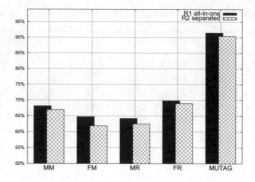

Fig. 2. Comparison of the accuracy rates obtained for all databases using the two proposed configurations R_1 and R_2 of the molecular embedding

Table 2. Comparison of *leave-one-out* results for different datasets using several methods. Accuracy rates in %. The best method on each dataset in printed bold face.

	MM	FM	MR	FR	MUTAG
Pattern Discovery [9]	61.0	61.0	62.8	66.7	89.9
Walk kernel [9]	64.3	63.4	58.4	66.1	85.1
Best 1D kernel [14]	66.4	63.0	57.6	67.0	85.6
Best 2D kernel [14]	66.4	64.5	**65.7**	66.9	87.8
Best 3D kernel [14]	59.8	61.0	60.8	64.4	81.9
Proposed (φ, R_1)	**68.15**	**64.75**	64.24	**69.80**	**91.48**
Proposed (φ, R_2)	66.96	61.89	62.50	68.94	90.42

non-zero ones. This is a plausible explanation that the SVM is capable to better learn the positive and negative classes for the R_1 representation than for the R_2.

In Table 2 a comparison between the reference methods and our two configurations of the graph of words embedding is shown for all databases. In four out of the five considered two-class classification problems it is actually superior to the other techniques. Moreover, since the proposed embedding has a low computational complexity, the whole system is worth considering.

4 Conclusions

In this paper, we have introduced a new embedding procedure of graph molecular compounds for the problem of structure-activity relationship analysis. The embedding is based on the idea of bag of words for document classification in which a document is represented by a histogram of appearing keywords in the text. Our approach takes the atomic elements appearing in the database and proceeds similarly to the bag of words methods. In order to take profit of the atomic bonds in molecules, we transform the molecule graph into the graph of words representation, in which not only the node histogram information is stored but also how the atomic vocabulary is structurally related. As the underlying vocabulary is uniquely given, the arrangement of the new graph representation into a vector is a straightforward step, resulting in a feature vector for each molecular compound.

Results with two different configurations of the embedding have been shown, as well as a comparison with several state-of-the-art molecules classification techniques. The results reveal that the proposed procedure is at the same level as such techniques, while avoiding the computational complexity problems typically encountered in graph-based problems.

References

1. Conte, D., Foggia, P., Sansone, C., Vento, M.: Thirty years of graph matching in pattern recognition. International Journal of Pattern Recognition and Artificial Intelligence 18(3), 265–298 (2004)
2. Gao, X., Xiao, B., Tao, D., Li, X.: A survey of graph edit distance. Pattern Analysis and Applications 13(1), 113–129 (2010)
3. Riesen, K., Bunke, H.: Graph Classification and Clustering Based on Vector Space Embedding. World Scientific, Singapore (2010)
4. Bunke, H., Shearer, K.: A graph distance metric based on the maximal common subgraph. Pattern Recognition Letters 19(3), 13–25 (1998)
5. Bunke, H., Allerman, G.: Inexact graph matching for structural pattern recognition. Pattern Recognition Letters 1, 245–253 (1983)
6. Fernandez, M.L., Valiente, G.: A graph distance metric combining maximum common subgraph and minimum common supergraph. Pattern Recognition Letter 22(6-7), 753–758 (2001)
7. Helma, C., King, R., Kramer, S., Srinivasan, A.: The Predictive Toxicology Challenge 2000-2001. Bioinformatics 17, 107–108 (2001)
8. Helma, C., Kramer, T., Kramer, S., De Raedt, L.: Data Mining and Machine Learning Techniques for the Identification of Mutagenicity Inducing Substructures and Structure-Activity Relationship of Noncongeneric Compounds. Journal of Chemical Information and Computer Sciences 44(4), 1402–1411 (2004)
9. Kashima, H., Tsuda, K., Inokuchi, A.: Marginalized Kernels Between Labeled Graphs. In: Proceedings of the 20th International Conference on Machine Learning, pp. 321–328. AAAI Press, Menlo Park (2003)
10. Kramer, S., De Raedt, L.: Feature construction with version spaces for biochemical application. In: Proceeding of the 18th International Conference on Machine Learning, pp. 258–265 (2001)
11. Lewis, D.: Naive (Bayes) at Forty: The Independence Assumption in Information Retrieval. In: Proceedings of the 10th European Conference on Machine Learning, vol. (1398), pp. 4–15 (1998)
12. Schölkopf, B., Smola, A.J.: Learning with Kernels: Support Vector Machines, Regularization, Optimization, and Beyond. MIT Press, Cambridge (2001)
13. Srinivasan, A., Muggleton, S., King, R.D., Sternberg, M.: Theories for mutagenicity: a study of first-order and feature based induction. Artificial Intelligence 85, 277–299 (1996)
14. Swamidass, S.J., Chen, J., Bruand, J., Phung, P., Ralaivola, L., Baldi, P.: Kernels for small molecules and the prediction of mutagenicity, toxicity and anti-cancer activity. Bioinformatics 21, 359–368 (2005)

A Hypergraph Reduction Algorithm for Joint Segmentation and Classification of Satellite Image Content*

Alain Bretto[1,2], Aurélien Ducournau[3], and Soufiane Rital[2]

[1] GREYC, Bd Marechal Juin BP 5186, Caen, France
[2] Telecom ParisTech, TSI, 46, 46 rue Barrault, Paris, France
[3] ENISE-DIPI, 74 rue des Aciéries, Saint-Etienne, France

Abstract. In this paper, we introduce a novel hypergraph reduction algorithm, and we evaluate it in an innovative method for joint segmentation and classification of satellite image content. It operates in 3 steps. First, we compute an Image Neighborhood Hypergraph representation (INH). Second, we reduce the INH model and we exploit a morphism from INH to Reduced INH (RINH) to generate superpixels. Then, we perform a superpixels supervised classification according to their features. Our approach is very fast and can deal with great sized images. Its reliability has been tested on several satellite images with comparison to single pixelwise classification.

Keywords: Hypergraph, Superpixel, Hypergraph Reduction, Satellite Image, Supervised Classification.

1 Introduction

Graph/Hypergraph based methods have played an important role in Computer Vision and Pattern Recognition due to their ability to represent relational patterns [14]. In many situations the graph representation is incomplete, as only binary relations between nodes can be represented through graph edges. An extension is provided by hypergraphs, where each edge is a subset of the set of nodes [4]. Hence higher-order relations between nodes can be directly modeled in a hypergraph, by the means of hyperedges. A large body of theoretical work on hypergraphs has been published [4]. However, not many applications in the field of satellite image analysis and pattern recognition involving hypergraphs have been reported. Refs. [1,6] list a number of applications of hypergraphs in low and high levels of image processing, [2] lists a number of solutions using hypergraph in partitioning large masses of data, in VLSI design [9], parallel scientific computing, software engineering, database design, and [15] describes a 3-D object recognition system using hypergraphs. In general, all contributions using hypergraph are focused on hypergraph representation and/or the use of hypergraph

---

* This work has been supported by the COC collaboration between CNES/DLR/ TéléCOM-ParisTech under the CNES R-S10/OT-0004-052 R&D action.

I. Bloch and R.M. Cesar, Jr. (Eds.): CIARP 2010, LNCS 6419, pp. 38–45, 2010.

properties. The drawbacks of most of these approaches are twofold: the loss of information and the computational complexity resulting respectively on how a hypergraph representation is computed (due to the hypergraph-to-graph conversion) and how the hypergraph properties are exploited (without a reduction step). We notice in particular that not much attention has been payed to the problem of reduction of hypergraphs. Having introduced a hypergraph theory in comptuer vision domain, we have clearly identified a new strategy for supervised satellite image segmentation. In this paper, we consider the two problems cited above, and we propose a new strategy for supervised joint segmentation and classification of satellite image content. The basic idea of the proposed algorithm can be described as follows: we first build a hypergraph representation of a digital image. Then, we reduce this representation using a new hypergraph reduction algorithm. Next, we exploit a morphism from the original hypergraph to the reduced one to estimate image structure through dense region segmentation, which provides superpixels. Finally, we perform supervised classification of each superpixel according to its features. The latter step is performed by the Support Vector Machine (SVM) learning classifier [3]. The organization of this paper is as follows: in section 2, the new hypergraph reduction algorithm is introduced. The supervised image classification framework is illustrated in section 3. The experimental results concerning a set of satellite images demonstrating the validity of our proposed approach appear in section 4. Finally, conclusions and perspectives are given in section 5.

2   Hypergraph Reduction and Properties

A *hypergraph* on a finite set V is a family $(e_i)_{i \in I}$, $I = \{1, 2, \ldots, l\}, (l \geq 1)$ of non-empty subsets of V called hyperedges with: $\bigcup_{i \in I} e_i = V$, we will denote it by: $H = (V; (e_i)_{i \in I})$. A *simple hypergraph* is a hypergraph $H = (V; E = (e_i)_{i \in I})$ such that: $e_i \subset e_j \implies i = j$. A hypergraph is without *repeated hyperedge* if the family $(e_i)_{i \in I}$ is a set. In the sequel, we will consider that any hypergraph is without repeated hyperedge. Let $H_1 = (V_1; E_1)$ and $H_2 = (V_2; E_2)$ be two hypergraphs. A map f from V_1 to V_2 is a *morphism* or *homomorphism* if it verifies the following properties: $e_1 \in E_1 \implies f(e_1) = \{f(x), x \in e_1\} \subset e_2 \in E_2$.

Numerous approaches have been adopted for hypergraph reduction [9,2]. However, many of these algorithms do not take advantage of the hypergraph properties. After hypergraph-to-graph conversion, they exploit only graph algorithms. The full proposed hypergraph reduction algorithm is described in Algorithms 1,2, for a hypergraph $H = (V, E)$ where E is ordered. The basic idea of the proposed algorithm can be summarized as follows : we first compute the set of intersecting hyperedges W of H. For each hyperedge $e_i \in E$, we generate W_{e_i} as the set of hyperedges intersecting with e_i. $W = \cup_{\forall e_i \in E}\{W_{e_i}\}$ is the set of intersecting hyperedges. Then, from W we keep only a subset B of W that covers the hypergraph H. From B, we generate the Reduced Hypergraph $RH = (RV, RE)$. All W_{e_i} of B stand for the vertices of RH. From RH and using the W_{e_i}, we generate RE.

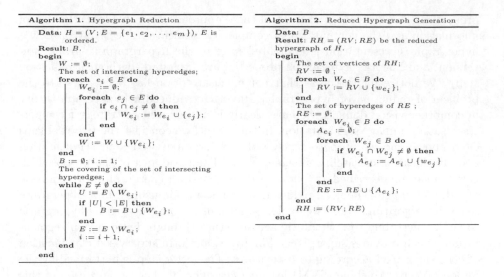

Algorithm 1. Hypergraph Reduction

Data: $H = (V; E = \{e_1, e_2, \ldots, e_m\})$, E is ordered.
Result: B.
begin
  $W := \emptyset$;
  The set of intersecting hyperedges;
  foreach $e_i \in E$ do
    $W_{e_i} := \emptyset$;
    foreach $e_j \in E$ do
      if $e_i \cap e_j \neq \emptyset$ then
        $W_{e_i} := W_{e_i} \cup \{e_j\}$;
      end
    end
    $W := W \cup \{W_{e_i}\}$;
  end
  $B := \emptyset$; $i := 1$;
  The covering of the set of intersecting hyperedges;
  while $E \neq \emptyset$ do
    $U := E \setminus W_{e_i}$;
    if $|U| < |E|$ then
      $B := B \cup \{W_{e_i}\}$;
    end
    $E := E \setminus W_{e_i}$;
    $i := i + 1$;
  end
end

Algorithm 2. Reduced Hypergraph Generation

Data: B
Result: $RH = (RV; RE)$ be the reduced hypergraph of H.
begin
  The set of vertices of RH;
  $RV := \emptyset$;
  foreach $W_{e_i} \in B$ do
    $RV := RV \cup \{w_{e_i}\}$;
  end
  The set of hyperedges of RE ;
  $RE := \emptyset$;
  foreach $W_{e_i} \in B$ do
    $A_{e_i} := \emptyset$;
    foreach $W_{e_j} \in B$ do
      if $W_{e_i} \cap W_{e_j} \neq \emptyset$ then
        $A_{e_i} := A_{e_i} \cup \{w_{e_j}\}$
      end
    end
    $RE := RE \cup \{A_{e_i}\}$;
  end
  $RH := (RV; RE)$
end

Proposition 1. *The algorithms 1,2 create a neighborhood hypergraph; its complexity is in $O(m^2)$, where m is the cardinality of hyperedge set of the hypergraph.*

Proof. We can build a graph Γ in the following way: (1) the set of vertices is RV. (2) Let $w_{e_i}, w_{e_j} \in RV$, we put an edge between w_{e_i} and w_{e_j} iff $W_{e_i} \cap W_{e_j} \neq \emptyset$, (excepted when $i = j$). So we obtain a graph $\Gamma = (RV; A)$.
Let A_{e_i} be a hyperedge of RH, $A_{e_i} = \{w_{e_i}; w_{e_j}$, such that $W_{e_i} \cap W_{e_j} \neq \emptyset\}$. Consequently $A_{e_i} = \{w_{e_i}\} \cup \Gamma(w_{e_i})$.
Now let $w_{e_i} \in RV$; $w_{e_j} \in \Gamma(w_{e_i}) \Longleftrightarrow W_{e_i} \cap W_{e_j} \neq \emptyset \Longleftrightarrow \{w_{e_i}\} \cup \Gamma(w_{e_i}) = A_{e_i}$.
It is easy to see that the complexity of our algorithm is in $O(m^2)$. $\qquad\square$

Because E is ordered B is. This order will be called Reduction Algorithm Order, (RAO). This one is linear: $e_i \leq e_j \Longleftrightarrow W_{e_i} \leq_{RAO} W_{e_j}$. So $(B; \leq_{RAO})$ is a poset totally ordered. We will denote by $V(W_{e_i}) = \bigcup_{e_j \in W_{e_i}} \{x; x \in e_j\}$.

Proposition 2. *Let $H = (V; E)$ and $RH = (RV; RE)$ be its reduction, then there is a morphism from H to RH.*

Proof. Let h be defined by:

$$h : V \longrightarrow B$$
$$x_i \longmapsto \min_{j \in \{1,2,\ldots|B|\}} \{W_{e_j}, x_i \in V(W_{e_j})\}$$

Because B is linearly ordered and H is without repeated hyperedge h is a map. There is a bijection g from B onto RV, consequently $f = g \circ h$ is a map from V to RV. Let $e_i \in E$ and $x_j \in e_i$; hence $f(x_j) = \min_{l \in \{1,2,\ldots|B|\}} \{W_{e_k}, x_j \in V(W_{e_k})\} = W_{e_l}$. Because $x_j \in V(W_{e_t})$ we have $e_i \in W_{e_t}$. Let $x_q \in e_i$, $x_j \neq x_q$; $f(x_q) = \min_{l \in \{1,2,\ldots|B|\}} \{W_{e_k}, x_j \in V(W_{e_k})\} = W_{e_l}$. Because $x_q \in V(W_{e_l})$, $e_i \in W_{e_l}$. Consequently $W_{e_t} \cap W_{e_l} \neq \emptyset$ and $W_{e_t}, W_{e_l} \in A_{e_h}$. By reasoning in the same way for all vertices of e_i we can show that $f(e_i) = \{f(x_i), x_i \in e_i\} \subset A_{e_h}$.
$\qquad\square$

3   Application: Joint Segmentation and Superpixels Classification

In the current section we will discuss possible use of hypergraph reduction algorithm in image analysis domain and more particularly in a supervised image content classification. The proposed application can be summarized as follows: (i) from image we compute the INH representation,(ii) we reduce the INH representation and we obtain the RINH hypergraph, (iii) we generate a set of superpixels from RINH using Proposition 2, (iv) generate a set of features for each superpixel and classify them using a SVM framework.

- **From Image to INH model.** The image will be represented by $I : V \subseteq \mathbb{Z}^2 \longrightarrow C \subseteq \mathbb{Z}^n$. Vertices of V are called pixels, elements of C are called colors. A distance d on V defines a grid (a connected, regular graph, without both loop and multi-edge). Let d' be a distance on C, we have a neighborhood relation on a satellite image defined for each pixel v on the grid by: $\Gamma_{\alpha,\beta}(v) = \{v \neq v' \in V, d'(I(v), I(v')) \leq \alpha$ and $d(v, v') \leq \beta\}$. To each satellite image I we associate a hypergraph called *Image Neighborhood Hypergraph* (INH) [13]:

$$H_{\alpha,\beta}(I) = (V, E_{\alpha,\beta}(v)), \quad and \quad E_{\alpha,\beta}(v) = (\{v\} \cup \Gamma_{\alpha,\beta}(v))_{v \in V}. \qquad (1)$$

- **Superpixelization.** Numerous approaches have been adopted for superpixels generation [12,7,8,10]. Our hypergraph reduction algorithm is applied to the resulting INH. The algorithm can be further applied to the so-obtained reduced hypergraph (RINH), and so on. The iterations are stopped when the ratio between the size of two successive coarser hypergraphs, i.e. $\frac{|H|}{|RH|}$, falls under a fixed real value, that we refer as the *reduction factor r*.

  In order to get a proper over-segmentation of the image, each pixel must be assigned to a single superpixel. However, the vertices in RINH represents a sets of hyperedges of the original hypergraph. So a pixel v of the original image can be shared by multiple vertices of the RINH. Each element of RV is a superpixel. Thanks to the morphism described in Proposition 2, we can associate to each v a single superpixel $w_{e_i} \in RV$. We can remark that the morphism f construct in Proposition 2 is not a surjection. Hence, only a subset S of RV is used to represent the set of superpixels.

- **Supervised Classification.** Given a set $S = \{w_{e_1}, \ldots, w_{e_n}\}$ of superpixels, we can associate to each w_{e_i} a feature vector $\mathbf{F}(w_{e_i})$. We consider the problem of satellite image content classification as a machine learning problem: we suppose that the labels of some of the superpixels of S are known, i.e. they have been previously hand-labeled. The objective is then to predict the labels of the remaining superpixels with the information provided by the hand-labeled superpixels features, leading to a supervised content classification. For this purpose, a SVM classifier [3] has been trained by the feature vectors of the hand-labeled superpixels, and the remaining superpixels are considered as the test set.

Table 1. Number of iterations, number of remaining vertices, elapsed time and SED values for proposed reduction approach, and algorithms from [9], namely First Choice (FC), Hyperedge Coarsening (HC), Modified Hyperedge Coarsening (MHC), Edge Coarsening (EC)

	Nb iter.	k	Time (s)	SED		Nb iter.	k	Time (s)	SED
Proposed	**2.5**	**33562**	**4.34**	**103721**	MHC	11.25	35144	14.12	115211
FC	4.5	33625	8.91	110540	EC	10.75	33754	25.12	143529
HC	12	35163	14.06	116358					

4   Experimental Results

We shall present a set of experiments in order to assess the performance of our hypergraph reduction algorithm and joint segmentation and pixelwise classification approach. All of the experiments take place under a machine with the following characteristics: Intel Xeon 2.67 GHz, 4 GB RAM, and all reported run-times are displayed in seconds. In all of our experiments, the RAO is naturally given by the order of the building of the hyperedges (the same as the browsing order of the image pixels. The hypergraph reduction algorithm is compared to other hypergraph and graph based coarsening algorithms [9] according to the total number of iterations of the algorithms, the computation time and the *Sum of External Degrees*(SED), as defined in [13]. Low values of SED indicate that the quality of the partitioning is good for a given hypergraph, and so that in our case the reduction algorithm has accurately maintained the properties of the original hypergraph. The color distance d' used in all our experiments is computed by $d'(I(v), I(v')) = |I(v) - I(v')|$ in panchromatic band, where $I(v)$ denotes the gray level of pixel v. The INH has been generated with four different values of α (5, 10, 15 and 20) and with $\beta = 1$ for three Quickbird XSP satellite images[1] (resolution $2.4m$) of size 800×800 pixels. The table 1 presents the average values of the resulting number k of vertices in the reduced hypergraph, the number of iterations, the elapsed time and the SED value for each of the five considered approaches. The number k of resulting vertices is directly controlled by the α parameter, where lower values indicate a sparser INH representation, and then a bigger k after some iterations. In order to obtain a comparable k over all the reductions of a same SINH, the reduction factor r has been fixed to 1.2 for FC and proposed approach, and 1.05 for the other algorithms. From these results, we can see that the proposed reduction algorithm preserves well the hypergraph structure, since it displays the lowest average SED value. In addition, our algorithm is at least about 2 times faster than the other approaches, as it needs a lower number of iterations to sufficiently reduce the hypergraph.

We now compare the reliability of the image superpixels generation derived from our hypergraph reduction algorithm. A set of 10 images from the Berkeley Segmentation Database (BSDB) [11] has been used. The performance of the superpixels approaches are evaluated according to the under-segmentation error

---

[1] Image ©DigitalGlobe, 2003.

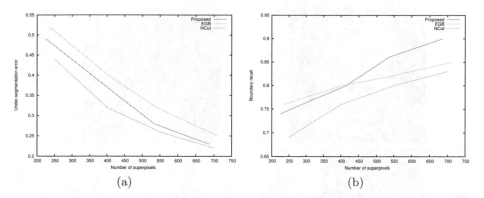

Fig. 1. (a) Under-segmentation error and (b) boundary recall for proposed, EBG and NCut frameworks as a function of the number of superpixels

and boundary recall [10] compared to ground truth segmentations available in the BSDB. Figure 1 displays the under-segmentation error and boundary recall as a function of the superpixels density for three considered algorithm: proposed, efficient graph-based (EGB) algorithm [7][2], and multiscale NCut framework [5][3]. All of these algorithms have been parametrized to get comparable numbers of superpixels. These results shows that our approach outperforms EGB algorithm in terms of under-segmentation error (since we produce superpixels of roughly regular size), and the NCut framework in terms of boundary recall. This last result highlights particularly the advantages of a hypergraph-based representation, since the NCut method finds quasi-optimal solutions of a graph-based partitioning problem. In addition, our algorithm becomes better when the number of superpixels increase, because lower values of α have been used in this case, and consequently more details of the image have been captured in the hypergraph model. In terms of computation time, our algorithm takes in general between 2 and 3 seconds to generate the superpixels (less than 2 seconds for EGB), and outperforms the NCut framework, since the last takes between 3 and 25 minutes (it depends of the number of superpixels) for images of size 321×481 pixels.

Figure 2 presents the results of supervised classification using the proposed framework. Classification objective has been set to 5 classes (see fig. 2.b where a few pixel samples have been hand-labeled). Results from fig. 2.c have been obtained with the SVM classification of the superpixels displayed in fig. 2.a. The feature vector of each superpixel consists of the normalized RGB histogram computed over the superpixel patch. Fig. 2.d presents the result of a simple pixelwise SVM classification, where the feature vector of each pixel is also a normalized RGB histogram, computed over a 5×5 window around the pixel. Standard parameters of the libSVM package[4] have been used in our experiments. These

---

[2] http://people.cs.uchicago.edu/~pff/segment/
[3] http://www.seas.upenn.edu/~timothee/software/ncut_multiscale/ncut_multiscale.html
[4] http://www.csie.ntu.edu.tw/~cjlin/libsvm/

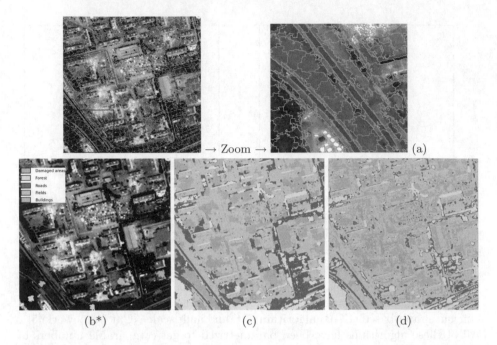

Fig. 2. (a) Superpixels map ($\alpha = 5$, $\beta = 1$, $r = 1.2$, $k = 7965$) of a Quickbird XSP satellite image from the Boumerdès database (2003-06-13). (b) Training data. Results of classification with (c) superpixels features, (d) pixels features. *Dataset Boumerdès ©SERTIT, 2009 ; distribution CNES.

results show that we get approximatively the same classification with a pixelwise and a superpixelwise classification. All the pixels in a same superpixel share a color homogeneity, so it is relevant to classify this set of pixels as a same entity. We should observe that without superpixelization, the framework is more prone to misclassifications (in particular with the class "Field" for example), because superpixels allow us to compute features over homogeneous patches, reducing the misclassification errors. Furthermore, it drastically reduces the amount of data to consider (from 640000 pixels to only 7965 superpixels in our example), and then makes the SVM classifier more computationally efficient: for a classification of all the pixels, the total time is up to 110 seconds in our experiments and depends highly on the feature vectors dimensionality. As a comparison, a superpixels classification takes less than 0.01 seconds when a superpixel map is available. In addition, the superpixels generation takes in general less than 5 seconds, and can be operated as a preprocessing step only once. Finally, we should observe that some of the classes are ambiguous (particularly the class "Buildings" for instance), due to the use of only color features.

5   Conclusions and Perspectives

In this paper, we proposed a hypergraph reduction algorithm and we evaluate it in a supervised superpixelwise image classification. The effectiveness of the proposed method was demonstrated with experimental results using various generic and satellite images. Our approach is an open system and several solutions can be made to improve the proposed framework such as reducing the hypergraph $H(V, E)$ without imposing E to be ordered. In future work, we will add more information in superpixels and more particularly neighborhood information, as well as other visual features like shape or texture information.

References

1. Agarwal, S., Lim, J., Zelnik-Manor, L., Perona, P., Kriegman, D., Belongie, S.: Beyond pairwise clustering. In: CVPR 2005, vol. 2, pp. 838–845 (June 2005)
2. Aykanat, C., Cambazoglu, B.B., Uçar, B.: Multi-level direct k-way hypergraph partitioning with multiple constraints and fixed vertices. J. Parallel Distrib. Comput. 68(5), 609–625 (2008)
3. Boser, B.E., Guyon, I.M., Vapnik, V.N.: A training algorithm for optimal margin classifiers. In: COLT 1992, pp. 144–152. ACM, New York (1992)
4. Bretto, A.: Introduction to Hypergraph Theory and its Applications to Image Processing. Mongraphy in: Advances in Imaging and Electron Physics, vol. 131, pp. 1–64. Academic Press, London (2004)
5. Cour, T., Benezit, F., Shi, J.: Spectral segmentation with multiscale graph decomposition. In: CVPR, vol. 2, pp. 1124–1131 (June 2005)
6. Ding, L., Yilmaz, A.: Interactive image segmentation using probabilistic hypergraphs. Pattern Recognition 43(5), 1863–1873 (2010)
7. Felzenszwalb, P.F., Huttenlocher, D.P.: Efficient graph-based image segmentation. Intl. Journal of Computer Vision 59(2), 167–181 (2004)
8. Hanbury, A.: How do superpixels affect image segmentation? In: Ruiz-Shulcloper, J., Kropatsch, W.G. (eds.) CIARP 2008. LNCS, vol. 5197, pp. 178–186. Springer, Heidelberg (2008)
9. Karypis, G., Aggarwal, R., Kumar, V., Shekhar, S.: Multilevel hypergraph partitioning: applications in vlsi domain. IEEE Trans. Very Large Scale Integr. Syst. 7(1), 69–79 (1999)
10. Levinshtein, A., Stere, A., Kutulakos, K.N., Fleet, D.J., Dickinson, S.J., Siddiqi, K.: Turbopixels: Fast superpixels using geometric flows. IEEE Trans. Pattern Anal. Mach. Intell. 31(12), 2290–2297 (2009)
11. Martin, D., Fowlkes, C., Tal, D., Malik, J.: A database of human segmented natural images and its application to evaluating segmentation algorithms and measuring ecological statistics. In: ICCV, vol. 2, pp. 416–423 (July 2001)
12. Ren, X., Malik, J.: Learning a classification model for segmentation. In: ICCV, pp. 10–17 (2003)
13. Rital, S.: Hypergraph cuts & unsupervised representation for image segmentation. Fundamenta Informaticae Journal 96(1-2), 153–179 (2009)
14. Torsello, A., Escolano, F., Brun, L. (eds.): GbRPR 2009. LNCS, vol. 5534, pp. 42–51. Springer, Heidelberg (2009)
15. Wong, A.K.C., Lu, S.W., Rioux, M.: Recognition and shape synthesis of 3-d objects based on attributed hypergraphs. IEEE Trans. Pattern Anal. Mach. Intell. 11(3), 279–290 (1989)

A Static Video Summarization Method Based on Hierarchical Clustering

Silvio Jamil F. Guimarães and Willer Gomes

Audio-Visual Information Processing Laboratory (VIPLAB)
Institute of Informatics - Pontifícia Universidade Católica de Minas Gerais
Belo Horizonte, MG, Brazil
{sjamil,willer}@pucminas.br
http://www.viplab.inf.pucminas.br

Abstract. Video summarization is a simplification of video content for compacting the video information. The video summarization problem can be transformed to a clustering problem, in which some frames are selected to saliently represent the video content. In this work, we use a graph-theoretic divisive clustering algorithm based on construction of a minimum spanning tree to select video frames without segmenting the video into shots or scenes. Experimental results provides a visually comparison between the new approach and other popular algorithms from the literature, showing that the new algorithm is robust and efficient.

Keywords: Video summarization, Minimum spanning tree, Video analysis.

1 Introduction

The increasing number of video files has become the task of searching a specific content very expensive, because it is necessary to index the video information. Usually, there are two approaches to cope with the index problem: (i) manual notation; and (ii) automatic notation. The former is expensive and subjective, since it depends on the experts to perfom this notation. The second one is objective and is directly related to the visual contents, however it depends on the features which are used to index. The cost to find a specific content related to a video depends on the size of the index, thus instead of considering all video content, we summarize it in order to reduce the search space. In literature, there are many approaches to simplify the video content [8,9,11,7,1,6,3,2]. Thus, video summarization is a simplification of video content for compacting the video information, also the feature or similarity measure used to this simplification depends on the application. The video summarization problem can be transformed to a clustering problem, in which some frames are selected to saliently represent the video content, as illustrated in Fig. 1. In [1] was proposed an approach to cope with the video summarization problem in which the clustering is achieved by a k-means algorithm, but it is necessary to know a priori the number of clusters. In [2] was proposed the use of graph-theoretic FCM algorithm for video summarization, however the graph creation is directly related to number of centers. In [6] it was used a Delaunay triangulation to automatically identify the frame clusters, however this approach is expensive and produces very compressed summaries. VISTO [3] is based on low-level video frames color

I. Bloch and R.M. Cesar, Jr. (Eds.): CIARP 2010, LNCS 6419, pp. 46–54, 2010.

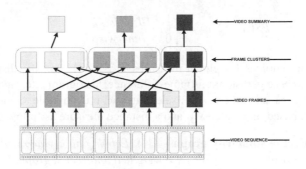

Fig. 1. Steps for video summarization (adapted from [6])

feature extraction and on a modification of furtherest point-first algorithm to cluster the frames. This approach is fast but the summaries is big.

In this work, we use a graph-theoretic divisive clustering algorithm based on construction of a Minimum Spanning Tree (MST) to select video frames without segmenting the video into shots or scenes, i.e., our approach eliminates pre-processing steps. It is important to note that according to [4] the MST approach for clustering is hierarchical, and thanks to this property, it is easy to compute a video summary regarding the specified number of keyframes.

The paper is organized as follows. Section 2 describes the clustering problem using minimum spanning tree and, also, it is defined many concepts used in our work. Section 3 describes our methodology to solve the video summarization problem. Section 4 describes the performed experiments together to a comparative analysis between our approach and the others methods. Finally, we give some conclusions in Section 5.

2   Clustering by Minimum Spanning Tree Approach

Let $\mathbb{A} \subset \mathbb{N}^2$, $\mathbb{A} = \{0, \ldots, H - 1\} \times \{0, \ldots, W - 1\}$, where H and W are the width and height of each frame, respectively, and, $\mathbb{T} \subset \mathbb{N}$, $\mathbb{T} = \{0, \ldots, N - 1\}$, in which N is number of frames of a video.

Definition 1 (Frame). *A frame f is a function from $\mathbb{A}$ to $\mathbb{Z}$, where for each spatial position (x, y) in $\mathbb{A}$, $f(x, y)$ represents the color value at pixel location (x, y).*

Definition 2 (Video). *A video V_N, in domain $\mathbb{A} \times \mathbb{T}$, can be seen as a sequence of frames f. It can be described by*

$$V_N = (f)_{t \in \mathbb{T}} \tag{1}$$

where N is the number of frames contained in the video.

Definition 3 (Frame similarity). *Let f_{t_1} and f_{t_2} be two video frames at locations t_1 and t_2, respectively. Two frames are similar if a distance measure $\mathcal{D}(f_{t_1}, f_{t_2})$ between them is smaller than a specified threshold (δ). The frame similarity is defined as*

$$FS(f_{t_1}, f_{t_2}, \delta) = \begin{cases} 1, & \text{if } \mathcal{D}(f_{t_1}, f_{t_2}) \leq \delta \\ 0, & \text{otherwise} \end{cases} \quad (2)$$

There are several choices for global measures $\mathcal{D}(f_{t_1}, f_{t_2})$, i.e., the distance measure between two frames, e.g. histogram/frame difference, histogram intersection, difference of histograms means, and others. After selecting one, it is possible to construct a frame similarity graph based on a video V_N and a distance measure as follows.

Definition 4 (Frame similarity graph – G^δ). *Let V_N be a video with N frames. A frame similarity graph $G^\delta = (N, E^\delta)$ is a weighted undirected graph. Each node $v_{t_1} \in N$ represents a frame $f_{t_1} \in V_N$. There is an edge $e \in E^\delta$ with weight $\mathcal{D}(f_{t_1}, f_{t_2})$ between two nodes v_{t_1} and v_{t_2} if frame similarity of associated frames is equal to 1:*

$$E^\delta = \{ (v_{t_1}, v_{t_2}, \mathcal{D}(f_{t_1}, f_{t_2})) \mid v_{t_1} \in N, v_{t_2} \in N,$$
$$FS(f_{t_1}, f_{t_2}, \delta) = 1\} \quad (3)$$

Fig. 2(a) illustrates a frame similarity graph of a real video in which only the frames 1, 501, 1001, 1501, 2001, 2501 and 3001 are sampled. The similarity measure used is the histogram intersection of HSV color space and is in the range $[0, 100]$.

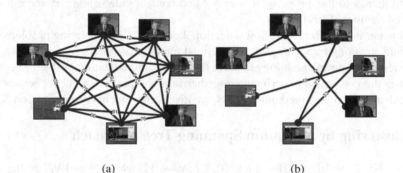

(a)   (b)

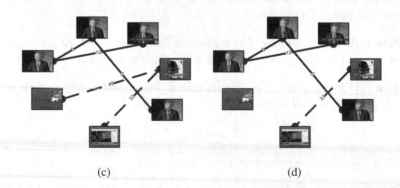

(c)   (d)

Fig. 2. Examples of video summarization. (a) frame similarity graph; (b) minimum spanning tree of frames; (c) deleting edge with weight equals to 72; (d) deleting edge with weight equals to 49.

In order to perform the video summarization, without considering a video partitioning (or segmentation) step, we propose the use of a divisive clustering algorithm. According to [4], the best-known graph-theoretic divisive clustering algorithm is based on construction of the minimum spanning tree of the data [10]. In this work, we define the minimum spanning tree of frames as a graph structure that preserves the video content and the relationship between all video scenes.

Definition 5 (Minimum spanning tree of frames - $f\mathrm{MST}_{G^\delta}$). *Let $G^\delta = (N, E^\delta)$ be a frame similarity graph. The minimum spanning tree of frames $f\mathrm{MST}_{G^\delta} = (N, E_1^\delta)$ is a subgraph of G^δ that minimizes the sum of weights of the edges E^δ.*

According to [5], a k-clustering divides the elements into k non-empty groups, in which the insertion of an element into a group depends on distance measure between this element and the elements already in the group. In order to compute the video summarization a k-clustering divides the video sequence into k video scenes, and consequently, it is necessary to eliminate $k - 1$ edges from the MST. To follow, the ordered edge sequence and the value transform are defined in order to simplify the frame clustering algorithm.

Definition 6 (Ordered edge sequence – $S^{E_1^\delta}$). *Let $f\mathrm{MST}_{G^\delta}$ be the minimum spanning tree of frames. Let $E_1^\delta = \{e = (a, b, c)\}$ be the collection of weight edges of $f\mathrm{MST}_{G^\delta}$. Let $S_i^{E_1^\delta}$ be the i-th edge $e_i = (a_i, b_i, c_i) \in E_1^\delta$ between two frames a_i and b_i with weight c_i. The ordered edge sequence $(S^{E_1^\delta})$ with respect to the weight is define by $S^{E_1^\delta} = (S_i^{E_1^\delta})_{i \in [1,N]}$ in which $S_i^{E_1^\delta} \leq S_{i+1}^{E_1^\delta}$ if $c_i \leq c_{i+1}$.*

Definition 7 (Value transform – $T(\Delta)$). *Let $f\mathrm{MST}_{G^\delta}$ be the minimum spanning tree of frames. Let $S^{E_1^\delta}$ be the ordered edge sequence of the $f\mathrm{MST}_{G^\delta}$. The value transform $T(\Delta)$ is define by*

$$T(\Delta) = \{||S^{E_1^\delta}|| - i + 2 \mid w(S_{i-1}^{E_1^\delta}) < \Delta \text{ and}$$
$$w(S_{i+1}^{E_1^\delta}) \geq \Delta\} \tag{4}$$

in which $w(S_i^{E_1^\delta})$ means the weight of the edge $S_i^{E_1^\delta}$.

If all values in the ordered edge sequence are different, $T(\max\{S^{E_1^\delta}\})$ is equal to 2. Thus, to compute a 2-clustering is necessary to eliminate the edge in $f\mathrm{MST}_{G^\delta}$ with the highest weight value. Finally, to identify the video scenes from minimum spanning tree of frames is necessary to delete some edges according to a specified criterium.

The edge deletion operation, when applied to a tree, produces two connected components. Here, each connected component is called *frame cluster*, as defined to follow. The process of edge deletion must be agreed to a specified criterium. In this work, we can use two different one: (i) deletion of largest weight edges; or (ii) deletion of edges with weight greater than or equal to a specified threshold. The former is useful when the number of clusters (defined before) is pre-determined. The second one can be considered when the minimum similarity measure between clusters is specified, and can be considered a special case of the first one when the weights are different. For example, the deletion in Fig. 2 of all edges with weight greater than or equal to a 49 produces the same result when we eliminate the 2 largest weight edges.

Definition 8 (Frame cluster – $C^{*,k}$). *Let $f\mathrm{MST}_{G^\delta}$ be a minimum spanning tree of frames. Let $C^{*,k}$ denote the k connected components $C_1^{*,k}, C_2^{*,k}, \cdots, C_k^{*,k}$ formed by deleting the $k-1$ largest edges of $f\mathrm{MST}_{G^\delta}$ in which $C_i^{*,k} = (N_i, E_i^\delta)$. $C^{*,k}$ is a k-clustering of max spacing.*

The number of clusters, and consequently, the number of video scenes is directly related to the number of edge deletion operations. Also, the process to compute the frame cluster is hierarchical in the sense that the edge deletion divides a cluster into two different groups. However, the saliency of a frame cluster component may depend on its size, since components with a small number of frames may represent noise. For example, a black frame or a flashlight frame are probably very dissimilar of all other frames and consequently, the adjacent edges will be the largest weight edges of the $f\mathrm{MST}_{G^\delta}$. The frame cluster produced by edge deletion will present a very small number of frames, and consequently, it could be ignored by our analysis.

3 Video Summarization Using Minimum Spanning Tree

In this work, we propose a new approach to video summarization in which the clustering of video frames are based on minimum spanning tree of frames. In Fig 3 is illustrated our method.

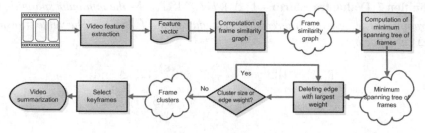

Fig. 3. Methodology for video summarization using minimum spanning tree

Thanks to the minimum spanning tree approach, our method eliminates the pre-processing to compute the number of clusters, and also, eliminates the video segmentation step. Thus, we compute the minimum spanning tree of frames from the frame similarity graph that was computed from the video sequence. Afterwards, we delete edges until stability. The concept of stability is related to two approaches: (i) number of desired clusters; and (ii) frame similarity in a cluster. While the former can be related to compress factor of the video summary, the second approach to stability establishes maximum (dis)similarity into a cluster. In both cases, only a keyframe for each cluster is selected. For now, the keyframe selection is done by the frame in the middle time of the cluster.

(a)

(b)

(c)

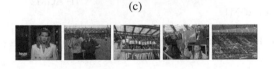

(d)

Fig. 4. Examples of video summarization applied to video "News.mpg" composed by 5 (five) shots: (a) T(35)-clustering; (b) 3-clustering; (c) T(34)-clustering; and (d) T(25)-clustering

Table 1. Experimental results compared to OpenVideo according to [6]

Method	Total Clips	Category 1 (Same Keyframes)	Category 2 (Fewer Keyframes)	Category 3 (More Keyframes)	Category 4 (Mismatched Keyframes)
AGM1	50	18	3	29	24
AGM2	50	28	3	19	3
Visto [3]	50	14	5	31	50
DT [6]	50	30	8	12	10
VSUMM1 [1]	50	20	3	27	5

To present some examples, in Fig. 4(a), Fig. 4(c) and Fig. 4(d) are illustrated the results of application of our method for $T(35) = 2$, $T(34) = 4$ and $T(25) = 5$. It is important to notice that the values 25, 34 and 35 in Fig. 4 represent three highest weight values in minimum spanning tree of frames, however there are 1, 2 and 1 edges with these weights, respectively. Thus, there exist two different options for computing a 3-clustering. The Fig. 4(b) illustrates a 3-clustering.

4   Experiments

In our experiments, we use some video extracted from the repository *Open Video*[1]. To visually compare our approach with others, we consider the dataset used in [3] composed by 50 videos in different genres (documentary, lectures, ephemeral, historical, educational). With respect to a comparative analysis, we consider a similar approach to [6] in which we compare the methods according to the summary size and also, the

---

[1] www.open-video.org

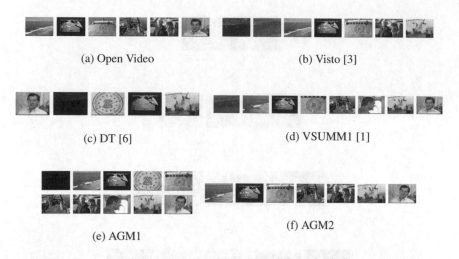

Fig. 5. Examples of static video summary (Video *Oceanfloor Legacy, segment 02*)

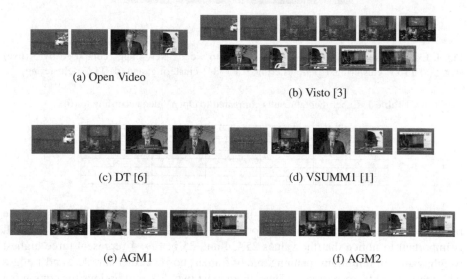

Fig. 6. Examples of static video summary (Video *Senses And Sensitivity, Introduct. to Lecture 2*)

number of mismatched frames, both related to OpenVideo summary. It is important to note that we consider the same approaches used in [1].

In order to illustrate the tuning of parameters for the proposed method, we consider two different sets of values (δ for clustering, α for connected component size and ϵ for sampling): (i) $\delta = 25$, $\alpha = 10$, $\epsilon = 1$; and (ii) $\delta = 25$, $\alpha = 10$, $\epsilon = 10$. Here, we consider a global measure in order to compute the similarity measure, we consider the histogram intersection from HSV color space, however for some applications, it is necessary to choice similarity measures that saliently represent the frame content like matching of interested points. To facilitate our description, AGM1 and AGM2 denote the proposed methods with the set of parameters described before, respectively. Also, to realize a visually comparative analysis, we consider the other methods: VSUMM [1], DT [6] and VISTO [3]. In Table 1 we divide our results in four categories (same keyframes, fewer keyframes, more keyframes, mismatched keyframes).

As can be seen, the VSUMM [1] and our approach (AGM2) present similar results. The Fig. 5 and Fig. 6 illustrate examples of video summaries computed by different methods. It is important to note the summaries are compared to the OpenVideo approach. The Fig. 5 illustrated a video summary with more keyframes for both, however the VSUMM computed a redundant frame. The Fig. 6 illustrated a video summary with more keyframes in which the quality of the summary is the same.

5   Conclusion and Further Works

In this work, we propose a divisive and hierarchical method to compute a static video summary without considering segmentation step. Our method is based on computation of MST of the frames. It is well-know that the algorithm to generate the MST is efficient and fast. The analysis of the video summary quality is subjective, however there is no redundancy and only the most salient scenes are represented. From our approach, it is possible to indicate the degree of desired compression. The proposed method try to eliminate the redundancy and non representative scenes, however the tunning of parameters influences the quality of video summary. We expect, in future work, improve the selection of keyframe and also, to automatically tune the parameters.

Acknowledgments

The authors are grateful to PUC Minas (Pontifícia Universidade Católica de Minas Gerais), MIC BH (Microsoft Innovation Center Belo Horizonte), CT-Info/MCT/CNPq (Project 551005/2007-6) and FAPEMIG (Project CEX PPM 126/08) for the financial support of this work.

References

1. de Avila Jr., S.E.F., da Luz Jr., A., de Araújo, A.A., Cord, M.: Vsumm: An approach for automatic video summarization and quantitative evaluation. In: SIBGRAPI 2008: Proceedings of the 2008 XXI Brazilian Symposium on Computer Graphics and Image Processing, pp. 103–110. IEEE Computer Society, Washington (2008)
2. Besiris, D., Fotopoulou, F., Economou, G., Fotopoulos, S.: Video summarization by a graph-theoretic fcm based algorithm. In: 15th International Conference on Systems, Signals and Image Processing, IWSSIP 2008, 25-28, pp. 511–514 (2008)
3. Furini, M., Geraci, F., Montangero, M., Pellegrini, M.: Visto: visual storyboard for web video browsing. In: Proceedings of the 6th ACM International Conference on Image and Video Retrieval, CIVR 2007, pp. 635–642. ACM, New York (2007)
4. Jain, A.K., Murty, M.N., Flynn, P.J.: Data clustering: A review. ACM Comput. Surv. 31(3), 264–323 (1999)
5. Kleinberg, J., Tardos, É.: Algorithm Design. Addison-Wesley, Reading (2006)

6. Mundur, P., Rao, Y., Yesha, Y.: Keyframe-based video summarization using delaunay clustering. Int. J. on Digital Libraries 6(2), 219–232 (2006)
7. Rui, Y., Huang, T.S., Mehrotra, S.: Browsing and retrieving video content in a unified framework. In: 1998 IEEE Second Workshop on Multimedia Signal Processing, 7-9, pp. 9–14 (1998)
8. Tan, Y.P., Lu, H.: Video scene clustering by graph partitioning. Electronics Letters 39(11), 841–842 (2003)
9. Yeung, M., Yeo, B.L.: Video visualization for compact presentation and fast browsing of pictorial content. IEEE Transactions on Circuits and Systems for Video Technology 7(5), 771–785 (1997)
10. Zahn, C.: Graph-theoretical methods for detecting and describing gestalt clusters. IEEE Transactions on Computers C-20(1), 68–86 (1971)
11. Zhu, S.H., Liu, Y.-C.: Automatic video partition for high-level search. IJCSES International Journal of Computer Sciences and Engineering Systems 2(3), 163–172 (2008)

Histopathological Image Classification Using Stain Component Features on a pLSA Model

Gloria Díaz and Eduardo Romero*

Bioingenium Research Group, National University of Colombia,
Bogotá, Colombia
{gmdiazc,edromero}@unal.edu.co

Abstract. Semantic annotation of microscopical field of views is one of the key problems in computer assistance of histopathological images. In this paper a new method for extracting patch descriptors is proposed and evaluated using a probabilistic latent semantic analysis (pLSA) classification model. The proposed approach is based on the analysis of the different dyes used to stain the histological sample. This analysis allows to find local regions that correspond to cells in the image, which are then described by the SIFT descriptors of the stain components. The proposed approach outperforms the conventional sampling and description strategies, proposed in the literature.

Keywords: Semantic annotation, Histopathological Images, Color decomposition, pLSA, SIFT descriptors.

1 Introduction

Computer-aided diagnosis (CAD) for histopathology images is an emerging research field, which has become popular because of the recent advances in capturing devices as well as in the increasing computational capacities that not only have facilitated digitization, storing and distribution of microscopic samples, but also has allowed the development of image analysis tools that support diagnosis, teaching and research processes [1]. In particular, computer aided image analysis can help pathologists to identify suspicious areas so that they can dedicate their analysis time to these areas, whereby their workload can be highly reduced and therefore the response delays of health systems.

One main challenge when developing histopathology CADs consists in building an effective model for extracting information that allows to determine the semantic meaning from the visual content of the image. This task has been twofold approached as a classification problem: either as classes assigned to the whole image, according to global descriptors, or as classes assigned to histological structures previously segmented [2]. In the former case, global descriptors are hardly able to extract relevant visual features from specific cytological components, a key factor

* This work was supported by the Colombian Administrative Department of Science and Technology (COLCIENCIAS).

I. Bloch and R.M. Cesar, Jr. (Eds.): CIARP 2010, LNCS 6419, pp. 55–62, 2010.

for the semantic description, while in the latter case the classification performance is straightforwardly related to the segmentation accuracy, a very difficult job when one considers the complexity of histopathological images.

Recently, patch-based representation schemes and probabilistic hidden models have shown excellent performance for unsupervised semantic description of images [3]. Specifically, the probabilistic latent semantic analysis (pLSA) [4], a generative model which tries to learn latent concepts or topics from a bag-of-features (BOF). Main challenges in such representations are extraction of the most discriminative patches and descriptors, which capture main statistical properties and therefore semantic categorization approaches can be improved. Caicedo et al. evaluated the BOF representation in histopathological images [5]. Interestingly, they found that this representation can be related to semantic concepts in histopathology images, but its performance is dependent on both the region selection and description.

In this paper a new method for extracting patch descriptors in histopathological images is proposed and evaluated on a pLSA classification model. This approach takes advantage of a specific image characteristic, obtained from histopathological slides, which are stained with Hematoxylin-Eosin. Hematoxylin stains cell nuclei in blue-purple, while Eosin stains cytoplasm and connective tissue in pink. These colors constitute the base upon which pathologists are able to distinguish cellular tissue components. Likewise, we used these properties for finding distinctive image markers that correspond to cell nuclei, and generate discriminative descriptors that amount to the stain absorbed by tissues.

2   Latent Topics Annotation Model

2.1   pLSA model

Probabilistic Latent Semantic Analysis (pLSA) is a generative model, which probabilistically describes how words, in a document, might be generated using latent variables [4]. This model assumes that a document d and a word w are conditionally independent given the unobserved topic z, by which each document d_i is a mixture of latent topics, a process modeled by a multinomial distribution $P(z|d_i)$, and each latent topic z_l is also modeled by an additional multinomial distribution $P(w|z_l)$. The process of generating the set of observations (w, d) can be described by the probabilistic model defined by eq. 1.

$$P(d_i, w_j) = P(d_i)P(w_j|d_i), \quad P(w_j|d_i) = \sum_{l=1}^{k} P(w_j|z_l)P(z_l|d_i) \qquad (1)$$

As the topic distribution is not an observed variable, the unobservable probability distribution $P(z_l|d_i)$ and $P(w_j|z_l)$ can be learned from the likelihood of the observed data given by the eq. 2.

$$L = \prod_{i=1}^{M} \prod_{j=1}^{N} P(w_i|d_j)^{n(w_i, d_j)} \qquad (2)$$

where N is the number of documents, M is the number of words in the vocabulary, $n(w_i, d_j)$ is the number of occurrences of a word w_i in document d_j and $P(w_i|d_j)$ is given by eq. 1. Best model parameters are found using the Expectation Maximization (EM) algorithm, which iteratively estimate the posterior probabilities for the latent variables $P(z_k|d_i, w_j)$ (expectation step) and optimize this estimation $P(w_j|z_k)$ and $P(z_k|d_i)$ (maximization step) until convergence.

The latent concept probabilities, from the observed words, are estimated for a new document d_{test}, using a partial version of the EM algorithm described previously, but the conditional probability distribution $P(w_j|z_k)$ is kept fixed i.e. this is not updated at each M-step.

2.2 Representing Images as Bag of Words

The pLSA model represents documents as a set of words. From an image analysis standpoint, the image semantic may be captured when the global scene is expressed in terms of its components. The Bag-of-Features representation aims to follow this principle when documents amount to whole images and words correspond to quantized local image descriptors named visual words [6]. The BoF is generated by selecting a set of local image regions, which are characterized in a feature space. Then, instances in the feature space are grouped using a conventional clustering algorithm (e.g. k-means), defining a fixed number of groups that corresponds to words in the visual vocabulary. K-clusters are finally used for representing the image by a histogram of visual words, resulting from assigning each local region to the nearest k-cluster center.

2.3 Image Annotation Based on the pLSA Model

Once the posterior probability distribution of concepts $P(z|d_i)$ is computed, image annotation can be twofold performed: 1)if images can be labeled with a unique concept, the number of latent concepts is set to the number of class labels, and the annotation process consists in finding the concept that has higher conditional probability $P(z|d_i)$. This case requires that image concepts are highly correlated, and that there exists only a single type of background, specific for each class label. 2)if image can not be uniquely labeled, the number of concepts can be different of the number of class labels, and the concept probability distribution is used as a feature vector (eq. 3) for training a discriminative classification model. In this work the latter approach was evaluated using the k-nn rule as classification model.

$$d_i = \{P(z_1|d_i), P(z_2|d_i), ..., P(z_k|d_i)\} \tag{3}$$

3 Local Region Description Based on the Staining Component Analysis

Histopathological concepts are mainly characterized by cells that are visually identified by their color, which result from the affinity of tissue components to particular dyes. Our aim was to find the most discriminative local regions for the classification task. For so doing, we propose to find the cell nuclei and describe the regions around them. The extraction of local regional descriptors consists in: color normalization, cell based local region detection and local region description of the staining components.

3.1 Color Normalization

The obserbed color at each pixel is proportional to the strength of a chemical reaction between a dye and the biological substances. Many factors such as environment illumination conditions, relative dye quantity or film inhomogeneities produced by the subsequent slide storage and handling, result in a high luminance and color variability, wich strongly affects the staining component based analysis. This problem was solved by applying the color normalization approach proposed by Reinhard et al. [7].

3.2 Local Region Selection

Decomposing the image in main stain factors. The main goal was to accurately separating the image into the colors that corresponded to the actual contribution of each stain (Hematoxylin-eosin). For doing so, it was assumed that each RGB color can be described as a linear combination of the two stain factors. Deconvolution process consisted on separating the two stain contributions as described in eq. 4, under the physical restriction that negative stain contribution were not possible. So, D and S were found using the non-negative matrix factorization method [8]. Images were converted to optical density (OD) values before than deconvolution process was applied.

$$\begin{bmatrix} R \\ G \\ B \end{bmatrix} = \begin{bmatrix} D1_1 & D2_1 \\ D1_2 & D2_2 \\ D1_3 & D2_3 \end{bmatrix} \begin{bmatrix} S_1 & S_2 \end{bmatrix}$$

where $D1$, $D2$ correspond to the two stain vectors, and S_1, S_2 indicate the stain contribution. Figure 1 show results from deconvolution process of selected images. First row, corresponds to input images, second row corresponds to the first stain component, which show the eosin dye contribution at each pixel. Finally, the hematoxylin dye contribution is drawn in the third row.

Extracting visual patches. Once the stain contribution was determined, the cell nuclei were detected on the Hematoxylin component using a simple Otsu threshold, followed by a morphological grey-scale opening filter using a 2×2 structuring element. On the other hand, the clumped cells were split as much as possible applying a morphological grey-scale closing filter on the segmented regions with areas larger than 100 pixels. Finally, circular patches were extracted around the centre of the detected nuclei, as shown in the four row of Figure 1.

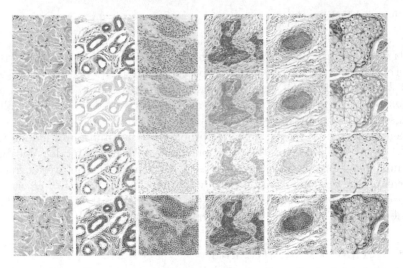

Fig. 1. Stain decomposition of selected samples from the training dataset

3.3   Local Region Description

Local patches were represented using the SIFT descriptor proposed by Lowe [9], which describes the texture of local regions, using edge orientation histograms. Traditionally, SIFT descriptor is computed under light intensity changes. However, color information is critical in histopathological image analysis. So, the use of color information inside the SIFT descriptors was evaluated. Images were decomposed in representative color spaces (rgSIFT, cSIFT and stnSIFT), and the SIFT descriptor for each color component was computed using a common parameter configuration i.e. 4×4 blocks and 8 orientations, resulting in a $128-$dimensional feature vector for each color component.

- **rgSIFT descriptor** that results from the concatenation of SIFT descriptors computed under r and g chromaticity components of the normalized RGB color space (eq. 4).

$$r_n = \frac{R}{R+G+B} \quad g_n = \frac{G}{R+G+B} \tag{4}$$

- **cSIFT descriptor**, corresponding to the concatenation of SIFT descriptors computed under the two components of the normalized opponent color space.

$$C_1 = \frac{C_1}{C_3}, C_2 = \frac{C_2}{C_3} \tag{5}$$

$$with, \quad C_1 = \frac{R-G}{\sqrt{2}}, \quad C_2 = \frac{R+G-2B}{\sqrt{6}}, \; C_3 = \frac{R+G+B}{\sqrt{3}}$$

- **stnSIFT descriptor**, corresponding to the concatenation of SIFT descriptors computed under the two stain channels obtained from the deconvolution process.

3.4   Model Evaluation

The proposed local region detection and description methods were compared with traditional grid based and sift point detection sampling strategies [10]. In the former case images were split in a regular grid of 21×21 pixels per block. In the latter, SIFT points were detected according to Lowe [9]. In both cases, circular local regions defined in a radius of 10 pixels were described as explained in the section 3.3 and processed by the pLSA model.

Images represented by the posterior probability distribution of hidden topics $P(z|d_i)$ were classified using the traditional $K - nn$ learning model. Vocabulary size, number of topics and k parameters of the learning model were evaluated. Performance of the classification tasks was quantified in terms of effectiveness measure F_β computed as $F_\beta = \frac{2*PR*RC}{PR+RC}$, with PR and RC the well known precision and recall performance measures.

4   Experiments and Results

4.1   Data Set

A total of 540 images acquired from histopathological skyn biopsies, stained with Hematoxylin-Eosin, were used. Each was annotated by experts, with one from nine possible class labels, resulting in 54 Pilosebaceous anexa (PA),71 Nodular, 62 basal cell carcinoma (NBC), 62 Micro-nodular basal cell carcinoma (MnBC), 51 Morpheiphorm basal cell carcinoma (MBC), 68 Epidermis (EP), 60 Sebaceous glands (SG), 51 Eccrine glands (EG), 58 Lymphocyte infiltration (LI) and 76 Collagen (CO) images. The dataset was randomly divided into training (80%) and test (30%) image sets. Images were cropped for containing only one of foreground concepts.

4.2   Results and Discussion

The first evaluation focused on the markers detection stage. Local regions extracted with the proposed approach, with the sift point detector and with the regular grid partition, were used for constructing a visual vocabulary that was input to the pLSA analysis. Local regions were described using the conventional SIFT descriptor. Although different vocabulary sizes were evaluated (50, 100, 200, 300 and 500) we report results obtained with 300 clusters, because they produced the best average performance for each parameter set (results not shown). Figure 2-(a) shows a plot of F_β measure reported per each sampling strategy with $k = 9$, for the different number of topics. The proposed point detection strategy reports better performance that points obtained from regular grid partition and SIFT detector in about 20%. Interestingtly, in this experiment the number of topics is not critical for performance, i.e. standar deviation reported was 0.06.

The second evaluated factor was the effect of using color information in the region descriptor. Figures 2-(b-d) show plots of F_β measures reported by varying the region description in the three sampling strategies: SIFT detector in

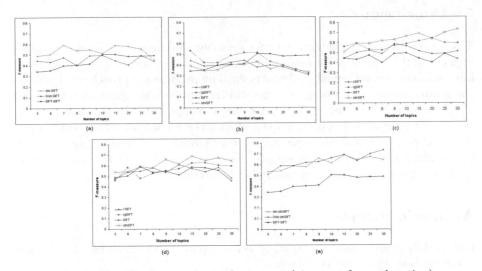

Fig. 2. Classification results in the test set (view text for explanation)

2-(b), regular grid partition in 2-(C) and the proposed approach in 2-(d). In these experiments the number of clusters and k parameter were set to 300 and 9, respectively. As expected, the results show that description computed from the illumination channel has in general poorer performance with respect to the color based description, except when regions are located around SIFT detected points. In that case, the color information effect is not clear, although rgSIFT and CSIFT descriptors report better performance than the illumination channel, when the number of concepts is smaller than the number of class labels. This bias changes when the number of topics increases, probabilly because SIFT points were detected under the illumination channel, whereby this component's contribution, for describing these points, is larger. On the other hand, in both regular grid partition and the proposed region selection, the color contribution is remarkable. Furthermore, the description based on the tissue components, defined by the staining contribution, outperforms the other color based descriptors with a maximal F_β measure of 0.73 for the regular grid partition and 0.69 for the staining based detected regions. Finally, Figure 2-(e) summarizes the results, plotting the best performance obtained for each point detection-descriptor combination. The black line, the poorest performance, corresponds to the results with regions obtained by conventional SIFT detector and descriptor. The red line corresponds to the results obtained by the proposed approach and they are comparable with those obtained from a regular grid partition described by the staining composition (blue line). However, the proposed approach is more efficient in terms of extraction of features and learning of the model, because a smaller number of regions is sampled, especially for images with a very small number of cells.

5   Conclusions

This paper presented a new strategy for selecting and describing local regions for improving the classification performance of histopathological images in a probabilistic latent semantic analysis framework. The proposed approach was based on the decomposition of histological images in their main stain contributions, which ideally allows to describe the biological tissue components. Image classification, based on the proposed approach, outperforms the conventional methods as regular grid partition and SIFT point detector. Moreover, describing local regions by measurement of stain components increased the classification performance based on the regular grid partition doing that comparable with our results.

Acknowledgments

Histopathology slides used in this study were supplied by the Pathology Department of the National University of Colombia.

References

1. Romero, E., Gomez, F., Iregui, M.: Virtual Microscopy in Medical Images: a Survey. In: Modern Research and Educational Topics in Microscopy. Formatex (2007)
2. Gurcan, M., Boucheron, L., Can, A., Madabhushi, A., Rajpoot, N., Yener, B.: Histopathological image analysis: A review. IEEE Reviews in Biomedical Engineering 2, 147–171 (2009)
3. André, B., Vercauteren, T., Perchant, A., Buchner, A.M., Wallace, M.B., Ayache, N.: Endomicroscopic image retrieval and classification using invariant visual features. In: Proceedings of International Symposium on Biomedical Imaging (2009)
4. Hofmann, T.: Unsupervised learning by probabilistic latent semantic analysis. Machine Learning 42, 177–196 (2001)
5. Caicedo, J.C., Cruz-Roa, A., Gonzalez, F.A.: Histopathology image classification using bag of features and kernel functions. In: Combi, C., Shahar, Y., Abu-Hanna, A. (eds.) AIME 2009. LNCS, vol. 5651, pp. 126–135. Springer, Heidelberg (2009)
6. Sivic, J., Zisserman, A.: Video google: A text retrieval approach to object matching in videos. In: International Conference on Computer Vision (2003)
7. Reinhard, E., Ashikhmin, M., Gooch, B., Shirley, P.: Color transfer between images. IEEE Transactions on Computer Graphics and Applications 21, 34–41 (2001)
8. Lee, D.D., Seung, H.S.: Algorithms for nonnegative matrix factorization. Advances in Neural Information Processing Systems 13, 556–562 (2001)
9. Lowe, D.: Distinctive image features from scale-invariant keypoints. International Journal of Computer Vision 60, 91–110 (2004)
10. Nowak, E., Jurie, F., Triggs, B.: Sampling strategies for bag-of-features image classification. In: Leonardis, A., Bischof, H., Pinz, A. (eds.) ECCV 2006. LNCS, vol. 3954, pp. 490–503. Springer, Heidelberg (2006)

Modified Expectation Maximization Algorithm for MRI Segmentation*

Ramiro Donoso, Alejandro Veloz, and Héctor Allende

Departamento de Informática, Universidad Técnica Federico Santa María,
Valparaíso-Chile
rdonoso@inf.utfsm.cl, avelozb@inf.utfsm.cl, hallende@inf.utfsm.cl

Abstract. Magnetic Resonance Image segmentation is a fundamental task in a wide variety of computed-based medical applications that support therapy, diagnostic and medical applications. In this work, spatial information is included for estimating paramaters of a finite mixture model, with gaussian distribution assumption, using a modified version of the well-know Expectation Maximization algorithm proposed in [3]. Our approach is based on aggregating a transition step between E-step and M-step, that includes the information of spatial dependences between neighboring pixels.

Our proposal is compared with other approaches proposed in the image segmentation literature using the *size and shape test*, obtaining accurate and robust results in the presence of noise.

Keywords: Expectation Maximization algorithm, Finite Mixture models, spatial information, Magnetic Resonance Imaging segmentation.

1 Introduction

Magnetic Resonance Imaging (MRI) has a special interest in computer-based biomedical applications due to the inherent high definition, contrast and resolution of soft tissues. In this sense, image segmentation techniques make possible computer-based quantitative analysis methods able to support diagnosis and decission making in clinical settings, thus improving medical outcomes (see, e.g., [1], [6] and [8]).

This work is focussed in the segmentation of brain anatomical structures on MRI for which a wide variety of methods have been proposed. Parametric statistical approaches are employed commonly for labeling pixels that are assigned according to probability values determined by the intensity distribution of the image. With a suitable assumption about the underlying distribution of the image regions, statistical approaches attempt to solve the problem of estimating the associated class label, given only the intensity of each pixel. In this sense, maximum *a posteriori* (MAP) or maximum likelihood are two widely used criteria for estimating the class or label of a pixel.

---

* This work was supported by Research Grant Basal FB0821, "Centro Científico-Tecnológico de Valparaíso", UTFSM.

I. Bloch and R.M. Cesar, Jr. (Eds.): CIARP 2010, LNCS 6419, pp. 63–70, 2010.

Finite mixture models that assume gaussian distributions for the mixture components, are one of the commonly used models for image segmentation. However, being this method a histogram-based approach, spatial information is not taken into account for estimating model parameters because the pixel intensities are considered to be independent samples drawn from a given gaussian random variable that represents a tissue type. This approach produces unreliable results in most MR images due to noise and to artifacts as the partial volume effect and bias field distortion (see [10]).

In order to address this problem, spatial dependences between pixels can be implicitly introduced by using the pixels coordinates as an extra feature. Also, Markov Random Fields (MRF) have been employed to take into account spatial dependences between pixels, but these approaches introduce a high computational cost for parameter estimation. Other approaches include spatial relationships between pixels for estimation the mixture model parameters. In [2] a modification of the well-know Expectation Maximization (EM), called Neighborhood EM (NEM), is proposed. In this approach, the spatial information is incorporated penalizing the log-likelihood function. Similar approaches are proposed in [10], where prior probabilities of the image classes from a mixture model are modeled as a random variable given by a MRF. In [5] Hybrid EM (HEM) algorithm is introduced based on both EM and NEM algorithms. The latter is used for fine tunning of the finite model parameters.

In order to address the segmentation of high amount of MRI images generated from patients in most medical centers, a simple method for estimating the parameters of a gaussian finite mixture model is proposed in this work. This method is based on the EM algorithm, and is called ETM algorithm, where spatial information is considered from neighboring pixels for the MRI segmentation. The ETM algorithm includes a transition step (T-step), between E-step and M-step, that increases the likelihood for certain pixels based on local relationships in a predefined neighborhood. The E-step is performed without changes and a modified M-step is derived form the T-step.

This work is organized as follows. In section 2 the mixture-model-based approach for image segmentation and the proposed method, called ETM algorithm, are presented. In section 3 a comparison between the proposed ETM algorithm and other segmentation methods are presented using the *sizes and shapes test* applied in [11]. The methods considered here for comparison are the classical EM algorithm [7], Neighborhood EM (NEM) [2], Hybrid EM (HEM) [5], Fuzzy C-Means (FCM) and Modified Fuzzy C-Means (FCMM) [9]. Finally, some discussions and conclusions are reported in section 4 and 5, respectivelly.

2   Methodology

2.1   Mixture Model-Based Image Segmentation

Let $I = \{\mathbf{x}_i \in \mathbb{R}^p | i = 1, ..., n \text{ and } p \in \mathbb{N}\}$ be the set of pixels forming an image. Each pixel value is a realization of random variable X, which density function is determined by the weigthed sum of K components. Each one of these components correspond to the density functions of the K regions from which it is suspected that the image is composed. Let $R_k = \{\mathbf{x}_j \in \mathbb{R}^p | j = 1, ..., n_k \text{ and } p \in \mathbb{N}\}$ be the set of pixels that compose the k-th region of the image; these pixels are a realization of a random variable $X_k, k = 1, ..., K$, whose probability density function is denoted by $g_k(X_k|\theta_k)$. In this sense, the density function of random variable X is given by:

$$f(x_i|\phi) = \sum_{k=1}^{K} p_k * g_k(x_i|\theta_k) \tag{1}$$

where $\phi = \{p_1, ..., p_K, \theta_1, ..., \theta_K\}$ are the set of unknown parameters of the mixture model, that are estimated in such way that the (log)likelihood function represented by the joint probability of having a particular set of pixel values $\{\mathbf{x}_1, ..., \mathbf{x}_n\}$ is maximized, given the set of parameters ϕ, i.e., $L(\mathbf{x}_1, ..., \mathbf{x}_n|\phi) = \prod_i f(\mathbf{x}_i|\phi)$. There is no requirement that the components $g_k(x_i|\theta_k)$ should all belong to the same parametric family, but in most MRI segmentation approaches the same functional form for each region but with different parameters is assumed (see, e.g., [10]). In this work, a multivariate gaussian distribution with parameters $\theta_k = (\mu_k, \Sigma_k)$ for $g_k(x_i|\theta_k)$ is assumed.

The maximum likelihood estimate (MLE) of ϕ can be found numerically using various optimization algorithms. A very important approach widely used in mixture modeling is the Expectation Maximization (EM). This is an iterative method for optimizing the likelihood function when some information is missing. In our case, the missing information is the region to which pixels belong. The MLE of ϕ using EM algorithm is obtained iterating two steps until convergence. In the first step (E-step) the posterior probability that a pixel $\mathbf{x}_i$ belong to each region is computed using the Bayes formula. In the second step (M-step), the parameters of the mixture model are estimated by maximizing the likelihood function. For instance, assuming a normal mixture the mean vector μ_k, the covariance matrix Σ_k and the weigth p_k for the normal mixture component of the k-th region of the image should be estimated.

2.2 ETM Algorithm

In this work a modified Expectation Maximization algorithm is proposed. This modification is based on increasing the likelihood of the mixture model for pixels that are homogeneous within the region with higher probability. These pixels have a better fit to its underlying probability distributions, and therefore increase the likelihood of the mixture model. The increment of the likelihood is achieved by weighting *free* or *homogeneous* pixels, during a step of transition (called T-step) that is performed between E-step and M-step. In the T-step, *free* pixels have a higher weight than the pixels that are not. The steps of the proposed ETM algorithm are explained below.

E-step (expectation): As suggested in the classical EM algorithm [7], in this step the expected value of the likelihood is obtained. For this purpose the following formula is used:

$$Pr(\theta_k|\mathbf{x}_i) \equiv c_{ik} = \frac{p_k * g_k(\mathbf{x}_i|\theta_k)}{\sum_{l=1}^{K} p_l * g_l(\mathbf{x}_i|\theta_l)} \tag{2}$$

where the value c_{ik} is an element of a matrix C and represents the probability that the pixel $\mathbf{x}_i \in I$ belongs to the region k in the image.

T-step (transition): In this step the probability of assigning a pixel $\mathbf{x}_i$ in the class k is modified. Let PA be a matrix of size $n \times K$, whose elements are given by:

$$pa_{ik} = \frac{c_{ik} + \sum_{\mathbf{x}_j \in N_8(\mathbf{x}_i)} c_{jk} * v_{ij}}{1 + \sum_{\mathbf{x}_j \in N_8(\mathbf{x}_i)} v_{ij}} \tag{3}$$

where v_{ij} takes a value $\alpha > 0$ if $\mathbf{x}_j \in N_8(\mathbf{x}_i)$, and 0 otherwise, i.e., v_{ij} represents the influence of the neighbor $\mathbf{x}_j$ on $\mathbf{x}_i$, and pa_{ik} is calculated as the weighted average of the probabilities of membership of the 8-neighbors $\mathbf{x}_j \in N_8(\mathbf{x}_i)$ of $\mathbf{x}_i$. It is clear that pa_{ik} represents the modified probability that a pixel $\mathbf{x}_i$ belongs to the class k taking into acount the influence of all neighbors. After this calculation, the elements of the probability matrix C are updated by replacing the value c_{ik} by pa_{ik} if $\mathbf{x}_i$ is a *non-free pixel*. A pixel $\mathbf{x}_i$ is considered a *free pixel* if the class assigned to c_{ik}, i.e., $\arg\max_k[c_{ik}]$ is the same class obtained according the matrix pa_{ik}, i.e., $\arg\max_k[pa_{ik}]$.

With the updated probability matrix C, the weight for each pixel of the image is calculated in order to increase the likelihood of the mixture model for *free pixels*. In this sense, a higher weight is assigned to *free pixels*, respect to *non-free pixels*. We propose to do this using two variants, a crisp weighting (see equation (4)) and a fuzzy weighting (see equation (5)).

$$ph_i = \begin{cases} 1 \text{ if } \mathbf{x}_i \text{ is a } free\ pixel \\ 0 \text{ otherwise} \end{cases} \tag{4} \qquad ph_i = \frac{\max_k[c_{ik}]}{\max_k\left[\frac{\sum_{\mathbf{x}_j \in N_8(\mathbf{x}_i)} c_{jk}*v_{ij}}{\sum_{\mathbf{x}_j \in N_8(\mathbf{x}_i)} v_{ij}}\right]} \tag{5}$$

where the values v_{ij} have the same behavior as in equation (3). In the equation (5) the element ph_i, i.e., the weight of the pixel $\mathbf{x}_i$, takes values greater than 1 if the higher probability of assignment of this pixel in certain class is greater than the weighted average of the probabilities of membership of all of their 8-neighbors in each class. In this sense, pixels that better fit to its underlying class, have a higher influence (i.e., higher weight) in the mixture model parameter estimation process.

M-step (maximization): In this step, the mixture model parameters are calculated. For this purpose the likelihood function is used including the weights for each pixel calculated in the previous step. Therefore, the set of parameters of the mixture model is obtained using a modification formulae presented in [7], which are shown below:

$$\widehat{p}_k = \frac{\sum_{i=1}^n c_{ik} * ph_i}{\sum_{i=1}^n ph_i} \tag{6} \qquad \widehat{\mu}_k = \frac{\sum_{i=1}^n c_{ik} * \mathbf{x}_i * ph_i}{\sum_{i=1}^n c_{ik} * ph_i} \tag{7}$$

$$\widehat{\Sigma}_k = \frac{\sum_{i=1}^n c_{ik} * ph_i * (\mathbf{x}_i - \widehat{\mu}_k)(\mathbf{x}_i - \widehat{\mu}_k)'}{\sum_{i=1}^n c_{ik} * ph_i} \tag{8}$$

3   Results

To make an appropriate evaluation of the segmentation algorithms, the *Sizes and Shapes Test* [11] was implemented. This test consists in segmenting a group of 12 synthetic images with different intensities of background and objects, where the first 8 images correspond to circles of different sizes (referred as *Set of Sizes*) and the last 4 correspond to ellipses with different eccentricities but maintaining approximately the same area (referred as *Set of Shapes*). In addition, with the purpose to make the images more realistic, a low-pass filter was applied and a gaussian additive noise component was introduced to the P percents of pixels of the image.

In order to measure quantitatively the performance of the proposed ETM algorithm, we calculate the accuracy, the RUMA index (relative ultimate measurement accuracy of object area [11]), the *Total Difference* (TD), the *Low Segmentation* (LS) or false negatives, and the *Over Segmentation* (OS) or false positives. These indices are given by:

$$\text{Accuracy} = \frac{Area(O \cap \overline{O})}{Area(O)} * 100 \qquad \text{RUMA} = \frac{|x_r - x_s|}{x_r} * 100$$

$$TD = LS + OS \qquad LS = \frac{Area(O \backslash \overline{O})}{Area(O)} \qquad OS = \frac{Area(B \backslash \overline{B})}{Area(O)}$$

where, O and B represent the region of the object and the background in the reference image, respectively. Analogously, $\overline{O}$ and $\overline{B}$ represent the same regions in the segmented image. The terms x_r and x_s correspond to the intensity value of the pixels in the reference image and the segmented image, respectively. Finally, the operation $R_1 \backslash R_2$ is defined by $R_1 \backslash R_2 = p \backslash p \in R_1, p \notin R_2$.

The ETM algorithm was compared with the EM, NEM, HEM, FCM and FCMM algorithms in 3 configurations of the *sizes and shapes test* and 3 experimental runs for each of these configurations, obtaining the mean and standard deviation of each index previously explained. The configurations used are defined by the intensity I_f of the background, the intensity I_o of the object, the diameter D or eccentricity e which defines a circle or ellipse respectively, the percentage P of pixels corrupted by gaussian noise and the standard deviation σ of this noise. The results for the 3 configurations used are presented below, in table 1.

Experiments with real T1-weighted MR images (with contrast agent *gadolinium*) were also conducted in a set of 32 MRI images with Brain Tumor, also used in [8]. These image data set were segmented with the ETM, EM, NEM, HEM, FCM, FCMM, region growing (RG) [8] and Genetic Algorithms (GA) [4] with 4 regions or classes defined a priori (tissues types in the image). The comparison of the results were performed using the Gold Standard (GS) of the image data set, provided by Carlos Van Buren Hospital of Valparaíso-Chile. We performed 5 experimental runs for each algorithm, obtaining the median and mean of the accuracy, the mean of the false positive (FP) and false negative (FN) errors and the mean of the time (in seconds) needed to produce the segmented image (see table 2). All indexes are shown with their respectives standard deviations. In figure 1 2 instances of segmented MR images are shown as example.

Table 1. Results obtained with synthetic images

Algorithm	LS (sd)	OS (sd)	TD (sd)	RUMA (sd)	Accuracy (sd)
Configuration 1 with $I_f = 20$, $I_o = 102$, $D = 128$, $P = 25\%$ and $\sigma = 40$.					
ETM	**0** (0)	**0,0225** (0,0001)	**0,0225** (0,0001)	**7,2903** (0,0086)	**100** (0)
EM	0,0156 (0,0004)	0,1662 (0,0013)	0,1818 (0,0015)	26,6559 (0,0155)	98,4426 (0,0385)
NEM	0,0126 (0,0002)	0,1362 (0,0021)	0,1488 (0,0019)	22,5671 (0,0035)	98,7382 (0,0229)
HEM	0,0157 (0,0004)	0,1647 (0,0012)	0,1804 (0,0015)	26,3491 (0,0154)	98,4273 (0,0385)
FCM	0,037 (0,001)	0,0744 (0,0038)	0,1114 (0,0028)	11,7085 (0,0053)	96,2988 (0,0994)
FCMM	0,0373 (0,001)	0,074 (0,0038)	0,1113 (0,0029)	11,8891 (0,0023)	96,2708 (0,1038)
Configuration 2 with $I_f = 182$, $I_o = 130$, $e = 0.7$, $P = 10\%$ and $\sigma = 80$.					
ETM	0,001 (0,0003)	**0,0017** (0,0001)	**0,0028** (0,0003)	**1,2695** (0,0001)	99,8977 (0,0251)
EM	**0** (0)	0,2124 (0,0005)	0,2124 (0,0005)	3,9775 (0,0002)	**100** (0)
NEM	0,028 (0,0005)	0,0543 (0,0027)	0,0823 (0,0027)	2,7221 (0,0006)	97,1974 (0,0536)
HEM	0,0312 (0,0043)	0,0583 (0,009)	0,0895 (0,0132)	2,8962 (0,0022)	96,8763 (0,4278)
FCM	0,0363 (0,0004)	0,0651 (0,0022)	0,1014 (0,0026)	2,1042 (0,0005)	96,3719 (0,0436)
FCMM	0,0364 (0,0004)	0,0648 (0,0022)	0,1012 (0,0026)	3,083 (0,0006)	96,3576 (0,043)
Configuration 3 with $I_f = 20$, $I_o = 223$, $e = 0.9$, $P = 10\%$ and $\sigma = 80$.					
ETM	**0** (0)	0,0359 (0,0008)	**0,0359** (0,0008)	13,3558 (0,0032)	**100** (0)
EM	**0** (0)	0,278 (0,0018)	0,278 (0,0018)	70,0654 (0,0035)	**100** (0)
NEM	0,0005 (0,0002)	0,1374 (0,0011)	0,1379 (0,0012)	41,4617 (0,0025)	99,9508 (0,0201)
HEM	0,0011 (0,0003)	0,1417 (0,0005)	0,1428 (0,0008)	42,7161 (0,0009)	99,8871 (0,0347)
FCM	0,0115 (0,0006)	**0,0279** (0,0019)	0,0395 (0,0024)	**13,1291** (0,0048)	98,8475 (0,0578)
FCMM	0,0115 (0,0006)	0,0281 (0,0018)	0,0396 (0,0024)	16,11 (0,0041)	98,8533 (0,0602)
Resume of the three configurations.					
ETM	**0,0003** (0,0006)	**0,0200** (0,0172)	**0,0194** (0,0234)	**7,3052** (6,0432)	**99,9659** (0,0591)
EM	0,0052 (0,0090)	0,2189 (0,0562)	0,2452 (0,0464)	33,5663 (33,5815)	99,4809 (0,8992)
NEM	0,0137 (0,0138)	0,1093 (0,0476)	0,1101 (0,0393)	22,2503 (19,3717)	98,6288 (1,3800)
HEM	0,0160 (0,0151)	0,1216 (0,0560)	0,1162 (0,0377)	23,9871 (20,0148)	98,3969 (1,5056)
FCM	0,0283 (0,0145)	0,0558 (0,0246)	0,0705 (0,0438)	8,9806 (5,9973)	97,1727 (1,4509)
FCMM	0,0284 (0,0146)	0,0556 (0,0243)	0,0704 (0,0436)	10,3607 (6,6466)	97,1606 (1,4666)

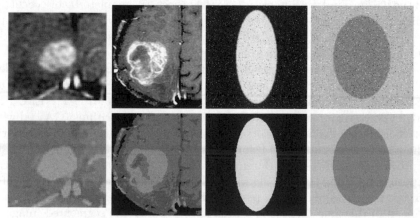

Fig. 1. Examples of segmented synthetic and real MR images (original images (upper row) and their corresponding segmented images (bottom row))

Table 2. Results obtained with real MR images with 4 classes

Algorithm	Median	Mean (sd)	FN (sd)	FP (sd)	Time (sd)
ETM	97,6031	**95,1324** (10,36)	**4,8676** (10,36)	9,5436 (7,89)	1,6435 (0,74)
EM	97,1843	94,3037 (10,99)	5,6963 (10,99)	6,8459 (6,62)	1,0957 (0,38)
NEM	95,3293	88,8553 (20,8)	11,1447 (20,8)	2,9788 (2,24)	2,3603 (1,15)
HEM	96,1029	93,2426 (12,29)	6,7574 (12,29)	5,358 (5,22)	1,2006 (0,53)
FCM	91,4426	86,6887 (17,33)	13,3113 (17,33)	2,8059 (4,79)	0,8612 (0,22)
FCMM	91,5879	87,6018 (14,17)	12,3982 (14,17)	**2,6723** (3,33)	0,688 (0,13)
GA	94,3389	89,8554 (13,72)	10,1446 (13,72)	4,8939 (9,25)	1,1288 (0,11)
RG	**97,6669**	92,8924 (13,27)	7,1076 (13,27)	9,1703 (15,63)	**0,6821** (0,09)

4 Discussion

As shown in Table 1 the proposed ETM algorithm succeeds in obtaining the lowest value for the TD index (only 1,9%) respect to other algorithms, which indicates that in most cases the ETM algorithm performs a more appropriate segmentation, with the lowest error respect to other segmentation techniques. As shown in resume of table 1, ETM algorithm obtains an accuracy of 99,96% without an important over segmentation (the ETM algorithm never gets more than 3.6% for OS, compared to other EM-based methods that get more than 10%).

Moreover it is observed that generally the RUMA rate obtained by the ETM algorithm is always one of the lowest, except in configuration 3 of Table 1, which means that the segmentation performed by this algorithm in terms of intensity, sometimes does not match the original image. However, since the proposed algorithm was designed primarily for the purpose of segmenting MRI, we aim to obtain a segmentation of homogeneous regions as connected as possible.

As shown in figure 1 for synthetic images, the proposed algorithm is robust to noise, mainly because the ETM algorithm includes spatial information of pixels when calculating the mixture model parameters, that is why we recommend using this method on images with high noise (see Configuration 1) and low contrast (see Configuration 2).

The ETM algorithm gets the best results for segmentation of the 32 real MR images, obtaining 95,13% of accuracy with a standard deviation of 10,36 (see Table 2). Moreover, with the ETM algorithm the lowest rates of false negatives were obtained, and also the lowest standard deviation, compared to the other approaches. Nevertheless, the false positives errors were not that good, but comparable with other approaches considered in this work.

With the inclusion of T-step, the ETM algorithm is more efficient compared with other techniques including spatial information data, because this modification does not increase the complexity significantly. ETM, EM, NEM and HEM have the same complexity in M-step, $O(nK)$. As for E-step complexity, ETM and EM is $O(nK)$, NEM is $O(mn^2K)$ (m is the number of iterations of E-step), HEM is $O(nK)$ in selective hard EM and $O(n^2K)$ in later NEM [5]. In T-step, ETM have a complexity of $O(8nk)$. The fastest is EM, closely followed by HEM and ETM, and NEM is the worst. This is corroborated by *a posteriori* temporal efficiency obtained in Table 2.

5   Conclusion

In this work, we introduced a modified Expectation Maximization algorithm to estimate mixture model parameters in a very simple way, taking into account spatial relationships between pixels. The proposed method outperforms other approaches proposed in the literature and constitute a reliable approach to segment MR images of the brain.

Further work is needed in order to provide more flexibility in the spatial relationships dependences modelling or to incorporate the bias field estimation to correct or compensate the intensity inhomogeneities introduced during the acquisition process in MRI. The proposed ETM algorithm is intensity-based, but incorporating spatial dependences between pixels, hence the segmentation do not depend on the region size as is the case with region-based approaches, so it could be applied to segment other brain anatomical structures, such as White Matter or Gray Matter, without requiring additional time.

References

1. Gering, D., Nabavi, A., Kikinis, R., Hata, N., O'Donnell, L., Grimson, W., Jolesz, F., Black, P., Wells, W.: An Integrated Visualization System for Surgical Planning and Guidance Using Image Fusion and an Open MR. Journal of Magnetic Resonance Imaging 13, 967–975 (2001)
2. Ambroise, C., Govaert, G.: Spatial Clustering and the EM Algorithm, Tech. report, Université de technologie de Compiègne, France (1996)
3. Dempster, A.P., Laird, N.M., Rubin, D.B.: Maximum likelihood from incomplete data via the EM algorithm. Journal of The Royal Statistical Society, Series B 39(1), 1–38 (1977)
4. Gil, P., Torres, F., Ortiz, F.G.: Detección de objetos por segmentación multinivel combinada de espacios de color, Tech. report, Dpto. Física, Ingeniería de Sistemas y Teoría de la Señal. Universidad de Alicate (Septiembre 2004)
5. Hu, T., Sung, S.Y.: Clustering Spatial Data with a Hybrid EM Approach, Tech. report, Department of Computer Science, National University of Singapore (2005)
6. Kaus, M.: Contributions to the Automated Segmentation of Brain Tumors in Magnetic Resonance Images, Ph.D. thesis, Der Technischen Fakultat der Universitat Erlangen-Nurnberg (1999)
7. Mostafa, M.G., Tolba, M.F., Gharib, T.F., Megeed, M.A.: Medical Image Segmentation Using a Wavelet-Based Multiresolution EM Algorithm. In: IEEE International Conference on Industrial Electronics, Technology and Automation, December 19-21 (2001)
8. Veloz, A., Chabert, S., Salas, R., Orellana, A., Vielma, J.: Fuzzy Spatial Growing for Glioblastoma Multiforme Segmentation on Brain Magnetic Resonance Imaging. In: Rueda, L., Mery, D., Kittler, J. (eds.) CIARP 2007. LNCS, vol. 4756, pp. 861–870. Springer, Heidelberg (2007)
9. Yang, Z., Chung, F.-L., Shitong, W.: Robust fuzzy clustering based image segmentation. Applied Soft Computing 9, 80–84 (2008)
10. Zhang, Y., Brady, M., Smith, S.: Segmentation of Brain MR Images Through a Hidden Markov Random Field Model and the Expectation-Maximization Algorithm. IEEE Transactions on Medical Imaging 20(1), 45-57 (2001)
11. Zhang, Y., Gerbrands, J.: Segmentation Evaluation Using Ultimate Measurament Accuracy. Image Processing Algorithms and Techniques III 1657, 449–460 (1996)

Generation of Synthetic Multifractal Realistic Surfaces Based on Natural Model and Lognormal Cascade: Application to MRI Classification

Mohamed Khider[1], Abdelmalik Taleb-Ahmed[2], and Boualem Haddad[1]

[1] Université des Sciences et de la Technologie Houari Boumedienne, LTIR, Algeria
[2] Université de Valenciennes et du Hainaut Cambrésis, LAMIH, FRE 3304, France
taleb@univ-valenciennes.fr

Abstract. This paper presents a method of generating realistic synthetic multi-fractals surfaces, constructed with multiplicative cascades, that follow lognormal probability density function. The conservation of the natural image gradient direction, and the variance of the difference minimization at each scale between natural image multipliers and those of the selected lognormal model, preserves the initial texture structure. Validation of the model is made with wavelet leader based multifractal analysis, we also propose an application to MRI classification of trabecular bone texture, to differentiate between healthy and osteoporotic cases.

Keywords: lognormal cascade, Discrete Wavelet Transform, wavelet leader, multifractal analysis, Monte-Carlo sampling, Iterative Conditional Modes (ICM), Markov Random Fields (MRF), probabilistic model and Bayesian classification.

1 Introduction

Over the past few decades, an important number of texture classification approaches have been explored, and numerous applications relating to computer vision and pattern recognition have been found, including industrial, remote sensing and medical imaging. These approaches can be divided into four categories: statistical, structural methods, modelbased, and signal processing methods [1]. In this work, the classification is performed in two steps : 1. firstly, we begin by generating the realistic multifractal surfaces from our serie of image, with a fixed predominant Holder exponent, 2. secondly, we calculate the percentage of correspondence between the original image and their multifractal version. Therefore, in our application of MRI trabecular bone texture classification, we begin by generating the multifractal version of the ROI (region of interest) as explained in section two, the validation of the model is performed by using wavelet leader based multifractal analysis in section three.To generate several prototypes from the multifractal version of our image, Markov random

I. Bloch and R.M. Cesar, Jr. (Eds.): CIARP 2010, LNCS 6419, pp. 71–78, 2010.
© Springer-Verlag Berlin Heidelberg 2010

fields are used as shown in section four. In this paper, detection of similarity is performed by Bayesian classification and comparison of coincidence between valley's pixel from trabecular texture is presented in section four.

2   Generation of the Natural Multifractal Model

Kolmogorov and Obukhov [2,3] have proposed the lognormal model that reveals multifractal behavior, afterward created from a W random multiplicative cascade process in Yalgom's work to generate intermittent [4,5,6]. Parallel to that, in the turbulence analysis, since the first works of Obukhov [7], the decomposition of signals into high and low-frequency parts did not cease to find favorable ground. Advent of Daubechies wavelet with compact support and fast algorithm implementation, on dyadic scales has made conceivable the synthesis of multifractal surfaces based on lognormal and log-poisson cascades in the relevant Arneodo et al articles of 2D-WTMM multifractal analysis [8]. We start by choosing the model, for example a Brodatz's texture, the product of convolution between the $f_m(x,y)$ model and the $\psi^m_{j,k,l}$ wavelet give us the coefficients according to the m direction, (j,k) position and the scale of analysis l :

$$C^m_{j,k,l} = \langle f_m(\mathrm{x,y}), \psi^m_{j,k,l} \rangle \tag{1}$$

The 2D-DWT modulus are expressed by :

$$d_{j,k,l} = \sqrt{\sum_{m=1}^{3} \left[C^m_{j,k,l} \right]^2} \tag{2}$$

The directions of the real model $f_m(x,y)$ coefficients must be preserved, hence the angles φ and θ are estimated by using the arguments :

$$\varphi_{j,k,l} = arg(\sqrt{\sum_{m=1}^{2} \left[C^m_{j,k,l} \right]^2} + iC^2_{j,k,l}) \tag{3}$$

$$\theta_{j,k,l} = arg(C^1_{j,k,l} + iC^2_{j,k,l}) \tag{4}$$

Let w_l be the multipliers at scale l that follow a lognormal law, by minimizing the variance of difference between w_m multipliers and those generated randomly w_i following a lognormal probability density function, this calculation is repeated many times until stability of the result :

$$d_{j,k,l} = d_{j,k,l-1} w_{m-1} \tag{5}$$

$$var(w_m - w_l) = \min_{w_i} \left[var(w_m - w_i) \right] \tag{6}$$

Then, we proceed as in Decoster et all works [9], with the iteration from the coarser to the finer scale :

$$M_{j,k,l} = M_{j,k,l-1} w_{l-1} \tag{7}$$

The wavelet coefficients of synthetic surface $G_{j,k,l}$ are written according to the $M_{j,k,l}$ modules through :

$$G^1_{j,k,l} = \cos(\varphi_{j,k,l})\cos(\theta_{j,k,l})M_{j,k,l}$$

$$G^2_{j,k,l} = \cos(\varphi_{j,k,l})\sin(\theta_{j,k,l})M_{j,k,l}$$

$$G^3_{j,k,l} = \sin(\theta_{j,k,l})M_{j,k,l} \tag{8}$$

The construction of the synthetic surface $f_s(\mathrm{x}, \mathrm{y})$ is performed with the following addition (N is the total number of scale) :

$$f_s(\mathrm{x},\mathrm{y}) = \sum_{j=0}^{+\infty}\sum_{k=0}^{+\infty}\sum_{l=0}^{N}\sum_{m=1}^{3} G^m_{j,k,l}\psi^m_{j,k,l}(\mathrm{x},\mathrm{y}) \tag{9}$$

Such in the case of our surfaces $f_s(\mathrm{x}, \mathrm{y})$, a generated surface by lognormal cascade is characterized with the multifractal spectrum :

$$D(h) = -\frac{(h + \mu/\ln(2))}{2\sigma^2/\ln(2)} + 2 \tag{10}$$

When μ and σ^2 denote respectively the mean and the variance from the w_l lognormal law.

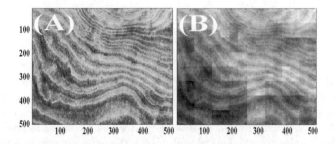

Fig. 1. (A) Brodatz's texture, and in **(B)** its multifractal version $h(q = 0) = 0.38$, $\mu = -0.38log(2)$ and $\sigma^2 = 0.03log(2)$ lognormal cascade parameter obtained by the first order Daubechies wavelet

3   Validation of the Model

To estimate the multifractal spectrum, the leading coefficients method of S. Jaffard [10] is used, and we employ the same notation as B. Lashermes [11]. In the case of one dimension for example, $d_f(j, k)$ indicate the discrete wavelet transform coefficient for each dyadic interval in scale 2^j, then $l_f(j, k)$the leading coefficient is obtained by the relation :

$$l_f(j,k) = \sup_{\lambda' \subset 3\lambda(j,k), j' \leqslant j} |d_f(\lambda')| \tag{11}$$

The structure function is given by the following equation $(d = 2)$:

$$S_f^l(q,j) = \frac{1}{n(j)} \sum_{\{k_i\}} \frac{1}{2^d - 1} \sum_m (l_f(j, k_i, m))^q \tag{12}$$

If we note, by q the moment and $n(j)$ the number of leading coefficients at the octave j, the scale function is specified by $\zeta_l^f(q)$ and satisfies the relation :

$$S_f^l(q,j) \sim 2^{j\zeta_f^l(q)} \tag{13}$$

The Legendre spectrum $D(h)$ is given by the multifractal formalism :

$$D_f^l(h) = \min_q (d + qh - \zeta_f^l(q)) \tag{14}$$

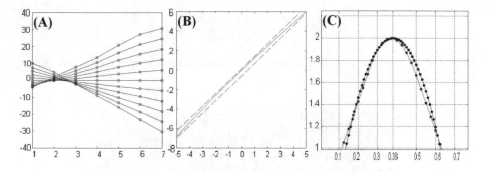

Fig. 2. Multfractal analysis of image (1.B) in **(A)** Partition functions $-5 \leq q \leq +5$ with axis $(x, y) = (j, S_f^l(q, j))$, **(B)** Scale function with axis $(x, y) = (q, \zeta_l^f(q))$, and in **(C)** The Legendre spectrum with multifractal behavior and axis $(x, y) = (h, D_f^l(h))$, wavelet leader based multifractal analysis is performed by second order Daubechies wavelet, in black color the theoretical and in blue the experimental spectrum

4   Application: MRI Classification

We present a method of bone texture classification based on Monte-Carlo sampling, following a uniform probability distribution. A great similarity is observed in the texture structure between the original image and the multifractal model when we generate a multifractal model with the most frequent Holder exponent close to the exponent of the original image. In addition, we have used Markov's chains for restoration. In the beginning Markov has developed his theory to analyze the Pushkin's literary text [12], then the appearance of Markov random fields is due to statistical physics in the work of Ising, and its theoretical basis were described by Preston and Spitzer [13].

4.1 The Proposed Method

Trabecular structures pixels and valleys pixels are detected by Bayesian classification, this requires a learning step to define the prior probability of gray levels (according to the mode of acquisition, one image is enough for a whole series). Next, the estimation of coincidence between pixels of the same nature is performed. Furthermore, we propose the combination of Markov random fields (MRF) restoration method of second order and the iterative conditional modes (ICM) with 6 cycles and β=1.5, this allow the production of several prototypes of our multifractal model, and increases at lower cost (in number of operations) the statistical population. The preliminary results are very encouraging and showing 100% of good classification on 10 MRI images (Table.1), and a dramatically reduced in computing time by using Monte Carlo sampling is observed. The algorithm can be implemented in parallel (multi processing). To generate the prototype, ICM and MRF are used, we proceed as follows : for any scene x^* which represents the central pixel obtained by Monte Carlo sampling and the second order MRF neighbors, We calculate the mean $\mu(x_i^*)$ and the variance σ^2, and generate the y_i variable from Gaussian probability distribution function with the same mean and variance as x^* scene. The y_i variable represents the generated gray level. The probability that the k gray level is associated with pixel at the position i is such that [14] :

$$P_i(k/.) = e^{\beta u_i(k)} / \sum_{l=1}^{c} e^{\beta u_i(l)} \qquad (15)$$

The variable $u_i(l)$ indicate the number of i neighbors possessing l gray level, β is a fixed parameter with a 1.5 value and 6 ICM cycles such as in Besag et al article. The ICM corresponds to a succession of successful expression reduction (improving) :

$$\frac{1}{2\sigma^2}\{y_i - \mu(x_i)\}^2 - \beta u_i^*(x_i) \qquad (16)$$

With $u_i^*(x_i)$ which gives the current number of i neighbors that have the same gray level as the pixel i. To estimate the correspondence of pixels (trabecular structures, valleys), we use a probabilistic model and a Bayesian classification, y indicates the gray level, T and V illustrate respectively trabecular structures and valleys pixels. The conditional a posteriori probabilities are obtained by [15]:

$$P(T/y) = \frac{P(T)P(y/T)}{P(T)P(y/T) + P(V)P(y/V)}$$

$$P(V/y) = \frac{P(V)P(y/V)}{P(T)P(y/T) + P(V)P(y/V)} \qquad (17)$$

The a priori probabilities $P(T)$, $P(V)$, $P(y/T)$ and $P(y/V)$ are estimated with a learning step performed by an expert (a doctor indicates the trabecular structures and valleys regions for best results, to do this, we suggest a pathological

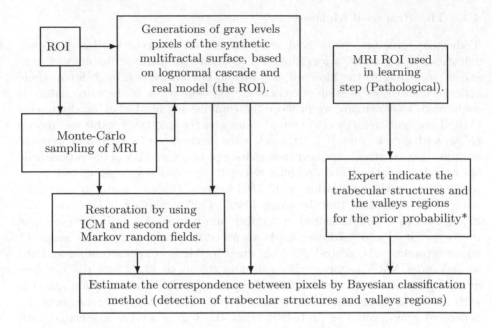

Fig. 3. Block diagram of the method, and the principal steps to follow. (*) this step is needed for training to estimate the prior probabilities.

ROI (fig.4)), a trabecular structure pixel is detected if $P(T/y) > \alpha P(V/y)$, in our case, we took $\alpha = 1$, it can be modified for example to reduce the risk of considering a valley pixel as a trabecular structure pixel, we must choose $0 < \alpha < 1$.

4.2 Results and Discussion

In our application, the method of Monte Carlo is employed with 10^4 samples, and the first order Daubechies wavelets are used during the reconstruction step with lognormal cascade multipliers, it requires a range of 8 octaves, for a ROI of 512x512 pixels. Ten MRI images are used, the choice of the most frequent exponent is performed with $h(q = 0) = 0.1$ value that best reflects the pathological ROI structure, indeed, the rate of coincidence of pixels in the regions of same nature (trabecular structure or valleys) is higher than in the case of trabecular texture of normal patient (Table.1). If we consider the totality of the ROI, using the ICM restoration method improve the homogeneity of the texture by reducing artifacts (due to the DWT dyadic grid)(fig.5 and fig.6). We can generate several prototypes from the same image (the table shows the result after one operation of restoration). We can distinguish unambiguously the two case of studies, furthermore, using MRF allowed us to increase the difference between average of the two classes. We should note, that the a priori probability is obtained after a training step by using a pathological ROI, since in this case, it's easier to distinguish between the two regions trabecular structures and valleys.

Table 1. The pathological ROI cases and its results are represented in bold characters, we give the percentage of coincidence between trabecular structures pixels and valleys pixels detected by Bayesian classification. MF indicates that the comparison is made between the ROI and its multifractal version. MF ICM indicates that the comparison is made between the ROI and its multifractal version restored by ICM method.

ROI	B	**C**	**E**	G	**K**	**M**	O	S	T	**U**
MF	19.24	**45.78**	**45.74**	26.21	**44.94**	**42.64**	26.23	28.72	22.13	**43.7**
MF ICM	18.6	**42.55**	**44.1**	26.49	**41.19**	**39.01**	22.26	22.39	18.23	**42.32**

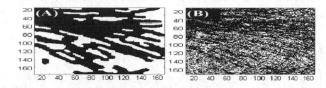

Fig. 4. (A) Training step, in black color the trabecular structures pixels region, the first figure from left illustrate the regions chosen by an expert (to estimate the a priori probabilities), and **(B)** indicate the detected regions by Bayesian classification of the same pathological ROI (the a posteriori probabilities)

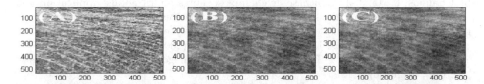

Fig. 5. (A) pathological MRI ROI, **(B)** its multifractal version $h(q = 0) = 0.1$, $\mu = -0.1log(2)$ and $\sigma^2 = 0.01log(2)$, and in **(C)** the same multifractal version restored with ICM

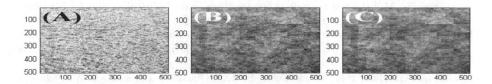

Fig 6. (A) healthy MRI ROI, **(B)** its multifractal version $h(q = 0) = 0.1$, $\mu = -0.1log(2)$ and $\sigma^2 = 0.01log(2)$, and in **(C)** the same multifractal version restored with ICM

5   Conclusions

This paper concerns the use of multifractal surfaces generation method based on the extraction of attributes from natural images such as cascade multipliers and the gradients directions from the wavelet of decomposition, what makes the synthetic image more realistic. An application of texture classification is derived, an osteoporotic bone texture and a healthy one are compared with their multifractals versions resulting from lognormal cascade with a fixed predominant Holder exponent, a greater similarity is observed between original texture and that generated with lognormal cascade when the Holder exponents are close together (pathological case in our application). Preliminary results are very promising and as perspective an automatic method is envisaged and it would be interesting to apply to other types of textures for classification or segmentation.

References

1. Bharati, M.H., Liu, J.J., MacGregor, J.F.: Image texture analysis: methods and comparisons. J. Chemometrics and Intelligent Laboratory Systems 72, 57–71 (2004)
2. Kolmogorov, A.N.: A refinement of previous hypotheses concerning the local structure of turbulence. J. Fluid Mech. 13, 83–85 (1962)
3. Obukhov, A.M.: Some specific features of atmospheric turbulence. J. Fluid Mech. 13, 77–81 (1962)
4. Bacry, E., Muzy, J.F.: Log-infinitely divisible multifractal processes. Comm. In Math. Phys. 236, 449–475 (2003)
5. Chainais, P., Li, J.-J.: Synthése de champs scalaires multifractals: application à la synthése de texture. In: GRETSI 2005, Louvain-la-Neuve, Belgique (2005)
6. Schmitt, F.G.: Intermittence et turbulences; analyse de données, validation de modéles et applications, HDR, Université Paris 6 (2001)
7. Frisch, U.: Turbulence. The legacy of A.N. Kolmogorov. Cambridge University Press, Cambridge (1995)
8. Arneodo, A., Decoster, N., Roux, S.G.: A wavelet-based method for multifractal image analysis. I. Methodology and test applications on isotropic random rough surface. European Physical Journal B 15, 567–600 (2000)
9. Arneodo, A., Decoster, N., Roux, S.G.: A wavelet-based method for multifractal image analysis. II. Applications to synthetic multifractal rough surface. European Physical Journal B 15, 739–764 (2000)
10. Jaffard, S.: Multifractal formalism for function, part 1: Results valid for all functions. S.I.A.M: Journal of Mathematical Analysis 28, 944–970 (1997)
11. Lashermes, Analyse multifractale pratique: coefficients dominants et ordres critiques. applications à la turbulence pleinement développé. effets de nombre de reynolds fini, Ph.D. thesis (2005)
12. Duda, R.O., Hart, P.E., Stork, D.G.: Pattern Classification. Edition Wiley Inter-Science, New York (2001)
13. Kindermann, R., Laurie Snell, J.: Markov Random Fields and their applications. American Mathematical Society, Providence (1980)
14. Besag, J.: On the statistical analysis of dirty pictures. Journal of Royal Statistical Society. Series B (Methodological) 48, 259–302 (1986)
15. Pieczynski, W.: Modèles de Markov en traitements d'images. Traitement Du Signal 20, 255–278 (2003)

Content-Based Emblem Retrieval Using Zernike Moments

Ezequiel Cura, Mariano Tepper, and Marta Mejail

Departamento de Computacion, Facultad de Ciencias Exactas y Naturales,
Universidad de Buenos Aires, Argentina

Abstract. The problem of content-based image retrieval is becoming essential in many real-world applications, mostly due to the growth in size of modern image databases. In particular, this work addresses the retrieval of trademark emblems, which is key for detecting trademark infringement. A common approach that proved suitable for this task, is to encode emblems using shape descriptors and Zernike complex moments. This work focuses on their study, proposing a two-fold contribution. First, we present some modifications to Zernike complex moments and then we explore the use of different comparison metrics. Both have shown to report improvements in retrieved results and in execution time.

1 Introduction

With the growth in size of modern image databases, the problem of content-based image retrieval is becoming crucial in many real-world applications. For some applications, determining duplicates, or look-alike images, is an essential task. The detection of trademark infringement is one of them, with deep commercial and monetary implications. Already registered trademark logos, or emblems, have to be protected against hundreds of new ones that are created every day. Fig. 1 depicts some examples of similar emblems.

The trademark infringement problem can be very simply stated: given a database of registered emblems, does a new emblem look similar to any of them? Unfortunately this problem cannot be solved in a fully automatic way by any state-of-the-art method. In practice, the new emblem is used as a query which retrieves the most similar emblems from the database. Then a human expert performs the final recognition test by only observing these remaining emblems.

Direct image comparison methods such as correlation fail to account for the perceptual similarity between two emblems. A successful approach is to regard emblems as shapes. Each shape in the database is then encoded by using some descriptor and these descriptors are ultimately used for comparison. Specifically, a query consists on sorting the emblems from the most similar to the least similar to the query emblem and then returning the first ones among them.

In general, when requirements impose real-time queries, only global methods are considered at the expense of possibly missing similar emblem subparts. For example, Shape Context [1] is commonly used for this task.

I. Bloch and R.M. Cesar, Jr. (Eds.): CIARP 2010, LNCS 6419, pp. 79–86, 2010.

Fig. 1. Examples of look-alike emblems. In the first example, NBC agreed to pay a compensation fee to Nebraska ETV Network for using a similar emblem.

An alternative and popular approach is derived from the use of image moments [2]. Zernike Moments (ZMs) are an interesting choice as they provide rotation and translation invariance, minimal redundancy and limited robustness to noise [3,4]. Although it used to be computationally prohibitive to compute higher order ZMs, nowadays it has become not only possible but also fast and numerically precise [5]. Our paper builds upon these approaches, improving the accuracy and the performance of ZMs-based image retrieval.

First, we propose a modification to ZMs base on an appropriate weighting and on PCA. The second contribution of this paper is to show that by a simle two-stage method for comparing ZMs, high efficiency and accuracy are achieved. The first stage, relies on a fast pruning technique, that allow to quickly retrieve a small set of likely candidates. The second stage performs more accurate and time demanding comparisons but, by applying it to the small ouput of the first stage, high speed is achieved.

This paper is organized as follows. Zernike Moments are reviewed in Section 1.1. In Sections 2 and 3 we propose a modification to Zernike Moments and a fast composite distance, respectively. Section 4 presents results that demonstrate the pertinence of our approach and provides final remarks.

1.1   Previous Work on Zernike Moments

Starting from a complete set of complex polynomials defined by Zernike, Khotanzad and Hong [3] introduce complex Zernike Moments.

Definition 1. *A Zernike polynom* $V_{nm} : \mathbb{R}^2 \to \mathbb{C}$ *is defined as*

$$V_{nm}(x,y) = V_{nm}(\rho,\theta) = R_{nm}(\rho)\exp(im\theta) \qquad (1)$$

where $0 \le n$, $|m| \le n$, $n - |m|$ *is even,* $\rho = |x + iy|$, $\theta = \arg(x + iy)$ *and*

$$R_{nm}(\rho) = \sum_{s=0}^{\frac{n-|m|}{2}} (-1)^s \; \frac{(n-s)!}{s!(\frac{n+|m|}{2} - s)! \, (\frac{n-|m|}{2} - s)!} \; \rho^{n-2s}.$$

The input for computing ZMs consists of a binary image, represented by a function $I : \mathbb{R}^2 \to \{0,1\}$. Of course not every emblem is binary and it must consequently be binarized. Binarization methods are outside the scope of this work and will not be covered: it is sufficient to state that any such method is suitable.

Definition 2. *Given a binary image I, a Zernike Moment A_{nm} is defined as*

$$A_{nm} = \frac{n+1}{\pi} \iint\limits_{x^2+y^2 \leq 1} I(x,y) V_{nm}^*(x,y) \; dx \; dy \tag{2}$$

where $V_{nm}^*(x,y)$ is the complex conjugate value of $V_{nm}(x,y)$.

From the above definition it can be trivially deduced that ZMs are translation invariant. Additionally, the image can be reconstructed from its ZMs [5]. Li *et al.* [4] show how to modify ZMs to obtain fully rotation invariance.

Definition 3. *A rotation invariant Zernike Moment A'_{nm} is defined as*

$$A'_{nm} = A_{nm} \exp(-im\theta_{n_0 1}), \tag{3}$$

where $V_{nm}^*(x,y)$ is the complex conjugate value of $V_{nm}(x,y)$ and $\theta_{n_0 1} = \arg(A_{n_0 1})$.

The value of n_0 is global, in the sense that it must be remain the same for all emblems in the database. Otherwise, comparisons will not be consistent.

2   Zernike Moments as Image Descriptors

In this section we present methods for using Zernike complex moments as image descriptors. Following Def. 2, given $n, m \in \mathbb{N}_0$ we say A_{nm} is valid if $m \leq n$ and $n - |m|$ is even.

Definition 4. *Given $N, M \in \mathbb{N}_0$ such that A_{NM} is valid, we define #dmz as*

$$\#\mathrm{dmz}(N, M) = \# \{A_{nm} \text{ is valid} \mid 0 \leq n \leq N, \; 0 \leq m \leq M\}$$

$$= \frac{\frac{N(N+1)}{2} - \lceil \frac{N}{2} \rceil}{2} + N + 1 - \frac{N - M}{2}. \tag{4}$$

We also denote $\#\mathrm{dmz}(N) = \#\mathrm{dmz}(N, N)$.

Definition 5. *Given an image I and $N \in \mathbb{N}_0$, we define a Zernike Moment Descriptor (ZMD) as a vector $\mathbf{Z}_{I,N} \in \mathbb{C}^{\#\mathrm{dmz}(N)}$ where*

$$(\forall n, m \leq N, A_{nm} \text{ is valid}) \quad \mathbf{Z}_{I,N}(\#\mathrm{dmz}(n,m)) = A_{nm}$$

2.1   First Modification: Higher Order Weighting

Using higher order ZMs allows to obtain a more precise description of the image. In fact, the reconstruction of an image from approximately 50 ZMs is very precise [5]. However, higher order ZMs are more sensitive to noise and prone to numerical errors [3].

The key idea behind this modification is that higher order ZMs are useful for encoding fine details, but, at the same time, more importance must be assigned

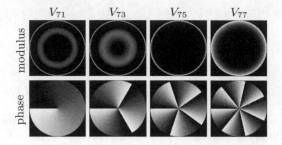

Fig. 2. Values taken by Zernike polynoms of order V_{7m}, $m = 1, 3, 5, 7$, on the unit circle

to lower order ZMs, which encode coarser details. In other words ZMs must be weighted, assigning more weight to lower order ZMs than to higher order ZMs.

Following Def. 4, valid ZMs describe a lower diagonal sparse matrix. By observing the values taken by Zernike polynoms (Def. 1) inside the unit circle in Fig. 2, we note that (1) the number of phase cycles depends only and is equal to m and (2) the number of weighted rings is equal to $\frac{n-m}{2} + 1$. In fact, given a fixed n, a larger value for m will result in a more sensitive ZMs. The direct implication is that when weighting ZMs we must not only take into account n but also m.

Definition 6. *We define a weighted Zernike Moment Descriptor (wZMD) as a vector* $\mathbf{Z}_{I,N}^w \in \mathbb{C}^{\#\mathrm{dmz}(N)}$ *such that*

$$(\forall n, m \leq N, A_{nm} \text{ is valid}) \quad \mathbf{Z}_{I,N}^w(k) = A_{nm} \cdot \exp(-k \cdot m \cdot |\sin(\theta_{n01})|), \quad (5)$$

where $k = \#\mathrm{dmz}(n, m)$.

2.2 Second Modification: PCA ZMs

PCA is a classical technique that transforms a number of possibly correlated variables into a smaller number of uncorrelated variables. PCA has been also extended to work with complex numbers [6]. A vector $v \sim \mathrm{N}(\mu, \Sigma)$, is transformed into a vector $\tilde{v} \sim \mathrm{N}(0, \mathrm{I})$ where I is the identity matrix, by using

$$\tilde{v} = (\Phi \, \Lambda^{-\frac{1}{2}})^T \, v \tag{6}$$

where Φ and Λ are the eigenvectors and eigenvalues matrices of Σ, respectively. The eigenvalues in Φ are sorted in decreasing order and the columns of Λ are arranged accordingly.

This process relies in an accurate estimation of Σ from the samples in our database. In our work, we compute Σ with the method proposed by Turk and Pentland [7]. Given a set of samples $\gamma_0, \gamma_2, \cdots, \gamma_n$, Σ is calculated as

$$\Sigma = \frac{1}{n} \sum_{i=0}^{n} \phi_i \, \phi_i^T \quad \text{where} \qquad \psi = \frac{1}{n} \sum_{i=0}^{n} \gamma_i \qquad \phi_i = \gamma_i - \psi$$

In our setting, the samples are simply the wZMD in the database.

Definition 7. *We define the PCA Zernike Moments Descriptors (PCA ZMD) as a vector* $\mathbf{Z}_{I,N}^{P} \in \mathbb{C}^{\#\mathrm{dmz}(N)}$ *where*

$$\mathbf{Z}_{I,N}^{wP} = (\Phi \, \Lambda^{-\frac{1}{2}})^T \, \mathbf{Z}_{I,N}^{w}. \tag{7}$$

We also note $\mathbf{Z}_{I,N}^{wP(n)}$ *the vector composed of the first n dimensions of* $\mathbf{Z}_{I,N}^{wP}$.

3   Metrics for Comparing Zernike Moments

Classically, two ZMD were compared by reconstructing both images and directly comparing them, i.e. using correlation or L_2 distance. Li *et al.* [4] proposed the use of a distance that takes into account phase and modulus.

Definition 8. *Let us define the* $D_\rho : \mathbb{C}^N \times \mathbb{C}^N \to \mathbb{R}$ *and* $D_\phi : \mathbb{C}^N \times \mathbb{C}^N \to \mathbb{R}$

$$D_\rho(X,Y) = \left(\sum_{i=1}^{N} (|X_i| - |Y_i|)^2 \right)^{\frac{1}{2}} \quad D_\phi(X,Y) = \left(\sum_{i=1}^{N} (\arg X_i - \arg Y_i)^2 \right)^{\frac{1}{2}}$$

The distance $D_\alpha : \mathbb{C}^N \times \mathbb{C}^N \to \mathbb{R}$ *is defined as* $D_\alpha = \alpha D_\rho + (\alpha - 1) D_\phi$

Our tests with different values for α indicate, as suggested in Li *et al.* [4], that the best results are obtained with $\alpha = 0.5$. Although other distance functions have been proposed to compare ZMs [3,8], during experimentation we found better results using D_α and consequently we use it as our reference metric.

For the sake of computational efficiency, we define a combination of two simple metrics. This allow us to perform real-time and accurate queries. The first metric performs a fast pruning of the database, retrieving a small set of good look-alike candidate images

$$d_{\|\cdot\|}(u,v) = |(\|u\|_2 - \|v\|_2)|. \tag{8}$$

As the norm of all ZMD in the database can be precomputed, the k nearest ZMD can be retrieved in $O(\max(\log(N), \, k))$. These neighboring ZMD can then be more carefully examined with

$$d_e(u,v) = \|u - v\|_2 \tag{9}$$

In synthesis, our algorithm will first prune the database using a threshold on $d_{\|\cdot\|}$ and then apply d_e on the smaller retrieved subset.

4   Results and Final Remarks

It is extremely hard to obtain real-world emblem datasets which are internally divided into similar classes. Therefore experimentation was performed on the following datasets:

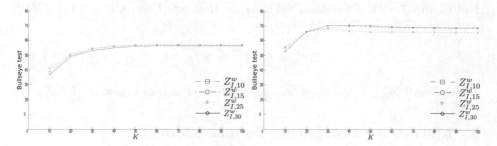

Fig. 3. Performance as the number of candidates K varies using wZMD of different dimensions. Left, on the MPEG-7 CE Shape 1 dataset. Right, on the ALOI dataset.

MPEG-7 CE Shape 1: 70 conceptual classes of 20 silhouettes [9].
ALOI: 20 classes of 74 images [10]. Each class is a set of silhouettes of some object taken from different views.
MNIST: 10 classes of 1000 binarized handwritten digits [11].

The performance is measured using the so-called "bullseye test". Given a dataset S_n^c, where c is the number of classes in S and n the number of images per class, each image in S_n^c is used as a query and one counts the number of correct images (i.e. belonging to the same class than the query) in the top $2n$ matches. A perfect score is achieved when n^2c positive cases are found across all the dataset.

The main parameter of our method is the number of candidates K retrieved using $d_{\|\cdot\|}$ (Eq. 8). Defining the number of suitable look-alike image candidates will determine the retrieval performance. Fig. 3 depicts the change in score as K varies. The optimal value for K is tied to the characteristics of each dataset. However, in general, small datasets will require a larger K (around 50% of the dataset size), while K can be safely reduced to 10% on larger datasets.

Table 1 shows the performance of the methods dsicussed in this work. Following Li *et al.* [4], we use $D_{\alpha=0.5}$.

On the first part, when comparing performance using $D_{\alpha=0.5}$ versus $d_{\|\cdot\|} + d_e$, two phenomena can be observed. First, in all cases our approach outperforms the one by Li *et al.* [4]. Second, increasing the number dimensions in ZMD does not necessarily imply better results (e.g. on the MNIST dataset).

Table 1. Bulls-eye test scores. For each method best results are highlighted.

Dataset	Metric	$\mathbf{Z}_{I,10}$	$\mathbf{Z}_{I,15}$	$\mathbf{Z}_{I,25}$	$\mathbf{Z}_{I,30}$	$\mathbf{Z}_{I,30}^{wP(20)}$	$\mathbf{Z}_{I,30}^{wP(15)}$	$\mathbf{Z}_{I,30}^{wP(10)}$	$\mathbf{Z}_{I,30}^{wP(5)}$
MPEG-7	$D_{\alpha=0.5}$	36.09	39.02	38.02	36.82	–	–	–	–
	$d_{\|\cdot\|} + d_e$	56.96	60.43	61.21	61.71	61.19	61.35	60.12	56.89
ALOI	$D_{\alpha=0.5}$	63.24	65.94	65.45	64.81	–	–	–	–
	$d_{\|\cdot\|} + d_e$	68.16	69.98	70.67	70.34	64.91	66.32	70.46	66.35
MNIST	$D_{\alpha=0.5}$	38.32	36.66	36.08	36.81	–	–	–	–
	$d_{\|\cdot\|} + d_e$	57.2	55.26	55.6	53.56	48.54	50.87	55.06	56.36

The second part of the table focuses on the result of using PCA. The performance of using PCA and $D_{\alpha=0.5}$ was very poor and results are not shown. Although dependent on the dataset, usually fixing $n = 15$ is sufficient. In our experiments with $\mathbf{Z}_{I,30}^{wP(n)}$, best results were obtained when n was chosen such that the cumulated standard desviation of the first n dimensions of $\mathbf{Z}_{I,N}^{wP}$ was around 90%. Note also that the best results obtained using PCA are almost as good as the best results obtained without it. However, comparing PCA ZMs is considerably faster because distance calculations involve fewer terms.

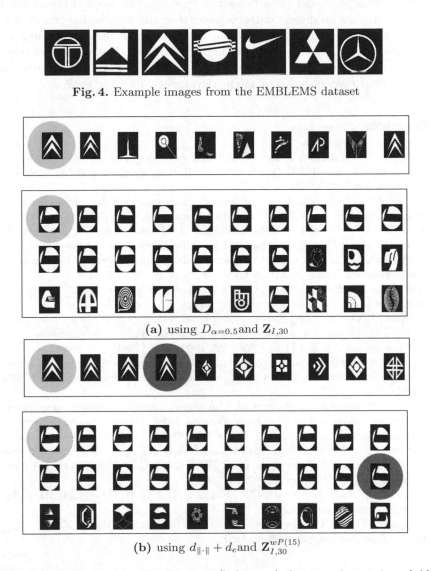

Fig. 4. Example images from the EMBLEMS dataset

(a) using $D_{\alpha=0.5}$ and $\mathbf{Z}_{I,30}$

(b) using $d_{\|\cdot\|} + d_e$ and $\mathbf{Z}_{I,30}^{wP(15)}$

Fig. 5. EMBLEMS dataset results. In green (light grey) the query image, in red (dark grey) the farthest ranked "equal to the query" image.

Additionally, we tested the proposed method on a dataset of 8 thousand binary images of real trademark (Fig. 4) . This dataset includes several slightly distorded images for each emblem. Two query examples over the EMBLEMS dataset are shown in Fig. 5. Li *et al.*'s approach [4] retrieves the farthest "equal to the query" emblem on the 36th and 72th position in each test. All "equal to the query emblems" are ranked first by the proposed method. Note that some of the subsequent retrieved emblems are similar to the query.

To conclude, this paper introduces (1) a composite modification to Zernike Moments Descriptors and (2) a two-stage time efficient method for comparing ZMs. Experiments on diverse datasets show that the proposed approach significantly and consistently improves the accuracy of the content-based image retrieval based on ZMs. Being based on simpler distance calculations, considerable speed is gained. Such combination allows the proposed approach to outperform state-of-the-art content-based image retrieval methods based on ZMs.

References

1. Belongie, S., Malik, J., Puzicha, J.: Shape matching and object recognition using shape contexts. IEEE Transactions on Pattern Analysis and Machine Intelligence 24, 509–522 (2002)
2. Kotoulas, L., Andreadis, I.: Image analysis using moments. In: Alexander Technological Educational Institute (ATEI) of Thessaloniki, Greece, pp. 360–364 (2005)
3. Khotanzad, A., Hong, Y.H.: Invariant image recognition by zernike moments. IEEE Transactions on Pattern Analysis and Machine Intelligence 12, 489–497 (1990)
4. Li, S., Lee, M.C., Pun, C.M.: Complex zernike moments features for shape-based image retrieval. Trans. Sys. Man Cyber. Part A 39, 227–237 (2009)
5. Amayeh, G.R., Erol, A., Bebis, G., Nicolescu, M.: Accurate and efficient computation of high order zernike moments. In: Bebis, G., Boyle, R., Koracin, D., Parvin, B. (eds.) ISVC 2005. LNCS, vol. 3804, pp. 462–469. Springer, Heidelberg (2005)
6. Horel, J.D.: Complex principal component analysis: Theory and examples. Journal of Climate and Applied Meteorology 23, 1660–1673 (1984)
7. Turk, M.A., Pentland, A.P.: Face recognition using eigenfaces. In: IEEE Computer Society Conference on Computer Vision and Pattern Recognition, pp. 586–591 (1991)
8. Revaud, J., Lavoué, G., Baskurt, A.: Improving zernike moments comparison for optimal similarity and rotation angle retrieval. IEEE Transactions on Pattern Analysis and Machine Intelligence 31, 627–636 (2009)
9. Latecki, L., Lakamper, R., Eckhardt, U.: Shape descriptors for non-rigid shapes with a single closed contour. In: Proc. IEEE Conf. Computer Vision and Pattern Recognition, vol. 2000, pp. 424–429 (2000)
10. Geusebroek, J.M., Burghouts, G.J., Smeulders, A.W.M.: The amsterdam library of object images. Int. J. Comput. Vision 1, 103–112 (2005)
11. Lecun, Y., Cortes, C.: The mnist database of handwritten digits (2004), http://yann.lecun.com/exdb/mnist/

A New Algorithm for Training SVMs Using Approximate Minimal Enclosing Balls

Emanuele Frandi[4], Maria Grazia Gasparo[3], Stefano Lodi[1],
Ricardo Ñanculef[2], and Claudio Sartori[1]

[1] Dept. of Electronics, Computer Science and Systems, University of Bologna, Italy
{claudio.sartori,stefano.lodi}@unibo.it
[2] Dept. of Informatics, Federico Santa María University, Chile
jnancu@inf.utfsm.cl
[3] Dept. of Energetics *Sergio Stecco*, University of Florence, Italy
mariagrazia.gasparo@unifi.it
[4] Dept. of Mathematics *Ulisse Dini*, University of Florence, Italy
emanuele.frandi@gmail.com

Abstract. It has been shown that many kernel methods can be equivalently formulated as minimal enclosing ball (MEB) problems in a certain feature space. Exploiting this reduction, efficient algorithms to scale up Support Vector Machines (SVMs) and other kernel methods have been introduced under the name of Core Vector Machines (CVMs). In this paper, we study a new algorithm to train SVMs based on an instance of the Frank-Wolfe optimization method recently proposed to approximate the solution of the MEB problem. We show that, specialized to SVM training, this algorithm can scale better than CVMs at the price of a slightly lower accuracy.

1 Introduction

Support Vector Machines (SVMs) are currently a well known set of methods to address classification and other machine learning problems with successful results in several application fields. SVMs are usually formulated as the solution of a convex quadratic programming problem (QP), for which a naive implementation requires $O(m^2)$ space and $O(m^3)$ time in the number of examples m [15,18], complexities that are prohibitively expensive for large scale problems. Major research efforts have been hence directed towards scaling up SVM algorithms to large datasets.

Due to the typically dense structure of the matrices involved in the QP, large SVM problems are usually adressed using an *active set method* where at each iteration only a small number of variables are allowed to change [14,8,13]. The most prominent example is Sequential Minimal Optimization (SMO [4,13]), where only two variables are selected for optimization each time. The main disadvantage of these methods is that they tend to have slow convergence when getting closer to the solution and performance results in practice are very sensitive to the size of the active set, the way to select the active variables and other implementation

I. Bloch and R.M. Cesar, Jr. (Eds.): CIARP 2010, LNCS 6419, pp. 87–95, 2010.

details like the caching strategy used to avoid the repetitive computation of the kernel function [14]. Other attempts to scale up SVM methods consist in adapting *interior point methods* to some classes of the SVM QP [5]. For large-scale problems however the resulting rank of the kernel matrix can still be too high to be handled efficiently [18]. The reformulation of the SVM objective function [6], sampling methods to reduce the number of variables in the problem [11,10] and the combination of small SVMs using ensemble methods [12] have also been explored.

A key observation exploited in [18] is that the QP underlying many SVMs is equivalent to the QP defining a *minimal enclosing ball* (MEB) problem, that is, the problem of computing the ball of smallest radius containing a set of points. Recent advances in computational geometry have demonstrated that there are algorithms capable to approximate a MEB with any degree of accuracy ϵ in $O(1/\epsilon)$ iterations independently of the number of points and the dimensionality of the space [18]. Based on these ideas, [18] obtains an algorithm to train SVMs which exhibits linear time-complexity in the number of examples m approximating the solution with any desired accuracy. Experiments in [18] confirm that this approach can be faster than SMO in large-scale problems [4,13].

In this paper, we study a new algorithm to exploit the reduction of SVMs to MEBs, which can still approximate the solution with any degree of accuracy ϵ but is considerably simpler than [18]. The algorithm completely avoids the resolution of reduced QP problems at each iteration and the corresponding computation and storage of reduced gram matrices that [18] need to by-pass using SMO and a caching strategy. Experiments in small, medium and large-scale classification problems show that, specialized to SVMs, this algorithm to compute MEBs is slightly less accurate than [18] but can significatively improve the complexity and actual running times of this algorithm.

2   MEB Problems and Support Vector Machines

As pointed out first by [18] and then generalized by [19], several SVM methods can be equivalently formulated as MEB problems in a certain feature space, that is, as the computation of the ball of smallest radius containing the images of the dataset under a mapping into a dot-product space $\mathcal{Z}$.

Consider a dataset $S = \{\mathbf{x}_i : i \in I\} \subset \mathcal{X}$ indexed by $I = \{1, 2, \ldots, m\}$ and a mapping $\phi : \mathcal{X} \to \mathcal{Z}$, such that $\tilde{k}(\mathbf{x}_i, \mathbf{x}_j) = \phi(\mathbf{x}_i)^T \phi(\mathbf{x}_j) \ \forall i, j \in I$ for a given kernel function $\tilde{k}$. The closed ball of center $\mathbf{c} \in \mathcal{Z}$ and radius $r \in \mathbb{R}^+$ is denoted by $\mathcal{B}(\mathbf{c}, r)$. The MEB $\mathcal{B}(\mathbf{c}^*, r^*)$ of $\phi(S)$ can hence be defined as the solution of the following optimization problem

$$\min_{r^2, \mathbf{c}} r^2 \qquad (1)$$
$$\text{st: } \|\phi(\mathbf{x}_i) - \mathbf{c}\|^2 \leq r^2 \ \forall i \in I,$$

whose Lagrange dual is given by [20]

$$\max_{\boldsymbol{\alpha}} \; \Phi(\boldsymbol{\alpha}) = \sum_{i \in I} \alpha_i \tilde{k}(\mathbf{x}_i, \mathbf{x}_i) - \sum_{i,j \in I} \alpha_i \alpha_j \tilde{k}(\mathbf{x}_i, \mathbf{x}_j) \qquad (2)$$
$$\text{st:} \sum_{i \in I} \alpha_i = 1, \;\; \alpha_i \geq 0 \;\; \forall i \in I \,.$$

If we denote by $\boldsymbol{\alpha}^*$ the solution of (2), the center $\mathbf{c}^*$ and the squared radius r^{*2} of the MEB of $\phi(S)$ follow from strong duality:

$$\mathbf{c}^* = \sum_{i \in I} \alpha_i^* \phi(\mathbf{x}_i) \;\; ; \;\; r^{*2} = \Phi(\boldsymbol{\alpha}^*) \,. \qquad (3)$$

Problem (2) coincides with the formulation of a number of kernel methods by correspondingly setting the kernel function $\tilde{k}$. For L2-SVMs [18] for example, we are given a set of labels $\{y_i : i \in I\}$ for the set of training inputs $\{\mathbf{x}_i : i \in I\}$ and we are aimed to implement a decision function to predict the class of new inputs $\mathbf{x} \in \mathcal{X}$. If the problem is two-class we can suppose without loss of generality that $y_i = +1$ if $\mathbf{x}_i$ belongs to the first class and $y_i = -1$ if $\mathbf{x}_i$ belongs to the other class. SVMs implement a decision function of the following form [15]

$$h(\mathbf{x}) = \text{sign} \left(\sum_{i \in I} \alpha_i y_i k(\mathbf{x}_i, \mathbf{x}) + b \right) , \qquad (4)$$

where k is a kernel function used to implement non-linear classification boundaries in non-linearly separable cases and the weights α_i are determined by minimizing a risk functional. This functional takes the form of problem (2) if we set $\tilde{k}$ to

$$\tilde{k}(\mathbf{x}_i, \mathbf{x}_j) = y_i y_j \left(k(\mathbf{x}_i, \mathbf{x}_j) + 1 \right) + \delta_{ij}/C \,, \qquad (5)$$

where C is a regularization parameter used within the SVM to handle noisy data. Details can be found in [18]. The kernel k is required to satisfy the following normalization condition

$$k(\mathbf{x}_i, \mathbf{x}_i) = \Delta^2 = \text{constant} \,, \qquad (6)$$

which is automatically satisfied for SVM kernels of the form $k(\mathbf{x}_i, \mathbf{x}_j) = g(\|\mathbf{x}_i - \mathbf{x}_j\|)$. Equivalent constructions for other kernel methods including regression and novelty detection are presented in [18] and [19]. Refer also to [19] for studies on kernels which do not satisfy the normalization condition.

3   Approximate MEBs and Core Vector Machines

The problem of computing the minimal enclosing ball of a set of points has a long history in computational geometry [20]. Traditional algorithms to find exact MEBs scale exponentially in the space dimension and hence could not be applied to SVM problems in which the feature space induced by the kernel is high-dimensional. Recent advances have been obtained by shifting the attention to approximation algorithms capable to output a ball near the MEB by a given degree of precision.

Given $\epsilon > 0$, a ball $\mathcal{B}(\mathbf{c}, r) \subset \mathcal{Z}$ is said to be an $(1 + \epsilon)$-*approximation* to the MEB $\mathcal{B}(\mathbf{c}^*, r^*)$ of $A \subset \mathcal{Z}$ (or more shortly an $(1 + \epsilon)$-*MEB* of A) if $r \leq r^*$ and $A \subset \mathcal{B}(\mathbf{c}, (1 + \epsilon)r)$.

In [1] and [20], algorithms to compute $(1 + \epsilon)$-MEBs that scale independently of the dimension of $\mathcal{Z}$ and the cardinality of A have been provided. These algorithms are built on the concept of ϵ-*core set* for A, that is, a subset $C \subset A$ whose MEB is a $(1 + \epsilon)$-MEB of A. In particular, the algorithm described in [1] is able to provide an ϵ-core set of a set A in no more than $O(1/\epsilon)$ iterations. We denote with C_k the core set approximation obtained at the k-th iteration and its MEB as $B_k = \mathcal{B}(\mathbf{c}_k, r_k)$. Starting from a given C_0, at each iteration C_{k+1} is defined as the union of C_k and the point of A furthest from $\mathbf{c}_k$. The algorithm then computes B_{k+1} and stops if $\mathcal{B}(\mathbf{c}_{k+1}, (1 + \epsilon)r_{k+1})$ contains A.

Exploiting these ideas, Tsang and colleagues introduced in [18] the CVM (Core Vector Machine) for training SVMs supporting a reduction to a MEB problem. CVM is described in Algorithm 1, where each C_k is identified by the index set $I_k \subset I$. The expression for the radius r_k follows easily from (3). Moreover, it is easy to show [18] that step 10 exactly looks for the point $\mathbf{x}_{i^*}$ whose image $\phi(\mathbf{x}_{i^*})$ is the furthest from $\mathbf{c}_k$. The index i^* is then included in the index set and the reduced QP corresponding to the MEB of the new approximate core set is solved.

Data: $S = \{(\mathbf{x}_i, y_i) : i \in I\}$, indexed by $I = \{1, 2, \ldots, m\}$, ϵ, I_0, $\boldsymbol{\alpha_0}$.

1   For any $\boldsymbol{\alpha} \in \mathbb{R}^k$, define $R(\boldsymbol{\alpha}) = \sum_{i,j \in I_k} \alpha_i \alpha_j \tilde{k}(\mathbf{x}_i, \mathbf{x}_j)$;

2   $\Delta^2 \longleftarrow \tilde{k}(\mathbf{x}_1, \mathbf{x}_1)$;

3   $r_0^2 \longleftarrow \Delta^2 - R(\boldsymbol{\alpha}_0)$;

4   $i^* \longleftarrow \arg\max_{i \in I} \delta^2(i, \boldsymbol{\alpha}_0) = \Delta^2 + R(\boldsymbol{\alpha}_0) - 2\sum_{j \in I_0} \alpha_{0,j} \tilde{k}(\mathbf{x}_j, \mathbf{x}_i)$;

5   $k \longleftarrow 0$;

6   **while** $\delta^2(i^*, \boldsymbol{\alpha}_k) > (1 + \epsilon)^2 r_k^2$ **do**

7      $k \longleftarrow k + 1$;

8      $I_k \longleftarrow I_{k-1} \cup \{i^*\}$;

9   Find $\boldsymbol{\alpha_k}$ by solving the reduced QP
     $\min_{\boldsymbol{\alpha} \in \mathbb{R}^m} R(\boldsymbol{\alpha})$ s.t. $\sum_{i \in I_k} \alpha_i = 1$, $\alpha_i \geq 0 \, \forall i \in I_k$;

10      $r_k^2 \longleftarrow \Delta^2 - R(\boldsymbol{\alpha}_k)$;

11      $i^* \longleftarrow \arg\max_{i \in I} \delta^2(i, \boldsymbol{\alpha}_k) = \Delta^2 + R(\boldsymbol{\alpha}_k) - 2\sum_{j \in I_k} \alpha_{k,j} \tilde{k}(\mathbf{x}_j, \mathbf{x}_i)$;

12 **end**

13 Output $I_S = I_k$, $\boldsymbol{\alpha} = \boldsymbol{\alpha}_k$.

Algorithm 1. Training SVMs using Approximate MEBs (MEB-SVMs)

Algorithm 1 has two main sources of computational overhead: the computation of the furthest point in step 10, which is linear in m, and the solution of the optimization problem in step 8. Complexity of step 10 can be made constant and independent of m by suitable sampling techniques [18]. As regards the optimization step 8, CVMs adopt a SMO method [4,13], where only two variables are selected for optimization at each iteration. It is known that the cost of each SMO iteration is not too high, but the method can require a large number of iterations in order to satisfy reasonable stopping criteria [13].

4   The New Algorithm for MEB-SVMs

In this section we provide a new algorithm to train SVMs based on approximate MEBs, which avoids the resolution of the reduced QP problem at each iteration of Algorithm 1. For this purpose we adopt a variant of the Frank-Wolfe algorithm, recently studied in [3] and [20]. The Frank-Wolfe method (see Algorithm 2, where $\mathbf{e}_i$ denotes the i-th vector of the canonical basis of $\mathbb{R}^m$) solves the general problem of maximizing a concave function $g(\boldsymbol{\alpha})$ on the unit simplex.

---

1   $\boldsymbol{\alpha} \longleftarrow \mathbf{e}_{i_0}$ with $i_0 = \arg \max_{i \in I} g(\mathbf{e}_i)$;

2   **for** $k = 0, 1, \ldots$ *until a stopping criterion is satisfied,* **do**

3   $\quad i^* \longleftarrow \arg \max_{i \in I} \nabla g(\boldsymbol{\alpha}_k)_i$;

4   $\quad \lambda^* \longleftarrow \arg \max_{\lambda \in [0,1]} g\left((1 - \lambda)\boldsymbol{\alpha}_k + \lambda \mathbf{e}_{i^*}\right)$;

5   $\quad \boldsymbol{\alpha}_{k+1} \longleftarrow (1 - \lambda^*)\boldsymbol{\alpha}_k + \lambda^* \mathbf{e}_{i^*}$;

6   **end**

Algorithm 2. The Frank-Wolfe Algorithm

Consider now the problem defined in (2). The gradient of $\Phi(\boldsymbol{\alpha})$ is given by

$\nabla \Phi(\boldsymbol{\alpha})_i = \tilde{k}(\mathbf{x}_i, \mathbf{x}_i) - 2 \sum_{j \in I} \alpha_j \tilde{k}(\mathbf{x}_i, \mathbf{x}_j) = \phi(\mathbf{x}_i)^T \phi(\mathbf{x}_i) - 2\phi(\mathbf{x}_i)^T \left(\sum_{j \in I} \alpha_j \phi(\mathbf{x}_j)\right)$. Furthermore, given any $\boldsymbol{\alpha}_k$, we can define the ball $B_k = \mathcal{B}(\mathbf{c}_k, r_k)$, where $\mathbf{c}_k = \sum_{j \in I} \alpha_j \phi(\mathbf{x}_j)$ and $r_k^2 = \Phi(\boldsymbol{\alpha}_k)$. In this way, step 3 of Algorithm 2 corresponds to

$$\arg \max_{i \in I} \left(\phi(\mathbf{x}_i)^T \phi(\mathbf{x}_i) - 2\phi(\mathbf{x}_i)^T \mathbf{c}_k\right) = \arg \max_{i \in I} \|\mathbf{c}_k - \phi(\mathbf{x}_i)\|^2 , \qquad (7)$$

that is, step 3 selects the point maximizing the distance from the center of B_k, as does step 10 of Algorithm 1. Moreover, the updating formula for $\boldsymbol{\alpha}$ shows that only the i^*-th entry of $\boldsymbol{\alpha}$ can become nonzero at each iteration. The optimization step 4 is analytic: indeed, it can be shown [3,20] that

$$\lambda^* = \frac{1}{2} - \frac{r_k^2}{2\|\mathbf{c}_k - \phi(\mathbf{x}_{i^*})\|^2} . \qquad (8)$$

In [20], it has been proved that $\{r_k\}$ is a monotonically increasing sequence. On the other hand, r_k is bounded by the radius r_* of the optimal MEB. Therefore, if we stop the Frank-Wolfe procedure with the same criterion as in Algorithm 1, then we have $r_k \leq r_*$, that is, I_k identifies a core set for $\phi(S)$ and B_k a

$(1 + \epsilon)$-MEB. In conclusion, we can preserve the main structure of Algorithm 1, substituting step 8 with a step 8' defined as follows:

$$\boldsymbol{\alpha}_{k+1} \longleftarrow (1 - \lambda^*)\boldsymbol{\alpha}_k + \lambda^* \mathbf{e}_{i^*}, \quad \text{with} \quad \lambda^* \longleftarrow \left(\frac{1}{2} - \frac{r_k^2}{2\delta^2(i^*, \boldsymbol{\alpha}_k)}\right).$$

This way, we are able to avoid the solution of reduced QP problems. The cost of each iteration of the algorithm is now dominated only by the computation of the furthest point from $\mathbf{c}_k$. The new algorithm hence offers considerably lighter iterations, whose complexity does not depend on additional numerical routines. Moreover, a theoretical bound in terms of ϵ on the total number of iterations, exactly identical to that of CVMs, holds. Indeed, Yildirim [20] proved that the method computes an ϵ-core set in $O(1/\epsilon)$ iterations.

Remark. From a numerical optimization point of view, the following remark might be of interest. From Theorem 2.2 of [3], we have that $\Phi(\boldsymbol{\alpha}^*) - \Phi(\boldsymbol{\alpha}_k) \leq 4C_f/(k+3)$, where C_f is a constant, bounded by the squared diameter of the MEB of S, that is, $4\Phi(\boldsymbol{\alpha}^*)$. Therefore, $\Phi(\boldsymbol{\alpha}^*) - \Phi(\boldsymbol{\alpha}_k) \leq 16\Phi(\boldsymbol{\alpha}^*)/(k+3)$. It follows that the relative error $(\Phi(\boldsymbol{\alpha}^*) - \Phi(\boldsymbol{\alpha}_k))/\Phi(\boldsymbol{\alpha}^*)$ is smaller than any fixed tolerance τ after $(16/\tau - 3)$ iterations.

5   Experiments and Conclusions

We provide experiments on 13 datasets listed in Table 1. The size of each problem is quantified by considering the number of training examples m and the number of classes K. Since we employ a one-versus-one method for multi-category classification [9], the number of binary submodels to compute is given by $s_K = K(K-1)/2$ [15]. The average number of examples for submodel is denoted by $\bar{m}_K$. The datasets *Kdd-full*, *Ijcnn* and *extended Usps* (abbreviated as *Usps-ext*) were used as in previous research to test the large-scale capabilities of CVMs [18] and are available at [17]. The other problems are available at [7] or [2]. For problems without a predefined test-set (*Iris*, *Wine*, *Glass* and *Kdd-10pc*) a 20% of the data was randomly selected and reserved to assess prediction accuracy.

SVMs were trained using a gaussian kernel $k(\mathbf{x}_1, \mathbf{x}_2) = \exp(-\|\mathbf{x}_1 - \mathbf{x}_2\|^2/\sigma^2)$. For datasets *Kdd-full*, *Usps-ext* and *Ijcnn* we used the hyper-parameter values reported at [18,16]. For the small datasets ($\leq 10^4$ examples) hyper-parameters were determined using 10-fold cross-validation. For the remaining datasets σ^2 was set to the average squared distance among training patterns and C was determined on a logarithmic grid $[2^0, 2^{12}]$ using a validation-set (30% of the training-set). In order to compute I_0 and $\boldsymbol{\alpha}_0$ for Algorithm 1 we adopted the initialization procedure of [17]. We also adopted the LRR caching strategy designed in [17] for CVMs to avoid the computation of recently used kernel values.

Tables 1 and 2 summarize the experimental results obtained after training with the parameters determined by the model-selection procedure. The proposed algorithm is denoted here as FVM (acronym of Frank-Wolfe Vector Machine). In Table 1 we present accuracy and running times obtained on a 2.40GHz Intel

Table 1. Dataset features (first 4 columns) and Performance of the two algorithms (last 4 columns)

Dataset	m	K	$\bar{m}_K$	Accuracy (%)		Time (secs)	
				CVM	FVM	CVM	FVM
Glass	1.4E+02	6	2.3E+01	67.93	55.81	1.5E-01	8.0E-03
Wine	1.1E+02	3	3.8E+01	97.49	97.49	5.0E-02	3.5E-03
Iris	1.2E+02	3	4.0E+01	96.24	94.62	5.5E-03	3.0E-03
Letter	1.5E+04	26	5.8E+02	97.44	95.98	3.2E+01	1.2E+01
Usps	7.3E+03	10	7.3E+02	95.76	95.37	6.3E+00	6.0E+00
Pendigits	7.5E+03	10	7.5E+02	98.40	97.91	5.3E-01	1.1E+00
Protein	1.8E+04	3	5.9E+03	69.84	60.91	8.7E+03	3.0E+02
Mnist	6.0E+04	10	6.0E+03	98.53	97.82	4.0E+02	3.0E+02
Shuttle	4.4E+04	7	6.2E+03	99.77	98.41	2.1E+00	3.3E-01
Ijcnn	5.0E+04	2	2.5E+04	98.55	95.17	1.3E+03	1.0E+02
Kdd-10pc	4.0E+05	5	7.9E+04	99.92	98.84	1.3E+03	2.5E+00
Usps-ext	2.7E+05	2	1.3E+05	99.50	99.25	1.8E+01	6.7E+00
Kdd-full	4.9E+06	2	2.4E+06	90.88	91.66	1.4E+00	4.7E+00

Table 2. Detailed measures of complexity

Dataset	Number of Support Vectors		Kernel Evals (with Cache)		Kernel Evals (without Cache)		SMO-It
	CVM	FVM	CVM	FVM	CVM	FVM	CVM
Glass	1.2E+02	1.4E+02	2.8E+04	2.8E+04	1.3E+07	5.6E+05	2.8E+05
Wine	5.6E+01	6.4E+01	1.0E+04	1.0E+04	4.7E+06	4.0E+05	1.5E+05
Iris	1.4E+01	7.0E+01	5.3E+03	9.3E+03	4.7E+05	3.8E+05	1.7E+04
Letter	6.8E+03	9.4E+03	3.6E+07	6.6E+07	2.5E+09	2.1E+09	2.6E+07
Usps	1.6E+03	2.1E+03	6.6E+06	8.4E+06	1.8E+08	1.5E+08	1.7E+06
Pendigits	7.6E+02	1.7E+03	2.3E+06	8.2E+06	2.7E+07	8.7E+07	4.5E+05
Protein	1.5E+04	1.4E+04	3.2E+08	2.7E+08	7.9E+11	7.2E+09	1.5E+08
Mnist	1.0E+04	1.2E+04	1.9E+08	2.3E+08	1.5E+10	1.1E+09	3.1E+07
Shuttle	3.1E+02	7.7E+02	8.8E+05	3.0E+06	1.7E+08	5.5E+06	2.0E+06
Ijcnn	8.0E+03	7.1E+03	6.5E+08	7.2E+08	1.2E+11	2.4E+09	3.1E+07
Kdd-10pc	1.1E+04	1.4E+03	1.9E+09	1.4E+07	6.9E+10	2.7E+07	2.2E+07
Usps-ext	5.4E+02	5.6E+02	1.6E+07	9.3E+06	5.4E+08	9.7E+06	1.1E+06
Kdd-full	1.6E+01	7.0E+02	6.6E+04	1.5E+07	7.0E+06	1.5E+07	1.7E+05

Core 2 Duo with 2GB RAM running openSUSE 11.1. In Table 2 we present platform-independent measures of complexity: the number of Support Vectors in the resulting model, which determines model complexity, and the number of kernel evaluations, that is, the number of times that the kernel function is evaluated on a pair of examples, which is frequently used as the measure of algorithmic complexity for kernel methods. Table 2 presents both the total number of kernel evaluations required by the algorithm and the values effectively computed after checking the cache: *Kernel Evals (without Cache)* and *Kernel Evals (with Cache)* respectively. Finally, we report the total number of SMO-iterations (*SMO-It*) carried out by the CVM algorithm.

Experiments show that FVM exhibits a slightly lower accuracy than CVM but a quite better algorithmic complexity, measured as the number of kernel evaluations. Even if the caching strategy benefits significatively more to CVM than FVM, by reducing by some orders of magnitude the number kernel evaluations that CVM effectively computes, our method exhibits much better actual running times in all the cases but two (on one of them CVM is faster at expenses of the classification accuracy).

Note that the number of support vectors (training points taking part in the final model) is of the same order for both algorithms. However, CVM computes on average between 10^3 and 10^4 SMO iterations for each support vector in the model while for FVM the inclusion of a new active point in the model involves the evaluation of a single analytical rule (see section 4). The overall runtime disadvantage of the CVM algorithm can hence be explained by the additional cost of the SMO iterations, which are completely avoided in the proposed algorithm.

References

1. Bădoiu, M., Clarkson, K.: Smaller core-sets for balls. In: Proceedings of the SODA 2003, pp. 801–802. SIAM, Philadelphia (2003)
2. Chang, C.-C., Lin, C.-J.: LIBSVM: a library for support vector machines (2010)
3. Clarkson, K.: Coresets, sparse greedy approximation, and the Frank-Wolfe algorithm. In: Proceedings of SODA 2008, pp. 922–931. SIAM, Philadelphia (2008)
4. Fan, R.-E., Chen, P.-H., Lin, C.-J.: Working set selection using second order information for training support vector machines. Journal of Machine Learning Research 6, 1889–1918 (2005)
5. Fine, S., Scheinberg, K.: Efficient SVM training using low-rank kernel representations. Journal of Machine Learning Research 2, 243–264 (2002)
6. Fung, G., Mangasarian, O.: Finite newton method for lagrangian support vector machine classification. Neurocomputing 55(1-2), 39–55 (2003)
7. Hettich, S., Bay, S.: The UCI KDD Archive (2010), http://kdd.ics.uci.edu
8. Joachims, T.: Making large-scale support vector machine learning practical, pp. 169–184. MIT Press, Cambridge (1999)
9. Kressel, U.: Pairwise classification and support vector machines. In: Advances in Kernel Methods: Support Vector Learning, pp. 255–268. MIT Press, Cambridge (1999)
10. Kumar, K., Bhattacharya, C., Hariharan, R.: A randomized algorithm for large scale support vector learning. In: Advances in Neural Information Processing Systems, vol. 20, pp. 793–800. MIT Press, Cambridge (2008)
11. Lee, Y.-J., Huang, S.: Reduced support vector machines: A statistical theory. IEEE Transactions on Neural Networks 18(1), 1–13 (2007)
12. Pavlov, D., Mao, J., Dom, B.: An improved training algorithm for support vector machines. In: Proceedings of the 15th International Conference on Pattern Recognition, vol. 2, pp. 2219–2222. IEEE, Los Alamitos (2000)
13. Platt, J.: Fast training of support vector machines using sequential minimal optimization, pp. 185–208 (1999)
14. Scheinberg, K.: An efficient implementation of an active set method for SVMs. Journal of Machine Learning Research 7, 2237–2257 (2006)

15. Schölkopf, B., Smola, A.J.: Learning with Kernels: Support Vector Machines, Regularization, Optimization, and Beyond. MIT Press, Cambridge (2001)
16. Tsang, I., Kocsor, A., Kwok, J.: Simpler core vector machines with enclosing balls. In: ICML 2007, pp. 911–918. ACM, New York (2007)
17. Tsang, I., Kocsor, A., Kwok, J.: LibCVM Toolkit (2009)
18. Tsang, I., Kwok, J., Cheung, P.-M.: Core vector machines: Fast SVM training on very large data sets. J. of Machine Learning Research 6, 363–392 (2005)
19. Tsang, I., Kwok, J., Zurada, J.: Generalized core vector machines. IEEE Transactions on Neural Networks 17(5), 1126–1140 (2006)
20. Yildirim, E.A.: Two algorithms for the minimum enclosing ball problem. SIAM Journal on Optimization 19(3), 1368–1391 (2008)

A Hybrid Face Recognition Approach Using GPUMLib

Noel Lopes[1,2] and Bernardete Ribeiro[1]

[1] CISUC - Center for Informatics and Systems of University of Coimbra, Portugal
[2] UDI/IPG - Research Unit, Polytechnic Institute of Guarda, Portugal
noel@ipg.pt, bribeiro@dei.uc.pt

Abstract. We present a hybrid face recognition approach which relies on a Graphics Processing Unit (GPU) Machine Learning (ML) Library (GPUMLib). The library includes a high-performance implementation of the Non-Negative Matrix Factorization (NMF) and the Multiple Back-Propagation (MBP) algorithms. Both algorithms are combined in order to obtain a reliable face recognition classifier. The proposed approach first applies an histogram equalization to the original face images in order to reduce the influence from the surrounding illumination. The NMF algorithm is then applied to reduce the data dimensionality, while preserving the information of the most relevant features. The obtained decomposition is further used to rebuild accurate approximations of the original data (by using additive combinations of the parts-based matrix). Finally, the MBP algorithm is used to build a neural classifier with great potential to construct a generalized solution. Our approach is tested in the Yale face database, yielding an accuracy of 93.33% thus demonstrating its potential. Moreover, the speedups obtained with the GPU greatly enhance real-time implementation face recognition systems.

Keywords: GPU computing, Non-Negative Matrix Factorization, Multiple Back-Propagation, Hybrid systems, Face Recognition.

1 Introduction

Face recognition has many potential applications in various distinct areas, such as military, law-enforcement, anti-terrorism, commercial and human-computer interaction [8]. Typically, solving this problem involves several phases: (*i*) segmentation of the faces, (*ii*) extraction of relevant features from the face regions, (*iii*) recognition and (*iv*) verification [10]. In this paper, we concentrate on the last phases, leaving out the segmentation phase. Over the past decades, face recognition has become an increasingly important area of research, attracting researchers from pattern recognition, neural networks, image processing, computer vision, Machine Learning (ML) and psychology among others [8,10]. However, this is still a very challenging and complex problem, because the appearance of the individuals is affected by a numerous factors (e.g. illumination conditions, facial expressions, usage of glasses) and current systems are still no match for

I. Bloch and R.M. Cesar, Jr. (Eds.): CIARP 2010, LNCS 6419, pp. 96–103, 2010.

the human perception system [10]. A detailed survey on existing techniques and methods for face recognition can be found in Zhao et al. [10].

In this paper, we propose a hybrid method for the face recognition problem, relying on a Graphics Processing Unit (GPU) Machine Learning Library (GPUMLib) high-performance implementation of Non-Negative Matrix Factorization (NMF) and Multiple Back-Propagation (MBP) algorithms.

NMF is an unsupervised technique for discovering a parts-based representation of objects [11]. Essentially, it decomposes a matrix, containing only non-negative coefficients, into the product of two matrices (also containing non-negative coefficients), usually with reduced ranks, thus reducing the number of characteristics in the database, while preserving the relevant information that allows for the reconstruction of the original data. Since negative coefficients are not allowed, the original data is reconstructed through additive combinations of the parts-based factorized matrix representation, which is consistent with psychological and physiological evidence for parts-based representations in the brain [2]. On the other hand, MBP is a neural networks supervised algorithm, being able to offer potentially greater generalization capabilities than the well known Back-Propagation (BP) algorithm [3]. Over time, neural networks have proven to solve complex problems in many different domains (e.g. pattern recognition, image processing, intelligent control and time series prediction systems) [7]. By combining both algorithms, we are able to take advantage of the superior generalization capabilities of neural networks, while retaining the possibility of having a parts-based representation of the facial images provided by the NMF algorithm.

The remainder of this paper is organized as follows: The next section covers the GPUMLib implementation of the NMF and MBP algorithms. Section 3 details the proposed hybrid method for face recognition. Section 4 analyses the results obtained with the referred method for the Yale face database. Finally, in section 5 conclusions and future work are addressed.

2   GPU Machine Learning Library

GPUMLib is an open source ML library, aiming to provide machine learning researchers and practitioners with a high-performance library by taking advantage of the GPU enormous computational power [5]. Currently, the GPUMLib fully implements the BP, MBP and NMF algorithms. Furthermore an implementation of the Radial Basis Functions (RBF) neural networks is being developed and the implementation of other ML algorithms is being planned. The library is released under the GNU General Public License and its source code, documentation and examples can be obtained at http://gpumlib.sourceforge.net/.

2.1   Non-Negative Matrix Factorization

Given a matrix $V \in \mathbb{R}_+^{n \times m}$ containing only non-negative coefficients ($V_{ij} \geq 0$) and a pre-specified positive integer, $r < min(n, m)$, NMF finds two matrices, with non-negative coefficients, $W \in \mathbb{R}_+^{n \times r}$ and $H \in \mathbb{R}_+^{r \times m}$ whose product approximates V (as closely as possible):

$$V \approx WH . \tag{1}$$

The value of r is generally chosen to satisfy $(n + m)r < nm$, so that the approximation WH can be viewed as a compressed form of the original data [9].

The non-negativity constrains imposed to the elements of W and H are compatible with the intuitive notion of combining parts to form a whole, which is how NMF learns a parts-based representation [11]. In our case, each column of V represents a human face. Thus, the basis elements of W, may contain facial features, such as eyes, noses and lips [1].

In order to measure the quality of the approximation defined in (1) the Euclidean distance can be used:

$$\|V - WH\|^2 = \sum_{ij} \left(V_{ij} - (WH)_{ij} \right)^2 . \tag{2}$$

Minimizing (2) subject to the constrains $W_{ij} \geq 0$ and $H_{ij} \geq 0$ leads to an optimization problem that can be solved by iteratively applying (3) and (4) until a good approximation is found:

$$H_{a\mu} \leftarrow H_{a\mu} \frac{(W^T V)_{a\mu}}{(W^T W H)_{a\mu}} , \tag{3}$$

$$W_{ia} \leftarrow W_{ia} \frac{(V H^T)_{ia}}{(W H H^T)_{ia}} . \tag{4}$$

To determine the speedups granted by the GPU parallel implementation of the NMF algorithms, the face database #1 from the MIT Center for Biological & Computational Learning, available at http://cbcl.mit.edu/cbcl/software-datasets/FaceData2.html, was used. This database includes a total of 2429 face images of $19 \times 19 = 361$ pixels. Thus, matrix V is composed by 361 rows and 2429 columns. Figure 1 presents the speedups yielded by an NVIDIA GTX 280 GPU (relatively to a Core 2 Quad Q9300 2.5 GHz CPU), considering the Euclidian distance metric and the multiplicative update rule described earlier (according to the value of r chosen) [6].

2.2   Multiple Back-Propagation

MBP is a generalization of the BP algorithm that can be used to train Multiple Feed-Forward (MFF) networks. Together, MFF networks and the MBP algorithm form an architecture that is in most cases preferable to Feed-Forward (FF) networks trained with the BP algorithm [3]. MFF networks are obtained by integrating two FF networks: a main network and a space network. The main network contains selective activation neurons that differ from standard ones by an importance factor. This parameter is adjusted according to the pattern presented to the

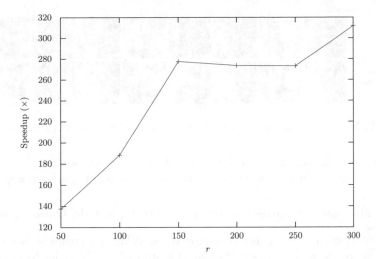

Fig. 1. Speedups provided by the GPU relatively to the CPU, for the NMF algorithm

network, enabling fine-tuning in a given set of patterns. In other words, it is responsible by the network response to specific *stimulus* while ignoring the rest. The importance factors are determined by the space network, which receives the same inputs as the main network. Both networks will thus function in a collaborative manner and must be trained together [3].

The MBP algorithm implementation in GPUMLib[1] has been tested with several benchmarks and real-world applications demonstrating the impressive speedups (up to 180×) that in some problems are responsible for reducing the running time from weeks to hours [4].

3   Face Recognition Based on a Hybrid Classifier

The proposed method consists of four steps. In the first step the facial images are pre-processed in order to reduce the influence of the different ambient illumination conditions. In the next step the parts-based representation of the faces dataset are obtained with the NMF algorithm. In the following step, using this information, a classifier is trained with the MBP algorithm. Finally, its performance is evaluated on the test data to validate the designed classifier. Eventually, the previous steps can be repeated with different configurations, until a classifier that meets the goals expectations is found.

3.1   Image Pre-processing

In order to reduce the influence of the surrounding illumination, an histogram equalization can be applied to the face images. This method improves the contrast

---

[1] The Multiple Back-Propagation software, available at http://dit.ipg.pt/MBP, shares the same GPU implementation and has been extensively tested and widely used by neural networks researchers and practitioners.

Original
image

Image after
histogram
equalization

Fig. 2. Yale face database images before and after the histogram equalization

of the images by changing its gray levels [11]. Figure 2 depicts some of the Yale face database images before and after the histogram equalization has been applied.

3.2 Parts-Based Representation of the Images Yale Data Base

Once the contrast of the images is enhanced, the NMF algorithm is then applied to the training database. As said before, this step is used in order to reduce the data dimensionality and to gather the main characteristics of the individuals faces. Thus, we build the $V \in \mathbb{R}_+^{n \times m}$ matrix by placing one image in each column of the matrix. Therefore the number of rows will be equal to the number of pixels of the images. As a result we will end up with the matrix $W \in \mathbb{R}_+^{n \times r}$ containing r parts-based faces representations and the matrix $H_{train} \in \mathbb{R}_+^{r \times m}$ containing the respective codification that must be added in order to obtain the correct approximations of the original m images. For the test database, the process is similar. First we must build a $V_{test} \in \mathbb{R}_+^{n \times m'}$ matrix. Then the NMF algorithm is applied to the new matrix, this time the parts-based matrix, W, must remain invariable. Thus, only the matrix $H_{test} \in \mathbb{R}_+^{r \times m'}$ gets updated. Once this process is completed, matrix H_{test} will contain the codification of the parts-based images that must be added in order to obtain the approximations of the m' images in the test database. Figure 3 shows the sequence of steps needed to obtain the desired matrices.

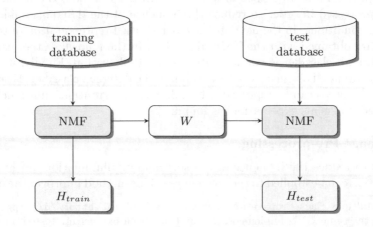

Fig. 3. Applying the NMF algorithm to the training and test databases

3.3   Building and Evaluating the Classifier

As soon as the matrices are computed, the H_{train} matrix can be used to train a MFF network with the MBP algorithm. The quality of the resulting neural network can then be asserted by using H_{test} matrix.

Every time new data is gathered to be used by the classifier, a new H matrix (containing the codification of the parts-based images that approximate the new data) needs to be created by using the NMF algorithm. Although only the H matrix needs to be computed as the parts-based matrix W remains constant, the time consumed in the process can prevent this method from being used in real-world applications. Thus the GPU implementation of the NMF algorithm is crucial for this method to be used in real-world scenarios.

4   Results and Discussion

To test the proposed method we used the Yale face database, consisting of 165 gray-scale face images (with 64×64 pixels) of 15 individuals. Each individual appears in 11 images, representing different facial expressions (happy, normal, sad, sleepy, surprised, wink) or configurations (center-light, left-light, right-light, with glasses, without glasses). In order to build the training dataset we randomly choose eight images of each person. The remainder three images were placed on the test dataset. Thus, the training dataset contains 120 images and the test dataset 45. An histogram equalization was applied to all the images.

Thereafter, the NMF algorithm was applied to the training dataset in order to determine the parts-based matrix, W, representation of the faces and the matrix H_{train} that will later be used to create (train) a classifier. The number of parts-based images (r) was chosen to be 45, so that each individual can potentially have three part-based images. In practice, because NMF is an unsupervised algorithm there is no guarantee that each individual will have three parts-based images associated or that the parts-based images will not end up being sharing by several individuals. Figure 4 shows the first 40 images of W. Once the matrix W was computed, we used the NMF algorithm again, this time on the test dataset in order to obtain the H_{test} matrix, necessary to assert the quality of the resulting neural network classifiers.

Finally, in order to train the neural networks, we developed a preliminary Autonomous Training System (ATS) that actively searches for better solutions, by adjusting the topology of the networks. The ATS makes use of the GPUMLib parallel implementation of the MBP algorithm. Essentially, after training a neural network the ATS evaluates its performance and compares it with the best performance achieved so far. The results of the performance comparison are then used to determine the number of hidden neurons of a new neural network and the process is repeated until a predefined specified stopping criteria is meet. For the problem at hand, the ATS took less than 16 hours to train a total of 100000 MFF networks. Figure 5 shows the number of networks trained by the ATS according to number of hidden neurons. The best network (with 12 hidden neurons) presents an accuracy of 93.33% on the test dataset and of 100% on

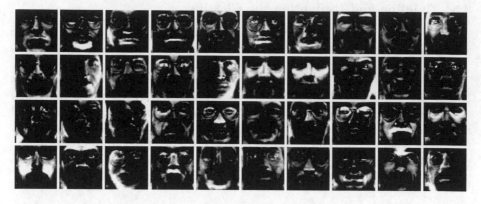

Fig. 4. Parts-based faces representations (W)

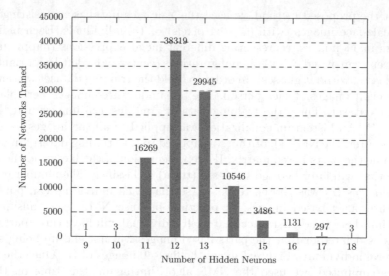

Fig. 5. Number of networks trained by the ATS, according to the number of neurons

the training dataset. Only three images (of different persons) on the test dataset were misclassified and among those one had 46.11% probability of belonging to the correct individual. Thus, the results obtained validate the proposed method, demonstrating its potential. Moreover the ATS approach is very promising, since it was able to find high-quality solutions without any human-intervention (aside from the initial configuration).

5   Conclusions and Future Work

A hybrid method, combining the NMF and MBP algorithms, for for face recognition is proposed. The proposed approach was tested in the Yale face database, yielding an accuracy of 93.33%, thus demonstrating its viability and power. However a key factor for its success in real-world applications, may rely on the use of the GPU to support for high-performance implentations of the NMF algorithm, because when presenting new data to the classifier it is necessary to calculate the matrix containing the codification of the parts-based images that approximate the new data. Nevertheless, GPUMLib already presents a GPU implementation of both the NMF and MBP algorithms, making the proposed method very attractive for use in real-world scenarios. Future work will address determining the impact of changing the number of parts-based images (r) in the quality of the resulting solutions. Moreover, another line of work consists in comparing the proposed method with other reported methods in the literature.

References

1. Gillis, N., Glineur, F.: Using underapproximations for sparse nonnegative matrix factorization. Pattern Recogntion 43(4), 1676–1687 (2010)
2. Lee, D.D., Seung, H.S.: Learning the parts of objects by non-negative matrix factorization. Nature 401, 788–791 (1999)
3. Lopes, N., Ribeiro, B.: An efficient gradient-based learning algorithm applied to neural networks with selective actuation neurons. Neural, Parallel & Scientific Computations 11(3), 253–272 (2003)
4. Lopes, N., Ribeiro, B.: GPU implementation of the multiple back-propagation algorithm. In: Corchado, E., Yin, H. (eds.) IDEAL 2009. LNCS, vol. 5788, pp. 449–456. Springer, Heidelberg (2009)
5. Lopes, N., Ribeiro, B.: GPUMLib: a new library to combine machine learning algorithms with graphics processing units. In: 10th International Conference on Hybrid Intelligent Systems, Atlanta, USA (2010)
6. Lopes, N., Ribeiro, B.: Non-negative matrix factorization implementation using graphic processing units. In: Fyfe, C., Tino, P., Charles, D., Garcia-Osorio, C., Yin, H. (eds.) IDEAL 2010. LNCS, vol. 6283, pp. 275–283. Springer, Heidelberg (2010)
7. Tang, H., Tan, K.C., Yi, Z.: Neural Networks: Computational Models and Applications. Studies in Computational Intelligence. Springer, New York (2007)
8. Wang, J., Zhang, B., Wang, S., Qi, M., Kong, J.: An adaptively weighted subpattern locality preserving projection for face recognition. Journal of Network and Computer Applications 33(3), 323–332 (2010)
9. Xu, B., Lu, J., Huang, G.: A constrained non-negative matrix factorization in information retrieval. In: IEEE International Conference on Information Reuse and Integration, IRI 2003, pp. 273–277 (2003)
10. Zhao, W., Chellappa, R., Phillips, P.J., Rosenfeld, A.: Face recognition: A literature survey. ACM Computing Surveys 35(4), 399–458 (2003)
11. Zilu, Y., Guoyi, Z.: Facial expression recognition based on NMF and SVM. International Forum on Information Technology and Applications 3, 612–615 (2009)

Self-training for Handwritten Text Line Recognition

Volkmar Frinken and Horst Bunke

Institute for Computer Science and Applied Mathematics
University of Bern, Switzerland
{frinken,bunke}@iam.unibe.ch

Abstract. Off-line handwriting recognition deals with the task of automatically recognizing handwritten text from images, for example from scanned sheets of paper. Due to the tremendous variations of writing styles encountered between different individuals, this is a very challenging task. Traditionally, a recognition system is trained by using a large corpus of handwritten text that has to be transcribed manually. This, however, is a laborious and costly process. Recent developments have proposed semi-supervised learning, which reduces the need for manually transcribed text by adding large amounts of handwritten text without transcription to the training set. The current paper is the first one, to the knowledge of the authors, where semi-supervised learning for unconstrained handwritten text line recognition is proposed. We demonstrate the applicability of self-training, a form of semi-supervised learning, to neural network based handwriting recognition. Through a set of experiments we show that text without transcription can successfully be used to significantly increase the performance of a handwriting recognition system.

1 Introduction

Off-line handwriting recognition (HWR) is the task of recognizing a handwritten text from a sheet of paper that was scanned, photographed or digitized otherwise. Opposed to on-line handwriting recognition where temporal and spatial information about each stroke is available, the off-line recognition task is performed using only the image of the written text. Many important applications are based on off-line handwriting recognition, e.g. postal address identification [3], Bank check processing [15], prescreening of handwritten notes [20], or the creation of digital libraries of historical documents [8]. After several decades of ongoing research, however, off-line handwritten text recognition is still considered a difficult problem that is only partially solved [4,17].

To create an automatic handwriting recognition system, a set of images of handwritten text along with their correct transcription is needed for training. As it turns out, one of the key problems encountered when building a writer independent recognition system[1] is the great variety in writing styles between

---

[1] A writer independent system is one that recognizes text from writers that have not contributed to the training set.

I. Bloch and R.M. Cesar, Jr. (Eds.): CIARP 2010, LNCS 6419, pp. 104–112, 2010.
© Springer-Verlag Berlin Heidelberg 2010

different persons. Hence, the amount of training data needed is extremely large. Unfortunately, the transcription of the handwritten text has to be done manually which makes the acquisition of training data costly and time consuming. On the other hand, collecting handwritten samples itself can be done very efficiently. Consequently, unlabeled data can be made easily available in large amounts. Hence the question arises whether such unlabeled data can be helpful for handwriting recognition systems. It has been shown that in various classification scenarios unlabeled examples can indeed significantly improve the recognition accuracy using semi-supervised learning [5]. Most of the existing works, however, deal with the standard classification scenario where a single point in a feature space has to be mapped into the label space [16,21]. In the current paper, a more general problem is considered in the sense that a (possibly long) sequence of feature vectors has to be mapped to a (usually much shorter) sequence of labels, or characters. Some research has been done on sequential semi-supervised learning, mostly with Hidden Markov Models, but only moderate success has been achieved following this approach [11,12]. Only few publications exist that deal specifically with semi-supervised learning for handwritten word recognition. In [1,2] the authors adapt a recognition system to a single person by using unlabeled data. This system is highly specialized after the adaptation and not suitable for general handwriting recognition, though. The task of unconstrained writer independent single word recognition was addressed in [6,7]. In this paper, we extend this approach by not restricting the focus on single, manually segmented words, but considering entire text lines.

The semi-supervised learning approach addressed in this paper is self-training. Under this paradigm, one starts with an initial recognizer trained on the available labeled data. This recognizer then classifies all unlabeled data and sorts them according to their recognition confidence. The most confidently recognized samples are assumed to be correct and added to the training set. Using the augmented training set, a new recognizer is created. This procedure of enlarging the training set can be continued for several iterations. A crucial point in this process, however, is to decide which elements should be added and which not. If, on the one hand, the data is selected too strictly, not enough samples might be added to change the training set substantially. On the other hand, if large amounts of incorrectly labeled data are added, the recognition accuracy of the created systems might decrease. For the task of text line recognition, we investigate the use of different confidence thresholds and their effect on self-learning. To the knowledge of the authors, this paper is the first to deal with semi-supervised learning for text-line recognition.

The rest of the paper is structured as follows. In Section 2, details of the task of handwritten word recognition are presented together with the recognizer used in this work. Semi-supervised learning and self-training are discussed in Section 3. The experiments are presented in Section 4 and the paper concludes with Section 5.

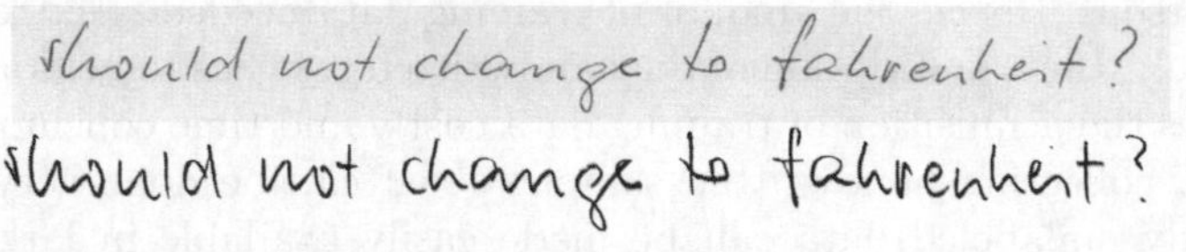

should not change to fahrenheit?

should not change to fahrenheit?

Fig. 1. A visualization of the effects of the preprocessing steps

2   Handwritten Text Line Recognition

2.1   Preprocessing

The database used in this paper consists of 1,539 pages of handwritten English text, written by 657 writers[2] [14]. All pages of the database are already segmented into individual text lines. The segmented text lines are normalized prior to recognition in order to cope with different writing styles. First, the skew angle is determined by a regression analysis based on the bottom-most black pixel of each pixel column. Then, the skew of the text line is removed by rotation. Afterwards the slant is corrected in order to normalize the directions of long vertical strokes found in characters like 't' or 'l'. After estimating the slant angle based on a histogram analysis, a shear transformation is applied to the image. Next, a vertical scaling is applied to obtain three writing zones of the same height, i.e., lower, middle, and upper zone, separated by the lower and upper baseline. To determine the lower baseline, the regression result from skew correction is used, and the upper baseline is found by vertical histogram analysis. Finally the width of the text is normalized. For this purpose, the average distance of black/white transitions along a horizontal straight line through the middle zone is determined and adjusted by horizontal scaling. The result of the preprocessing steps can be seen in Fig. 1. For more details on the text line normalization operations, we refer to [13].

2.2   The HWR System

The recognizer used in this paper is a recently developed recurrent neural network, termed *bidirectional long short-term memory* (BLSTM) neural network [10]. A hidden layer is made up of so called *long short-term memory* blocks instead of simple nodes. These memory blocks are specifically designed to address the *vanishing gradient problem* which describes the exponential increase or decay of values as they cycle through recurrent network layers. This is done by nodes that control the information flow in and out of each memory block.

The network is made up of two separate input layers, two separate recurrent hidden layers, and one output layer. Each input layer is connected to one hidden layer. The hidden layers are both connected to the output layer. The network is *bidirectional*, i.e. a sequence is fed into the network in both the forward and the backward mode. The input layers consist of one node for each feature. One

---

[2] http://www.iam.unibe.ch/fki/databases/iam-handwriting-database

input and one hidden layer deal with the forward sequence, the other input and hidden layer with the backward sequence. At each position p of the input sequence of length l, the output layer sums up the values coming from the hidden layer that has processed positions 1 to p and the hidden layer that has processed the positions l down to p. The output layer contains one node for each possible character in the sequence plus a special ε node, to indicate "no character". At each position, the output activations of the nodes are normalized so that they sum up to 1, and are treated as probabilities that the node's corresponding character can occur at this position.

The output of the network is therefore a matrix of probabilities for each letter and each position. A likelihood is assigned to each path through the matrix by multiplying all probability values along the path. The letters visited along the optimal path, i.e. the one with maximum likelihood, give the recognized letter sequence. Note, however, that the optimal path may not correspond to any existing word. Given a dictionary of all recognizable words, the Connectionist Temporal Classification (CTC) token passing algorithm returns a sequence of words from the dictionary whose likelihood is (locally) optimal. This sequence is the final output of the recognizer. For more details about BLSTM networks and the CTC token passing algorithm, we refer to [9,10].

3   Self-training

3.1   Overview

The way semi-supervised learning is applied in this paper is self-training. It is a methodology widely applicable due to its general and abstract formulation. It states that all available labeled data should be utilized to train an initial recognizer in a classic supervised manner. This recognizer is then used to classify the unlabeled data. Each classification result is stored along with its recognition confidence. The most confidently recognized elements are considered as correctly recognized and hence added to the already existing training set which is then used to create a new recognizer. These steps are repeated until some criterion is met, e.g. the convergence of the recognition accuracy.

Applying this scheme, a decision has to be made at each iteration which elements are to be added to the training set and which not. This can be done by comparing the recognition confidence to some threshold. Using a very strict threshold ensures that as few as possible falsely recognized elements are added to the new training set, but also that not many elements are added at all. This may lead to a training set that is not substantially different from the original training set and produces recognizers that are not much different from the initially created one. When the threshold is too loose, more data is added to the training set at the cost of misclassified data. Therefore a trade-off has to be found between data quality and quantity.

nominating any more Labour life Poors

dominating	any	more	Labour	the	Few
nominative	a	none	Labour	the	Peru
nominal	in c	more	Labour	the	Dr
dominating	any	more	Labour	with	Peru
mining	any	one	labour	the	Ten
dominating	any	more	labour	like	e
dominating	any	more	labour	the	Dr
nomination	any	one	Labour	the	Kerr
morning	any	more	Labour	He	or
noting	any	more	Labour	the	Few

dominating	any	more	Labour	the	Few
$\frac{4}{10}$	$\frac{8}{10}$	$\frac{7}{10}$	$\frac{7}{10}$	$\frac{7}{10}$	$\frac{2}{10}$

Fig. 2. A text line, the aligned outputs of 10 neural networks, and the resulting recognition confidences. Note that the recognition of the best network is used as the final transcription (given in the first line of the table).

3.2 Recognition Confidence

In order for the entire process to work, a reliable measure of the recognition confidence is crucial since it specifies what elements are used to train a new recognizer. A simple approach in the case of text recognition using BLSTM neural networks would be to use the likelihood of the path though the letter probability matrix. However, preliminary experiments have shown, this method does not serve well as an overall reliability measure of the output.

Therefore we exploit the fact that the BLSTM neural network is initialized with random weights and create an ensemble of several neural networks by random initialization. Clearly, each network of this ensemble produces a different recognition result for a given input text in general. Therefore, we count how often a word occurs in the set of produced transcriptions, and use this count as a confidence measure. Of course, the individual neural networks may output word sequences of different lengths. Consequently, the word sequences of all outputs have to be aligned with each other. Since finding an optimal alignment is NP-complete [19] we use an approximation algorithm that works well for the considered application.

To create the alignment, the networks are ranked according to their performance on the validation set first. Then, the best network's output is fixed and the other word sequences are sequentially aligned to it. By this procedure, an adequate recognition with a reliable confidence measure for each word is efficiently generated. An example of the procedure can be seen in Fig. 2.

In Fig. 3, a sample plot can be seen that shows the number of words being correctly as well as incorrectly recognized as a function of the recognition confidence. This function can be evaluated on the validation set and used to define the threshold that is applied when deciding what elements are used for retraining. For an optimal increase in the recognizer's accuracy, the threshold should

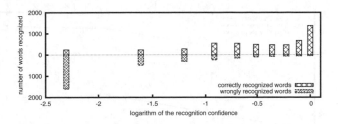

Fig. 3. The number of correctly and incorrectly recognized words as a function of the logarithm of the recognition confidence. Since the recognized confidence is calculated from the numbers of networks agreeing with the transcription, the confidence takes on only a few distinct values.

maximize the number of correct elements that are added, while at the same time minimizing the number of wrong elements. Obviously, this is not an easy task. In this paper, we investigate three different threshold selection methods.

3.3 Confidence Thresholds

The first threshold is called *High Threshold* and is set to 0 (See Fig. 3). It means that a word is added to the retraining set only if all networks agree on the output. A second, more refined threshold is the *Medium Threshold*. It is set so that all elements added are more likely to be correct than wrong. This threshold is found by choosing the lowest value returning more correctly that incorrectly recognized samples in the validation set. (In Fig. 3, a possible value is *Medium Threshold* = −1). The last threshold investigated is the *Low Threshold*. It is set to −∞ so that all words, regardless of their recognition confidence, are added to the training set.

4 Experimental Evaluation

To analyze the effects of self-training on the recognition accuracy, we performed experiments on the IAM database [14] using the thresholds described in 3.3. The database is split up into a working set of 6161 text lines, a validation set of 920 text lines and a writer independent test set of 929 text lines. These three sets are writer disjoined, i.e. a person who has contributed to any of the three sets did not contribute to any of the other sets. Therefore, we test the applicability of the method for writer independent recognition instead of adapting to a specific style of writing as done in [1,2]. The working set is randomly split up into a training set consisting of 1000 labeled text lines and a set of 5161 unlabeled text lines.

  Initially, we trained 10 neural networks on the training set. The networks then transcribed the unlabeled text lines and the transcriptions were sorted according to the networks' performance on the validation set. In the next step, the transcriptions were aligned and used to compute a new confidence measure for each word. Then we applied the confidence threshold and added the appropriate

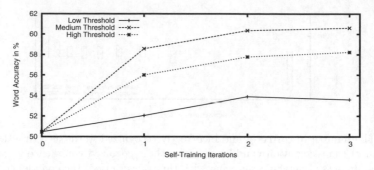

Fig. 4. The average recognition accuracy of 10 neural network based recognition systems on the test set as a function of the self-training iterations

words to the initial training set. The initial neural networks were then retrained on the extended training set. We repeated this process for several iterations. Due to the high computational costs, we did not wait for the accuracy to converge but instead fixed the number of iterations.

For recognition of text lines, the accuracy is defined by $Acc = \frac{n-S-D-I}{n}$ where n is the number of words in the ground truth, S is the number of mis-recognized words (substitutions), D is the number of words that don't appear in the recognized text (deletions) and I is the number of words that appear in the recognized text but not in the ground truth (insertions) [18].

We evaluated the word accuracy of the initial system and the system obtained after each iteration. The results can be seen in Fig. 4. The initial system has an average accuracy of 50.47%. During the course of the iterations, an increase in accuracy can clearly be observed. Using the *Low Threshold* retraining rule, an increase up to 53.89% on average was observed. A larger increase achieved the *High Threshold* retraining rule of 58.24% on average. The largest increase, however, was achieved using the *Medium Threshold* retraining rule. Using this rule, the average accuracy of the system after three iteration was at 60.61%. Note that each single increase in each iteration is statistically significant at the $\alpha = 95\%$ level. As a comparison and to evaluate how good such a system can get, we additionally trained ten neural networks on the entire working set of 6161 labeled text lines and reached an accuracy of 71%.

The *High Threshold* retraining rule added mostly correct elements to the training set, but only a few words from a text line and not even from each of the lines of the unlabeled set was chosen. Hence, there are not many samples that are added and the training set changes only slightly. The *Low Threshold* rule ensures that each word from each text line is added. This produces enough correct data as not to impede the recognition accuracy, but the large amount of noise also hinders a larger increase. A good trade-off appears to be the *Medium Threshold*, which picks words from each text line that are likely to be correct. Therefore the *Medium Threshold* rule adds more data than the *High Threshold* rule with less noise than the *Low Threshold* retraining rule.

5   Conclusion

We have presented strategies for self-training in the field of handwritten text line recognition. These strategies decrease the need of manually labeled training data and reduce the cost of building recognition systems. Furthermore, by focusing on text line recognition as opposed to single word recognition, not even a segmentation into distinct words is necessary. To the knowledge of the authors, this is the first time that such an approach has been proposed. In a set of experiments we demonstrated the applicability of the procedure and compared the proposed thresholding strategies among each other. In each experiment we evaluated the average recognition accuracy of different recognition systems after each self-training iteration. The highest increase in recognition accuracy, from about 50% to 60%, was observed when making a compromise between including too much noisy data and excluding too much correctly labeled data. Although the increase is remarkable, it still leaves room for further improvements which will be investigated in the future. Next steps include investigations into larger ensembles of diverse recognizers such as HMMs and single word recognizers after an automatic segmentation of the text line into words. Co-training with different recognizers will also be along our line of research.

While previous approaches to using semi-supervised learning in handwriting recognition were restricted to either single writer scenarios or to single word recognition, the system described in this paper is quite general. It can successfully deal with multiple writers and complete text lines. Consequently, it can potentially be applied to many real world tasks, such as transcription of handwritten notes or historical manuscripts.

Acknowledgments

We thank Alex Graves for kindly providing us with the BLSTM Neural Network source code.

References

1. Ball, G.R., Srihari, S.: Prototype Integration in Off-Line Handwriting Recognition Adaptation. In: Proc. Int'l. Conf. on Frontiers in Handwriting Recognition, pp. 529–534 (2008)
2. Ball, G.R., Srihari, S.N.: Semi-supervised Learning for Handwriting Recognition. In: 10th Int'l Conf. on Document Analysis and Recognition (2009)
3. Brakensiek, A., Rigoll, G.: Handwritten Address Recognition Using Hidden Markov Models. In: Dengel, A.R., Junker, M., Weisbecker, A. (eds.) RL 2004. LNCS, vol. 2956, pp. 103–122. Springer, Heidelberg (2004)
4. Bunke, H.: Recognition of Cursive Roman Handwriting - Past, Present and Future. In: Proc. 7th Int'l Conf. on Document Analysis and Recognition, vol. 1, pp. 448–459 (August 2003)
5. Chapelle, O., Schölkopf, B., Zien, A.: Semi-Supervised Learning. MIT Press, Cambridge (2006)

6. Frinken, V., Bunke, H.: Evaluating Retraining Rules for Semi-Supervised Learning in Neural Network Based Cursive Word Recognition. In: 10th Int'l Conf. on Document Analysis and Recognition, pp. 31–35 (2009)
7. Frinken, V., Bunke, H.: Self-Training Strategies for Handwritten Word Recognition. In: Perner, P. (ed.) ICDM 2009. LNCS, vol. 5633, pp. 291–300. Springer, Heidelberg (2009)
8. Govindaraju, V., Xue, H.: Fast Handwriting Recognition for Indexing Historical Documents. In: First Int'l Workshop on Document Image Analysis for Libraries, pp. 314–320. IEEE Computer Society, Los Alamitos (2004)
9. Graves, A., Fernández, S., Gomez, F., Schmidhuber, J.: Connectionist Temporal Classification: Labelling Unsegmented Sequential Data with Recurrent Neural Networks. In: 23rd Int'l Conf. on Machine Learning, pp. 369–376 (2006)
10. Graves, A., Liwicki, M., Fernández, S., Bertolami, R., Bunke, H., Schmidhuber, J.: A Novel Connectionist System for Unconstrained Handwriting Recognition. IEEE Transaction on Pattern Analysis and Machine Intelligence 31(5), 855–868 (2009)
11. Inoue, M., Ueda, N.: Exploitation of Unlabeled Sequences in Hidden Markov Models. IEEE Transactions on Pattern Analysis and Machine Intelligence 25(12), 1570–1581 (2003)
12. Ji, S., Watson, L.T., Carin, L.: Semisupervised Learning of Hidden Markov Models via a Homotopy Method. IEEE Transactions on Pattern Analysis and Machine Intelligence 31(2), 275–287 (2009)
13. Marti, U.V., Bunke, H.: Using a Statistical Language Model to Improve the Performance of an HMM-Based Cursive Handwriting Recognition System. Int'l Journal of Pattern Recognition and Artificial Intelligence 15, 65–90 (2001)
14. Marti, U.V., Bunke, H.: The IAM-Database: An English Sentence Database for Offline Handwriting Recognition. Int'l Journal on Document Analysis and Recognition 5, 39–46 (2002)
15. Palacios, R., Gupta, A., Wang, P.S.: Handwritten Bank Check Recognition of Courtesy Amounts. Int'l Journal of Image and Graphics 4(2), 1–20 (2004)
16. Seeger, M.: Learning with Labeled and Unlabeled Data. Tech. rep., University of Edinburgh, 5 Forest Hill, Edinburgh, EH1 2QL (2002)
17. Vinciarelli, A.: A Survey On Off-Line Cursive Word Recognition. Pattern Recognition 35(7), 1433–1446 (2002)
18. Vinciarelli, A., Bengio, S., Bunke, H.: Offline Recognition of Unconstrained Handwritten Texts Using HMMs and Statistical Language Models. IEEE Trans. on Pattern Analysis and Machine Intelligence 26(6), 709–720 (2004)
19. Wang, L., Jiang, T.: On the complexity of multiple sequence alignment. Journal of Computational Biology 1(4), 337–348 (1994)
20. Ye, M., Viola, P.A., Raghupathy, S., Sutanto, H., Li, C.: Learning to Group Text Lines and Regions in Freeform Handwritten Notes. In: Ninth Int'l Conf. on Document Analysis and Recognition, pp. 28–32. IEEE Computer Society, Los Alamitos (2007)
21. Zhu, X.: Semi-Supervised Learning Literature Survey. Tech. Rep. 1530, Computer Science, University of Wisconsin-Madison (2005),
http://www.cs.wisc.edu/~jerryzhu/pub/ssl_survey.pdf

Improving the Dynamic Hierarchical Compact Clustering Algorithm by Using Feature Selection

Reynaldo Gil-García and Aurora Pons-Porrata

Center for Pattern Recognition and Data Mining
Universidad de Oriente, Santiago de Cuba, Cuba
{gil,aurora}@cerpamid.co.cu

Abstract. Feature selection has improved the performance of text clustering. In this paper, a local feature selection technique is incorporated in the *dynamic hierarchical compact* clustering algorithm to speed up the computation of similarities. We also present a quality measure to evaluate hierarchical clustering that considers the cost of finding the optimal cluster from the root. The experimental results on several benchmark text collections show that the proposed method is faster than the original algorithm while achieving approximately the same clustering quality.

1 Introduction

Managing, accessing, searching and browsing large repositories of text documents require efficient organization of the information. In dynamic information environments, such as the World Wide Web or the stream of newspaper articles, it is usually desirable to apply adaptive methods for document organization such as clustering. Dynamic algorithms have the ability to update the clustering when data are added or removed from the collection. These algorithms allow us dynamically tracking the ever-changing large scale information being put or removed from the web everyday, without having to perform complete re-clustering.

Hierarchical clustering algorithms have an additional interest, because they provide data-views at different levels of abstraction, making them ideal for people to visualize and interactively explore large document collections. In the context of hierarchical document clustering, the high dimensionality of the data and the large size of collections are the major challenges facing researchers today.

In [1], a hierarchical clustering algorithm, namely *dynamic hierarchical compact (DHC)* was introduced. It is not only able to deal with dynamic data while achieving a similar clustering quality than static state-of-the-art hierarchical algorithms, but also has a linear computational complexity with respect to the number of dimensions. It uses a multi-layered clustering to update the hierarchy when new documents arrive (or are removed). The process in each layer involves two steps: the updating of similarity-based graphs and the obtaining of the connected components for these graphs. The graph updating requires to compute the similarities between clusters, which is the most time-consuming operation.

Feature selection for text clustering is the task of disregarding irrelevant terms, aiming to find the smallest subset of terms that reveals "natural" clusters from

---

I. Bloch and R.M. Cesar, Jr. (Eds.): CIARP 2010, LNCS 6419, pp. 113–120, 2010.

text data. Different measures such as scatter separability, entropy and document or term frequency have been proposed [2,3]. Unsupervised feature selection can be categorized as global or local approaches. The global feature selection chooses the relevant features once according to a ranking criterion, and uses the same feature subset in the whole clustering process. On the contrary, in local feature selection a different subset of features is chosen for each cluster.

The main contribution of this paper is twofold. Firstly, we present a version of DHC algorithm for clustering of dynamic document collections, in which a local feature selection strategy is incorporated to reduce the cost of computing similarities. Secondly, we present a new quality measure to evaluate hierarchical clustering solutions that considers the cost of finding the optimal cluster from the root. The experimental results on several benchmark text collections show that the proposed method is faster than DHC algorithm while achieving approximately the same clustering quality.

2   Feature Selection in Dynamic Hierarchical Compact Algorithm

DHC is an agglomerative method based on graph. It uses a multi-layered clustering to produce the hierarchy. The process in each layer involves two steps: updating of similarity-based graphs and obtaining the connected components for these graphs. Each connected component represents a cluster.

DHC algorithm uses two graphs. The first one is the β-similarity graph, which is an undirected graph whose vertexes are the clusters and there is an edge between vertexes i and j, if the cluster j is β-similar to i. Two clusters are β-similar if their similarity is greater than or equal to β, where β is a user-defined parameter. Analogously, i is a β-isolated cluster if its similarity with all clusters is less than β. As inter-cluster similarity measure we use group-average. In the vector space model, the cosine similarity is the most commonly used measure to compare the documents. By using the cosine measure, we can take advantage of a number of properties involving the composite vector of a cluster (i.e., the sum of document vectors of the cluster) [4]. In particular, the group-average similarity between clusters i and j is equal to the fraction between the scalar product of the composite vectors of these clusters and the product of clusters' sizes.

The second graph relies on the maximum β-similarity relationship (denoted as max-S graph) and it is a subgraph of the first one. The vertices of this graph coincide with vertices in the β-similarity graph, and there is an edge between vertices i and j, if i is the most β-similar cluster to j or vice verse.

Given a cluster hierarchy previously built by the algorithm, each time a new document arrives (or is removed), the clusters at all levels of the hierarchy must be revised (see Figure 1). When a new document arrives (or is removed), a singleton is created (or deleted) and the β-similarity graph at the bottom level is updated. Then, the max-S graph is updated too, which produce (or remove) a vertex and can also produce new edges and remove others. These changes on the max-S graph lead to the updating of the connected components. When

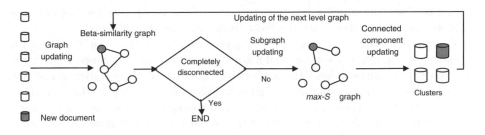

Fig. 1. Dynamic hierarchical compact algorithm

clusters are created or removed from a level of the hierarchy, the β-similarity graph at the next level must be updated. This process is repeated until this graph is completely disconnected (all vertices are β-isolated). It is possible that the β-similarity graph became completely disconnected before the top level of the hierarchy is reached. In this case, the next levels of the hierarchy must be removed. Notice that the algorithm uses the same β value in all hierarchy levels.

Algorithm 1. DHC with Local Feature Selection

---

1. Arrival of a document to cluster (or to remove).
2. Put the new document in a cluster on its own (or remove the single cluster to which the document belongs).
3. $level = 0$ and update the β-similarity graph at the bottom level, G_0.
4. While G_{level} is not completely disconnected:
   (a) Update the *max-S* graph at *level*.
   (b) Update the connected components for the *max-S* graph. Let N be the set of the new clusters and R be the set of the removed clusters.
   (c) For each new cluster c in N:
       i. Calculate the composite vector $\vec{c}$ of the cluster c as the sum of the composite vectors of its subclusters.
       ii. Select the most $f \cdot dt(\vec{c})$ relevant terms of $\vec{c}$ and remove the remaining terms from it.
   (d) Update the β-similarity graph at the next level, $G_{level+1}$.
   (e) $level = level + 1$
5. If there exist levels greater than *level* in the hierarchy, remove them.

The updating of the β-similarity graph in *DHC* is trivial. For each vertex to add, the similarities with the remaining vertices are calculated and the corresponding edges are added to the graph. On the contrary, for each vertex to remove, all its edges are removed too. Notice that *DHC* needs to compute the similarities between the new document and all existing documents at the bottom level. Also, for each level of the hierarchy the similarities between the new clusters created at the previous level and the existing clusters at the corresponding level must be calculated too. The composite vector of each cluster is used to compute these similarities. The computation of the composite vectors and the similarities between them are the most time-consuming operations.

Our proposal focuses on improving the performance of the β-similarity graph updating by applying a simple local feature selection criterion. Since DHC is an agglomerative method, both the size of the clusters and the number of distinct terms (features) in its composite vectors increase as we go up in the hierarchy. Thus, a feature selection criterion is applied to choose the most relevant terms for each cluster. The relevance of a term t in the cluster c is calculated as $w(t,c) = \sum_{d \in c} tf(t,d)$, where $tf(t,d)$ is the number of occurrences of t in the document d. Notice that $w(t,c)$ coincides with the weigth of term t in the composite vector $\overrightarrow{c}$. The local selection is performed by using a variable number of features according to $dt(\overrightarrow{c})$, which is the number of distinct terms in the composite vector of the cluster c. The number of selected features in the cluster c is $f \cdot dt(\overrightarrow{c})$, where $f \in [0,1]$. Notice that each cluster is represented by a different subset of features. Since the dynamic nature of our algorithm, a global feature selection criterion can not be applied.

The steps are shown in Algorithm 1. A detailed description of steps 4(a) and 4(b) can be seen in [1,5].

3   F1-Travel Quality Measure

Evaluation of clustering is usually done by comparing system-generated clusters to a "gold standard" (i.e., the manually labeled topics). Several measures have been proposed to evaluate the quality of flat clustering. However, the evaluation of hierarchical approaches is still an open problem. The manually labeled topics of the most standard text collections have currently a flat structure. It is due to historical reasons and the difficulties for humans to build the topic hierarchy.

The most widely used measure is *overall F1* [6], which compares the system-generated clusters at all levels of the hierarchy with the manually labeled topics. It is calculated as: $Overall\ F1 = \frac{\sum_{i=1}^{|T|} |t_i| F1(t_i, \sigma(t_i))}{\sum_{i=1}^{|T|} |t_i|}$, where T is the set of manual topics and $\sigma(t_i)$ is the "best matching" cluster with the topic t_i, i.e., the cluster that maximizes $F1(t_i, c_j) = 2 |t_i \cap c_j| / (|t_i| + |c_j|)$.

The *extended F1-BCubed* measure to evaluate hierarchical clustering was recently proposed in [7]. Extended F1-BCubed is the F1-measure evaluated over extended BCubed precision and recall. It takes into account the multiplicity of document occurrences in clusters and topics.

Let us suppose that we have a collection of 8 documents and the manual topics are {1,2}, {3,4}, {5,6} and {7,8}. Figure 2 shows three possible hierarchies obtained by clustering algorithms. As we can observe, extended F1-BCubed considers the hierarchy (a) better than (b) despite it does not contain any "perfect" cluster. It is due to that the number of document pairs that occur in the clusters of the hierarchy (a) is more similar to that in the topics than to that in the hierarchy (b). For example, the pair (1,2) occurs twice in (a) and four times in (b), while occurs only once in the topics. Both extended F1-BCubed and overall F1 measure can not distinguish the hierarchy (b) from (c).

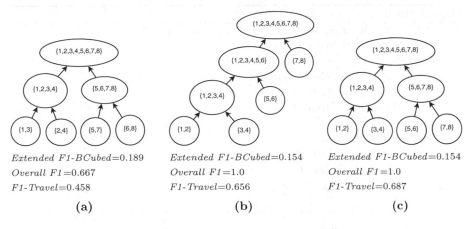

Extended $F1\text{-}BCubed$=0.189   Extended $F1\text{-}BCubed$=0.154   Extended $F1\text{-}BCubed$=0.154

Overall $F1$=0.667   Overall $F1$=1.0   Overall $F1$=1.0

$F1\text{-}Travel$=0.458 $F1\text{-}Travel$=0.656 $F1\text{-}Travel$=0.687

(a)   **(b)**   **(c)**

Fig. 2. Example of hierarchy evaluation by using different measures

We see the hierarchy as providing paths for traveling between topics. Deep hierarchies may not be suitable for browsing, since a user may require a high number of navigation steps to finding the topics of her interest. However, if a hierarchy is too flat, a parent topic may contain too many subtopics and it would increase the time and difficulty for the user to locate her target. Therefore, we expect that the number of explored nodes to find the "best matching" clusters be as small as possible. In this sense, the hierarchy (c) is preferable.

In the context of Topic Detection and Tracking, Allam et al. [8] proposed the minimal cost measure, which is defined as a linear combination of detection cost and travel cost. The former cost is expressed in terms of missed and false alarm rates, while the latter is defined as the search cost to find the optimal cluster from the root. Following this idea, we propose the $F1\text{-}Travel$ measure. It is very similar to overall F1-measure, but differs in that we add a travel cost to the measure. Thus, we defined *overall F1-Travel* as follows:

$$Overall\ F1\text{-}Travel = \frac{\sum_{i=1}^{|T|} |t_i|\ F1\text{-}Travel(t_i)}{\sum_{i=1}^{|T|} |t_i|}$$

To evaluate each topic t_i, we use a best-first search to find the optimal cluster (see Algorithm 2). That is, $F1\text{-}Travel(t_i) = F1(t_i, \sigma(t_i))(1 - \frac{v}{2n})$, where n is the number of documents in the collection, $\sigma(t_i)$ is the "best-matching" cluster with t_i found by the best-first search, and v denotes the number of visited clusters while looking $\sigma(t_i)$. Notice that $2n$ represents the worst case (i.e., all clusters of the largest hierarchy are visited). The greater number of visited clusters required to find the "best matching" clusters, the smaller F1-Travel is.

As we can observe in Figure 2, unlike extended F1-BCubed and overall F1, our measure considers the hierarchy (c) better than (b), because 20 clusters are visited to find all topics in (c), whereas 22 clusters are explored in (b).

Algorithm 2. F1-Travel for the topic t

---

1. Let Q be a null queue of nodes, sorted by decreasing $F1$
2. $v = 1$, $BestF1 = 0$, and insert $root$ into Q
3. while $Q \neq \emptyset$:
   - (a) Extract the first cluster c from Q
   - (b) if $F1(t, c) > BestF1$:
       - i. $BestF1 = F1(t, c)$
   - (c) $v = v + |c.childs|$ // $|c.childs|$ is the number of childs of c in the hierarchy
   - (d) for each child c' of c:
       - i. if $F1(t, c') > BestF1$:
           - A. Insert c' into Q
4. $F1\text{-}Travel(t) = BestF1(1 - \frac{v}{2n})$

---

4   Experimental Results

The performance of the proposed version of dynamic hierarchical compact algorithm has been evaluated using six benchmark text collections, whose general characteristics are summarized in Table 1. They are heterogeneous in terms of document size, number of topics and document distribution. Human annotators identified the flat topics in each collection. In our experiments, the documents are represented using the traditional vector space model. Document terms represent the lemmas of the words appearing in the texts (stop words are disregarded) and they are statistically weighted using TF (term frequency in the document).

The experiments were focused on comparing the proposed version against the original *DHC* algorithm in terms of clustering quality and time efficiency. From the results reported in [5], we fix the parameter $\beta = 0.02$, which produces good hierarchies for all text collections.

To quantitatively compare the relative performance of both methods, we divided the overall F1 score obtained by the proposed method by the corresponding score obtained by *DHC*. We referred to this ratio as *relative overall F1* score. In the same way, we calculated *relative extended F1-BCubed* and *relative overall F1-Travel* scores. We also computed the speedup obtained by the proposed method, that is, the ratio between the execution times of *DHC* and our method.

Table 1. Description of document collections

Collection	Source	Docs	Terms	Topics
eln	TREC-4 (http://www.trec.nist.gov)	5829	83434	50
hitech	San Jose Mercury (http://glaros.dtc.umn.edu)	2301	13170	6
new3	San Jose Mercury (http://glaros.dtc.umn.edu)	9559	83487	44
oshcal	Ohsumed-233445 (http://glaros.dtc.umn.edu)	11162	11465	10
reu	Reuters-21578 (http://kdd.ics.uci.edu)	10369	35297	119
tdt	TDT2 (http://www.nist.gov/speech/test/tdt.html)	9824	55112	193

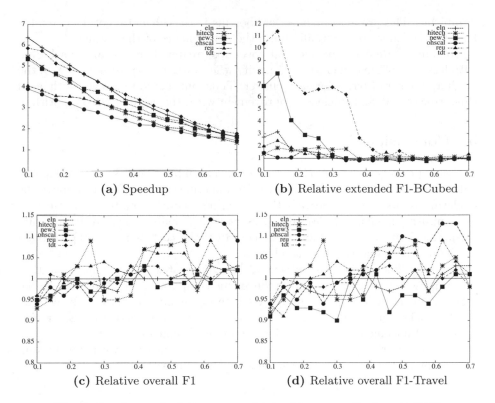

Fig. 3. Speedup and relative scores obtained by our method w.r.t. *DHC*

Figure 3 shows the speedups and the relative quality scores, when we vary the fraction of relevant terms (f) from 0.1 to 0.7 for each text collection. At a glance, we can observe in Figure 3(a) that speedups between 2 and 6 are achieved for all collections when $f \leq 0.5$. As expected, the greater reduction, the higher speedups are obtained.

From the Figures 3(c) and 3(d), we can see that the overall F1 and overall F1-Travel scores slightly decrease (about 5%) or even improve in all collections while reducing the number of features per cluster in the fraction between 0.2 and 0.5. The slight decrease in the relative overall F1-Travel score w.r.t. the relative overall F1 score demonstrates that the number of navigation steps to finding the "best matching" clusters is not significantly increased with the feature selection.

The extended F1-BCubed measure shows a different behavior (see Figure 3(b)). In this case, our method obtains better scores than those obtained by the original *DHC* algorithm for all feature reductions. The smaller the number of selected terms per cluster, the higher extended F1-BCubed scores are achieved, specially when few features are selected (about 10-20%). This can be explained by the fact that both the number of hierarchy levels and clusters' size decrease, which causes that the number of document pairs that occur in the clusters diminishes. This produces an effect of boosting in the calculation of the extended F1-BCubed values that actually hides the performance of the method.

To sum up, we can conclude that speedups greater than 2.5 can be achieved with less than 5% loss in clustering quality when we select between 20-45% of the original number of terms for each cluster. Thus, our method achieves both good clustering quality and efficiency improvement w.r.t. the original DHC algorithm.

5   Conclusions

In this paper, a version of DHC algorithm has been proposed. Since the dynamic nature of the method, a local feature selection criterion is applied to remove the irrelevant terms that may degrade the clustering accuracy, and to reduce the cost of computing similarities. We also present a new quality measure to evaluate hierarchical clustering solutions that considers the cost of navigating through the hierarchy to find the optimal clusters.

The experimental results on several benchmark text collections show that the proposed method significantly reduces the computation times of the original DHC algorithm while maintaining the clustering quality. Thus, we advocate its use for tasks that require dynamic clustering of large text collections, such as creation of document taxonomies and hierarchical topic detection.

As future work, we plan to combine the proposed method with the speedup version presented in [9], to further improve DHC algorithm.

References

1. Gil-García, R., Badía-Contelles, J.M., Pons-Porrata, A.: Dynamic Hierarchical Compact Clustering Algorithm. In: Sanfeliu, A., Cortés, M.L. (eds.) CIARP 2005. LNCS, vol. 3773, pp. 302–310. Springer, Heidelberg (2005)
2. Dy, J.G., Brodley, C.E.: Feature selection for unsupervised learning. Journal of Machine Learning Research 5, 845–889 (2004)
3. Ribeiro, M.N., Neto, M.J.R., Prudêncio, R.B.C.: Local feature selection in text clustering. In: Köppen, M., Kasabov, N., Coghill, G. (eds.) ICONIP 2008. LNCS, vol. 5507, pp. 45–52. Springer, Heidelberg (2008)
4. Zhao, Y., Karypis, G.: Evaluation of hierarchical clustering algorithms for document datasets. In: 11th CIKM, pp. 515–524. ACM Press, New York (2002)
5. Gil-García, R., Pons-Porrata, A.: Dynamic hierarchical algorithms for document clustering. Pattern Recognition Letters 31(6), 469–477 (2010)
6. Larsen, B., Aone, C.: Fast and Effective Text Mining Using Linear-time Document Clustering. In: KDD 1999, pp. 16–22. ACM Press, New York (1999)
7. Amigó, E., Gonzalo, J., Artiles, J., Verdejo, F.: A comparison of extrinsic clustering evaluation metrics based on formal constraints. Inform. Retrieval 12, 461–486 (2009)
8. Allan, J., Feng, A., Bolivar, A.: Flexible intrinsic evaluation of hierarchical clustering for tdt. In: 12th CIKM, pp. 263–270. ACM Press, New York (2003)
9. Gil-García, R., Pons-Porrata, A.: A speed-up hierarchical compact clustering algorithm for dynamic document collections. In: Bayro-Corrochano, E., Eklundh, J.-O. (eds.) CIARP 2009. LNCS, vol. 5856, pp. 379–386. Springer, Heidelberg (2009)

Background Division, A Suitable Technique for Moving Object Detection

Walter Izquierdo-Guerra and Edel García-Reyes

Advanced Technologies Application Center (CENATAV), 7a ♯ 21812 e/ 218 y 222,
Rpto. Siboney, Playa, C.P. 12200, La Habana, Cuba
{wizquierdo,egarcia}@cenatav.co.cu

Abstract. Nowadays, background model does not have any robust solution and constitutes one of the main problems in surveillance systems. Researchers are working in several approaches in order to get better background pixel models. This is a previous step to apply the background subtraction technique and results are not as good as expected. We concentrate our efforts on the second step for segmentation of moving objects and we propose background division to substitute background subtraction technique.This approach allows us to obtain clusters with lower intraclass variability and higher inter-class variability, this diminishes confusion between background and foreground,pixels. We compared results using our background division approach versus wallflowers algorithm [1] as the baseline to compare.

1 Introduction

Surveillance systems are interested in the problem of segmenting moving objects in video sequences. Background subtraction technique is one of the most widely used approaches. This algorithm compares the current image versus a background image obtained by a previous processing of the pixel history. Pixels where the difference is greater than a threshold are marked as foreground pixels. That is the main principle for this technique. In our opinion this kind of algorithms may be separate in two main steps: background maintenance and segmenting criteria.

The background maintenance is the step where the background is modeled. Next, an expected image according to his model is predicted. In general, this is the main feature that distinguishes methods. The current models report a lot of errors when predicting the background. Some researchers have produced state of the art of the existent methods in recent years [1], [2],[3] and [4].

The second step (segmenting criteria) has evolved since a simple priori threshold [5] to a more complex system as [1]. Some variables are inferred from the background maintenance phase in order to obtain an automatic threshold to segment foreground pixels. One of the most popular algorithms for moving object detection is the Gaussian mixture model. In [6], the authors explain a detailed version of it. At present, there are authors trying to improve this method because it has a great number of advantages. For example, the authors of [7] propose an

I. Bloch and R.M. Cesar, Jr. (Eds.): CIARP 2010, LNCS 6419, pp. 121–127, 2010.

approach that combines the Gaussian mixture model with a Markov random fields smoothness. That algorithm has a great computational cost. It fixes a lot of parameters. That turns the method into a scene-dependant method. A survey with a great amount of approaches can be found in [8]. Most of them try to solve the problem of robust background maintenance, but the number of situations that can be observed in an image sequence is colossal.

In general, researchers have accepted the background subtraction technique as the basis of all the a posteriori processing. Our point is that background division is the most appropriate technique in order to do this work because it diminishes confusion between background and foreground pixels. This constitutes the second part of our work.

The main problems that affect the segmentation of moving objects are presented in [1]. We are going to focus our work on seven of them: moved object, time of day, light switch, waving trees, camouflage, bootstrap and foreground aperture. There are works which try to solve other problems. For example [9] shows an algorithm to solve the shadows in the image.

This paper is divided into 5 sections. Section 1 is an overview of this work. Section 2 describes the theoretical topics about the physical nature images. Section 3 presents our proposal of background division and explains why we prefer this technique. Section 4 shows the comparison of our results versus wallflowers algorithm and SACON's algorithm. Lastly, section 5 contains the conclusions.

2   Fresnel Reflection

The Fresnel equations describe the behavior of light when moving between mediums of different refractive indexes. The reflection of light that the equations predict is known as Fresnel reflection. When light moves from a medium of a

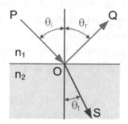

Fig. 1. Reflection and Refraction representation

given refractive index n_1 into a second medium with refractive index n_2, both reflection and refraction of the light may occur(see Figure 1). The angles of incident, reflected and refracted rays with respect to the normal of the surface that separate the mediums are given as Θ_i, Θ_r and Θ_t, respectively. Relationship among these angles is given by the law of reflection and Snell's law [10]. The fraction of the incident energy that is reflected from the surface is given by the reflectance R and the fraction that is refracted is given by the transmittance T, where $R = R(\Theta_i, n_1, n_2)$. In this way, the coefficient R depends on the refraction indexes of the materials and the angle between the source and the object. We talk about Fresnel equations because it describes the theoretical behavior of the real world. In the next section we are going to observe how background subtraction and background division work for theoretical assumptions.

3   Background Division

As it was shown above, the coefficient R depends on the incident angle and refractive indexes of the mediums. It means that we are going to work with an R coefficient $R(\Theta_i, n_1, n_2, x, y)$ being (x, y) the position of the pixel in the image. This is the physics behind the problem, but we are going to take into consideration some topics. In general,Θ_i can be variable(example the sun light). The sun is moving the entire day; but if we take into account small movement of the sun and the algorithm update speed, we can consider this source as fixed for small time intervals. In the case of indoor environments the light sources are fixed. Now we can ensure, that for our purposes, the reflection coefficient does not depend on Θ_i.

R also depends on the refraction indexes. In the case of n_1, it is always going to represent the air refraction index. In this way, it will be fixed in all the video. n_2 only changes if an object in the scene was moved(in this case R changes too) and this is a situation we want to detect. Then we can characterize our scene by its reflectance. We are going to have one point x, y with a reflectance value. But, we only observe the light intensity reflected by image I.

$$I(x, y, t) = I_o(x, y, t) * R(x, y) \tag{1}$$

where t is the time and

$$I_o(x, y, t) = I_o(t) + \epsilon(x, y, t) \tag{2}$$

Where $I_o(t)$ is the proper source illumination. Here $\epsilon(x, y, t)$ is a natural noise that affects the three variables. It represents a gaussian distribution. So when we collect a big number of ϵ_k its expected value is 0:

$$\lim_{N \to \infty} \sum_{k}^{N} \epsilon_k(x, y, t) = 0 \tag{3}$$

where $k = x, y$ or t. so,

$$I(x, y, t) = [I_o(t) + \epsilon(x, y, t)] * R(x, y) \tag{4}$$

Usually, the background(B) is estimated as the expected value of $I(x, y, t)$ [1] [4]. The are a lot of approaches to estimate the background. The most widely used are the mean value over t, median value, gaussian mixture models(GMM) among others. We are going to concentrate our efforts in the mean value in order to explain easily the problem.

$$B(x, y) = \sum_{t=0}^{N} \frac{I(x, y, t)}{N} = \frac{R(x, y)}{N} * [\sum_{t=0}^{N} I_o(t) + \sum_{t=0}^{N} \epsilon_t] \tag{5}$$

We consider N very big in order to suppress the noise. Then, according to equation 3:

$$\sum_{t=0}^{N} \epsilon_t = 0 \tag{6}$$

So,

$$B(x, y) = R(x, y) * \overline{I}_o \tag{7}$$

where $\overline{I}_o$ is the mean value of $I_o(t)$

When a new frame is coming($I(x, y, t+1)$) background subtraction technique is applied:

$$S(x, y, t) = I(x, y, t+1) - B(x, y) = [I_o(t+1) + \epsilon(x, y, t+1) - \overline{I}_o] * R(x, y) \tag{8}$$

Usually it is accept that the expected value of $S(x, y, t)$ is a matrix of zeros. This is only right when $I_o(t+1) = \overline{I}_o$(An illumination change did not occur) and under certain conditions of $R(x, y)$. If background division technique is applied the following expression is obtained:

$$D(x, y, t) = \frac{I(x, y, t+1)}{B(x, y)} = \frac{I_o(t+1) + \epsilon(x, y, t+1)}{\overline{I}_o} * \frac{R(x, y)}{R(x, y)} \tag{9}$$

$$D(x, y, t) = \frac{I_o(t+1)}{\overline{I}_o} + \frac{\epsilon(x, y, t+1)}{\overline{I}_o} \tag{10}$$

Notice that $D(x, y, t)$ maintains the original gaussian distribution. The expected value of $D(x, y, t)$ is:

$$C(t) = \frac{I_o(t+1)}{\overline{I}_o} \tag{11}$$

and the noise:

$$\frac{\epsilon(x, y, t+1)}{\overline{I}_o} \tag{12}$$

Computing the mean value over x and y of the matrix $D(x, y, t)$(this is an observable magnitude) we obtain the value of $C(t)$.

When we use background division technique we obtain an expected value for the matrix $D(x, y)$ and we can use this value as a center of a gaussian, etc. This is the main advantage of background division. There are others, it is easy to predict the shadow and the magnitude of illumination change, as the mean of the divided image. But those topics are going to be discussed in future works.

As a conclusion, background subtraction is affected by the illumination change while background division is not affected.

In order to apply our algorithm to the wallflower's dataset [1], for the modeling phase, we used the approximated median filter [11]. This is a very simple method. In this way, we have a background image.

We have a second background to model the sudden illumination changes. It is used when the algorithm classifies more than 80 per cent of the pixels as foreground. This background is obtained in a training phase.[12]

Now, when a new frame is coming we use the background to apply background division technique.

$$D(x, y, t) = \frac{I(x, y, t + 1)}{B(x, y)} \tag{13}$$

In this way we are going to obtain a matrix $D(x, y, t)$ where certain value is predominant. Now, we consider there is not only one predominant value, we are going to suppose there are 5 most probably values in order to classify all pixels in the image. We apply k-means algorithm to find this 5 values. We initialize with the seeds (0 0.8 1 1.2 2). The value near 1 is a background value. The other four clusters are going to be classified as foreground.

We also take into account another advantage of the method. When we have shadows in the scene, these are poorer illuminated places than the rest of the image. When we apply background division, we can predict this shadows as values minor than 1 but near to it.

In our paper we classify a second cluster as background if it is close enough to the cluster centered on 1.

The processing continues applying a connected components algorithm. We keep the regions greater or equal than a size estimated for a person (suitable for each scene).

We apply a segmenting criteria similar to the explained in [12]:

Let $A(x, y)$ be the binary image at this point of processing.

We compute the distant transform$(d(x, y))$ of A [13]. We are going to classify a pixel as foreground in $F(x, y)$ only if $D_t(x, y) * d_t(x, y) < \tau$.

Where $F(x, y)$ is the final binary image that our algorithm return.

4   Results

We compare our results versus wallflower's results [1]. Wallflower's algorithm is a very famous method and its dataset is one of the most widely used to compare algorithms. We compare our results vs. [12] results too. It is an algorithm where background subtraction technique is applied.

The visual results are shown in figure 2 and error rates are shown on Table 1.

As we can observe in Table 1, our algorithm works better than the wallflower algorithm. It reduces to 56 % the total of errors they reported for background subtraction and to 53 % for background division.

In light switch image, there is a great amount of false negative pixels. In our opinion, this does not constitute an error of our algorithm because most of them are pixels belonging to a chair, that wallflower dataset reports as an object. We consider that the chair is background in the scene.

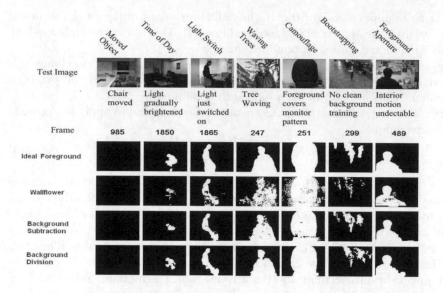

Fig. 2. Visual results. The first row of pictures is hand-segmented images.

Table 1. Numeric results

Algorithm	Error Type	moved object	time of day	light switch	waving trees	camouflage	bootstrap	foreground aperture	Total Errors
Wallflower[1]	false neg.	0	961	947	877	229	2025	320	11448
	false pos.	0	25	345	1999	2706	365	649	
Background subtraction [12]	false neg.	0	1030	1308	164	518	907	236	5906
	false pos.	0	3	385	333	384	565	73	
Background division	false neg.	0	638	1059	108	164	1287	152	5579
	false pos.	0	64	417	192	379	833	286	

It is possible to see that the noise in the silhouettes is lower for background division. However, a small trend to rise the false positive rate was observed, especially with bootstrapping problem. The advantage of background division is that interclass variability is lower than for background subtraction, then the confusion between background and foreground pixel is lower. This way a clustering algorithm may separate moving objects and shadows in different connected components.

5   Conclusions

In this paper, we present a novel approach to the moving object detection problem. We use the background division approach to obtain a model suitable to illumination changes. The global threshold used to segment the moving objects is dependent on the current image noise level and it is automatically calculated applying an empirical formula[12].

We experimentally compared our approach against the wallflower algorithm and we obtained better results, as showed visually in figure 2, and numerically in Table 1. Our future research direction is to combine our algorithm with a more robust tool to model the pixel history.

On the other hand, to the best of our knowledge, this is the first time approaches of background subtraction and background division for segmentation of moving object have been compared taking into account different problems affecting the segmentation. In general, for the wallflower dataset, the background division outperforms background subtraction, especially when the light gradually changes. This was visual and numerically observed in the experiments, and the total error rate was better than previous published results.

References

1. Toyama, K., Krumm, J., Brumitt, B., Meyers, B.: Wallower: Principles and practice of background maintenance. In: Seventh International Conference on Computer Vision, vol. 1, p. 255 (1999)
2. Sen, Kamath, C.: Robust techniques for background subtraction in urban traffic video, vol. 5308, pp. 881–892. SPIE, San Jose (2004)
3. Ribeiro, H.N., Hall, D., Nascimento, J., Ribeiro, P., Andrade, E., Moreno, P., Pesnel, S., List, T., Emonet, R., Fisher, R.B., Santos Victor, J., Crowley, J.L.: Comparison of target detection algorithms using adaptive background models. In: Proc. 2nd Joint IEEE Int. Workshop on Visual Surveillance and VisLab-TR 13/2005, pp. 113–120 (2005)
4. Mcivor, A.M.: Background subtraction techniques. In: Proc. of Image and Vision Computing, pp. 147–153 (2000)
5. Heikkilä, J., Silvén, O.: A real-time system for monitoring of cyclists and pedestrians. Image and Vision Computing 22(7), 563–570 (2004)
6. Power, P.W., Schoonees, J.A.: Understanding background mixture models for foreground segmentation. In: Proceedings Image and Vision Computing, New Zealand, p. 267 (2002)
7. Schindler, K., Wang, H.: Smooth foreground-background segmentation for video processing (2006)
8. Bouwmans, T., Baf, F.E., Vachon, B.: Background modeling using mixture of gaussians for foreground detection - a survey. Recent Patents on Computer Science 1, 219–237 (2008)
9. Kaewtrakulpong, P., Bowden, R.: An improved adaptive background mixture model for realtime tracking with shadow detection. In: Proc. 2nd European Workshop on Advanced Video Based Surveillance Systems, AVBS 2001, VIDEO BASED SURVEILLANCE SYSTEMS: Computer Vision and Distributed Processing (2001)
10. Frish, S., Timoreva, A.: Curso de Física General, vol. 3. MIR, Moscow (1973)
11. Bécsi And, T., Péter, T.: A mixture of distributions background model for traffic video surveillance. Periodica Polytechnica Ser. Transp. Eng. 34, 109–117 (2006)
12. Izquierdo-Guerra, W., García-Reyes, E.B.: A novel approach to robust background subtraction. In: Bayro-Corrochano, E., Eklundh, J.-O. (eds.) CIARP 2009. LNCS, vol. 5856, pp. 69–76. Springer, Heidelberg (2009)
13. Gonzalez, R.C., Woods, R.E., Eddins, S.L.: Digital Image Processing Using MATLAB. Prentice-Hall, Inc., Upper Saddle River (2003)

Concept Formation Using Incremental Gaussian Mixture Models

Paulo Martins Engel and Milton Roberto Heinen

UFRGS – Informatics Institute
Porto Alegre, CEP 91501-970, RS, Brazil
engel@inf.ufrgs.br, mrheinen@inf.ufrgs.br

Abstract. This paper presents a new algorithm for incremental concept formation based on a Bayesian framework. The algorithm, called IGMM (for Incremental Gaussian Mixture Model), uses a probabilistic approach for modeling the environment, and so, it can rely on solid arguments to handle this issue. IGMM creates and continually adjusts a probabilistic model consistent to all sequentially presented data without storing or revisiting previous training data. IGMM is particularly useful for incremental clustering of data streams, as encountered in the domain of moving object trajectories and mobile robotics. It creates an incremental knowledge model of the domain consisting of primitive concepts involving all observed variables. Experiments with simulated data streams of sonar readings of a mobile robot shows that IGMM can efficiently segment trajectories detecting higher order concepts like "wall at right" and "curve at left".

Keywords: Concept Formation, Incremental Learning, Unsupervised Learning, Bayesian Methods, EM Algorithm, Finite Mixtures, Clustering.

1 Introduction

In this paper, we focus in the so called unsupervised incremental learning [1, 2], which considers building a model, seen as a set of concepts of the environment describing a data flow, where each data point is just instantaneously available to the learning system [3, 4]. In this case, the learning system needs to take into account these instantaneous data to update its model of the environment. An important issue in unsupervised incremental learning is the stability-plasticity dilemma, i.e., whether a new presented data point must be assimilated in the current model or cause a structural change in the model to accommodate the new information that it bears, i.e., a new concept. We show that our algorithm, the so called IGMM (standing for Incremental Gaussian Mixture Model), uses a probabilistic approach for modeling the environment, and so, it can rely on solid arguments to handle this issue [5, 6].

We are interested in problems like the ones encountered in autonomous robotics. To be more specific, we consider the so called perceptual learning that allows an embodied agent to understand the world [7]. Here an important task is the detection of concepts such as "corners", "walls" and "corridors" from the sequence of noisy sensor readings of a mobile robot. The detection of these regularities in data flow allows the robot to localize its position and to detect changes in the environment [8]. In the past, different approaches were presented to this end, but they have scarce means to handle the

I. Bloch and R.M. Cesar, Jr. (Eds.): CIARP 2010, LNCS 6419, pp. 128–135, 2010.

stability-plasticity dilemma and to appropriately model the data. As a typical example of these approaches, Nolfi and Tani [9] proposed a hierarchical architecture to extract regularities from time series, in which higher layers are trained to predict the internal state of lower layers when such states change significantly. In this approach, the segmentation was cast as a traditional error minimization problem [10], which favors the most frequent inputs, filtering out less frequent input patterns as being "noise". The result is that this system recognizes slightly differing walls, that represent frequent input patterns, as distinguish concepts, but is unable to detect corridors or corners that are occasionally (infrequently) encountered.

Focusing in change detection, Linåker and Niklasson [11, 12] proposed an adaptive resource allocating vector quantization (ARAVQ) network, which stores moving averages of segments of the data sequence as vectors allocated to output nodes of the network. New model vectors are incorporated to the model if a mismatch between the moving average of the input signal and the existing model vectors is greater than a specified threshold and a minimum stability criterion for the input signal is fulfilled. However, like other distance based clustering algorithm, the induced model is equivalent to a set of equiprobable spherical distributions sharing the same variance, what barely fits to a data flow with temporal correlation, better described by elongated elliptical distributions [5, 6].

Our approach can be seen as an incremental solution for the problem of probability density estimation, a very important research field in statistical pattern recognition [13, 14]. As the EM algorithm [15, 16], IGMM follows the mixture distribution modeling. However, its model can be effectively *expanded* with new components (i.e. concepts) as new relevant information is identified in the data flow. Moreover, IGMM adjusts the parameters of each distribution after the presentation of every single data point according to recursive equations that are approximate incremental counterparts of the batch-mode update equations used by the EM algorithm. Although in the past several attempts have been made to create an algorithm to learn Gaussian mixture models incrementally [17, 18, 19, 20], most of these attempts require several data points to the correct estimation of the covariance matrices and/or does not handles the stability-plasticity dilemma. The IGMM algorithm, on the other hand, converges after the presentation of few training samples and does not require a predefined number of distributions.

The promising results obtained with IGMM applied to sonar signal flows from a robot simulator, described later on in this text, point out that it fits the requirements of the so called Embodied Statistical Learning, a desired but still scarce set of statistical methods compatible to the design principles of Embodied AI [7]. The rest of this paper is organized as follows. Section 2 presents in details the proposed algorithm. Section 3 describes an experiment performed to evaluate the proposed model. Finally, Section 4 provides some final remarks and perspectives.

2   The Incremental Gaussian Mixture Model

This section describes the proposed model, called IGMM [5], which was designed to learn Gaussian mixture models from data flows in an incremental and unsupervised way. IGMM assumes that the probability density of the input data $p(\mathbf{x})$ can be modeled by a linear combination of component densities $p(\mathbf{x}|j)$ corresponding to independent probabilistic processes, in the form

$$p(\mathbf{x}) = \sum_{j=1}^{M} p(\mathbf{x}|j)p(j) \tag{1}$$

This representation is called a *mixture model* and the coefficients $p(j)$ are called the mixing parameters, related to the *prior* probability of $\mathbf{x}$ having been generated from component j of the mixture. The priors are adjusted to satisfy the constraints

$$\sum_{j=1}^{M} p(j) = 1 \tag{2}$$

$$0 \leq p(j) \leq 1 \tag{3}$$

Similarly, the component density functions $p(\mathbf{x}|j)$ are normalized so that

$$\int p(\mathbf{x}|j)d\mathbf{x} = 1 \tag{4}$$

The probability of observing vector $\mathbf{x} = (x_1, \ldots, x_i, \ldots, x_D)$ belonging to the jth mixture component, is computed by a multivariate normal Gaussian, with mean $\boldsymbol{\mu}_j$ and covariance matrix $\mathbf{C}_j$:

$$p(\mathbf{x}|j) = \frac{1}{(2\pi)^{D/2}\sqrt{|\mathbf{C}_j|}} \exp\left\{-\frac{1}{2}(\mathbf{x} - \boldsymbol{\mu}_j)^T \mathbf{C}_j^{-1}(\mathbf{x} - \boldsymbol{\mu}_j)\right\} \tag{5}$$

IGMM adopts an incremental mixture distribution model, having special means to control the number of mixture components that effectively represent the so far presented data. We are interested in modeling environments whose overall dynamics can be described by a set of persistent concepts which will be incrementally learned and represented by a set of mixture components. So, we can now rely on a novelty criterion to overcome the problem of the model complexity selection, related to the decision whether a new component should be added to the current model. The mixture model starts with a single component with unity prior, centered at the first input data, with a baseline covariance matrix specified by default, i. e., $\boldsymbol{\mu}_1 = \mathbf{x}^1$, meaning the value of $\mathbf{x}$ for $t = 1$, and $(\mathbf{C}_1)^1 = \sigma_{ini}^2 \mathbf{I}$, where σ_{ini} is user-specified configuration parameter.

New components are added by demand. IGMM uses a *minimum likelihood* criterion to recognize a vector $\mathbf{x}$ as belonging to a mixture component. For each incoming data point the algorithm verifies whether it minimally fits any mixture component. A data point $\mathbf{x}$ is not recognized as belonging to a mixture component j if its probability $p(\mathbf{x}|j)$ is lower than a previously specified *minimum likelihood-* (or *novelty-*) *threshold*. In this case, $p(\mathbf{x}|j)$ is interpreted as a *likelihood function* of the jth mixture component. If $\mathbf{x}$ is rejected by all density components, meaning that it bears new information, a new component is added to the model, appropriately adjusting its parameters. The novelty-threshold value affects the sensibility of the learning process to new concepts, with higher threshold values generating more concepts. It is more intuitive for the user to specify a minimum value for the acceptable likelihood, τ_{nov}, as a *fraction* of the maximum value of the likelihood function, making the novelty criterion independent of the covariance matrix. Hence, a new mixture component is created when the instantaneous data point $\mathbf{x} = (x_1, \ldots, x_i, \ldots, x_D)$ matches the *novelty criterion* written as

$$p(\mathbf{x}|j) < \frac{\tau_{nov}}{(2\pi)^{D/2}\sqrt{|\mathbf{C}_j|}} \quad \forall j \tag{6}$$

An instantaneous data point that does not match the novelty criterion needs to be assimilated by the current mixture distribution, causing an update in the values of its parameters due to the information it bears. IGMM follows an incremental version for the usual iterative process to estimate the parameters of a mixture model based on two steps: an estimation step (E) and a maximization step (M). The update process begins computing the posterior probabilities of component membership for the data point, $p(j|\mathbf{x})$, the *estimation* step. These can be obtained through Bayes' theorem, using the current component-conditional densities $p(\mathbf{x}|j)$ and priors $p(j)$ as follows:

$$p(j|\mathbf{x}) = \frac{p(\mathbf{x}|j)p(j)}{\sum_{j=1}^{M} p(\mathbf{x}|j)p(j)} \quad \forall j \tag{7}$$

The posterior probabilities can then be used to compute new estimates for the values of the mean vector $\boldsymbol{\mu}_i^{new}$ and covariance matrix $\mathbf{C}_j^{new}$ of each component density $p(\mathbf{x}|j)$, and the priors $p^{new}(j)$ in the *maximization* step. Next, we derive the recursive equations used by IGMM to successively estimate these parameters.

The parameters $\boldsymbol{\theta} = (\theta_1, \ldots, \theta_M)^T$, corresponding to the means, $\boldsymbol{\mu}_j$, covariances matrices, $\mathbf{C}_j$, and priors $p(j)$ of a mixture model involving D-dimensional Gaussian distributions $p(\mathbf{x}|j)$, can be estimated from a data sequence of t vectors, $\mathbf{X} = \{\mathbf{x}^1, \ldots, \mathbf{x}^n, \ldots, \mathbf{x}^t\}$ assumed to be drawn independently from this mixture distribution. The estimates of the parameters are random vectors whose statistical proprieties are obtained from their joint density function. Starting from an initial "guess", each observation vector is used to update the estimates according to a successive estimation procedure.

IGMM follows the Robbins-Monro stochastic approximation method to derive the recursive equation used to successively estimate the priors [21]. For this, in the maximization step the parameters of the current model are updated based on the maximization of the likelihood of the data.

In this case, the *likelihood* of $\boldsymbol{\theta}$ for the given $\mathbf{X}$, $L(\boldsymbol{\theta})$, is the joint probability density of the whole data stream $\mathbf{X}$, given by

$$L(\theta) \equiv p(\mathbf{X}|\theta) = \prod_{n=1}^{t} p(\mathbf{x}^n|\theta) = \prod_{n=1}^{t} \left[\sum_{j=1}^{M} p(\mathbf{x}^n|j)p(j) \right] \tag{8}$$

The technique of maximum likelihood sets the value of $\boldsymbol{\theta}$ by maximizing $L(\boldsymbol{\theta})$.

Although the maximum likelihood technique for estimating the priors is straightforward, it becomes quite complex when applied to estimate the mean vector and the covariance matrix directly from (5). Instead, we follow the natural conjugate technique to estimate these parameters [22]. When $\boldsymbol{\mu}$ and $\mathbf{C}$ are estimated by the sample mean vector and sample covariance matrix, and $\mathbf{X}$ is a normally distributed random vector, the joint density function $p(\boldsymbol{\mu}, \mathbf{C}|\mathbf{x}^1, \ldots, \mathbf{x}^i, \ldots, \mathbf{x}^n)$ is known to be the reproducible Gauss-Wishart distribution, the natural conjugate density for the model of (5) [22]. In this case, when we estimate both the expected vector and the covariance matrix of a single distribution, starting with a priori distribution with an expected vector $\boldsymbol{\mu}^0$ and covariance matrix $\mathbf{C}^0$, these parameters are transformed through n observations in the following manner [22, 13]:

$$\omega^1 = \omega^0 + n \quad v^1 = v^0 + n$$

$$\boldsymbol{\mu}^1 = \frac{\omega^0 \boldsymbol{\mu}^0 + n \langle \mathbf{X} \rangle}{\omega^0 + n} \tag{9}$$

$$\mathbf{C}^1 = \frac{\left(v^0 \mathbf{C}^0 + \omega^0 \boldsymbol{\mu}^0 \left(\boldsymbol{\mu}^0\right)^T\right) + n \langle \mathbf{X} \rangle \langle \mathbf{X} \rangle^T - \omega^1 \boldsymbol{\mu}^1 \left(\boldsymbol{\mu}^1\right)^T}{v^0 + n} \tag{10}$$

where ω^0 and v^0 reflect the confidence about the initial estimates of $\boldsymbol{\mu}^0$ and $\mathbf{C}^0$ respectively, corresponding to the number of samples used to compute these initial estimates.

On the other hand, when the probability density of the input data is a Gaussian Mixture Model with M components, an observation $\mathbf{x}^t$ is probabilistic assigned to a distribution j by the corresponding posterior probability $p(j|\mathbf{x}^t)$. In this case, the equivalent number of samples used to compute the parameter estimates of the jth distribution component corresponds to the sum of posterior probabilities that the data presented so far were generated from component j, the so called 0th-order moment of $p(j|\mathbf{x})$ over the data, or simply the 0th-order data moment for j. IGMM stores this summation as the variable sp_j which is periodically restarted to avoid an eventual saturation.

The recursive equations used by IGMM to update the model distributions are:

$$sp_j = sp_j + p(j|\mathbf{x}) \tag{11}$$

$$\boldsymbol{\mu}_j = \boldsymbol{\mu}_j + \frac{p(j|\mathbf{x})}{sp_j} (\mathbf{x} - \boldsymbol{\mu}_j) \tag{12}$$

$$\mathbf{C}_j = \mathbf{C}_j - (\boldsymbol{\mu}_j - \boldsymbol{\mu}_j^{old})(\boldsymbol{\mu}_j - \boldsymbol{\mu}_j^{old})^T + \frac{p(j|\mathbf{x})}{sp_j} \left[(\mathbf{x} - \boldsymbol{\mu}_j)(\mathbf{x} - \boldsymbol{\mu}_j)^T - \mathbf{C}_j\right] \tag{13}$$

$$p(j) = sp_j / \sum_{q=1}^{M} sp_q \tag{14}$$

where $p(j|\mathbf{x})$ $\boldsymbol{\mu}_j^{old}$ refers to the value of $\boldsymbol{\mu}_j$ at time $t - 1$ (i.e., before updating). One important property of these update equations is the fact that they continuously compute a instantaneous approximation of the parameters that represent the mixture distribution.

The IGMM algorithm has just two configuration parameters, σ_{ini} and τ_{nov}. The σ_{ini} parameter is not critical – its only requirement for σ_{ini} is be large enough to avoid singularities. In our experiments we have simply used $\sigma_{ini} = (\mathbf{x}_{max} - \mathbf{x}_{min})/10$. The τ_{nov} parameter, on the other hand, is more critical and must be defined carefully. It indicates how distant $\mathbf{x}$ must be from $\boldsymbol{\mu}_j$ to be consider a non-member of j. For instance, $\tau_{nov} = 0.01$ indicates that $p(\mathbf{x}|j)$ must be lower than one percent of the Gaussian height (probability in the center of the Gaussian) for $\mathbf{x}$ be considered a non-member of j. If $\tau_{nov} < 0.01$, few pattern units will be created and the regression will be coarse. If $\tau_{nov} > 0.01$, more pattern units will be created and consequently the regression will be more precise. In the limit, if $\tau_{nov} = 1$ one unit per training pattern will be created.

3   Experimental Results

This section describes the experiments devised to evaluate IGMM using data obtained from simulated mobile robot sonars. In these experiments, the data consist of a sequence of 4 continuous values (s_1, s_2, s_3, s_4) corresponding to the readings of a sonar array located at the left/right side (s_1, s_4) and at $-10°/+10°$ from the front (s_2, s_3) of a robot, generated using the Pioneer 3-DX simulator software ARCOS (Advanced Robot Control & Operations Software). The first experiment was accomplished in an environment composed of six corridors (four external and two internal), and the robot performed a complete cycle in the external corridors. Fig. 1 shows the segmentation of the trajectory obtained by IGMM when the robot follows the corridors of this environment. IGMM created four clusters corresponding to the concepts of "corridor" (red), "wall at right" (blue), "corridor / obstacle front" (black) and "curve at left" (cyan). The colored filled dots in this figure correspond to the location where each cluster was created. A square represents a robot position and has the same color of the cluster with the largest posterior probability for the corresponding data point.

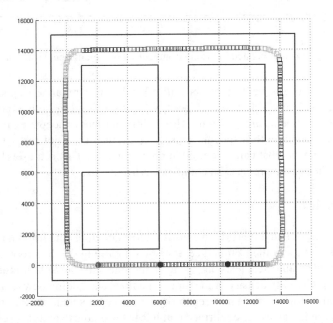

Fig. 1. Concepts created in the environment composed of six corridors

The next experiment was performed in an environment with two different sized rooms connected by a short corridor. This more complex environment is inspired in those used in [9] and [11, 12]. Fig. 2 shows the segmentation of the trajectory of a robot following the walls in this environment. IGMM created seven clusters corresponding to the concepts "wall at right" (1: red), "corridor" (2: blue), "wall at right / obstacle front" (3: black), "curve at left" (4: cyan), "bifurcation / obstacle front" (5: magenta), "bifurcation / curve at right" (6: green) and "wall at left / curve at right" (7: yellow).

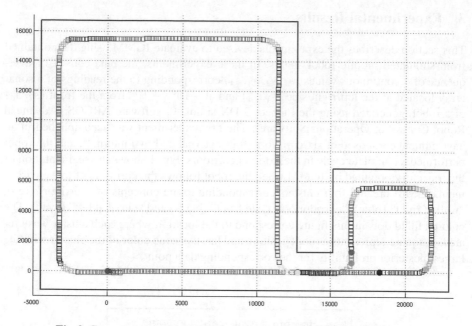

Fig. 2. Concepts created in the environment with two different sized rooms

Comparing the experiments, it can be noticed that some similar concepts, like "curve at left" (cyan) and "obstacle front" (black), were discovered in both experiments, although the environments are different. This points out that concepts extracted from a data flow corresponding to a specific sensed environment are not restricted to it, but they form an alphabet that can be reused in other contexts. This is a useful aspect, that can improve the learning process in complex environments.

4   Conclusion

In this paper we presented IGMM, an algorithm for modeling data flows that fulfills the requirements of the so called Embodied Statistical Learning [7]. It is rooted in the well established field of statistical learning, using an incremental Gaussian Mixture Model to represent the probability density of the input data flow, and adding new density components to the model whenever a new regularity, or concept, is identified in the incoming data. The experimental results confirmed that IGMM was able to extract useful concepts of the data flow from just a single iteration over the training data. This experiment have also shown the representational power of the generated statistical model, since from the values of the computed parameters and the corresponding plots one could readily interpret and label each extracted concept.

Acknowledgment

This work is supported by CNPq, an entity of the Brazilian government for scientific and technological development.

References

1. Arandjelovic, O., Cipolla, R.: Incremental learning of temporally-coherent Gaussian mixture models. In: Proc. 16th British Machine Vision Conf. (BMVC), Oxford, UK, pp. 759–768 (September 2005)
2. Kristan, M., Skocaj, D., Leonardis, A.: Incremental learning with Gaussian mixture models. In: Proc. Computer Vision Winter Workshop, Moravske Toplice, Slovenia, pp. 25–32 (2008)
3. Fisher, D.H.: Knowledge acquisition via incremental conceptual learning. Machine Learning 2, 139–172 (1987)
4. Gennari, J.H., Langley, P., Fisher, D.: Models of incremental concept formation. Artificial Intelligence 40, 11–61 (1989)
5. Engel, P.M., Heinen, M.R.: Incremental learning of multivariate Gaussian mixture models. In: Proc. 20th Brazilian Symposium on AI (SBIA), São Bernardo do Campo, SP, Brazil. Springer, Heidelberg (October 2010)
6. Heinen, M.R., Engel, P.M.: An incremental probabilistic neural network for regression and reinforcement learning tasks. In: Diamantaras, K., Duch, W., Iliadis, L.S. (eds.) ICANN 2010, Part II. LNCS, vol. 6353, pp. 170–179. Springer, Heidelberg (2010)
7. Burfoot, D., Lungarella, M., Kuniyoshi, Y.: Toward a theory of embodied statistical learning. In: Asada, M., Hallam, J.C.T., Meyer, J.-A., Tani, J. (eds.) SAB 2008. LNCS (LNAI), vol. 5040, pp. 270–279. Springer, Heidelberg (2008)
8. Thrun, S., Burgard, W., Fox, D.: Probabilistic Robotics. In: Intelligent Robotics and Autonomous Agents. MIT Press, Cambridge (2006)
9. Nolfi, S., Tani, J.: Extracting regularities in space and time through a cascade of prediction networks: The case of a mobile robot navigating in a structured environment. Connection Science 11(2), 125–148 (1999)
10. Haykin, S.: Neural Networks and Learning Machines, 3rd edn. Prentice-Hall, Upper Saddle River (2008)
11. Linåker, F., Niklasson, L.: Time series segmentation using an adaptive resource allocating vector quantization network based on change detection. In: Proc. IEEE-INNS-ENNS Int. Joint Conf. Neural Networks (IJCNN 2000), Los Alamitos, CA, USA, pp. 323–328 (2000)
12. Linåker, F., Niklasson, L.: Sensory flow segmentation using a resource allocating vector quantizer. In: Amin, A., Pudil, P., Ferri, F., Iñesta, J.M. (eds.) SPR 2000 and SSPR 2000. LNCS, vol. 1876, pp. 853–862. Springer, Heidelberg (2000)
13. Fukunaga, K.: Introduction to Statistical Pattern Recognition, 2nd edn. Academic Press, London (1990)
14. Bishop, C.: Neural Networks for Pattern Recognition. Oxford Univ. Press, New York (1995)
15. Dempster, A.P., Laird, N.M., Rubin, D.B.: Maximum likelihood from incomplete data via the EM algorithm. Journal of the Royal Statistical Society 39(1), 1–38 (1977)
16. Tan, P.N., Steinbach, M., Kumar, V.: Introduction to Data Mining. Addison-Wesley, Boston (2006)
17. Titterington, D.M.: Recursive parameter estimation using incomplete data. Journal of the Royal Statistical Society 46(2), 257–267 (1984)
18. Wang, S., Zhao, Y.: Almost sure convergence of titterington's recursive estimator for mixture models. Statistics & Probability Letters (76), 2001–2006 (2006)
19. Neal, R., Hinton, G.: A view of the EM algorithm that justifies incremental, sparse, and other variants. In: Learning in Graphical Models, pp. 355–368. Kluwer Academic Publishers, Dordrecht (1998)
20. Cappé, O., Moulines, E.: Online EM algorithm for latent data models. Journal of the Royal Statistical Society (September 2008)
21. Robbins, H., Monro, S.: A stochastic approximation method. Annals of Mathematical Statistics 22, 400–407 (1951)
22. Keehn, D.G.: A note on learning for Gaussian proprieties. IEEE Trans. Information Theory 11, 126–132 (1965)

Integrating Phonological Knowledge in ASR Systems for Spanish Language

Javier Mikel Olaso and María Inés Torres

Universidad del País Vasco
{javiermikel.olaso,manes.torres}@ehu.es

Abstract. In this paper we undertake the use of phonological features applied to speech recognition in Spanish language. We investigate two different ways to integrate these phonological features into an HMM based speech recognition system. We also propose a method to integrate these features using an architecture that uses independent feature streams. In the experimental results we find that higher recognition accuracies and less computational cost can be obtained.

Keywords: speech recognition, acoustic modeling, phonological features.

1 Introduction

The majority of speech recognition systems are currently based on the use of the acoustic properties of speech to establish its characteristics. This method has to tackle various difficulties, such as, [2], [3], [12], phonation differences due to the diversity of speakers, coarticulation effects, spontaneous speech, problems with pronunciation dictionaries, mainly in the English language or ambient noise and interferences.

Other approaches have alternatively been proposed. One such approach seeks to incorporate information relating to the way speech is produced in terms of articulatory gestures. This approach is considered to be highly beneficial for automatic speech recognition systems, mainly due to the invariance of critical articulators, those mostly involved in sound production, and the lower susceptibility of the articulatory space to the effects of coarticulation, [1],[2]. This approach has to deal with two main problems. On the one hand, the speaker's utterances need to be represented in terms of these articulatory gestures, and on the other hand a system is needed to interpret such representation. Some studies have attempted to solve these problems. The seemingly most successful method has been the use of Recurrent Time Delay Neural Networks (RTDNN) [5] for articulatory gestures detection, and the re-scoring of lattices obtained using a system based on HMMs defined over Mel Frequency Cepstral Coefficients (MFCC) [1].

This paper is twofold. On one hand, we want to undertake the use of phonological features applied to the Castilian variety of Spanish, investigating two methods to integrate these features into an HMM based speech recognition system. The first method used vectors representing phonological information as

I. Bloch and R.M. Cesar, Jr. (Eds.): CIARP 2010, LNCS 6419, pp. 136–143, 2010.

observation vectors of HMM models and the second used acoustic vectors based on MFCC. On the other hand, we propose a method to integrate these features into a speech recognition system.

The structure of the article is as follows. Section 2 provides a short description of the different methods studied to obtain articulatory information and describes how we decided to implement this phase. Section 3 describes the architecture of the speech recognizer used in our experiments. Section 4 contains the results of our experiments. And the paper ends with the concluding remarks and acknowledgements in Sections 5 and 5, respectively.

2   Phonological Feature Extraction

Several methods have been proposed for the extraction of the phonological features. These methods fall into one of two approaches. On the one hand, there are the methods based on extraction of information directly from the measurement of the positions or the articulatory organs responsible for speech generation, such as those presented in [6] where measures of the articulator's positions taken with X ray are used. On the other hand, there are the methods based on indirect measurements. Examples of the indirect methods can be found in [7], where visual information of the mouth is used, or in [8], [10], [11], where the phonological information is taken from the surface waveform. The most common of these two approaches seems to be the indirect one, and more specifically when information is taken from the surface waveform. This is mainly due to the fact that direct measurements require expensive and invasive devices, such as an electropalatograph. On the other hand, different methods are used to extract phonological information from the surface waveform, such as, the use of artificial neural networks [8], [10], dynamic Bayesian networks [4], [9] or Hidden Markov Models [13], among others.

We used neural networks in this study, and more specifically, RTDNN [5], a type of neural networks that combines time-delay windows and recurrent connections to capture the dynamic information of the speech signal.

We therefore needed to define the set of sounds (phonemes) used in our experiments and how they were described in terms of articulatory features. Basing on the theoretical classification shown in Table 1, and after a set of tests to maximize the classification accuracy, we defined the articulatory feature sets shown in Table 2, where we can see that it corresponds to the theoretical classification, plus a class *silence* in all features except sonority, a class *vowel* in manner and place of articulation, and a *non-vowel* class for vowel/non-vowel features, see [15] for a more detailed description.

3   Speech Recognizer Architecture

Different systems have been developed that make use of the phonological features. For example, a system is presented in [1], [10], that uses phonological features to re-score the lattices generated by a MFCC based HMM phone recognizer.

Table 1. Theoretical classification for phonemes in spanish language

Place of articulation	Manner of articulation						
	Plosive	Fricative	Affricate	Lateral	Trill	M. Trill	Nasal
	unvoiced	voiced	unvoiced	voiced			
Bilabial	p	b						m
Labiodental			f					
Linguodental			z					
Alveolar	t	d	s	ch	l	r	rr	n
Palatal					ll			ñ
Velar	k	g	j					

	Front	Central	Back
Close	i		u
Close-Mid	e		o
Open		a	

Table 2. Classification used for the phonological features

Sonority	
Voiced	a,e,i,o,u,b,d,g,l,ll,r,rr,m,n,ñ
Unvoiced	p,t,k,f,z,s,j,ch

Vowel - Non Vowel			
Front	i,e	Open	a
Central	a	Mid-Close	e,o
Back	o,u	Close	i,u
Non Vowel	rest	Non Vowel	rest
Silence	SIL	Silence	SIL

Manner	
Plosive	p,t,k,b,d,g
Fricative	f,z,s,j
Affricate	ch
Lateral	l,ll
Trill	r
M. Trill	rr
Nasal	m,n,ñ
Vowel	a,e,i,o,u
Silence	SIL

Place	
Bilabial	p,b,m
Labiodental	f
Linguodental	z
Albeolar	t,d,s,ch,l,r,rr,n
Palatal	ll,ñ
Velar	k,g,j
Vowel	a,e,i,o,u
Silence	SIL

In this paper, we propose a system based on a classical acoustic speech recognition system, based on HMMs, with two main differences. On one hand, we introduce phonological information in the system architecture. On the other hand, we followed an approach of integrating the feature vectors using independent feature streams.

Let,

$$O = o_1, o_2, ..., o_T \qquad (1)$$

be a sequence of observations where o_t is the speech vector observed at time t. When o_t are elements of a continuous observation alphabet, and in case of using Gaussian mixtures as probability distribution function, the observation symbol probability matrix, $b_j(o_t)$, for an HMM can be written as:

$$b_j(o_t) = \sum_{m=1}^{M} c_{jm} \mathcal{N}(o_t; \mu_{jm}, \Sigma_{jm}) \qquad (2)$$

where $\mathcal{N}(o_t, \mu_{jm}, \Sigma_{jm})$ denotes m'th Gaussian, with μ_{jm} mean vector and Σ_{jm} variance matrix, for state j. M is the number of Gaussians in the mixture and c_{jm} is the weight of the m'th component in the mixture, that compliments:

$$\sum_{m=1}^{M} c_{jm} = 1 \qquad (3)$$

Well, now we propose to use an architecture with independent feature streams.[1] Let S be the number of independent feature streams and O_{st} a vector defined as:

$$O_{st} = o_{st}^1, o_{st}^2, \ldots, o_{st}^n \qquad (4)$$

that represents an observation in stream s and time t, and with n its dimension, which may vary for each feature stream. With this approach the observation symbol probability matrix, $b_j(o_t)$, can be rewritten as:

$$b_j(o_t) = \prod_{s=1}^{S} \left(\sum_{m=1}^{M_s} c_{jms} \mathcal{N}(O_{st}; \mu_{jms}, \Sigma_{jms}) \right) \qquad (5)$$

where M_s is the number of Gaussians in the mixture of stream s, which may be different in each stream.

Likewise, in the case of using discrete symbol streams, the matrix, $b_j(o_t)$, can be rewritten as:

$$b_j(o_t) = \prod_{s=1}^{S} b_{js}(O_{st}) \qquad (6)$$

where $b_{js}(O_{st})$ is the observation symbol probability matrix of stream s.

4   Experimental Evaluation

This section is dedicated to a more detailed description of the implementation of the system presented. First, we provide a short description of the corpus used. The process for the phonological feature extraction is then described, and finally the different configurations, and the recognition results are given.

4.1   Database Description

The speech corpus used in this paper was Albayzin [14]. This is a corpus in the Castilian variety of Spanish recorded at 16KHz divided in three sub-corpus: a phonetic corpus without syntactic-semantic restrictions, which was used in this study, a second corpus including those restrictions and a third corpus designed for noisy environments. The phonetic corpus consists of sentences of read text and is divided in a training set of 200 sentences pronounced by 4 speakers and 25 sentences more pronounced by 160 speakers, making a total of 4800 sentences, 42144 words (712 different) and 187848 phonemes, along with a test set with 50 sentences pronounced by 40 speakers, making a total of 2000 sentences, 21052 words (1856 different) and 93696 phonemes. Table 3 contains a short description of the phonetic corpus.

---

[1] Most speech recognition systems use as observation vectors a concatenation of different types of feature vectors (e.g. MFCC, energy, and it's first and second derivatives). We propose to treat the different types of feature vectors independently and denote each independent feature as a *feature stream*.

Table 3. Summary of the phonetic subcorpus of Albayzin speech corpus

	Speakers	Sentences	Words	Different Words	Phonemes
Training	164	4800	42144	712	187848
Test	40	2000	21052	1856	93696

On the other hand, the representation of the corpus in terms of the phonological features needed to be obtained prior to training the HMM models. This representation was obtained by making previously trained networks, see section 4.2, act on the acoustic representation of the corpus. Finally, the corpus was transcribed using a set of 24 phonetic units, 23 phonemes and 1 silence, and therefore 24 HMM models were trained.

4.2 Phonological Feature Extraction

For the case of use a phonological representation space we need a way to obtain such representation. Based on the study in [5], we used RTDNN for phonological feature detection. Five neural networks were used to detect each of the features presented in Table 2, that is, sonority, manner and place of articulation, vowel-nonvowel in front-central-back axis and vowel-nonvowel in open-close-midclose axis. These neural networks had multiple outputs and the classes to be detected for each feature were those described in Section 2. The inputs of all the neural networks were 12 first MFCC plus energy, which were extracted in 25 ms Hamming windowed frames with an overlapping of 10 ms. The outputs of the neural networks were real values ranging from 0 to 1. Although these values could be treated as the posterior probabilities of the features, we applied a more basic implementation and used them as simple observation vectors.

4.3 Comparing Phonological and Acoustic Representation Spaces

To compare the different representation spaces used we made three different experiments.

In the first experiment, we used an acoustic representation space in which the observation vectors were a concatenation of MFCC, energy and it's first and second derivatives. To include the phonological knowledge we proceeded as follows: we used a Gaussian function to model each of the classes presented in Table 2. To construct each of the Gaussian functions we obtained the mean and variance vectors of all the vectors belonging to each of the classes and used these as mean and variance for each of the Gaussian function. We used two different implementations. The first with a feature stream for each of the phonological features and the second integrating all the phonological features in an unique stream. Resulting in mixtures of 2, 5, 5, 9 and 8 Gaussians, respectively, for each of the streams in the case of independent feature streams and a mixture of 24 Gaussians in the case of an unique stream. Finally, and to maintain the phonological information in the training process we keep the values of the Gaussian functions fixed and only reestimate it's weights in the mixture.

For the second experiment, we used a phonological representation space based on using as observation vectors for the HMM states those obtained as outputs of the phonological feature detectors, see Section 4.2. Two different implementations were used. The first used independent feature streams for each of the phonological features with mixtures of 2, 5, 5 ,9 and 8 Gaussians respectively, and the second used a unique feature stream resulting from the concatenation of the vectors of each of the independent streams and which used a mixture of 128 Gaussians.

Finally, we made a last experiment combining both phonological and acoustic information. In this case, we used the same two types of observation vectors of the second experiment for the phonological space, and for the acoustic space we used four independent feature streams for each of the following features: 12 first MFCC, it's first and second derivative, and energy and it's first and second derivative. Mixtures of 32 Gaussians were used for each of the acoustic streams.

We also used discrete models when using phonological representation space only and combination of phonological and acoustic spaces. To obtain the codebooks for the phonological space, in the case of an unique stream, it was generated using the LBG algorithm to the concatenation of the independent feature vectors. For the various streams case, for each independent feature, the representative vector for each class was obtained as the mean vector of all the vectors belonging to that class. And were these representative vectors what we used as the codebook's vectors.

Finally, say that the topology of the HMM models used was the classical left-to-right of three states with transitions from one state to itself and to the adjacent one.

We then proceeded to train and test the models. Table 4 contains the phone recognition accuracies (PRA) obtained, together with the PRA for the acoustic based baseline system. The topology of this baseline system was identical to the topology of the system presented, with four independent feature streams corresponding to MFCC, it's first and second derivatives, and energy and it's first derivative, respectively. A codebook of 1024 classes in the case of discrete models and 32 mixture Gaussians in the case of continuous models were used for each of the streams.

When using the phonological representation space, we can see that better recognition accuracies was obtained in the case of discrete HMM models than in the case of continuous models. We believe that this could be due to the fact that the phonological space is highly discretized which favours the use of discrete models. On the other hand, when using the acoustic representation space the results obtained are not as good as in the previous case, and we can conclude that is better to use the phonological representation space.

Also can see that only when combining phonological and acoustic information we obtain recognition accuracies similar to the baseline system. On the other hand, and comparing the systems with just phonological information and with both phonological and acoustic information, it can be seen that the systems combining both types of information have better recognition accuracies.

Table 4. Phone recognition accuracies for baseline and presented systems. S is the number of independent feature streams. When Ph.+Ac. we have $S = S_{ph} + S_{ac}$ and $S_{ac} = 4$.

	Ac. Space		Ph. Space				Ph. + Ac. Space			
	CHMM		DHMM		CHMM		DHMM		CHMM	
	$S=1$	$S=5$	$S=1$	$S=5$	$S=1$	$S=5$	$S_{ph}=1$	$S_{ph}=5$	$S_{ph}=1$	$S_{ph}=5$
Ac. baseline	75.15		69.40		75.15		69.40		75.15	
PRA	48.92	47.67	72.93	72.46	70.35	70.23	75.83	75.72	75.06	74.24

Table 5. Normalized computation times for baseline and discrete HMM models

	$S_{ph}=1$	$S_{ph}=5$
DHMM	0.13	0.03
BASELINE	1	

We find that the results obtained for the discrete models are pretty good because they have proved to be computationally faster than continuous ones. In Table 5 we show computation times for the recognition process of the continuous HMM models based baseline system and the different implementations used with discrete HMM models, normalized with the value of the baseline system. It also can be seen that when speaking of computational cost is better to use phonological features in independent streams rather than concatenate them in one stream.

5   Concluding Remarks

In this work we have undertaken the problem of using phonological features for speech recognition in Castilian variety of Spanish. Also we have proposed a method for integrate these features in a speech recognition system based on HMM models. We have used two different representation spaces, phonological and acoustic, to integrate phonological features in a speech recognition system and have found that is better to use the phonological space. Also have found that the use of phonological features could be highly beneficial above all in the case of using discrete HMM models where we have obtained better results than the baseline system used, both in accuracy rate and in computational cost.

Acknowledgements

This work has been partially supported by the University of the Basque Country under grant GIU07/57, Spanish CICYT under grant TIN2008-06856-C05-01 and by the Spanish program Consolider-Ingenio 2019 under grant CSD2007-00018.

References

1. Rose, R., Momayyez, P.: Integration of multiple feature sets for reducing ambiguity in ASR. In: ICASSP 2007, vol. 4, pp. 325–328 (2007)
2. Rose, R., et al.: An investigation of the potential role of speech production models in automatic speech recognition. In: Proceedings ICSLP 1994, pp. 575–578 (1994)
3. Koreman, J., Andreeva, B.: Can we use the linguistic information in the signal? Phonus (Institute of Phonetics, University of the Saarland) 5, 47–58 (2000)
4. Livescu, K., et al.: Articulatory Feature-based Methods for Acoustic and Audio-Visual Speech Recognition: 2006 JHU Summer Workshop Final Report, Technical Report, Center for Language and Speech Processing, Johns Hopkins University (2007)
5. Strom, N.: Phoneme probability estimation with dynamic sparsely connected artificial neural networks. The Free Speech Journal 1(#5) (1997)
6. Blackburn, C.S., Young, S.J.: Pseudo-Articulatory speech synthesis for recognition using automatic feature extraction from X-Ray data. In: Proceedings ICSLP 1996, pp. 969–972 (1996)
7. Saenko, K., et al.: Articulatory features for robust visual speech recognition. In: ICMI 2004 (2004)
8. King, S., Taylor, P.: Detection of phonological features in continuous speech using neural networks. Computer Speech & Language, 333–353 (2000)
9. Frankel, J., et al.: Articulatory feature recognition using dynamic Bayesian networks. Computer Speech and Language Archive 21(4), 620–640 (2007)
10. Parya, M., et al.: Exploiting complementary aspects of phonological features in automatic speech recognition. In: IEEE Workshop on Automatic Speech Recognition & Understanding, pp. 47–52 (2007)
11. Stouten, F., Martens, J.P.: On the use of phonological features for pronunciation scoring. In: Proceedings ICASSP, pp. 229–232 (2006)
12. BenZeghiba, M., et al.: Automatic speech recognition and intrinsic speech variation. In: 31st International Conference on Acoustics, Speech, and Signal Processing ICASSP 2006, May 14-19 (2006)
13. Abu-Amer, T., Carson-Berndsen, J.: HARTFEX: A multi-dimentional system of HMM based recognisers for articulatory features extraction. In: Proceedings NOLISP 2003, paper009 (2003)
14. Casacuberta, F., et al.: Desarrollo de corpus para investigación en tecnologías del habla (Albayzin). Procesamiento del Lenguage Natural 12, 35–42 (1992)
15. Olaso, J.M., Torres, M.I.: Speech production models for ASR in Spanish language. Paper Submmited to FALA 2010 (2010)

Inference of Restricted Stochastic Boolean GRN's by Bayesian Error and Entropy Based Criteria

David Correa Martins Jr.[1], Evaldo Araújo de Oliveira[2],
Vitor Hugo Louzada[2], and Ronaldo Fumio Hashimoto[2]

[1] Center for Mathematics, Computation and Cognition - Federal University of ABC,
Brazil
david.martins@ufabc.edu.br
[2] Institute of Mathematics and Statistics – University of São Paulo, Brazil
{evaldo,louzada,ronaldo}@vision.ime.usp.br

Abstract. This work compares two frequently used criterion functions in inference of gene regulatory networks (GRN), one based on Bayesian error and another based on conditional entropy. The network model utilized was the stochastic restricted Boolean network model; the tests were realized in the well studied yeast cell-cycle and in randomly generated networks. The experimental results support the use of entropy in relation to the use of Bayesian error and indicate that the application of a fast greedy feature selection algorithm combined with an entropy-based criterion function can be used to infer accurate GRN's, allowing to accurately infer networks with thousands of genes in a feasible computational time cost, even though some genes are influenced by many other genes.

Keywords: feature selection, gene regulatory networks inference, stochastic restricted Boolean network models, entropy, Bayesian error.

1 Introduction

Gene regulatory networks (GRN) models help us to study biological phenomena (e.g. cell cycle) and diseases (e.g. cancer). Therefore, the inference of such networks is an important problem to be addressed. Unfortunately, the GRN inference problem usually involves data with a large number of variables and small number of observations, making the problem particularly hard due to error estimation issues. In this context, many inference algorithms have been proposed. A survey of GRN inference methods can be found in [1].

In this context, we compare two feature selection criteria commonly used for inference of gene regulatory networks, one based on Bayesian error (non-linear coefficient of determination) and another based on mean conditional entropy (uncertainty coefficient). The experiments considered the stochastic model of the yeast cell cycle provided by Zhang *et al*, which is based on restricted Boolean networks [2]. Besides the network topology of the yeast cell cycle model, other randomly generated topologies following a similar parametrization were included

I. Bloch and R.M. Cesar, Jr. (Eds.): CIARP 2010, LNCS 6419, pp. 144–152, 2010.
© Springer-Verlag Berlin Heidelberg 2010

in the experiments. Applying exhaustive search and a classical and fast feature selection algorithm (Sequential Forward Selection - SFS) to the transition matrices corresponding to such networks, it can be observed a significantly better performance of the entropy over the Bayesian error in recovering the groundtruth connections. Besides, the application of SFS guided by the entropy based criterion leaded to surprisingly good results, which is a valid alternative to become feasible the inference of GRNs considering thousands of genes with nice quality. These findings are the main contribution of this work.

Next section presents a brief background on feature selection, the algorithms and criterion functions used. In Section 3, the restricted Boolean network model of the yeast cell-cycle is presented. Section 4 discusses the GRN inference results obtained by the application of the considered algorithms criterion functions. Finally, the conclusion of this work along with future perspectives are found in Section 5.

2   Feature Selection

Feature selection techniques are composed by two main parts: a search algorithm and a criterion function that guides the algorithm. In feature selection, the only way to guarantee that the optimal solution be achieved is by exploring all possible subsets of all dimensions (exhaustive search), although depending on the behavior of the criterion function, it is possible to design branch-and-bound algorithms that obtain the optimal solution without the need to investigate the whole space of solutions [3, 4]. Greedy algorithms like Best Individual Features or Sequential Forward Selection (SFS) are very fast, although do not guarantee the optimal solution due to the *nesting effect*, i.e. a phenomenon in which the inclusion of the best features according to a given criterion may not lead to the optimal subset [5]. Yet, this phenomenon can be explained by the intrinsically multivariate prediction concept [6], also known as synergy [7], which states that it is possible to obtain a very good predictor set with regard to a considered target even that all its properly contained subsets do not offer any prediction about the target. Due to the nesting effect, many floating search algorithms that try to alleviate it by trying to successively add elements to and remove elements from the current solution have been proposed.

Here the attention is given to the SFS, a genuinely greedy feature selection algorithm [8]. It starts with the empty set and includes the best feature according to the criterion function. In every step i, it adds the i-th feature that forms the best set with the already included $i - 1$ features in the partial solution. This process continues until reaching a stop condition, which usually either is based on a fixed dimensionality given as input or based on the evaluation of the improvement of the criterion function (if the improvement by adding the next feature is smaller than a certain threshold, it stops).

With regard to the criterion functions, the focus is given on two commonly used criteria in GRN inference. One of them is the coefficient of non-linear determination (CoD), which considers the error committed by a subset in classifying the target value (Bayesian error) [9, 10, 11]. The CoD of the target Y given the knowledge of $\mathbf{X} = (X_1, ..., X_n)$ is given by:

$$CoD_Y(\mathbf{X}) = \frac{\varepsilon(Y) - \varepsilon(Y|\mathbf{X})}{\varepsilon(Y)} \tag{1}$$

where $\varepsilon(Y) = 1 - \max_{y \in Y} P(y)$ is the prior error, i.e. the error by predicting Y in the absence of other observations, and $\varepsilon(Y|\mathbf{X}) = \sum_{\mathbf{x} \in \mathbf{X}} P(\mathbf{x})(1 - \max_{y \in Y} P(y|\mathbf{x}))$ is the average error by predicting Y based on the observation of $\mathbf{X}$.

Criterion functions based on entropy (H), such as mutual information or mean conditional entropy, are frequently adopted for GRN inference as well [12, 13]. The Uncertainty Coefficient (UC) is similar to CoD, but instead of using Bayesian error, it employs entropy [14]. Its equation is given by:

$$UC_Y(\mathbf{X}) = \frac{H(Y) - H(Y|\mathbf{X})}{H(Y)} \tag{2}$$

where $H(Y) = -\sum_{y \in Y} P(y) log P(y)$ is the entropy of predicting Y in the absence of other observations, and $H(Y|\mathbf{X}) = \sum_{\mathbf{x} \in \mathbf{X}} P(\mathbf{x}) H(Y|\mathbf{x})$ is the mean conditional entropy of Y given the observation of $\mathbf{X}$.

3   Yeast Cell-Cycle Stochastic Restricted Boolean Model

Following the yeast cell-cycle model with 11 genes proposed by Li *et al* [15] and its stochastic version [2], a *Restricted Boolean Network* is defined as a graph where each node is represented by a Boolean variable $s_i \in \{0, 1\}$ and its dynamics is given by the following transition probabilities:

$$P(s_1(t+1), s_2(t+1)...s_{11}(t+1)|s_1(t), s_2(t)...s_{11}(t)) =$$
$$\prod_i P(s_i(t+1)|s_1(t), s_2(t)...s_{11}(t)), \tag{3}$$

where

$$P(s_i(t+1) = \sigma_i|s_1(t), ...s_{11}(t)) = \frac{\exp\{-\beta(1 - 2\sigma_i)\sum_j w_{ij}s_j\}}{\exp\{-\beta\sum_j w_{ij}s_j\} + \exp\{\beta\sum_j w_{ij}s_j\}}, \tag{4}$$

if $\sum_j w_{ij}s_j \neq 0$ or
$$P(s_i(t+1) = s_i(t)|s_1(t), ...s_{11}(t)) = 1/(1 + \exp\{-\alpha\}) \tag{5}$$

otherwise.

In the context of gene regulatory networks, $s_i(t)$ represents the expression of gene i at the moment t; w_{ij} sets the influence of gene i on gene j ($w_{ij} \in \{-1, 0, 1\}$ for $i \neq j$ and $w_{ij} \in \{-0.1, 0\}$ for $i = j$). The parameters α and β are positive and related to intrinsic and input noises, respectively. They work as inverse temperatures, *i.e.* the probability of the system to follow the deterministic pathway increases with their values. These deterministic pathways are the trajectories of the system in the state space of the noiseless case. In the Zhang *et al* model, these pathways are the trajectories of the network state in the deterministic yeast cell-cycle model [15].

For a network with N nodes, there are 2^N distinct states. Naturally, some of these states are not allowed in the dynamics of the deterministic model (noiseless case). But in the presence of noise, the system eventually can be found in some of the "forbidden" states.

The model proposed by Equations 4 and 5 comes from the assumption in which all nodes are under the same kind of noise and that the transition function does not change in time, which means that it is a time homogeneous Markovian process. Besides, as can be noted, all states are accessible, $i.e.$ the Markov chain is ergodic and, therefore, there is a time-invariant probability distribution $\pi = (\pi_0, \pi_1, ..., \pi_{2^N-1})$ to which the system converges:

$$\lim_{r \to \infty} p_{mn}(r) = \pi_n, \quad 0 \leqslant m, n < 2^N \tag{6}$$

where $p_{mn}(r)$ is the element on the row m and column n of P^r, with P being the transition matrix defined by Eq. 3.

4   Experimental Results

Using the model described in Section 3, we have all state transition probabilities of the Markov chain process given in a matrix P. As this is an ergodic matrix (see Section 3), we have the limit probability distribution of all states given by the vector π. With P and π, it is possible to obtain the joint probability distribution table (JPD) for all possible subsets of variables, allowing to apply criterion functions to evaluate any subset of genes as predictor candidates for any gene considered as target [16].

Here we considered two feature selection algorithms: the exhaustive search (which examines all possible subsets of all dimensions, returning the optimal subset with the smallest dimension) and the SFS (see Section 2 for a brief description) with a stop condition that is based on the improvement of the criterion (if the addition of the n-th gene does not improve the result obtained by the current subset of dimension $n - 1$, the process returns the last one as result). Each algorithm was applied considering two criterion functions: CoD (Bayesian error based, see Equation 1) and UC (entropy based, see Equation 2). Therefore, four methods were considered for comparison: exhaustive search with CoD (ES-CoD), exhaustive search with UC (ES-UC), SFS with CoD (SFS-CoD) and SFS with UC (SFS-UC).

In the first experiment, we set the w_{ij}'s as the Zhang $et\ al$ model [2] and applied the four methods aforementioned to the inference of the network in the case of small ($\alpha = 5, \beta = 6$) and large temperature ($\alpha - 0.05, \beta = 0.06$). The accuracy was perfect in both cases, $i.e.$ the network was fully recovered, presenting neither false positives nor false negatives for all methods used (ES-CoD, ES-UC, SFS-CoD and SFS-UC).

In order to compare the inference performance obtained by the CoD and the UC criteria in more situations, we generate random networks with a parametrization close to that presented by the cell-cycle network of the budding yeast using

Table 1. Tables containing the numbers of false negatives (FN) and false positives (FP) obtained by the application of ES-CoD, ES-UC, SFS-CoD and SFS-UC to infer each one of the 10 randomly generated topology samples considering small temperature ($\alpha = 5, \beta = 6$) and large temperature ($\alpha = 0.05, \beta = 0.06$).

		Sample 1							
		ES-CoD		ES-UC		SFS-CoD		SFS-UC	
α	β	FN	FP	FN	FP	FN	FP	FN	FP
5	6	12	0	3	0	12	0	3	0
0.05	0.06	0	0	0	0	12	0	0	0

		Sample 2							
		ES-CoD		ES-UC		SFS-CoD		SFS-UC	
α	β	FN	FP	FN	FP	FN	FP	FN	FP
5	6	0	0	0	0	7	0	0	1
0.05	0.06	0	0	0	0	17	0	0	0

		Sample 3							
		ES-CoD		ES-UC		SFS-CoD		SFS-UC	
α	β	FN	FP	FN	FP	FN	FP	FN	FP
5	6	3	0	0	0	8	0	0	0
0.05	0.06	3	0	0	0	17	0	0	0

		Sample 4							
		ES-CoD		ES-UC		SFS-CoD		SFS-UC	
α	β	FN	FP	FN	FP	FN	FP	FN	FP
5	6	0	0	0	0	3	0	0	0
0.05	0.06	0	0	0	0	20	0	0	0

		Sample 5							
		ES-CoD		ES-UC		SFS-CoD		SFS-UC	
α	β	FN	FP	FN	FP	FN	FP	FN	FP
5	6	0	0	0	0	8	0	0	1
0.05	0.06	0	0	0	0	18	0	0	0

		Sample 6							
		ES-CoD		ES-UC		SFS-CoD		SFS-UC	
α	β	FN	FP	FN	FP	FN	FP	FN	FP
5	6	1	0	0	0	12	0	0	0
0.05	0.06	0	0	0	0	18	0	0	0

		Sample 7							
		ES-CoD		ES-UC		SFS-CoD		SFS-UC	
α	β	FN	FP	FN	FP	FN	FP	FN	FP
5	6	14	0	11	0	17	0	11	0
0.05	0.06	0	0	0	0	22	0	0	0

		Sample 8							
		ES-CoD		ES-UC		SFS-CoD		SFS-UC	
α	β	FN	FP	FN	FP	FN	FP	FN	FP
5	6	0	0	0	0	2	0	0	0
0.05	0.06	4	0	0	0	9	0	0	0

		Sample 9							
		ES-CoD		ES-UC		SFS-CoD		SFS-UC	
α	β	FN	FP	FN	FP	FN	FP	FN	FP
5	6	30	0	18	0	30	0	18	0
0.05	0.06	5	0	0	0	20	0	0	0

		Sample 10							
		ES-CoD		ES-UC		SFS-CoD		SFS-UC	
α	β	FN	FP	FN	FP	FN	FP	FN	FP
5	6	18	0	13	0	18	0	13	0
0.05	0.06	0	0	0	0	25	0	0	0

the model given by Equation 3. For each generated network, the connection matrix w is randomly set in the following way. Firstly, as occurs with the yeast model, we consider $N = 11$ genes, fixing one of the genes (gene 1) as the source of the network (input degree equals to zero) by making $w_{11} = w_{21} = ... = w_{N1} = 0$. As there are 29 connections present in yeast model, 30 cells from $w_{ij}, 1 \leq i, j \leq N$ are randomly chosen. For these randomly chosen cells, each one has a probability of 0.5 to be represented by activation (+1) or inhibition (-1), while all other cells remain zero. Also, considering that in yeast model, 4 out of 11 genes suffer self-degradation (approximately one third), each gene has probability $\frac{1}{3}$ to be self-degradated. If a gene i suffers self-degradation, then $w_{ii} = -0.1$.

We applied the random network generation procedure presented above to generate 10 random network topology samples. For each network topology, the transition matrix P and the limit distribution π were computed considering both large temperature ($\alpha = 5$ and $\beta = 6$) and small temperature ($\alpha = 0.05$ and $\beta = 0.06$). Finally, these transition matrices and limit distributions were supplied as inputs to the four inference methods considered (ES-CoD, ES-UC, SFS-CoD, SFS-UC). The numbers of false negatives (FN) and false positives (FP) obtained for each method applied to each considered sample are shown in Table 1. Table 2 summarizes these results presenting the mean and standard deviation values.

Table 2. Averages and standard deviations of the results presented in Table 1

	ES-CoD		ES-UC		SFS-CoD		SFS-UC	
	FN	FP	FN	FP	FN	FP	FN	FP
($\alpha = 5, \beta = 6$) averages	7.8	0	4.5	0	11.7	0	4.5	0.2
($\alpha = 5, \beta = 6$) std. dev.	10.4	0	6.8	0	8.3	0	6.8	0.4
($\alpha = 0.05, \beta = 0.06$) averages	1.2	0	0	0	17.8	0	0	0
($\alpha = 0.05, \beta = 0.06$) std. dev.	2.0	0	0	0	4.6	0	0	0

The first important observation that can be drawn from Tables 1 and 2 is that the inference accuracy of the uncertainty coefficient for both exhaustive search and SFS is significantly better than the accuracy obtained by the application of CoD. In fact, CoD performs very poorly especially when embedded in the SFS algorithm, since in average, the percentage of recovery is around 50% (15 out of 30) of the connections. Moreover, for the sample 9 considering $\alpha = 5$ and $\beta = 6$, CoD was incapable to identify any connection even when exhaustive search was applied (i.e., CoD was zero for all possible subsets of all genes considered as targets). On the other hand, SFS performed nicely when guided by the uncertainty coefficient, having a very small number of false negatives in average, although it obtained one false positive in two cases.

These results can be explained by the fact that, in many cases, the Bayesian error does not decrease by adding features, even that such features offer some gain of information about the target behavior (i.e., the average entropy decreases). Table 3 refers to an example where the prior Bayesian error of the target Y is not improved by including the feature X ($CoD_Y(X) = 0$), while the prior entropy of Y is decreased by the information of X ($UC_Y(X) = 0.065$). Figure 1 illustrates this same example in graphics with the Bayesian error and entropy values for $P(Y = 1)$, $P(Y = 1|X = 0)$ and $P(Y = 1|X = 1)$. As $P(X = 0) = P(X = 1)$, the mean conditional entropy of Y given X becomes smaller than the prior entropy, since $|H(Y|X = 1) - H(Y)|$ is smaller than $|H(Y|X = 0) - H(Y)|$, which leads to a positive $UC_Y(X)$. On the other hand, since $|\varepsilon(Y|X = 1) - \varepsilon(Y)| = |\varepsilon(Y|X = 0) - \varepsilon(Y)|$, the Bayesian error of Y given X remains the same as the prior Bayesian error, which leads to $CoD_Y(X) = 0$.

Table 3. Example that illustrates a case where $CoD_Y(X) = 0$ and $UC_Y(X) > 0$. (a) Probability distribution of the target Y ($\varepsilon(Y) = 0.2$ and $H(Y) = 0.722$); (b) Joint probability distribution of X and Y ($\varepsilon(Y|X) = 0.2 \rightarrow CoD(Y|X) = \frac{0.2-0.2}{0.2} = 0$ and $H(Y|X) = 0.675 \rightarrow UC_Y(X) = \frac{0.722-0.675}{0.722} = 0.065$).

$P(Y=0)$	$P(Y=1)$
0.2	0.8

(a)

X	$P(X, Y=0)$	$P(X, Y=1)$
0	0.05	0.45
1	0.15	0.35

(b)

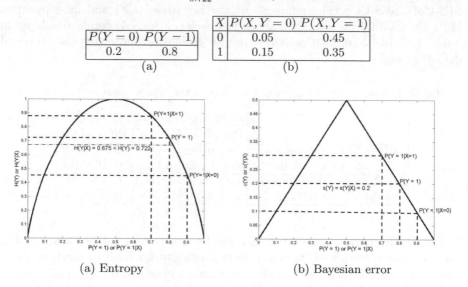

(a) Entropy   (b) Bayesian error

Fig. 1. These graphics illustrate why the mean conditional entropy of Y given X is smaller than the prior entropy of Y and the Bayesian error of Y given X is the same as the prior Bayesian error of Y for the joint probability distributions presented on Table 3.

5   Conclusion

Considering an ideal setting where all state transition probabilities of a gene regulatory network are known, experiments using stochastic restricted Boolean networks have shown that the adoption of a feature selection criterion based on conditional entropy (uncertainty coefficient) performed a significantly better inference than that obtained by the application of a Bayesian error based criterion (non-linear coefficient of determination). This happens because, in many situations, the prior error of the target feature is not improved by the knowledge of other features even that there is some information provided by such features (i.e. the prior entropy decreases). More importantly, the SFS algorithm had very nice results when guided by the uncertainty coefficient, which could be an indicative that this approach may be used to accurately infer a network containing thousands of genes in a small time interval, even when hubs are present, i.e. genes influenced by five or more genes.

However, real microarray experiments do not provide all state transition probabilities. In fact, only a few dozens of samples are available and the error estimation becomes an important issue to address. Certainly, inference of networks from limited number of data samples could imply a qualitative change in the results presented here. In this sense, a future step of this research is to consider the same comparison in small sets of temporal gene expression signals. But, in principle, there is no reason to think that entropy-based criteria could perform worse than Bayesian error criteria in such situations.

We also plan to extend the comparison to more general stochastic Boolean networks, since the restricted Boolean networks do not allow some specific Boolean logic functions that can not be expressed by linear functions (e.g. exclusive-or and its negated version, considering logics with two predictor features).

Acknowledgments

This work was supported by FAPESP, CNPq and CAPES.

References

1. Sima, C., Hua, J., Jung, S.: Inference of gene regulatory networks using time-series data: A survey. Current Genomics 10, 416–429 (2009)
2. Zhang, Y., Qian, M., Ouyang, Q., Deng, M., Li, F., Tang, C.: Stochastic model of yeast cell-cycle network. Physica D 219(1), 35–39 (2006)
3. Somol, P., Pudil, P.: Fast branch & bound algorithms for optimal feature selection. Pattern Analysis and Machine Intelligence 26(7), 900–912 (2004)
4. Ris, M., Martins Jr., D.C., Barrera, J.: U-curve: A branch-and-bound optimization algorithm for u-shaped cost functions on boolean lattices applied to the feature selection problem. Pattern Recognition 43(3), 557–568 (2010)
5. Somol, P., Pudil, P., Novovicová, J., Paclk, P.: Adaptive floating search methods in feature selection. Pattern Recognition Letters 20, 1157–1163 (1999)
6. Martins Jr., D.C., Braga-Neto, U., Hashimoto, R.F., Dougherty, E.R., Bittner, M.L.: Intrinsically multivariate predictive genes. IEEE Journal of Selected Topics in Signal Processing 2(3), 424–439 (2008)
7. Anastassiou, D.: Computational analysis of the synergy among multiple interacting genes. Molecular Systems Biology 3(83) (2007)
8. Pudil, P., Novovicová, J., Kittler, J.: Floating search methods in feature-selection. Pattern Recognition Letters 15(11), 1119–1125 (1994)
9. Hashimoto, R.F., Kim, S., Shmulevich, I., Zhang, W., Bittner, M.L., Dougherty, E.R.: Growing genetic regulatory networks from seed genes. Bioinformatics 20(8), 1241–1247 (2004)
10. Dougherty, E.R., Brun, M., Trent, J., Bittner, M.L.: A conditioning-based model of contextual regulation. IEEE/ACM Transactions on Computational Biology and Bioinformatics (August 2007)
11. Ghaffari, N., Ivanov, I., Qian, X., Dougherty, E.R.: A CoD-based reduction algorithm for designing stationary control policies on boolean networks. Bioinformatics 26(12), 1556–1563 (2010)
12. Liang, S., Fuhrman, S., Somogyi, R.: Reveal: a general reverse engineering algorithm for inference of genetic network architectures. In: Pacific Symposium Biocomputing, PSB, pp. 18–29 (1998)

13. Zhao, W., Serpedin, E., Dougherty, E.R.: Inferring connectivity of genetic regulatory networks using information-theoretic criteria. IEEE/ACM Transactions on Computational Biology and Bioinformatics 5(2), 262–274 (2008)
14. Theil, H.: Statistical Decomposition Analysis. North-Holland Publishing Company, Amsterdam (1972)
15. Li, F., Long, T., Lu, Y., Ouyang, Q., Tang, C.: The yeast cell-cycle network is robustly designed. Proc. Natl. Acad. Sci. USA 101(14), 4781–4786 (2004)
16. Higa, C., Hashimoto, R., Hirata, R., Hirata, N., Santos, C.: Inference of gene regulatory network using temporal coefficient of determination obtained from ergodic markov chains. In: IEEE International Workshop on Genomic Signal Processing and Statistics, GENSIPS 2009, pp. 1–4 (May 2009)

Grid Smoothing: A Graph-Based Approach

Guillaume Noel, Karim Djouani, and Yskandar Hamam

French South African Institute of Technology
Tshwane University of Techology, Pretoria, South Africa

Abstract. In the past few years, mesh representation of images has attracted a lot of research interest due to its wide area of applications in image processing. In the mesh framework, an image is represented by a graph in which the nodes represent the pixels and the edges reflect the connectivity. The definition of the most adapted mesh for a given image is a challenge in terms of computation cost and information representation. In this paper, a new method for content adaptive mesh representation of gray scale images, called grid smoothing, is presented. A cost function is defined using the spatial coordinates of the nodes and the gray levels present in the image. The minimisation of the cost function leads to new spatial coordinates for each node. Using an adequate cost function, the grid is compressed in the regions with large gradient values and relaxed in the other regions. The result is a grid which better fits the objects in the image. The mathematical framework of the method is introduced in the paper. An in-depth study of the convergence is presented as well as results on real gray scale images.

Keywords: Content adaptive mesh, grid smoothing, image coding, non-linear optimisation.

1 Introduction

Mesh representation of images has received a lot of attention in the recent years due to its wide range of applications in the image processing domain such as image compression and coding [1], low rate video coding[2], [3] and image processing for medical application [4]. In the mesh representation of a gray scale image, the information is no longer coded into a matrix of real numbers. Instead, a graph is defined, in which the nodes represent the pixels and the edges reflect the connectivity between the pixels. The main challenges faced when generating the mesh representation of an image is the accuracy of the representation of the information contained in the image, the size of the mesh and the computation time. Various methods have been proposed for content adaptive mesh generation, the common trend between them being to select particular pixels in the image (the one carrying the largest part of the information) and to create a mesh based on this set of point using a Delaunay triangulation scheme. For example, Yang [5] analysed the second order derivative of a pixel to consider it as a significant pixel and then a node in the mesh while Ramponi [6] selected the meaningful pixels by looking at their normalized skewness. Using a different

I. Bloch and R.M. Cesar, Jr. (Eds.): CIARP 2010, LNCS 6419, pp. 153–160, 2010.

methodology, Sarkis [7] generated the mesh by dividing, in a recursive manner, an initial triangle. The decision of dividing a triangle into two is based on its ability to represents the lying pixels in the triangle. The method presented in this paper differs in the approach. The main idea of the grid smoothing is, starting from a uniform grid, composed by squares or triangles depending on the connectivity chosen, to reshape the grid according to the information (gray levels) contained in the image. The grid smoothing relies on the minimisation of a cost function leading to a compression of the grid in the regions with large gradient values and a relaxing in the other regions. Section 2 of this paper presents the graph-based representation of an image while section 3 exposes the mathematical framework of the grid smoothing as well as the convergence. Simulations results and example of grid smoothing on real images may be found in Section 4. Conclusion and recommendations are underlined in section 5.

2   Graph-Based Image Representation

Our input data is a graph $G = (V, E)$, embedded in the 3D Euclidian space. Each edge e in E is an ordered pair (s, r) of vertices, where s (resp. r) is the sending (resp. receiving) end vertex of e [8]. To each vertex v is associated a triplet of real coordinates x_v, y_v, z_v. Let C_{ve} be the node-edge incidence matrix of the graph G, defined as:

$$C_{ve} = \begin{cases} 1 \text{ if } v \text{ is the sending end of edge } e \\ -1 \text{ if } v \text{ is the receiving end of edge } e \\ 0 \text{ otherwise} \end{cases} \tag{1}$$

In the rest of the paper, the node-edge matrix C_{ve} will also be denoted C.

Considering an image with M pixels, X, Y and Z respectively represent $[x_1, ..., x_M]^t$, $[y_1, ..., y_M]^t$ and $[z_1, ..., z_M]^t$. X and Y are at first uniformly distributed (coordinates of the pixels in the plane), while Z represents the gray level of the pixels. Each pixel in the image is numbered according to its column and then its rows. We define L as the number of edges in the graph. C is consequently a matrice with L rows and M columns.

3   Optimisation-Based Approach to Grid Smoothing

3.1   General Framework

A cost function is introduced to fit the object of the image with the grid. The main idea is that the regions where the variance is small (low gradient) require fewer points than the regions with a large variance (large gradient). The grid smoothing techniques will move the points of the grid from small variance regions to large variance regions. To achieve this goal, a cost function J is defined as follows:

$$J = J_X + J_Y \tag{2}$$

where

$$J_X = \frac{1}{2}\left[\left(X - \hat{X}\right)^t Q\left(X - \hat{X}\right) + \theta\left(X^t A X\right)\right] \tag{3}$$

and

$$J_Y = \frac{1}{2}\left[\left(Y - \hat{Y}\right)^t Q\left(Y - \hat{Y}\right) + \theta\left(Y^t A Y\right)\right] \tag{4}$$

where $\hat{X}$ and $\hat{Y}$ are respectively the initial values of X and Y, A being equal to $C^t \Omega C$.

The matrix Ω is defined as follows:

$$\Omega_{k,k} = (z_i - z_j)^2 \tag{5}$$

where node i is the sending end of the edge k and node j the receiving end. Ω and Q are square diagonal matrices which dimensions are respectively $L \times L$ and $M \times M$.

The first term in the expression of the cost function is called the *attachment* as it penalises the value of the cost function if the coordinates are too far from the original values. It is introduced to avoid large movement in the grid [8]. θ is a real number and is acting as weighing factor between the terms of the cost function. As a result of the definition of Ω, the minimisation of J is leading to the reduction of the areas of the triangle formed by two connected points and the projection of one of the point on the Z-axis. The edges in the image act as attractors for the points in the grid. As a consequence, the edges are better defined in terms of location and steepness in the smoothed grid.

3.2   Convergence of the Cost Function

The following sub-sections present the proof of convergence in two scenari: minimisation of a cost function with attachment and a cost function with attachment and fixed points.

Cost function with attachment. This section focuses on proving the existence of a unique solution for the minimisation problem presented above. The solution is presented for J_X only. The proof for J_Y can be derived in a similar manner. The cost function of the first order with attachment may be expressed as:

$$J_X = \frac{1}{2}\left[\left(X - \hat{X}\right)^t Q\left(X - \hat{X}\right) + \theta\left(X^t A X\right)\right] \tag{6}$$

The gradient of the first order cost function J_X with attachment is:

$$\nabla_x J_X = Q\left(X - \hat{X}\right) + \theta A X \tag{7}$$

At the optimum, the gradient is equal to zero. Let X_{opt} be the optimal solution for X. X_{opt} may be expressed as:

$$X_{opt} = (Q + \theta A)^{-1} Q \hat{X} \tag{8}$$

The above equation shows that a unique optimal solution (it may be shown that $Q + \theta A$ is inversible) exists for the minimisation problem and that for small scale problem, the solution may be obtained easily. For large scale problem, a gradient descent method may be used. Let X_{n+1} and X_n be respectively the values of X at iteration $n + 1$ and n. X_{n+1} is equal to

$$X_{n+1} = X_n - \alpha_n \nabla_x J_X = X_n - \alpha_n \left(Q \left(X - \hat{X} \right) + \theta A X \right) \tag{9}$$

α_n is the step and may be chosen optimal or not. An optimal step leads to a smaller number of iterations while increasing the processing power required for the optimisation. The optimal step α_n may be expressed by:

$$\alpha_n = \frac{\nabla_x J^t \nabla_x J}{\nabla_x J^t \left(Q + \theta A \right) \nabla_x J} \tag{10}$$

Cost with fixed points and attachment. The cost function with attachment results in a grid whose size might differ from the original grid size. A solution to conserve the original size is to fix the coordinates of the outer points of the grid. Let the X coordinates be partitioned into two parts, variable coordinates 'x' and fixed coordinates 'a' giving

$$X = \begin{bmatrix} x \\ a \end{bmatrix} \tag{11}$$

Then the first order cost function without attachment is

$$J_x = \frac{1}{2} \left(\left[(x - \hat{x})^t \; 0 \right] Q \begin{bmatrix} (x - \hat{x}) \\ 0 \end{bmatrix} + \theta \left[x^t \; a^t \right] \begin{bmatrix} C_x^t \\ C_a^t \end{bmatrix} \Omega \left[C_x \; C_a \right] \begin{bmatrix} x \\ a \end{bmatrix} \right) \tag{12}$$

Expanding the above equation gives

$$J_x = \frac{1}{2} \left[(x - \hat{x})^t Q_x (x - \hat{x}) + \theta x^t C_x^t \Omega C_x x + 2\theta x^t C_x^t \Omega C_a a + \theta a_t C_a^t \Omega C_a a \right] \tag{13}$$

The gradient of J_x with respect to x is

$$\nabla_x J_x = Q_x (x - \hat{x}) + \theta C_x^t \Omega C_x x + \theta C_x^t \Omega C_a a \tag{14}$$

Setting the gradient to zero gives

$$x = - \left[Q_x + \theta C_x^t \Omega C_x \right]^{-1} \left[Q_x \hat{x} - \theta C_x^t \Omega C_a a \right] \tag{15}$$

This gives the exact solution for the coordinates x.
Let x_{n+1} and x_n be x at iteration $n + 1$ and n then

$$x_{n+1} = x_n - \alpha_n \nabla_x J_x \tag{16}$$

The gradient of J_x at the point x_{n+1} is equal to

$$\nabla_x J_{x_{n+1}} = \nabla_{x_n} J_x - \alpha_n Q_x \nabla_x J_{x_n} - \alpha_n \theta C_x^t \Omega C_x \nabla_x J_{x_n} \tag{17}$$

The optimal step condition may by expressed by $\nabla_x J_{x_n}^t . \nabla_x J_{x_{n+1}} = 0$
It leads to:

$$\alpha_n = \frac{\nabla J^t \nabla J}{\nabla J^t \left(Q_x + \theta C_x^t \Omega C_x \right) \nabla J} \tag{18}$$

Stopping criterion. As mentioned earlier, for large scale problem, the minimisation uses a gradient descent algorithm as it is computationally expensive to inverse very large matrices. Three gradient methods are used for the simulation, namely the steepest descent gradient with fixed step, the steepest descent gradient with optimal step and the conjugate gradient with optimal step. The descent gradient methods are iterative process and require a stopping criterion ϵ to stop the iterations. The chosen criterion is the simulation is the norm of the gradient ∇J. The iterative process continues while $\nabla J^t \nabla J \geq \epsilon$. When it is possible, the comparison between the exact coordinates given by the inversion of the matrix and the result of the gradient descent algorithm is small and is of the order of ϵ. For example, if $\epsilon = 10^{-3}$, the difference between the exact coordinates (matrix inversion) and the coordinates obtained through the gradient descent is 10^{-3} of the width of a pixel.

4 Simulations

The simulations were performed using a standard laptop (1.87 GHz processor, 2GB RAM and *Windows Vista SP1* as operating system) and *Matlab R14 Service Pack 2*. The algorithms are tested on an image coming from the *Matlab* library. The computing time is obtained for 15 executions of the program and the mean value is indicated. Tables 1 and 2 show that the conjugate gradient with optimal step performs much better than the fixed step and optimal step descent gradient methods. For example, for an image of 300×300 pixels (90000 nodes), the number of iterations is limited to 76 while the computing time is 5s. The number of iterations for the optimal step gradient descent is almost ten times this figure while the fixed step method requires 20 times more iterations. The computation times for the fixed and optimal step methods are in the same range. The computation of the optimal step at each iteration doubles the time of the fixed-step iteration. The conjugate gradient descent is consequently the most suitable method out of the three tested for the grid smoothing. Consequently, the rest of the simulations uses the conjugate gradient descent. Table 3 shows that the stopping criterion has little effect on the number of iterations and the computation time. From a qualitative point of view, and $\epsilon = 10^{-4}$ looks like a good compromise between the result and the computing time. Table 4 displays the number of iteration and the computing time required for various values of θ. It may be seen that θ influences deeply the convergence. Small values of θ lead to speedy convergence whereas large values require more iteration. θ is the weighing factor between the two terms of the cost function. With θ small, the attachment term dominates the cost function and very little displacement of the points is allowed (quick convergence). The opposite effect is obtained with a large θ. From a qualitative point of view, $\theta = 0.05$ looks like a convenient value. This however depends on the application. Fig. 1 shows the results of the grid smoothing on two images for various values of θ. It may be seen that the level of compression (and noise) in the grid increases with θ. In both cases, it may be observed that the grid fits the object present in the images.

Table 1. Convergence in iterations for $\epsilon = 10^{-4}$ and $\theta = 0.005$

Number of points	Fixed step	Optimal step	Conjugate gradient
100	363	190	23
2500	543	282	37
10000	1174	593	60
90000	1440	707	76

Table 2. Convergence in seconds for $\epsilon = 10^{-4}$ and $\theta = 0.005$

Number of points	Fixed step	Optimal step	Conjugate gradient
100	1.9×10^{-4}	2.3×10^{-4}	1.8×10^{-4}
2500	8.3×10^{-1}	9.0×10^{-1}	5.9×10^{-2}
10000	6.8	7.6	3.3×10^{-1}
90000	1.2×10^2	1.3×10^2	5.0

Table 3. Convergence of the conjugate gradient in iterations and seconds for $\theta = 0.05$

	$\epsilon = 10^{-3}$	$\epsilon = 10^{-4}$	$\epsilon = 10^{-5}$	$\epsilon = 10^{-6}$
Iterations	240	263	287	312
Time (s)	15.1	16.4	17.9	19.7

Table 4. Convergence of the conjugate gradient in iterations and seconds for $\epsilon = 10^{-4}$

Number of points	θ	Iterations	Time (s)
2500	5×10^{-3}	37	7.4×10^{-2}
	5×10^{-2}	126	1.6×10^{-1}
	5×10^{-1}	432	5.1×10^{-1}
	5	1116	1.3
10000	5×10^{-3}	60	3.3×10^{-1}
	5×10^{-2}	206	1.3
	5×10^{-1}	701	3.6
	5	2162	1.1×10^1
40000	5×10^{-3}	66	1.8
	5×10^{-2}	228	5.7
	5×10^{-1}	784	1.9×10^1
	5	2660	6.8×10^1
90000	5×10^{-3}	76	5.0
	5×10^{-2}	263	1.6×10^1
	5×10^{-1}	920	6.1×10^1
	5	3183	2.1×10^2

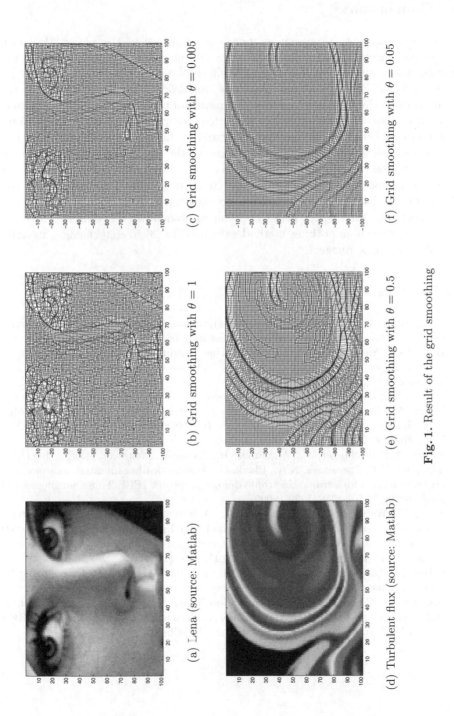

(a) Lena (source: Matlab)

(b) Grid smoothing with $\theta = 1$

(c) Grid smoothing with $\theta = 0.005$

(d) Turbulent flux (source: Matlab)

(e) Grid smoothing with $\theta = 0.5$

(f) Grid smoothing with $\theta = 0.05$

Fig. 1. Result of the grid smoothing

5   Conclusions

A new framework to represent an image is presented in the paper. Based on the graph representation of an image, the grid smoothing process modifies the coordinates of the points in the grid to fit the objects in the image. The convergence is shown and the conjugate gradient descent is recommended for the optimisation in large scale problems. The results obtained are promising and may be used in many applications (edge detection, compression or super-resolution). The main challenge of the method presented is the choice of the parameter θ. This parameter should be chosen according to the desired application, keeping in mind the computation time implication of this choice. The computational cost of the grid smoothing approach is high even when working with sparse matrices. Properties af the various matrices will be analysed in detail to achieve a faster grid smoothing. Finally, the grid smoothing approach will be combined with the graph-based mesh smoothing method presented in [8] to detect edges in noisy complex grayscale images.

References

1. Demaret, L., Dyn, N., Iske, A.: Image compression by linear splines over adaptive traingulations. IEEE Trans. on Signal Processing 86(7), 1604–1616 (2006)
2. Han, S.-R., Yamasaki, T., Aizawa, K.: Time-varying mesh compression using an extended block matching algorithm. IEEE Trans. on Circuits and Systems for Video Technology 17(11), 1506–1518 (2007)
3. Bu, S., Shiina, T., Yamakawa, M., Takizawa, H.: Adaptive dynamic grid interpolation: A robust, high-performance displacement smoothing filter for myocardial strain imaging. In: Ultrasonics Symposium, IUS 2008, vol. 2(5), pp. 753–756. IEEE, Los Alamitos (2008)
4. Prassl, A.J., Kickinger, F., Ahammer, H., Grau, V., Schneider, J.E., Hofer, E., Vigmond, E.J., Trayanova, N.A., Plank, G.: Automatically generated, anatomically accurate meshes for cardiac electrophysiology problems. IEEE Trans. on Biomedical Engineering 56(5), 1318–1329 (2009)
5. Yang, Y., Wernick, M.N., Brankov, J.G.: A fast approach for accurate content-adaptive mesh generation. IEEE Trans. on Image Processing 12(8), 866–880 (2003)
6. Ramponi, G., Carrato, S.: An adaptive sampling algorithm and its application to image coding. Image Vis. Comput. 19(7), 451–460 (2001)
7. Sarkis, M., Dieplod, K.: Content adaptive mesh representation of images using binary space partitions. IEEE Trans. on Image Processing
8. Hamam, Y., Couprie, M.: An Optimisation-Based Approach to Mesh Smoothing: Reformulation and Extension. In: Torsello, A., Escolano, F., Brun, L. (eds.) GbRPR 2009. LNCS, vol. 5534, pp. 31–41. Springer, Heidelberg (2009)

A Quality Analysis on JPEG 2000 Compressed Leukocyte Images by Means of Segmentation Algorithms

Alexander Falcón-Ruiz[1], Juan Paz-Viera[1],
Alberto Taboada-Crispí[1], and Hichem Sahli[2]

[1] Center for Studies on Electronics and Information Technologies, Universidad Central de Las Villas, Carretera a Camajuaní km 5 ½, Santa Clara, VC, CP 58430, Cuba
{afalcon,jpaz,ataboada}@uclv.edu.cu
[2] VrijeUniversiteitBrussel, Dept. Electronics & Informatics, VUB-ETRO,
B-1050 Brussels, Belgium
sahli@etro.vub.ac.be

Abstract. Reducing image file size by means of lossy compression algorithms can lead to distortions inimage contentaffectingdetection of fine detail structures, either by human orautomated observation. In the case of microscopic images of blood cells, which usually occupy large amounts of disk space, the use of such procedures is justified within a controlled quality loss. Although JPEG 2000 remains as the accepted standard for lossycompression, still a set of guidelines need to be established in order to use this codec in its lossy mode and for particular applications. The present paper deals with a quality analysis of reconstructed microscopic leukocytes images after they have beenlossy compressed. The quality loss is investigated near the lower compression boundby evaluating the performance of several segmentation algorithms together with objective quality metrics. The value of compression rate of142:1 is estimated from the experiments.

Keywords: microscopicimages, leukocytes, segmentation, JPEG 2000, compression.

1 Introduction

Images produced by digital microscopy techniques are characterized by large file sizes due,not only to the bit depths employed, but also to the high resolution properties of the digital acquisition devices. The amount of such images obtained in daily practice, also depending on the type of studies required for every particular detection task, can be huge, leading to problems of storage and transmission of the image data through communication networks [1], [2].

Reducing file size of microscopic images by means of lossy compression algorithms, such as the JPEG 2000 codec, can lead to image distortions and therefore, to affect their value for diagnosis. Preservation of imagequality is essential, for example, the count of white blood cell(leukocyte) structures within the observed field of view can lead to identification and/or diagnosis of several pathologies,such as acquired immunodeficiency syndrome,cancers, or chronic infections. Fig. 1a) shows a typical image where leukocytes are indicated. The fine detail structures, which

I. Bloch and R.M. Cesar, Jr. (Eds.): CIARP 2010, LNCS 6419, pp. 161–168, 2010.

identify or differentiate among the different leukocyte types, are sensitive to distortions, such as noise or artifacts introduced by *lossy* codecs.

The JPEG 2000 codec (ISO 15444-1) uses the Wavelet Transform as the kernel transformation surpassing the performance of its predecessor, the JPEG codec, based on Discrete Cosine Transform [3], [4]. *Lossy* codecshave been reported as having compression ratio (CR) of one order of magnitude higher thanthose obtained with *lossless* ones.

Although JPEG2000 has been adopted by DICOM standard, there are still no regulations for the use of its *lossy*mode where the higher the CRs are, the more distortion is introduced in the image, affecting particularly edge definition and therefore, jeopardizing the correct identification of the structures and the diagnosis made through these images [5]. Fig. 1 show Regions of Interest (ROIs) containing two different types of leukocytes, i.e. monocyte and lymphocyte, extracted from image in Fig. 1a) after compression at different CRs.

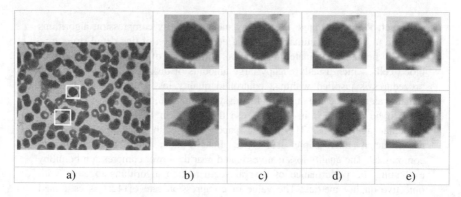

Fig. 1. Image in a) shows a bitmap of 1536V x 2048H pixel size, which occupies 9.00 MB of disk space. White squares indicate two different types of leukocytes, i.e. lymphocyte andmonocyte. Images in columns b) to e) show the two leukocytes extracted from image in column a)compressed at different CRs; b) no compression, c) CR=250:1, d) CR=500:1 and e) CR=1000:1. The edges, texture and contrast are severely distorted as compression rate increases.

Several researches have been carried out in order to establish a CRlimit for specific image types where the overall perceived image quality is not perceptually affected when using alossycodec [6], [7], [8]. In this paper, we propose a strategy to estimate the maximum allowable CR where deterioration introduced in the images by the codec, does not affect the quality of leukocytes images. The estimation is based on the performance of several segmentation algorithms.

2   Materials and Methods

2.1   The Images

Images were acquired using a Micrometrics 318CU CMOS digital camera, resulting in 24-bit color pictures of 2048H x 1536V size. The camera was attached to an

Accu-scope 3016PL trinocular microscope with 100x oil immersion objective and 10x eyepieces. For the test, we selected 15 images per leukocyte class, where the classes of interest were: lymphocytes, monocytes, neutrophils, basophils and eosinophils.Some manually cropped images are shown in Fig.2.

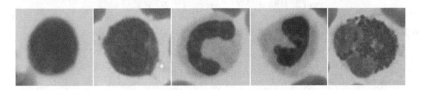

Fig. 2. Leukocytes. Left to right: lymphocyte, monocyte, neutrophil, basophil, eosinophil

2.2 Compression with JPEG 2000 Codec

For achieving JPEG2000 compression,the*JasPer*software [9]was employed.Images as in Fig. 1a) were compressed at 30 different compression factor (CF=1/CR), from 0.001 (CR=1000:1) to 0.03(CR=33:1), with a step of 0.001. Then, ROIs were extracted from the uncompressed and the 30 compressed images.

The CR was calculated as the necessary memory space (in bytes) for allocating uncompressed image divided by the number of bytes necessary for allocating the same image in its compressed format.

2.3 The Segmentation Algorithms and Distance Measures

Typically, leukocytes identification is based on visual inspection of individual images with fields of view wider than the size of individual cells and containing other structures as well as noise and/or artifacts. The approach of having experts dedicated to this task is time consuming, exhausting and prone to human error, requiring frequent repetitions to validate results [11]. These situations, altogether with the great amount of images necessary to achieve a diagnosis, encourage scientists to develop segmentation algorithms as an early stage for automated classification.

Three automatic segmentation algorithms were tested over a set of leukocytes images each one compressed at 30 different CFs. These were theOtsu's method [12], Active Contours (AC) method [13] and the Mixture of Gaussians (MoG) method [14]. For assessing the segmentation results, of each of the proposed methods, applied at a specific CF, the contour basedHausdorff distance [15] and the region based Vinet distance [16], between Ground Truths (GTs) and segmentation results have been estimated. GTsweremanually selected in each ROI at initial state, i.e. without compression.

Given two finite point sets $A = \{a_1,...,a_p\}$and $B = \{b_1,..., b_q\}$, the Hausdorff distance is defined as

$$H(A,B) = \max \left(h(A,B), h(B,A) \right) \tag{1}$$

where

$$h(A,B) = \max_{a \in A} \min_{b \in B} \|a - b\|, \tag{2}$$

and$\|.\|$ is some underlying norm on the points of A and B (e.g., the L_2 or Euclidean norm). Thus, it measures the maximum mismatch between two sets by measuring the distance of the point of A that is farthest from any point of B and vice versa.

The Vinet distance between two images is computed as

$$s(L_i^n, R_j^n) = \sum_{p=1}^{q} \omega_p s_p(L_i^n, R_j^n),\tag{3}$$

for weight $\omega_p$and various resemblance functions between regions

$$s_p(L, R) = 1 - \frac{min(A_p(L),\ A_p(R))}{max(A_p(L),\ A_p(R))},\tag{4}$$

whereL_i^n, $R_j^n$are regions in the left (L) and right (R) images respectively and $A_p$is some attribute of a region, for example, intensity mean, intensity variance, special moment, etc.

2.4 Quantitative Measures

For our particular research the following bi-variate measures were calculated in order to have an estimate of image quality according to CF[1], [2], [10]:

- The Peak Signal-to-Noise Ratio $(PSNR)$:considering $X(i,j)$as the uncompressed image and $Y(i,j)$the restored one, $PSNR$is defined as:

$$PSNR(dB) = 10 \cdot \log_{10}\left(\frac{MAXp^2}{MSE}\right),\tag{5}$$

where$MAXp=2^B-1$,B is the image bitdepth and MSE (mean square error) is defined as:

$$MSE = \frac{1}{m \cdot n}\sum_{i=1}^{m}\sum_{j=1}^{n}(X(i,j) - Y(i,j))^2,\tag{6}$$

where$m$ and n are the number of rows and columns in the image, respectively.

- The spectral distance (SD):a measure of distance between uncompressed and reconstructed Fourier domainimages given by:

$$SD = \frac{1}{m \cdot n}\sum_{i=1}^{m}\sum_{j=1}^{n}(|\varphi(i,j)| - |\hat{\varphi}(i,j)|)^2,\tag{7}$$

where$\varphi(i,j)$and$\hat{\varphi}(i,j)$are the imaginary parts ofFourier transforms of uncompressed and restored images, respectively.

- The gain in Contrast to Noise ratio$(gCNR)$ is defined as:

$$gCNR(dB) = 10 \cdot \log_{10}\left(\frac{CNR_X}{CNR_Y}\right),\tag{8}$$

whereCNR_X and CNR_Y are the contrast-to-noise ratios in the uncompressed and reconstructed images respectively calculated as $CNR_i = (\bar{X}_{i2} - \bar{X}_{i1})/\sigma_i$, with $\bar{X}_{i1}$ and $\bar{X}_{i2}$ being the mean values of intensity from two different regions in the i-thimage and σ_i the standard deviation of noise in the same image.

- The structural similarity index $(MSSIM)$:a powerful measure proposed by Wang et $al.$ [10] was also employed. It can be calculated as:

$$MSSIM(X,Y) = \frac{1}{M}\sum_{i=1}^{M} SSIM(x_i,y_i),$$ (9)

where M is the number of image blocks x_i and y_i of uncompressed and reconstructed image respectively and $SSIM$ calculated as:

$$SSIM(X,Y) = \frac{(2\mu_X\mu_Y+C_1)(2\tau_{XY}+C_2)}{(\mu_X^2+\mu_Y^2+C_1)(\tau_X^2+\tau_Y^2+C_2)},$$ (10)

where μ_X and μ_Y are the luminance values, τ_X and τ_Y the contrast estimation values for uncompressed and reconstructed images respectively, and $\tau_{XY} = \frac{1}{N-1}\sum_{i=1}^{N}(x_i - \mu_x)(y_i - \mu_y)$. The constants C_1 and C_2 are placed to avoid instability: $C_i=(K_iL)^2$ where $L= 255$, for 8bpp images and $K_i << 1$.

All bi-variate calculations are made between the uncompressed image and every reconstructed image after being compressed at each CF value in the interval studied.

3   Results

The normalized Hausdorff distances for the three segmentation algorithms tested are shown in Fig. 3. As we can see, the three methods show a similar behavior as quality metrics, with Otsu's method having lower Hausdorff distance to the GT in general. The Hausdorff distance for CF higher than 1/142, has a standard deviation below 5% of the Hausdorff distance for the maximum CR tested.

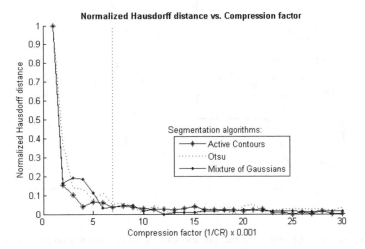

Fig. 3. Normalized Hausdorff distance (HD) for the three segmentation algorithms tested. Dotted line at CF=0.007(CR=142:1) indicates the estimated lower bound, at this point not normalized $HD_{AC} = 10.3$, $HD_{Otsu} = 4.5$ and $HD_{MoG} = 8.3$ Hausdorff distance units.

Fig. 4 shows the normalized Vinet distances for the three segmentation algorithms. In this case, the curves are smoother; due to Vinet distance capture better perturbation in edge (introduced by JPEG2000 Codec) than Hausdorff distance, which is more tolerant to those variations, because it measures proximity rather than exact superposition.

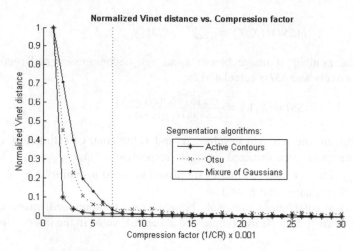

Fig. 4. Normalized Vinet distance (VD) for the three segmentation algorithms tested. Dotted line at CF=0.007(CR=142:1) indicates the estimated lower bound, at this point not normalizedHD$_{AC}$ = 1.0, VD$_{Otsu}$ = 1.1 and VD$_{MoG}$ = 2.3 Vinet distance units.

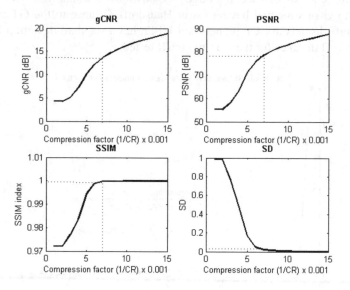

Fig. 5. The calculated objective metrics are shown in a compression interval from 1 to 15. At CF=0.007(CR=142:1), *gCNR*=13.7 dB, *PSNR*=78.7 dB, *SSIM* = 0.99 and *SD*=0.02.

The nick point in the curves at CF=0.007 (CR=142:1) suggests a lower CR bound. For CR values bigger than this, image quality is severely distorted, as we can corroborate in Fig. 5 with quantitative measures.At this CR, file size is reduced from 9 MB to approximately 65 KB. Metrics such as PSNR and gCNR show a stronger dependency with variation in CR while metrics such as SD and SSIM show less dependence with CR.

4 Conclusions

The analysis with the automatic segmentation algorithms tested suggestedan interval of CR values from 33:1 up to 142:1 where is *safe* to use JPEG 2000. This initial and partial result is later confirmed by objective metrics,which agrees in the upper most CR value of 142:1.

Both, metrics for evaluating the performance of segmentation algorithms and objective quality distortion, are considered representative for estimating quality degradation caused by the *lossy* codec.

The result presented are preliminary and lack of subjective experience in interpreting this type of images. A more complex investigation including subjective evaluation should be carried out in order to precise the bounds for *lossy* compression. Nevertheless, a CR limit of 142:1 was estimated through both metric types as a limit for using JPEG 2000 compression in leukocytes identification tasks.

Acknowledgements

The authors would like to thank, the Canadian International Development Agency Project Tier II-394-TT02-00 and the Flemish VLIR-UOS Programme for Institutional University Cooperation (IUC) for partly supporting this investigation.

References

1. Acharya, T., Ray, A.K.: Image Processing Principles and Applications. John Wiley & Sons, Inc., Hoboken (2005)
2. Lau, C., et al.: Telemedicine. In: Kim, Y., Horri, S. (eds.) Handbook of Medical Imaging, vol. 3, pp. 305–331. SPIE, Bellingham (2000)
3. Clunie, D.A.: DICOM Supplement 61: JPEG 2000 Transfer Syntaxes (2002),
   ftp://medical.nema.org/medical/dicom/final/sup61_ft.pdf
4. Rabbani, M., Joshi, R.: An overview of the JPEG 2000 still image compression standard. 1, Signal Processing: Image Communication 17, 3–48 (2002)
5. Foes, D.H., et al.: JPEG 2000 compression of medical imagery. In: Proc. SPIE, San Diego, California, vol. 3980 (2002)
6. Penedo, M., Lado, M.J., Tahoces, P.G., Souto, M., Vidal, J.J.: Effects of JPEG 2000 data compression on an automated system for detecting clustered microcalcifications in digital mammograms. IEEE Trans. on Information Technology in Biomedicine 10(2) (2006)
7. Zhang, Y., Pham, B., Eckstein, M.P.: Evaluation of JPEG 2000 encoder options: human and model observer detection of variable signals in X-Ray coronary angiograms. IEEE Trans. On Med. Imaging 23(5) (2004)
8. Paz, J., Pérez, M., Schelkens, P., Rodríguez, J.: Impact of JPEG 2000 Compression on Lesion Detection in MR Imaging. Journal of Medical Physics 36(11), 4967–4976 (2009)
9. Adams, M., Kossentini, F.: JasPer: a software based JPEG 2000 codec implementation. In: Proc. of IEEE International Conference on Image Processing, vol. 2, pp. 53–56. Institute of Electrical and Electronics Engineers, Vancouver, British Columbia, Canada (2002)
10. Wang, Z., Bovik, A.C., Sheikh, H.R., Simoncelli, E.P.: Image Quality Assessment: From Error Visibility to Structural Similarity. IEEE Trans. on Image Proc. 13(4) (2004)

11. Lee, J.K.T.: Interpretation accuracy and pertinence. American College of Radiology 4 (2002)
12. Otsu, N.: A Threshold Selection Method from Gray-Level Histograms. IEEE Transactions on Systems, Man and Cybernetics 9(1), 62–66 (1979)
13. Kass, M., Witkin, A., Terzopoulos, D.: Snakes: Active contour models. International Journal of Computer Vision 1(4), 321–331 (1988)
14. Gupta, L., Sortrakul, T.: A gaussian-mixture-based image segmentation algorithm. Pattern Recognition 31(3), 315–325 (1998)
15. Huttenlocher, D., Klanderman, G.A., Rucklidge, W.J.: Comparing Images Using the Hausdorff Distance. IEEE Transactions on Pattern Analysis and Machine Intelligence 15(9), 850–863 (1993)
16. Cohen, L., Vinet, L., Sander, P.T., Gagalowicz, A.: Hierarchical Regional Based Stereo Matching. In: Proc. Computer Vision and Pattern Recognition, pp. 416–421 (1989)

Comments on Matrix-Based Secret Sharing Scheme for Images

Esam Elsheh and A. Ben Hamza

Concordia Institute for Information Systems Engineering
Concordia University, Montréal, QC, H3G 2W1, Canada
{e_elsh,hamza}@ciise.concordia.ca

Abstract. Several attempts have been made to propose efficient secret sharing schemes for 2D images. Rey M.D (Iberoamerican Congress on Pattern Recognition, 2008) proposed a relatively fast image secret sharing scheme based on simple binary matrix operations. In this work, we show that care should be taken when choosing the matrices that corresponding to the shares, in particular if the rank of these singular matrices is not low enough then one can recover the secret image from only one share. Experimental results are provided to demonstrate the practicality of the recovery procedure on various 2D images.

Keywords: Secret sharing; Image processing; Cryptanalysis.

1 Introduction

The continuing advancements in computer technologies and the rapid increase in internet users have led to the increasing usage of network-based data transmission. In numerous applications, such as military documents and sensitive business data, this information must be kept secret and safe. Recently, 2D images are considered as important as any other text sensitive information. As a result, several 2D image-protection techniques, such as data encryption in [1, 2] and steganography in [3, 4], have been proposed to insure the security of secret images. One major disadvantage of the traditional protection techniques, such as encryption, is their policy of centralized storage, in that an entire protected model is usually maintained in a single information storage. If an intruder detects security vulnerability in the information storage in which the protected images resides, then s/he may attempt to decipher the secret model inside, or simply damage the entire information storage. Hence, the secret sharing is a defense mechanism to protect the secret that does not suffer from these problems. It works by splitting the secret into n shares that are transmitted and stored separately. One can then reconstruct the original secret if at least a preset number t $(1 \leqslant t \leqslant n)$ of these n shares are obtained. However, knowledge of less than t shares is insufficient for revealing the secret.

The first secret sharing scheme was introduced independently in [5] and [6]. Both schemes are based on the use of Lagrange interpolation polynomial and the intersection of affine hyperplanes, respectively. Since after, several studies

I. Bloch and R.M. Cesar, Jr. (Eds.): CIARP 2010, LNCS 6419, pp. 169–175, 2010.

have investigated different implementations of the (t, n)-threshold schemes and their usage in the keys communication of the cryptosystems. The majority of these schemes are based on different mathematical primitives, such as matrix theory and prime numbers [7]. These protocols are specifically designed for text and numeric data. Due to the main distinctive nature of multimedia, in the sense that they have a large amount of data and the difference between two neighboring values is typically very small, it is considerably difficult to apply directly traditional secret sharing schemes to digital images. Thus, various secret sharing protocols have been designed exclusively for digital images, some based on vector quantization [9], Shamir-based schemes [10,11,12], sharing circle [7,8], binary matrices [13], or cellular automata [1,2]. In this paper, we show that the scheme proposed in [13] is not an ideal image secret sharing scheme due to the fact that any participant is able to recover the secret image using only his share.

The rest of the paper is organized as follows. In Section 2 , we briefly review the description of the image secret sharing scheme proposed in [13]. In Section 3, we present the theoretical steps to recover the secret image from a single share only. In Section 4, we provide experimental results on different images to validate the effectiveness of the recovering process. Finally, we conclude in Section 5.

2   Description of $(2, n)$-Threshold Image Secret Sharing Scheme Proposed by Rey.M.D

The proposed secret sharing scheme in [13] is based on binary operations of two matrices $\boldsymbol{A}$ and $\boldsymbol{B}$ that satisfy the following algebraic property, let $\boldsymbol{A}$ and $\boldsymbol{B}$ two binary matrices such that $\boldsymbol{A} \oplus \boldsymbol{B} = \boldsymbol{Id}$, then the following theorem holds,

Theorem 1. $\boldsymbol{A}^m \oplus \boldsymbol{B}^m = \boldsymbol{Id}$ *if and only if* $m = 2^e$, *with* $e \in Z^+$

The reader can refer to [13] for the proof of theorem 1.

The steps of the image secret sharing scheme proposed in [13] are described as follows,

The setup phase. Let the matrix $\boldsymbol{J} = (p_{i,j})$ be a gray-level image defined by $n \times n$ pixels such that $p_{i,j}$ is the numeric value of the gray color of the (i, j)-th pixel, where $p_{i,j} = (q_{i,j}^1, q_{i,j}^2, \cdots, q_{i,j}^8) \in \mathbb{Z}_2^8$, with $1 \leq i, j \leq n$. Consequently, eight binary matrices with coefficients in $\mathbb{Z}_2$ are extracted from $\boldsymbol{J} = (q_{i,j}^k)$, where $1 \leq k \leq 8$. For simplicity, we write $\boldsymbol{J} = \boldsymbol{J}^1 \| \boldsymbol{J}^2 \| \ldots \| \boldsymbol{J}^8$ as a concatenation of eight binary matrices, where each of them represents a black and white subimage. Fig. 1 and Fig. 2 correspond to Lena gray image defined by 128×128 pixels and its eight subimages, respectively.

The sharing phase. We choose two singular binary matrices $\boldsymbol{A}$ and $\boldsymbol{B}$ satisfying Theorem 1. Then, we randomly choose $n/2$ integer numbers $e_1 \leq e_2 \leq \ldots \leq e_{n/2}$ and computes $m_i = 2^{e_i}$. The shares $\mathbb{S}_i^1, \mathbb{S}_i^2$, where $1 \leq i \leq n/2$, are computed as follows,

$$\mathbb{S}_i^1 = \boldsymbol{A}^{m_i} \cdot \boldsymbol{J}^1 \| \boldsymbol{A}^{m_i} \cdot \boldsymbol{J}^2 \| \cdots \| \boldsymbol{A}^{m_i} \cdot \boldsymbol{J}^8,$$
$$\mathbb{S}_i^2 = \boldsymbol{B}^{m_i} \cdot \boldsymbol{J}^1 \| \boldsymbol{B}^{m_i} \cdot \boldsymbol{J}^2 \| \cdots \| \boldsymbol{B}^{m_i} \cdot \boldsymbol{J}^8. \tag{1}$$

The recovery phase. The users P_i^1 and P_i^2 combine their shares, $\mathbb{S}_i^1$, $\mathbb{S}_i^2$, and computes the original image as follows,

$$\boldsymbol{J} = (\boldsymbol{A}^{m_i} \cdot \boldsymbol{J}^1) \oplus (\boldsymbol{B}^{m_i} \cdot \boldsymbol{J}^1) \| (\boldsymbol{A}^{m_i} \cdot \boldsymbol{J}^2) \oplus (\boldsymbol{B}^{m_i} \cdot \boldsymbol{J}^2) \| \cdots \| (\boldsymbol{A}^{m_i} \cdot \boldsymbol{J}^8) \oplus (\boldsymbol{B}^{m_i} \cdot \boldsymbol{J}^8).$$

The drawback of this scheme is that every participant P_i^1 has only one qualified participant from the pool of participants that s/he can collude to recover the original image. If the share of the qualified participant P_i^2 is altered or modified, the participant P_i^1 will never be able to recover the original image. Obviously, this scheme does not provide the basic property of the secret sharing idea, which is the safe, that is, the original secret can be recovered even if more than one share were destroyed.

Thus, the author in [13] proposed a generalization of the protocol. Such that any participant P_i^1, $1 \le i \le n/2$, can combine his share with any other participant P_j^2, $1 \le j \le n/2$ to recover the secret image. The generalization of the protocol is exactly the same as in the basic proposal except for the sharing phase where the data $\{\mathbb{S}_i^1, m_i = 2^{e_i}\}$, $\{\mathbb{S}_i^2, m_i = 2^{e_i}\}$ are distributed to the participants P_i^1, P_i^2 respectively. Finally, in the recovery phase the participants P_i^1, P_j^2 recover the secret $\boldsymbol{J}$ image as follows:

i) They compare the integer numbers m_i and m_j.
If $m_i < m_j$, P_i^1 computes

$$\boldsymbol{A}^{m_i + m_j - m_i} \cdot \boldsymbol{J}^1 \| \cdots \| \boldsymbol{A}^{m_i + m_j - m_i} \cdot \boldsymbol{J}^8 = \boldsymbol{A}^{m_j} \cdot \boldsymbol{J}^1 \| \cdots \| \boldsymbol{A}^{m_j} \cdot \boldsymbol{J}^8.$$

otherwise, if $m_i > m_j$, P_j^2 computes

$$\boldsymbol{B}^{m_j + m_i - m_j} \cdot \boldsymbol{J}^1 \| \cdots \| \boldsymbol{B}^{m_j + m_i - m_j} \cdot \boldsymbol{J}^8 = \boldsymbol{B}^{m_i} \cdot \boldsymbol{J}^1 \| \cdots \| \boldsymbol{B}^{m_i} \cdot \boldsymbol{J}^8.$$

ii) The recovery of the original image is carried as follows

$$\boldsymbol{J} = (\boldsymbol{A}^{m_j} \cdot \boldsymbol{J}^1) \oplus (\boldsymbol{B}^{m_j} \cdot \boldsymbol{J}^1) \| \cdots \| (\boldsymbol{A}^{m_j} \cdot \boldsymbol{J}^8) \oplus (\boldsymbol{B}^{m_j} \cdot \boldsymbol{J}^8)$$

or

$$\boldsymbol{J} = (\boldsymbol{A}^{m_i} \cdot \boldsymbol{J}^1) \oplus (\boldsymbol{B}^{m_i} \cdot \boldsymbol{J}^1) \| \cdots \| (\boldsymbol{A}^{m_i} \cdot \boldsymbol{J}^8) \oplus (\boldsymbol{B}^{m_i} \cdot \boldsymbol{J}^8)$$

We should highlight here that in order for the participants P_i^1 and P_j^2 to carry out the recovery phase of the generalized scheme, they must know the matrices $\boldsymbol{A}$ and $\boldsymbol{B}$.

We should also note that the most significant bits of the 8-bit values of grey images are the most important bits. One can distinguish the original image from the first subimages. For instance, if we can recover $\boldsymbol{J}^1$ or $\boldsymbol{J}^2$ even partly we can recognize the original image. Recall that in cryptography, the distinguishing attack is an attack in which the attacker is given an encrypted secret, which is here the secret image, and try to determine if this secret is random or it comes from a specific cryptosystem.

Fig. 1. 128×128 Lena gray image

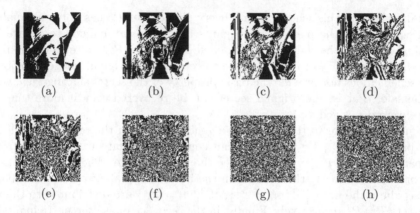

(a)   (b)   (c)   (d)

(e)   (f)   (g)   (h)

Fig. 2. (a) Subimage $\boldsymbol{J}^1$ (b) Subimage $\boldsymbol{J}^2$ (c) Subimage $\boldsymbol{J}^3$ (d) Subimage $\boldsymbol{J}^4$ (e) Subimage $\boldsymbol{J}^5$ (f) Subimage $\boldsymbol{J}^6$ (g) Subimage $\boldsymbol{J}^7$ (h) Subimage $\boldsymbol{J}^8$

3   Recovering the Original Image from a Single Share

It is proven in ([14], Ch. A.3.3) that a real-valued matrix filled with independent and identically distributed random variables, with continuous probability distribution function, will be singular with probability zero. On the contrary, in $GF(2)$ the probability a square random binary matrix is singular as its dimension tends to infinity is 71.1 [15].

The scheme proposed in [13] stated that the random matrices $\boldsymbol{A}$ and $\boldsymbol{B}$ must be singular without specifying the value of the ranks. Furthermore, generating a singular binary matrix randomly will produce a matrix that has high rank with high probability. Consequently, solving a set of linear equations when the coefficient matrix has a high rank will result in decreasing the number of independent/depended variables and increasing the number of determined variables.

The main weakness in the generalization of the image secret sharing scheme proposed in [13] is that for the participants to reconstruct the secret image they must know $\boldsymbol{A}$ and $\boldsymbol{B}$ along with the integer numbers m_i and m_j. For instance, the participants P_i^1 and P_j^2 must know $(\boldsymbol{A}, \boldsymbol{B}, m_i, m_j)$ to perform the comparison between m_i and m_j and the computation $\boldsymbol{A}^{m_i+m_j-m_i} \cdot \boldsymbol{J}^1 \| \cdots \| \boldsymbol{A}^{m_i+m_j-m_i} \cdot \boldsymbol{J}^8$ or $\boldsymbol{B}^{m_j+m_i-m_j} \cdot \boldsymbol{J}^1 \| \cdots \| \boldsymbol{B}^{m_j+m_i-m_j} \cdot \boldsymbol{J}^8$, as stated in the generalization of the scheme.

To recover the original $n \times n$ gray image from a single share, the participant P_i^1 has his share $\mathbb{S}_i^1 = \boldsymbol{A}^{m_i} \cdot \boldsymbol{J}^1 \| \cdots \| \boldsymbol{A}^{m_i} \cdot \boldsymbol{J}^8$ and knows $\boldsymbol{A}$ and m_i. Then, he perform the following to recover $\boldsymbol{J}^1$,

Let $\boldsymbol{A} = (a_{i,j})$, $\boldsymbol{J}^1 = (J_{i,j})$ and $\boldsymbol{A}^{m_i} \cdot \boldsymbol{J}^1 = (s_{i,j})$, calculate $\boldsymbol{A}^{m_i} = (\hat{a}_{i,j})$, $1 \leq i, j \leq n$ and form the set of linear Boolean equations as follows,

For $k = 1$ to n

$$
\begin{aligned}
\bigoplus_{i=1}^{n} \hat{a}_{k,i} J_{i,1} &= s_{k,1} \\
\bigoplus_{i=1}^{n} \hat{a}_{k,i} J_{i,2} &= s_{k,2} \\
\vdots \qquad \vdots \qquad &\quad \vdots \\
\bigoplus_{i=1}^{n} \hat{a}_{k,i} J_{i,n-1} &= s_{k,n-1} \\
\bigoplus_{i=1}^{n} \hat{a}_{k,i} J_{i,n} &= s_{k,n}
\end{aligned}
\tag{2}
$$

We have $n \times n$ binary linear equations with $n \times n$ variables. Solving this set of linear equations will produce determined variables (pixels) with specific values, depended variables, and independent variables which we can assign any value to them. Due to the nature of the image, there is no need to find the exact values of all the pixels, with only small percentage of the correct values of the pixels we can distinguish the original image, as we can see from the recovered $\boldsymbol{J}^1$ and $\boldsymbol{J}^2$ in Fig 3. To recover the original gray image, we perform the previous recovery steps to all eight subimages and then concatenate them together.

4   Experimental Results

We applied the recovery technique on different 128×128 gray images, namely, Lena, F16 and Fishing boat. The singular binary matrix $\boldsymbol{A}$ was chosen randomly with a rank equals 127 and the integer number m_i equals 2.

It is worthy to mention that we used the BooleanPolynomial class from the SAGE [16] package to do the fast calculations for solving the set of linear Boolean equations depending on 128×128 binary variables.

As an example in the case of Lena, after solving the set of linear binary equations, the number of undetermined variables was 12928, which were set to zeros. On the other hand, the number of determined variables for each of $\boldsymbol{J}^1, \boldsymbol{J}^2 \cdots, \boldsymbol{J}^8$ was 3456, which is the number of bits (pixels) that were recovered exactly. Although this number seems too small comparing to 128×128 bits, it is enough to recognize the original image easily as shown in Fig.3.

One can see from Fig. 4 and Fig. 5 the similarity between the recovered images and the corresponding original images.

To see the Matlab code used in the implementation and the experimental results, look at: http://users.encs.concordia.ca/~e_elsh/ImageSecretSharing/.

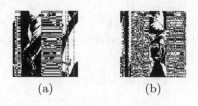

Fig. 3. The recovered subimages of Lena (a) J^1 (b) J^2

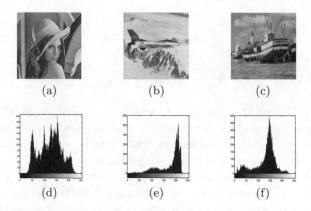

Fig. 4. Original images of (a) Lena (b) F16 (c) Fishing boat (d)-(f) their histograms

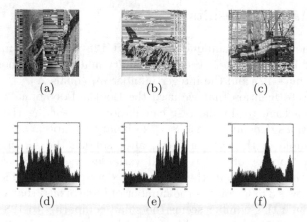

Fig. 5. Recovered images of (a) Lena (b) F16 (c) Fishing boat (d)-(f) their histograms

5   Conclusions

In this paper, we showed the proposed scheme for image secret sharing by Rey M.D is insecure. This is because any participant in the scheme can recover the original image without the need to combine his share with any other participant. Specifically, the main flaw is the generalization of the protocol, where both matrices A and B are known to all participants.

References

1. Cheng, H., Xiaobo, L.: Partial encryption of compressed images and videos. IEEE Trans. Signal Process. 48(8), 2439–2451 (2000)
2. Bourbakis, N., Dollas, A.: Scan-based compression-encryption hiding for video on demand. IEEE Multimedia Mag. 10, 79–87 (2003)
3. Marvel, L.M., Boncelet, C.G., Retter, C.T.: Spread spectrum image steganography. IEEE Trans. Image Process. 8(8), 1075–1083 (1999)
4. Petitcolas, F.A.P., Anderson, R.J., Kuhn, M.G.: Information hiding-a survey. Proc. IEEE, Special Issue on Protection of Multimedia Content 87(7), 1062–1078 (1999)
5. Shamir, A.: How to share a secret. ACM Comm. 22(11), 612–613 (1979)
6. Blakley, G.R.: Safeguarding cryptography keys. In: Proc. of the AFIPS 1979 National Computer Conference, vol. 48, pp. 313–317 (1979)
7. Menezes, A., Van Oorschot, P., Vanstone, S.: Handbook of Applied Cryptography. CRC Press, Boca Raton (1997)
8. Tsai, D., Chen, T., Horng, G.: A cheating prevention scheme for binary visual cryptography with homogeneous secret images. Pattern Recogn. 40, 2356–2366 (2007)
9. Chang, C., Hwang, R.: Sharing secret images using shadow codebooks. Inform. Sciences 111, 335–345 (1998)
10. Wang, R.Z., Su, C.H.: Secret image sharing with smaller shadow images. Pattern Recognition Letters 27(6), 551–555 (2006)
11. Thien, C.C., Lin, J.C.: Secret image sharing. Computers and Graphics 26(1), 765–770 (2002)
12. Wu, Y., Thien, L., Lin, J.: Sharing and hiding secret images with size constrain. Pattern Recogn. 37, 1377–1385 (2004)
13. Rey, M.D.: A matrix-based secret sharing scheme for images. In: Ruiz-Shulcloper, J., Kropatsch, W.G. (eds.) CIARP 2008. LNCS, vol. 5197, pp. 635–642. Springer, Heidelberg (2008)
14. Bard, G.: Algorithms for the solution of linear and polynomial systems of equations over finite fields, with applications to cryptanalysis. PhD thesis, Department of Applied Mathematics and Scientific Computation, University of Maryland at College Park (2007)
15. Studholme, C., Blake, I.F.: Random Matrices and Codes for the Erasure Channel. Algorithmica 56(4), 605–620 (2010)
16. William, S.: Sage Mathematics Software (Version 4.4.2). The Sage Group (2010), http://www.sagemath.org

A Very Low Bit-Rate Minimalist Video Encoder Based on Matching Pursuits

Vitor de Lima and Helio Pedrini

Institute of Computing - University of Campinas
Campinas, SP, Brazil, 13084-971

Abstract. This work proposes and implements a simple and efficient video encoder based on the compression of consecutive frame differences using sparse decomposition through matching pursuits. Despite its minimalist design, the proposed video codec has performance compatible to H.263 video standard and, unlike other encoders based on similar techniques, is capable of encoding videos in real time. Average PSNR and image quality consistency are compared to H.263 using a set of video sequences.

1 Introduction

Video compression at very low bit-rates is needed for applications that operate using low bandwidth communication channels, for instance, video transmission in mobile equipments. Some techniques that have been suggested for such applications include hybrid-DCT coding [6], wavelet-based coding [20], model-based coding [2], and fractal coding [11].

Extreme compression rates demanded by low bit-rate video applications require unusual video encoding techniques. One possible approach is the matching-pursuit video coding, however, it involves a very time-consuming encoding process [15] due to its exhaustive image scan in order to find patterns that can be represented efficiently.

The approach proposed in this paper is extremely simple and capable of compressing video sequences in real time. The video encoder compresses only the difference between two consecutive frames through matching pursuits. No motion compensation algorithm [9] is used in the process and the quantization is performed by rounding the coefficients to the nearest integer. An innovation of the proposed method is the subdivision of the frame into blocks and application of matching pursuit to each block instead of scanning the entire image looking for regions that have relevant characteristics that can be compressed and then applying matching pursuits to those regions.

A dictionary generated by K-SVD algorithm [1] is used to create sparse decompositions of the processed frame sub-blocks, which are compressed by a context-adaptive arithmetic encoder [18].

Compared to H.263 video codec [10], which has a motion compensation algorithm, more sophisticated quantizers and mechanisms for rate-distortion

I. Bloch and R.M. Cesar, Jr. (Eds.): CIARP 2010, LNCS 6419, pp. 176–183, 2010.

optimization, the proposed method achieves compatible PSNR values, as demonstrated in the experiments using well-known benchmark video sequences at several average bit rates per second.

The text is organized as follows. Section 2 describes the main algorithms used in the proposed solution, as well as reviews of some relevant encoders based on matching pursuits found in literature. Details of the proposed methodology are presented and discussed in Section 3. Experimental results obtained with our video codec are shown in Section 4. Finally, conclusions of the work and future directions are presented in Section 5.

2 Related Work

This section briefly describes some relevant concepts and techniques related to the proposed video encoder.

2.1 Matching Pursuits

Transforms, such as DCT [5], decompose signals as a linear combination of mutually orthogonal elements belonging to a predetermined basis. This basis contains a minimum number of elements sufficient to express any vector belonging to a particular vector space.

A possible generalization for such type of transform involves using more than the minimum required number of elements within the basis, thus forming an overcomplete dictionary, In this case, a single vector has several possible decompositions and, for data compression purpose, the most interesting decompositions are those that have the largest possible number of linear coefficients equal to zero.

Finding such decompositions is a NP-hard problem [7], so that matching pursuits [12] is a greedy heuristic for finding a very sparse decomposition of a signal using low processing time. Given an overcomplete dictionary $D = \{g_\gamma\}_{\gamma \in \Gamma}$, a signal f to be decomposed and a threshold of the decomposition error ϵ, Algorithm 1 determines which elements of D and linear coefficients are used in a sparse decomposition of f. Term R^k is the signal residue not yet represented by the chosen bases until step k.

Algorithm 1. Matching pursuit algorithm.

$R^0 f = f$
$n = 0$
repeat
  $i = \arg \max_{k \in \Gamma} \langle R^n f, g_k \rangle$
  $R^{n+1} = R^n f - \langle R^n f, g_i \rangle g_i$
  $n = n + 1$
until $n < n_{max}$ OR $|R^{n+1} f| < \epsilon$

2.2 Optimized Orthogonal Matching Pursuits

A more powerful heuristic for searching for sparse signal representations using overcomplete dictionaries was employed in the proposed video codec, known as optimized orthogonal matching pursuit [17].

At each step of the encoding process, after choosing an element g_i of the dictionary by the same criterion of the conventional matching pursuit, such search heuristic orthogonalizes the entire dictionary with respect to g_i. Therefore, the chosen element in the following step is orthogonal to all elements used previously. The heuristic ensures more sparse representations at a higher computational cost.

2.3 K-SVD

A well generated overcomplete dictionary ensures more sparse decompositions, provides a higher convergence speed in matching pursuits, is capable of representing only psychovisually significant features and ignores minor irrelevant details. It is possible to develop such dictionaries through machine learning algorithms [19], among them the K-SVD, which is a generalization of the algorithm for solving the K-means problem.

Two alternating steps are performed during its execution. In the first step, data from the training set is decomposed according to the initial overcomplete dictionary to be optimized using any algorithm capable of doing it. In the second step, each element of the dictionary is replaced by a new one, calculated to minimize the error of each data from the training set that used it in its sparse decomposition, as described in Algorithm 2.

Algorithm 2. K-SVD algorithm.

Input: initial set $Y = \{y_i\}_{i=1}^N$ of training signals, an initial dictionary D with normalized columns, a target sparsity T and the total number of iterations k.

Output: an approximate solution to $min_{D,X}\{||Y - DX||_F^2\}$ subject to $\forall i, ||x_i||_0 \leq T$ and $\forall j, ||D_j||_2 = 1$.

for $n = 1$ to k **do**

    $\forall i, x_i = \arg\min_\gamma\{||y_i - D\gamma||_2^2\}$ subject to $||\gamma||_0 \leq T$

    for each column j in D **do**

        $D_j - 0$

        $I = \{$indices of the signals in Y whose decompositions use $D_j\}$

        $E = Y_I - DX_I$

        $\{d, g\} = \arg\min_{d,g} ||E - dg^T||_F^2$ subject to $||d||_2 = 1$

        $D_j = d$

        $X_{j,I} = g^T$

    end for

end for

2.4   Matching Pursuit Video Coding

The absolute majority of video codecs based on matching pursuits [3,14,21,22] have their origins in [15]. The method uses an inner-product search to decompose motion residual signals over an overcomplete dictionary of 2D separable Gabor functions.

Despite the high computational cost of such search, the approach avoids artificial block edges and presents both better perceptual image quality and higher PSNR than DCT-based methods for low bit rates video coding. However, the dictionary must be efficiently built to allow fast inner-product computation between its elements and various regions of the residue.

The proposed encoder avoids performing costly searches working similarly to DCT-based coders, where the difference between two consecutive frames is partitioned into non-overlapping blocks that are independently coded using matching pursuits. This allows encoding parallelization of the sub-blocks, however, it does not prevent artifact appearance at the intra-block edges.

3   Proposed Video Codec

Initially, the encoder calculates the difference between the frame to be processed and the previous uncompressed frame. If the norm of this subtraction is greater than a certain threshold, the entire frame is used in the next step, otherwise only the difference between these two frames is used.

The image generated in the previous step is then subdivided into blocks of 8×8 pixels without overlapping. Each block is decomposed as a sparse linear combination of the dictionary elements through the Optimized Orthogonal Matching Pursuit algorithm [17]. The average bit rate is controlled by manually varying the error threshold ϵ used in the algorithm.

The overcomplete dictionary used in our encoding method is the same used by Elad and Aharon [8] for image denoising. The learned dictionary contains 256 elements and was trained using K-SVD algorithm using a number of several photographs as a training set.

In the final step, a flag is coded to indicate whether what is being transmitted is only the difference between two consecutive frames or an entire frame.

For each block of the current frame decomposed in the previous step, its sparse representations are transmitted through an arithmetic encoder using four distinct symbols, each one containing its proper adaptive context. The first symbol indicates the number of elements of the dictionary used in the decomposition of that block. For each used element, sign and magnitude of the linear coefficient associated with that element and its index are transmitted in different symbols.

4   Experimental Results

The proposed video codec was implemented on a graphics processing unit (GPU) with CUDA [16]. Our codec was compared to the implementation of the H.263 video standard present in the open-source `libavcodec` library [4].

Several video sequences were used in the experiments [13]. Results for three video samples are reported in this work. The videos have resolution of 176×144 pixels and 10 frames per second with subsampled chrominance (format 4:2:2).

All videos were compressed both with our codec and H.263 at different average rates of kilobits per second. The comparison was based on peak signal-to-noise ratio (PSNR) value, expressed by

$$PSNR = 10 \log_{10} \left(\frac{255^2}{MSE} \right) \tag{1}$$

where MSE is the mean squared error between the resulting image after compression and uncompression steps and the original image.

Average PSNR values for all frames and three color channels of the tested video sequences are shown in Table 1.

Table 1. Average PSNR (in decibels) obtained by using the proposed codec (MP) and H.263

kbps	Akiyo		Salesman		Hall Monitor	
	H.263	MP	H.263	MP	H.263	MP
15	30.70	30.71	29.41	28.74	29.54	29.07
20	31.67	31.73	30.01	29.38	30.22	30.18
30	33.60	33.38	31.21	30.55	31.60	32.11
40	35.20	34.66	32.29	31.55	32.88	33.56
50	36.54	35.77	33.18	32.30	34.06	34.80

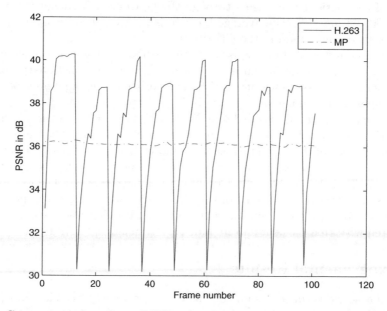

Fig. 1. Comparison of per-frame PSNR values between the proposed encoder and H.263 for Akiyo sequence at 50 kbps

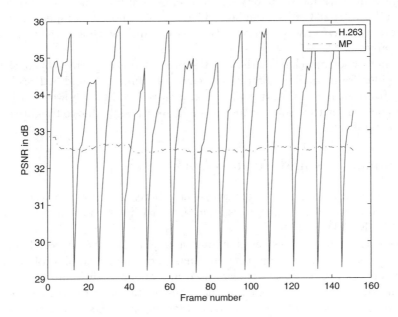

Fig. 2. Comparison of per-frame PSNR values between the proposed encoder and H.263 for Salesman sequence at 50 kbps

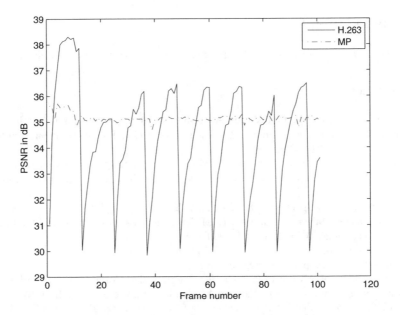

Fig. 3. Comparison of per-frame PSNR values between the proposed encoder and H.263 for Hall monitor sequence at 50 kbps

Despite the extreme simplicity of the proposed approach, its performance is very similar to H.263 video standard. The lack of a motion compensation algorithm prevented effective use of statistical redundancy present in the consecutive video frames.

Another important characteristic of the presented approach is its consistency in the video frame quality. As can be seen in Figures 1, 2 and 3, PSNR value of each frame changed abruptly when compressed by H.263, however, it is kept almost constant by the proposed algorithm. This is mainly due to the rate control mechanism of H.263.

5   Conclusions and Future Work

A video encoder is proposed to compress the difference between two consecutive frames through the matching pursuit approach using a dictionary previously trained by K-SVD method.

Unlike other video codecs based on matching pursuits, the proposed approach is able to encode video in real time and has performance compatible to H.263 when tested for some video sequences used in standard benchmarks.

Future directions for work include the implementation of refined motion compensation methods, a filter for removing blocking artifacts, a better quantization scheme of the sparse decomposition coefficients and other forms of prediction residue coding using both matching pursuits and dictionaries created by K-SVD. Such changes can significantly improve the resulting image quality.

Acknowledgments

The authors are grateful to FAPESP and CNPq for their financial support.

References

1. Aharon, M., Elad, M., Bruckstein, A.: K-SVD: An Algorithm for Designing Overcomplete Dictionaries for Sparse Representation. IEEE Transactions on Signal Processing 54(11), 4311–4322 (2006)
2. Aizawa, K., Harashima, H., Saito, T.: Model-Based Analysis Synthesis Image Coding (MBASIC) System for a Person's Face. Signal Processing: Image Communications 1(2), 139–152 (1989)
3. Al-Shaykh, O., Miloslavsky, E., Nomura, T., Neff, R., Zakhor, A.: Video Compression using Matching Pursuits. IEEE Transactions on Circuits and Systems for Video Technology 9(1), 123–143 (1999)
4. avcodec: libavcodec: A Library containing Decoders and Encoders for Audio/Video Codecs (2010), http://www.ffmpeg.org/
5. Bhaskaran, V., Konstantinides, K.: Image and Video Compression Standards: Algorithms and Architectures. Kluwer Academic Publishers, Norwell (1997)
6. CCITT: Video Codec for Audiovisual Services at p × 64 kbit/s, CCITT Recommendation H.261, CDM XV-R 37-E (August 1990)
7. Davis, G.: Adaptive Nonlinear Approximations. Ph.D. thesis, Department of Mathematics, New York University (1994)

8. Elad, M., Aharon, M.: Image Denoising Via Sparse and Redundant Representations Over Learned Dictionaries. IEEE Transactions on Image Processing 15(12), 3736–3745 (2006)
9. Furht, B., Furht, B.: Motion Estimation Algorithms for Video Compression. Kluwer Academic Publishers, Norwell (1996)
10. H263: ITU-T Recommendation H.263, Video Coding for Low Bit Rate Communication (September 1997)
11. Jacquin, A.: Image Coding Based on a Fractal Theory of Iterated Contractive Image Transformations. IEEE Transactions on Image Processing 1(1), 18–30 (1992)
12. Mallat, S., Zhang, Z.: Matching Pursuit with Time-Frequency Dictionaries. IEEE Transactions on Signal Processing 41, 3397–3415 (1993)
13. Media, X.T.: Video Sequences (2010), http://media.xiph.org/video/derf/
14. Neff, R., Nomura, T., Zakhor, A.: Decoder Complexity and Performance Comparison of Matching Pursuit and DCT-based MPEG-4 Video Codecs. In: International Conference on Image Processing, Chicago, IL, USA, pp. 783–787 (October 1998)
15. Neff, R., Zakhor, A.: Very-Low Bit-Rate Video Coding Based on Matching Pursuits. IEEE Transactions on Circuits and Systems for Video Technology 7(1), 158–171 (1997)
16. NVIDIA: CUDA - Parallel Computing Architecture (2010), http://www.nvidia.com/
17. Rebollo-Neira, L., Lowe, D.: Optimized Orthogonal Matching Pursuit Approach. IEEE Signal Processing Letters 9(4), 137–140 (2002)
18. Said, A.: Arithmetic Coding. Communications, Networking, and Multimedia. In: Lossless Compression Handbook. Academic Press, London (2003)
19. Sculley, D., Brodley, C.: Compression and Machine Learning: A New Perspective on Feature Space Vectors. In: Data Compression Conference, Snowbird, UT, USA, pp. 332 (March 2006)
20. Shapiro, J.: Application of the Embedded Wavelet Hierarchical Image Coder to Very Low Bit Rate Image Coding. In: IEEE International Conference on Acoustics, Speech, and Signal Processing, Minneapolis, MN, USA, vol. 5, pp. 558–561 (April 1993)
21. Wang, B., Wang, Y., Yin, P.: A Two Pass H.264-Based Matching Pursuit Video Coder. In: IEEE International Conference on Image Processing, Atlanta, GA, USA, pp. 3149–3152 (October 2006)
22. Zhang, H., Wang, X., Huo, W., Monro, D.: A Hybrid Video Coder Based on H.264 with Matching Pursuits. In: IEEE International Conference on Acoustics, Speech and Signal Processing, Toulouse, France, vol. 2, pp. 889–892 (July 2006)

An Unified Transition Detection Based on Bipartite Graph Matching Approach

Zenilton Kleber Gonçalves do Patrocínio Jr., Silvio Jamil F. Guimaräes, Henrique Batista da Silva, and Kleber Jacques Ferreira de Souza

Audio-Visual Information Processing Laboratory (VIPLAB)
Institute of Informatics - Pontifícia Universidade Católica de Minas Gerais
Belo Horizonte, MG, Brazil
{zenilton,sjamil,henriquebat,kleberjac}@pucminas.br
http://www.viplab.inf.pucminas.br

Abstract. This paper addresses transition detection which consists in identifying the boundary between consecutive shots. In this work, we propose an approach to cope with transition detection in which we define and use a new dissimilarity measure based on the size of the maximum cardinality matching calculated using a bipartite graph with respect to a sliding window. The experiments have used two video datasets which presents a variety of different video genres with 3079 transitions. Our method achieves performance measures similar to the best results found in the literature with a much simpler classification approach.

Keywords: Bipartite graph matching, cut, gradual transition.

1 Introduction

An hierarchical model for video analysis and segmentation is usually divided into four levels based on its temporal resolution. At the lowest level one can find the most basic unit, i.e., a single video frame. Several of those frames are gathered into a shot that represents a continuous camera recording. Some shots present a storytelling coherence and they are grouped into distinct scenes. Finally an assembly of different scenes constitute a digital video. Amongst the problems related to video analysis and indexing, sometimes video segmentation can be considered as an essential first step. This paper addresses transition detection which is part of video segmentation problem, and consists in identifying the boundary between consecutive shots. The most common approach to cope with transition detection is based on the use of a dissimilarity measure [1]. A review of the most popular methods for cut (abrupt transition) detection (such as pixel-wise comparison, histogram comparison, etc) can be found in [2, 3]. If two frames belong to the same shot, then their dissimilarity measure should be small. Two frames belonging to different shots generally yield a high dissimilarity measure. In the same way, a dissimilarity measure concerning the frames of a gradual transition is difficult to define and the quality of this measure is very important for the whole segmentation process.

I. Bloch and R.M. Cesar, Jr. (Eds.): CIARP 2010, LNCS 6419, pp. 184–192, 2010.

Another approach to the video segmentation problem is to transform the video into a 2D image [4], and apply image processing methods on this image to extract the different patterns related to each transition. Some works on gradual transitions detection can be found in [5–7]. Zabih et al. [5] proposed a method based on edge detection which is very costly due to the computation of edges for each frame of the sequence. Fernando et al. [6] used a statistical approach that considers features of the luminance signal. This approach presents high precision on long fades. Zhang et al. [7] introduced the twin-comparison method in which two different thresholds are considered. In [4], Ngo et al. applied Markov models for shot transition detection which fails in the presence of low contrast between textures of consecutive shots. Recently, Bescós et al. [8] proposed a unified framework with very good results for detecting both cuts and gradual transitions. The major drawback of this method is the large number of parameters (thresholding) that are needed to adjust the classification algorithm. Finally, Grana et al. [9] proposes a linear transition detector for both cuts and linear gradual transitions. Their method searches for the transition center and transition length using different values of frame step. However, this algorithm assumed that the feature information is computable, discriminating, and constant within the shots. In this work, we propose an unified approach to cope with transition detection. In this paper, we define and use a new dissimilarity measure based on the size of the maximum cardinality matching calculated using a bipartite graph with respect to a sliding window. In [10], an approach based on a bipartite graph was used only for cut detection in which a dissimilarity measure between two consecutive frames was calculated from maximum cardinality matching. The main contribution of this work is the application of a new simple and efficient dissimilarity measure unifiedly to solve the cut and gradual transition detection problem.

This paper is organized as follows. In Section 2 we define a new dissimilarity measure and the transition detection problem resolution using that measure. In Section 3 our methodology is fully presented. In Section 4 we perform an analysis for transition detection involving our method using three different quality measures. Some conclusions and a summary of future works are given in Section 5.

2 A Dissimilarity Measure

In [10], it was defined some concepts used here, like point similarity graph and list of frame points. Unformally, the point similarity graph $G^{\delta,\lambda}(t_1, t_2)$ is created from a list of frame points, L_{t_1} and L_{t_2}, computed from a visual rhythm which is a simplification of the frame. The graph vertex is the frame points (pixels) and the weighted edge is the similarity value between two points.

Definition 1 (Matching – $M^{\delta,\lambda}$). *Let $G^{\delta,\lambda}(t_1, t_2)$ be a point similarity graph between the frames f_{t_1} and f_{t_2} represented by their list of frame points L_{t_1} and L_{t_2} [10]. A subset $M^{\delta,\lambda} \subseteq E^{\delta,\lambda}$ is a matching if any two edges in $M^{\delta,\lambda}$ are not adjacent. The size of matching $M^{\delta,\lambda}$, $|M^{\delta,\lambda}|$, is the number of edges in $M^{\delta,\lambda}$.*

Definition 2 (Maximum cardinality matching – $\overline{M^{\delta,\lambda}}$). *Let $\overline{M^{\delta,\lambda}}$ be a matching in a point similarity graph $G^{\delta,\lambda}(t_1, t_2)$. So, $\overline{M^{\delta,\lambda}}$ is the maximum* *cardinality matching if there is no other matching* $\mathrm{M}^{\delta,\lambda}$ *in* $\mathrm{G}^{\delta,\lambda}(t_1, t_2)$ *such that* $|\mathrm{M}^{\delta,\lambda}| > |\overline{\mathrm{M}^{\delta,\lambda}}|$. Solving the maximum cardinality matching on a bipartite graph could done with $O(E\sqrt{V})$ operations, in which V and E represent the number of nodes and edges, respectively. Based on the size of maximum cardinality matching we can define an interframe dissimilarity measure in the following manner:

Definition 3 (Dissimilarity measure $\mathrm{DIS}^{\delta,\lambda}(t_1, t_2)$**).** *Let* $\overline{\mathrm{M}^{\delta,\lambda}}$ *be a maximum cardinality matching in a point similarity graph* $\mathrm{G}^{\delta,\lambda}(t_1, t_2)$. *So, the dissimilarity measure* $\mathrm{DIS}^{\delta,\lambda}(t_1, t_2)$ *can be calculated as* $\mathrm{DIS}^{\delta,\lambda}(t_1, t_2) = 1 - \dfrac{|\overline{\mathrm{M}^{\delta,\lambda}}|}{\max\{|\mathrm{L}_{t_1}|, |\mathrm{L}_{t_2}|\}}$.

Two consecutive frames that are similar are considered to belong to the same shot, and consequently a high similarity score (computed using the size of the maximum cardinality matching) should be encountered. Our search procedure uses dissimilarity measurements calculated between frames in a sliding window W. This sliding window is divided into two disjoint parts whose size is equal to r frames (see Fig. 1). More specifically, for the sliding window W of size $2r$, which is centered between frames f_k and f_{k+1}, we compute $2r$ lists of frame points $\mathrm{L}_{k-r+1}, \ldots, \mathrm{L}_k, \mathrm{L}_{k+1}, \ldots, \mathrm{L}_{k+r}$. Then, we generate point similarity graphs between lists of frame points which do not belong to the same part of the sliding window W (see Fig. 1). Finally, for a given sliding window W with radius r, the dissimilarity measure $\mathrm{DIS}^{\delta,\lambda}$ is calculated for each those graphs and used to compute the r-cumulative dissimilarity measure as follows.

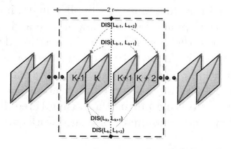

Fig. 1. Computation of cumulative dissimilarity for a sliding window W whose size is equal to 4 (i.e., with radius $r = 2$) and centered between frames f_k and f_{k+1}. The cumulative dissimilarity for frame f_k will be the summation of dissimilarity measures between frames from disjoint parts of the sliding window, i.e, $2\text{-CDIS}^{\delta,\lambda}_k = \mathrm{DIS}^{\delta,\lambda}(\mathrm{L}_k, \mathrm{L}_{k+1}) + \mathrm{DIS}^{\delta,\lambda}(\mathrm{L}_k, \mathrm{L}_{k+2}) + \mathrm{DIS}^{\delta,\lambda}(\mathrm{L}_{k-1}, \mathrm{L}_{k+1}) + \mathrm{DIS}^{\delta,\lambda}(\mathrm{L}_{k-1}, \mathrm{L}_{k+2})$.

Definition 4 (r-Cumulative dissimilarity $- r\text{-CDIS}^{\delta,\lambda}_k$). *Let* f_k *be the frame at location* k, $k \in [0, N-1]$ *and* L_k *be the list of frame points associated with that frame. So, for a $2r$-sized sliding window centered between frames* f_k *and* f_{k+1}, *the r-cumulative dissimilarity $r\text{-CDIS}^{\delta,\lambda}_k$ can be calculated as*

$$r\text{-CDIS}^{\delta,\lambda}_k = \sum_{i=k-r+1}^{k} \sum_{j=k+1}^{k+r} \mathrm{DIS}^{\delta,\lambda}(\mathrm{L}_i, \mathrm{L}_j). \tag{1}$$

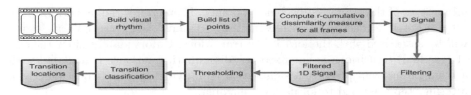

Fig. 2. Workflow for transition detection

Fig. 1 illustrates the computation of $r\text{-CDIS}_k^{\delta,\lambda}$. Finally, the transition detection problem can be stated as follows.

Definition 5 (Transition detection – TD). *The transition detection (TD) problem corresponds to the identification of all content changes on a video sequence. Thus, transition detection at any frame f_k can be defined as*

$$TD(\mathrm{V}_N, r, \lambda, \delta, \Delta) = \{k \in \mathbb{T} | f_k \in \mathrm{V}_N, r\text{-CDIS}_k^{\delta,\lambda} \geq \Delta\} \qquad (2)$$

where $r\text{-CDIS}_k^{\delta,\lambda}$ is the r-cumulative dissimilarity measure for a sliding windows W of radius r centered between frames f_k and f_{k+1}; and three specified thresholds λ, δ and Δ. λ corresponds to the maximum distance between two point locations, δ corresponds to the maximum dissimilarity allowed between two point values; and Δ corresponds to the minimum cumulative dissimilarity score needed to classify the location as transition.

One should notice that Δ may be either specified or an adaptive threshold can be used. To specify a single value for Δ that is best suitable for a given situation is not an easy task. Moreover, depending on parameter values, the transition detection approach stated by Equation 2 identifies all types of transitions.

3   Our Method for Transition Detection

As described before, the main goal of transition detection problem is to identify changes on a video sequence, such as cuts, dissolves, fades, and wipes, among others. In the proposed workflow, as described in Fig. 2, the first step of the process is the extraction of frame points from a visual rhythm [4] in order to construct lists of frame points for a specified window with $2r$ frames.

The main idea of our method is to compute the r-cumulative dissimilarity measure for a sliding window centered between two frames. It is important to remark that window size, i.e. $2r$ frames, where r is the radius parameter, is directly related to the gradual transition size that may be identified. For instance, let T be the length in frames of a transition. According to [8, 9, 11], for an ideal (gradual) transition (i.e. a linear dissolve between two almost still shots ends), the 1-dimensional signal obtained from sequence of dissimilarity values results in a *plateau* (an isosceles trapezoid) with width of $2r + T + 1$ (with a minor top base of $|2r - (T + 1)|$ frames and two slopes of $\min(2r, T + 1)$ frames) with maximum height for $2r = T + 1$ (when it degenerates into a triangle since the minor base of the trapezoid becomes a point). Therefore, if radius parameter is set to $(T+1)/2$ a set of local maxima in the 1-dimensional dissimilarity signal will be associated with the location of transitions. Unfortunately, since the size of (gradual) transitions is not fixed our dissimilarity measure (calculated with a fixed radius) will produce a signal with high dynamics; and, consequently, a filtering step is needed to locate local maxima.

Once the r-cumulative dissimilarity measure $r\text{-CDIS}_k^{\delta,\lambda}$ is calculated for each frame at location k, the sequence of dissimilarity values is then stored as an 1-dimensional signal (see Fig. 3). Due to the hypothesis that the computation of the dissimilarity measure produces a local maximum with high dynamics into a 1-dimensional signal, morphological filters – (i) closing; and (ii) white top hat – can be applied in order to find or enhance these maxima (see Fig. 3).

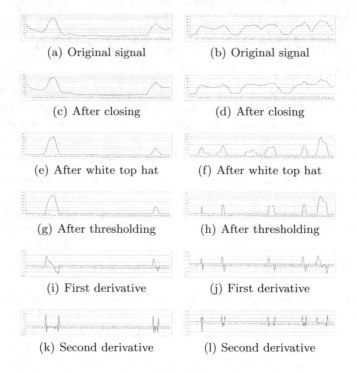

(a) Original signal   (b) Original signal

(c) After closing   (d) After closing

(e) After white top hat   (f) After white top hat

(g) After thresholding   (h) After thresholding

(i) First derivative   (j) First derivative

(k) Second derivative   (l) Second derivative

Fig. 3. Signal filtering, thresholding and classification of a transition: (left column) the first transition of this signal is gradual since $t_e - t_s \geq 3$; and (right column) the first transition of this signal is abrupt since $t_e - t_s \leq 2$

After the filtering step, a transition is associated with a local maximum that is larger than a specified threshold value (Δ), in order to prevent a great number of false positives related to effects, such as flashes and object/camera motions. Finally, the transition center is located where the first derivative of the 1-D signal changes sign (crosses zero) and the corresponding points have negative values of the second derivative. After identifying the maxima of the signal, we search

Table 1. Overall Values of F1 Score

Minimum cumulative	F1 Score			
dissimilarity (Δ)	Min	Max	Avg	Std Dev
05%	87.00%	91.45%	90.21%	0.94%
10%	88.09%	92.02%	90.25%	0.96%
15%	85.28%	90.94%	88.49%	1.13%

around the maximum for the start t_s and end t_e time instant of the transition (transition boundaries). Boundaries are detected as the points left/right of the maximum where the second derivative crosses zero in the so called inflection points. Since, a gradual transition has a certain duration, we consider that at least three frames should be involved to declare a gradual transition, i.e., $t_e - t_s \geq 3$ (see Fig. 3). If this condition does not hold, i.e., if $t_e - t_s \leq 2$ then an abrupt transition (cut) is declared (see Fig. 3).

4 Experiments

In our experiments, we have used two video datasets which presents a variety of different video genres. The first video dataset contains 20 videos – 1069 seconds (31796 frames) of MPEG-1 testing material with 570 transitions (47 cuts and 523 graduals). The second dataset contains 10 videos from TRECVID 2006 related to shot detection track, with 15160 seconds (467895 frames) of MPEG-1 testing material with 2509 transitions (1770 cuts and 759 graduals). In order to evaluate the results, we consider the precision, recall and F1 measure. According to [12], F1 is a combination of precision and recall and is maximized at the intersection of the two distributions. For that reason, F1 score is also called by [12] the best overall performance measure.

Several experiments, applied to the first dataset, have been conducted for 3 (three) different values of minimum dissimilarity score (Δ), i.e., for $\Delta = 05\%, 10\%, 15\%$, for 3 (three) values of radius (r), i.e., $r = 09, 12, 15$, for 4 (four) values of maximum point dissimilarity (δ), i.e., $\delta = 05, 10, 15, 20$, and for 4 (four) values of maximum point distance allowed (λ), i.e., $\lambda = 05, 10, 15, 20$. Table 1 presents overall average values of F1 score obtained for those tests, together with minimum and maximum values and standard deviation for each value of minimum dissimilarity score (Δ). One can easily verify that best results found are associated with $\Delta = 10\%$, while the set of tests with $\Delta = 15\%$ produces the lowest overall average value of F1 score.

Table 2 presents a detailed view of these three quality measures (recall (R), precision (P), and F1 score) for the proposed method for several parameter settings (with $\Delta = 10\%$). The proposed method achieves more than 92% recall with almost 92% precision (see Table 2 for window radius $r = 12$, $\delta = 10$ and $\lambda = 15$). Even the dataset is different for literature, our results are similar to (and even better than) the best results presented in [8] (their results are only

Table 2. Results for video dataset 1 and $\Delta = 10\%$

Point distance (λ)	Window radius $r = 12$ Point dissimilarity (δ)											
	5			10			15			20		
	R	P	F1	R	P	F1	R	P	F1	R	P	F1
5	0.891	0.904	0.897	0.905	0.900	0.903	0.893	0.902	0.897	0.894	0.902	0.898
10	0.912	0.910	0.911	0.919	0.916	0.917	0.919	0.916	0.917	0.894	0.910	0.902
15	0.921	0.911	0.916	**0.924**	**0.916**	**0.920**	0.921	0.914	0.918	0.894	0.909	0.902
20	0.921	0.913	0.917	0.866	0.913	0.889	0.912	0.912	0.912	0.894	0.901	0.898

(a) False positive cut   (b) False positive gradual transition

Fig. 4. Examples of abrupt and gradual transitions that do not appear in groundtruth of TRECVID 2006

better for abrupt transitions), but our method uses a much simpler classification approach. Moreover, the number of gradual transitions in our first dataset is almost 92% (523 gradual transitons), while in [8] only 14% from the total number of transition are graduals (262 gradual transitions and 1571 cuts).

In our first dataset, since the transition average size is 23 frames, the best results (i.e., higher F1 scores) are associated with radius $r = 12$ ($= (23 + 1)/2$) – as it should be expected. In our dataset, the shot average size is only 31 frames, so for larger values of r there is a great probability that two consecutive plateaus (i.e. transitions) merge into a single one. We consider the first dataset to tune the parameters. The proposed method, applied to the second dataset, achieves more than 75% recall with 68% precision and F1=71% for window radius $r = 12$, $\delta = 15$ and $\lambda = 15$). In order to understand the reasons behind this reduction in both recall and precision rates, we have to take a closer look into video content added to the dataset. The average size of gradual transitions is 15.4 frames, and consequently, the window radius must be $r = 8$ instead of $r = 12$ in order to decrease the dissimilarity measure and increase the precision rate. Also, as one reexamines TRECVID 2006 groundtruth, he might have some doubts about some false positives detected by our method. Fig. 4 presents a example of 2 video sequences that were detected by our method. The first one shows a "video-in-video" (in which there is a cut), which is a very hard problem to cope with during transition detection. The other is an example of effects that are very hard to classify (even for humans). One could claim that they are again examples of "video-in-video", but they also could be taken as gradual transitions. Many teams of TRECVID 2006 have reported those same problems.

Also, the quality of video sequences is poor, that is very different of our first dataset in which there is no doubt about boundary classification. Unfortunately, the dissimilarity measure adopted does not allow our method to identify those effects.

5   Conclusion and Further Works

In this work, the size of the maximum cardinality matching calculated using a bipartite graph with respect to a sliding window is used as a dissimilarity measure in order to identify locations of abrupt and gradual transitions. The main contribution of our work is the application of a simple and efficient distance to solve a problem of video segmentation. According to experimental results, the performance of our method, when applied to the first dataset (more than 92% recall with almost 92% precision), is similar to (and even better than) the one proposed by [8] with lower computational cost since its classifications step is much simpler. In our experiments, we have used a "not so large" dataset – but it presents a huge number of gradual transitions (almost one transition for each two seconds), which makes the problem of abrupt and gradual transition detection even harder. However, transition detection results can be highly dependent on the testing material, which is usually scarce and not especially representative. So, as a future work, we plan to apply our approach to a large and representative video database in which the average shot size will be much greater than the size of the specified window. We also intend to investigate further strategies to cope with hard effects such as "video-in-video".

Acknowledgments

The authors are grateful to PUC Minas (Pontifícia Universidade Católica de Minas Gerais), MIC BH (Microsoft Innovation Center Belo Horizonte), CT-Info/MCT/CNPq (Project 551005/2007-6) and FAPEMIG (Project CEX PPM 126/08) for the financial support of this work.

References

1. Naphade, M.R., Mehrotra, R., Ferman, A.M., Warnick, J., Huang, T.S., Tekalp, A.M.: A high-performance shot boundary detection algorithm using multiple cues. In: Proc. Int. Conf. Image Processing - ICIP, pp. 884–887 (1998)
2. Yuan, J., Wang, H., Xiao, L., Zheng, W., Li, J., Lin, F., Zhang, B.: A formal study of shot boundary detection. IEEE Transactions on Circuits and Systems for Video Technology 17(2), 168–186 (2007)
3. Wang, Y., Liu, Z., Huang, J.-C.: Multimedia content analysis. IEEE Signal Processing Magazine, 12–36 (2000)
4. Ngo, C.-W., Pong, T.-C., Chin, R.T.: Detection of gradual transitions through temporal slice analysis. In: CVPR, pp. 1036–1041. IEEE Computer Society, Los Alamitos (1999)

5. Zabih, R., Miller, J., Mai, K.: A feature-based algorithm for detecting and classifying production effects. Multimedia Syst. 7(2), 119–128 (1999)
6. Fernando, W.A.C., Canagarajah, C.N., Bull, D.R.: Fade and dissolve detection in uncompressed and compressed video sequences. In: ICIP, vol. (3), pp. 299–303 (1999)
7. Zhang, H., Kankanhalli, A., Smoliar, S.W.: Automatic partitioning of full-motion video. Multimedia Syst. 1(1), 10–28 (1993)
8. Bescos, J., Cisneros, G., Martinez, J., Menendez, J., Cabrera, J.: A unified model for techniques on video-shot transition detection. IEEE Transactions on Multimedia 7(2), 293–307 (2005)
9. Grana, C., Cucchiara, R.: Linear transition detection as a unified shot detection approach. IEEE Transactions on Circuits and Systems for Video Technology 17(4), 483–489 (2007)
10. Guimarães, S.J.F., Patrocínio Jr., Z.K.G., de Paula, H.B.: A rotation and translation invariant algorithm for cut detection using bipartite graph matching. In: Proc. of the Tenth IEEE International Symposium on Multimedia (ISM 2008), pp. 104–110. IEEE Computer Society Press, Los Alamitos (2008)
11. Yeo, B.-L., Liu, B.: A unified approach to temporal segmentation of motion jpeg and mpeg compressed video. In: Proceedings of the International Conference on Multimedia Computing and Systems, pp. 81–88 (May 1995)
12. Whitehead, A., Bose, P., Laganiere, R.: Feature based cut detection with automatic threshold selection. In: Enser, P.G.B., Kompatsiaris, Y., O'Connor, N.E., Smeaton, A., Smeulders, A.W.M. (eds.) CIVR 2004. LNCS, vol. 3115, pp. 410–418. Springer, Heidelberg (2004)

A New Dissimilarity Measure for Trajectories with Applications in Anomaly Detection

Dustin L. Espinosa-Isidrón and Edel B. García-Reyes

Advanced Technologies Application Center (CENATAV), 7a # 21812 e/ 218 y 222,
Rpto. Siboney, Playa, C.P. 12200, La Habana, Cuba
{despinosa,edel}@cenatav.co.cu

Abstract. Trajectory clustering has been used to very effectively in the detection of anomalous behavior in video sequences. A key point in trajectory clustering is how to measure the (dis)similarity between two trajectories. This paper deals with a new dissimilarity measure for trajectory clustering, giving the same importance to differences and similarities between the trajectories. Experimental results in the task of anomalous detection via hierarchical clustering shows the validity of the proposed approach.

Keywords: Trajectory Clustering, Dissimilarity, Anomaly Detection.

1 Introduction

Video surveillance is a research field that has received much interest over the last years. Parking lot surveillance, traffic monitoring, and crime prevention are among the applications of video surveillance systems. A key task that could help improve the effectiveness of these systems is the automatic detection of anomalous behaviors. Trajectory clustering has been established as an effective tool to address the task. A fundamental issue in trajectory clustering is how to measure the (dis)similarity between the trajectories.

In this work we propose a new dissimilarity measure for trajectories, namely Dissimilarity for Trajectories(DT). The core of DT is a non-symmetric dissimilarity which yields the same importance to differences and similarities between the trajectories. All measures are tested in the task of anomaly detection via trajectory clustering. The selected data sets contain different amounts of normal trajectories with different amounts of abnormal trajectories.

The remainder of this paper is organized as follows. Sec. 2 describes the representation and dissimilarity for trajectories, including the proposed dissimilarity measure. Anomaly detection via trajectory clustering is presented alongside experimental results in Sec. 3. Finally, Sec. 4. concludes the paper.

2 (Dis)Similarity Measures for Trajectories

Trajectory Representation: Usually a trajectory is represented as a sequence $S = (s_1, s_2, \ldots, s_h)$, where each s_i, $1 \leq i \leq h$, is a point in a multidimensional space containing information about the moving object at time i. Most

I. Bloch and R.M. Cesar, Jr. (Eds.): CIARP 2010, LNCS 6419, pp. 193–201, 2010.

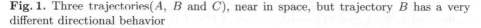

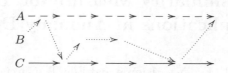

Fig. 1. Three trajectories(A, B and C), near in space, but trajectory B has a very different directional behavior

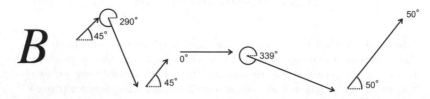

Fig. 2. Calculation of the direction in each point of the trajectory B. In each point b_i, the direction is represented as the angle clockwise with the right horizontal of (x_{bi}, y_{bi}). To subtract two directions d_{bi}, d_{aj} we take the minimum between $|d_{bi} - d_{aj}|$ and $|360 - d_{bi} - d_{aj}|$

of the research done until now for trajectory analysis, is only based on the position($s_i = (x_{si}, y_{si})$) at time i[1][2]. Note that time information is used implicitly, since in general, trajectories are sampled at equal time rates. Other features one should consider are the direction and the velocity of the objects. Obtaining both features depends on the tracker and not all tracking algorithms records this information. The significance of using direction comes from the fact that two trajectories can be very close in the space domain, but have a very different directional behavior (see figure 1). The direction at time i can be estimated using the position at time $i + 1$, as the angle clockwise with the right horizontal of (x_{si}, y_{si}) as shown in figure 2. For the case of the velocity you also need to know the sampling rate. In this work we represent s_i as a point in a 4 dimensional space $s_i = (x_{si}, y_{si}, t_{si}, d_{si})$, encoding information about the position(x_{si}, y_{si}), time(t_{si}) and direction(d_{si}) of the moving object. In addition, each feature is normalized dividing by its standard deviation.

Previous Work: The Euclidian dissimilarity for trajectories, the Longest Common SubSequence(LCSS) and the Dynamic Time Warping(DTW) are the three most widely studied (dis)similarity measure for trajectories in the literature[1][4]. This section introduces these widely used (dis)similarity measures and discusses their main features.

Euclidean(EU) Dissimilarity is defined as the sum of the distances between corresponding points: $Eu(S, T) = \sum_{i=1}^{h} D(s_i, t_i)$, where h is the length of the trajectories and D is the Euclidean distance between s_i and t_i[3]. Note that this measure assumes that both trajectories have the same length. This is not a common scenario due to speed variations and occlusions[5]. Another known problem of the Euclidean Measure is that it cannot handle local time shifting[1]. However it is simple to implement and very fast $O(h)$.

Longest Common Subsequence(LCSS) Similarity is a variation of the Edit Distance on strings[3]. Let $S = (s_1, s_2, \ldots, s_h)$ and $T(t_1, t_2, \ldots, t_l)$ two trajectories, δ and ϵ two user-defined parameters, then LCSS is defined as:

$$Lcss(S,T) = \begin{cases} 0 & \text{if } |S| = 0 \text{ or } |T| = 0 \\ 1 + Lcss(Rest(S), Rest(T)) & \text{if } |t_{s1} - t_{t1}| \leq \delta \text{ and} \\ & |x_{s1} - x_{t1}| \leq \epsilon \text{ and } |y_{s1} - y_{t1}| \leq \epsilon \\ \max(Lcss(Rest(S), T), & \text{otherwise} \\ \quad Lcss(S, Rest(T))) \end{cases}$$

where $Rest(S) = (s_2, \ldots, s_h)$.

The main idea of LCSS is to allow the trajectories to stretch and to allow some points to remain *unmatched*[1]. The value of $Lcss(S,T)$ is the length of the longest matching subsequence of S and T as indicated by its name. This measure has proven great effectiveness in the presence of noisy points[3]. The main drawback of $Lcss(S,T)$ is that it does not penalize unmatched subsequences, given no information of how separated the unmatched subsequences are. Work in [3] tries to solve this, but they use a fixed penalty, no matter the difference of the subsequences. In addition, $Lcss(S,T)$ in its original form, doesn't take the direction into account, and may fail to separate two trajectories near in space but very different directional behavior (see figure 1). Also, it should be noticed that the user needs to define ϵ and δ parameters. Last, the time complexity of $Lcss(S,T)$ is $O(|S| + |T|)$ applying dynamic programming techniques and with a small δ[1].

Dynamic Time Warping(DTW) Dissimilarity as LCSS allows warping in time, but contrary to LCSS doesn't allow points to remain unmatched[1]. DTW is defined as:

$$Dtw(S,T) = \begin{cases} 0 & \text{if } |S| = 0 \text{ and } |T| = 0 \\ \infty & \text{if } |S| = 0 \text{ or } |T| = 0 \\ D(s_1, t_1) + \min(Dtw(Rest(S), Rest(T)), & \text{otherwise} \\ Dtw(Rest(S), T), Dtw(S, Rest(T))) \end{cases}$$

The main idea of DTW is to duplicate some points to handle local time shifting. The general criticism to DTW in the literature is its sensitivity to noisy points, since all points need to be matched[3][1]. In addition, we point out that DTW penalize long trajectories. Two very similar long trajectories may have similar DTW value that two dissimilar but much smaller trajectories. As all of above measures if information about the direction is not included in the trajectories representation, DTW may fail to separate two trajectories near in space but very different directional behavior. The time complexity of $Dtw(S,T)$ is $O(|S||T|)$ applying dynamic programming as with LCSS.

2.1 Proposed Approach

With the purpose of solving the above mentioned problems, we developed a new dissimilarity measure for trajectories. This measure should be able to handle trajectories of different lengths. Moreover, it shouldn't be influenced by the length of the given trajectories, in the sense that a pair of long (dis)similar trajectories should have an analogous dissimilarity value as another pair of smaller ones. Besides, similar subsequences should be rewarded, and dissimilar ones penalized.

Given two trajectories S and T, and a boolean user-defined parameter m, the Dissimilarity for Trajectories(DT) is defined as:

$$DT(S,T,m) = \begin{cases} \min(ADT(S,T)/|S|, ADT(T,S)/|T|) & \text{if } m = true \\ \max(ADT(S,T)/|S|, ADT(T,S)/|T|) & \text{if } m = false \end{cases}$$

where:

$$ADT(S,T) = \begin{cases} Nearest(s_1,T) & \text{if } |S| = 1 \\ \sum_{i=1}^{|S|} D(s_i,t_1) & \text{if } |T| = 1 \\ \min(D(s_1,t_1) + ADT(Rest(S),T), & \text{otherwise} \\ \quad ADT(S,Rest(T)) \end{cases}$$

and $Nearest(s,T) = \min_{t \in T} D(s,t)$

$Nearest(s,T)$ returns the distance of the nearest point to s in the sequence T. The function $ADT(S,T)$(Asymmetric Dissimilarity for Trajectories) is a nonsymmetric dissimilarity measure that quantifies how far S is from T. This is done by finding the subsequences of T(allowing replication of points in T as in DTW, as well as allowing some points of T remain unmatched as in LCSS) passing nearest to S, and summing the Euclidean distances of corresponding points (see figures 3 and 4). If S is a subsequent of T, then $ADT(S,T)$ is 0. On the other hand, $DT(S,T)$ normalizes the result of $ADT(S,T)$ and $ADT(T,S)$ dividing by the size of S and T respectively. Furthermore, let the user to chose what is more relevant, the differences(max)[1] or the similarities(min) among the trajectories. The time complexity of $DT(S,T)$ is $O(|S||T|)$ applying similar dynamic programming techniques as with DTW and LCSS.

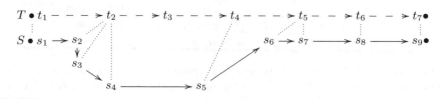

Fig. 3. Resultant matching points in $ADT(S,T)$. The dissimilarity value is equivalent to $Eu(S,T')$, where $T' = (t_1,t_2,t_2,t_2,t_4,t_5,t_5,t_6,t_7)$. The points t_2 and t_5 were duplicated and t_3 was left unmatched.

---

[1] For anomaly detection differences will be more relevant.

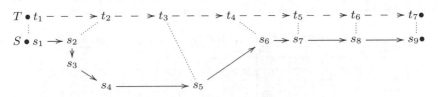

Fig. 4. Resultant matching points in $ADT(T, S)$. The dissimilarity value is equivalent to $Eu(S', T)$, where $S' = (s_1, s_2, s_5, s_6, s_7, s_8, s_9)$. The points t_3 and t_4 were left unmatched.

To sum up briefly, the new measure is able to work with trajectories of different sizes(contrary to EU), it is not influenced by the size of the trajectories, since the value is normalized(contrary to DTW, LCSS), and allows the user to specify the relevance of differences and similarities. Besides, only the less dissimilar(most similar) subsequences are used in the computation of the dissimilarity(contrary to EU, DTW), and Euclidian measure is used to penalize the differences(contrary to LCSS).

3   Experimental Results in Anomaly Detection

The automatic anomaly detection task implies finding objects moving with an unusual(abnormal, infrequent) pattern. Trajectory clustering provides a practical approach for the detection of this unusual(abnormal) motion patterns in video sequences. The main idea is that larger groups are considered as normal trajectories while singletons or very small groups are considered as abnormal trajectories. In this section a trajectory clustering algorithm is selected for the task of anomaly detection. The (dis)similarity measures presented above are tested with a selected clustering algorithm, in a previously used data set, and experimental results are shown.

Single-Link(SL)[6] is a well known and widely used hierarchical clustering algorithm. Given a set of objects O, a dissimilarity measure d, and a stopping criteria θ, the SL algorithm is defined as:

1. Represent each object of O as a singleton cluster.
2. Select the two objects with minimum d that are in different clusters.
3. Join the corresponding clusters.
4. Stop if θ is true, else go to step 2.

This algorithm has several desirables properties that make it a practical choice for anomaly detection. First, it has a very easy implementation. Moreover, it can discover clusters of any shape and size. Furthermore, it has a very easy interpretation: objects separated from the rest(i.e. anomalies) are joined last, this

Table 1. Results using **EU**. For each entry (rows = anomalies; columns = groups of normal trajectories) ten runs were performed and the results averaged.

FALSE POSITIVES. The total average over 100 cases: 6.06%									
Anomalies	Groups of normal trajectories								
	1	2	3	4	5	6	7	8	9	10
1	0.30	0.00	0.00	0.00	0.00	0.00	0.00	0.00	0.00	0.00
2	0.50	6.80	4.20	1.65	7.35	6.45	4.40	8.35	6.25	6.95
3	9.00	2.90	14.03	7.23	6.90	3.57	2.30	5.07	1.53	3.57
4	8.70	5.43	4.83	8.25	6.65	5.78	5.83	6.35	11.20	5.05
5	7.96	2.90	10.08	6.16	7.56	5.48	10.20	7.66	3.76	3.54
6	9.38	5.32	8.22	6.87	5.25	5.93	8.43	6.67	3.33	9.90
7	5.14	7.37	11.27	8.53	6.00	8.40	6.89	7.30	9.46	5.03
8	6.85	8.46	6.68	10.01	8.53	11.08	7.04	6.53	7.94	5.74
9	7.49	4.79	5.78	7.86	7.70	4.27	6.73	6.07	8.80	7.84
10	11.34	4.92	7.00	6.39	10.10	3.95	8.26	8.48	5.91	6.51
TRUE POSITIVES. The total average over 100 cases: 96.73%									
Anomalies	Groups of normal trajectories								
1	90.00	100.00	100.00	100.00	100.00	100.00	100.00	98.75	100.00	100.00
2	100.00	100.00	96.67	100.00	100.00	98.33	100.00	98.75	93.33	99.00
3	100.00	100.00	96.67	95.00	96.00	98.33	98.57	98.75	97.78	99.00
4	100.00	90.00	100.00	100.00	100.00	100.00	100.00	98.75	96.67	97.00
5	80.00	100.00	96.67	92.50	98.00	98.33	95.71	98.75	96.67	95.00
6	90.00	100.00	100.00	95.00	94.00	95.00	97.14	92.50	97.78	98.00
7	100.00	95.00	100.00	97.50	96.00	90.00	95.71	97.50	96.67	97.00
8	80.00	100.00	96.67	95.00	100.00	95.00	95.71	97.50	97.78	98.00
9	100.00	100.00	96.67	100.00	88.00	98.33	88.57	95.00	97.78	97.00
10	100.00	90.00	93.33	95.00	92.00	90.00	92.86	95.00	98.89	96.00

is very important since minimizes the risk of false positives. The main drawback is that it suffers from the chaining effect, but if the clusters are well separated(the dissimilarity measure should be able to separate the anomalies from the rest), the algorithm performs well[6].

Experimental Results: A synthetic data set, first introduced in [2], was selected to test the effectiveness of the (dis)similarity measures presented in this work, for the task of anomaly detection. It contains *"100 different experimental cases, each one with a different number of groups of 100 normal trajectories (ranging from 1 to 10) and outliers (from 1 to 10). For each test, ten different training/test sets were created, for a total of 2000 data sets...Note that outliers in the test sets are drawn from the same distribution used for outliers in the corresponding training sets, in order to ease the detection of anomalous training patterns being included in the normality class."* [2].

The experiment was conducted in the following way: For each measure[2], the SL algorithm was applied over the test sets. Trajectories in clusters with size greater than 2, were classified as normal and the rest was classified as anomaly. The stopping criteria was selected by the following approach: A threshold ϵ was selected using the corresponding training set, and the SL algorithm stopped before joining the pair of objects with the minimum dissimilarity greater than ϵ. To compute ϵ in the corresponding training set: For each normal cluster C_i: the mean of the dissimilarities between every pair of objects in C_i was calculated,

---

[2] LCSS was tested with several choices of ϵ and δ. $\epsilon = 0.45$ and $\delta = 2$ gave the best results.

Table 2. Results using **LCSS**. For each entry (rows = anomalies; columns = groups of normal trajectories) ten runs were performed and the results averaged.

FALSE POSITIVES. The total average over 100 cases: 0.004%										
Anomalies	Groups of normal trajectories									
	1	2	3	4	5	6	7	8	9	10
1	0.00	0.00	0.00	0.00	0.00	0.00	0.00	0.00	0.00	0.00
2	0.00	0.05	0.00	0.00	0.00	0.00	0.00	0.00	0.00	0.00
3	0.00	0.03	0.00	0.00	0.00	0.00	0.00	0.00	0.00	0.00
4	0.00	0.05	0.00	0.00	0.00	0.00	0.00	0.03	0.00	0.00
5	0.02	0.02	0.02	0.04	0.00	0.00	0.00	0.00	0.02	0.00
6	0.02	0.00	0.00	0.02	0.00	0.00	0.00	0.00	0.00	0.00
7	0.00	0.03	0.00	0.00	0.01	0.00	0.00	0.01	0.00	0.01
8	0.00	0.00	0.00	0.00	0.00	0.00	0.00	0.00	0.00	0.00
9	0.00	0.00	0.02	0.00	0.00	0.00	0.02	0.00	0.00	0.00
10	0.00	0.00	0.00	0.00	0.00	0.00	0.01	0.00	0.01	0.00
TRUE POSITIVES. The total average over 100 cases: 91.35%										
Anomalies	Groups of normal trajectories									
1	90.00	95.00	83.33	97.50	98.00	83.33	97.14	95.00	97.78	95.00
2	90.00	100.00	100.00	90.00	92.00	95.00	94.29	92.50	91.11	98.00
3	100.00	100.00	96.67	95.00	94.00	91.67	90.00	95.00	93.33	95.00
4	90.00	85.00	96.67	92.50	92.00	98.33	98.57	93.75	93.33	90.00
5	80.00	90.00	90.00	92.50	96.00	95.00	84.29	96.25	91.11	91.00
6	90.00	100.00	100.00	85.00	86.00	88.33	92.86	88.75	95.56	96.00
7	80.00	95.00	86.67	95.00	92.00	85.00	92.86	93.75	94.44	89.00
8	70.00	95.00	96.67	85.00	94.00	85.00	90.00	92.50	93.33	93.00
9	90.00	90.00	93.33	85.00	66.00	90.00	82.86	93.75	88.89	91.00
10	80.00	90.00	90.00	90.00	86.00	86.67	87.14	93.75	92.22	86.00

Table 3. Results using **DTW**. For each entry (rows = anomalies; columns = groups of normal trajectories) ten runs were performed and the results averaged.

FALSE POSITIVES. The total average over 100 cases: 2.02%										
Anomalies	Groups of normal trajectories									
	1	2	3	4	5	6	7	8	9	10
1	0.30	0.00	0.00	0.00	0.00	0.00	0.00	0.00	0.00	0.00
2	0.35	1.45	1.35	1.10	1.40	5.35	1.85	0.95	1.25	2.85
3	3.23	0.83	3.67	2.30	2.60	0.77	0.97	1.47	0.63	0.63
4	4.13	1.73	2.68	3.15	2.63	1.58	1.88	2.25	4.43	1.60
5	2.32	0.88	3.64	1.78	3.96	1.68	5.08	1.56	0.80	1.20
6	2.57	1.62	2.20	2.08	2.32	2.03	2.80	2.47	0.60	3.23
7	2.00	3.07	3.74	2.26	1.53	2.40	3.01	2.10	2.90	1.67
8	2.05	2.19	2.46	2.98	3.14	3.75	2.11	2.19	3.06	1.58
9	2.53	2.00	1.90	3.00	2.50	1.59	1.86	2.34	3.46	2.32
10	3.87	1.48	2.03	1.76	2.96	1.13	3.10	2.54	1.34	2.18
TRUE POSITIVES. The total average over 100 cases: 96.73%										
Anomalies	Groups of normal trajectories									
1	90.00	100.00	100.00	100.00	100.00	100.00	100.00	98.75	100.00	100.00
2	100.00	100.00	96.67	100.00	100.00	98.33	100.00	98.75	94.44	99.00
3	100.00	100.00	96.67	95.00	96.00	98.33	98.57	98.75	97.78	99.00
4	100.00	90.00	100.00	100.00	100.00	100.00	100.00	98.75	97.78	96.00
5	80.00	100.00	96.67	92.50	98.00	96.67	95.71	98.75	96.67	96.00
6	90.00	100.00	100.00	95.00	94.00	95.00	97.14	93.75	97.78	98.00
7	100.00	95.00	100.00	97.50	96.00	90.00	95.71	97.50	96.67	97.00
8	80.00	100.00	96.67	95.00	100.00	95.00	94.29	97.50	97.78	97.00
9	100.00	100.00	96.67	100.00	86.00	98.33	88.57	95.00	97.78	97.00
10	100.00	90.00	93.33	95.00	94.00	90.00	92.86	95.00	98.89	96.00

Table 4. Results using the **DT**. For each entry (rows = anomalies; columns = groups of normal trajectories) ten runs were performed and the results averaged.

FALSE POSITIVES. The total average over 100 cases: 1.27%									
Anomalies	Groups of normal trajectories								
	1	2	3	4	5	6	7	8	9	10
1	0.30	0.00	0.00	0.00	0.00	0.00	0.00	0.00	0.10	0.00
2	0.30	1.10	0.90	0.80	1.25	4.05	1.00	0.90	0.60	1.60
3	1.93	0.40	1.67	1.13	1.43	0.37	0.70	0.87	0.27	0.53
4	1.95	1.15	1.60	1.73	1.65	1.15	1.13	1.58	2.78	0.90
5	1.56	0.70	2.18	1.24	2.74	1.04	2.64	0.82	0.58	0.86
6	1.62	1.40	1.28	1.67	1.43	1.18	1.58	1.77	0.48	1.80
7	1.47	1.80	2.47	1.39	1.06	1.47	2.17	1.20	2.19	1.20
8	1.48	1.30	1.64	1.70	1.66	2.33	1.30	1.20	2.03	0.84
9	1.62	1.19	1.03	1.80	1.44	0.91	1.21	1.67	2.36	1.53
10	2.38	1.07	1.28	1.16	1.86	0.77	2.04	1.72	0.92	1.59
TRUE POSITIVES. The total average over 100 cases: 96.65%									
Anomalies	Groups of normal trajectories								
1	90.00	100.00	100.00	100.00	100.00	100.00	100.00	98.75	100.00	100.00
2	100.00	100.00	96.67	100.00	98.00	100.00	100.00	98.75	94.44	99.00
3	100.00	100.00	96.67	95.00	96.00	98.33	98.57	98.75	97.78	99.00
4	100.00	90.00	100.00	100.00	100.00	100.00	100.00	98.75	97.78	96.00
5	80.00	100.00	93.33	92.50	98.00	96.67	92.86	98.75	96.67	96.00
6	90.00	100.00	100.00	92.50	94.00	95.00	97.14	93.75	97.78	98.00
7	100.00	95.00	100.00	97.50	96.00	90.00	95.71	97.50	96.67	96.00
8	80.00	100.00	96.67	95.00	98.00	95.00	94.29	97.50	97.78	96.00
9	100.00	100.00	96.67	100.00	88.00	98.33	88.57	96.25	97.78	97.00
10	100.00	95.00	93.33	92.50	94.00	88.33	92.86	96.25	97.78	97.00

and the minimum of the calculated means was selected as ϵ. Tables 1 through 8 show the results in terms of false positives (FP = % of normal trajectories misclassified as anomalies) and true positives (TP = % of abnormal trajectories correctly classified as anomalies).

The EU shows very good results detecting TP with an overall above 96% of effectiveness, but misclassifies many normal trajectories. This is very undesirable in real world applications, since many false alarms could lead human operators to a loss of confidence on the automatic system. On the contrary, LCSS has near zero FP, but stays more than 5% behind in TP detection. This behavior could be expected since LCSS is the only that does not penalizes the differences(section 2). DT and DTW behave very good in both aspects, but DTW have some particular cases where it misclassifies around 5% of normal trajectories. For the above mentioned reasons, the proposed dissimilarity measure shows better overall performance(FP,TP) than the others widely used measures.

4   Conclusions

In this paper, a new dissimilarity measure for trajectories was proposed and compared with three (dis)similarity measures widely used in the literature. The experiments for anomaly detection in video sequences via trajectory clustering (Single-Link), show that the proposed measure achieves the best results in overall performance.

References

1. Vlachos, M., Hadjieleftheriou, M., Gunopulos, D., Keogh, E.: Indexing Multidimensional Time-Series. The VLDB Journal 15, 1–20 (2006)
2. Piciarelli, C., Micheloni, C., Foresti, G.L., Keogh, E.: Trajectory-Based Anomalous Event Detection. IEEE Transactions on Circuits And Systems For Video Technology 18, 1544–1554 (2008)
3. Chen, L., Tamer, M., Oria, V.: Robust and Fast Similarity Search for Moving Object Trajectories. In: 2005 ACM SIGMOD, pp. 491–502. ACM, New York (2005)
4. Zhang, Z., Huang, K., Tan, T.: Comparison of Similarity Measures for Trajectory Clustering in Outdoor Surveillance Scenes. In: 18th International Conference on Pattern Recognition, pp. 1135–1138. IEEE Computer Society, Los Alamitos (2006)
5. Morris, B.T., Trivedi, M.M.: A Survey of Vision-Based Trajectory Learning and Analysis for Surveillance. IEEE Transactions on Circuits and Systems For Video Technology 18, 1114–1127 (2008)
6. Xu, R., Wunsch II, D.C.: Clustering. IEEE Press, NJ (2009)

Modelling Postures of Human Movements

Djamila Medjahed Gamaz, Houssem Eddine Gueziri, and Nazim Haouchine

Computer Science Departement, USTHB University,
BP 32 El Alia, 16 000, Algiers Algeria
Tel.: +213 21 24 79 50 to 60
dmedjahed@usthb.dz, dmedjahedgamaz@yahoo.com

Abstract. The goal of this paper is to present a novel modelling of postures of human activities such us walk, run... Effectively, human action is, in general, characterized by a sequence of specific body postures. So, from an incoming sequence video, we determine the postures (key-frames) which will represent the movement. We construct the prototypes corresponding to these key-frames by thinning these postures, and then we use this skeleton as a starting point for building the model. Some results are presented to validate our models.

Keywords: Human Activities, Modelling, Shape Matching, Skeleton, thinning.

1 Introduction

Lot of papers present an overview of human motion estimation and recognition [1] [2] [3]. The video of measuring shape deformation relative to prototypes has a long history in pattern recognition and computer vision [4] [5]. The work in [6] [7] present an algorithm for computing correspondence between arbitrary shapes. Based on skeletons directly, many approaches have been developed for shape matching [8] [9] [10]. The benefits of applying skeleton-based methods are its natural consistency with human intuition and capability to describe the local geometrical features, allowing the performance of articulated matching [11] [15] [16]. In this paper, we present a novel modelling of human activities postures.

Inspired by works of [12] [13] [14] [18], we propose to hide (superimposed) the skeleton (of different body poses) on models representing human activities in a predefined database, to recognize the motion in the input video made by a single person. So, we first, construct prototypes of postures which describe a movement from an incoming sequence video. We determine automatically the postures which will represent the movement, we skeletal these postures then we use this skeleton as a starting point for building the model.

We test the relevance of the models constructed by calculating the degree of correspondence between key-frames of an unknown motion with the models in the database. The originality of this modelling is that the posture of a person is represented by a weighting silhouette representing the pose; weights which materialize variations of postures (As movement is executed in a different way from a person to

I. Bloch and R.M. Cesar, Jr. (Eds.): CIARP 2010, LNCS 6419, pp. 202–211, 2010.

another). The advantage of this approach is its simplicity and ease of processing and calculations. The selection of key positions is done automatically which is not always the case in other work [13].

2   System Overview

Human action is, in general, characterized by a sequence of specific body postures. So, the problem that we proposed to solve is to determine models representing these poses, to take them as references in order to recognize human action of everyday life with a fixed camera. The system implementation consists of three parts shown in figure 1. After the background subtraction, we have a human silhouette, then we centre this silhouette in a frame with predefined size, and as the last phase of pre-processing we select a set of frames (key-frames) that will represent the movement achieved in a video sequence. This last step, allows us to process just a fewer number of frames (the key-frames) instead of the entire input sequence frames. In modelling phase, we first calculate skeleton of silhouette in the key-frames. Then we use this skeleton as a starting point for building the model of the posture associated (weighting module). The out put of the modelling phase is a database of models representing movements (run, walk...). The last part of the implementation is the activity recognition module. This module use as input, a database cited above, and an unknown video sequence.

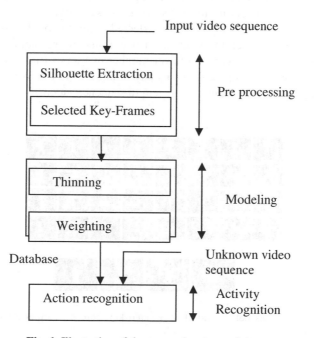

Fig. 1. Illustration of the processing stage of the system

3 Selected Key-Frames

An action is often described as a sequence of discrete postures. For determining which postures are the ones which can represent the movement, we treat the frames (given after the background subtraction) in pairs. This step is dependent on the accuracy of the tracking step (tracking process is not performed in this work) and is very important for the next process. So, we calculate the percentage of pixels (*perc*) that is different between two successive frames. Then we compare this value to a predefined threshold. If *perc* is upper than the threshold then the frame is selected to be a key-frame; otherwise it is not selected and we process the same treatment between the next frame and the last key-frame selected (See fig.2). The percentage is calculated as follows:

$$Perc = Diff / Add \qquad (1)$$

Where **Diff** is the number of common pixels of two consecutives frames (given by the XOR operation between two frames).

 Add is the number of all pixels in the two consecutives frames (given by the OR operation between two frames).

 Perc is the percentage of pixels which is different between the two frames. This process allows us to quantify the difference in pixels using percentages to avoid relying on the number of image pixels (which change from one image to another).

   This step allows us to define the keys postures (keys-frames) of a given movement. All these postures will therefore be selected to represent the movement. So, instead of processing the entire input sequence frame to recognize an unknown movement, we have to process just a fewer number of frames (the key-frames) (See figure 2.b). Note that this step can give us any number of key-frames in accordance with the velocity of the movement and the length sequence video.

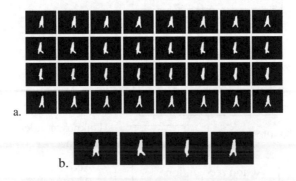

a.

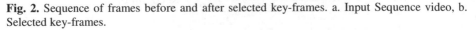

b.

Fig. 2. Sequence of frames before and after selected key-frames. a. Input Sequence video, b. Selected key-frames.

4 Modelling

The idea of creating weighted models of postures comes from the fact that a movement is executed by several people in a similar manner. Indeed, the different postures representing a movement for a given person are almost the same for any other person with slight deformations. These deformations are represented in models through the weights assigned to their pixels. The weight distribution in the frame model will be such that the skeleton pixels will receive the highest weight and distance from this position the more we will assign lower weights.

4.1 Building Models

The key-frames given by the postures selection step, on the input sequence video, are processed for building the models. The building models occur on two steps: thinning the silhouette then weighting the obtained skeleton.

Thinning. A skeleton is a geometric representation of an object in a dimension less than the input object. It can describe a compact way the properties of an object, especially its shape [19][20]. The algorithm we use is based on the topological thinning. The image analysis is to find simple points of the object of interest. To enjoy the benefits of parallel methods of thinning and conservation topological skeleton of sequential methods, we implement a hybrid algorithm. This algorithm is thinning the silhouette of two sides, north-east and south-west alternating direction at each iteration so as to obtain a skeleton centred in the image (See figure 3.b). We can divide the 16 cases of simple points in two groups: On one side the points which represent the north and/or east of the subject of interest. They are found in the following cases:

```
x 1 x   x 1 x   x 1 x   0 0 x   x 1 x
0 p 1   1 p 1   0 p 1   0 p 1   1 p 0
x 1 x   x 0 x   0 0 x   x 1 x   x 0 0

1 1 x   x 1 1   0 0 1   0 0 x
0 p 0   0 p 0   0 p 1   0 p 1
0 0 0   0 0 0   0 0 x   0 0 1
```

On the other side the points representing the south and / or west of the object of interest:

```
x 1 x   x 0 x   x 0 0   0 0 x   x 1 x
1 p 0   1 p 1   1 p 0   0 p 1   1 p 0
x 1 x   x 1 x   x 1 x   x 1 x   x 0 0

0 0 0   0 0 0   1 0 0   x 0 0
0 p 0   0 p 0   1 p 0   1 p 0
1 1 x   x 1 1   x 0 0   1 0 0
```

Some pixels may belong to both cases; this does not affect the course of the algorithm. The pixels removed are those located in opposite of the scanning direction of the image. This operation is repeated until no more simple point is detected.

The skeleton obtained is sometimes beyond the skeletal branches called "barbules". We call a branch; any set of pixels forming an eight-connected path whose elements

Fig. 3. Thinning a- Input silhouette, b- Skeleton, c-Skeleton after removing barbules

have strictly two neighbours (except for the two end pixels). Several criteria exist to remove the barbules (branches). The most used and easiest to implement is the size criterion. All arcs of the skeleton whose length is less than a given threshold are considered noise (barbules) and are removed. Several iterations are sometimes necessary (see figure 3).

Weighting. The weighting is a process of assigning weights, represented by symbols (Z, Y... in figure 4), to pixels in an image. These weights are used to specify the relative importance of each pixel compared to others. Weighting is used in the classification of postures, to calculate the degree of similarity (or correlation) between an unknown form and a model in the database.

For building models from the skeleton we process the following steps:

Step1: Distribution of maximum values of weighting on the skeleton.

Let Z be the maximum weight assigned to all pixels of the skeleton (see Figure 4.b).

Step 2: Second layer .

Each pixel 8-neighbor related to Z is associated with weighted value Y. The weight of Y is smaller than that of Z. Y values represent a layer covering the skeleton (see Figure 4.c).

Step3: Third layer (and more).

We repeat the "Step 2" with lower weight values (X, W,...) to the previous layer until we reach a thickness desired for shape (this processing is, always, done on the last layer obtained by the previous step).

The difference in values between each layer remains constant. A direct relationship between weight and number of layer is represented by:

$$NbL = Val\_max - Val\_min / Step \tag{2}$$

Where **NbL** is the number of layers, **Val_max** is maximum weight, **Val_min** is minimum weight, **Step:** difference between each weight of layer (step = Z – Y = Y – X...). These parameters are determined experimentally.

This treatment gives us almost the same gait (look) as that of the input posture. But the pixels of the image model are weighted (see figure 5).

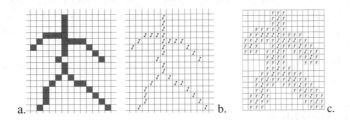

Fig. 4. Distribution of weights on the model a- Skeleton, b- Weights of the skeleton, c- Layer covering the skeleton

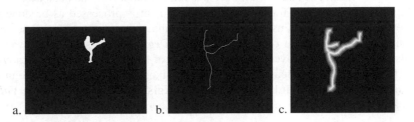

Fig. 5. A key-frame with his corresponding model, a-Input key-frame, b- Skeleton Key-frame, c- Corresponding model

4.2 Construction of Database of Models

The models are obtained after several treatments on selected images, namely: the normalization of size, thinning and weighting. For overlay models and skeleton, the frames must have the same size; a scaling is necessary. In this first work we are limited to process images that have relatively the same size. So we did not standardization of dimensions (scaling) on the images, but just add margins for the silhouette. We determine the endpoint of the object of interest for the four sides of the image. Then add columns and rows, on both sides of the object for getting a silhouette centred in an image of fixed dimensions.

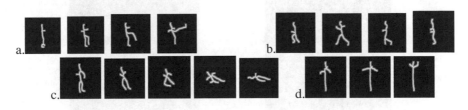

Fig. 6. Some models of the database, a. Models of 'kick', b. Models of 'run', c. Models of 'Collapse Right', d. Models of 'hand wave'

From a video sequence of motion data, we select the key-frames representing the movement. Then, each of these key-frames undergoes treatment for scaling, thinning and finally weighted. Our database has been constructed from seven input video representing different movements such as walk, run, punch, give a kick, collapse right, standup right and hand waving. Each movement is represented in the database by a set of image models of selected key-frames (see figure 6).

This first phase of the chain of recognition of human motion is, by analogy with other methods, the learning module.

5 Shape Matching

To validate the models we built, we propose to calculate a degree of correspondence between key-frames of unknown movement and the models in the database.

Input video sequences for an unknown movement is processed as be done for the sequence video which be used to build the database (select key-frames, scaling and thinning). We call degree of correspondence (***Deg_cor***) the sum of the weights of pixels in the model that overlap with the pixels of the skeleton of the unknown posture (figure 7.d.e). We calculate the number of pixels of the skeleton, in the unknown posture, and we multiply it by the maximum weight (Z), we obtain a value ***Val_max***. We calculate then the Rate correspondence (***Rat_cor***) by:

$$Rat\_cor = (Deg\_cor / Val\_max) * 100 \qquad (3)$$

The above calculation allows for comparison between two images: a model with an input image. But to make the recognition of a movement, we need to match a sequence of an unknown motion picture with a sequence of models (representing a movement) in the database.

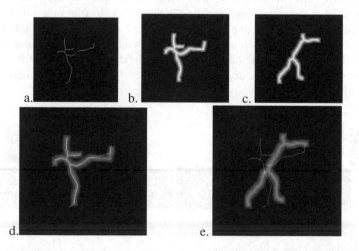

Fig. 7. Superimpose of skeleton on models. a- Skeleton of a posture, b- Corresponding Model, c- Non Corresponding model, d- superimpose of a skeleton on the corresponding model, e- superimpose of a skeleton on non corresponding model

6 Tests and Results

We have performed experiments on different video sequence actions. The system was trained using only one person for constructing the database. For the time being, the total number of activities in the database is seven (07). We give here an example of result obtained with an unknown input sequence.

We present (see figure 8.b) the results of the correlation calculated on an example of an unknown movement sequence "walking" (Four key postures: 1, 2, 3, 4; see figure 8.a) with the models of movements of the database "walk", "run" and "Kick". The first line of the matrix (respectively second, third and fourth) represents the correlations between the key position 1 (respectively 2, 3 and 4) movement to recognize with the different postures of the models.

a-   Movement to recognize (with four key postures)

Walk				
1	**58.4746 %**	44.1702 %	54.5556 %	41.5484 %
2	22.7684 %	**66.8085 %**	30.5556 %	24.9677 %
3	40.8475 %	28.7660 %	**75 %**	38.7097 %
4	45.4237 %	42.9574 %	23.8889 %	**98.8390 %**
Run				
1	29.2181 %	28.0615 %	18.6517 %	34.4545 %
2	**53.4979 %**	**28.5164 %**	**55.8052 %**	42.6364 %
3	21.0700 %	15.1385 %	10.6367 %	**45.1818 %**
4	30.4527 %	19.0154 %	23.2210 %	21.4545 %
Kick				
1	27.9661 %	20.8833 %	17.5084 %	**24.7879 %**
2	35.7628 %	26.1199 %	**18.9226 %**	19.7576 %
3	**37.8814 %**	20.7571 %	10.7071 %	14 %
4	17.6271 %	**33.8170 %**	17.3064 %	16.9091 %

b-

Fig. 8. The rats' correlation between an unknown sequence key frames with the models (walk, run and kick) in the database

From the results obtained, we can see that the degree of correspondence, between an unknown movement (figure 8.a) and his corresponding model, (figure 8.b, values in bold) give us higher values than those given for others models.

We used the video database given in [17] and our own sequence video. These first results encourage us to develop an approach for human motion recognition, which take, as a basis of knowledge, the models we built.

7 Conclusion

A novel modelling of human activities postures has been presented. The experiment, based on a simple compute of degree of correspondence shows encouraging results. For the future work, we envisage developing a recognition approach. Currently the implementation has some restrictions. The viewing direction is somewhat fixed and the background is assumed to be uniform making the segmentation of the silhouette easy. In addition, we assume that there is only one person in the field of view and that there is no occlusion. We plane to conduct more extensive tests to establish the limitation of our system.

References

1. Moeslund, T.B., Granum, E.: A Survey of computer vision-based human motion capture. Computer Vision and Image Understanding 81, 231–268 (2001)
2. Gavrila, D.M.: The visual analysis of human movement: a survey. Computer Vision and Image Understanding 73(1), 82–98 (1999), http://www.idealibrary.com
3. Aggarwal, J.K., Cai, O.: Human motion analysis: a review. Computer Vision and Image Understanding 73(3) (1999)
4. Bermermann, H.J.: Cybernetic functional and fuzzy sets. In: IEEE Systems, Man and Cybernetics Group Annual Symposium, pp. 248–254 (1971)
5. Sclaroff, S.: Deformable prototypes for encoding shape categories in image databases. Pattern Recognition 30(4), 627–640 (1996)
6. Belongie, S., Malik, J.: Matching with shape contexts. In: IEEE Workshop on Content-based Access of Image and Video Libraries (June 2000)
7. Carlson, S.: Order structure, correspondence and shape based categories. In: Forsyth, D., Mundy, J.L., Di Gesú, V., Cipolla, R. (eds.) Shape, Contour, and Grouping in Computer Vision. LNCS, vol. 1681, pp. 58–71. Springer, Heidelberg (1999)
8. Liu., T.L., Geiger, D.: Approximate tree matching and shape similarity. In: Proceeding of the IEEE International Conference on Computer Vision, Corfu, Greece, pp. 456–462 (1999)
9. Sharvit, D., Chan, J., Tek, H., Kimia, B.B.: Symmetry-based indexing of image database. J. Visual Commun. Image Representation 9(4), 366–380 (1998)
10. Siddiqi, K., Bouix, S., Tannenbaum, A., Zuker, S.W.: The Hamilton-Jacobi Skeleton. In: Proceeding of the IEEE International Conference on Computer Vision, Corfu, Greece, pp. 828–834 (1999)
11. Xie, J., Heng, P.A., Shaha, M.: Shape matching and modelling using skeletal context. Pattern Recognition 41, 1756–1767 (2008)
12. Goh, W.-B.: Strategies for shape matching using skeletons. Computer Vision and Image Understanding 110, 326–345 (2008)

13. Carlsonn, S., Sullivan, S.: Action Recognition by shape matching to Key Frame. In: Workshop on Models versus Exemplars in Computer Vision at CVPR (2001)
14. Kellokumpu, V., Pictikanen, M., Heikkila, J.: Human Activity Recognition Using Sequences of Postures. In: IAPR Conference on Machine Vision Applications (MVA 2005), Tsukuba Science City, Japan, pp. 570–573 (2005)
15. Huang, L., Wan, G., Liu, C.: An improved parallel thinning algorithm. In: ICDAR, vol. 02, p. 780 (2003)
16. Jang, B.K., Chin, R.T.: One-pass parallel thinning: analysis, properties, and quantitative evaluation. IEEE Transactions Pattern Analysis and Machine Intelligence 14(11), 1129–1140 (1992)
17. Schuldt, Laptev, Caputo: Proc. ICPR 2004, Cambridge, UK (2004)
18. Achard, C., Qu, X., Mokhber, A., Milgram, M.: A novel approach for recognition of human actions with semi-global features. Machine Vision and Applications 19, 27–34 (2008)
19. Ronse, C.: Pixel simple et nombres de Yokoi, LSIIT URM 7005 CNRS-ULP, Département d'informatique (2007),
    http://arthure.u-strasbg.fr/~ronse/TIDOC/index.html
20. Djahromi, A.K.: Binary Image Processing, Department of Electrical Engineering University of Texas at Arlington,
    http://www-ee.uta.edu/Online/Devarajan/ee6358/BinaryImage.pdf

Detection and Tracking of Driver's Hands in Real Time

Raúl Crespo, Isaac Martín de Diego, Cristina Conde, and Enrique Cabello

Face Recognition and Artificial Vision Group, Universidad Rey Juan Carlos.
C. Tulipan, S/N, 28934, Mostoles, España
{raul.crespo.soto,isaac.martin,cristina.conde,
enrique.cabello}@urjc.es

Abstract. In this paper a complete driver's hands detection and tracking system suitable for working in real time conditions has been developed. The proposed system has been successfully tested in close-real world conditions in different scenarios on a very realistic and immersive cabin truck simulator. A database of 24 video sequences monitoring the driving task in different circuits, illumination conditions and video resolutions has been obtained. The hands detection rate and the computational times needed to process each frame are presented. The proposed system has proven to be high accurate and fast enough to work in real time conditions. In the future, the selected algorithm will be included as part of an automotive compliance embedded system placed in a real truck cabin.

Keywords: Image Processing, Real Time, Tracking, Automotive Application.

1 Introduction

Driver's distraction is involved in 30% of the car accidents and is responsible of a lot of fatalities every year [1]. To study driver's distractions is a very difficult problem due to the high number of factors involved in the distraction-related accidents [2]. One of the most important of these parameters is the driver behavior that could be study analyzing the position of his/her hands.

There are three elements that compose an accident: vehicle, road, and driver. Among these three elements, human factor is the one that has received least attention in the past. Vehicle manufacturers have increased security measures, both active and passive. Roads have improved its quality: received new layers of asphalt, better signaling, together with more appropriate driving design. Several approaches to supervise the driving task using computer vision techniques have been presented during the last years. A driver hand supervising system based on artificial vision techniques has been presented in [3]. The hands were detected by fitting a geometrical model to them and tracking was done based on an extended Kalman Filter. Although graphical results were shown in some videos, no numerical data were presented. In addition the tests were obtained with a parked car with changes in lighting. In [4], a vision system has been proposed for the analysis of the driver's behavior based on 3D tracking of the driver's head and hands. In this case, several cameras were used. First, basic information regarding hands position was retrieved, whether the hands were placed on the wheel or not, and where the driver's gaze is set: left, right, or forward. This basic

I. Bloch and R.M. Cesar, Jr. (Eds.): CIARP 2010, LNCS 6419, pp. 212–219, 2010.

information was put together to generate a high level response. In order to determine the position of the hands, a semi supervised system was used. This system removed the background from color images and has been completely described in [5]. A method for head tracking has been developed in [6]. The main idea was to combine a static model with a 3D estimation in real time based on a tracking system. Various graphic results were presented, showing that the tests were undergone outdoors. Although it was indicated that the algorithm performs in real time, hand detection tests only reached six frames per second (fps). The objective of this the present work is to develop a hand driver supervision system with a low computational cost that allows the system to work in real time conditions, and to test it in realistic conditions. This supervision is done with a non-intrusive technical setup, using an infrared lighting system (invisible to the human eye) and a charge-coupled device (CCD) camera. The output of this system will be a signal indicating if the hands are placed on the steering wheel or in other areas of interest. Most of the alternative hands detection methods are based on the skin detection using color information. However, in our problem the color information is lost due to the special light conditions of our framework.

The rest of the paper is organized as follows: in Section 2, we describe the technical setup and the database acquisition. Section 3 presents the proposed algorithms to hand detection and tracking. The results on several videos sequences obtained from a cabin truck simulator are described in Section 4. Finally, Section 5 summarizes the conclusions and future work.

2 Technical Setup

CABINTEC ("Intelligent cabin truck for road transport") is an ongoing project focused on risk reduction for traffic safety [7]. One of the main objectives of CABINTEC is to identify driver's unsuitable behavior and lacks of attention. The data base considered in this paper was obtained in a very realistic and immersive cabin truck simulator (see [8] for a complete description). The cabin is a real cabin truck placed over pneumatically devices, so real movements are reproduced. The frontal and lateral views are covered by scene projectors synchronized with the driving activities. The rear mirrors are computer screens showing the rear objects. Sound simulation helps to be focused on driving actions, recreating a natural driving situation. The acquisition setup is shown in Figure 1. The whole system is very compact and is placed in the top of the truck cabin. Although in the experimental configuration shown all elements are visible, in the final configuration all elements were covered. The proposed system consists of three infrared illuminators and a CCD camera. One of the illuminators is focused on the left hand of the driver and the other two are placed up of the steering wheel with the CCD camera between them. Each of these two illuminators has a white diffuser in front of it. Illuminators emit a continuous beam of infrared light (850 nm wavelength), so it is not visible by the human eye. CCD camera captures only in its infrared-acquisition peak, using a filter that removes visible information and allows only the pass of infrared wavelength. CCD camera is a five megapixels resolution complementary metal-oxide-semiconductor (CMOS) sensor and has a maximum

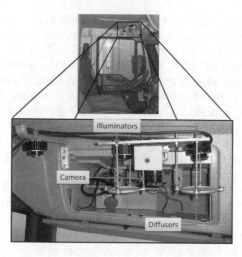

Fig. 1. Experimental setup of the camera, the illuminators and diffusers

Fig. 2. Sample image taken from camera

bandwidth of 14 frames per second at full resolution. Resolution of the camera can be selected between several standard formats, in our case 352x288, 640x480 and 1024x768 are allowed modes.

Figure 2 shows a sample image acquired by the camera. Camera height is 80 cm on the driving wheel but its field of view includes the complete steering wheel, gear change and hand brake levers, GPS, instrument panel and part of the copilot seat.

2.1 Data Base Description

In order to collect the database, an experimental design considering four factors was built: driving scenario, number of illuminators, number of diffusers, and resolution sizes. Two driving scenarios were selected in the simulator: an urban path and a road between two cities (interurban path). Following the indications of the professional driver, no gloves were considered during the experiment. Hands motion while driving strongly depends on the kind of scenario, so the system response was deeply analyze in each case. Half of the sequences come from each scenario. Four illumination conditions were tested: three illuminators with two diffusers (3I2D), three illuminators with no diffusers (3I0D), two illuminators with two diffusers (2I2D) and two illuminators with no diffusers (2I0D). For each illumination condition, three resolution sizes were selected: 352x288, 640x480 and 1024x768. Each video sequence can be easily identified knowing the scenario (urban-interurban); illumination conditions (3I2D, 3I0D, 2I2D, 2I0D) and image resolution (352x288 - 640x480 - 1024x768). A total of 24 video sequences were obtained. The time length of each sequence was at least seven minutes. The average number of fps acquired is 25.6 for 352x288 image size, 12.4 for 640x480 and 5.7 for 1024x768.

To obtain the "ground truth", that is, the real position of the driver's hands, all images were manually labeled by two independent experts. The number of driver hands in each region was stored. When contradictory labels were obtain (for example, the first expert determines two hands on the steering wheel area, but the second expert determines only one hand), the opinion of a third expert was considered.

3   Detection and Tracking Methods

Three algorithms to detect the driver's hands have been developed. The first algorithm, *Global Threshold Detection* (GDT), makes a sequential search in the regions of interest (ROI) previously defined. It has been considered that the most important ROI is the steering wheel region. The most efforts (such as fit of relevant parameters) are focused on this region. The main difference between GDT and the second proposed algorithm, *Local Threshold Detection* (LTD), is the information taking into account to binaries the steering wheel area. In the GDT method a global adaptive threshold that considers the whole image is done. In the LTD method the steering wheel area has been divided into four quadrants, and a different local threshold is considered for each quadrant. Finally, in the third proposed algorithm, *Local Threshold Detection with Tracking* (LTD-T), a tracking module has been added to the LTD method.

3.1   Global Threshold Detection (GDT)

This algorithm performs a search of the hands on the steering wheel ROI, and if no-hands are detected, a search on other ROIs such as gear charge and hand brake levers. First, a binarization on the steering wheel ROI is calculated. Next, a logical "and" operator is applied to the mask of the steering area and the binarized image. As a result, the occlusions on the steering area are obtained. Notice that the number of these occlusions is, in general, higher than two (the desirable number). Next, for each occlusion, we search the associated area in the binarized image. These areas are called candidates. Usually, this step eliminates errors such as shine from the steering wheel. To calculate the final points, called endpoints, several methods of discrimination between candidates are used. The candidates with size lower than a threshold were eliminated. If the distance between adjacent candidates were lower than a threshold, the candidates were merged in a unique candidate. If only one candidate remains, it is considered an endpoint, that is, a hand has been detected. If two candidates remain, it is necessary to determinate whether they correspond to one or two hands. To do that, the centers of the ellipses containing each candidate are obtained. The ellipse which major axis is the distance between these centers is built. If the percentage of the area inside the new ellipse corresponding to candidates is higher than a threshold, it means that the two candidates correspond to the same hand. For instance, this is the case of a hand and an arm "separated" for a watch. If the percentage of the area inside the new ellipse corresponding to candidates is lower than the threshold, it means that the two candidates correspond to different hands. This is the case of two hands placed in separated steering wheel areas. In the particular case when two hands were not detected, a search in other ROIs was carried out: the gear lever and the truck hand brake were the considered ROIs. To develop such searches we calculate the difference between the image in the ROI and the background image calculated when the hands were on the steering wheel. An illustrative example of the GDT algorithm is presented in Figure 3.

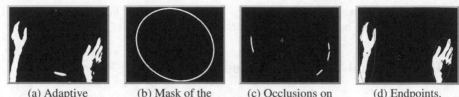

| (a) Adaptive Threshold result. | (b) Mask of the steering wheel area. | (c) Occlusions on the steering wheel. | (d) Endpoints. |

Fig. 3. Steps of the GDT algorithm for a sample image

3.2 Local Threshold Detection (LTD)

In this algorithm a new method to binarize the steering wheel area is proposed. In this case local thresholds are considered for each part of the wheel, making the system more adaptive to changing illumination. The ROI of the steering wheel is divided into four quadrants as shown in Figure 4(a). Different thresholds are calculated for each quadrant. Then, each of these quadrants is locally binarized with their local thresholds. As experiments will show in Section 4, this change reduces the processing time of the algorithm without worsening the GDT detection results. Furthermore, the LTD method obtains candidates with more smooth edges than those obtained when GDT algorithm was used (see Figure 3(d) and Figure 4(c), as example).

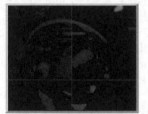
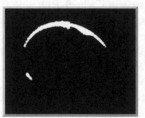

| (a) ROI divided in four quadrants. | (b) Initially the segmentation fail because the threshold levels are unknown. | (c) Binarization with the correct threshold. |

Fig. 4. Steps of the LDT algorithm for a sample image

3.3 Local Threshold Detection with Tracking (LTD-T)

In order to improve the LTD algorithm, a simple and soft tracking module based on Camshift algorithm [9] has been integrated. As a first step of the LTD-T algorithm, we detect the hands with the LTD method previously described. Once we know the hand positions, the well known Camshift algorithm is used for the tracking step. If hands are lost during the tracking step, the LTD method is used to detect them again. In order to define the model of the object to track, the Camshift algorithm needs a segmented image as parameter. To obtain this image the difference between the actual frame and the image mode is used. To control the performance of the algorithm, the detection step is executed even when the hands are not missed in the tracking step. This control is developed each 20 frames, that is, approximately once per second.

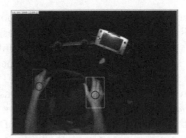

Fig. 5. The tracking windows of LTD-T algorithm

Given the robustness of the LTD algorithm, if the detection step and the tracking step locate the hands in different positions, only the detection step location is considered.

4 Experiments and Results

The performance of the three proposed algorithms was analyzed in the close-real world conditions of the 24 video sequences described in Section 2. The hand detection results are presented in Table 1. For each frame of the videos, the ground truth defined in Section 2 was compared with the detection results (number of hands in the ROI) of each algorithm for that frame.

Table 1. Hands detection results, percentage of success, for GDT, LTD and LTD-T algorithms in all the proposed configurations (2I0D: 2 illuminators and 0 diffusers, 2I2D: 2 illuminators and 2 diffusers, 3I0D: 3 illuminators and 0 diffusers, 3I2D: 3 illuminators 2 diffusers)

		Interurban				Urban			
		2I0D	2I2D	3I0D	3I2D	2I0D	2I2D	3I0D	3I2D
GDT									
	352 x 288	7	13	90	87	43	23	83	84
	640 x 480	75	12	98	93	69	81	86	88
	1024 x 768	92	19	93	90	71	43	90	85
LTD									
	352 x 288	88	70	91	90	70	58	83	82
	640 x 480	96	96	98	93	68	83	81	88
	1024 x 768	92	76	77	61	56	42	81	52
LTD-T									
	352 x 288	79	71	91	94	61	64	83	83
	640 x 480	96	97	94	91	75	76	84	85
	1024 x 768	89	83	88	86	76	43	89	94

In general, 3 illuminators schemes outperform 2 illuminators schemes. No significative differences were observed between 0 and 2 diffusers. In the interurban circuit 0D configuration seems to be better, but in the urban circuit 2D configuration seems to outperform 0D. As expected, the results in the interurban circuit are slightly better than the results in the urban circuit. The driver moved his hands most frequently in the urban than in the interurban scenario in order to response to the circuit design: curves, traffic signs, etc. Regarding image size, the best results were obtained for the 640x480 configuration. As a global conclusion the best configuration corresponds to: 3I0D and 640x480 image size. For the GDT method the best overall detection result for interurban circuit was achieved for 3I0D and 640x480 image size configuration (98%). For the urban circuit case, the best accuracy was achieved for 3I0D and 1024x762 image size (90%). As in the GDT algorithm, for the LTD method the best detection result for interurban circuit was achieved for 3I0D and 640x480 image size configuration (98%). For the urban circuit case, the best result was achieved for 3I2D and 640x480 image size (88%). For the LTD-T method the best result for interurban circuit was achieved for 2I2D and 640x480 image size configuration (97%). For the urban circuit case, the best result was achieved for 3I2D and 1024x762 image size (94%). Notice that increasing the image resolution the performance is not generally improved.

As a resume, the LTD-T method obtains better results than GDT method in 14 of 24 configurations. In addition the LTD-T method is better than LTD method in 16 of 24 sequences. If we considered as significative difference between detection percentages those higher than 5%, LTD-T algorithm outperforms GDT algorithm in 9 configurations. GDT outperforms LTD-T only in 1 configuration. In 14 configurations no significative differences were observed. Using the same definition of significative difference, the LTD-T method outperforms LTD method in 8 configurations. LTD outperforms LTD-T only in 3 configurations. In 13 configurations no significative differences were observed. That is, LTD-T algorithm improves GDT and LTD algorithms in most of the configurations analyzed.

The average computational times needed to process each frame in a PC (CORE 2 DUO 3.00 GHz) are presented in Table 2. For all the image sizes, the faster algorithm is LTD, and the slowest algorithm is GTD. As expected, the LTD-T algorithm is slightly slower than the LTD algorithm. The main reason of this difference is that when the LTD-T algorithm misses some of the hands during the tracking step, an additional detection step is needed to recover the hands. That is, for the same frame, two procedures are performed.

Table 2. Average time in milliseconds needed to process each frame

	352 x 288	640 x 480	1024 x 768
GDT	12	23	102
LTD	3	7	18
LTD-T	8	17	41

5 Conclusions and Future Work

In this paper, a complete system of driver's hands detection and tracking is presented. Three different algorithms have been developed and tested in a large database acquired in a high realistic truck simulator, close to real world conditions. The performance of each algorithm has been tested in different illumination conditions and image resolutions. The LTD-T algorithm gives the most complete information: not only allows the detection of the hands on the ROIs but the position of the hands on the complete image is known in each frame. The algorithm can automatically detect and track the hands in real time. Regarding the detection task, the LTD-T improves the GDT and the LTD methods. With the appropriate illumination and resolution, the accurate of the system is higher than 90%. Most of the errors were due to hands passing over each other during heavy turns of the steering wheel. As future work, the LTD-T algorithm will be included as part of an automotive compliance embedded system to be set in a real truck cabin. An alert will be given when the LTD-T algorithm detects a lack of attention regarding the hands position. In addition, the system will consider other signals such as head position in face images.

Acknowledgements

Supported by the Minister for Science and Innovation of Spain through the projects CABINTEC: PSE-37010-2007-2 and VULCANO: TEC2009-10639-C04-04.

References

1. Dingus, T., et al.: The 100-Car Naturalistic Driving Study. Virginia Tech Transportation Institute, NHTS (2006)
2. Zhang, H., Schreiner, C., Zhang, K., Torkkola, K.: Naturalistic use of cell phones in driving and context-based user assistance. In: Lew, M., Sebe, N., Huang, T.S., Bakker, E.M. (eds.) HCI 2007. LNCS, vol. 4796, pp. 273–276. Springer, Heidelberg (2007)
3. McAllister, G., McKenna, S.J., Ricketta, I.W.: Tracking a driver's hands using computer vision. In: IEEE International Conference on Systems, Man, and Cybernetics (2000)
4. Tran, C., Trivedi, M.M.: Driver Assistance for "Keeping Hands on the Wheel and Eyes on the Road". In: IEEE International Conference on Vehicular Electronics and Safety (2009)
5. Tran, C., Trivedi, M.M.: Introducing XMOB: Extremity Movement Observation Framework for Upper Body Pose Tracking in 3D. In: IEEE Int. Symp. on Multimedia (2009)
6. Murphy-Chutorian, E., Trivedi, M.M.: HyHOPE: Hybrid Head Orientation and Position Estimation for Vision-based Driver Head Tracking. In: IEEE Int. Vehicles Symposium (2008)
7. Brazalez, A., Delgado, B., Sevillano, M., Garcia, I., Matey, L.: Cabintec: Cabina inteligente para el transporte por carretera. In: Proc. VIII Cong. Esp. Sist. Int. de Transporte (2008)
8. Siordia, O.S., Martín de Diego, I., Conde, C., Reyes, G., Cabello, E.: Driving risk in, classification based on experts evaluation. In: Proceedings of the 2010 IEEE Intelligent Vehicles Symposium, IV 2010 (2010)
9. Bradski, G.R.: Computer vision face tracking for use in a perceptual user interface. Intel Technology Journal, 2nd Quarter (1998)

Speaker Verification in Noisy Environment Using Missing Feature Approach

Dayana Ribas[1], Jesús A. Villalba[2], Eduardo Lleida[2], and José R. Calvo[1]

[1] Advanced Technologies Application Center (CENATAV), 7a ♯ 21812 e/ 218 y 222,
Rpto. Siboney, Playa, C.P. 12200, La Habana, Cuba
[2] Communications Technology Group (GTC), Aragon Institute for Engineering
Research (I3A), University of Zaragoza, Spain
{dribas,jcalvo}@cenatav.co.cu, {villalba,lleida}@cenatav.co.cu

Abstract. In order to handle speech signals corrupted by noise in speaker verification and provide robustness to systems, this paper evaluates the use of missing feature (MF) approach with a novel combination of techniques. A mask estimation based on spectral subtraction is used to determine the reliability of spectral components in a speech signal corrupted by noise. A cluster based reconstruction technique is used to remake the damaged spectrum. The verification performance was evaluated through a speaker verification experiment with signals corrupted by white noise under different signal to noise ratios. The results were promising since they reflected a relevant increase of speaker verification performance, applying MF approach with this combination of techniques.

1 Introduction

Dealing with noisy signals is a fact in real life, background noise can markedly degrade performance of any speaker verification system. In order to handle environmental noise to improve the robustness of verification performance, many techniques have been proposed [1]. Most of them were originally designed and applied in speech verification application. MF method [2] is an example of that.

MF approach is a group of techniques developed to compensate for noise. Unlike other compensation methods MF does not require to know a priori the characteristics of noise to handle unknown noise. Because of that, it has a lot of potential to ensure robustness in speaker verification applications which process speech signals acquired in noisy environmental conditions with unknown features. This situation is very frequent in real applications.

The MF approach has two steps. The first determines the level of noise corruption in each time-frequency region of speech spectrum to set up a map of binary labels called spectrographic mask. The mask tags as unreliable *(U)* the time-frequency spectral components that are so corrupted by noise that can cause poor verification performance, and tags as reliable *(R)* the time-frequency spectral components that are not very corrupted by noise. The second step is compensation of unreliable region, it could be bypassing the spectral unreliable locations in the verification process, known as marginalization, or reconstructing

I. Bloch and R.M. Cesar, Jr. (Eds.): CIARP 2010, LNCS 6419, pp. 220–227, 2010.

unreliable spectrum location and keeping the verification process with the new reconstructed spectrum.

Until now, most of the MF development has occurred on the speech verification field, while only a few works have been done on speaker verification [3][4][5][6]. This work presents a novel combination of MF techniques for robust speaker verification with noisy speech. To estimate the MF mask we proposed the use of SNR criterion. For MF compensation we proposed to use a reconstruction method which estimates U components from R ones. This kind of reconstruction has not been previously used for speaker verification. We evaluate the performance impact of this MF setup through speaker verification experiment in noisy environments.

From now on, this paper is organized as follows. Section 2 describes mask estimation technique. Section 3 explains the MF compensation technique used. Section 4 presents speaker verification experiments and results. Finally, section 5 a discussion of results and conclusions.

2   Mask Estimation

The success of the MF approach in providing robustness to speaker verification system will depend on the mask accuracy [2]. To estimate the masks, the SNR criterion is the most widely used in previous works because of SNR-based masks are very easy to compute [7].

In this paper we proposed, as MF detector, the identification of U spectral components based on spectral enhancement technique used frequently in speech processing. This approach was applied to MF mask estimation in the previous work [8]. This is an effective technique in the detection of corrupted components that is known as Negative Energy Criterion.

This method uses a frame by frame spectral subtraction algorithm as MF detector and is based on an estimated noise spectrum. The reliability decision of spectral components is done following this rule:

$$\begin{array}{llll} |Y(f,s)|^2 \leq |\hat{N}(f,s)|^2 & then & Y(f,s) \leftarrow U \\ |Y(f,s)|^2 > |\hat{N}(f,s)|^2 & then & Y(f,s) \leftarrow R \end{array} \tag{1}$$

where, f and s are the frame (time) and subband (frequency) spectrographic representation of the signal power spectrum, respectively. If the power spectrum in a component is less than the estimated noise power spectrum in it, this component is assumed as U, otherwise the component is tagged as R.

3   Cluster-Based Reconstruction

Until now, most speaker verification systems using the MF approach, to improve performance in noisy environments, have been based on modifying the classifier to work with the reliable components of the spectrographic representation of the speech signal. That is the case of the works of Drygajlo et al. [8] or Padilla et al.

[3]. In these systems, the unreliable log-Mel spectral components are integrated out of the GMM distributions to get the speaker likelihood. This technique is known as marginalization.

Marginalization has several drawbacks. On the one hand, recognizers are constrained to use Mel spectral features that are known to produce worse performance than Mel frequency cepstral coefficients (MFCC). On the other side, by using incomplete spectrographic data we are not able to apply certain feature processing steps that are known to improve considerably the results. These processing steps include mean normalization, feature warping [9] or added time derivatives .

For these reasons, in this paper we are taking an alternative approach by trying to estimate the true values of the unreliable spectrographic components from the reliable ones. Once we get the complete time frequency representation of the signal, we are able to compute MFCC features, and apply whatever postprocessing step to the features. Besides, we do not need to modify the recognizer so we can use anyone at our disposal. The algorithm we have chosen to compensate for the U components is cluster-based reconstruction which has proven to be very effective in speech verification tasks as it is reported in the work of Raj et al. [10] [11].

3.1   The Algorithm

The Cluster-based Reconstruction (CBR) algorithm estimates the U components of the spectral vector from the R ones of the same vector using a statistical model that relates both of them. This method is based on the assumption that the sequence of observations is an independent, identically distributed random process. This assumption is used by the most successful text independent speaker verification approaches too. Therefore, it is expected to have good results for MF compensation in speaker verification systems.

This algorithm models the distribution of log-Mel spectral vectors for clean signals as a mixture of Gaussian distributed clusters. The mean, covariance and a priori probability of each cluster can be estimated from a training corpus using maximum likelihood estimation via the expectation maximization (EM) algorithm [12].

Let Y be the noisy spectral vector and X the reconstructed spectral vector and let Y_r, X_r and Y_u, X_u be their R and U components respectively. The first step to compensate for the U components is to determine the noisy vector probability of belonging to each cluster. This is given by

$$P(k|Y) = \frac{w_k P(Y|k)}{\sum_{j=1}^{k} w_j P(Y|j)} \tag{2}$$

where w_k is the a priory cluster probability.

To calculate the term $P(Y|k)$ we have to take into account that Y has R and U components, and that $X_r = Y_r$ and $X_u \leq Y_u$ for additive noises. Therefore we can evaluate the Gaussian distribution in the R components and integrate out the U ones. This integration supposes additive noise so, the estimated U components need to be less than the measured components

$$P(Y|k) = P(X_r, X_u \leq Y_u|k) = \int_{-\infty}^{Y_u} P(X_r, X_u|k)dX_u \qquad (3)$$

If we suppose that the covariance matrices are diagonal this can be written as

$$P(Y|k) = \Pi_{i|X_i \epsilon X_r} \frac{1}{\sqrt{2\pi}\sigma_{ki}} exp(-\frac{1}{2}\frac{(X_i - \mu_{ki})^2}{\sigma_{ki}^2}) \times$$
$$\Pi_{i|X_i \epsilon X_u} \frac{1}{2}(1 + erf(\frac{Y_i - \mu_{ki}}{\sqrt{2}\sigma_{ki}})) \qquad (4)$$

where erf is the Gauss error function.

We can get an estimation of the clean value of the unreliable components from each cluster based on its distribution maximizing its likelihood given the measured reliable and unreliable components as

$$\hat{X}_u^k = \arg \max_{X_u} \{P(X_u|k, X_u \leq Y_u, X_r = Y_r)\} \qquad (5)$$

Assuming diagonal covariance matrices this can be reduced to

$$\hat{X}_u^k = min(Y_u, \mu_{kr}) \qquad (6)$$

where μ_{kr} is the Gaussian means of the unreliable components of the associated cluster.

Finally, we can get the overall unreliable components using the posterior membership probabilities to combine, by a weighted sum, the unreliable components estimations given by each cluster.

$$\hat{X}_u = \sum_{k=1}^{K} P(k|Y)\hat{X}_u^k \qquad (7)$$

Once we have recovered the full Mel spectral vector, we are able to calculate the MFCC with their time derivatives and apply any preprocessing technique we need prior to the recognizer input.

4   Experiments and Results

In order to evaluate the behavior of the MFs techniques combination in front of corrupted signals, a speaker verification experiment was carried out using the 1conv4w-1conv4w task of the 2006 NIST SRE [13].

4.1   Detection and Compensation of Unreliable Components

To implement the mask estimator based on spectral subtraction we used the classical algorithm of Berouti et al. [14] and the noise estimator of Martin work [15].

The noisy signals were segmented with 25 msec. Hamming window overlapped 15 msec. and passed through 24 Mel filters bank. Then, noise estimator was applied, taking decision of reliability presented in equation 1, to obtain the un-reliable components of the noise corrupted speech.

Once the mask estimation was done, the Cluster-based Reconstruction algo-rithm makes an estimation of the unreliable components. These reconstructed log-Mel spectra are then used to calculate the MFCC features that will be the input to the speaker verification system.

4.2   Speaker Verification Protocol

In this task, the enrollment and test utterances contain around 2 minutes of speech after voice activity detection. There are a total of 810 target models with 3176 true trials and 42079 false trials. It has used clean speech to train the target models and contaminated test signals with different levels of white noise selected to get several mean SNR, from 5 to 20 dB.

Our acoustic features are 15 MFCC plus first and second derivatives and C0 derivatives resulting in a total of 47 features. On the one hand, we have got results using no feature normalization at all to prove the capacity of our MF approach to cope with noise on its own. On the other hand, we have repeated the experiments using feature warping over 3 seconds in order to proof the benefits of being able to use feature normalization techniques together with the MF approach.

A gender dependent Universal Background Model (UBM) of 512 Gaussians is used. This model is trained using NIST SRE 2004 database containing 124 male and 184 female speakers with several utterances each one of them. The means of target models are adapted from the UBM using relevance MAP [16]. Classi-fication is performed evaluating the log-likelihood ratio between the target and the UBM model for the test signal. Gender dependent cluster models for CBR are trained from the same dataset as UBM using different number of Gaussians.

4.3   Results

The first experiment we have conducted was intended to determine the optimal number of Gaussians needed for reconstruction. For that purpose, we have got results comparing baseline and MF cluster-based reconstruction with different number of clusters between 64 and 1024 using test signals contaminated with a SNR of 10 dB. The experiment has been repeated using feature warping and no feature normalization. In Table 1, we show the equal error rate (EER) and improvement percentage relative to the baseline of this experiment.

Figure 1 shows DET curves using no feature normalization and feature warp-ing respectively, results with number of cluster over 256 are not plotted in order to preserve clarity.

We have got an amazing improvement when no feature normalization is ap-plied nearly reaching clean signal performance. When using feature warping the challenge is bigger, but MF achieves a considerable improvement. The great ca-pacity of feature warping of increasing robustness against channel mismatch,

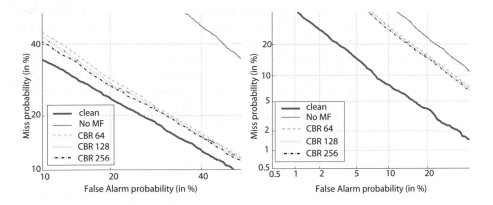

Fig. 1. DET curves to SNR=10 dB (left), with features normalization (right)

Table 1. EER and Improvements to SNR = 10 dB

	No Feat. Norm.		Feat. Warp.	
	EER(%)	Δ(%)	EER(%)	Δ(%)
clean	22.3		8.7	
No MF	42.9	0	21	0
CBR 64	25.2	41.2	17.7	15.4
CBR 128	24.7	42.4	17.4	17.1
CBR 256	24.2	43.6	17.1	18.6
CBR 512	24.9	41.9	16.8	20
CBR 1024	24.3	43.5	17.3	17.6

Table 2. EER and Improvements to SNR = 5-20 dB

SNR(dB)	20	15	10	5
EER(%) No MF	29.8	36.9	42.9	46.8
EER(%) MF	21.8	22.5	24.2	29.5
Δ(%)	26.8	39	43.6	36.9
Feature Norm.				
EER(%) No MF	13.37	16.95	21	27.2
EER(%) MF	11.5	13.5	17.1	22.5
Δ(%)	14.5	20.3	18.6	17.28

additive noise or even headset non-linearity it is well known. As a matter of fact, most sites participating in NIST evaluations use it in their systems. As we can see in Table 1, feature warping on its own is able to provide better results than MF compensation alone. That means it does a great deal of the same job as MF does. However, the benefits of using both techniques together are not negligible producing around a 17 percent of improvement compared to using feature warping only. This encourages us to think reconstruction of missing spectral component is the right path to follow in order to take advantage easily of the existing techniques to build robust speaker verification systems.

Results show there is little improvement as we increase the number of clusters getting the best performance with 256 with no feature normalization and 512 with feature warping. We have found there is no improvement if we use more clusters. This could be explained by the fact that if we increase the number of clusters, they become more similar among them. Considering that cluster membership is estimated using only the reliable components of the spectrogram, it becomes more difficult to select precisely the best cluster as the number of clusters rises.

We have repeated the experiment using signals contaminated with SNR between 5 and 20 dB. This time we have used only 256 clusters, what seems a good choice given the previous results. In Table 2, we give a summary of the obtained results. We have got interesting improvements for all SNR tested. Something curious we note is that with no feature normalization and a SNR of 20 dB EER outperforms clean signal one. We expected a more important decrease of the improvement with low SNR due to the fact that we have less reliable components to make the spectral reconstruction but results are quite good.

5   Conclusions and Future Work

In this paper the proposed MF techniques combination has shown its potentiality in providing robustness for speaker verification systems. The results obtained with MF alone or in combination with feature normalization produced an important increase of verification performance. It is convenient to highlight some ideas:

Improvement obtained in speaker verification results show that SNR criterion is an effective method when trying to obtain the reliability of the corrupted speech spectral components. However the enhancement of SNR contributes to increase speech quality, but does not necessarily ensure the improvement of verification performance, so in the future we will focus on criteria that use representative speaker features. We will evaluate mask estimation methods based on spectral features classification such as Seltzer et. al work [11].

Since mask estimation is the prior step in MF approach, we do not lose sight of the MF compensation step. In this work we have used a reconstruction technique originally designed for speech verification. We must take into account the fact that we have used speaker independent cluster models. This means that reconstructed features will be made more speaker independent too. In speaker verification applications this is a great drawback. Despite that, results show improvements since noise compensation is more important than the effect of using speaker independent models. Nevertheless, we think we could get even better results using cluster models adapted to the test signal. Future work will be oriented in that direction.

On the other side, we must take into account the fact that GMM distributions with diagonal covariance matrices have limited correlation information between features. In future work, we plan to perform MF reconstruction using more complex distributions that should be able to perform a more precise estimation of the U components values. Examples of these models are GMM with full covariance matrices or graphical models [17]. Graphical models have the capacity of modeling correlations between features or groups of features at any level of complexity, what can be very promising for the MF approach.

Acknowledgements

This work has been supported by the Spanish Government through national project TIN2008-06856-C0504.

References

[1] Benesty, J., Chen, J., Huang, Y., Cohen, I.: Noise Reduction in Speech Processing. Springer Topics in Signal Processing 2 (2009)

[2] Raj, B., Stern, R.: Missing-Feature Approaches in Speech Recognition. In: IEEE Signal Proc. Magazine (2005)

[3] Padilla, M., Quatieri, T., Reynolds, D.: MF Theory with Soft Spectral Subtraction for Speaker Verification (2006)

[4] Ming, J., Hazen, T., Glass, J.R., Reynolds, D.A.: Robust Speaker Recognition in Noisy Conditions. IEEE Trans. on Speech and Audio Proc. 15, 1711–1723 (2007)

[5] Pullella, D., Kuhne, M., Togneri, R.: Robust Speaker Identification Using Combined Feature Selection and Missing Data Recognition. In: ICASSP (2008)

[6] Kuhne, M., Pullella, D., Togneri, R., Nordholm, S.: Towards the use of full covariance models for missing data speaker recognition. In: ICASSP (2008)

[7] Cerisara, C., Demange, S., Haton, J.-P.: On noise masking for automatic missing data speech recognition: a survey and discussion. Computer Speech and Language 21(3), 443–457 (2007)

[8] Drygajlo, A., El-Maliki, M.: Speaker Verification in Noisy Enviroments with Combined Spectral Subtraction and MF Theory. In: Signal Proc. Laboratory, Swiss Federal Institute of Technology at Lausanne (1998)

[9] Pelecanos, J., Sridharan, S.: Feature warping for robust speaker verification. Speaker Odyssey (2001)

[10] Raj, B., Seltzer, M., Stern, R.M.: Reconstruction of MFs for robust speech recognition. Speech Communication 43 (2004)

[11] Seltzer, M., Raj, B., Stern, R.M.: A Bayesian classifier for spectrographic mask estimation for MF speech recognition. Speech Communication 43 (2004)

[12] Dempster, A.P., Laird, N.M., Rubin, D.B.: Maximum likelihood from incomplete data via the EM algorithm. Journal of the Royal Statistical Society (1977)

[13] The NIST year, speaker recognition evaluation plan (2006), http://www.nist.gov/speech/tests/spk/2006/index.htm

[14] Berouti, M., Schwartz, R., Makhoul, J.: Enhancement of speech corrupted by acoustic noise. In: IEEE ICASSP (1979)

[15] Martin, R.: Noise Power Spectral Density Estimation Based on Optimal Smoothing and Minimum Statistics. IEEE Trans. on Speech and Audio Proc. 9 (2001)

[16] Reynolds, D., Quatieri, T., Dunn, R.: Speaker Verification Using Adapted Gaussian Mixture Models. Digital Signal Proc. 10 (2000)

[17] Bilmes, J.: Graphical Models and Automatic Speech Recognition. Mathematical Foundations of Speech and Language Proc., 191–235 (2004)

Fast k-NN Classifier for Documents Based on a Graph Structure

Fernando José Artigas-Fuentes[1], Reynaldo Gil-García[1],
José Manuel Badía-Contelles[2], and Aurora Pons-Porrata[1]

[1] Center of Pattern Recognition and Data Mining
Universidad de Oriente, Santiago de Cuba, Cuba
{artigas,gil,aurora}@csd.uo.edu.cu
[2] Computer Science and Engineering Department
Universitat Jaume I, Castelló, Spain
badia@uji.es

Abstract. In this paper, a fast k nearest neighbors (k-NN) classifier for documents is presented. Documents are usually represented in a high-dimensional feature space, where their terms are treated as features and the weight of each term reflects its importance in the document. There are many approaches to find the vicinity of an object, but their performance drastically decreases as the number of dimensions grows. This problem prevents its application for documents. The proposed method is based on a graph index structure with a fast search algorithm. Its high selectivity permits to obtain a similar classification quality than the exhaustive classifier, with a few number of computed distances. Our experimental results show that our method can be applied to problems of very high dimensionality, such as Text Mining.

Keywords: nearest neighbor classifier, fast nearest neighbor search, text documents.

1 Introduction

Text classification is the task of assigning documents to one or more predefined classes. This task relies on the availability of an initial set of text documents classified under these classes (known as training data). Classification falls at the crossroads of information retrieval, pattern recognition and data mining, that involves very large data sets. Moreover, the dimensionality of the text documents is usually large. Therefore, it is crucial to design algorithms which scale well with the dimension.

The k nearest neighbor (k-NN) classifier is a very simple and popular approach used in classification [1], but it has the problem of the exhaustive computation of distances to training objects. Several methods have been proposed in order to avoid this problem. One approach involves improving the access methods combining appropriate index structures, such as trees or graphs, with fast search algorithms. But, in the most of cases, their performance drastically decrease

I. Bloch and R.M. Cesar, Jr. (Eds.): CIARP 2010, LNCS 6419, pp. 228–235, 2010.

as the number of dimensions grows. This problem is known as "the curse of dimensionality" [2], and prevents its application for text documents.

Several exact methods have been proposed for objects with high dimensionality, such as VA-File [2], VA+-File [3], IQ-tree [4] and more recently VQ-index [5]. The main purpose of those methods is to overcome the I/O disk bottleneck, which is crucial in large databases. Those methods were tested on relative high dimensional spaces, with 32, 64, 200 and 500 dimensions. However the main purpose of our proposal is to work over spaces with several thousands of dimensions, as arise in the case of text documents. In this case we can deal with more than 30.000 dimensions with a relatively small set of text documents.

On the other hand, several fast search algorithms have been proposed by Arya et. al in [6], and others, such the optimal nearest neighbor algorithm for data structures that are stored in main memory.

However, for very high dimensionality most of those methods have a performance as bad as a linear scan, or even worse. Recall that a linear scan does not scale well when the set of objects to search is large or the relationship function (distance, similarity or dissimilarity function) is hard to compute.

Different relaxations on the precision of the result have been proposed in order to obtain a computationally feasible solution in those cases. This kind of methods perform an inexact proximity searching, as opposed to the classical exact proximity searching. Inexact proximity searching is possible in many applications because the preprocessing of data already involves an approximation to reality, and therefore a second approximation at search time is acceptable. Examples of those methods can be found in [7,8].

In [9] an approximated classifier for mixed data was presented. This method uses a tree index structure and a fast search algorithm. It obtains the information necessary to classify while searching. Even when the accuracy of the classification obtained for mixed data is high, it decreases when applied to documents.

In this paper, we introduce a fast k-NN classifier for text documents based on a graph index structure with an approximate k nearest neighbors fast search algorithm. Its high selectivity and precision permits to obtain a similar classification quality than the exhaustive classifier, with a few number of computed relationships. Our experimental results show that it is feasible the use of the proposed method in problems of very high dimensionality, such as Text Mining.

The rest of the paper is organized as follows: Our proposed classifier is presented in Section 2. The obtained experimental results over Reuters Corpus Version 1 (RCV1-v2) are presented in Section 3. Finally, in Section 4, we present some conclusions and future work.

2   Proposed Classifier

In this section, an approximate fast k-NN classifier for documents is introduced. The classifier consists of two phases. In the first phase, the graph structure, using training set T, is constructed. In the second phase, novel documents are classified.

2.1 Preprocessing Phase

The main idea of this phase is to build an index structure based on a connected graph. This graph must fulfils the following conditions:

- Each vertex corresponds to a different and unique training document (represented by it features vector).
- Each edge represents a relationship value between two vertices calculated by a similarity, dissimilarity or distance function Ψ.
- Each vertex v has, at least, ϕ adjacent vertices, were ϕ is an integer value preset by the user. Those vertices correspond with the ϕ nearest neighbors of v.
- Vertices are connected forming triangles of minimum area.
- A small number of vertices are fixed and used as possible entry points to the structure during the search phase.

In [10] the algorithm to build the graph index structure was introduced, whereas in [11] some improvements in order to reduce the time cost to build it were presented.

It is important to describe how the triangles of the graph are built. For this access method, there are two ways to perform this task.

The simple way is to connect first the most Ψ-related pair of documents in the training set TS. This pair of documents are used to obtain the first two vertices and the first edge of the graph. Then, the rest of documents in TS are candidates to be connected to this pair in order to obtain the third vertex of the first triangle. To do that we calculate the *media object* of this pair of vertices. It is obtained by adding each dimension of original objects and inserted into the set of media objects MOS. Then, the most Ψ-related pair formed by a candidate and a member of MOS is computed, and the candidate of this pair is selected as the next vertex. Following a similar iterative process new media objects for the new edges are calculated and inserted into MOS, and the rest of documents become candidates to be connected into the graph.

The second method to build the triangles reduces the number of candidates to be considered in each iteration to obtain the new vertex to be connected into the graph. This improvement also reduces the total time to generate the index structure. In this case, the documents in TS are previously sorted by their relationship with the global centroid GC. This centroid is calculated in the same way of media objects, but using all documents in TS.

Then, the sorted set of documents is divided into a number of equal sized subsets. As result we obtain a sequence of subsets ordered by its decreasing relationship with GC. Next, the first subset is selected as the current one (CS). In this way, on each iteration, we only consider as candidates to become new vertices those belonging to CS. When all candidates have been connected, the next subset becomes CS, and the next iteration begins. This process continues until all documents are connected into the graph.

To guaranty the ϕ condition, if any vertex results with less than n of adjacent vertices, that vertex is connected with its other $\phi - n$ nearest neighbors. The ϕ nearest neighbors of all documents are calculated and kept in a previous stage.

Finally, vertices belonging to the borders of the region defined by the graph are selected as entry points to the structure (See [10,11] for details). Those vertices are called as Entry Points Set (EPS). This is the main difference of this access method: the index structure has several entry points, while methods based on trees have only one entry point to the structure, the root.

2.2 Classification Phase

In this phase, given the index structure G previously built, the classes associated with the documents in the training set, and a novel document d to be classified, our classifier finds its k nearest neighbors, according with Ψ, and assigns to d its majority class.

The classification involves three main stages:

1. The k nearest neighbors of the novel document are searched.
2. The votes of classes are counted, using a vote rule.
3. Finally, the classification is performed using a decision rule.

In the first main stage, the fast search algorithm proposed in [10] and improved in [11] is used. It has three steps, in the first one a proper entry point EP_d to G for the current search d is selected. This choice can be different for each d and it must be the most Ψ-related to d of the members of EPS. EP_d is calculate in an exhaustive way, and it becomes the current solution (NN).

In the second step of the search the current nearest neighbor vertex to d is found. This task is performed by traversing the index structure following the edges of graph. The next solution is the most Ψ-related adjacent vertex of NN to d, if it is better than the current one. The process ends when there is no new NN. The problem is that it is not always possible to obtain the nearest neighbor. In a few cases an approximated one must be obtained.

In order to improve the quality of k-NN, a variation of the search algorithm and a prune rule were introduced in [11]. The variation involves selecting the best results of three independent searches of the k-NN, using three different entry points to the index structure. This solution increases the number of comparisons computed during searches. To avoid this problem the pruning rule that increases the selectivity of the search algorithm, avoiding extra computations was used.

In the last step of the search, if $k > 1$, the other $k - 1$ neighbors of d are obtained. This task is performed using another algorithm described in [10]. It also traverses the edges of the graph, but using as initial point the actual (or approximated) NN calculated in the previous step. Besides, the algorithm keeps in each iteration a vector with the current list of k nearest neighbors.

After finding k-NN, the votes of each class are counted and the majority class is assigned to d.

3 Experimental Results

In this section, the results of applying the proposed fast approximate k-NN classifier are presented.

To perform our experiments, we use the well-known benchmark collection Reuters Corpus Version 1 (RCV1-v2) [12]. This collection has a set of documents represented as vectors. The feature vector for each document was produced from the concatenation of text in the <headline> and <text> XML elements. Text was reduced to lower case characters, after which tokenization, punctuation removal and stemming, stop word removal, term weighting, feature selection, and length normalization was applied. The LYRL2004 partition, with 23.149 training, and 781.265 testing vectors, was used.

Classes files of both training and test sets were modified to avoid overlapping among classes. The resulting sets belong only to four non-overlapped classes: ECAT, CCAT, MCAT and GCAT. This modification was necessary because the other fast approximated classifier implemented (FC) to compare with our proposal (FGC) do not support class overlapping. A k-NN exhaustive classifier (EC) was implemented too, and was used as base line of the comparison.

First, a 10% of training documents (692) documents were randomly chosen to build index structures for both FC and FGC classifiers, while maintaining the distribution of the class probabilities in the original training and test sets. The representation space obtained has 8.731 dimensions.

FC is a k-NN classifier [9] that uses an index structure based on a tree. Each node of the tree contains a certain number of elements selected using a grouping algorithm. In the original paper, the authors present and use a new clustering algorithm called *CMFS*, which is an extension of the C-Means algorithm [13], but in our experiments we used both *CMFS* and the well-known *K-Means* [14].

Besides, FC requires additional parameters to build the tree. The minimal number of objects in a node was fixed to 20, the maximum number of clusters by level was fixed to 5, and the maximum number of iterations of the clustering algorithm was fixed to 10. The authors used three stop conditions to determine the leaf nodes. But, we use only the last two conditions based on non-homogeneous (noHomo) and homogeneous (Homo) nodes. In the case of our proposal, the value of ϕ was fixed to 50.

We select a small number of training documents due to the cost of *CMFS* when applied to grouping objects with an elevate number of dimensions.

The Ψ used was a distance function based on the well-known cosine similarity ($\Psi(d_1, d_2) = \sqrt{1 - cos(d_1, d_2)}$), were d_1 and d_2 are the documents to be compared, which is the most widely used to compare documents in text mining. This measurement reaches its minimum value at 0 and maximum at 1. All the classifiers use the same vote rule.

All the algorithms were implemented using Python 2.5 over an Intel(R) Core(TM)2 Quad CPU, 2.50 GHz and 3GB of RAM with Linux Mandriva 2009 OS.

For the classification phase, 500 documents from the test set were randomly selected. The classification was carried out using the three classifiers: FC, FGC and EC. For FC, its authors offer two algorithms to search the approximates k-NN. But, we only show the results obtained using the KMSNLocal algorithm, because the results for the other were very similar.

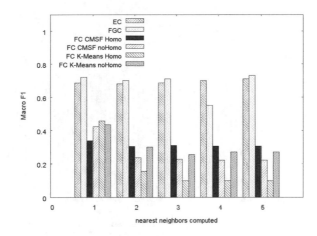

Fig. 1. A comparison of the quality of the implemented classifiers varying the number of nearest neighbors calculated

To compare the quality of classifiers, macro F1-measure was used. It is the average on the F1 scores of all the topics. The F1 score $(F1 = 2 \cdot \frac{precision.recall}{precision+recall})$ can be interpreted as a weighted average of the precision and recall, where an F1 score reaches its best value at 1 and its worst score at 0. Precision is the proportion of documents classified into a class that indeed belong to it, and recall is the proportion of documents belonging to a class that are indeed classified into this class. When quality is computed for several categories, the results for individual categories must be averaged in some way. Two methods may be adopted: micro-averaging and macro-averaging. Micro-averaging gives equal weight to every document, while macro-averaging gives equal weight to each category.

Figure 1 shows the macro-average F1 values obtained with the classifiers varying the number of nearest neighbors computed from 1 to 5. It can be seen that our classifier was better than FC in all cases. Surprisingly, our proposal even improves the EC classifier, although this uses an exact method to obtain the vicinity of document queries.

In order to investigate the cause of this behavior, we implemented a fourth classifier βFGC, based on FGC. Despite of the original, in the voting phase, for βFGC only those nearest neighbors with a relationship value greater than a certain threshold β are taken into account. We do the same change to EC and obtain a new base line classifier (βEC).

Figure 2 shows the quality of results when β has the values 0.75, 0.80, 0.85 and 0.90. For β values less than 0.90 the quality of βFGC are slightly worse than those of βEC. On the contrary, for β values greater than 0.90 it is slightly better. This results means that the previous strange behavior was provoked by the elements of the k-NN more distant to the queries. When all k-NN are taken into account, in most of the approximate results, the last elements found by our search algorithm belongs to the actual classes of queries despite of the elements found by EC.

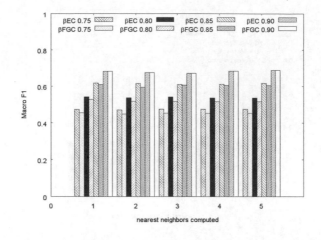

Fig. 2. A comparison between βEC and βFGC varying β parameter

Another aspect that we consider to evaluate our proposal, was the time required to classify documents. The best improvement obtained as consequence to use our access method based on a graph was the dramatical reduction of the number of distances computed to obtain the k-NN against the 100% needed by the EC. Table 1 shows the time cost and the best quality in classification obtained by EC, FC and our proposal FGC.

Table 1. Summary of best results for each classifier

Parameter	EC	FC	FGC
Time (s)	60.06	1.20	14.53
Macro-average F1	0.71	0.45	0.73

As you can see, FC is very fast, but its results are not good for documents classification. On the other hand, our proposal obtains good results in a reasonable time.

4   Conclusions

In this work, an approximated fast k-NN classifier for text documents, a problem with a very high dimensionality, was proposed. In order to compare our method, different variants of a fast k-NN classifier were implemented using the same distance function to compare documents, and the same vote and decision rules for classification. An exhaustive classifier was used as base line. Experimental results show that our proposal obtains high quality results, better than the state-of-the-art classifiers presented.

Our method reduces drastically the time of the exhaustive classifier, while obtaining very similar or even better classification quality results. This behaviour is due to the use of an index structure based on a connected graph and a fast search algorithm.

References

1. Myles, J.P., Hand, D.J.: The Multi-Class Metric Problem in Nearest Neighbor Discrimination Rule. Pattern Recognition 23, 1291–1297 (1990)
2. Schek, H., et al.: A quantitative analysis and performance study for similarity-search methods in high-dimensional spaces. In: VLDB 1998, New York, USA, pp. 194–205 (1998)
3. Ferhatosmanoglu, H., et al.: High dimensional nearest neighbor searching. Information Systems 31, 512–540 (2006)
4. Berchtold, S., et al.: Independent quantization: An index compression technique for high-dimensional data spaces. In: Proc. 16th Int. Conf. on Data Engineering, San Diego, CA, pp. 577–588 (2000)
5. Tuncel, E., et al.: VQ-Index: An Index Structure for Similarity Searching in Multimedia Databases. In: 10th ACM International Conf. on Multimedia 2002, Juan Les Pins, France, pp. 543–552 (2002)
6. Arya, S., et al.: An optimal algorithm for approximate nearest neighbor searching. In: 5th Ann. ACM-SIAM Symposium on Discrete Algorithms, pp. 573–582 (1994)
7. Chávez, E., et al.: Effective proximity retrieval by ordering permutation. In: IEEE Trans. on Pattern Analysis and Machine Intelligence, TPAMI 2007, vol. 30(9), pp. 1647–1658 (2008)
8. Figueroa, K., Fredriksson, K.: Speeding up permutation based indexing with indexing. In: SISAP 2009, pp. 107–114. IEEE Computer Society, Los Alamitos (2009)
9. Hernández-Rodríguez, S., et al.: Fast Most Similar Neighbor Classifier for Mixed Data Based on a Tree Structure. In: Rueda, L., Mery, D., Kittlel, J. (eds.) CIARP 2007. LNCS, vol. 4756, pp. 407–416. Springer, Heidelberg (2007)
10. Artigas-Fuentes, F., et al.: Vicinity calculation with graph in text mining. In: Genolet, F. (ed.) UCT, vol. 48, pp. 1–10 (2008)
11. Artigas-Fuentes, F., et al.: A High-dimensional Access Method for Approximated Similarity Search in Text Mining. In: ICPR 2010 Congress, Istanbul, Turkey (2010)
12. Lewis, D.L., et al.: RCV1: A new benchmark collection for text categorization research. Journal of Machine Learning Research 5, 361–397 (2004)
13. Yu, J.: General C-Means Clustering Model. IEEE Trans. on Pattern Analysis and Machine Intelligence 27(8), 1197–1211 (2005)
14. MacQueen, J.: Some Methods for Classification and Analysis of Multivariate Observations. In: Proc. 5th Berkeley Symp. Math. Statistics and Probability, vol. 1, pp. 281–297 (1967)

Comparative Analysis between Wavelets for the Identification of Pathological Voices

Náthalee Cavalcanti[1], Sandro Silva[1], Adriano Bresolin[2],
Heliana Bezerra[1], and Ana Maria G. Guerreiro[1]

[1] UFRN, Federal University of Rio grande do Norte, Brazil
nathalee.telecom@gmail.com, sandro@ct.ufrn.br,
heliana@ufrnet.br, anamaria@dca.ufrn.br
[2] UTFPR, Federal Technological University of Paraná, Brazil
aabresolin@utfpr.edu.br

Abstract. This study presents a comparative analysis of wavelets, in order to find a descriptor that provides a better classification of voice pathologies. Different types of Wavelet Packet Transform were used as a tool for feature extraction and Support Vector Machine (SVM) to classify vocal disorders. Tests were conducted with 23 wavelets types in two SVMs, the first using the strategy "one vs. all" to classify normal and pathological voices and the second, using the strategy "one vs. one" to classify pathologies: edema and nodules. The best results were obtained using Daubechies family, especially Daubechies 5 (db5) wavelet.

Keywords: Vocal disorder, Wavelet Packet Transform, Support Vector Machine (SVM).

1 Introduction

Pathological voices have become a social concern, since the voice and speech are important in certain professions as teachers, speakers, singers, and quality of life in general. Moreover, the voice is an important tool of communication.

There is a great range of diseases that causes modifications in the voice. They could appear as a modification of the excitation morphology (the distribution of mass on vocal fold is increased). These are classified as organic pathologies as nodules, polyps, cysts and edemas. Voice disorders can also be caused by other pathologies which are provoked by neuro-degenerative diseases [1], [2].

The presence of pathologies in the vocal folds such as nodules, polyps, cysts and paralysis of laryngeal nerves can be corrected by: voice therapy, surgery, and in some cases, radiotherapy [3]. But not always vocal diseases cause necessarily changes in voice quality level perception of listeners.

Digital signal processing techniques have been used by acoustic analysis, as an effective noninvasive tool for diagnosing changes in sound production caused by diseases of the larynx, the voice classification of diseases and their pre-detection, aiding, this way, the development of the therapeutic process [4].

I. Bloch and R.M. Cesar, Jr. (Eds.): CIARP 2010, LNCS 6419, pp. 236–243, 2010.

The aim of this paper is to present a comparative analysis of wavelets, used as input attributes of support vector machines, which will be responsible for classification of pathological voices. The vocal pathologies considered in this study were edemas and nodules.

Several studies on pattern recognition have used wavelet packet descriptors in the stage of feature extraction [5]-[7], but have not yet conducted studies on which the wavelets perform better in the classification of laryngeal pathologies.

The wavelet transform has been an important tool in signal and imaging processing to determine not just "which" frequency, but also "where" these frequencies are located [8].

The Wavelet Packet Transform has been used in recent years in signal processing allowing better classification of signs. This technique is used as a tool to extract features of signals from one or more dimensions improving the performance of the classifiers to extract relevant features through decomposition of signals in different frequency bands. In this work, we decide to use the Packet Wavelet Transform, which is a generalization of Discrete Wavelet Transform.

The SVM has aimed at building optimal hyperplanes which have the largest margin of separation between classes. The generated hyperplane is determined by a subset of points in classes, named support vectors. SVMs were used as a tool for classification of normal and pathological voices.

The main contribution of this paper is the application of these tools in the classification of pathological voices.

This paper is organized as follows: Section 2 presents the signal pre-processing phase. Section 3 shows the speech feature extraction through Wavelet Packet Transform. In Section 4, is the procedure of training and validation SVM. Section 5 shows the experiments and results in 10 tests with 23 types of wavelets.

2 Signal Pre-processing

The signal pre-processing is composed of several processes such as filtering, pre-emphasis, normalization and windowing. The aim of this step is to eliminate noise, discontinuities and any effects that might affect system performance.

The speech signals used in this work are a sustained vowel /a/. Initially, the voice signal is passed through a bandpass filter with a cutoff frequency of 80 Hz and 9 kHz, which will eliminate the signal frequencies above 9 kHz and the noise of the electric grid (60 Hz). After that, the speech signal is pre-emphasized to equalize the spectrum of the speech signal and improve the spectral analysis performance [9]. The value of pre-emphasis filtering in time domain is 0.97. In the normalization step, the speech signal is normalized by the maximum value of its amplitude.

Finally, the speech signal is broken into time frames at intervals of 16 to 32 ms, so that the signal during this interval is considered stationary. Aiming to standardize and reduce the amount of processing and storage, the window width was set at 20 ms, overlapping 33 percent. According to Stephen Levison [10], overlapping 25 percent is mathematically optimal, but experiments in this study the superposition of 33.3% had a better cost benefit due to reduced numbers of windows and the consequent reduction of processing time without significant loss of performance. Each frame is multiplied by Hamming window in order to minimize any signal discontinuities in the time domain, i.e to reduce abrupt transitions at the end of the signal.

3 Wavelet Packet Transform

The Wavelet Transform is used to analyze the non-stationary phenomena, such as voice. The bases of this transform are analyzed in the time domain and frequency domain and their algorithms process information at different scales, managed to get an image or a sign of a general and detailed way [11].

Through the wavelet can be seen that there are significant differences between normal voices and voices with nodules as shown in Fig. 1.

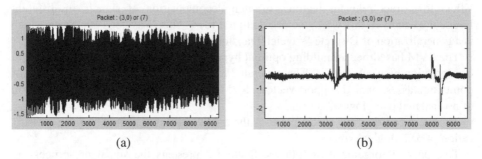

(a)   (b)

Fig. 1. (a) Signal of normal voice and (b) Voice Signal with Nodule

The Wavelet Transform Packet type used in this work is a generalization of the Discrete Wavelet Transform. Discrete Wavelet analysis on the signal is divided into approximation and detail coefficients, although only the approximation coefficients are divided again [12]. In both Wavelet Packet coefficients of approximation and the details are decomposed at each level as shown in Fig 2.

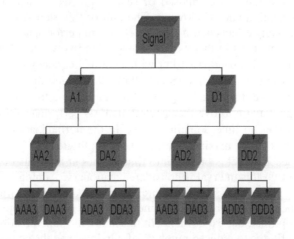

Fig. 2. Binary tree Wavelet Packet Transform with 3 levels of decomposition

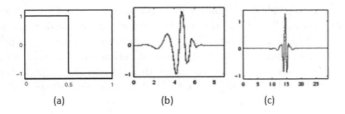

Fig. 3. Wavelets Mothers: (a) Haar; (b) *Daubechies* 5; (c) *Coiflet* 5

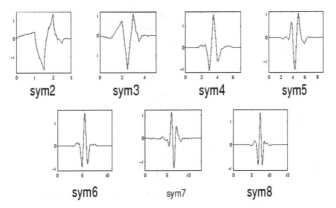

Fig. 4. Symlets Wavelets Examples

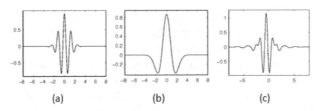

Fig. 5. (a) Morlet; (b) Mexican Hat; (c) Meyer

With this transform is possible to extract relevant characteristics of the signal, improving the classifiers performance by decomposing the speech signal into different frequency bands.

Depending on the characteristics of the signal to be analyzed, a different mother wavelet can be used. In Fig 3, 4 and 5 show kinds of wavelets used in the experiments. They are: Haar, Daubechies (db), Coiflets, Symlets, Morlet, Mexican Hat and Meyer.

4   SVM Classifier

Support Vector Machines (SVMs) is a technique based on statistical learning theory. This strategy was introduced by Vapnik in [13].

The SVM finds a single hyperplane with maximum margin of separation is denoted by δ. This hyperplane lines located between H1 and H2, and will be great if the distance to the two lines is maximum. The H1 line defines the edge or border of objects of class +1, while H2 line determines the edge or border with the objects of the class -1. Two objects Class +1 define the boundary line H1 and H2 to the border there are three objects of class -1. These objects are called Support Vectors (Fig. 6).

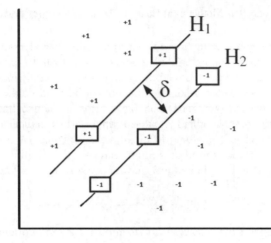

Fig. 6. Formation of the separation hyperplane through the support vectors

Basically, SVM maps the input space into a high dimensional space and from the calculation of an optimal separating hyperplane in this new space, the SVM learns the boundary between regions belonging to two classes. This separation hyperplane is chosen so that it maximizes the separation between the closest training samples [14].

Fig. 7. shows the SVMs used for pathological voices classification, where the first machine uses the strategy "one vs. all" (normal x all) and the second machine is used if the first machine has classified certain voice to "All", i.e, unable to determine the type of pathology. This second machine uses the strategy "one vs. one" (edema x nodule).

Each of the two machines can be considered as a binary classifier, they present as a result only 2 hypotheses: (+1) that corresponds to the first class and (-1) corresponding to the second class trained.

If the first machine (normal against all) presents the result +1 then the unidentified pattern is classified as normal. On the other hand, if the answer machine is -1 then the unknown pattern is classified as "all" or "not normal".

To identify pathologies is used machine 2 with strategy "one against one" that is "edema against nodule". The same as machine 1, if the SVM 2 presents +1 as result, the pathology is classified as edema, if the result is -1, nodule is the correct classification of the pathologies.

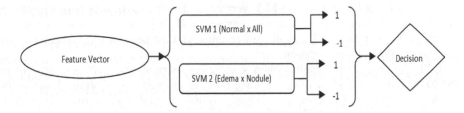

Fig. 7. SVM for three classes classification: Normal, Edema and Nodules

5 Experiments and Results

In this article are considered three classes: normal (normal voice, with no pathology in the vocal folds), edema (voices with vocal folds edema) and nodule (voices affected with nodules on vocal cords).

The database consists of 26 voices among which 10 with healthy voices, 10 presenting edemas in the vocal folds and 6 with nodules.

To form the feature vector were used coefficients obtained through the Wavelet Packet Transform. These data were used as input of SVMs. For each test performed, a new mother wavelet was tested to find that had better results.

Table 1. Performance Evaluation of two support vector machines

Wavelet type	SVM 1 %SR mean	SVM 2 %SR mean
Daubechies 1	97,7	98,44
Daubechies 2	96,62	98,32
Daubechies 3	97,81	97,46
Daubechies 4	98,46	98,66
Daubechies 5	98,68	98,75
Daubechies 6	98,14	97,68
Daubechies 7	98,36	98,04
Daubechies 8	97,89	98,46
Coiflet 1	92,74	96,81
Coiflet2	90,97	97,04
Coiflet3	91,03	97,08
Coiflet4	92,53	96
Coiflet5	97,03	96,57
Symlet 2	92,93	93,83
Symlet 3	96,95	94,8
Symlet 4	95,04	94,86
Symlet 5	91,46	94,18
Symlet 6	94	94,06
Symlet 7	91,56	95,18
Symlet 8	93,60	93,01
Morlet	93,81	92,48
Mexican Hat	92,57	85,99
Meyer	97,38	97,01

Two machines SVM 1 and SVM 2 were created. For each of these machines were carried out 10 tests with 23 different wavelets and their samples were chosen randomly, with 50 percent of samples for training and 50 percent for validation. This process is called cross-validation.

Table 1 shows the results when comparing normal and pathological voices (SVM 1) and pathological voices together (edema and nodules). Column 1 shows the mother wavelet used features descriptors. Columns 2 and 3 show the average performance of the device obtained after carrying out 10 tests. All results are expressed in success rate percentage (%SR).

The best results of classification for the two machines were obtained using wavelet Daubechies 5 with 98.68% in the first machine and 98.75% in the second machine. On machine 1, were obtained good results with the Daubechies wavelets (4, 7, 6, 8, 3 and 1) in ascending order of performance, followed by Meyer and Coiflet 5. On the second machine, the other Daubechies wavelets (4, 8, 1 and 2), followed by Coiflet 5 Wavelets.

These results show that the Daubechies families are a good descriptor of voice pathologies classification, especially Daubechies 5. Moreover, it can be observed that the Daubechies 5 is also quite effective in speech recognition as in [15].

6 Conclusions

This paper analyzes different types of mother wavelets as feature descriptors in the classification of voice pathologies.

The main objective of this paper was to find the mother wavelet which best classifies normal and pathological voices. We performed extensive testing with voices from different patients with normal voice, edema and nodules. Through the mean shown in Table I can be seen that that the best results were obtained using Wavelet Daubechies Familie, especially Daubechies 5 for both machines. With other types of wavelets, we obtained good results with Meyer and Coiflet 5.

Acknowlegment

The authors thank to CAPES by support financed given.

References

1. Davis, S.B.: Acoustic Characteristics of Normal and Pathological Voices. Speech and Language: Advances in Basic Research and Practice 1, 271–335 (1979)
2. Quek, F., Harper, M., Haciahmetoglou, Y., Chen, L., Raming, L.O.: Speech pauses and gestural holds in Parkinson's disease. In: Proc. of International Conference on Spoken Language Processing, pp. 2485–2488 (2002)
3. Martinez, C.E., Rufiner, H.L.: Acoustic Analysis of Speech for Detection of Laryngeal Pathologies. In: Proceedings of the 22nd Annual International Conference of IEEE Engineering in Medicine and Biology Society, Chicago, EUA, vol. 3, pp. 2369–2372 (2000)

4. Costa, S.C., Correia, S., Falcão, H., Almeida, N., Assis, F.: Uso da Entropia na Discriminação de Vozes Patológicas. In: II Congresso de Inovação da Rede Norte Nordeste de Educação Tecnológica, João Pessoa, Paraíba (2007)
5. Soares, H.B., Neto, A.D.D., de Carvalho, M.A.G.: Extration and Selection of Characteristics in Skin Lesions Images Using Wavelet in Multiresolution Analysis. In: ASME 2007 Summer Bioengineering Conference, SBC 2007 (2007)
6. Bresolin, A.A., Neto, A.D.D., Alsina, P.J.: Brasilian Vowels Recongnition using a New Hierarchical Decision Structure with Wavelet Packet and SVM. In: IEEE Intern. Conf. on Acoustics, Speech and Signal Processing. ICASSP 2007, vol. 2, pp. 493–496 (April 2007)
7. Kim, J., Cho, S., Choi, J.: Iris Recognition Using Wavelet Features. Journal of VLSI Signal Processing 38, 147–156 (2004)
8. de Almeida, N.C., Barros, J.D., Soares, H.B., Bresolin, A.A., Guerreiro, A.M.G., Brandão, G.B.: A new computational tool for voice analysis based on FFT, Wavelet Transform and Spectrogram. In: Proceedings of the ASME 2009 Summer Bioengineering Conference, SBC 2009 (2009)
9. Yang, S., Er, M.J., Gao, Y.: A high performance neural-networks-based speech recognition system. In: International Joint Conference on Neural Networks, IJCNN 2001, vol. 2, pp. 1527–1531 (July 2001)
10. Levison, S.C.: Mathematical Models for Speech Technology. John Wiley & Sons Ltd., West Sussex (2005)
11. Júnior, A.J.P., Castilho, J.E.: Um estudo comparative entre a Análise de Fourier e Análise Wavelet. FAMAT em Revista – Número 05- Setembro (2005)
12. Parraga, A.: Aplicação da Transformada Wavelet Packet na Análise e Classificação de vozes patológicas. UFRGS, Porto Alegre (2002)
13. Vapnik, V.N.: Principles of risk minimization for learning thoery. In: Advances in Neural Information Processing Systems, San Mateo, CA, vol. 4, pp. 831–838 (1992)
14. Haykin, S.: Redes Neurais: Princípios e Prática. 2a Edição, Porto Alegre, Editora Bookman (2001)
15. Bresolin, A.A., Neto, A.D.D., Alsina, P.J.: Digit recognition using wavelet and SVM in Brazilian Portuguese. In: Proceedings of IEEE International Conference on Acoustics, Speech and Signal Processing, ICASSP 2008, Las Vegas, USA, pp. 1545–1548 (2008)

Comparison of HMM and DTW for Isolated Word Recognition System of Punjabi Language

Kumar Ravinder

Department of Computer Science & Engineering,
Thapar Univeristy, Patiala – 147004 (India)
ravinder@thapar.edu

Abstract. Issue of speech interface to computer has been capturing the global attention because of convenience put forth by it. Although speech recognition is not a new phenomenon in existing developments of user-machine interface studies but the highlighted facts only provide promising solutions for widely accepted language English. This paper presents development of an experimental, speaker-dependent, real-time, isolated word recognizer for Indian regional language Punjabi. Research is further extended to comparison of speech recognition system for small vocabulary of speaker dependent isolated spoken words in Indian regional language (Punjabi) using the Hidden Markov Model (HMM) and Dynamic Time Warp (DTW) technique. Punjabi language gives immense changes between consecutive phonemes. Thus, end point detection becomes highly difficult. The presented work emphasizes on template-based recognizer approach using linear predictive coding with dynamic programming computation and vector quantization with Hidden Markov Model based recognizers in isolated word recognition tasks, which also significantly reduces the computational costs. The parametric variation gives enhancement in the feature vector for recognition of 500-isolated word vocabulary on Punjabi language, as the Hidden Marko Model and Dynamic Time Warp technique gives 91.3% and 94.0% accuracy respectively.

Keywords: Dynamic programming (DP), dynamic time warp (DTW), hidden markov model (HMM), linear predictive coding (LPC), Punjabi language, vector quantization (VQ).

1 Introduction

Research in automatic speech recognition has been known for many years, various researchers have tried to analyze the different aspects of speech in Indian languages. Existing literature reveals that Punjabi (ਪੰਜਾਬੀ in Gurmukhi script) is highly phonetic language as compared to other national and international languages. Punjabi language is one of the popular and used north western India and in Pakistan. Gurmukhi script alphabet consists of 41 consonants and 10 vowels (laga matra), two symbols for nasal sounds (bindī and ṭippī), and one symbol which duplicates the sound of any consonant (addak) with writing style from left to right. Three consonants are used in Punjabi as conjuncts.

I. Bloch and R.M. Cesar, Jr. (Eds.): CIARP 2010, LNCS 6419, pp. 244–252, 2010.

Recently "British researchers have used the Punjabi language to help narrow down the identity of writers and develop a technique that could profile criminal authors of documents [1]. In consecutive phoneme that has immense variation, end point detection is highly difficult. However in time-domain equation the deviation of preemphasis filter enhances filtering of end point detection.

As indicated in figure 1, the speech recognition system contains four components: end point detection, linear predictive coding (LPC) processor, statistical-pattern-recognition techniques HMM /DTW and recognition process [2] [3]. The speech recognition has two algorithmic procedures to deal with the non-stationary speech signals: the temporal alignment technique and markov modeling. The time warping technique is combined with linear predictive coding analysis in DTW approach. In HMM approach, well known techniques of vector quantization and hidden markov modeling are combined with a linear predictive coding analysis. The DTW approach uses the nearest neighbor (NN) decision rule and HMM uses the maximum likelihood (ML) decision rule.

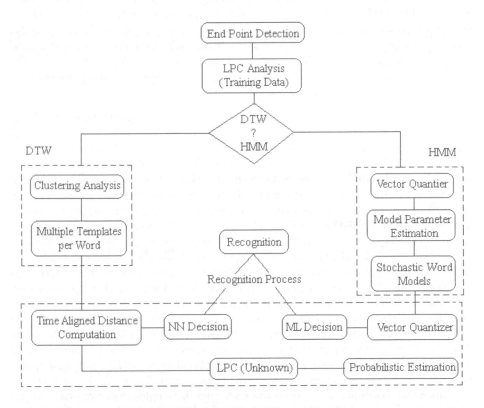

Fig. 1. Block diagram of Speech Recognition System

These methods display certain superficial similarities, as a result of which, it has occasionally been claimed that they are identical. From the simulation, it is clear that the methods are not identical. While their overall performances are comparable, they appear to make different errors, and involve different amounts of computation and different complexities of training. This recognition system is implemented using Visual C++ with Multimedia API in Windows environment. The speech is recorded in the form of wave file using RIFF structure. The proposed system speech has to be sampled at 6.67 kHz, 16 kHz sampling frequency, sampling size 8 bit on mono channel and recording of a single word within limit 3000 milliseconds. Threshold energy 10.1917 dB is used in the word detection [4] [5] [6].

The organization of this paper is as follows. In section II, the system model is used for endpoint detection and feature extraction. Further, section III elaborates working of HMM and DTW approaches on Punjabi language. In section IV, experimental performance has been conducted and compared. Finally section V provides the concluding remarks.

2 System Model

2.1 End point Detection

The significant effort on the implementation of speech recognition is the problem of extricating background silence before and after the input speech. To find, the energy of the speech signal *Wave (s) s=48000*, it is formatted into blocks of 10 ms and each block, we define *Wave (n) is, n(1..160)* to be the nth sample in the block. The log energy E_s of a block of length N samples is

$$E_s = 10*\log 10(\in + \frac{1}{N}\sum_{n=1}^{N} Wave^2(n)) \qquad (1)$$

Where $\in = 1.0\ e - 007$ is a small positive constant added to prevent the computing of log zero. Hence, log energy E_s is used for end point detection [7].

2.1 LPC Feature Analysis

To compute LPC feature analysis involves the following operation for each speech frames [2].

Preemphasis: The digitized speech signal is processed by a first order digital network in order to spectrally flatten the recorded signal *Wave(s)*.

$$pre(s) = Wave(s) - \alpha Wave(s-1) \qquad (2)$$

$$Where\ \alpha = 0.9731$$

Blocking into frames: Here N is consecutive speech samples (we use N=320 corresponding to 20 ms of signal) are used as a single frame. Consecutive frames are spaced M sample apart (we use M = 160 corresponding to 10ms frame spacing or 20ms frame overlap) and L is the number of frames in voiced speech word.

$$X(\ell)(n) = pre(M\ell + n) \qquad (3)$$

Frame Windowing: Each frame is multiplied by an N-samples window (we use Hamming window) so as to minimize the adverse effect of chopping N-sample out of the running speech signal.

$$W(\ell)(n) = (0.54 - 0.46\cos(\frac{2\pi n}{N-1}))X(\ell)(n), \tag{4}$$

Where $0 \leq n \leq N-1$ *and* $0 \leq \ell \leq L-1$

Autocorrelation Analysis: Each windowed set of speech samples is autocorrelated to a given a set of $(p + 1)$ coefficient, where p is the order of the desired LPC analysis (we use $p = 11$).

$$R(\ell)(k) = \sum_{n=0}^{N-1-k} W(\ell)(n)W(\ell)(n+k) \tag{5}$$

Where $0 \leq k \leq p$, $0 \leq n \leq N-1$ *and* $0 \leq \ell \leq L-1$

LPC/Cepstral Analysis: For each frame, a vector of LPC coefficients is computed from the autocorrelation vector using a Levinson-Durbin recursion method. An LPC derived cepstral vector is then computed up to the Qth component, where Q is the order of the cepstral coefficients and Q > k, Q = 11 used in this work.

Weighted Cepstral Coefficient: After computing cepstral coefficients, weight is given to them by multiplying them with cepstral weight. It will enhance the portion of the cepstrum in vocal tract information. The computation involved at this step is:

$$W_C(k) = 1 + \frac{Q}{2}\sin\left(\frac{\pi k}{Q}\right) \tag{6}$$

Where $0 \leq k \leq p$

$$WC_C(\ell)(k) = W_C(k) \cdot C_C(\ell)(k) \tag{7}$$

Where $0 \leq k \leq p$ *and* $0 \leq \ell \leq L-1$

Delta Cepstrum: The time derivative of the sequence of the weighted cepstral vectors is approximated by a first order orthogonal polynomial over a finite length window of $(2k+1)$ frames centered on the current vector. The value of $k = 2$ i.e., 5 frame window is used for computing the derivative). The cepstral derivative (i.e., the delta cepstral vector) is computed as

$$D_C(\ell)(m) = \left[\sum_{k=-K}^{K} k WC_C(\ell-k)(m)\right] \cdot G \tag{8}$$

Where $0 \leq m \leq Q$

Where *G* is a gain term chosen to make the variances of weighted cepstral coefficient and delta cepstral coefficient equal (A value of G of 0.375 was used.) [8] [9].

2.2 Vector Quantization

The VQ codebook is a discrete representation of speech. We will generate the codebook by using LBG algorithm. This algorithm has used two times, one is on training time and other is testing time. In training time we will generate codebook for delta cepstrum coefficients. In testing we will use stored codebook for getting the indices of codebook that give minimum distortion. The VQ will find a codebook index corresponding to the vector that best represents a given spectral vector, for an input vector sequence *V{v(1), v(2), v(3), ..., v(N)}*, VQ will calculate the vector distance between each vector in codebook *C{c(1), c(2), c(3), ..., c(P)}* and each vector *v(n)*, and the codebook index with minimum distance will be chosen as output. After VQ, a sequence of codebook indexes *I{i(1), i(2), i(3),...., i(N)}* will be produced. The vector distance between an input vector *v(n)* and each vector in codebook are calculated as follows:

$$Distance\ (p) = \sum_{k=1}^{k=11} [v(n)(k) - c(p)(k)]^2 \qquad (9)$$

$$i(n) = \arg\min_p (Distance\ (p)) \qquad (10)$$

The vector quantization codebook of size *p = 256* and vector length *k = 11* are used. This size selection is based on the experimental results [8] [10].

3 HMM and DTW for Isolated Word Recognition

Dynamic Time Warp approach and Hidden Markov approach for isolated word recognition of small vocabulary are implemented. The time warping technique is combined with linear predictive coding analysis and HMM approach used with vector quantization and hidden markov modeling are combined with a linear predictive coding analysis.

3.1 Hidden Markov Model

LPC analysis followed by the vector quantization of the unit of speech, gives a sequence of symbols (VQ indices). HMM is one of the ways to capture the structure in this sequence of symbols. In order to use HMM in speech recognition, we should have some means to achieve the following.

Evaluation: Given the observation sequence O=O_1, O_2,..., O_T, and the model λ =(A, B, π), how we compute Pr (O| λ), the probability of the observation sequence. The evaluation problem is efficient way of computing this probability using forward and backward algorithm.

Decoding: Given the observation sequence O=O_1, O_2 ,..., O_T, how we choose a state sequence I=i_1, i_2,..., i_T, which is optimal in some meaningful sense. The decoding helps to find the best matching state sequence given an observation sequence and solve using Viterbi algorithm.

Training: How we adjust the model parameters λ =(A, B, π) to maximize Pr (O| λ). The training problem resolved by Baum-Welch algorithm [11] [12][15].

3.2 Dynamic Time Warping

The DTW deals with features and distances (local and global) concept. To obtain a global distance between two speech patterns (represented as a sequence of vectors) a time alignment must be performed. Dynamic time warp alignment that simultaneously provides a distance score associated with the alignment. Consider a matrix with $N \times n$ (N reference, n input signal) and a local distance $l(i, j)$ which returns a distance associated with i, j (where i template of reference, j of input signal). Compute the shortest path with minimum distance from each cell of $N \times n$ matrix. This problem exhibits optimal substructure. The solution to the entire problem relies on solutions to sub problems. Let us define a function $g(i, j)$ as

$$g(i, j) = the\ minimum\ distance\ to\ reach\ at\ final\ (i,\ j)\ in\ N \times n$$

$$g(i,j) = \begin{cases} \infty & j < 1 \quad or \quad j > n \\ l(i,j) & i = 1 \\ \min(g(i-1,j-1), g(i-1,j), g(i-1,j+1)) + l(i,j) & otherwise \end{cases}$$

This is recursive process and global distance is the value at top most cell of the last column in matrix. On training time the database of the features LPC Coefficients of the training data is created. In testing time, the input pattern (features vector of the test token) is compared with each reference pattern. The distance scores for all the reference patterns are sent to a decision rule, which gives the word with least distance as recognized word. The distance measure between two feature vectors is calculated using Euclidean distance metric [13] [14][15].

4 Experimental Performance

4.1 Performance Based on Punjabi Numerals

The recordings were done for one male speaker. The experimental result gives incremented accuracy as increases the size of the codebook, but constantly increasing the complexity and time of recognition increases. So the codebook size of 256 for the comparison between DTW and VQ/HMM techniques is used. (Tested various size of code book but give more accuracy/time results optimized on only size of 256). The train the system for Punjabi numerals is the five times. The recognition results of numerals are show in figure 2.

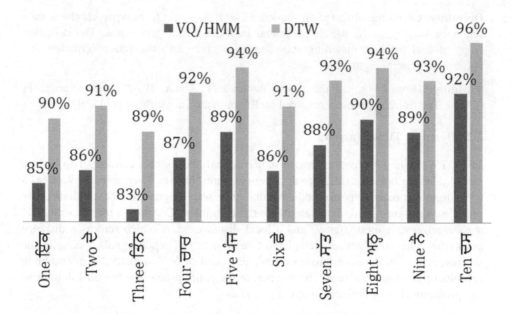

Fig. 2. Performance comparison of Punjabi numerals between DTW and VQ/HMM

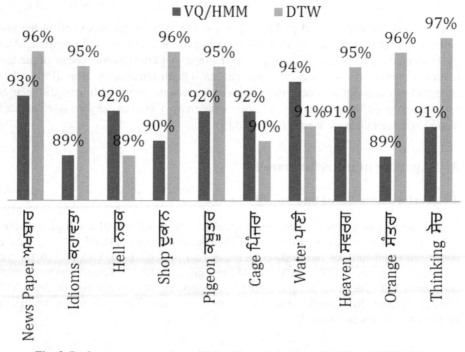

Fig. 3. Performance comparison of Punjabi words between DTW and VQ/HMM

4.2 Performance Based on Randomly Selected Words

The recognition vocabulary of Punjabi words (the English word "Newspaper" is translated and pronounced as "ਅਖਬਾਰ" in Punjabi language). The system for each of the words was trained with 10 utterances of the same word. The comparison for the performance of the VQ/HMM recognizer with DTW recognizer, a sub set of 10 randomly selected words from 500 trained words set was tested on both of the recognizers. The recognition accuracies of the VQ/HMM recognizer vs. DTW recognizer are as shown in figure 3.

5 Conclusion

Results carried out by above experiments reveal that performance of HMM recognizer is somewhat poorer than the DTW based recognizer because of the insufficiency of the HMM training data. However with the increase in the size of the codebook, the accuracy of the HMM based recognizer may improve but that will increases the complexity of the system. The time and space complexity of the HMM approach is less as compared to the DTW approach for same size of codebook because during HMM testing we have to compute the probability of each model to produce that observed sequence. In DTW testing, the distance of the input pattern from every reference pattern is computed, which is computationally more expensive. In experimental result the system gives very impressive performance for Punjabi language numerals with DTW is 92.3% and with HMM is 87.5%. The experimental research reveals that DTW approach is more appropriate for Punjabi numerals and isolated spoken words. Further, the results have also shown that the errors made by the two recognizers are largely disjoint. Hence there exist the potential of DTW using some fairly standard techniques for Punjabi Language as compared to HMM approach for better accuracy because is more phonetic as compared to other languages.

References

1. Prasun, S.: British experts use Gurmukhi to aid forensic research. In: Indo-Asian News Service, London. Hindustan Times (September 21, 2007)
2. Rabiner, L.R.: A Tutorial on Hidden Markov Models and Selected Applications in Speech Recognition. Proceedings of the IEEE 77(2), 257–286 (1989)
3. George, M.W., Richard, B.N.: Speech Recognition Experiments with Linear Prediction, Bandpass Filtering, and Dynamic Programming. IEEE Transaction on Acoustics, Speech, and Signal Processing ASSP-24(2), 183–188 (1976)
4. Bovbel, E.L., Kheidorov, I.E.: Statistical recognition methods, application for isolated word recognition. IEEE Transaction on Digital Signal Processing, 821–823 (June 1997)
5. Guan, C., Zhu, C., Chen, Y., He, Z.: Performance Comparison of Several Speech Recognition Methods. In: 1994 International Symposium on Speech, Image Processing and Neural Networks, Hong Kong, pp. 13–16 (April 1994)
6. Levinson, S.E., Rabiner, L.R., Sondhi, M.M.: Speaker Independent Isolated Digit Recognition Using Hidden Markov Models. In: International Conference on Acoustics, Speech, and Signal Processing, Paper 22.8, pp. 1049–1052 (April 1983)

7. Picone, J.W.: Signal Modeling Techniques in Speech Recognition. Proceedings of the IEEE 81(9), 1214–1245 (1993)
8. Rabiner, L., Juang, B.-H.: Fundamentals of Speech Recognition. Prentice Hall PTR, Englewood Cliffs (1993)
9. Bahl, L.R., Brown, P.F., de Souza, P.V., Mercer, R.L., Picheny, M.A.: A Method for the Construction of Acoustic Markov Models for Words. IEEE Transaction on Speech and Audio Processing 1(4), 443–452 (1993)
10. Soong, F.K., Rosenberg, A.E., Rabiner, L.R., Juang, B.H.: A Vector Quantization Approach to Speaker Recognition. In: Conference Record 1985 IEEE International Conference on Acoustics, Speech, and Signal Processing, Paper 11.4.1, pp. 387–390 (March 1985)
11. Rabiner, L.R., Juang, B.H., Levinson, S.E., Sondhi, M.M.: Recognition of Isolated Digits Using Hidden Markov Models with Continuous Mixture Densities. Bell System Tech. Jour. 64(6), 1211–1234 (1985)
12. Rabiner, L.R., Juang, B.H.: An Introduction to Hidden Markov Models. IEEE ASSP Magazine 3(1), 4–16 (1986)
13. Rabiner, L.R., Schmidt, C.E.: Application of Dynamic Time Warping to Connected Digit Recognition. IEEE Trans. on Acoustics, Speech, and Signal Processing ASSP 28(4), 377–388 (1980)
14. Myers, C.S., Rabiner, L.R., Rosenberg, A.E.: Performance Tradeoffs in Dynamic Time Warping Algorithms for Isolated Word Recognition. IEEE Trans. on Acoustics, Speech, and Signal Processing ASSP 28(6), 623–635 (1980); Smith, T.F., Waterman, M.S.: Identification of Common Molecular Subsequences. J. Mol. Biol. 147, 195–197 (1981)
15. Axelrod, S., Maison, B.: Combination of hidden markov model with dynamic time warping for speech recognition. In: Proceedings of the ICASSP, pp. 173–176 (2004)

A Combination of Classifiers for the Pronominal Anaphora Resolution in Basque

Ana Zelaia Jauregi, Basilio Sierra, Olatz Arregi Uriarte, Klara Ceberio, Arantza Díaz de Illarraza, and Iakes Goenaga

University of the Basque Country
ana.zelaia@ehu.es

Abstract. In this paper we present a machine learning approach to resolve the pronominal anaphora in Basque language. We consider different classifiers in order to find the system that fits best to the characteristics of the language under examination. We apply the combination of classifiers which improves results obtained with single classifiers. The main contribution of the paper is the use of bagging having as base classifier a non-soft one for the anaphora resolution in Basque.

1 Introduction

Pronominal anaphora resolution is related to the task of identifying noun phrases that refer to the same entity mentioned in a document.

According to [5], *anaphora, in discourse, is a device for making an abbreviated reference (containing fewer bits of disambiguating information, rather than being lexically or phonetically shorter) to some entity (or entities).*

Anaphora resolution is crucial in real-world natural language processing applications e.g. machine translation or information extraction. Although it has been a wide-open research field in the area since 1970, the work presented in this article is the first dealing with the subject for Basque, especially in the task of determining anaphoric relationship using a machine learning approach.

Recently, an annotated corpus has been published in Basque with pronominal anaphora tags [2] and thanks to that, this work could be managed.

Although the literature about anaphora resolution with machine learning approaches is very large, we will concentrate on those references directly linked to the work done here. In [10] they apply a noun phrase (NP) coreference system based on decision trees to MUC6 and MUC7 data sets. It is usually used as a baseline in the coreference resolution literature. Combination methods have been recently applied to coreference resolution problems. In [11] the authors use bagging and boosting techniques in order to improve single classifiers results.

The state of the art of other languages varies considerably. In [8] they propose a rule-based system for anaphora resolution in Czech. They use the Treebank data, which contains more than 45,000 coreference links in almost 50,000 manually annotated Czech sentences. In [12] the author uses a system based on a loglinear statistical model to resolve noun phrase coreference in German texts.

I. Bloch and R.M. Cesar, Jr. (Eds.): CIARP 2010, LNCS 6419, pp. 253–260, 2010.
© Springer-Verlag Berlin Heidelberg 2010

On the other hand, [6] and [7] present an approach to Persian pronoun resolution based on machine learning techniques. They developed a corpus with 2,006 labeled pronouns.

The paper we present describes a baseline framework for Basque pronominal anaphora resolution using a machine learning approach. In Section 2 some general characteristics of Basque pronominal anaphora are explained. Section 3 shows the results obtained for different machine learning methods. The combination of classifiers is presented in Section 4, and finally, in Section 5, we present some conclusions and point out future work lines.

2   Pronominal Anaphora Resolution in Basque

2.1   Main Characteristics of Pronominal Anaphora in Basque

Basque is not an Indo-European language and differs considerably in grammar from languages spoken in other regions around. It is an agglutinative language, in which grammatical relations between components within a clause are represented by suffixes. This is a distinguishing characteristic since morphological information of words is richer than in the surrounding languages. Given that Basque is a head final language at the syntactic level, the morphological information of the phrase (number, case, etc.), which is considered to be the head, is in the attached suffix. That is why morphosyntactic analysis is essential.

In this work we specifically focus on the pronominal anaphora; concretely, the demonstrative determiners when they behave as pronouns. In Basque there are not different forms for third person pronouns and demonstrative determiners are used as third person pronominals. There are three degrees of demonstratives that are closely related to the distance of the referent: hau (this/he/she/it), hori (that/he/she/it), hura (that/he/she/it). As we will see in the example of Section 2.3 demonstratives in Basque do not allow to infer whether the referent is a person (he, she) or it is an impersonal one (it).

Moreover, demonstrative determiners do not have any gender in Basque. Hence, the gender is not a valid feature to detect the antecedent of a pronominal anaphora because there is no gender distinction in the Basque morphological system.

2.2   Determination of Feature Vectors

In order to use a machine learning method, a suitable annotated corpus is needed. We use part of the Eus3LB Corpus[1] which contains approximately 50.000 words from journalistic texts previously parsed. It contains 349 annotated pronominal anaphora.

In this work, we first focus on features obtainable with the linguistic processing system proposed in [1]. We can not use some of the common features used by

---

[1] Eus3LB is part of the 3LB project [9].

most systems due to linguistic differences. For example the gender, as we previously said. Nevertheless, we use some specific features that linguistic researchers consider important for this task.

The features used are grouped in three categories: features of the anaphoric pronoun, features of the antecedent candidate, and features that describe the relationship between both.

- Features of the anaphoric pronoun
    - f_1 - *dec_ana*: The declension case of the anaphor.
    - f_2 - *sf_ana*: The syntactic function of the anaphor.
    - f_3 - *phrase_ana*: Whether the anaphor has the phrase tag or not.
    - f_4 - *num_ana*: The number of the anaphor.
- Features of the antecedent candidate
    - f_5 - *word*: The word of the antecedent candidate.
    - f_6 - *lemma*: The lemma of the antecedent candidate.
    - f_7 - *cat_np*: The syntactic category of the NP.
    - f_8 - *dec_np*: The declension case of the NP.
    - f_9 - *num_np*: The number of the NP.
    - f_{10} - *degree*: The degree of the NP that contains a comparative.
    - f_{11} - *np*: Whether the noun phrase is a simple NP or a composed NP.
    - f_{12} - *sf_np*: The syntactic function of the NP.
    - f_{13} - *enti_np*: The type of entity (PER, LOC, ORG).
- Relational features
    - f_{14} - *dist*: The distance between the anaphor and the antecedent candidate in terms of number of Noun Phrases.
    - f_{15} - *same_sent*: If the anaphor and the antecedent candidate are in the same sentence.
    - f_{16} - *same_num*: Besides to singular and plural numbers, there is another one in Basque: the indefinite. Thus, this feature has more than two possible values.

In summary we would like to remark that we include morphosyntactic information in our pronoun features such as the syntactic function it accomplishes, the kind of phrase it is, and its number. We also include the pronoun declension case. We use the same features for the antecedent candidate and we add the syntactic category and the degree of the noun phrase that contains a comparative. We also include information about name entities indicating the type (person, location and organization). The word and lemma of the noun phrase are also taken into account. The set of relational features includes three features: the distance between the anaphor and the antecedent candidate, a Boolean feature that shows whether they are in the same sentence or not, and the number agreement between them.

2.3   Generation of Training Instances

The method we use to create training instances is similar to the one explained in [10]. Positive instances are created for each annotated anaphor and its antecedent. Negative instances are created by pairing each annotated anaphor with each of its preceding noun phrases that are between the anaphor and the antecedent. When the antecedent candidate is composed, we use the information of the last word of the noun phrase to create the features due to the fact that in Basque this word is the one that contains the morphosyntactic information.

In order to clarify the results of our system, we introduce the following example: **Ben Amor** *ere ez da Mundiala amaitu arte etorriko Irunera,* **honek** *ere Tunisiarekin parte hartuko baitu Mundialean.*

(**Ben Amor** *is not coming to Irun before the world championship is finished, since* **he** *will play with Tunisia in the World Championship*).

The word *honek* (he) in bold is the anaphor and *Ben Amor* its antecedent. The noun phrases between them are *Mundiala* and *Irunera*. The next table shows the generation of training instances from the sentence of the example.

Antecedent Candidate	Anaphor	Positive
Ben Amor	honek (he/it)	1
Mundiala	honek (he/it)	0
Irunera	honek (he/it)	0

Generating the training instances in that way, we obtained a corpus with 968 instances; 349 of them are positive, and the rest, 619, negatives.

3   Experimental Setup

In order to evaluate the performance of our system, we use the above mentioned corpus. Due to the size of the corpus, a 10 fold cross-validation is performed. It is worth to say that we are trying to increase the size of the corpus.

3.1   Learning Algorithms

We consider different machine learning paradigms from Weka toolkit [4] in order to find the best system for the task. On one hand, we use some typical classifiers like SVM, Multilayer Perceptron, Naïve Bayes, k-NN, and simple decision trees like C4.5 and REPTree. On the other hand, we use classifiers not so frequently used such as Random Forest (RF), NB-Tree and Voting Feature Intervals (VFI).

The SVM learner was evaluated by a polynomial kernel of degree 1. The k-NN classifier, $k = 1$, uses the Euclidean distance as distance function in order to find neigbours. Multilayer Perceptron is a neural network that uses backpropagation to learn the weights among the connections, whereas NB is a simple probabilistic classifier based on applying Bayes' theorem, and NB-Tree generates a decision tree with Naïve Bayes classifiers at the leaves. C4.5 and REPTree are well known decision tree classifiers. Random Forest and VFI are traditionally less used algorithms; however, they produce good results for our corpus. Random forest is a combination of tree predictors, such that each tree depends on the values of a random vector sampled independently and with the same distribution for all trees in the forest. VFI constructs feature intervals for each feature. An interval represents a set of values for a given feature, where the same subset of class values is observed. Two neighbouring intervals contain different sets of classes.

3.2   Results for Single Classifiers

The results obtained with these classifiers are shown in Table 1. The best result is obtained by using the Multilayer Perceptron algorithm, an F-measure of 68.7%.

Table 1. Results for different algorithms

	Precision	Recall	F-measure
VFI	0.653	0.673	0.663
Perceptron	0.692	0.682	**0.687**
RF	0.666	**0.702**	0.683
SVM	**0.803**	0.539	0.645
NB-tree	0.771	0.559	0.648
NB	0.737	0.587	0.654
k-NN	0.652	0.616	0.633
C4.5	0.736	0.438	0.549
REPTree	0.715	0.524	0.605

In general, precision obtained is higher than recall. The best precision is obtained with SVM (80.3%), followed by NB-tree (77.1%). Althought C4.5 and REPTree are traditionally used for this task, they do not report good results for our corpus, as it can be observed in the table.

These results are not directly comparable with those obtained for other languages such as English, but we think that they are a good baseline for Basque language. We must emphasize that only the pronominal anaphora is treated here, so actual comparisons are difficult.

4   Experimental Results

In this section the experimental results obtained are shown. It is worth to mention that one of the main contributions of this paper is concerned with the selection of single classifiers in order to perform the combination.

4.1   Combination of Classifiers

Classifier combination is very used in the Machine Learning community. The main idea is to combine some paradigms from the supervised classification trying to improve the individual accuracies of the component classifiers.

According to the architecture used to combine different single classifiers, there are three possible configurations: cascaded, parallel and hierarchical. In this paper we use two parallel combinations of classifiers. One of the ways to combine the classifiers in parallel consists of using several base classifiers, applying them to the database, and then combining their predictions using a vote process. But even with a unique base classifier, it is still possible to build an ensemble, applying it to different training sets in order to generate several different models. A way to get several training sets from a given dataset is bootstrap sampling, which is used in bagging [3].

4.2 Results Obtained

We tried both vote and bagging combination approaches based on the results obtained in the previous section for the single classifiers. We selected five single classifiers, which belong to different paradigms, and which obtain good results for our corpus: Multilayer Perceptron, Random Forest, VFI, NB and k-NN. We performed the experiments in the following way:

- We make a votation with those five classifiers. Three different voting criteria were used: Majority, average of probabilities and product of probabilities.
- We apply the bagging multiclassifier with those five single classifiers, using different number of classifiers: 10, 15, 20, 30 and 40.

Results obtained by applying the vote combination schema are shown in Table 2. As it can be seen a slight increase in results is obtained with the majority voting achieving an F-measure of 69.2%.

Table 2. Results for different voting criteria

Classifier voting criteria	F-measure
Majority voting	0.692
Vote: average of probabilities	0.684
Vote: product of probabilities	0.636

The bagging multiclassifier is supposed to obtain better results when "soft" base classifiers are used. Classification trees are a typical example of soft classifier. That is why, for comparison reasons, we applied a bagging combination of C4.5 and REPTree trees. In Table 3 just the best results obtained from the bagging process for each classifier are shown. Although it is not recommended, we applied bagging to the selected classifiers, some of which are not considered to be "soft". As it can be seen, results obtained using classification trees are worse than those obtained with the selected classifiers. However, they are the single classifiers which obtain the highest benefit from the combination.

The best result is obtained by the multilayer perceptron classifier as the base one, obtaining an F-measure of 70.3%.

Table 3. Results for the bagging multiclassifier

	Single	Bagging
C4.5	0.549	0.654
REPTree	0.605	0.657
VFI	0.663	0.664
Perceptron	0.687	**0.703**
RF	0.683	0.702
NB	0.654	0.654
k-NN	0.633	0.634

5 Conclusions and Future Work

This paper presents a study carried out on resolution of pronominal anaphora in Basque using a machine learning multiclassifier. The results obtained from this work will be helpful for the development of a better anaphora resolution tool for Basque.

We considered nine machine learning algorithms as single classifiers in order to decide which of them select to combine in a parallel manner. Two different classifier combination approaches were used: vote and bagging. The main contribution of the paper is the use of bagging having as base classifier a non-soft one for the anaphora resolution in Basque.

There are several interesting directions for further research and development based on this work. The introduction of other knowledge sources to generate new features and the use of composite features can be a way to improve the system.

We plan to expand our approach to other types of anaphoric relations with the aim of generating a system to determine the coreference chains for a document.

Finally, the interest of a modular tool to develop coreference applications is unquestionable. Every day more people research in the area of the NLP for Basque and a tool of this kind can be very helpful.

Acknowledgments

This work was supported in part by KNOW2 (TIN2009-14715-C04-01) and Berbatek (IE09-262) projects.

References

1. Aduriz, I., Aranzabe, M.J., Arriola, J.M., Daz de Ilarraza, A., Gojenola, K., Oronoz, M., Uria, L.: A cascaded syntactic analyser for basque. In: Gelbukh, A. (ed.) CICLing 2004. LNCS, vol. 2945, pp. 124–134. Springer, Heidelberg (2004)
2. Aduriz, I., Aranzabe, M.J., Arriola, J.M., Atutxa, A., Daz de Ilarraza, A., Ezeiza, N., Gojenola, K., Oronoz, M., Soroa, A., Urizar, R.: Methodology and steps towards the construction of EPEC, a corpus of written Basque tagged at morphological and syntactic levels for the automatic processing. In: Wilson, A., Archer, D., Rayson, P. (eds.) Language and Computers, Corpus Linguistics Around the World, Rodopi, Netherlands, pp. 1–15 (2006)
3. Breiman, L.: Bagging predictors. Machine Learning 24(2), 123–140 (1996)
4. Hall, M., Frank, E., Holmes, G., Pfahringer, B., Reutemann, P., Witten, I.H.: The WEKA Data Mining Software: An Update. SIGKDD Explorations 11(1) (2009)
5. Hirst, G.: Anaphora in Natural Language Understanding. Springer, Berlin (1981)
6. Moosavi, N.S., Ghassem-Sani, G.: Using Machine Learning Approaches for Persian Pronoun Resolution. In: Workshop on Corpus-Based Approaches to Conference Resolution in Romance Languages, CBA 2008 (2008)
7. Moosavi, N.S., Ghassem-Sani, G.: A Ranking Approach to Persian Pronoun Resolution. Advances in Computational Linguistics. Research in Computing Science 41, 169–180 (2009)

8. Nguy, G.L., Zabokrtský, Z.: Rule-based Approach to Pronominal Anaphora Resolution Method Using the Prague Dependency Treebank 2.0 Data. In: Proceedings of DAARC 2007, 6th Discourse Anaphora and Anaphor Resolution Colloquium (2007)
9. Palomar, M., Civit, M., Díaz, A., Moreno, L., Bisbal, E., Aranzabe, M.J., Ageno, A., Mart, M.A., Navarro, B.: 3LB: Construcción de una base de datos de árboles sintáctico-semánticos para el catalán, euskera y español. In: XX. Congreso SEPLN, Barcelona (2004)
10. Soon, W.M., Ng, H.T., Lim, D.C.Y.: A Machine Learning Approach to Coreference Resolution of Noun Phrases. Computational Linguistics 27(4), 521–544 (2001)
11. Vemulapalli, S., Luo, X., Pitrelli, J.F., Zitouni, I.: Using Bagging and Boosting Techniques for Improving Coreference Resolution. Informatica 34, 111–118 (2010)
12. Versley, Y.: A Constraint-based Approach to Noum Phrase Coreference Resolution in German Newspaper Text. In: Konferenz zur Verarbeitung Natrlicher Sprache KONVENS (2006)

Text Segmentation by Clustering Cohesion

Raúl Abella Pérez and José Eladio Medina Pagola

Advanced Technologies Application Centre (CENATAV), 7a #21812 e/ 218 y 222, Rpto.
Siboney, Playa, C.P. 12200, Ciudad de la Habana, Cuba
{rabella,jmedina}@cenatav.co.cu

Abstract. An automatic linear text segmentation in order to detect the best topic boundaries is a difficult and very useful task in many text processing systems. Some methods have tried to solve this problem with reasonable results, but they present some drawbacks as well. In this work, we propose a new method, called ClustSeg, based on a predefined window and a clustering algorithm to decide the topic cohesion. We compare our proposal against the best known methods, with a better performance against these algorithms.

1 Introduction

Text segmentation is the task of splitting a document into syntactical units (paragraphs, sentences, words, etc.) or semantic blocks, usually based on topics. The difficulty of text segmentation mainly depends on the characteristics of documents which will be segmented (i.e. scientific texts, news, etc.) and the segmentation outputs (e.g. topics, paragraphs, sentences, etc.). There are different approaches to solve this problem; one is a linear segmentation, where the document is split into a linear sequence of adjacent segments. Another approach is a hierarchical segmentation; the outputs of these algorithms try to identify the document structure, usually chapters and multiple levels of sub-chapters [6].

There are many applications for text segmentation. Many tools for automatic text indexing and information retrieval can be improved by a text segmentation process. For example, when segmenting news of broadcast story transcriptions, a topic segmentation takes a crucial role, because a topic segmentation can be used for retrieving passages more linked to the query made by the user, instead of the full document [9], [11]. In tasks of summary generation, text segmentation by topics can be used to select blocks of texts containing the main ideas for the summary requested [9].

Analyzing the performance of different methods of text segmentation by topics [7], [8], [9], [10] we observed some difficulties as, for instance, wrong interruptions of segments, leaving out sentences or paragraphs which belong to the segments, and generating segments with incomplete information. When these situations happen, spurious segments are obtained. Another difficulty we observed is that those methods are not able to identify the true relations amongst paragraphs of each segment considering natural topic cohesion.

In this work we propose an algorithm for linear text segmentation of multi-paragraphs based on topics, called ClustSeg, defined as a solution of the aforementioned difficulties. This method is based on a window approach to identify boundaries of

I. Bloch and R.M. Cesar, Jr. (Eds.): CIARP 2010, LNCS 6419, pp. 261–268, 2010.
© Springer-Verlag Berlin Heidelberg 2010

topics. Each paragraph is represented using the vector space model, similar to other methods [6], [7], [9]. But, unlike these methods, we assumed that the paragraph cohesion is obtained from a clustering method, generating segments containing paragraphs from one topic or a mixture of them.

We have structured the present work as follows. In Section 2 we briefly explain some previous works to solve the segmentation problem and their drawbacks. In Section 3 we describe the proposed method. In the last section we present the experimental results by using a textual corpus which we prepared with articles selected from the ICPR'2006 proceedings.

2 Related Work

The study of the linear text segmentation methods by topics must be initiated by the TextTilling algorithm. This method was proposed by Hearst and it is considered one of the most interesting and complete studies on the identification of structures of sub-topics [7]. In this paper, Hearst proposed a method which tries to split texts into discourse units of multiple paragraphs. This algorithm uses a sliding window approach and for each position two blocks are built; one preceding and the second succeeding each position. To determine the lexical punctuation between these two blocks, it uses the term repetition as a lexical cohesion mechanism. These blocks are formed by a specified amount of pseudo-sentences which are represented by the vector space model and the cosine as the similarity measure. Considering the lexical values calculated, this method splits the text from the valleys, or points with low lexical scores.

Unlike Hearst, Heinone proposed a method which uses a sliding window to determine, for each paragraph, which the most similar paragraph inside the window is [8]. The sliding window is formed by several paragraphs on both sides (above and below) of every processed paragraph. This segmentation method is especially useful when it is important to control the segment length. The author uses a dynamic programming technique that guarantees getting segments of minimum cost. The segment cost is obtained by a lexical cohesion curve among the paragraphs, a preferential segment size specified by the user, and a defined parametric cost function.

Another approach of linear text segmentation by topic is TextLec, proposed in 2007 [9]. This method, like TextTiling, uses word repetition as a lexical cohesion mechanism. Each paragraph is represented by the vector space model, as in Hearst's and Heinonen's work. The authors of this work assume that all the sentences which belong to a paragraph are about a same topic. This method also uses a sliding window approach but, unlike Hearst, it only uses a window of paragraphs which are below each position. This method consists of two stages; the first finds for each paragraph the farthest cohesive one within the window, using the cosine measure and a threshold. Finally, it searches the segment boundaries in a sequential process, in which a paragraph is included in a segment if it is the farthest cohesive one related to any other paragraph previously included in the segment.

The last method we have considered is the C99 algorithm proposed by Choi [3]. This method is strongly based on the lexical cohesion principle. C99 uses a similarity matrix of the text sentences. First projected in a word vector space representation, sentences are then compared using the cosine similarity measure. More recently, Choi improved C99 by using the Latent Semantic Analysis (LSA) achievements to reduce the size of the word vector space [4].

3   ClustSeg: A Method for Text Segmentation

In our approach, we assume a linear segmentation and consider paragraphs as the minimum text units. But, in spite of other methods, we assume that sentences belonging to a paragraph, and each paragraph *per se*, could be on several topics. Paragraph representation is based on the vector space model and the topic cohesion is calculated using the cosine measure. Nevertheless, the segment boundaries are defined from the results of a clustering algorithm, as we can see below.

The ClustSeg algorithm begins preprocessing the document. In this stage, the stop-words (prepositions, conjunctions, articles, pronouns) are eliminated, considering that these words are devoid of information to decide how similar paragraphs are amongst them. All punctuation marks, numbers and special characters are also removed. Next, the terms can be transformed by their lemmas. We have used in this work the TreeTager, which is a system with the possibility of extracting the lemmas in various languages.

After this preprocessing, the algorithm continues with three stages: the search for topic cohesion, the detection of topic segment boundaries, and the detection of the document segment boundaries.

3.1   Searching for Topic Cohesion

Although we consider the vector space model and the cosine measure, assuming that a vocabulary change could produce a topic change and also a beginning of a new segment, we do not take that model and measure directly to decide the segment boundaries, as the aforementioned methods do.

The main drawback that all those methods present is the assumption that if two paragraphs or textual units have a high similarity value, then there is a high confidence that these paragraphs belong to a significant topic and could belong to a same segment. We have observed that this assumption does not identify all the spurious segments and, also, it can create segments with paragraphs of weak topic cohesion.

Besides, all the methods we have analyzed assume that each paragraph or textual unit is about a unique topic, and the cosine similarity amongst paragraphs can link them, making up segments based on a topic-driven process. In this paper, we have considered that a paragraph could be about several topics, and the significant cohesion amongst them depends on the related topic and on its significance to the document.

Taking into consideration those drawbacks and hypotheses, we weigh up a clustering process applied to the set of paragraphs, without taking into account their order, as a way to obtain clusters of high topic cohesion. Besides, because of the hypothesis of multi-topic paragraphs, a convenient (or maybe necessary) restriction is that the clustering algorithm could produce overlapped clusters.

There are not so many clustering algorithms oriented to obtain cohesive and overlapped clusters. Examples of them are Star [1], Strong Compact (FCI) [14] and

ICSD [12]. We decided to use the static version of ICSD, considering a good performance (or better according to the authors) on overlapped clusters for topic discovery.

The selected algorithm, called (Incremental) Clustering by Strength Decision (ICSD), obtains a set of dense and overlapped clusters using a graph cover heuristic. It is applied over a thresholded similarity graph formed by the objects (paragraphs represented by the vector space model) as the vertices and the similarity values (using the cosine measure) amongst them. The threshold (defined by the user) is used to determining whether two paragraphs are similar.

So, when the static version of ICSD is applied, we can obtain a set of clusters, where each cluster represents a set of cohesive paragraphs belonging (presumably) to an independent topic. The paragraphs identified by the clustering are the only ones we will consider in the following stages.

3.2 Detecting the Topic Segment Boundaries

After obtaining the clustering from the static version of ICSD algorithm, we process every cluster in order to obtain all the segments which can be formed from each cluster.

As in other methods, we use a window (W) to define if two adjacent paragraphs in a cluster are close. Each segment is obtained linking adjacent paragraphs according to the predefined window.

The result of this stage is a set of segments defined by a set of pairs $\langle I, F \rangle$, where I and F represent the indexes of the initial and final paragraphs of the segment. The algorithm of this stage is shown in fig. 1.

Algorithm: Topic Segmentation
Input: C - Clustering of paragraph indexes;
W - A predefined window;
Output: SI - Set of $\langle I, F \rangle$ obtained from C;
1) **for each** $c \in C$ **do begin**
2) $j = 1$;
3) $c' = \{p_1, ..., p_k\}$ by sorting c in ascending order;
4)   **while** $j < k$ **do begin**
5) I = First $p_i \in c'$ / $p_{i+1} - p_i \leq W$ **and** $i \geq j$;
6)   **if** does not exist I **then** $j = k$
7)   **else begin**
8) $F = p_{i+1}$;
9) $j = i+2$;
10)   **while** $p_i - p_{i-1} \leq W$ **do begin**
11) $F = p_i$;
12) $j = j+1$;
13)   **end**
14) $SI = SI \cup \{\langle I, F \rangle\}$;
15)   **end**
16)   **end**
17) **end**

Fig. 1. Topic segment boundaries detection algorithm

3.3   Detecting the Document Segment Boundaries

As a result from the previous stage, we have obtained a set of topic segment boundaries. As these segments were obtained from different clusters, and they are overlapped, these segments could be also overlapped.

In this stage, we concatenate all the segments that have at least one common paragraph. Observe that, with this consideration, we obtain a linear segmentation satisfying the following condition: A document segment could be made up by a concatenation of a set of topic segments from different topics only if any topic segment has a non null intersection (at least one paragraph) with another one. The Fig. 2 shows this third stage.

Algorithm: Document Segmentation
Input: SI – Set of $\langle I, F \rangle$ from *Topic Segmentation*;
Output: SF – Set of $\langle I, F \rangle$ obtained from SI;
1)   **for each** $\langle I, F \rangle$ = $\underset{\langle I', F' \rangle}{\mathrm{MinArg}} \{ I' \, / \, \langle I', F' \rangle \in SI \}$ **do begin**
2) $\langle In, Fn \rangle = \langle I, F \rangle$;
3) $SI = SI \setminus \{\langle I, F \rangle\}$;
4)   **while exist** $\langle I1, F1 \rangle \in SI$ **and** $I1 \geq I$ and $I1 \leq Fn$ **do begin**
5) $Fn = \max(Fn, F1)$;
6) $SI = SI \setminus \{\langle I1, F1 \rangle\}$;
7)   **End**
8) $SF = SF \cup \{\langle In, Fn \rangle\}$;
9)   **End**

Fig. 2. Document segment boundaries detection algorithm

4   Evaluation

There are two main problems related to evaluation of text segmentation algorithms. The first one is given by the subjective nature when detecting the right boundaries of topics and sub-topics into texts; it turns the selection of reference segmentation for a fair and objective comparison into a very difficult task [13]. In order to solve this problem, usually artificial documents are created, concatenating different real documents, on the assumption that the limits between these documents are good breaking points [6], [9], [13]. Another way is to compare the results against a manual segmentation based on human judgments, which makes a "gold standard" [18].

The second problem is the selection of a measure to use in the evaluation; because, for different applications of text segmentation, different types of mistakes become more or less important. For example, in information retrieval, segment boundaries that differ from the real ones in some few sentences can be accepted. For evaluating a method with this goal, measures like Precision or Recall should not be used. However, when segmenting news of broadcast stories transcription, the accuracy of the boundaries is very important.

In our proposal, the accuracy of the boundaries is not important, because we are trying to automatically discover topic segmentations. One of the best measures to evaluate this task is WindowDiff, a measure proposed by Pevzner and Hearst in 2000 [13].

The WindowDiff measure uses a sliding window of length k to find disagreements between the reference and the algorithm segmentation. In this work we take k as the half of the average true segment size in the reference segmentation.

The amount of boundaries inside the window of both segmentations is determined for each window position; it is penalized if the amount of boundaries disagrees. Later, all penalizations found are added. This value is normalized and the metric takes a value between 0 and 1. WindowDiff takes a score of 0 if all boundaries are correctly assigned and it takes a score of 1 if there is a complete difference between the automatic segmentation and the reference one. The WindowDiff formal expression and other details of this measure can be seen in Pevzner and Hearst [13].

In this section we show the results of five segmentation algorithms: ClustSeg, TextLec, TextTiling, Heinone's and C99. The corpus that we used in the experimentation is the same as Hernandez&Medina's work [9]. This corpus was built joining 14 different papers taken from the ICPR'2006 proceedings. The resultant corpus has 305 paragraphs and an average of 22 paragraphs approximately for each paper. We took the segmentation output of our algorithm and we compared it with the results shown in Table 1 of Hernandez&Medina's work [9]. Besides, we included the C99 algorithm results. The C99 algorithm used was downloaded on May 26th from the following *url:http://sourceforge.net/projects/textsegfault/files/c99/C99-1.2-release.tgz/download.*

In Table 1 we can see the results of this experimentation. It was done with a window (W) equal to 10 and a threshold of 0.35 for deciding a significant cosine value between two paragraphs. We can notice a significantly better performance of ClustSeg. We also did other evaluations, varying the window size and the threshold, but these results can not be included here because of the page restrictions. Nevertheless, the ClustSeg algorithm achieved better results than the others for windows size in [9, 11] and threshold in [0.25, 0.38], with a best result of 0.11 for a windows of 11 and a threshold of 0.27 and 0.28.

Table 1. WindowDiff values

Algorithms	ClustSeg	TextLec	TextTilling	Heinone's	C99
WindowDiff	0.12	0.21	0.33	0.26	0.21

Although we did not accomplish any experimentation in terms of execution time, we ran our algorithm and measured the time consumption. The execution time was 1124 ms. Besides, the execution order of this algorithm is $O(m \times n \times \log_2 n)$, including the clustering stage, where m is the amount of clusters and n the amount of paragraphs.

5 Conclusion

The use of text methods of segmentation by topic would improve the results of many text processing tasks; for example, text summarization, information retrieval and others. We have proposed a new segmentation method for discovering topic boundaries.

Although we use the vector space model and the cosine measure, we consider that the paragraph cohesion can be better obtained from a clustering method, generating segments containing paragraphs from one topic or a mixture of them.

The ClustSeg algorithm was compared with four methods, obtaining more cohesive segments and increasing significantly its performance.

As future work, we propose to evaluate other clustering methods and to achieve a better integration of both strategies.

References

1. Aslam, J., Pelekhov, E., Rus, D.: The star clustering algorithm for static and dynamic information organization. Journal of Graph Algorithms and Applications 8(1), 95–129 (2004)
2. Beeferman, D., Berger, A., Lafferty, J.: Statistical Models for Text Segmentation. In: Second Conference on Empirical Methods in Natural Language Processing, pp. 35–46 (1997)
3. Choi, F.Y.Y.: Advances in domain independent linear text segmentation. In: NAACL 2000, pp. 26–33 (2000)
4. Choi, F.Y.Y., Wiemer-Hastings, P., Moore, J.: Latent semantic analysis for text segmentation. In: EMNLP, pp. 109–117 (2001)
5. Filippova, K., Strube, M.: Using Linguistically Motivated Features for Paragraph Boundary Identification. In: The 2006 Conference on Empirical Methods in Natural Language Processing (EMNLP 2006), pp. 267–274 (2006)
6. Ken, R., Granitzer, M.: Efficient Linear Text Segmentation Based on Information Retrieval Techniques. In: MEDES 2009, Lyon, France (2009)
7. Hearst, M.: TextTiling: Segmenting Text into Multi-paragraph Subtopic Passages. Computational Linguistics 23(1), 33–64 (1997)
8. Heinonen, O.: Optimal Multi-Paragraph Text Segmentation by Dynamic Programming. In: COLING-ACL 1998, Montreal, Canada, pp. 1484–1486 (1998)
9. Hernández, L., Medina, J.: TextLec: A Novel Method of Segmentation by Topic Using Lower Windows and Lexical Cohesion. In: Rueda, L., Mery, D., Kittler, J. (eds.) CIARP 2007. LNCS, vol. 4756, pp. 724–733. Springer, Heidelberg (2007)
10. Labadié, A., Prince, V.: Finding text boundaries and finding topic boundaries: two different tasks. In: Nordström, B., Ranta, A. (eds.) GoTAL 2008. LNCS (LNAI), vol. 5221, pp. 260–271. Springer, Heidelberg (2008)
11. Misra, H., et al.: Text Segmentation via Topic Modeling: An Analytical Study, Hong Kong, China (2009)
12. Pérez-Suáerez, A., Martínez, J.F., Carrasco-Ochoa, J.A.: A New Incremental Algorithm for Overlapped Clustering. In: Bayro-Corrochano, E., Eklundh, J.-O. (eds.) CIARP 2009. LNCS, vol. 5856, pp. 497–504. Springer, Heidelberg (2009)
13. Pevzner, L., Hearst, M.: A Critique and Improvement of an Evaluation Metric for Text Segmentation. Computational Linguistics 28(1), 19–36 (2002)

14. Pons-Porrata, A., Ruiz-Shulcloper, J., Berlanga-Llavori, R., Santiesteban-Alganza, Y.: Un algoritmo incremental para la obtención de cubrimientos con datos mezclados. In: CIARP 2002, pp. 405–416 (2002)
15. Schmid, H.: Probabilistic part-of-speech tagging using decision trees. In: International Conference on New Methods in Language Processing (1994)
16. Schmid, H.: Improvements in part-of-speech tagging with an application to german. In: ACL SIGDAT-Workshop (1995)
17. Shi, Q., et al.: Semi-Markov Models for Sequence Segmentation. In: Proc. of the 2007 Joint Conference on Empirical Methods in Natural Language Processing and Computational Natural Language Learning, pp. 640–648 (2007)
18. Stokes, N., Carthy, J., Smeaton, A.: SeLeCT: A Lexical Cohesion Based News Story Segmentation System. AI Communications 17(1), 3–12 (2004)

Multiple Clues for License Plate Detection and Recognition

Pablo Negri[1], Mariano Tepper[2], Daniel Acevedo[2],
Julio Jacobo[2], and Marta Mejail[2]

[1] PLADEMA-Universidad del Centro de la Provincia de Buenos Aires
Tandil, Argentina
pnegri@exa.unicen.edu.ar
http://www.plademadema.net
[2] Departamento de Computación-Facultad de Ciencias Exactas y Naturales
Universidad de Buenos Aires, Argentina
http://www-2.dc.uba.ar/grupinv/imagenes/

Abstract. This paper addresses a license plate detection and recognition (LPR) task on still images of trucks. The main contribution of our LPR system is the fusion of different segmentation algorithms used to improve the license plate detection. We also compare the performance of two kinds of classifiers for optical character recognition (OCR): one based on the *a contrario* framework using the shape contexts as features and the other based on a SVM classifier using the intensity pixel values as features.

1 Introduction

License plate recognition (LPR) currently finds other applications than the electronic payment systems (toll payment and parking fee payment) or traffic surveillance. Entrepreneurs discover the usefulness of identifying their clients, for example, by using this technology to study clients' shopping habits in a fast food drive-thru. The present work involves an application where the LPR solution is installed on a truck balance to identify incoming vehicles making it possible to record the truck's weight automatically.

Figure 1 shows some samples of the images captured by the camera system. The system has been installed outdoors and works during day and night. It can be seen from the samples that the distance between the camera and the vehicle is variable, and the license plate can be anywhere in the image. Finally, characters in the license plate can be distorted, noisy, broken or incomplete, challenging the simple methods used in the commercial systems.

The state of art in LPR systems is well summerized in the work of Anagnostopoulos [1]. They present the LPR algorithm as a three-step framework: 1) LP location; 2) characters segmentation; and 3) character recognition. In general, the first step should operate fast enough to fulfill the need of real time operations. For still images, which are the scope of our work, methods in the literature include techniques that take advantage of the high contrast in the license plate:

I. Bloch and R.M. Cesar, Jr. (Eds.): CIARP 2010, LNCS 6419, pp. 269–276, 2010.
© Springer-Verlag Berlin Heidelberg 2010

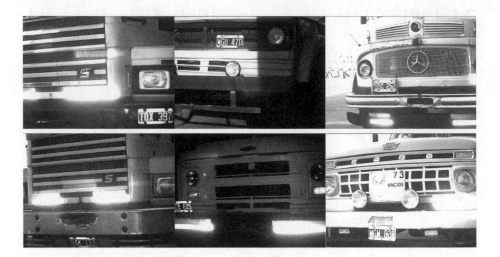

Fig. 1. Non deteriorated truck image samples in the first row. Second row shows three examples of deteriorated truck images: noisy, incomplete and broken characters.

morphological operations, edge detection [10], hierarchical representations [4], image transformations [7], etc. There are also detection algorithms based on AdaBoost [8] and support vector machine (SVM) [9] classifiers, using Haar-like features or the color and texture information.

The character segmentation step examines the potential LP locations to determine the character bounding boxes. The final step matches the extracted characters to a number or a letter. In this stage, different types of classifiers have been applied such as SVM [4], artificial neural networks (ANN) [12], etc.

This paper describes a three steps framework for robust license plate detection and recognition. The main contribution of our LPR system is the fusion of different kinds of segmentation algorithms to obtain a strong license plate detector.

The article is organized as follows: section 2 presents the detection and recognition framework, section 3 shows the results of our system, finalizing with conclusions and perspectives in section 4.

2   LPR Framework

In this section we introduce the three steps of the LPR framework: license plate detection, character segmentation and character recognition.

2.1   License Plate Detection

The first task of a LPR system is the detection of the license plate inside the image. The LP detection process starts generating several Regions of Interest (RoIs) using morphological filters. To validate the RoIs and choose the most

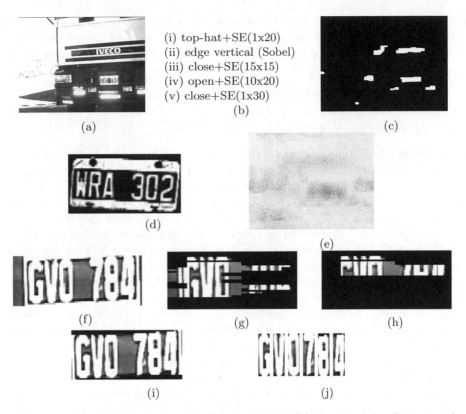

(i) top-hat+SE(1x20)
(ii) edge vertical (Sobel)
(iii) close+SE(15x15)
(iv) open+SE(10x20)
(v) close+SE(1x30)

(a)   (b)   (c)

(d)

(e)

(f)   (g)   (h)

(i)   (j)

Fig. 2. License plate detection. (a) Original image; (b) Pseudo code of the morphological operations; (c) resulting RoIs; (d) correlation pattern; (e) correlation map; (f) extracted RoI; (g) text segments; (h) text blocks; (i) choosen RoI and (j) characters extraction.

probable license plate region, we perform a more exhaustive evaluation: analysis of the presence of text and obtainment of a correlation map using the Fourier transform. These clues, being of different nature, help the system to obtain a strong and robust detection.

Morphological filters. A morphological top-hat filtering is applied to the input image to enhances the contrast in regions with great difference in intensity values. Then, the vertical contours are calculated using a Sobel operator. Successive morphological operations are then applied to connect the edges in potential LP regions. Fig. 2 (b) shows the pseudo-code of the morphological operations. Each line shows the structural element employed and its size, found empirically based on the expected license plate size. In that way, the morphological filters are a simple and rapid way to provide several potential RoIs and, at the same time, they have the responsibility not to miss the license plate in this step. The N resulting RoIs are showed in Fig. 2 (c): R_i, $i = 1, ..., N$.

Template matching. We calculate a correlation map of the occurrences of a license plate in the image using a FFT. Let be $\mathbf{I}$ the input image and $F(\mathbf{I})$ its FFT, $\mathbf{P}$ the correlation pattern, Fig. 2 (d), and $F(\mathbf{P})$ its FFT. Then, the correlation map M (see Fig. 2 (e)) is given by $M = F^{-1}\left(\frac{F(\mathbf{I})F(\mathbf{P})^*}{\|F(\mathbf{I})\|\|F(\mathbf{P})\|}\right)$ where F^{-1} is the inverse Fourier transform and F^* the complex conjugate of F. We get then a feature vector $\mathbf{scv} = (scv_1, \ldots, scv_N)$ of confidence values, where $scv_i = \frac{1}{|R_i|}\sum_{(x,y)\in R_i} M(x,y)$ and $|\cdot|$ is the area of R_i.

Text segments. From each region R_i, $i = 1, \ldots, N$, we calculate the potential text segments using Wong's method [5]. For that, the horizontal intensity gradient is calculated using a derivative mask [-1,1]. Then, at each $(x,y) \in R_i$, the Maximum Gradient Difference (MGD) is computed. This value is the difference between the maximum and minimum gradient values inside an horizontal segment s of width $n + 1$ centered at (x,y). In our application $n = 40$, which is slightly longer than the average size of two characters. Usually, text segments have large MGD values. The segments are then filtered preserving those with a MGD value larger than a certain threshold. A value of *200* has empirically been found to be the best choice for this parameter.

Next step gets the number of background-to-text $n_{b-t-t}(s)$ and text-to-background $n_{t-t-b}(s)$ transitions for each segment s, which should be close if s contains text. Also, the mean and variance of the horizontal distances between the background-to-text and text-to-background transitions in every segment s is computed. We define the following two conditions: $C^{(1)}(s) = \{n_{b-t-t}+n_{t-t-b} > \text{threshold}\}$ and $C^{(2)}(s)=\{$mean and variance of horizontal distances in s are inside a certain range$\}$. Then, $S_i = \{s \in R_i \,/\, C^{(1)}(s) \wedge C^{(2)}(s) \text{ holds}\}$, are the validated segments for every R_i, $i = 1, \ldots, N$. We define two features vectors: $\mathbf{nts} = (nts_1, \ldots, nts_N)$ and $\mathbf{mgd} = (mgd_1, \ldots, mgd_N)$, where $nts_i = \#S_i$ and $mgd_i = \frac{1}{nts_i}\sum_{s\in S_i} MGD(s)$.

Text blocks. In this step, the text segments validated previously are merged to form text blocks. For each text segment, the mean and the variance of the intensity values in the original image are calculated. Two continuous segments are merged if the mean and the variance are close using a two pass strategy, top-down and bottom-up. We define a text block feature $\mathbf{ror} = (ror_1, \ldots, ror_N)$, where ror_i is the confidence value indicating the RoI occupation ratio defined as $ror_i = \text{area}(\text{text blocks} \in R_i)/\text{area}(R_i)$, for $i = 1, \ldots, N$. Fig. 2 (h) presents two text blocks covering 23% of the area region.

Clues combination and decision. We get four feature vectors, $\mathbf{nts}$, $\mathbf{mgd}$, $\mathbf{ror}$ and $\mathbf{scv}$ of different nature, each of them having a confidence value for each RoI. We need to merge their information in order to decide which of the N regions have obtained the highest values in the vectors. To do so, we create four sorting index vectors: $\mathbf{nts^{si}}$, $\mathbf{mgd^{si}}$, $\mathbf{ror^{si}}$ and $\mathbf{scv^{si}}$. These vectors give an index to each R_i that depends on an ascending sorting: the R_i with the lowest value in the feature vector gets index 1, and the R_i with the highest value gets index N. Then, we define a vector $\mathbf{votes}$ with length N:

$\mathbf{votes}(i) = \mathbf{nts^{si}}(i) + \mathbf{mgd^{si}}(i) + \mathbf{ror^{si}}(i) + \mathbf{scv^{si}}(i)$, for $i = 1, \ldots N$.

The region R_m, with $m = \arg\max_{1 \le i \le N} \mathbf{votes}(i)$ is retained as the license plate. R_m will always be in the latest positions in the sorted vectors receiving the greatest votes. See Fig. 2 (i) for the chosen region in our example.

2.2   Character Segmentation

The RoI R_m detected as the license plate is thresholded in order to obtain a binary image, where high intensity values correspond to the foreground color. To identify the characters, the algorithm groups the connected foreground pixels in regions and calculates its bounding boxes. In order to filter the non-character bounding boxes, the algorithm evaluates the width and height ratio and the spatial position, being also capable to split connected characters. The final bounding boxes will establish the validated characters (see Fig. 2 (j)).

2.3   Classification

A LP is composed of two groups of three characters. The first group of characters are letters and the second group are numbers (see Fig. 2). If the number of segmented characters is at least four, it is possible to associate their index position on the license plate. The bounding boxes are sent to a classifier specialized in letters or a classifier specialized in numbers. Two types of classifiers are compared in this work: an edge based method and a template based method.

Edge based method

The first classification method is based on the work of Tepper et al. [13]. They employ the shape context [2] as descriptor and the *a contrario* framework [3] to perform the shape context matching.

Let $\mathcal{T} = \{t_1, \ldots, t_n\}$ be the set of points of the contour obtained using the Canny's algorithm. For each $t_i \in \mathcal{T}$, we model the distribution of the positions of $n - 1$ remaining points in $\mathcal{T}$ relative to t_i. We call this distribution the Shape Context of t_i (SC_{t_i}). In order to render the SC_{t_i} useful, we discretize the values in a log-polar space obtaining a coarse histogram of 180 bins. Each bin of the histogram corresponds to a cell on the partition and their value is calculated as the number of edge points lying inside the cell.

We use the *a contrario* framework, developed as part of the Computational Gestalt project (see [3] for a complete description).

Let $\{SC_i | 1 \le i \le n\}$ and $\{SC'_j | 1 \le j \le m\}$ be two sets of shape contexts from two different shapes. We want to see if both shapes look alike. The distances between SC_i and SC'_j can be seen as observations of a random variable D that follows some unknown random process. Formally, let $\mathcal{F} = \{F^k | 1 \le k \le K\}$ be a database of K shapes. For each shape $F^k \in \mathcal{F}$ we have a set $\mathcal{T}^k = \{t_j^k | 1 \le j \le n_k\}$ where n_k is the number of points in the shape. Let $SC_{t_j^k}$ be the shape context of t_j^k, $1 \le j \le n_k$, $1 \le k \le M$. We assume that each shape context is split in C independent features that we denote $SC_{t_j^k}^{(i)}$ with $1 \le i \le C$. Let Q be a query shape and q a point of Q. We define

$$d_j^k = \max_{1 \leq i \leq C} d_j^{k(i)}, \text{ where } d_j^{k(i)} = d(SC_q^{(i)}, SC_{t_j^k}^{(i)})$$

where $d(\cdot, \cdot)$ is some appropriately chosen distance. We can state the *a contrario* hypothesis: $\mathcal{H}_0$: *the distances d_j^k are observations of identically distributed independent random variables D that follows some stochastic process.* The number of false alarms of the pair (q, t_j^k) is $\text{NFA}(q, t_j^k) = N \cdot \prod_{i=1}^{C} P(D \leq d_j^k | \mathcal{H}_0)$, where $N = \sum_{k=1}^{K} n_k$, and $P(D \leq d_j^k | \mathcal{H}_0)$ is the probability of false alarms (further details to obtain P can be founded in [13]). If $\text{NFA}(q, t_j^k) \leq \varepsilon$ then the pair (q, t_j^k) is called ε-meaningful match.

The classifier decides which character from the database corresponds to the query counting the number of ε-meaningful matches between the shape query and each shape from the database. The database shape that produces the biggest number of matches is selected. In case that there are no ε-meaningful matches for any database shape, a no-match decision is returned. We have only one shape in the base for each class.

Template based method

In the template based method, the pixel intensity values of the character feed a classifier trained with the Support Vector Machine (SVM) algorithm.

In this work, we train the SVM using the algorithm proposed for Platt: the Sequential Minimal Optimization (SMO) [11]. SMO is a simple algorithm (the pseudocode is available at [11]) that solves the SVM quadratic problem analytically inside an iterative process. Its advantage lies in the fact that solving the dual maximization problem for two Lagrange multipliers can be done analytically and very quickly.

The strategy for the classification is the *One Against All* approach. We construct N binary SVM classifiers, each of which separates one class from the rest. The positive samples for the k-th SVM classifier correspond to those of the k-th class. The negative samples are the samples of the other classes. In the training phase, the training samples are resized to a pattern of 16x10 pixels and their intensity values normalized between -1 and 1. In the testing phase, an input sample, resized and normalized, is the input of the N classifiers. It will be classified as the class whose classifier produces the highest value.

3   Experimental Results

Dataset

The dataset is composed of 623 images captured by an infrared camera system placed at a truck entrance gate. Captures are taken at any time of the day (there are day and night captures). The dataset is split into two databases. The first base is composed of 151 images and is used to extract the training samples for the SVM training and the patterns for the shape context matching. The second base (472 images) is our test database. There are two labels for each test sample indicating the license plate numbers and the nature of the LP: non-deteriorated or deteriorated. License plates that are deformed, noisy, broken or incomplete are labeled as deteriorated. There are 356 non deteriorated samples and 116 deteriorated.

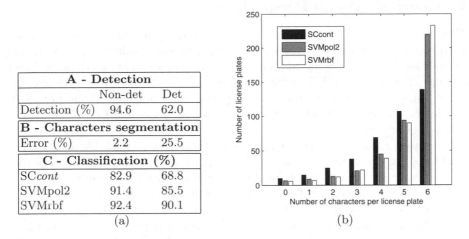

A - Detection		
	Non-det	Det
Detection (%)	94.6	62.0
B - Characters segmentation		
Error (%)	2.2	25.5
C - Classification (%)		
SC*cont*	82.9	68.8
SVMpol2	91.4	85.5
SVMrbf	92.4	90.1

(a)   (b)

Fig. 3. Results of the LPR system. Table (a) shows the detection results in A, error percentage in characters segmentation in B and classification results in C. Figure (b) presents the quantity of characters recognized in the detected LPs.

Results

Fig. 3 (a) shows the results of the LPR system. Table **A** presents the detection results with a 94.6 % in the non-deteriorated LPs images and 62 % for the deteriorated. A detection is validated if the license plate is entirely inside the RoI and the character segmentation found at least four characters. The average executing time of the detection step using MATLAB running on a PC with 3.16GHz processor is 700 ms. In general, the system misses the samples when there are strong vertical edges in the truck front, which can defeat the LP region in the clues fusion decision. This situation often happens in the case of the deteriorated samples, when the LPs are noisy or deteriorated.

Row **B** exposes the character segmentation errors. We observe the difficult task of this step on the deteriorated images, when there are missing characters or bounding boxes validated out of the boundaries of the LP.

Row **C** exhibits the classification results of the two classifiers on the well extracted characters. For the SVM classifier we use two kind of kernels: SVMpol2, polynomial function (2nd degree) and SVMrbf, radial basis function. The latter obtains the best score. The edge based classifier SC*cont* obtains the worst performance. This is a natural result if we consider that there is only one shape for each class in the database.

Finally, the last bars in Fig. 3 (b) present the number of LPs in which the system recognizes the six characters well. LPs giving five characters means that one character was missed or erroneously classified. Certainly we can expect the LPR system to make some mistakes. In order to improve the system performance, a list of LPs can be used to verify the LPR response and to validate it or change it for the most probable LP in the base.

4   Conclusions and Perspectives

This paper presented a LPR system for still outdoor truck images. We obtained good results in the detection phase by using a fusion of different segmentation algorithms. For the recognition phase, we compared an edge based method and a template based method. The former, using the *a contrario* framework and the shape context features, has the advantage that uses only one shape per class. The latter, based on a SVM classifier and pixel values as features, obtained the best performance.

We consider, however, that further research is necessary to tackle deteriorated LP images on the detection and character segmentation phases. Consequently, we plan on applying new clues to minimize erroneous detection results, especially for deteriorated images. As far as it is possible, we expect to make use of the number of segments inside each region extracted using the Hough transform. More detailed research can also be done in the characters segmentation phase in order to improve the performance of the system. Finally, classification results using the edge based method could be improved generating shapes in a different way that better generalize each class.

References

1. Anagnostopoulos, C., et al.: License plate recognition from still images and video sequences: A survey. Inteligent Transportation Systems 9(3), 377–391 (2008)
2. Belongie, S., Malik, J., Puzicha, J.: Shape matching and object recognition using shape contexts. Pattern Analysis and Machine Intelligence 24(4), 509–522 (2002)
3. Desolneux, A., Moisan, L., Morel, J.: From Gestalt Theory to Image Analysis: A Probabilistic Approach. Springer, Heidelberg (2008)
4. Donoser, M., Arth, C., Bischof, H.: Detecting, tracking and recognizing license plates. In: Yagi, Y., Kang, S.B., Kweon, I.S., Zha, H. (eds.) ACCV 2007, Part II. LNCS, vol. 4844, pp. 447–456. Springer, Heidelberg (2007)
5. Wong, E.K., Chen, M.: A new robust algorithm for video text extraction. Pattern Recognition 36, 1397–1406 (2003)
6. Hongliang, B., Changping, L.: A hybrid license plate extraction method based on edge statistics and morphology. In: ICPR, pp. 831–834 (2004)
7. Hsieh, C.T., Juan, Y.S., Hung, K.M.: Multiple license plate detection for complex background. In: AINA, pp. 389–392 (2005)
8. Huaifeng, Z., et al.: Learning-based license plate detection using global and local features. In: ICPR, pp. 1102–1105 (2006)
9. Kim, K.I., Jung, K., Kim, J.: Color Texture-Based Object Detection: An Application to License Plate Localization. In: Lee, S.-W., Verri, A. (eds.) SVM 2002. LNCS, vol. 2388, pp. 321–335. Springer, Heidelberg (2002)
10. Mello, C.A.B., Costa, D.C.: A Complete System for Vehicle License Plate Recognition, In: WSSIP, pp. 1–4 (2009)
11. Platt, J.C.: Sequential minimal optimization: A fast algorithm for training support vecthor machines. Tech. Rep. MSR-TR-98-14, Microsoft Research (1998)
12. Rahman, C.A., Badawy, W., Radmanesh, A.: A real time vehicle's license plate recognition system. In: AVSS, pp. 163–166 (2003)
13. Tepper, M., Acevedo, D., Goussies, N., Jacobo, J., Mejail, M.: A decision step for shape context matching. In: ICIP, pp. 409–412 (2009)

Non Local Image Denoising Using Image Adapted Neighborhoods

Álvaro Pardo

Department of Electrical Engineering, Faculty of Engineering and Technologies,
Universidad Católica del Uruguay
apardo@ucu.edu.uy

Abstract. In recent years several non-local image denoising methods were proposed in the literature. These methods compute the denoised image as a weighted average of pixels across the whole image (in practice across a large area around the pixel to be denoised). The algorithm non-local means (NLM) proposed by Buades, Morel and Coll showed excellent denoising capabilities. In this case the weight between pixels is based on the similarity between square neighborhoods around them. NLM was a clear breakthrough when it was proposed but then was outperformed by algorithms such as BM3D. The improvements of these algorithms are very clear with respect to NLM but the reasons for such differences are not completely understood. One of the differences between both algorithms is that they use adaptive regions to compute the denoised image. In this article we will study the performance of NLM while using image adapted neighborhoods.

1 Introduction

In this work we assume that the observed image, x, is the result of adding a random noise component n to the original noiseless image z. Therefore, the relationship at pixel i becomes: $x_i = z_i + n_i$. The problem of image denoising is to estimate z while preserving its features such as edges and texture. To preserve these features several non-linear or locally adapted methods have been developed. Non-local methods are an example of non-local and non-linear denoising methods. In [4] Buades, Morel and Coll presented the Non Local Means (NLM) denoising method. The underlying idea of this method is to estimate, z_i, using a weighted average of all pixels in the image. Given the pixel to be denoised, i, the weights w_{ij} measure the similarity between neighborhoods centered at i and j. The trick is that corresponding neighborhoods are found all over the image imposing a non-local nature to the method. In practice, this is not computationally efficient and similar neighborhoods are looked in a search windows around pixel i. For more details on similar non-local methods see [1,2,6,5,3].

In this work we explore our claim that locally adaptive neighborhoods play an important role in the performance of non-local methods. To prove this claim we will compare the performance of NLM against a NLM with image adapted neighborhood configurations. First, for synthetic images, based on the local structure of the image an optimal neighborhood is selected. For natural images we will use Principal Component Analysis (PCA) to extract image adapted neighborhoods.

I. Bloch and R.M. Cesar, Jr. (Eds.): CIARP 2010, LNCS 6419, pp. 277–284, 2010.

2 Non Local Means Denoising

The NLM algorithm [4] estimates the denoised value at pixel i, $\hat{x}_i$, using a weighted average of all pixels in the search region R_i:

$$\hat{x}_i = \frac{\sum_{j \in R_i} w_{ij} x_j}{\sum_{j \in R_i} w_{ij}} \tag{1}$$

The weights w_{ij} reflect the similarity between pixels i and j based on the distance between neighborhoods N_i and N_j around them. In [4] the authors proposed to compute the weight as:

$$w_{ij} = \exp(-||N_i - N_j||_2^2/\sigma^2). \tag{2}$$

N_i, N_j are image neighborhoods of size $(2K+1) \times (2K+1)$ centered at pixels i and j respectively and $||N_i - N_j||_2^2$ is de squared distance between them. The parameter σ controls the weights; with a small sigma only points with close neighborhoods receive weights close to one.

In some cases the weights w_{ij} are not able to discriminate between different neighborhood classes. This is critical along edges since pixels along them have less corresponding neighborhoods in the image. The main difficulty is that in several cases, for instance when i lies over a corner, it is very difficult to find similar neighborhoods in R_i. So, even if we could segment the pixels in R_i based on its neighborhoods configuration, it will not be enough. Therefore, in order to solve this situation we need to modify the neighborhood configuration.

2.1 Neighborhood Selection for Synthetic Images

The idea here is to select the neighborhood configuration that best suits the local structure around each pixel i. This a classical idea that dates back to [7]. In Figure 1 we show the nine neighborhoods considered. If i is over a smooth region the configuration (9) should be selected. On the other hand, if i lies along a vertical edge configuration (3) or (4) should be used. The selection is based on the distance between the mean inside and outside the pixels in neighborhood.

When we plug the procedure described above into NLM algorithm we found that the best MSE for traditional NLM is outperformed by the modified NLM here proposed. For the image in Figure 2 the MSE for NLM is 4.38 and for the modified NLM here proposed is 2.12. So, adapting the neighborhood during similarity computation seems a promising idea. Unfortunately, when we applied the same algorithm to real images we found that the modified NLM, for the images un Figure 3, was outperformed by the traditional NLM. Observing the map that showed the selected neighborhood configuration for each pixel we found that it was very noisy. That means that the selection of the neighborhood was unstable. On one hand the noise present in the image makes it very difficult to correctly select the true neighborhood configuration. On the other hand, natural images rarely have local configurations as the ones shown in Figure 1. Therefore, to apply the same idea to natural images we need another way to introduce the local configurations into the neighborhoods similarity computation. The requirements

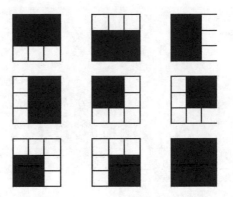

Fig. 1. Neighborhood configurations. From left to right and top to bottom the neighborhoods are numbered from 1 to 9.

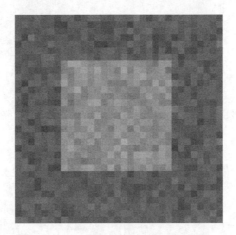

Fig. 2. Synthetic image corrupted with Gaussian noise

for this are stability against noise and the capability to extract the local configurations present in the image. In next section we will show that traditional Principal Component Analysis (PCA) fulfills both requirements and gives good results in terms of MSE.

3   PCA and NLM

The use of PCA in the context of non-local method was mainly used to reduce the computational complexity via dimensionality reduction. In [9] the author reviews the more relevant literature in this area. Also explores the use of PCA to compute what he calls the Principal Neighborhoods (the eigenvectors computed with PCA). We will also use PCA to compute image adapted neighborhoods. The main difference with his approach and ours is that in our case we use this idea to justify the need of image adapted neighborhoods. In this way we are looking the same problem from another

Fig. 3. Test images: Barbara, Couple, Einstein, GoldHill, House, Boat, Peppers, Baboon

point of view. Finally, the estimation of the parameters of NLM is done in a completely different way (see Section 4).

Our claim is that using PCA we can extract the local configuration of each neighborhood being processed. Using the correct neighborhood we compute the distance considering only the relevant information while being, at the same time, insensitive to noise. Instead of selecting the relevant information in the pixel space, as we did for synthetic images, for natural images we do it in the projected space obtained with PCA. PCA is well known for its stability in the computation of the principal components (eigenvectors) in the presence of noise in the data. Furthermore, the selection of the relevant information to compute the neighborhood similarity is image dependent (PCA is computed for each image being denoised). This is another advantage of PCA; although for every image we start with the same neighborhood configuration in the space of pixels the similarity is image dependent via the principal components. So far we considered that the original image z contains some structure and therefore the use of principal components will allow us to robustly compute the similarity between neighborhoods. As we will se in the Section 4 with textured images there is no clear benefit in using principal components to compute the similarity.

4   NLM Using PCA Neighborhoods

In this section we discuss the implementation of NLM using PCA image adapted neighborhoods.

The new algorithm has several parameters. First we have the parameters of NLM: the size of the neighborhoods, the size of the search windows and the width of the exponential kernel. In this work we fix the first two with values 3×3 and 7×7 respectively. For the setting of the width we follow the idea presented in [5,3] and set the width σ proportional to the noise variance. This can be justified using the following result. The expected distance for two identical neighborhoods with additive and independent gaussian noise with zero mean and variance σ_n results:

$$E\left\{\sum_{k=1}^{(2K+1)^2} (X_i^k - X_j^k)^2\right\} = \sum_{k=1}^{(2K+1)^2} E\left\{(N_i^k - N_j^k)^2\right\} = 2(2K+1)^2\sigma_n^2. \quad (3)$$

Based on this, first we estimate the σ_n using [8] and then set $\sigma = 3\sqrt{2}\sigma_n$ (for $2K+1 = 3$). The last parameter is the dimension of the projection and will be discussed in the reminder of this section.

The computation of the image adapted neighborhoods is done using PCA. Given the set X containing the n neighborhoods for the image, PCA is applied to obtain the principal components P and the projected information Y. Since we are using neighborhoods of size 3×3 the size of X is $n \times 9$, the size of P is 9×9 and the size of Y is $n \times 9$. The distance between two points in X can be computed using the corresponding

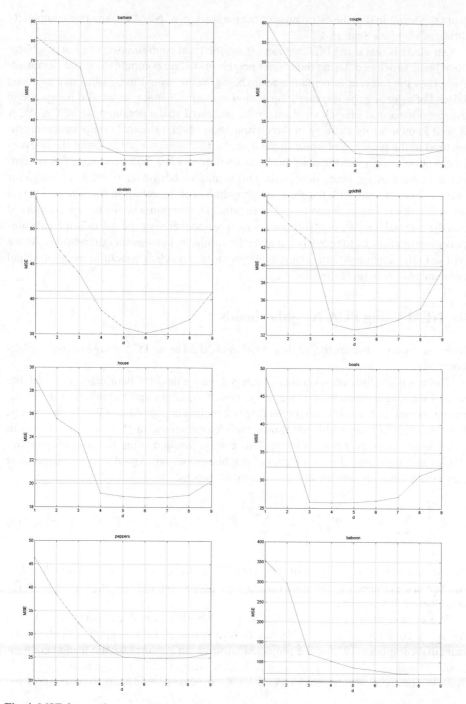

Fig. 4. MSE for test images while varying the number of components d in PCA. The red (horizontal) line indicates the result of traditional NLM. Images: Barbara, Couple, Einstein, Goldhill, House, Boat, Peppers, Baboon.

projected samples in Y. If the coordinates in Y are sorted in descending order with respect to the eigenvalues obtained from PCA, the distance can be approximated with the first d coordinates. This idea was traditionally used to speed up the computational time of NLM. Here we argue that not only this speeds the computations of NLM but also give improvements in terms of MSE since the distance is computed in another space where noise is reduced and the local structure of the image is introduced.

The distance between two neighborhoods N_i and N_j is computed using its corresponding projections in Y: Y_i and Y_j. If we use only d coordinates the we have an approximation of the distance:

$$||N_i - N_j||_2^2 \approx \sum_{k=1}^{d}(Y_i^k - Y_j^k)^2.$$

As we will show the approximation at the end improves the results. This reinforces our idea that for the computation of the distances between neighborhoods we must use the local structure of the image. Using PCA components we do it so and also we are immune to the effects of the noise. In Figure 4 we show the evolution of the MSE for different values of d. The red line shows the result of NLM (using all the coordinates in Y). We can observe that in all cases but one, the optimal results are obtained with $d < 9$. Thus, the adaptation of the neighborhoods to the image statistics improves the results of NLM. The only case where this is not true is for baboon, an extremely textured image. Additionally, the MSE is stable with d between 5 and 8. In these experiments artificial Gaussian noise with $\sigma_n = 10$ was added to each image.

5   Discussion, Conclusions and Future Work

As we showed in Figure 4 the MSE using the image adapted neighborhoods improves with respect to traditional NLM. So, not only we obtain a computationally improved algorithm but also we gain in terms of MSE. Based on this data we confirm our claim that the adaptation to the local structure of the image is important in this kind of algorithms. For synthetic images the adaptation can be done using naive neighborhoods. On the other hand, natural images need neighborhoods that reflect the statistics of the image itself. The only image where our proposal fails is Baboon. This is an extremely textured image where it is difficult to extract the structure. This stresses that discovering the structure of the image neighborhoods it is important for this kind of algorithms.

We believe that with this evidence we add some light to the study of non-local denoising algorithms. Although PCA has been studied before, here we study the problem from another perspective. For the future, we want to study the optimal estimation of d and its influence on the results. It is interesting to note that consistently in all the experiments performed the MSE is stable between d=5 and d=8. The work [9] studied this problem and would be an starting point in our work. Also, we expect to explore the possibility of defining binary masks in the PCA space as we did in the pixel space in the case of synthetic images.

References

1. Awate, S.P., Whitaker, R.T.: Unsupervised, information-theoretic, adaptive image filtering for image restoration. IEEE Trans. Pattern Anal. Mach. Intell. 28(3), 364–376 (2006)
2. Boulanger, J., Kervrann, C., Bouthemy, P.: Adaptive space-time patch-based method for image sequence restoration. In: Workshop on Statistical Methods in Multi-Image and Video Processing, SMVP 2006 (May 2006)
3. Buades, A., Coll, B., Morel, J.M.: The staircasing effect in neighborhood filters and its solution. IEEE Transactions on Image Processing 15(6), 1499–1505 (2006)
4. Buades, A., Coll, B., Morel, J.M.: Denoising image sequences does not require motion estimation. In: Proc. IEEE Conf. on Advanced Video and Signal Based Surveillance, pp. 70–74 (2005)
5. Buades, A., Coll, B., Morel, J.M.: A review of image denoising algorithms, with a new one. SIAM Multiscale Modeling and Simulation 4(2), 490–530 (2005)
6. Mahmoudi, M., Sapiro, G.: Fast image and video denoising via nonlocal means of similar neighborhodds. IEEE Signal Processing Letters 12(12), 839–842 (2005)
7. Nagao, M., Matsuyama, T.: A structural analysis of complex aerial photographs. Plenum Press, New York (1980)
8. Olsen, S.I.: Noise variance estimation in images. In: Proc. 8th SCIA, pp. 25–28 (1993)
9. Tasdizen, T.: Principal neighborhood dictionaries for nonlocal means image denoising. IEEE Transactions on Image Processing 18(12), 2649–2660 (2009)

A Quantitative Evaluation of Fixed-Pattern Noise Reduction Methods in Imaging Systems

Pablo Meza[1,3], César San Martin[2,3], Esteban Vera[1,3], and Sergio Torres[1,3]

[1] Depto. Ing. Eléctrica, Universidad de Concepción, Casilla 160-C, Concepción, Chile
[2] Depto. Ing. Eléctrica, Universidad de La Frontera, Casilla 54-D, Temuco, Chile
csmarti@ufro.cl
[3] Center for Optics and Photonics, Universidad de Concepción, Concepción, Chile

Abstract. Fixed pattern noise is a common feature in several uncalibrated imaging systems, and it typically appears as striping and grid-like nonuniformity artifacts in hyperspectral and infrared cameras. In this work, we present a quantitative and comparative analysis of fixed-pattern noise reduction, or calibrating techniques, by using several image quality indexes. A special emphasis is made in demonstrating the correspondence between the reference-free (blind) image quality indexes and the typical reference-based metrics, specially when using online calibration procedures where reference data is not available. We evaluate the performance of several classic scene-based calibrating algorithms applied to: multispectral images with simulated striping noise; and infrared image sequences with simulated nonuniformity. The results show that most of the tested reference-free indexes are useful indicators for tracking some of the real degradation of the calibrated or even uncalibrated imagery, but they are far from perfect to match an error or similarity measure if the clean or reference data is available.

1 Introduction

Digital imaging systems are often composed of a bundle of optical lenses and a focal-plane array (FPA) with its associated readout electronics. A FPA can be arranged in a one dimensional array, or linear detector, which might need to employ a scanning acquisition mode in order to form an image. On the other hand, a two dimensional FPA can directly form images without any moving parts, which is the case of most of the photographic and video cameras available on the market. However, in multi or hyperspectral cameras the two dimensional FPA is employed as an array of linear detectors, one for each wavelength band, so again there is a need for scanning in order to create the bidimensional images, which is the case from consumer RGB scanners up to state-of-the-art satellite cameras.

The fixed-pattern noise (FPN) corresponds to a degradation common to all FPA based imaging systems, and it is due to the intrinsic and uneven response of the individual detectors, or pixels, within the array. In the case of bidimensional staring arrays, such as in infrared cameras, the FPN is often spatially distributed

I. Bloch and R.M. Cesar, Jr. (Eds.): CIARP 2010, LNCS 6419, pp. 285–294, 2010.

in a grid-like appearance, known as nonuniformity (NU) noise. On the other hand, when dealing with a scanning device such as a hyperspectral imager, the FPN is seen as vertical or horizontal strip lines, known as striping noise, and the pattern is different between bands because each band is captured by a different line of the detector array.

Fortunately most of the detectors can be modeled by a linear model represented by a gain and an offset parameter. Therefore, the proper way of calibrating the FPA, and thus removing for the FPN, is by estimating such parameters and correct for their disparity or nonuniformity. Even though the FPN can be restored by a proper calibration of the detectors in order to estimate its intrinsic parameters, there are still two main issues. The first is related to the change on the environmental or operational conditions of the camera, so the parameters may drift. The second is related to the fact that the calibration may be unfeasible due to increased setup costs or complexity.

Nonetheless, several methods have been developed in order to calibrate the FPA and then reduce the striping and NU noise by using scene-based data or statistics. For the striping FPN, a moment matching (MM) method has been proposed in [3]. In this case, the mean and variance of the readout data is obtained and used to compensate the corrupted image. In [9] a method based on histogram matching with weighted least-squares filter is introduce in order to reduce the striping noise in MODIS data. The histogram matching is used to reduce the detector-to-detector stripe and mirror stripes, and the weighted least-squares filter is used to reduce the stripe noise. In [1] several methods are reviewed and compared such as the ones based on: low pass filtering, gray value substitution, and wavelet transforms. In this case, the best visual results were obtained using a wavelet approach, but the use of a low pass filter had a noticeable noise removal in despite of removing useful high pass information. From this point, in [8] is proposed a combination of wavelet transform and frequency filtering in a novel, fast and stable filter called the wavelet-FFT (WFT) filter. For vertical striping noise, the vertical detail band contains the principal striping artifacts. Therefore the filter operation is only selectively applied to this band by means of a Gaussian low-pass filter, and the denoised image is then reconstructed using the inverse wavelet transform. The results show a good performance in visual results and radiometric range preservation. In order to reduce the FPN in staring FPA, such as in infrared imaging system, several methods have been proposed in the literature called nonuniformity correction (NUC) methods. In this work, we are interested in scene-based methods, which only make use of the images captured during the normal operation of the camera to perform the NUC, and thus removing the NU noise. Among all NUC methods, the following two are highlighted due to their simplicity and because they allow a dynamic frame-by-frame operation. The constant statistics algorithm [5], which has a reminiscence of the MM approach previously reviewed for scanning imaging systems, and the neural-network approach [12,13] which has a extreme ability for adapting to the drift of the parameters.

Figures of merit for evaluating the performance of destriping or NUC methods can be divided in: reference-based and reference-free (or blind) performance metrics. Reference-based metrics require a set of reference images or video sequences. An example of this metric, which is used for laboratory calibration, is the correctability parameter [11]. This parameter, defined as the ratio between the magnitudes of the spatial and temporal noise, indicates when the spatial noise has been reduced to a magnitude below the magnitude of the temporal noise. Another kind of reference-based metrics are the image quality indexes based on measure of distance, traditionally used in image processing such as the mean-squared error (MSE), the mean-absolute error (MAE), the root-mean-square-error (RMSE), and the peak-signal-to-noise-ratio (PSNR). The main advantage of such metrics is that they provide a radiometric performance evaluation of the algorithms, although globally. Lately, the universal image quality index (UIQI) [15], the structural similarity index measure (SSIM) [16] and the feature based SSIM [7] have been used in order to assess the quality of images in a perceptual framework. When the reference images are not available, the applicability of reference-based metrics is confined to simulation scenarios where artificial noise is added to sets of clean or previously calibrated images. On the other hand, a reference-free metric may be able to recognize quantitatively, but blindly, if a image is getting better or worst after any denoising or restoration procedure, trying to emulate our own visual system mechanism for deciding wether an image has a good overall quality or not. Among them, the most suited for evaluating the removal of FPN are the roughness (ρ) index, the noise reduction (NR) ratio and the residual non-uniformity (RNU). The ρ metric was introduced by Hayat's group in [6], and it quantifies the tentative amount of NU in an image by using first order gradient filters in the horizontal and/or vertical directions. The ρ index is a clear indicator on the FPN removal, but it might produce confusion, leading to good (or low results) if real high frequency information from the original images is removed as well. A modified and enhanced version that accounts for some of the ρ index flaws is also proposed in [10]. The NR ratio was proposed and used in [2] in order to specifically evaluate the noise reduction achieved by the exemplified destriping method, and the index corresponds to the ratio between the mean frequency power of the raw image and the denoised one. Latest, the RNU index was defined in [14] to evaluate the ability of their own NUC method to reduce the FPN.

In this paper we use several image quality **indices** in order to compare and rank the performance of certain classic destriping and NUC methods using image data with simulated FPN. In Section 1 we present the striping noise problem and its reduction methods, and in Section 3 we explain the NU problem and the correction methods herein used. Section 4 contains a description of the quantitative indexes, and the results achieved by the simulations are summarized in Section 5. Finally, in Section 6 we present a discussion and some conclusions, as well as a outline of our future work.

2   Striping Noise and Its Reduction

When the image is formed by the scanning of a one dimensional sensor array, the produced FPN is known as striping noise. Formally, by assuming a linear model between the readout signal $Y_j(n)$ and the input irradiance $X_j(n)$ collected by the $(j)^{\text{th}}$ detector at a given time n, it is common to define the following image formation model:

$$Y_j(n) = A_j(n) \cdot X_j(n) + B_j(n), \tag{1}$$

where $A_j(n)$ and $B_j(n)$ are the gain and the offset of the jth detector. As the gain and offset are not necessarily equal along the detector array, then any disparity presented between their responsivity and bias levels triggers the generation of a striping noise at the scanning direction. Hopefully, as the gain and offset are often constant in time, they can be computed by performing a calibration procedure, and further used for compensating the acquired images. However, it is well known that at different operation conditions, and specially at longer wavelengths, the gain and offset parameters may drift and thus differ from the previously calibrated ones. In addition, calibration setups can be expensive, as well as time consuming, and they are not always available, as it is the case of space-based applications such as in satellite imaging. Nevertheless, there are calibration methods that purely rely on the acquired data for estimating the uneven parameters, and thus reduce the undesired FPN.

Assuming the model en Eq. 1, it is possible to obtain the temporal mean and standard deviation of the readout data as:

$$\mu_{Y_{nj}} = A_j \cdot \mu_{X_{nj}} + B_j, \tag{2}$$

$$\sigma_{Y_{nj}} = A_j \cdot \sigma_{X_{nj}}, \tag{3}$$

In addition, it is also feasible to assume that the input irradiance is of zero mean and unitary variance, obtaining that:

$$B_j = \mu_{Y_{nj}}, \tag{4}$$

$$A_j = \sigma_{Y_{nj}}. \tag{5}$$

Thus, the image with reduced striping noise is finally given by:

$$\hat{X}_{nj} = (Y_{nj} - \mu_{Y_{nj}})/\sigma_{Y_{nj}}. \tag{6}$$

This destriping noise reduction methods is known as the MM [3]. Now, if we apply the Fourier transform to the gain and offset images previously obtained we have that $FA(u,v) = \sum_{m=0}^{M-1} a_m e^{-jmv}\delta(u)$ and $FB(u,v) = \sum_{m=0}^{M-1} b_m e^{-jmv}\delta(u)$, representing that the gain and the offset is concentrated in the horizontal frequency components when vertical striping noise is present. Using this result, a WFT filter was proposed in [8], that applies a high pass filter to any vertical sub-band of a wavelet decomposition. For achieving good results, the WFT method relies on the adjustment of the two key parameters: the damping factor (of the high pass filter) and the decomposition level of the wavelet transform. In this paper, we use the best combination as reported in [8].

3   Nonuniformity and Its Correction

Assuming that each infrared detector is characterized by a linear model, the measured readout signal Y_{ij} at a given time n can be expressed as for the $(ij)^{\text{th}}$ detector in the form:

$$Y_{ij}(n) = A_{ij}(n) \cdot X_{ij}(n) + B_{ij}(n), \tag{7}$$

where $A_{ij}(n)$ and $B_{ij}(n)$ are the gain and the offset of the ij^{th} detector, and $X_{ij}(n)$ is the real incident infrared photon flux collected by the respective detector.

Harris $et.\ al$ in [4] developed a recursive version of the constant statistics NUC technique where the parameters are recursively estimated frame by frame as follows:

$$B_{ij}(n+1) = \hat{\mu}_{Y_{ij}}(n+1) = (Y_{ij}(n+1) + n\hat{\mu}_{Y_{ij}}(n))/(n+1)$$
$$A_{ij}(n+1) = \hat{\sigma}_{Y_{ij}}(n+1) = (|Y_{ij}(n+1) - \hat{\mu}_{Y_{ij}}(n+1)| + n\hat{\sigma}_{Y_{ij}}(n))/(n+1)$$

A second fundamental NUC method is the one proposed by Scribner $et.\ al$ in [12], where equation (7) is reordered as follows:

$$X_{ij}(n) = w_{ij}(n) \cdot Y_{ij}(n) + b_{ij}(n), \tag{8}$$

where the new parameters $w_{ij}(n)$ and $b_{ij}(n)$ are related to the real gain and offset parameters of each detector as follows:

$$w_{ij}(n) = g_{ij}^{-1}(n) \qquad b_{ij}(n) = -o_{ij}(n)g_{ij}^{-1}(n). \tag{9}$$

The expression presented in equation (8) is the responsible of performing the NUC on the readout data. Then, for each ij^{th} detector, the NUC model (8) can be considered as the simplest neural network structure, which consists of a single linear neuron node, with an estimate weight $(\hat{w}_{ij}(n))$ and an estimate bias $(\hat{b}_{ij}(n))$. For this reason we denoted this method as neural network (NN). A complete version of Scribner's NUC method can be found in [13].

4   Quality Indexes

In this section, the quality indexes are addressed. The RMSE reference-based index for a $L-$dimensional FPA is given by:

$$RMSE^2 = \frac{1}{size(L)} \sum_{L} (I_L - \hat{X}_L)^2, \tag{10}$$

where $\hat{X}$ is the corrected image and I is the real image. L is the dimension of the FPA array (1 or 2) where I denote a vector or matrix, respectively. The RMSE is higher when the correction is poor, and it is lower when the corrected image is closer to the real image.

Moving to reference-free indexes, the ρ index is described as:

$$\rho(\hat{X}) = (||h \otimes \hat{X}|| + ||h^T \otimes \hat{X}||)/||\hat{X}||, \tag{11}$$

where $\hat{X}$ is an $M \times N$ pixels compensated image, $||\hat{X}||$ is the ℓ_1 norm of $\hat{X}$, $\otimes$ represents the discrete 2D convolution, h is a horizontal edge-detector filter, which is defined as $[-1 \ 1]$, and T stands for vector transposition. Note that the roughness index measures the horizontal and vertical components of the FPN. If the stripe noise is presented in vertical direction, the ρ index only requires the horizontal component. By definition, the roughness index is always a non-negative real number, and $\rho(\hat{X}) = 0$ whenever $\hat{X}$ is constantly flat. Thus, according to the roughness index, the closer to zero the better the NUC performed on the raw image, but if it reaches a zero value, it means that the corrected image is a constant and uninformative image.

In [10] the effective roughness (ER) index is proposed as a redefinition of the roughness index, modifying the edge-detection filtering operation. The mathematical definition of the ER index is:

$$\text{ER}(\hat{X}) = \frac{||h \otimes (g \otimes \hat{X})|| + ||h^T \otimes (g \otimes \hat{X})|| - 2||g \otimes \hat{X}||}{||g \otimes \hat{X}||}, \tag{12}$$

where g is any edge-detector filter. The rationale for the filtering operation is twofold: diminish the low-frequency components of the image and accentuate the (residual) noise in the image. The ER index ranks a correction with the best performance when $\text{ER}(\hat{X}) = 0$.

Another method is the ratio of NR that has been used in several works [2]. This is defined as:

$$NR = N_0/N_1, \tag{13}$$

where N_0 and N_1 stand for the mean power spectrum of the corrupted and corrected image, respectively. In order to quantify the performance of the denoising method, $NR \to \infty$, i.e., the ideal is to remove as much noise as possible from the corrupted image. Finally, the RNU metric is given by:

$$RNU = \frac{1}{\mu}(\frac{1}{nm} \sum_i \sum_j (Y_{ij} - \mu))^{1/2} \times 100\%, \tag{14}$$

where μ is the spatial mean of the corrected image. The RNU must be lower in order to rank the best correction method.

Table 1. Statistical parameters to generate the simulated fixed-pattern noise test images and image sequences for both types of fixed pattern noise

	$\bar{g}$	σ_g	$\bar{o}$	σ_o	t	σ_t
Test Sequence 1	1	0,025	0	5%	0	0,5%
Test Sequence 2	1	0,05	0	10%	0	0,5%

5   Results

In order to quantify the image quality indexes behavior, we present results over simulated FPN of both striping and NU, providing the real image and the corrupted frame. We compute the RMSE, ρ, ER, NR, and RNU metrics for the original images, and for two FPN reduction algorithms considered for both simulations. The destriping is performed using MM and WFT, and the NUC is performed by the constant statistics (CS) and NN methods. Two levels of FPN were chosen to generate the simulated fixed gain and offset image masks to produce the desired FPN appearance over each kind of data, and the selected statistics are the same for both types of noise, as displayed in Table. 1. In addition, a small temporal noise component was added to simulate the common electronic/thermal noise.

For the stripping noise simulation we used a multispectral satellite image with three channels (red, green and blue), using a different strip noise pattern with the same statistics to each channel. The main reason for this is to demonstrate how the correction affects the combined image, making easy to visualize any radiometric problems in the denoised images. For the infrared NU noise, we used a sequence of 4000 frames that includes camera motion and moving targets, so helping to achieve the requirements needed for the NUC algorithms. Fig. 1 shows graphically the FPN generated for both kinds of noise.

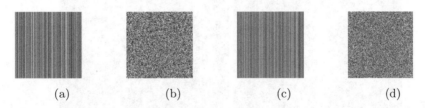

(a)   (b)   (c)   (d)

Fig. 1. Image of the simulated fixed pattern noise with $\overline{g} = 0.025$ and $\sigma_g = 5\%$: a) unidimensional and b) bidimensional gain; c) unidimensional and d) bidimensional offset

Table 2. Performance comparison of the striping reduction methods in terms of the different quality indexes

Gain					$\sigma = 0.02$			
Offset		$\sigma = 5\%$				$\sigma = 10\%$		
Method	Index	Ch1	Ch2	Ch3	Mean	Ch1	Ch2	Ch3	Mean
Noisy	RMSE	0.05	0.05	0.05	**0.05**	0.10	0.10	0.10	**0.10**
	ρ	0.35	0.27	0.33	**0.32**	0.48	0.42	0.50	**0.47**
	ER	0.54	0.58	0.59	**0.57**	0.67	0.73	0.71	**0.70**
	NR	1.00	1.00	1.00	**1.00**	1.00	1.00	1.00	**1.00**
	RNU	0.81	0.66	0.85	**0.77**	0.86	0.72	0.89	**0.82**
MM	RMSE	0.06	0.06	0.07	**0.06**	0.06	0.07	0.08	**0.07**
	ρ	0.27	0.20	0.28	**0.25**	0.29	0.22	0.29	**0.27**
	ER	0.32	0.37	0.39	**0.36**	0.33	0.37	0.39	**0.36**
	NR	0.94	0.93	0.86	**0.91**	0.88	0.85	0.80	**0.84**
	RNU	0.81	0.66	0.85	**0.77**	0.86	0.72	0.89	**0.82**
WFT	RMSE	0.02	0.02	0.02	**0.02**	0.02	0.02	0.02	**0.02**
	ρ	0.25	0.19	0.23	**0.22**	0.26	0.19	0.22	**0.22**
	ER	0.33	0.37	0.38	**0.36**	0.33	0.37	0.38	**0.36**
	NR	1.00	1.00	1.00	**1.00**	1.00	1.00	1.00	**1.00**
	RNU	0.78	0.64	0.82	**0.75**	0.78	0.64	0.79	**0.74**

Results obtained for the two destriping corrections used for each channel, and for different levels of FPN, are summarized in Table. 2, where the mean value obtained from the three channels is calculated to compare the methods. The RMSE analysis shows that the WFT correction produces a more similar image compared to the original one, and that the increase of the FPN affects in the same amount both corrections. When comparing the reference free indexes, ρ and ER fail to difference which correction generates a better result without indicating any change after applying the higher FPN mask. On the other hand, RNU presents mixed results, correctly interpreting the FPN reduction using the WFT technique, but does not reveals the increase in the FPN applied. The NR values cannot be correlated with the other results because it indicates that the destriping effects of the algorithms does not produce any different output whatsoever. It is necessary to highlight that in the test sequence 1 the MM-correction produce a worse image than the noisy one product of the change in the radiometric range but all the reference free indexes fail to indicate. Fig. 2 presents the noisy image and the FPNcorrected versions.

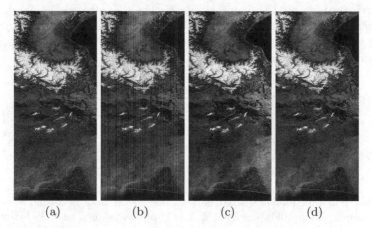

(a)   (b)   (c)   (d)

Fig. 2. Destriping results on simulated FPN (test sec. 2) in the reconstructed color image a) Reference Image b) Noisy Image c) MM-Correction and d) WFT-Correction

For the infrared case, the mean and standard deviation of every index calculated over 2000 frames after the algorithms have reached the stationary state are presented in Table. 3(a), and a sample for the frame 1602 is shown in Table. (b). The main observation for the indexes values is that they follow a similar behavior between the results reported for the bidimensional FPN case as in the one dimensional FPN case. The results in Table. 3(b) show a scenery where the indexes indicate incongruous results, where Harris NUC method produces a corrected image that is worse than the original, but the ρ and ER index indicate a minor effect of the FPN than the original. At the same time, the NR and RNU index are not delivering new information when the level of FPN is increased. Fig. 3 presents the noisy corrected frame 1602 of the infrared video sequence.

Table 3. a) Mean/standar deviation and b) Frame 1602 comparison performance of the non-uniformity reduction methods in terms of the different quality indexes

(a)

Gain		$\sigma = 0.02$	
Offset		$\sigma = 5\%$	$\sigma = 10\%$
Method	Index	mean/std	mean/std
Noisy	RMSE	0.05/ 0	0.10/ 0
	ρ	0.35/0.05	0.62/0.12
	ER	0.82/0.07	0.94/0.37
	NR	1.00/0.00	1.00/0.00
	RNU	0.37/0.04	0.43/0.05
Harris	RMSE	0.12/0.04	0.12/0.04
	ρ	0.20/0.10	0.20/0.11
	ER	0.22/0.05	0.23/0.06
	NR	1.13/0.09	1.36/0.18
	RNU	0.21/0.07	0.49/0.14
NN	RMSE	0.01/0.002	0.02/0.004
	ρ	0.13/0.02	0.14/0.02
	ER	0.21/0.05	0.27/0.06
	NR	1.12/0.04	1.36/0.11
	RNU	0.35/0.04	0.35/0.04

(b)

Gain		$\sigma = 0.02$	
Offset		$\sigma = 5\%$	$\sigma = 10\%$
Method	Index		
Noisy	RMSE	0.05	0.10
	ρ	0.28	0.48
	ER	0.8	0.94
	NR	1.00	1.00
	RNU	0.42	0.45
Harris	RMSE	0.11	0.11
	ρ	0.13	0.14
	ER	0.28	0.31
	NR	1.01	1.16
	RNU	0.35	0.35
NN	RMSE	0.02	0.03
	ρ	0.12	0.14
	ER	0.25	0.32
	NR	1.12	1.29
	RNU	0.40	0.39

The obtained results suggest that from all of the reference free metrics, the one that best track the evolution of the correction or denoising process is the ρ index, in despite of the fact that it fails when identifying low frequency noise components or radiometric changes in the resulting image. In addition, it is the one that better fits the tendency given by the RMSE.

(a)   (b)   (c)   (d)

Fig. 3. NUC results on simulated FPN (test sec. 2) in the frame 1602 a) Reference Image b) Noisy Image c) Harris Correction and d) NN-Correction

6   Conclusions

In this paper we contrast several state-of-the-art reference-free indexes which are commonly used to evaluate the effectiveness of the FPN reduction methods. The study was performed by simulating the FPN typically found in two different imaging systems, such as hyperspectral and infrared cameras. The results indicate a low level of confidence between the presented indices given the inconsistency found when they are compared to each other. Nevertheless, the ρ metric presents the best results as a good blind indicator when it is contrasted to a standard reference-based index, but unfortunately it is not able to reveal any modification to the radiometric or dynamic range of the corrected or calibrated images. Future work may include a deeper study for different types of indexes and FPN reduction methods, giving the foundations for the design of a new blind index for NUC purposes.

Acknowledgements

This work was partially supported by FONDECYT 11090034 and the Center for Optics and Photonics (CEFOP) FB0824/2008.

References

1. Chang-yan, C., Ji-xian, Z., Zheng-jun, L.: Study on Methods of Noise Reduction in a Stripped Image. Int. Arch. of P, RS, and SI Sciences 37, 213–216 (2008)
2. Chen, J., Shao, Y., Guo, H., Wang, W., Zhu, B.: Destriping CMODIS Data by Power Filtering. IEEE Trans. on Geoscience and Remote Sensing 41, 2119–2124 (2003)
3. Gadallah, F., Csillag, F.: Destriping Multisensor Imagery with Moment Matching. International Journal of Remote Sensing 21, 2505–2511 (2000)
4. Harris, J., Chiang, Y.: Nonuniformity correction using constant average statistics constraint: analog and digital implementation. In: Proc. of SPIE, vol. 3061, pp. 895–905 (1997)
5. Harris, J., Chiang, Y.: Nonuniformity correction of infrared image sequences using constant statistics constraint. IEEE Trans. on Image Proc. 8, 1148–1151 (1999)
6. Hayat, M., Torres, S., Amstrong, E., Cain, S., Yasuda, B.: Statistical algorithm for nonuniformity correction in focal plane arrays. Applied Optics 38, 773–780 (1999)
7. Liu, Z., Forsyth, D., Laganière, R.: A feature-based metric for the quantitative evaluation of pixel-level image fusion. C. Vision and Image Under. 109, 56–68 (2008)
8. Munch, B., Trtik, P., Marone, F., Stampanoni, F.: Stripe and ring artifact removal with combined wavelet Fourier filtering. Optics Express 17, 8567–8591 (2009)
9. Rakwatin, P., Takeuchi, W., Yasuoka, Y.: Stripe Noise Reduction in MODIS Data by Combining Histogram Matching With Facet Filter. IEEE Trans. on Geoscience and Remote Science 45(6), 1844–1856 (2007)
10. San Martn, C., Torres, S., Pezoa, J.: An Effective Reference-Free Performance Metric for Non-uniformity Correction Algorithms in Infrared Imaging Systems. In: Proc. of the IEEE LEOS 20th A. M., pp. 576–577 (2007)
11. Schulz, M., Caldwell, L.: Nonuniformity Correction and Correctability of infrared focal plane arrays. Infrared Phys. Technology 36, 763–777 (1995)
12. Scribner, D., Sarkady, K., Kruer, M.: Adaptive nonuniformity correction for infrared focal plane arrays using neural networks. In: Proc. of SPIE, vol. 1541, pp. 100–109 (1991)
13. Scribner, D., Sarkady, K., Kruer, M.: Adaptive retina-like preprocessing for imaging detector arrays. In: Proc. of the IEEE Int. Conf. on Neural Net., vol. 3, pp. 1955–1960 (1993)
14. Wang, B., Liu, S., Bai, L.: An enhanced non-uniformity correction algorithm for IRFPA based on neural network. Optics Communications 281, 2040–2045 (2008)
15. Wang, Z., Bovik, A.: A universal image quality index. IEEE SP L 9, 81–84 (2002)
16. Wang, Z., Bovik, A., Sheikh, H., Simoncelli, E.: Image quality assessment: from error visibility to structural similarity. IEEE T. on Image Proc. 13, 600–612 (2004)

Vessel Centerline Tracking in CTA and MRA Images Using Hough Transform

Maysa M.G. Macedo[1], Choukri Mekkaoui[2], and Marcel P. Jackowski[1]

[1] University of São Paulo, Department of Computer Science,
Rua do Matão 1010, São Paulo, Brazil
{maysa,mjack}@ime.usp.br
[2] Harvard Medical School, 25, Shattuck Street, Boston, MA, USA
mekkaoui@nmr.mgh.harvard.edu

Abstract. Vascular disease is characterized by any condition that affects the circulatory system. Recently, a demand for sophisticated software tools that can characterize the integrity and functional state of vascular networks from different vascular imaging modalities has appeared. Such tools face significant challenges such as: large datasets, similarity in intensity distributions of other organs and structures, and the presence of complex vessel geometry and branching patterns. Towards that goal, this paper presents a new approach to automatically track vascular networks from CTA and MRA images. Our methodology is based on the Hough transform to dynamically estimate the centerline and vessel diameter along the vessel trajectory. Furthermore, the vessel architecture and orientation is determined by the analysis of the Hessian matrix of the CTA or MRA intensity distribution. Results are shown using both synthetic vessel datasets and real human CTA and MRA images. The tracking algorithm yielded high reproducibility rates, robustness to different noise levels, associated with simplicity of execution, which demonstrates the feasibility of our approach.

Keywords: lumen segmentation, vessel tracking, Hough transform, angiographic images, CTA, MRA.

1   Introduction

Vascular diseases have reached a significant number of people in the world. Developed countries and more recently underdeveloped countries have shown an increase of aneurysms, stenosis, embolisms and arteritis [1]. In this context, successful detection and characterization of vessel anomalies by medical imaging modalities as Computed Tomography Angiography (CTA) and Magnetic Resonance Angiography (MRA), requires efficient computational tools for visualization and analysis. Vessel segmentation methods may provide useful surgical planning information and may aid in diagnostics [2,3]. There are important challenges involving the characterization of vascular architectures: high-resolution images that increases computational time and storage space; handling

I. Bloch and R.M. Cesar, Jr. (Eds.): CIARP 2010, LNCS 6419, pp. 295–302, 2010.

of bifurcations and successful detection of capillaries. According to [4] the analysis of vascular images can be divided into four steps : (i) feature extraction - detect vessel points and diameters; (ii) geometric model - connect the vessel points to form vascular trees; (iii) quantify properties of the vascular tree; and in the case of serial imaging; and (iv) quantify differences in these properties over time. In most cases, methods rely on the detection of local tubular structures based on the local intensity characteristics. The feature extraction process in 3D images can be performed by tracking the vessel centerlines [5,6] or by extracting the vessel wall [7]. While most centerline-based methods directly estimate vessel diameters, they may have limitations such as their inability to track more than one branch at a time. Model-based methods, on the other hand, estimate vessel diameter from boundary detection techniques and may suffer from discontinuities because of noise. They may also require non-trivial initialization procedures. Overviews on vessel lumen segmentation techniques are presented in [8] and [9], according to different categories.

In order to avoid common drawbacks of model-based methods, we propose a methodology that easily tracks vessel centerlines and estimate vessel diameters, has simple initialization and avoids cumbersome multiscale extraction techniques. The work presented in this paper focuses on the development of a technique to extract blood vessel morphological attributes from 3D medical images using Hessian matrix information coupled with Hough Transform (HT) in order to perform detection and tracking.

This paper proposes the use of the HT to determine vessel scale for successful tracking without resorting to time-consuming multiscale techniques. Successive circle detection on 2D cross-sections and prediction of vessel direction are performed in order to track along a branch. In the next section, the methodology is detailed, followed by synthetic and real datasets results. A discussion of the methodology followed by conclusions and future research directions are provided at the end.

2   Vessel Tracking Method

The goal of the proposed vessel tracking is to construct a vessel skeleton based on the extracted centerlines on several slices. CTA and MRA images show vessels as high intensity profiles, with maximum intensity near their centers. The idea is to model this maximum intensity location as the center of a circle. When the plane of extraction is completely orthogonal to the vessel, the vessel wall can be modeled as a circle and this process can be repeated by following the tangent of the vessel trajectory.

2.1   Initialization and Preprocessing

An extraction plane orthogonal to a given vessel is selected from a 3D image to start the tracking process. Following selection, the extracted plane is smoothed by an anisotropic diffusion filter [10,11] to reduce noise and enhance linear structures. Next, morphological opening and subtraction operators are applied to highlight maximum intensities and the Canny filter finally is employed in order to extract edges. Parameter values at each step of this pipeline is chosen depending on the modality.

2.2   Vessel Detection by Hough Transform

Once the edge image is obtained, the HT is computed to identify circle centers and their estimated diameters. If more than one vessel is found in the chosen plane of extraction, the best match is chosen. At end of this step, both centerline and vessel radius is acquired.

2.3   Vessel Tangent Estimation

Based on this centerline and on the detected radius taken as a vessel scale, eigen-values $(\lambda_1, \lambda_2, \lambda_3)$ and eigenvectors (e_1, e_2, e_3) are computed from a Hessian matrix computed at the centerline location. The eigenvector corresponding to the eigenvalue closer to 0 (λ_1) indicates the vessel direction (e_1). This direction is maintained by the multiplication of e_1 and the sign of the dot product of e_1 and the previous tangent direction t_{i-1} at centerline point x_i:

$$t_i = signal(e_1 \cdot t_{i-1})e_1 \qquad (1)$$

The direction t_i defines the normal to the next extraction plane in the 3D image. Image resampling according to the new direction is necessary to detect the circles in a perpendicular manner. This process finishes when it is not possible to detect a significant difference between the eigenvalues. The proposed tracking method consists of successive executions of the above steps to extract a vessel trajectory. Figure 1 depicts tracking process scheme. Initially, only one vessel will be detected for each 2D cross-section to start the tracking. The idea is detect all centerlines of a unique vessel branch and then go back to each branching point to continue the centerline detection.

According to Aylward [12] it is necessary recover from local discontinuities, so during the tracking we adopted the following heuristics:

1) If λ_2 and λ_3 of the local Hessian become negative, the tangent and the normal directions may temporarily change. We detect the next eigenvector that best matches the previous tangent direction modifying the equation (1) to (3).

2) If $|\lambda_1 - \lambda_2| < 0.02$ the tangent vessel direction is not well defined. It is necessary choose the eigenvector that best matches the previous tangent direction according to equation (3).

$$q = arg \max_{j \in 1...3} (|e_j \cdot t_{i-1}|) \qquad (2)$$

$$t_i = signal(e_q \cdot t_{i-1})e_q \qquad (3)$$

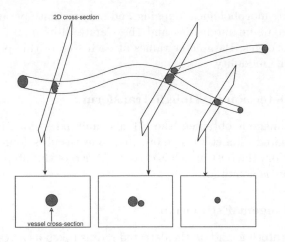

Fig. 1. Representative scheme of proposed method. The arrows indicate extracted planes according to the tangent direction identified by Hessian matrix.

2.4 Bifurcations

In a vessel network, a bifurcation is the branching of a vessel, which it can be further divided into several branches. This feature constitutes a challenge for most vessel tracking algorithm because the eigenvalues are not able to represent each individual bifurcation. However, when the tracking trajectory approaches a branching point, the vessel profile starts to change in shape, as well as its curvature (Fig. 2). The vessel shape changes from a convex configuration and becomes concave. This changing is employed to identify branching locations and determine follow-up directions for the subsequent extraction planes.

3 Preliminary Results

The methodology was implemented using C++ language and auxiliary libraries such as *Visualization Toolkit* and *Insight Toolkit*. Both synthetic images and a real CTA and MRA image was used in order to assess whether the centerlines and vessel tangent directions are correctly extracted.

3.1 Synthetic Images

Synthetic vessel images were constructed and corrupted by Gaussian noise in order to test for method's robustness to noise. In addition, to assess the tracking method's behavior on different vessel shapes, these images depict shapes with low and high curvature. Noise quantity depended on a normal random number and a percentage related to the maximum intensity image. In this case, images with 5%, 10% and 15% of noise were used. Synthetic images have size $128 \times 128 \times 128$, containing vessel of radius 2 voxels wide and cubic resolution ($1mm^3$). For

Fig. 2. Tracking sequence of a synthetic vessel with a branching point. From left to right, this sequence shows each slice when the tracking is approaching the bifurcation. A simple circle (convex curve) becomes a non trivial form (concave curve).

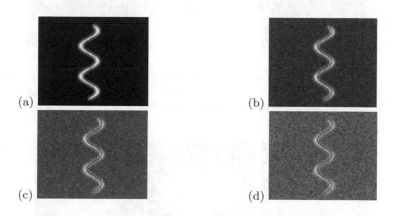

(a)   (b)

(c)   (d)

Fig. 3. Centerlines extracted from a simulated sinusoid. (a) Original image. (b) Image with 5% of noise. (c) Image with 10% of noise. (d) Image with 15% of noise.

our set of sinusoidal synthetic images, the average distance to the ground-truth centerlines was 1.5mm. Figures 3 and 4 show the extracted tube trajectories from noisy images.

3.2 Real Images

The real images represent a thoracic CTA and a cerebral MRA. Authors were blind in regard of the presence or not of possible vessel anomalies in either dataset. The CTA image was released by *Centre Hospitalier Universitaire - Hopital de la Timone* from a GE LightSpeed Pro 16 with size $512 \times 512 \times 256$, resolution $(0.78\text{x}0.78\text{x}0.78 \ mm^3)$. The MRA image was acquired by *Institute of Radiology - Hospital das Clínicas - University of São Paulo* in a Philips 3T with size $512 \times 512 \times 290$ and resolution $(0.39\text{x}0.39\text{x}0.50 \ mm^3)$. The goal is to extract the thoracic aorta from the CTA dataset and a segment of the internal carotid from the MRA image.

Preprocessing steps are ilustrated by Figure 5 (a)-(e). Following preprocessing, the HT is performed and the result is displayed by Figure 5 (f). After identifying the vessel center, the direction of the vessel cross-section is determined by computing the Hessian matrix. Figure 6 shows a sequence of resampled images according to the vessel direction characterizing the vessel tracking approach. Note that the aorta is at the middle of the image. As the 2D cross-section is

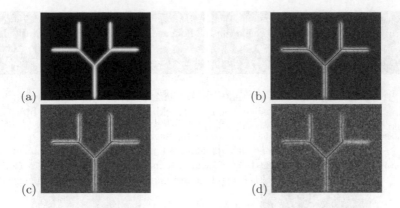

Fig. 4. Centerlines extracted from synthetic image with bifurcation points. (a) Original image. (b) Image with 5% of noise. (c) Image with 10% of noise. (d) Image with 15% of noise. In this case one of branches was not identified.

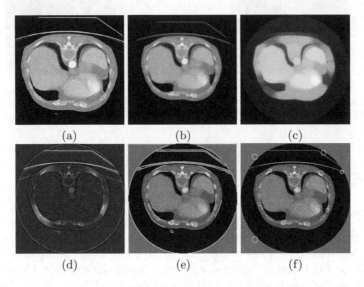

Fig. 5. Preprocessing steps of a CTA slice: (a) Input 2D cross-section (b) Anisotropic diffusion filtering (c) Opening operator result (d) Result of top-hat operator (e) Canny edges (f) Circle detection by Hough transform.

extracted perpendicularly to the vessel tangent, the vessel boundary resembles a circle. Figure 7 shows the extracted vessel trajectory. For the time, estimated diameter is not employed for visualization, although is immediately available after HT computation. Scale tests were performed after HT determination and vessel radius has been found to be off by +2 or -2 voxels.

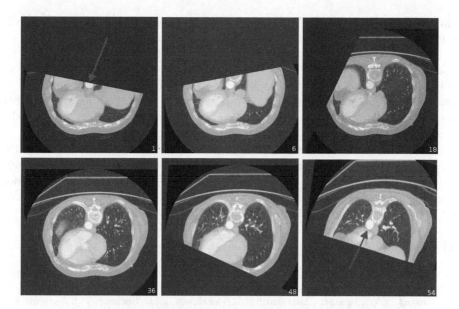

Fig. 6. From left to right, it is shown part of the sequence of 2D cross-sections extracted during the tracking of the thoracic aorta. The red arrow indicates the aorta cross-section.

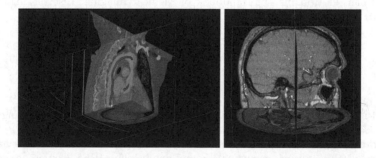

Fig. 7. (a) Thoracic aorta trajectory in CTA image track after 405 successive iterations (b) Carotid artery trajectory in MRA image after 310 iterations. Each centerline was extracted and represented as a cylinder. The step size between centerlines is $\delta=1$ voxel.

4   Discussion and Conclusions

In the present study, we have proposed a semi-automated method to detect and track vessel centerlines in CTA and MRA images. The initialization step is currently done interactively in order to select the starting plane for extraction. This interaction can be minimized by choosing a single point inside the vessel or selecting the most perpendicular plane to this vessel.

The methodology has shown to work well under significant amounts of noise, although a branch segment was not identified in the synthetic example corrupted with 15% Gaussian noise. A change in the tracking heuristics will be made in order to account for detecting an inverse direction from the seed point.

The main contribution of this work is the use of HT to define the seed point for tracking and detecting the vessel scale without resorting to multiscale analysis techniques, and in spite of the presence of anomalies, a mean diameter can be established. While branching in the synthetic datasets was handled according to the Section 2, it still remains to be thoroughly validated, given the complexity of real data bifurcations. Bifurcations were not handled in the real datasets.

Future work will focus on fine tuning the scale detection resulting from the HT, reconstructing the diameter of the extracted vessels, automatic bifurcation handling using analysis of curvature of the vessel profile at the cross-section when it approaches the branching point and use of ground-truth data to allow our method to be compared with established methods.

References

1. American Heart Association: Heart disease and stroke statistics - 2010 update. American Heart Association - Learn and Live (2010)
2. Zhuang, Z.W., Gao, L., Murakami, M., Pearlman, J.D., Sackett, T.J., Simons, M., Muinck, E.D.: Arteriogenesis: Non-invasive quantification with multi-detector row ct angiography and three-dimensional volume rendering in rodents. Radiology 240, 698–707 (2006)
3. Bankman, I., Hopkins, J.: Handbook of Medical Imaging. Elsevier, Amsterdam (2000)
4. Qian, X., Brennan, M.P., Dione, D.P., Dobrucki, W.L., Jackowski, M.P., Breuer, C.K., Sinusas, A.J., Papademetris, X.: A non-parametric vessel detection method for complex vascular structures. Medical Image Analysis 13, 49–61 (2009)
5. Metz, C.T., Weustink, A.C., Mollet, N.R., van Walsum, T., Niessen, W.J.: Coronary centerline extraction from ct coronary angiography images using a minimum cost path approach. Medical Physics 36(12) (2009)
6. Wink, O., Niessen, W.J., Viergever, M.A.: Multiscale vessel tracking. IEEE Transaction on Medical Imaging 23(1) (2004)
7. McIntosh, F., Hamarneh, G.: Vessel crawlers: 3d physically-based deformable organisms for vasculature segmentation and analysis. In: IEEE Conference on Computer Vision and Pattern Recognition, pp. 1084–1091 (2006)
8. Lesage, D., Angelini, E.D., Bloch, I., Funka-Lea, G.: A review of 3d vessel lumen segmentation techniques: Models, features and extraction scheme. Medical Image Analysis (2009)
9. Kirbas, C., Quek, F.: A review of vessel extraction techniques and algorithms. ACM Computing Surveys 36(2), 81–121 (2004)
10. Frangi, A.F., Niessen, W.J., Vincken, K.L., Viergever, M.A.: Multiscale vessel enhancement filtering. In: Wells, W.M., Colchester, A.C.F., Delp, S.L. (eds.) MICCAI 1998. LNCS, vol. 1496, pp. 130–137. Springer, Heidelberg (1998)
11. Manniesing, R., Viergever, A., Niessen, W.J.: Vessel enhancing diffusion. a scale space representation of vessel structures. Medical Image Analysis 10, 815–825 (2006)
12. Alyward, S., Bullitt, E.: Initialization, noise, singularities, and scale in height ridge traversal for tubular object centerline extraction. IEEE Transaction on Medical Imaging 21, 61–75 (2002)

Automatic Image Segmentation Optimized by Bilateral Filtering

Javier Sanchez, Estibaliz Martinez, Agueda Arquero, and Diego Renza

Polytechnic University of Madrid, DATSI, Informatics Fac. Campus de Montegancedo
28660 Boadilla del Monte, Madrid, Spain
jarsahe@hotmail.com,
{emartinez,aarquero}@fi.upm.es,
d.renza@alumnos.upm.es

Abstract. The object-based methodology is one of the most commonly used strategies for processing high spatial resolution images. A prerequisite to object-based image analysis is image segmentation, which is normally defined as the subdivision of an image into separated regions. This study proposes a new image segmentation methodology based on a self-calibrating multi-band region growing approach. Two multispectral aerial images were used in this study. The unsupervised image segmentation approach begins with a first step based on a bidirectional filtering, in order to eliminate noise, smooth the initial image and preserve edges. The results are compared with ones obtained from Definiens Developper software.

Keywords: Image segmentation, Bilateral filter, Self-calibrating framework.

1 Introduction

Remote sensing is an effective technology to acquire information about geographic objects. The automatic classification of remotely sensed data is an essential action within the process of generating or updating Geographical Information System (GIS) databases. The thematic mapping is a widely adopted method to obtain land cover information from satellite or aerial images and many classification algorithms have been extensively applied to. Increasing demands on the accuracy and thematic resolution of land cover maps from remote sensing imagery has created a need for novel image analysis techniques. During classical image classification, each pixel is assigned to a final class of the entire object according to their statistical properties, instead of determining the class label for each pixel separately (pixel-based methods). Pixel-based image classification encountered serious problem in dealing with high spatial resolution images. Therefore, object-based methods represent a good alternative [1] because the effect of the spectral variability, critical inconvenient present in these images, can be minimized.

One motivation for the object-oriented approach is the fact that, in many cases, the expected result of most image analysis tasks is the extraction of real world objects, proper in shape and proper in classification. The concept of "object" plays one of

I. Bloch and R.M. Cesar, Jr. (Eds.): CIARP 2010, LNCS 6419, pp. 303–310, 2010.
© Springer-Verlag Berlin Heidelberg 2010

central roles in image interpretation. This also has impact on the reliability of object recognition, which requires good whole-object segmentation. In this sense, image segmentation is critical for subsequent image analysis.

Segmentation subdivides an image into its constituent regions or objects. The level at which the subdivision is carried out depends on the problem being solved. That is, the segmentation should stop when the objects of interest in an application have been identified. Traditionally segmentation methods can be divided into methods based on pixel, on edge, and region-based methods. The last kind of segmentation methods includes region growing, region merging, region splitting and their combinations [2]. A world famous example of object oriented image analysis software is Definiens Developper [3], in which the multi-resolution image segmentation method [4] is key and a patented technology. But whatever the method, in remote sensed imagery, a critical task is the selection of segmentation parameters. In most cases, the parameters are selected by trial and error.

The primary focus of this paper is to introduce a new designed and implemented region-based image segmentation algorithm following self-calibrating idea proposed by Paglieroni [5], with an optimal initialization step based on a bidirectional filtering [6], which smoothes the initial image in order to reduce noise within regions while preserving edges between them. This method is validated by comparing the obtained results with ones obtained from Definiens Developper software.

2 Methodology

2.1 Study Scenes

Several remote sensed images with different spatial resolutions were used in this study, but only the obtained results with two selected multispectral aerial images (Scene 1 and Scene 2) are showed in this paper. The aerial image represents 8-bit RGB data with a high spatial resolution of 50 cm. In this case, the selection of segmentation parameters will be critical because you can end up with hundreds of thousands of objects.

The images cover an area of the order of 0.065 km^2. As with any remote sensing project, it is helpful if you have an idea of what you are looking at. In these scenes there are extensions of natural mediterranean forest partially or fully degraded, with the city-planning, industrial advance and road infrastructures that degrade natural zones in other times. The left corner is placed at 429581.98E, 4472991.21N and 428394.20E, 4474495.79 N (UTM geographic coordinates, h30) respectively.

2.2 Bilateral Filtering

This research proposes an initialization step where the image is filtered with a bilateral filter. Bilateral filtering is a non-linear filtering technique introduced by Tomasi [6], where the weight of each pixel is computed using a Gaussian in the spatial domain multiplied by an influence function in the intensity domain that decreases the weight of pixels with large intensity differences. Pixels that are very different in intensity from the central pixel are weighted less even though they may be in close proximity to the central pixel. Therefore, this is applied as two Gaussian filters at a localized pixel neighborhood, one in the spatial domain, named the domain filter (Fig.1a) which smoothes homogeneous areas, and one in the intensity domain, named the range filter (Fig.1b) which controls the smoothing for preserving edges. Thus, the main advantage of using bilateral filter (Fig. 1c) is the growth of large and homogeneous regions.

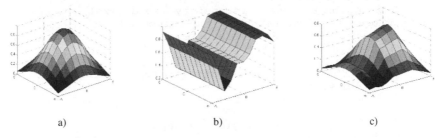

a)   b)   c)

Fig. 1. Domain (a), Range (b) and Bilateral (c) filters

2.3   Segmentation Process with Self-calibration Framework

Paglieroni [5] developed a self-calibration framework for automatically selecting parameter values that produce segmentations that most closely resemble a calibration edge map (derived separately using a simple edge detector), but there isn´t a commercial available implementation of this work. In order to implement our image segmentation software, it is proposed a new method based on its self-calibration framework for getting initial parameters but modifying some steps to try to optimize the quality of segmentation jointly with the computational efficiency.

After the initialization step where the image is processed with the bilateral filter described above, an adaptive Canny edge detection algorithm [7] is applied to obtain a calibration map. The Canny edge detector is employed to identify the mixed (edge) pixels in the image region and offers sub-pixel interpolation for detecting edges using a Gaussian filter. The algorithm is based on the computation of the image gradient. It works in a multistage process, which is summarized below. First, the image is smoothed by Gaussian convolution, then two-dimensional first derivatives are computed, the gradient magnitude (edge strength) and gradient direction are calculated. Traditionally, following steps consist of the non-maxima suppression, and the hysteresis thresholding by two parameters, low and high thresholds. These are used for estimating the population minimum parameter of region growing which is used to avoid small regions. These processes are applied with the objective of obtaining 1-pixel wide contours and to remove noisy maxima without breaking the contours, respectively.

In the methodology proposed, it is suggested erasing non-maxima suppression step because several experiments have showed that it is not critical for our goal, however this step would increase the execution time of the process. To obtain the region maps, the starting points of the segmentation, often referred to as 'seed' pixels, have to be identified. The regions are built around these pixels by joining the similar neighboring pixels to them. To compute the similarity the Euclidean distance is used. Once the regions have been obtained, a merging process is performed in order to eliminate small regions. The complete procedure is summarized in the next program code (region-growing pseudo-code)

```
Begin Region-growing:
    1. find seed pixel (not labeled and following a row-order)
    2. label it:
        2.1 seed_pixel = i
        2.2 region_average = intensisty (seed_pixel)
    3. explore its eight neighbors (8-connected):
        3.1 list = neighbors(seed pixel)
        3.2 while (length(list) > 0):
            remove first pixel y from L
            if      (euclidean_distance(y,      region_average)<
            distance):
                add y to L
                y = i
                update region average
Begin Region-merging:
    1. find region r with number of pixels < population_minimum
    2. list N = neighbors(r)
    3.  explore  its  neighbors  regions  looking  for  the  most
    similarity r_min:
        3.1 while (length(N) > 0):
            remove first region r' from N
            r_min = find_minimum(euclidean_distance(r, r'))
    4. merge(r, r_min)
End.
```

The automatically map generated prior to segmentation, is a calibration edge map that can be used to obtain the optimal region maps by means a measure of disparity (Figure 2). This disparity measure is calculated by comparing the maps of distances associated with edges maps of each region maps obtained during the segmentation process, with the map of distances from the calibration edge map. Note that this measure is obtained as described Paglieroni [5]. Consider a region map R and an associated binary border map B in which pixels of value 1 correspond to borders between different regions (specifically, $B(i,j) = 1$ if $R(i,j) \neq R(i-1,j)$ or $R(i,j-1)$). Let E be the calibration edge map with edge pixels of value 1 on a background of zeros (R, B and E all have the same number of rows and columns). The disparity Δ_{BE} between R and E is given by

$$
\begin{array}{ll}
\Delta_{BE} = 0 & n_B = n_E = 0 \\
\Delta_{BE} = 1 & n_B \text{ or } n_E = 0 \text{ but not both } 0 \\
\Delta_{BE} = (n_{BE}+n_{EB})/n_B+n_E & n_B, n_E \neq 0
\end{array}
\tag{1}
$$

In equation 1, n_B is the number of boundary pixels in B, n_E is the number of edge pixels in E, n_{BE} is the number of boundary pixels in B that are not associated with an edge pixels in E, and n_{EB} is the number of edge pixels in E not associated with a boundary pixel in B.

In order to evaluate this proposed segmentation methodology, the analysis of similarity factor (1-disparity factor) and the computation times has been carried out.

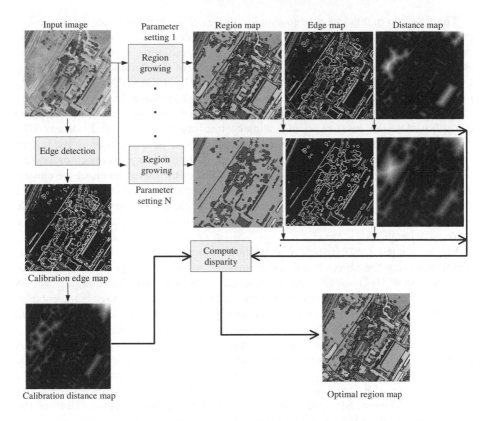

Fig. 2. Methodological scheme of self-calibration framework and segmentation

2.4   Segmentation Process with Definiens Developper Software

The segmentation technique used within Definiens Developer software for this investigation is the multi-resolution segmentation. This technique creates objects using an iterative algorithm, whereby objects (starting with individual pixels) are grouped until a threshold representing the upper object variance is reached. Critical parameters are used here to guide the segmentation result. The Scale parameter determines the maximum allowed heterogeneity for the resulting image objects. The Color criterion defines the weight with which the spectral values of the image layers contributes to image segmentation, as opposed to the weight of the Shape criterion. The relationship between Color and Shape criteria is: Color + Shape = 1. Maximum Color criterion 1.0 results in objects spectrally homogeneous; while with a value of less than 0.1, the created objects would not be related to the spectral information at all. Smoothness is used to optimize image objects with regard to smooth borders, and compactness allows optimizing image objects with regard to compactness [8]. The resulting objects also depend on the image data. For a given set of segmentation parameters, heterogeneous image data result in smaller image objects than homogeneous image data.

The first step in this image segmentation process has been to cluster the image and produce a low-level segmentation for further processing. This strategy permits to optimize the selection of parameters for the multi resolution segmentation (second step). The clustering step was carried out by means of the Iterative Self-Organizing Data Analysis Technique (ISODATA) [9]. Traditionally, ISODATA begins arbitrarily locating a given number of cluster centroids in the feature space. In this case, we have introduced in the process, the initial spectrally supervised centroids. Therefore, the algorithm classifies each pixel of an image into one of these initial clusters. The classification is carried out by assigning each pixel to the nearest cluster in the feature space. A Euclidean distance measure is applied. After the image has been processed, the cluster centers are recalculated as a mean vector of the observations of the cluster. This process continues iterating until one of the user-defined parameters; convergence threshold or the maximum number of iterations is reached. The convergence threshold is the percentage of those observations which remain in a same cluster during two successive iterations.

In the second step, image segmentation (multi resolution segmentation) was performed using the object-based image analysis software Definiens Developper for Earth Sciences [3]. The segmentation approach is a bottom-up region merging process based on heterogeneity of image objects, and controlled by three segmentation parameters: shape(S)/color, compactness/smoothness, and a scale parameter [10]. Shape/Color and compactness(C)/smoothness were set to 0.1/0.9 and 0.5/0.5 respectively, using as a guideline previous research with Supervised ISODATA Clustering (SIC) imagery in this study scenes. We segmented the images (each of the three layers, RGB has an equal weight) several times with different values for the scale parameter (SP) and choosing from 50 to 150 in increments of 50. At scales coarse than 150, some SIC individual class were being merged together, therefore 150 became the cut-off of the coarsest scale.

3   Results

First, the goodness of the new approach can be analyzed by comparing the visual interpretation of segmented images (Fig. 3). This method generates more real world objects or segments (RGB image supervision). The results from Definiens show a major number of segments than the obtained by the proposed methodology and thus an unreasonable segmentation of natural soil land cover is carried out (see Fig. 3c). If the Scale parameter is changed, the number of segments can decrease, but we will not get the proper segmentation of vegetation land covers (trees). This confirms that the selection of segmentation parameters is a critical task and in most cases, it has to be choosing by trial and error. However in this case, a previous low-level segmentation (ISODATA clustering) was carried out, in order to define the guidelines of the segmentation parameters.

On the other hand, the similarity factor obtained from disparity factor is shown as measure of images segmentation quality, in Table 1. These values indicate the goodness of the segmentation methodology proposed in this work.

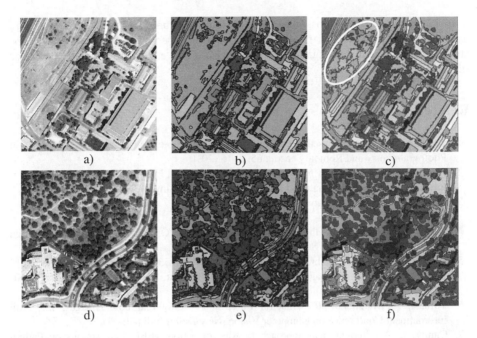

Fig. 3. Comparison of segmented images. a) and d) RGB images. b) and e) Segmented images by means the proposed methology. c) and f) Segmented images by multi resolution segmentation from Definiens Developper Software (SP = 50, S = 0.1 and C = 0.5).

Table 1. Evaluation parameters with a 2.1 GHz processor and 640 MB of RAM

	This work (Execution time / Similarity factor)	Definiens Developper (Execution time)
Scene 1	1.265 s / 88 %	5 s
Scene 2	1.297 s / 93 %	6 s

4   Conclusions

It was designed and implemented our image segmentation methodology for information extraction from remotely sensed imagery. We propose in this paper an unsupervised image segmentation approach with an optimal initialization step based on applying a bidirectional filter as a pre-processing step to eliminate noise, smooth the initial image and preserving edges.

Our segmentation method is validated with several experiments and the results show similar segmentation quality with ones obtained from Definiens Developer software, however in the self-calibration framework, the parameter values are automatically select, and this is a great advantage. Likewise the execution times for our segmentation algorithm are better than the obtained from multiresolution segmentation performed by Definiens Developper software.

In the future work, the possibility of adding new features such as color and texture as well as parallelization of the self-calibration process and the bilateral filter will be studied for optimizing the quality of segmentation and execution time on very large images.

References

1. Blashke, T.: Object based image analysis for remote sensing. ISPRS Journal of Photogrammetry and Remote Sensing 65, 2–16 (2010)
2. Pekkarinen, A.: A method for the segmentation of very high spatial resolution images of forested landscapes. International Journal of Remote Sensing 23, 2817–2836 (2002)
3. http://www.definiens.com/
   definiens-developer-for-earth-sciences_180_7_9.html
4. Baatz, M., Schape, A.: Multiresolution Segmentation an Optimization Approach for High Quality Multi-scale Image Segmentation, http://www.ecognition.com
5. Paglieroni, D.: A self-calibrating multi-band region growing approach to segmentation of single and multi-band images. In: SPIE Photonics West, Optical Engineering at LLNL (2003)
6. Tomasi, R., Manduchi, R.: Bilateral Filtering for gray and color images. In: Sixth International Conference on Computer Vision, New Delhi, India (1998)
7. Canny, J.: A computational approach to edge detection. IEEE Transactions on Pattern Analysis and Machine Intelligence 8, 679–698 (1986)
8. Baatz, M., Benz, U., Dehghani, S., Heynen, M., Holtje, A., Hofmann, P., Lingenfelder, I., Mimler, M., Sohlbach, M., Weber, M., Willhauck, G.: eCognition User's Guide,
   http://www2.definiens.com/central/default.asp
9. Tou, J.T., Gonzalez, R.C.: Pattern Recognition Principles. Addison-Wesley, Reading (1974)
10. Benz, U.C., Hofmann, P., Willhauck, G., Lingenfelder, I., Heynen, M.: Multi-resolution, object-oriented fuzzy analysis of remote sensing data for GIS-ready information. ISPRS Journal of Photogrammetry & Remote Sensing 58, 239–258 (2004)

Pansharpening of High and Medium Resolution Satellite Images Using Bilateral Filtering

Diego Renza, Estibaliz Martinez, Agueda Arquero, and Javier Sanchez

Polytechnic University of Madrid
d.renza@alumnos.upm.es,
{emartinez,aarquero}@fi.upm.es,
jarsahe@hotmail.com

Abstract. We provide and evaluate a fusion algorithm of remotely sensed images, i.e. the fusion of a panchromatic (PAN) image with a multi-spectral (MS) image using bilateral filtering, applied to images of three different sensors: SPOT 5, Landsat ETM+ and Quickbird. To assess the fusion process, we use six quality indexes, that confirm, along with visual analysis, good overall results for the three sensors.

Keywords: Bilateral filter, Image fusion, Pansharpening.

1 Introduction

The term "image fusion" usually implies the integration of images acquired by multiple sensors with the intention of providing a better perspective of a scene that contains more content. In remote sensing there are many sensors that have a set of multispectral bands and a co-registered higher spatial resolution panchromatic band. Examples of this sensors are SPOT, Landsat ETM+, QuickBird, or IKONOS. With appropriate algorithms it is possible to combine these data and produce multispectral imagery with higher spatial resolution. This concept is known as multispectral or multisensor merging, fusion or sharpening (of the lower-resolution image) [1].

In remote sensing, the fusion schemes can be grouped into three classes: (1) color related techniques, (2) statistical/numerical methods and (3) combined approaches [2]. The first covers the color composition of three image channels in the RGB color space as well as more sophisticated color transformations, e.g., HSV (hue-saturation-value), IHS (intensity-hue-saturation) [3]. The second group includes methods that use different mathematical tools, like channel statistics including correlation and filters. High pass filtering (HPF) [1], principal component analysis (PCA) [3] and multiresolution analysis (MRA) [4] belong to this category. The combined approaches include methods that are not limited to follow one approach.

In particular, fusion methods based on injection of high-frequency components into resampled versions of the MS bands have shown better spectral results, attracting the interest of researchers in recent years [5]. Within these methods

I. Bloch and R.M. Cesar, Jr. (Eds.): CIARP 2010, LNCS 6419, pp. 311–318, 2010.

can highlight the different variants of MRA (e.g. wavelets), or a less complex scheme, the high pass filtering, so we propose a new fusion scheme that makes use of bilateral filter as principal element for the extraction of features.

The next section describes a non-linear technique appropriate for image processing, known as bilateral filter (BF) which has been used for some image processing applications like denoising, texture editing or optical flow estimation [6]; also BF has been used for merging video (Visible (RGB) + IR) [7] and detail enhancement in multi-light image collections [8]. BF is an effective way to smooth an image while preserving its discontinuities and also to separate image structures of different scales, hence we propose its use in pansharpening.

2   Bilateral Filter

A bilateral filter is an edge-preserving smoothing filter. BF operates both in the domain and range of the image (i.e. pixel values). In the image domain, the core component of many filters is the kernel convolution. At each pixel position the filter estimates the local average of intensities, which corresponds to low-pass filtering. For instance, the Gaussian filtering (GF) is a weighted average of the intensity of the adjacent pixels where the weights decrease with the spatial distance to the center position; GF is a simple approach to smooth images, but with blurred edges, because pixels across discontinuities are averaged together.

Bilateral filter was proposed based on the definition of Gaussian convolution, taking into account both the image domain as the range image. BF is also defined as a weighted average of nearby pixels, the difference with GF is that BF takes into account the difference in value with the neighbors to preserve edges while smoothing. The key idea of the bilateral filter is that for a pixel influences another pixel, it should not only occupy a nearby location but also have a similar value [6]. The bilateral filter is simple: each pixel is replaced by a weighted average of its neighbors; BF depends only on two parameters that indicate the size and contrast of the features to preserve; furthermore, BF can be used in a non-iterative manner. Mathematically BF is given by [6]:

$$BF\left[I\right]_p = \frac{1}{W_p} \sum_{q \in S} G_{\sigma_s}\left(\|p - q\|\right) G_{\sigma_r}\left(|I_p - I_q|\right) I_q \tag{1}$$

$$W_p = \sum_{q \in S} G_{\sigma_o}\left(\|p - q\|\right) G_{\sigma_r}\left(|I_p - I_q|\right) \tag{2}$$

Where normalization factor W_p ensures pixel weights sum to 1.0.

$\sum_{q \in S}$ denotes a sum over all image pixels indexed. $|.|$ is used for the absolute value and $\|.\|$ for the L2 norm. G_σ denotes a 2D Gaussian Kernel.

G_{σ_r} is a range Gaussian function that decreases the influence of pixels q when their intensity values differ from I_p, therefore as the range parameter σ_r increases, the bilateral filter gradually approximates Gaussian convolution. G_{σ_s} is a spatial Gaussian weighting function that decreases the influence of distant pixels, therefore increasing the spatial parameter σ_s smooths larger features.

3   Image Fusion with Bilateral Filter

The potential benefit of a fused image is that the single resulting image both has a high spatial resolution and contains the spectral information, hence, the result of image fusion is a new image which is more suitable for human and machine perception or further image-processing tasks such a classification, segmentation, feature extraction or object recognition. For image fusion with BF, we first resample the MS image so that its bands have the same pixel size as the PAN image. These bands, along with PAN image are decomposed by means of BF.

The BF can split an image into two parts: (1) a filtered image, equivalent to low frequency component and in particular to spectral information, which holds only the large-scale features, as the bilateral filter smooths away local variations without affecting strong edges and (2) a "residual" image, made by subtracting the filtered image from the original, which holds only the image portions that the filter removed, i.e. detail or small-scale components that can represent texture or structures within image.

Therefore, the idea of applying the bilateral filter is to extract the details of the PAN image and the approximation (large-scale component) of the MS bands. A key factor when extracting these components is filter-parameters determination. Experimentally we obtained the best results with a $\sigma_s = R/2$, for both the PAN and MS images filter, where R is the scale ratio between PAN and MS images. In the case of σ_r, best results were obtained with $\sigma_r = 0.1(2^{nbits} - 1)$ for MS image and $\sigma_r = 0.4(2^{nbits} - 1)$ for the PAN image, where $nbits$ is the radiometric resolution of each image.

To combine these two components it is necessary to define an injection model to establish how high frequency information will be merged with the MS bands. Such a model can be global over the whole image or can depend on the spectral or spatial context [5]. In our case it was only necessary to apply a weight factor to the high frequency component, adding it to the low frequency component, thus minimizing spectral distortions. For the injection of these details the gain factor is defined by the ratio of standard deviation of each MS band approximation to the standard deviation of the PAN. The fusion process is showed in the Fig. 1.

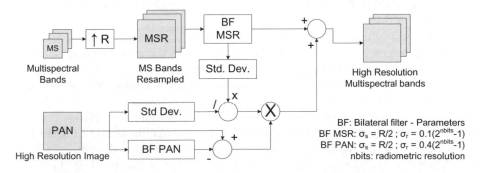

Fig. 1. Block diagram of bilateral filter-based image fusion approach (scale ratio 1:R)

4   Data and Methodology

4.1   Study Area

The proposed approach was applied to images from sensors of medium and high resolution: SPOT 5, Landsat ETM+ and Quickbird. The cases presented in this paper are:

1. Spot5: PAN 2048 x 2048 px (2,5 m), MS 512x512x4 (10 m). Madrid (Spain), 461990 E, 4480340 N (WGS84 UTM Zone 30)
2. Landsat ETM+: PAN 768 x 768 px (15 m), MS 384x384x6 (30 m) (Bands 1-5 & 7). Madrid (Spain), 409012,5 E, 4419247,5 N (WGS84 UTM Zone 30)
3. Quickbird: PAN 2048 x 2048 px (0,7 m), MS 512x512x4 (2,8 m). Madrid (Spain), 434753,2 E, 4479221,6 N (WGS84 UTM Zone 30)

4.2   Quality Determination - Comparison with Other Techniques

For comparison we employed four different image-fusion algorithms: two standard fusion techniques implemented in commercial software (ENVI), these were Gram-Schmidt spectral sharpening [9] and principal component (PC) fusion [10]. The third algorithm was a multiresolution analysis-based method, proposed recently [11,12]. The fourth method, bilateral filter-based fusion, is proposed in this work. All images were visually and statistically evaluated.

For quality evaluation, the first step was a visual analysis of the fused images. Therefor it was necessary take into account the color preservation of the fused image with respect to the original MS image. In the same way the quality evaluation took into account the spatial improvement of fused image compared to the original PAN image. Although the visual analysis is subjective and depends on the interpreter, it usually gives a first idea of spatial and spectral distortions.

To evaluate the quality of the merged image, it is usually compared against a reference image. In practice a true reference image does not exist, therefore, it is necessary to create it from the original PAN (with resolution h) and MS (with resolution l) images. Therefor, the PAN image is degraded to the low resolution l and the MS image is degraded to the resolution l^2/h. The fusion process is applied to new degraded images and the quality can be assessed using the original MS image as a reference image [13].

To assess the fusion process we use the following metrics [4,13]: (a) Relative Dimensionless Global Error (ERGAS), used to estimate the overall spectral quality of fused images. (b) Spectral Angle Mapper (SAM), which determines the degree of spectral similarity of an image against a known or reference image, expressed in terms of the average angle between the two spectra. (c) Mean bias (MB), which measures the difference in central tendency of two images. (d) Variance Difference (VD) for estimating the change in variance during the enhancement of the spatial resolution. (e) Standard deviation difference (SDD), which provides a global indication of the level of error at any pixel. (f) Correlation Coefficient (CC), which shows the similarity in small size structures between the original and synthetic images.

5   Results

Tables 1,2,3 show the quality measures for the whole image of three cases studied. Figures 2,3,4 show only a sub-scene of the corresponding merged images. The visual analysis shows a perceptible improvement in spatial quality for fused images compared with the original MS image. Although slight variations occur, all methods clearly sharpen the original image and improving the spatial quality.

By comparing the resulting images, one can also see that the fused images retain a high degree of spectral information. For color preservation, 432 and 321

Table 1. Test Case No. 1, SPOT5. Quality metrics. [a]Average for all four bands.

Type	ERGAS	SAM (*rad*)	MB[a]	VD[a]	SDD[a]	CC[a]
Ideal	0	0	0	0	0	1
Bilateral filter	**1,3316**	**0,0260**	**-6,38E-04**	**0,0375**	**0,0523**	**0,9736**
Gram-Schmidt	1,9021	0,0329	1,64E-04	0,1164	0,0756	0,9476
PCA	1,7581	0,0317	-2,96E-04	0,1405	0,0698	0,9549
DT-CWT	1,6392	0,0273	2,59E-05	0,0050	0,0642	0,9607

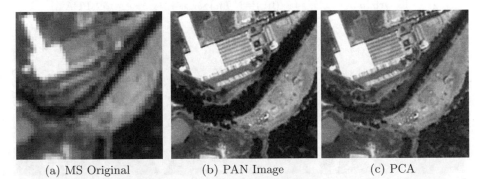

(a) MS Original   (b) PAN Image   (c) PCA

(d) BF   (e) DT-CWT   (f) Gram-Schmidt

Fig. 2. Test Case No. 1, SPOT5. A fragment of the original MS (10 m), PAN (2,5 m) and fused images (2,5 m). (200x200 pixels false color (NIR-Red-Green) composition).

Table 2. Test Case No. 2, Landsat ETM+. Quality metrics. [a]Average for all six bands.

Type	ERGAS	SAM (rad)	MB[a]	VD[a]	SDD[a]	CC[a]
Ideal	0	0	0	0	0	1
Bilateral filter	2,1755	0,0243	-1,02E-05	0,0691	0,0427	0,9800
Gram-Schmidt	4,0632	0,0352	4,34E-04	0,0722	0,0794	0,9329
PCA	4,5065	0,0368	-2,76E-04	0,0577	0,0878	0,9185
DT-CWT	2,3891	0,0294	-9,01E-06	0,0532	0,0473	**0,9749**

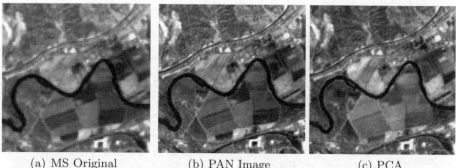

(a) MS Original   (b) PAN Image   (c) PCA

(d) BF   (e) DT-CWT   (f) Gram-Schmidt

Fig. 3. Test Case No. 2, Landsat ETM+. A fragment of the original MS (30 m), PAN (15 m) and fused images (15 m). (200x200 pixels false color 432 composition).

band RGB combinations are showed for spectral analysis. The spectral distortion of the PCA and Gram-Schmidt methods is most visible in the red color of vegetation (false color). The BF and DT-CWT methods produce an image whose colors better match the original image.

Regarding the quality indexes, (Tables 1,2,3) the values obtained for ERGAS, combined with the angles obtained by the SAM metric, were acceptable, so the spectral information is largely preserved, particularly according to BF and DT-CWT for SPOT and Landsat images. As for the mean bias, results close to ideal were obtained since the injection of spatial information resulted in a near-zero mean. The difference in variance suggests an advantage for the BF and

Table 3. Test Case No. 3, Quickbird. Quality metrics. [a]Average for all four bands.

Type	ERGAS	SAM (*rad*)	MB[a]	VD[a]	SDD[a]	CC[a]
Ideal	0	0	0	0	0	1
Bilateral filter	**3,8319**	**0,0908**	**-6,30E-04**	**0.1907**	**0.1476**	**0.9288**
Gram-Schmidt	4,4896	0.1067	4,54E-04	0,3162	0.1726	0.9069
PCA	4,5392	0.1015	8,36E-04	0.2458	0.1745	0.9032
DT-CWT	3,8623	0.0868	-7,40E-05	0.1378	0.1486	0.9290

(a) MS Original   (b) PAN Image   (c) PCA

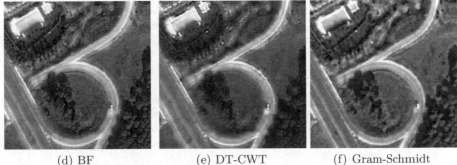

(d) BF   (e) DT-CWT   (f) Gram-Schmidt

Fig. 4. Test Case No. 3, Quickbird. A fragment of the original MS (2,8 m), PAN (0,7 m) and fused images (0,7 m). (200x200 pixels true color (RGB) composition).

DT-CWT, which preserve slightly more information. The overall estimate of error in a pixel (SDD) shows again better results for the BF and DT-CWT. Although visually the results are very similar in spatial quality, correlation coefficient shows slightly higher results for the BF in two of three cases.

6   Conclusion

The proposed fusion scheme showed good results applied to three different types of sensors. It was compared against traditional methods and showed that BF is an appropriate alternative for image fusion, presenting the best results for SPOT and Landsat images and results similar to a wavelet approach. In the Quickbird case it is necessary to study alternatives to the merger scheme adapted to the pixel size to preserve the spectral information more accurately. However, it is important to consider the influence of image degradation when implementing quality indices. A future work will consider alternatives such as multiscale approach and fast approximations of the bilateral filter.

References

1. Schowengerdt, R.A.: Remote Sensing: Models and Methods for Image Processing, 3rd edn. Academic Press, San Diego (2007)
2. Pohl, C., Van Genderen, J.L.: Multisensor image fusion in Remote sensing: concepts, methods and applications. Int. Journal of Remote Sensing 19, 823–854 (1998)
3. Gonzalez-A, M., Saleta, J.L., Garcia-C, R., Garcia, R.: Fusion of Multispectral and Panchromatic Images Using Improved IHS and PCA Mergers Based on Wavelet Decomposition. IEEE Trans. on Geos. and Rem. Sens. 42(6), 1291–1299 (2004)
4. Alparone, L., Wald, L., Chanussot, J., Thomas, C., Gamba, P., Bruce, L.M.: Comparison of Pansharpening Algorithms Outcome of the 2006 GRS-S Data-Fusion Contest. IEEE Trans. on Geoscience and Rem. Sensing 45(10) (2007)
5. Aiazzi, B., Baronti, S., Selva, M.: Image fusion through multiresolution oversampled decompositions. In: Stathaki, T. (ed.) Image Fusion: Algorithms and Applications. Academic Press, London (2008)
6. Paris, S., Kornprobst, P., Tumblin, J., Durand, F.: Bilateral Filtering: Theory and Applications. Foundations and Trends in Computer Graphics and Vision 4(1), 1–73 (2008)
7. Bennett, E.P., Mason, J.L., McMillan, L.: Multispectral Bilateral Video Fusion. IEEE Transactions on Image Processing 16(5), 1185–1194 (2007)
8. Fattal, R., Agrawala, M., Rusinkiewicz, S.: Multiscale Shape and Detail Enhancement from Multi-light Image Collections. In: ACM SIGGRAPH (2007)
9. Laben, C.A., Brower, B.V.: Process for enhancing the spatial resolution of multispectral imagery using pan-sharpening. US Patent No. 6,011,875. Eastman Kodak Company (2000)
10. Chavez, W.J., Sides, S.C., Anderson, J.A.: Comparison of three different methods to merge multiresolution and multispectral data. Phot. Eng. Rem. Sens. 57, 295–303 (1991)
11. Ioannidou, S., Karathanassi, V.: Investigation of the Dual-Tree Complex and Shift-Invariant Discrete Wavelet Transforms on Quickbird Image Fusion. IEEE Geoscience and Remote Sensing Letters 4(1), 166–170 (2007)
12. Renza, D., Martinez, E., Arquero, A.: Optimizing classification accuracy of remotely sensed imagery with DT-CWT fused images. In: Bayro-Corrochano, E., Eklundh, J.O. (eds.) CIARP 2009. LNCS, vol. 5856, pp. 1031–1038. Springer, Heidelberg (2009)
13. Wald, L.: Data fusion: Definitions and Architectures - Fusion of Images of Different Spatial Resolutions, Paris, ch. 8 (2002)

Color Image Segmentation by Means of a Similarity Function

Rodolfo Alvarado-Cervantes, Edgardo M. Felipe-Riveron[*],
and Luis P. Sanchez-Fernandez

Center for Computing Research, National Polytechnic Institute, Juan de Dios Batiz w/n,
Col. Nueva Industrial Vallejo, P.O. 07738, Mexico
Tel.: (52)-55-5729 6000; Ext. 56515
ateramex@gmail.com, edgardo@cic.ipn.mx, lsanchez@cic.ipn.mx

Abstract. An interactive, semiautomatic image segmentation method is presented which, unlike most of the existing methods in the published literature, processes the color information of each pixel as a unit, thus avoiding color information scattering. The process has two steps: 1) The manual selection of few sample pixels of the color to be segmented, 2) The automatic generation of the so called *Color Similarity Image* (CSI), which is a gray level image with all the tonalities of the selected color. The color information of every pixel is integrated by a similarity function for direct color comparisons. The color integrating technique is direct, simple, and computationally inexpensive. It is shown that the improvement in quality of our proposed segmentation technique and its quick result is significant with respect to other solutions found in the literature.

Keywords: Color image segmentation; Adaptive color similarity function; HSI parameter distances; Morphology in color images.

1 Introduction

Image segmentation consists of partitioning an entire image into different regions, which are similar in some predefined manner. Segmentation is an important feature of human visual perception, which manifests itself spontaneously and naturally. It is also one of the most important and difficult tasks in image analysis and processing [2] [6] [8] [9] [10]. All subsequent steps, such as feature extraction and objects recognition depend on the quality of segmentation. Without a good segmentation algorithm, objects of interest in a complex image are difficult (often impossible) to recognize using automated techniques [1] [2] [7] [8] [10]. At present, several segmentation techniques are available for color images, but most of them are just monochromatic methods applied on the individual planes in different color spaces where the results are combined later in different ways [5]. Their common problem is that when the color components of a particular pixel are processed separately the color information is so scattered in its components that most of the color information is lost [2] [5] [9].

In this work, an interactive, semiautomatic image segmentation method is presented which, in contrast with most of previously published algorithms, uses the color

---

[*] Corresponding author.

I. Bloch and R.M. Cesar, Jr. (Eds.): CIARP 2010, LNCS 6419, pp. 319–328, 2010.
© Springer-Verlag Berlin Heidelberg 2010

information for each pixel as a whole, thus avoiding color information scattering. In our method, the three color components (RGB) of every pixel transformed to the HSI color model are integrated in two steps: in the definitions of distances in hue, saturation and intensity planes $[\Delta_h, \Delta_s, \Delta_i]$ and in the construction of an adaptive color similarity function that combines these three distances assuming normal probability distributions.

To obtain a consistent color model for direct color comparisons, some simple but important modifications to the classical HSI color space were necessary. These modifications eliminated the discontinuities occurring in the red hue (in 0 and 360 degrees) and all the problems associated with them.

The segmentation method proposed basically relies on the calculation of a color similarity function for every pixel in a RGB 24-bit true color image, its automatic thresholding and finally the possible application of some simple morphological filters to introduce geometric characteristics in some cases where it is needed.

2   Previous Works

There has been a considerable amount of research dedicated to the problem of color image segmentation due to its importance and potential, and because color is an effective and robust visual cue for differentiating between objects in an image. The current available techniques and approaches vary widely from extensions of classical monochromatic techniques to mathematical morphology [2], clustering schemes [4] [12], wavelets [3] and quaternions [11], among others. Until recently, the majority of published approaches were based on monochromatic techniques applied to each color component image in different color spaces, and in different ways to produce a color composite [5].

Some color similarity measures and distances are presented in [10]. All these measures compare color pixels as units. They are all based in three dimensional vector representations of color in which each vector component corresponds to the RGB color channels components.

A technique that combines geometrical and color features for segmentation extending concepts of mathematical morphology (for gray images) is developed in [2] to process color images. The final segmentation is obtained by fusing a hierarchical partition image and a text/graphic finely detailed image.

In [15] the authors present a mathematic and physic solid framework for the local measure of texture in color images. They present a physic based color model using as a starting point three dimensional energy density functions $E(x, y, \lambda)$. From these energy density functions they derive color texture measures in the wavelength – Fourier domain using Gaussian derivative apertures integrating in this way texture and color information. In their implementation they start with RGB images transforming them to an opponent Gaussian color space $(E, E_\lambda, E_{\lambda\lambda})$ by a linear transform where they process with each channel separately with a set of Gabor filters and integrate later the results.

3 Description of the Method

The segmentation method proposed in this paper basically relies on the calculation of a color similarity function for every pixel in a RGB 24-bit true color image to form what we call a *Color Similarity Image* (CSI), which is a gray level image. A true color image usually contains millions of colors and many thousands of them represent the same perceived color of a single object due to the presence of additive noise, lack of definition between color borders and regions, shadows in the scene, etc., [1] [8] [10]. The color similarity function proposed allows the clustering of the many thousands colors representing the same perceived color in a single gray output image. This CSI image is then automatically thresholded and the output can be used as segmentation layer, or it can be used with morphological operators to introduce geometric enhancements if they are needed.

Firstly, we compute the color centroid and color standard deviation of a small sample consisting of few pixels. The computed centroid represents the desired color to be segmented using the technique we designed for that purpose.

Then, our color similarity function uses the color standard deviation calculated from the pixel sample to adapt the level of color scattering in the comparisons. The result of a particular similarity function calculation for every pixel and the color centroid (meaning the similarity measure between the pixel and the color representative value) generates the CSI. The generation of this image is the basis of our method and preserves the information of the color selected from the original color image. This CSI is a digital representation of a normalized function [0 - 1] extended to the range of [0 - 255].

The CSI can be thresholded with any automatic method like Otsu's [13] which was our selection for the results presented in this work. In those cases where color is a discriminating characteristic of objects of interest in a source image, only thresholding the CSI could be necessary to complete the segmentation.

To generate a CSI we need: 1. A color image in RGB 24-bit true color format; and 2. A small set of arbitrarily located pixels forming a sample of the color desired to be segmented. From this sample of pixels we calculate the statistical indicators according to our HSI modified color model (see Section 3.1). This information is necessary to adapt the color similarity function in order to obtain good results. To obtain the CSI we calculate for every pixel (i, j) in the image the following color similarity function S :

$$S_{i,j} = e^{(\frac{-\Delta_h^{\,2}}{2\sigma_h^{\,2}})} * e^{(\frac{-\Delta_s^{\,2}}{2\sigma_s^{\,2}})} * e^{(\frac{-\Delta_i^{\,2}}{2\sigma_i^{\,2}})} . \qquad (1)$$

where Δ_h is the hue Euclidean distance between $hue(i, j)$ and the *average_hue* ; Δ_s is the saturation Euclidean distance between *saturation* (i, j) and the *average_saturation* ; Δ_i is the intensity Euclidean distance between *intensity* (i, j) and the *average_intensity* ; σ_h is the hue standard deviation of the sample; σ_s is the Saturation standard deviation of the sample; σ_i is the Intensity standard deviation of the sample. In Eq. (1) the color information is integrated giving high importance to perceptual small changes in hue, as well as giving wide or narrow tolerance to the intensity and saturation values depending on the initial sample, which is representative to the desired color to be segmented.

The common disadvantages attributed to the cylindrical color spaces such as the irremovable singularities of hue in very low saturations or the periodical nature of hue [5] (which is lost in its standard representation as an $angle \in [0°, 360°]$ are overcome in our technique using vector representation in $\Re^2$ in the separation of chromatic and achromatic regions, and in the definition of the Δ_h, Δ_s and Δ_i distances.

Two modifications on standard HSI color space were necessary in order to create a consistent model to represent colors and color centroids:

1. *Representation of hue.* Instead of standard representation of hue as an angle in the range [0°-360°], hue is represented here as a normalized vector in $\Re^2$ (with magnitude 1 or 0). This representation has at least three advantages compared to an angle in the range [0°-360°] a) the existing discontinuity in 360 and 0 degrees is eliminated; b) the average hue of a group of pixels can be understood as the resulting angle of a vector addition of the color pixels in the chromatic region of the sample, giving a simple manner to calculate the average hue; c) setting magnitude to 0 or 1 works as a flag intended for distinction between chromatic or achromatic regions.

2. *Separation of chromatic and achromatic regions.* We use a separation of the region as described in [10] in order to calculate the average hue and Δ_h. Once calculated Δ_h, Δ_s and Δ_i this distinction is no longer necessary because in the formulation of $S_{i,j}$ (Eq. 1) all the cases of color comparison between zones are accounted for and it is a simple matter to maintain consistency. The use of Gaussians in the definition of $S_{i,j}$ (Eq. 1) reflects our belief that the color model modifications proposed in this paper allows normal distributions of the color characteristics in this modified HSI space according to the visual experience of color similarity.

The pixel sample is a representation of the desired color(s) to be segmented from a color image. From this pixel sample we obtain two necessary values to feed our segmentation algorithm: the color centroid and a measure of the dispersion from this centroid, in our case the standard deviation. These two values are represented accordingly to our modified HSI model.

The achromatic zone G is the region in the HSI color space where no hue is perceived by humans. This means that color is perceived only as a gray level because the color saturation is very low or intensity is either too low (near to black) or too high (near to white).

Given the three-dimensional HSI color space, we define the achromatic zone G as the union of the points inside the cylinder defined by *Saturation* $< 10\%$ of MAX and the two cones *Intensity* $< 10\%$ of MAX and *Intensity* $> 90\%$ of MAX, were MAX is the maximum possible value as presented in [10]. Pixels inside this region are perceived as gray levels.

3.1 Calculation of Average Hue

In order to obtain the average of the hue (H_m) of several pixels from a sample, we take advantage of the vector representation in $\Re^2$. Vectors that represent the hue values of individual pixels are combined using vector addition. From the resulting vector we obtain the average hue corresponding to the angle of this vector respected to the red axis. Thus H_m is calculated in the following manner:

1. For every pixel $P(x, y)$ in the sample the following $\Re^3$ to $\Re^2$ transformation is applied:

$$V_1(P) = \begin{bmatrix} 1 & -\cos(\pi/3) & -\cos(\pi/3) \\ 0 & \sin(\pi/3) & -\sin(\pi/3) \end{bmatrix} * \begin{bmatrix} R \\ G \\ B \end{bmatrix} = \begin{bmatrix} x \\ y \end{bmatrix} \quad \text{If } P \notin G \qquad (2)$$

and $V(P) = V_1(P) / |V_1(P)|$;

In other case:

$$V(P) = \begin{bmatrix} 0 \\ 0 \end{bmatrix} \qquad\qquad \text{If } P \in G$$

where $V(P)$ is the normalized projection of the RGB coordinates of the pixel P to the perpendicular plane to the Intensity axis of the RGB cube when the x axis is collinear to the Red axis of the chromatic circle. On the other hand G (see Section 3) represents the achromatic zone in the HSI space and $[RGB]^t$ is a vector with the color components of the pixel in the RGB color space.

To carry out this, the following code is executed:

```
Vector.x = 0;
 Vector.y = 0;                        // initialize vectors
 For (i = 1; i < = n; i++)            // for every pixel in
                                         the sample do
    {Vector.x = Vector.x + V(i).x;    // x-component of the
                                         accumulated vector
     Vector.y = Vector.y + V(i).y;}   // y-component of the
                                         accumulated vector
   Vs = [Vector.x Vector.y];          // Accumulated vector
```

In this code we have a vector in $\Re^2$, which accumulates the vector additions as index i increments. Each of the vectors being added corresponds to the previous $\Re^3$-to-$\Re^2$ transformation for every pixel in the sample made in step 1.

2. The angle of the accumulated vector (V_s) with respect to the X-axis is the average hue:

$$H_m = angle\,(V_s, 0)$$

where 0 represents the Red axis.

Using the vector representation of Hue obtained by the $\Re^3$-to-$\Re^2$ transformation of RGB space points expressed in Eq. (2), we can calculate the hue distance Δ_h between two colors pixels or color centroids C_1 and C_2, as follows:

$$\Delta_h(C_1, C_2) = |V_1 - V_2| \qquad \text{If } C_1 \text{ and } C_2 \notin G$$

$$= 0 \qquad \text{If } C_1 \text{ or } C_2 \in G$$

where G is the achromatic region; V_1 and V_2 are the vectors in $\Re^2$ calculated with the transformation on C_1 and C_2 given in Eq. (2).

Using the standard conversions for saturation and intensity from RGB space [10], normalized in the range [0, 1]:

$$saturation(P) = 1 - \left[\frac{3}{R+G+B} \min(R, G, B) \right] . \tag{3}$$

$$intensity(P) = \frac{1}{3}(R+G+B) .$$

we define saturation distance Δ_s and intensity distance Δ_i between two pixels or color centroids as:

$$\Delta_s = abs[saturation (C_1) - saturation (C_2)], \text{ and}$$
$$\Delta_i = abs[intensity (C_1) - intensity (C_2)],$$

where C_1 and C_2 are color pixels or color centroids, respectively, in RGB space.

In Eq. (3) we defined the saturation equal zero in case of the black color.

The statistical values needed in Eq. (1) are calculated as follows [14]:

$$Saturation\_average = S_c = \frac{1}{n} \sum_{i=1}^{n} saturation (i) .$$

$$Intensity\_average = I_c = \frac{1}{n} \sum_{i=0}^{n} intensity(i) .$$

$$Hue\_standard\_deviation = \sigma_h = \sqrt{\frac{\sum_{i=1}^{n} \Delta^2_h(i)}{n}} .$$

$$Saturation\_standard\_deviation = \sigma_s = \sqrt{\frac{\sum_{i=1}^{n} \Delta^2_s(i)}{n}} .$$

$$Intensity\_standard\_deviation = \sigma_i = \sqrt{\frac{\sum_{i=1}^{n} \Delta^2_i(i)}{n}} .$$

where n is the number of pixels in the sample; Δ_h is the hue distance between $hue(i, j)$ and $hue\_average$; Δ_s is the saturation distance between $saturation\ (i, j)$ and $saturation\_average$; Δ_i is the intensity distance between $intensity\ (i, j)$ and $intensity\_average$.

4 Results and Discussion

In this section we present the results of our segmentation method applied to two classical color images in RGB 24-bit true color format that are representative of many image processing and analysis applications. These experiments consisted of the segmentation of color regions according to the following three steps:

1) Selection of the pixel sample. In order to have a helping direction for this task the following considerations may be useful to select the number of pixels of the sample: If the color of the desired area to segment is solid (without additive noise) it is only necessary to have one pixel sample from the desired area. However, if we want to take in account the color lack of definition happening in the borders, we have to take a sample of the new colors that appear in that area due to the above condition. The pixels of the samples from the original images can be selected arbitrarily, that is, in any order, in any number and physically adjacent or not.

2) CSI calculation. This step is automatic; its output is a gray level image showing the similarity of each pixel of the RGB true color image to the color centroid formed with the chosen pixel sample taken from of the region of interest to be segmented, being white for 100% of similarity and black for 0%.

3) Thresholding and application of mathematic morphology. The user can threshold now the CSI and could be arranged as an automatic step by using, for example, the non-supervised Otsu's thresholding method [13]. After this step we can apply optionally any desired morphological tool if the thresholding results are not solid enough or geometric characteristics are needed to correctly separate the objects of interest.

Figure 1 shows a RGB color image (sized 200 x 200 pixels and with 33753 different colors) of the popular image of the baboon. In this image we can see four main hues of colors despite the many thousands of actual RGB values to represent them: The red part of the baboon's nose, the blue part of the nose, the orange eyes and the yellow-orange part of the fur.

Different pixel tonalities in the image depend on their particular saturation and on the unavoidable presence of additive noise. The proposed segmentation method is

Fig. 1. Baboon

practically immune to these conditions, although obviously there are some solutions to improve the quality of the segmented regions, as for example, preprocessing the image for smoothing noises of different types, applying some morphological operator to reduce objects with given characteristics, and so on.

In this experiment we took pixel samples for the blue color belonging to the edge of the perceived blue color. They are selected from an enlarged 21 x 21 pixels region as shown in Fig. 2. From this sample we calculated the color centroid and the standard deviation in our modified HSI space; with these two values we use the Eq. 1 to calculate for every pixel the pixel values of the CSI shown in Fig. 3. After applying Otsu's thresholding method and an area closing with a box of 3x3 to eliminate small holes, we obtain the final segmentation shown in Fig. 4.

For the blue part of the nose we repeated part of the process. Figure 5 shows the pixels sample, its corresponding CSI is shown in Fig. 6 and after applying Otsu's thresholding, an opening with a box of 3x3, a closing with the same box and eliminating remaining small areas, the final segmentation is shown in Fig. 7.

In Fig. 8 we show the pixel sample and in Fig. 9 the CSI for the orange color of the eyes. After thresholding the CSI, applying an opening with a disk 5x5 and eliminating the big area of the fur we obtain the final segmentation of the eyes shown in Fig. 10. The yellow-orange part of the fur shown in Fig. 11 was obtained as residue from the thresholding of the CSI and shown together in the composite of the segmentations of Fig. 4, 7 and 10.

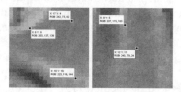

Fig. 2. Sample composed by 5 pixels located in two zones with red color

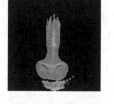

Fig. 3. The Color Similarity Image (CSI) of red   **Fig. 4.** Final segmentation of the red nose

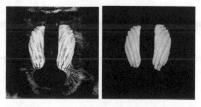

Fig. 5. Pixel sample for the blue nose   **Fig. 6.** CSI   **Fig. 7.** Final segmentation

Fig. 8. Pixel sample for the eyes   **Fig. 9.** CSI   **Fig. 10.** Final segmentation

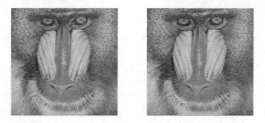

Fig. 11. Original image and a composite image achieved from the four previously segmented regions

5 Conclusions

The results in the previous section, demonstrate that the color segmentation method presented in this paper offers a useful and efficient alternative for the segmentation of objects with different colors in relatively complex color images with good performance in the presence of the unavoidable additive noise. The steps required to obtain a good segmentation of regions with different colors by using the proposed methodology are usually straightforward, simple and repetitive. If color is a discriminative characteristic in the layer of interest, only the selection of a given threshold to the color similarity function CSI is needed to obtain a good segmentation result. From many experiments we have observed that a good percentage of colors were obtained in a straightforward way only by thresholding the so called Color Similarity Image. In our method, the three RGB color components of every pixel transformed to the HSI color model are integrated in two steps: in the definitions of the Euclidean distances $[\Delta_h, \Delta_s, \Delta_i]$ in hue, saturation and intensity planes and in the construction of an adaptive color similarity function that combines these three distances assuming normal probability distributions. Thus the complexity is linear ($O[n]$) with respect to the number of pixels n of the source image. The method discriminates whichever type of different color objects independently on their shapes and tonalities in a very straightforward way.

Acknowledgments. The authors of this paper wish to thank the Computing Research Center (CIC), Mexico; Research and Postgraduate Secretary (SIP), Mexico, and National Polytechnic Institute (IPN), Mexico, for their support.

References

1. Alvarado-Cervantes, R.: Segmentación de patrones lineales topológicamente diferentes, mediante agrupamientos en el espacio de color HSI, M. Sc. Thesis, Center for Computing Research, National Polytechnic Institute, Mexico 1 (2006)
2. Angulo, J., Serra, J.: Mathematical morphology in color spaces applied to the analysis of cartographic images. In: Proceedings of International Congress GEOPRO, México (2003)
3. Bourbakis, N., Yuan, P., Makrogiannis, S.: Object recognition using wavelets, L-G graphs and synthesis of regions. Pattern Recognition 40, 2077–2096 (2007)
4. Chang, H., Yeung, D.Y.: Robust path-based spectral clustering. Pattern Recognition 41, 191–203 (2008)
5. Cheng, H., Jiang, X., Sun, Y., Wang, J.: Color image segmentation: Advances and prospects. Pattern Recognition 34(12), 2259–2281 (2001)
6. Felipe-Riverón, E.M., García-Ramos, M.E., Levachkine, S.P.: Problemas potenciales en la digitalización automática de los mapas cartográficos en colores. In: Proceedings of International Congress on Computation CIC IPN, Mexico City, Mexico (2000)
7. Felipe-Riverón, E.M., Garcia-Ramos, M.E.: Enhancement of digital color halftoning printed images. In: Proceedings of International Congress GEOPRO, México (2002) ISBN: 970-18-8521-X
8. Gonzalez, R.C., Woods, R.E.: Digital Image Processing, 3rd edn. Prentice Hall, USA (2008)
9. Hanbury, A., Serra, J.A.: 3D-polar coordinate colour representation suitable for image analysis, Technical Report PRIP-TR-77, Austria (2002)
10. Plataniotis, K.N., Venetsanopoulos, A.N.: Color Image Processing and Applications, 1st edn. Springer, Germany (2000)
11. Shi, L., Funt, B.: Quaternion color texture segmentation. Computer Vision and Image Understanding 107, 88–96 (2007)
12. Van den Broek, E.L., Schouten, T.E., Kisters, P.M.F.: Modeling human color categorization. Pattern Recognition Letters (2007)
13. Sezgin, M., Sankur, B.: Survey over image thresholding techniques and quantitative performance evaluation. Journal of Electronic Imaging 13(1), 146–165 (2003), doi:10.1117/1.1631315
14. Dodge, Y.: The Concise Encyclopaedia of Statistics, 1st edn. Springer, Germany (2008)
15. Hoang, M.A., Geusebroek, J.M., Smeulders, A.W.: Color texture measurement and segmentation. Signal Processing 85(2), 265–275 (2005)

Image Segmentation Using Quadtree-Based Similarity Graph and Normalized Cut

Marco Antonio Garcia de Carvalho, Anselmo Castelo Branco Ferreira,
and André Luis Costa

School of Technology - FT, State University of Campinas - UNICAMP
Rua Paschoal Marmo, 1888, Jd Nova Itália, Limeira, São Paulo, Brazil
magic@ft.unicamp.br

Abstract. The graph cuts in image segmentation have been widely used
in recent years because it regards the problem of image partitioning as
a graph partitioning issue, a well-known problem in graph theory. The
normalized cut approach uses spectral graph properties of the image representative graph to bipartite it into two or more balanced subgraphs,
achieving in some cases good results when applying this approach to image segmentation. In this work, we discuss the normalized cut approach
and propose a Quadtree based similarity graph as the input graph in
order to segment images. This representation allow us to reduce the cardinality of the similarity graph. Comparisons to the results obtained by
other graph similarity representation were also done in sampled images.

Keywords: image segmentation; quadtree; graph partitioning; spectral
graph.

1 Introduction

The image segmentation issue has been studied by many authors as a way to
distinguish different objects from a scene. Regarding this process as a graph
partitioning problem, a graph cut, is a promising area and there are a lot of
recent studies on this field. Graph cut is a measure that divides a graph into
two disjoints sets. Therefore, an initial challenge consists to carry out the image-
graph conversion adequately.

The Spectral Graph Theory (SGT) [3] studies the graph's matrix eigenvalues
and eigenvectors, their relation with the graph's features and the use of eigenvectors for graph bipartition. There are several applications on this field [7, 14, 16].
The concepts of SGT originated lots of graph partition techniques, such as the
Normalized Cut [12] and the Average Cut [13].

The Normalized Cut (NCut) image segmentation technique [12] segments an
image by minimizing the cut cost of a weighted graph. This cost is calculated as
a fraction of the total edge connections of each partition. One problem in this
technique is to defeat the high computational cost demanded as the graph size
increases. In order to avoid this problem, there are several ways of generating

I. Bloch and R.M. Cesar, Jr. (Eds.): CIARP 2010, LNCS 6419, pp. 329–337, 2010.

the input graph for the segmentation, with different results and applications [12, 10, 2, 5].

In this work, we propose an alternative graph representation as input for the NCut, instead of the commonly used pixel affinity graph. This graph, the Quadtree-based similarity graph, is generated from the quadtree leaves. It uses as decomposition criterion an edge detection operation. We show that this approach reduces the graph size and, consequently, the computational cost. The results are similar to the obtained by the other similarity graphs, using the same technique, the NCut.

This paper is organized as follows. Section 2 introduces the NCut technique and presents some related works. Some kinds of graphs that can be used as input for this technique, including our Quadtree based similarity graph are described in section 3. An overview of the proposed approach is given in section 4. Experiments in sampled images are done in section 5 and further comments of the experiments, conclusions, as well as suggestions of future work are done in section 6.

2 Related Works

The Normalized Cut technique [12] is a theoretic method for graph partitioning. Its goal is to find a balanced cut in a graph, in order to generate two or more subgraphs. Applying this method for image segmentation is possible with a proper image-graph representation. The subgraphs obtained from graph partitioning represents the image regions.

The Normalized Cut in a graph G is calculated by (1), as follows:

$$\text{NCut}(A, B) = \frac{\text{cut}(A, B)}{\text{SumCon}(A, G)} + \frac{\text{cut}(A, B)}{\text{SumCon}(B, G)}, \tag{1}$$

where A and B are subgraphs, subject to $A \cup B = G$ and $A \cap B = 0$; $\text{cut}(A, B)$ is defined as the total weight of the edges removed from the graph, $\text{SumCon}(A, G)$ is the total weight of the edges connecting nodes from a subgraph A to all nodes in the original graph G; and $\text{SumCon}(B, G)$ is similarly defined to a subgraph B. The optimal NCut is the one that minimizes (1), but minimizing it is a NP-Complete complexity problem [12]. However, by expanding (1), the authors noticed that it can be minimized using spectral graph properties of the graph's Laplacian Matrix described by Fiedler [6].

There is a wide range of recent work in image segmentation using the NCut technique. In [12], the similarity graph is built by taking each pixel as a node. Then, the node pairs within a given radius r are conected by an edge. Monteiro and Campilho [10] proposed the Watersheded Normalized Cut, which uses the regions from the Watershed image segmentation as nodes for the similarity graph. The Watershed region similarity graph is either used in [2] for comparison with the primitive pixel affinity graph in yeast cells images segmentation.

The primitive NCut enhancement was also studied and applied by many researchers. Cour *et al* [5] proposes a NCut adaptive technique that focus on the computational problem created by long range graphs. The authors suggested the use of multi-scale segmentations, decomposing a long range graph into independent subgraphs. The main contribution of this technique is that larger images can be better segmented with a linear complexity. Sun and He [15] purposed the use of the multiscale graph decomposition, partitioning the image graph representation at the finest scale level and weighting the graph nodes using the texture features.

3   Graph Representation

A graph representation of the image is needed to perform the NCut segmentation approach. Basically, this representation is done by an undirected weighted graph $G = (V, E, W)$, where: (i) V is the nodes set, where each node corresponds to a region or a pixel of the image; (ii) E is the edges set, where each edge links two nodes, and consequently, make a relationship between two regions or pixels of the image; (iii) and W is the weights set, where each weight is related to an edge and corresponds to a measure of similarity between the regions on the relationship. This structure is called the Similarity Graph.

There are several techniques to construct the similarity graph of a image. Some of these techniques, used by us in this work, are described in the following subsections.

3.1   Pixel Affinity Graph

Each pixel is taken as a graph node, and two pixels in a r distance are connected by an edge. The edges weights should reflect the similarity between the pixels connected by them. The grouping cue used in the similarity function will reflect the overall quality of the segmentation. Some of them are the intensity, position, and contours [12, 5, 8].

The intensity and position grouping cue assumes that close-by pixels with similar intensity are most probably to belong to the same object. The measure of similarity regarding this grouping cue is given by (2) [12, 5]:

$$
W_{\mathrm{IP}}(i, j) = \begin{cases} e^{-\left(\frac{\alpha^2}{d_p}\right)-\left(\frac{\beta^2}{d_i}\right)}, & \text{if } \alpha_2 < r\ , \\ 0, & \text{Otherwise} \end{cases} \tag{2}
$$

where $\alpha = ||P_i - P_j||$ and $\beta = ||I_i - I_j||$ are respectively the distance and the difference of intensity between pixels i and j; r is a given distance (also called graph connection radius); and d_p and d_i could be set with the variance of the image pixels positions and intensity. This grouping cue used separately often gives bad segmentations because some natural images are affected by the texture clutter.

The measure of similarity regarding the intervening contours grouping cue is given by (3) [5]:

$$W_C(i,j) = \begin{cases} e^{-\left(\dfrac{\max_{(x \,\in\, \text{line}(i,j))} \varepsilon^2}{d_c}\right)}, & \text{if } \alpha_2 < r \ , \\ 0, & \text{Otherwise} \end{cases} \tag{3}$$

where $\text{line}(i,j)$ is a straight line joining pixels i and j and $\varepsilon = \|\text{Edge}(x)\|$ is the image edge strength at location x.

These two grouping cues can be combined as shown by (4) [5]:

$$W_{IPC}(i,j) = \sqrt{W_{IP}(i,j)\,W_C(i,j)} + W_C(i,j). \tag{4}$$

Multiscale Graph Decomposition. The Multiscale Graph Decomposition algorithm [5] works on multiple scale of the image to capture coarse and fine level details. The construction of the image segmentation graph is given according to $W = W_1 + W_2 + \ldots + W_s$, where W represents the graph weights $\text{w}(i,j)$ and s, the scale, i.e., each W_s is an independent subgraph. Two pixels i,j are connected only if the distance between them is lower than G_r. As G_r value is a tradeoff between the computation cost and the segmentation result. W_s can be compressed using recursive sub-sampling of the image pixels. This compression is not perfect, but he has the advantage of the computational efficiency.

3.2   Quadtree-Based Similarity Graph

The term Quadtree is used to describe a class of hierarchical data structures whose common property is that they are based on recursive decomposition of space. They can be classified on the following bases [11]: (i) the type of data that they are used to represent, *i. e.*, points, regions, volumes, etc; (ii) the principle guiding the decomposition, that can be fixed or based on the input data; (iii) the resolution, that can be variable or not.

In order to represent an image through a Quadtree, its regions should be recursively decomposed into exact four new disjoint regions, when they satisfy a defined criterion. The initial region corresponds to the whole image and is associated to the tree root node [4, 11].

Defining the criterion to decompose the regions of the Quadtree is not a trivial task. There are different criteria that can be used, as standard deviation or entropy of image gray levels [4]. We found that using the image edges for guiding the regions decomposition was very adequated, because: (i) the edge detection operation drastically reduce the size of data to be processed, while at the same time preserves the structural information about object boundaries [1]; (ii) the edge detection results in a binary matrix. Then, became trivial to define that a region should be decomposed when it is not formed entirely by 1's or 0's [11].Figure 1 shows one grayscale image with 256 x 256 pixels, its edge detection by Canny filter and a reconstruction based on regions associated with

(a)   (b)   (c)

Fig. 1. (a) Original image with 65536 pixels (256 x 256) (b) edge detection resulting from applying Canny filter to 1a (c) image reconstruction with 14749 regions

the Quadtree leaves. Can be observed that the image reconstruction, showed in Fig. 1c, is very similar to the original one.

The main goal of using a Quadtree image representation is to reduce the similarity graph size, used as input to the NCut segmentation technique. For this purpose, the input graph will be generated with basis on the regions associated to the Quadtree leaves. Each region will be associated to a graph node. For instance, for the image showed in Fig. 1a, the resulting similarity graph using the Quadtree-based approach has 14749 nodes, about 22,5% of the total nodes obtained by using the Pixel Affinity approach (65536 nodes).

The number of regions obtained by the proposed technique will vary in function of the image data. Also, the parameters of the edge detection filter can be manually specified, in order to change its sensibility. It means that the number of nodes on the similarity graph can be influenced by the choice of the edge detector parameters.

4   Algorithm Overview

The segmentation based on NCut technique can be applied by two distinct methods: recursive 2-way NCut and k-way NCut. The first one uses the second smallest eigenvector of the graph Laplacian's matrix L, where $L = D - W$ with W being the weight matrix and D a diagonal degree matrix, to recursively bipartite the similarity graph [12]. The k-way NCut uses the K first eigenvectors of the graph Laplacian's matrix L to directly generate a number K of desired partitions [12].

The image segmentation process using k-way NCut is described in the following steps:

1. Given an input image, compute the Similarity Graph $G = (V, E, W)$ using one of the techniques described in section 3.
2. Build the weight matrix W and the degree matrix D from the Similarity Graph.
3. Solve $(D - W)x = \lambda D x$
4. Discretize the K first eigenvectors into X, where $X = [X_1, X_2, .., X_K]$ and $X_N[i] = 1$ iff node i belongs to the partition N.
5. Use X for the distribution of the graph nodes into the K partitions.

5   Experiments

We used in our experiments a set of 15 randomly chosen images from the Berkeley Image Database [9] and more 10 images from a particular database. In order to make a regular decomposition, the quadtree implementation requires squared images with size 2^n, where n is a positive integer. The images of the Berkeley Database needed to be cropped to 256 x 256 pixels due to this restriction.

The experiments were executed according to the steps described in section 4. For the Pixel Affinity Graphs and the Quadtree-based Similarity Graphs, the similarity between node's relations was calculated by (3), while for the Multiscale Decomposition Graphs it was calculated by (4). The connection radius was, respectively, $r = 10$, $r = 20$ and $r = \{2, 3, 7\}$. Note that for the Multiscale method was generated three scales, and there are one correspondent radius for each scale. Given the irregularity of the region's size, the connection radius between them on the Quadtree representation is given by (5)

$$Radius = \frac{\max{(RS_a, RS_b)}}{2} + r, \tag{5}$$

where RS_a and RS_b are the sizes of the two regions being connected and r is the radius given by the user. The k-way NCut was used with $K = 30$, yelding to 30 regions for each images segmentation. Fig. 2 shows five selected results.

We use the original implementations of the Pixel Affinity and Multiscale segmentation provided by the authors [12, 5].

As observed on experiments, the NCut with Quadtree-based Similarity Graph presented results as good as with the Pixel Affinity. There are minor differences on the resulting segmentations with these two techniques. However, our technique has a lower computational cost due to the reduced number of nodes on the similarity graph. For the 25 images used in the experiments, the average number of nodes on the similarity graph was 18755, about 28.62% of the total number of pixel on the images. Table 1 shows statistics about the nodes quantity for our particular database and from the Berkeley Database.

Table 1. Number of nodes for Quad-Tree Based Similarity Graph

	Mean	Higher	Lower
Particular Database	16177,6	24478	9040
Berkeley Database	20473,4	30751	9700

When comparing our technique with the Multiscale method, the differences on the results are more expressive for some images, see Fig. 2c and Fig. 2d, once, in this work, these technique uses different similarity functions. Nevertheless, these two techniques proposes a way to reduce the computational cost of NCut segmentation. The main advantage of our technique is that the similarity graph size can be controlled. However, this control is limited by impacts on the

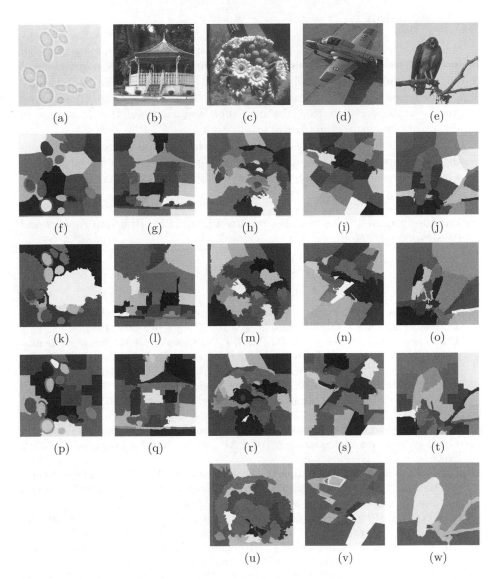

Fig. 2. Ncut image segmentation results obtained by different graph representations. (a-e) Original images, respectively: Yeast Cells and Coreto from particular database and 19021, 37073, 42049 from Berkeley Database. (f-j) Results from Pixel Affinity Graph. (k-o) Results from Multiscale Graph Decomposition. (p-t) Results from Quadtree-based Similarity Graph. (u-w) Ground Truth segmentations for the Berkeley images.

segmentation quality. It is important to note that the overall quality of the proposed technique rely on the edge detection filter efficience. The edge detection uses Canny filter.

6   Conclusion

In this paper we proposed a novel input similarity graph in order to segment images by NCut approach. We showed that the utilization of the Quadtree-based Similarity Graph provides similar results when compared to the two classical similarity graph representations. Experiments on real images (particular and Berkeley databases) show that the new representation had the advantage of significantly reducing the number of graph nodes.

Using regions instead of pixels seems to be a better strategy to segment images by NCut approach. We would like to explore the Quadtree-based Similarity Graph and compare its results with other obtained from regions similarity graphs.

Acknowledgments. This work is supported by CAPES Brazilian Agency and FAPESP (2009/10266-2).

References

1. Canny, J.: A computational approach to edge detection. IEEE Transactions on Pattern Analysis and Machine Intelligence PAMI-8(6), 679–698 (1986)
2. Carvalho, M.A.G., Ferreira, A.C.B., Pinto, T.W., Cesar Jr., R.M.: Image segmentation using watershed and normalized cuts. In: Proc. of 22th Conference on Graphics, Patterns and Images (SIBGRAPI). Rio de Janeiro, Brazil (2009)
3. Chung, F.: Spectral Graph Theory. CBMS Regional Conference Series in Mathematics, vol. 92. American Mathematical Society, Providence (1997)
4. Consularo, L.A., Cesar Jr., R.M.: Quadtree-based inexact graph matching for image analysis. In: Proceedings of the XVIII Brazilian Symposium on Computer Graphics and Image Processing (SIBGRAPI 2005), Natal - Brazil, pp. 205–212 (2005)
5. Cour, T., Bénézit, F., Shi, J.: Spectral segmentation with multiscale graph decomposition. In: Proc. of IEEE Computer Society Conference on Computer Vision and Pattern Recognition - CVPR 2005, vol. 2, pp. 1124–1131 (2005)
6. Fiedler, M.A.: Property of eigenvectors of nonnegative symmetric matrices and its applications to graph theory. Czech Math Journal 25(100), 619–633 (1975)
7. Malik, J.: Visual grouping and object recognition. In: Proc. of 11th International Conference on Image Analysis and Processing, pp. 612–621 (2001)
8. Malik, J., Belongie, S., Shi, J., Leung, T.: Textons, contours and regions: cue integration in image segmentation. In: Proc. of IEEE International Conference on Computer Vision, Corfu, Greece, pp. 918–925 (1999)
9. Martin, D., Fowlkes, C., Tal, D., Malik, J.: A database of human segmented natural images and its application to evaluating segmentation algorithms and measuring ecological statistics. In: Proc. of 8th Int'l Conf. Computer Vision, vol. 2, pp. 416–423 (July 2001)
10. Monteiro, F.C., Campilho, A.: Watershed framework to region-based image segmentation. In: Proc. of IEEE 19th International Conference on Pattern Recognition - ICPR, pp. 1–4 (2008)
11. Samet, H.: The quadtree and related hierarchical structures. ACM Computing Surveys 16(2), 187–261 (1984)

12. Shi, J., Malik, J.: Normalized cuts and image segmentation. IEEE Transactions on Pattern Analysis and Machine Intelligence PAMI-22(8), 888–905 (2000)
13. Soundararajan, P., Sarkar, S.: Analysis of mincut, average cut and normalized cut measures. In: Workshop on Perceptual Organization in Computer Vision (2001)
14. Spielman, D.: Spectral graph theory and its applications. In: Proc. of 48th Annual IEEE Symposium on Foudations of Computer Science, pp. 29–38 (2007)
15. Sun, F., He, J.P.: A normalized cuts based image segmentation method. In: Proc. of II International Conference on Information and Computer Science, pp. 333–336 (2009)
16. Tolliver, D.A., Miller, G.L.: Graph partitioning by spectral rounding: Applications in image segmentation and clustering. In: Proc. of IEEE Computer Society Conference on Computer Vision and Pattern Recognition - CVPR 2006, vol. 1, pp. 1053–1060 (2006)

A Genetic-Algorithm-Based Fusion System Optimization for 3D Image Interpretation

Lionel Valet[1], Beatriz S.L.P. de Lima[2], and Alexandre G. Evsukoff[2]

[1] LISTIC - Université de Savoie, BP 806, 74016 Annecy Cedex, France
`lionel.valet@univ-savoie.fr`
[2] COPPE/Federal University of RJ, P.O. Box 68506,
21941-972 Rio de Janeiro, Brazil
`bia@coc.ufrj.br`

Abstract. Information fusion systems are complex systems with many parameters that must be adjusted to obtain interesting results. Generally applied in specialized domains such as military, medical and industrial areas, these systems must work in collaboration with the experts of the domains. As these end-users are not specialists in information fusion, the parameters adjustment becomes a difficult task. In addition, to find a good set of those parameters is a hard and time consuming process as the search space is very large. In order to overcome this issue a genetic algorithm is applied to automatically search the best parameter set. The results show that the proposed approach produces accurate levels of the global performance of the fusion system.

1 Introduction

Cooperative fusion systems devoted to image interpretation are more and more complex [1]. These systems help experts in the difficult task of image interpretation which generally consists in detecting typical regions within the images. Fusion systems are composed of several steps. The first step concerns the extraction of a piece of pertinent information from the original image. Several image processing techniques could be used to characterize the different sought-after regions. Then the extracted information must be represented into a common and commensurable space in order to be aggregated in the following step. Finally, the output is expressed in an understandable space for the end-user. This step is achieved by the representation step.

Such systems generally imply in high computational cost. They also have many parameters that are not easy to use and to adjust by the end-users. The parameter setting and attributes selection are strongly necessary to obtain relevant results. Unfortunately, the end-users of this kind of fusion system are not specialists in computer sciences and they need help to interact with the system. This is reinforced by the fact that an optimized adjustment obtained for a given data is not compulsory the best one for other data.

The work presented in this paper is based on a local evaluation of the mission of the fusion system extraction step. The local evaluation turns possible to have

I. Bloch and R.M. Cesar, Jr. (Eds.): CIARP 2010, LNCS 6419, pp. 338–345, 2010.

a better identification of which extractor need to be adjusted. In a context of image interpretation, the extractors are based on image processing algorithms. They have technical parameters (filter coefficient, windows size, normalization, ...) that are not accessible to the end-user. However, the parameters must be adjusted and adapted to the input image and to the sought-after regions. The high computation time makes a manual setting very difficult even for experimented users in image processing techniques. In order to solve this problem, this paper employs a local evaluation combined to the use of genetic algorithms. In the literature, GA has already shown their interests for image processing. The obtained results show that it is an interesting way to automatically optimize parameters that should have some impact on the fused result.

2   Fusion System for 3D Image Interpretation

2.1   The Studied Fusion System

The cooperative fusion system concerned in this paper, was designed for 3D gray level image interpretation. This application concerns the analysis of electro-technical parts manufactured by Schneider Electric Company. The studied parts are mainly composed of glass fibers mixed with an organic matrix. The quality of the parts is directly correlated to the fiber organization. Experts (geophysics, part designers, ...) try to understand the inside part organization to find the best fabrication process (fiber length, injection point, baking time, ...). The method chosen by Schneider Electric to analyze the parts is based on X-ray computed tomography (CT). It is a reliable non-destructive evaluation technique. The CT results are 3D gray-scale images which provide data about the organization of the internal morphology. The sought-after regions are presented on figure 1. The first one is the *oriented region* (noted R_1) which has a regular and organized texture with a single preferential orientation of the glass fibers. They are made up of long white fibers giving the impression of a flow. The *Disordered regions* (noted R_2) do not appear organized on the images, locally "chaotic", i.e. for which there is not a clearly defined principal orientation. The regions called *Lack*

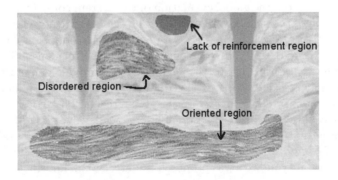

Fig. 1. The sought-after regions

of reinforcement (noted R_3) only contain resin (or paste) and no glass fibers. They appear in clear and homogeneous gray level on the images. These three regions need different measurements to be detected simultaneously (orientation, texture, morphology, ...). An information fusion system has been developed to aggregate the heterogeneous measurements.

In the concerned application, the experts introduce their knowledge by pointing references of the regions directly on the input image. To help them in the interpretation of the images (i.e. to detect the sought-after regions in all the images based on the pointing reference), the synoptic of the designed fusion system is presented on figure 2. The extraction steps involve three image processing measurements: local organisations based on principal component analysis of voxel intensity, texture measurements based on coocurrence matrix and morphological measurements based on morphology mathematics. The extracted information is then transformed into similarity map using possibility theory. Then, Choquet integral aggregates the similarity maps into a global one. The final decision on the belonging region of each voxel is obtained by a thresholding operation. The voxels that do not have enough similarity to any of the sought-after regions are labelled to a rejected class. More details on the system can be found in [2].

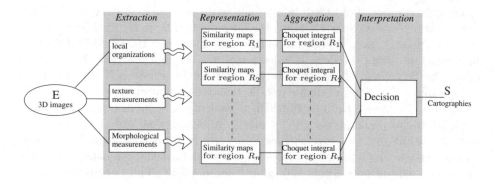

Fig. 2. Fusion system designed for 3D image analysis

In this application, the global evaluation of the system consists in verifying the correct decision of the voxels contained into the reference regions by computing a confusion matrix. Detection rate for each region (and a global one) are extracted from the matrix and serve to comment the global performance of the system. The global evaluation of the fused image does not provide enough explanation on the efficiency of each step. It is also difficult to explain the influence and the dependency of a parameter directly on the global result. Therefore there is a need for a local measure to adjust the parameters. A local evaluation of the extraction step was proposed in [4]. It is based on a mission achievement evaluation: *an extracted information must bring a better separability between the sought-after regions*. Separability indexes was proposed to detect weak informative attributes.

2.2   Importance of the Extraction Step

In the studied fusion system devoted to image interpretation, the extraction step have a great impact on the rest of the system. Indeed, most parameters are concentrated on this step. These parameters are difficult to adjust by a end-user not specialist in image processing. A first fusion of two attributes is proposed to illustrate the complexity of the system. The first attribute noted A_1 belongs to the local organisations family. It measures the main orientation of the fiber in the part. Its computation need the following parameter: α the Derich filter coefficient, W_x, W_y, W_z the window size of the principal component analysis, W_g the window size of the gradient calculation, N a normalisation coefficient. The second attribute noted A_2 belongs to the texture measurement family. The homogeneity index is computed on the coocurrence matrix evaluated on a windows W_x, W_y, W_z and for a direction vector (d_x, d_y, d_z). A_1 and A_2 were initially computed with the default parameters presented in table 1 with their separability indexes for each attribute. The separability indexes are all weak which mean that those attributes were not able to discriminate the regions. Only A_2 reached a better separability for region R_3. The detection rates are also weak even for the third region which is the best one detected. Therefore, the global detection rate is clearly insufficient.

Figure 3 presents the output cartography. White voxels correspond to region R_3, clear gray level voxels correspond to region R_2, dark grey level voxels correspond to region R_1. Black voxel are voxel belong to the rejected class because they have a weak similarity to the sought-after regions. The contour of the reference regions are also plot on the image and the hole in the part are hatched. This result clearly shows the weakness of the detection. Region are too fragmented and don't correspond to the result expected by the end-users.

To improve the detection, parameters of attribute A_1 are adjusted manually: the windows size used in the principal component analysis is increased and the α coefficient is decreased (growth of the smoothing effect). The new attribute is noted A_1' and the new separability indexes and detection rate are also presented on the table 1. Separability indexes have a small increase but not significantly. At the end, we even notice a slight improvement of the global rate, however, not considerable. The obtained cartography have also the same weakness. Manually it is extremely difficult and time-consuming to find interesting parameter according to the sought-after regions. The search space of the fusion system parameters is very large which describes a complex combinatorial optimization problem.

Table 1. Initial fusion

Attribute parameters

	α	W_x	W_y	W_z	W_g	N
A_1	0.5	9	9	9	15	10.0
A_1'	0.4	11	11	11	15	10.0

	W_x	W_y	W_z	d_x	d_y	d_z
A_2	8	8	8	2	2	2

Separability indexes and detection rates

	R_1	R_2	R_3	T_{Global}
S_{A_1}	0,32	0,35	0,66	
$S_{A_1'}$	0,35	0,37	0,67	
S_{A_2}	0,22	0,30	**0,74**	
$Fusion(A_1, A_2)$	0,45	0,69	**0,74**	0,52
$Fusion(A_1', A_2)$	0,51	0,53	0,77	0,54

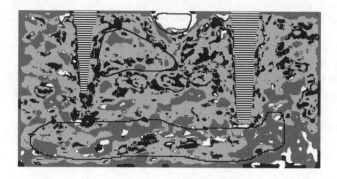

Fig. 3. Classification obtained with attributes A_1 and A_2

3   Genetic Algorithms

Evolutionary Algorithms (EA) have been considered as powerful search and optimization methods that prevail over the drawbacks of classical mathematical optimization methods. They are based in probabilistic searching, and do not need gradient information; therefore, they are more robust in locating global optima in multi-modal search space [5]. EAs have been widely applied in the last few years in computationally expensive applications and proved to be a strong optimization method in many types of combinatorial problems. Those successful applications of EAs involve scheduling [6], knowledge discovery [7], information fusion [8], etc.

3.1   Principle of Genetic Algorithm

Genetic Algorithms (GA) belong to the class of EA, it is a population-based model that uses various operators to evolve, such as selection, crossover and mutation. These operations correspond, respectively, to the principles of survival of the fittest; recombination of genetic material, and mutation observed in nature, following the mechanisms of natural selection [9].

In GAs, each optimization variable or parameter (x_n) is encoded by a gene using an appropriate representation, such as a real number or a string of bits. The corresponding genes for all parameters $x_1, x_2, \ldots, x_n$ form a chromosome, capable of describing an individual design solution. A set of chromosomes representing several individual solutions comprises a population, where the fittest individuals are selected to mate and reproduce. Mating is performed using crossover to combine genes from different parents to produce children (offspring). The children inherit features from both parents, and may be submitted to mutation, which confers some truly innovative features as well. The offspring are made to compete with each other, and possibly with their parents. Individuals are evaluated via the objective function that defines the problem. As a result of the evaluation, they are assigned a certain cost that dissociate them. This value, named fitness value, represents the quality of the solution. By the end of a generation, only the fittest individuals are selected to continue in the population, and the other ones are rejected.

Improvement in the population arises as a consequence of the repeated selection of the best parents, which are in turn more likely to produce good offspring, and the consequent elimination of low-performers. In the present work, the classical Genetic Algorithm is used, with binary codification, single point crossover, individual elitism and roulette-wheel selection with Genesis package[1].

3.2   Application to Image Processing Parameter Adjustments

In this work, GA was applied to optimize extraction step corresponding to attribute A_1 which has the weak separability for regions R_1. Genes must be declared and configured to well represent the image processing parameters. Six genes were used, one for each of the six parameters. Chromosomes x_i of the population are binary strings composed by the 6 genes. The gene declaration is presented in table 2. Chromosomes x_i are composed of 26 binary elements. For the window sizes, values can only be odd. The min and max value and the number of binary elements was selected in consequence. The attribute is thus obtained by a function of the chromosomes x_i: $A_1 = g(x_i)$ The objective function f is the separability index presented in section 2 for a given region. $f : (A_1, R_i) \rightarrow S_{R_i}$. This function is directly dependent to the x_i chromosomes. In this work, the main objective is to find the best set of parameters in the extraction step of image interpretation that maximizes the separability of the regions.

Table 2. Genes definition for attribute A_1

parameters	α	W_x	W_y	W_z	W_g	N
genes	1	2	3	4	5	6
binary string size	5	4	4	4	4	5
parameter values	$[0, 1.0]$	$\{3..33\}$	$\{3..33\}$	$\{3..33\}$	$\{3..33\}$	$[0, 200.0]$
number of possible values	32	16	16	16	16	32

3.3   Illustration on 3D Tomography Image Interpretation

The optimization is applied on attribute A_1 to improve the separability of this attribute to region R_1 which has the lowest detection rate. The population size of the GA is 20 individuals, the crossover Rate is set to 0.8 and the mutation Rate equal 0.01. Stopping criteria is maximum number of evaluations. The initial population is set randomly.

In this population, several individuals makes a complete separability of the region R_1 possible. Moreover, the final population also brought interesting information on the behavior of the parameters according to the sought-after regions. It shows that the Derich filter must be weak (a strong smoothing is necessary) and the gradient window size must also be weak (a windows size of 3 is enough).

---

[1] Genesis package can be found:
http://www.cs.cmu.edu/afs/cs/project/airepository/ai/areas/genetic/ga/systems/genesis/0.html

Table 3. Classification obtained after optimization

α	W_x	W_y	W_z	W_g	N	S_{R_1}
0.03	19	31	11	3	10.00	1.0000

	R_1	R_2	R_3	T_{Global}
$S_{A_1''}$	**1,0**	**0,91**	0,77	
$Fusion A_1'', A_2$	**0,93**	0,94	**0,81**	0,92

Concerning the window sizes principal component analyse, a large one ([31, 33]) is required for W_y, and finally more classical sizes have been encountered for W_z and W_x. Values for these two parameters are also established on a larger interval. It also means that these two parameters have less influence on the result.

The parameters for the optimized attribute (noted A_1'' in the following), its separabilities and the obtained cartography are given in figure 3. The fusion of the optimized attribute A_1'' with A_2 gives now good detection rates. The classification better presents a good correspondence to the sought-after regions and the detected regions are less fragmented. Many voxels remain classified into the rejected class (black voxel). It is an effect to the strong learning realized on the reference regions. It could have a perverse effect on the generalization of the classification (i.e. classification of the voxel for which we have no reference).

4   Conclusions

Cooperative fusion system for image interpretation are now complex systems. The complexity concerns both the system conception (choice of the inputs, choice of the aggregation function, . . .), the performance evaluation and the parameter adjustment. Based on an existing fusion system, this paper has proposed a way to locally adjust some parameters which could have a strong impact on the fused results. To help the end-users in the difficult task of the parameter adjustment, an optimization algorithm was proposed. Based on Genetic Algorithms, a set of best parameters can be found in a large search space. This algorithm appears interesting to find a stable local optimum that corresponds to a maximization of the objective function. Even though a set of possible interesting solution corresponding to different optima certainly exists, the main objective remains to find, at least, one situation that can improve the attribute. GA are specially interesting in this situation.

The proposed approach was applied on an attribute devoted to organisation measurement in the 3D images. The obtained parameters make it possible to have the maximum separability for a given sought-after region. Thanks to the new attributes, the global detection on the output of the fusion system can immediately considerably increase. The final parameter population brought information on the parameters (difference between the 3D dimension, variability of several one, unique value for other ones, . . .). They also would have been difficult to find manually. However, the success of such an optimization depends on two important factors: the objective function and the reference regions. The objective function must be pertinent for the application because it corresponds to the criteria to optimize. Work is under progress to improve the actual objective function to try and attempt to optimize attribute parameters according to the 3 sought-after regions (or only one without saying which one). The reference regions are also very important. They must be representative to the sought-after regions to keep interesting results in generalization.

Acknowledgment. The authors acknowledge financial support from the CAPES/COFECUB which made the collaboration possible. We also would like to thank Schneider Electric. The fusion system concerned in this paper has been fully developed in collaboration with the material research Laboratory of Grenoble.

References

1. Kokar, M.M., Tomasik, J.A., Weyman, J.: Formalizing classes of information fusion systems. Information Fusion 5(3), 189–202 (2004)
2. Jullien, S., Valet, L., Mauris, G., Bolon, P., Teyssier, S.: An attribute fusion system based on the choquet integral to evaluate the quality of composite parts. IEEE Trans. On Instrumentation and Measurement 57(4), 755–762 (2008)
3. Zhang, Y.: A survey on evaluation methods for image segmentation. Pattern Recognition 29(8), 1335–1346 (1996)
4. Lamallem, A., Valet, L., Coquin, D.: Local versus global evaluation of a cooperative fusion system for 3d image interpretation. In: International Symposium on Optomechatronic Technologies cdrom (2009)
5. Hammouche, K., Diaf, M., Siarry, P.: A comparative study of various meta-heuristic techniques applied to the multilevel thresholding problem. Engineering Applications of Artificial Intelligence (to appear)
6. Talbi, E., Geneste, L., Grabot, B., Previtalia, R., Hostachy, P.: Application of optimization techniques to parameter set-up in scheduling. Computers in Industry 55, 105–124 (2004)
7. Gabrys, B., Ruta, D.: Genetic algorithms in classifier fusion. Applied Soft Computing 6, 337–347 (2006)
8. Maslov, I., Gertner, I.: Multi-sensor fusion: an evolutionary algorithm approach. Information Fusion 7, 304–330 (2006)
9. Goldberg, D.: Genetic Algorithms in Search, Optimization and Machine Learning. Addison-Wesley, Reading (1989)
10. Chaibakhsh, A., Ghaari, A., Moosavian, S.A.A.: A simulated model for a once-through boiler by parameter adjustment based on genetic algorithms. Simulation Modelling Practice and Theory 15, 1029–1051 (2007)
11. Montero, G., Rodrguez, E., Montenegro, R., Escobar, J., Gonzalez-Yuste, J.: Genetic algorithms for an improved parameter estimation with local renement of tetrahedral meshes in a wind model. Advances in Engineering Software 36, 3–10 (2005)
12. Nougues, J.M., Grau, M.D., Puigjaner, L.: Parameter estimation with genetic algorithm in control of fed-batch reactors. Chemical Engineering and Processing 41, 303–309 (2002)

Quaternion Atomic Function Wavelet for Applications in Image Processing

E. Ulises Moya-Sánchez and Eduardo Bayro-Corrochano

CINVESTAV, Unidad Guadalajara
Electrical and Computer Sciences Department
{emoya,edb}@gdl.cinvestav.mx

Abstract. Atomic Functions are widely used in different applications in image processing, pattern recognition, computational physics and also in the digital interpretation of signal measurements. The main contribution of this work is to develop a Quaternionic Atomic Function Wavelet as a new quaternionic image wavelet transform. This filter have a real part and three imaginary parts (i, j, k) of the Quaternion Atomic Function, as a result we can extract more information from the image by the three phases (ϕ, θ, φ) of the quaternion representation. The experimental part shows clearly that the phase information of the image is not afected by illumination changes.

Keywords: Quaternion Algebra, Atomic functions, Image Processing, 2D Phase Information.

1 Introduction

One of the main fields of Atomic functions AFs application is pattern recognition and image processing [1]. This work presents the theory and some results of the Quaternion Atomic Function QAF, as a new quaternionic wavelet. We use the AF because, it is novel and versatile, easy to derivate (only a shift), it is compact in space domain, and it has the possibility of representing any polynomial by means of its translations. We develop the AF in a hypercomplex algebra (quaternion algebra H), this framework permits to extract the phase information of the image. The combination of this function AF with this framework H makes a new useful image filter.

We apply the QAF or qup on a test image (squares) in 3 ways as follows: firstly, convolution of each part (real, i, j, k) of QAF is applied on the test image, secondly, we calculate the three phases of the filtered image, thirdly and we uses a wavelet for multiscale image processing. We structure this work as follows, the first section is devoted to present the AF and the main characteristics, the subject of the second section is the quaternion algebra, the next section introduces the QAF, in the section four we present the Quaternion Atomic Wavelet Function, in the section five we present the results and finally the conclusions.

I. Bloch and R.M. Cesar, Jr. (Eds.): CIARP 2010, LNCS 6419, pp. 346–353, 2010.

2   Atomic Functions

By definition, AF are compactly supported infinitely differentiable solutions of differential equations with a shifted argument [1] i.e.

$$Lf(x) = \lambda \sum_{k=1}^{M} c(k)f(ax - b(k)), |a| > 1, \qquad (1)$$

where $L = \frac{d^n}{dx^n} + a_1 \frac{d^{n-1}}{dx^{n-1}} + ... + a_n$ is a linear differential operator with constant coefficients. In the AF class, the function $up(x)$ is the simplest and at the same time, the most useful primitive function to generate other kinds of atomic functions [1]. It satisfies the equation

$$f(x)' = 2\left(f(2x + 1) - f(2x - 1)\right), \qquad (2)$$

Function $up(x)$ is infinitely differentiable but non-analytical; $up(0) = 1$, $up(-x) = up(x)$. Other types of AF satisfying equation (1): $fup_n(x)$, $\Xi_n(x)$, $h_a(x)$ [6]. In this work we only use $up(x)$. In general the Atomic Function $up(x)$ is generated by infinite convolutions of rectangular impulses. The function $up(x)$ has the following representation in terms of the Fourier transform:

$$up(x) = \frac{1}{2\pi} \int_{\infty}^{\infty} e^{iux} \prod_{k=1}^{\infty} \frac{\sin(u2^{-k})}{u2^{-k}} du. \qquad (3)$$

Figure 1 shows the $up(x)$ and the Fourier Transform of $F(up)$. Atomic windows were compared with classic ones [1,6] by means of the system of parameters such as: the equivalent noise bandwidth, the 50% overlapping region correlation, the parasitic modulation amplitude, the maximum conversion losses (in decibels), the maximum side lobe level (in decibels), the asymptotic decay rate of the side lobes (in decibels per octave), the window width at the six-decibel level, the coherent gain. All atomic windows exceed classic ones in terms of the asymptotic decay rate [1,6].

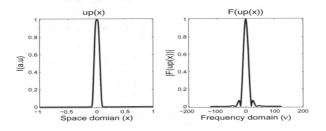

Fig. 1. Atomic function $up(x)$ and the Fourier Transform of $up(x)$

Figure 2 illustrate the first derivate, dup see equation (2) in convolution with the image, this function can be used as a oriented line detector with a simple rotation. We show three orientations 0°, 45°, 135°.

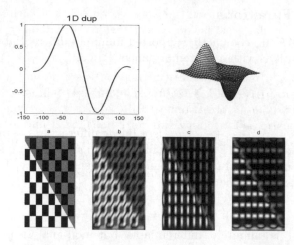

Fig. 2. Convolution of $dup(x,y)$ with the test image. a) Test Image, b)Result of the convolution of the image with $dup(x,y,0°)$, c)Result of the convolution of the image with $dup(x,y,45°)$, d)Result of the convolution of the image with $dup(x,y,135°)$.

3   Quaternion Algebra

The quaternion algebra is a framework we need to define the QAF. Quaternion algebra was invented by Hamilton in 1843. It is an associative non-commutative four-dimensional algebra [2,3].

$$q = a + bi + cj + dk \ a,b,c,d \ \epsilon \ \Re \tag{4}$$

The units i, j obey the relations

$$i^2 = j^2 = -1, ij = -k, \tag{5}$$

the norm of a quaternion is defined $|q| = \sqrt{q\bar{q}}$ where $\bar{q}$ is a conjugate of q. Similarly to the complex numbers. In 2D the phase component carries the main part of image information [4,5].

Since the quaternions constitute a 4D algebra we can represent q in a polar representation of the form equation (4) i.e. $(|q|, \phi, \theta, \psi)$, where $|q|$ is the magnitude and the angles (ϕ, θ, ψ) represent a novel kind of phase vector. By definition [3]:

$$q = |q|e^{i\phi}e^{k\psi}e^{j\theta} \tag{6}$$

the phase range are delimited $(\phi,\theta,\psi),[-\pi, \pi]\times[-\pi/2, \pi/2]\times[-\pi/4, \pi/4]$.

4   Quaternion Atomic Function

The $up(x)$ function is easily extendable to two dimensions. Since a 2D signal can be split into an even (e) and odd (o) parts [3]

$$f(x,y) = f_{ee}(x,y) + f_{oe}(x,y) + f_{eo}(x,y) + f_{oo}(x,y), \tag{7}$$

one can then separate the four components of equation (3) and represent it as a quaternion as follows:

$$QAF(x,y) = up(x,y)[\cos(w_x)\cos(w_y) + i(\sin(w_x)\cos(w_y)) + \qquad (8)$$
$$+ j(\cos(w_x)\sin(w_y)) + k(\sin(w_x)\sin(w_y))]$$
$$= QAF_{ee} + iQAF_{oe} + jQAF_{eo} + kQAF_{oo} \qquad (9)$$

Figure 3 shows a Quaternion Atomic Function QAF or qup in the space domain with its four components: real part QAF_{ee} is observed in a , and the imaginary parts $QAF_{eo}, QAF_{oe}, QAF_{oo}$ are illustrated in b, c, d respectively. We can see clearly the differences in each part of our filter.

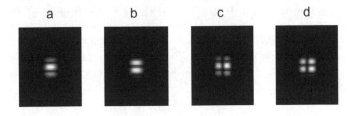

Fig. 3. Quaternion Atomic function up(x). a) QAF_{ee}, b) QAF_{oe}, c) QAF_{eo} and d) QAF_{oo}.

5   Quaternion Atomic Wavelet Function

In the Fourier Transform of a 2D signal, the phase component carries the main part of image information. We use this phase information in the quaternionic wavelet multiresolution analysis. This technique can be easily formulated in terms of the quaternion AF mother wavelet, for a more detail explanation see [2]. For the 2D image function $f(x,y)$, a quaternionic wavelet can be written as

$$f(x,y) = A_n^q f + \sum_{j=1}^{n} [D_{j,1}^q f + D_{j,2}^q f + D_{j,3}^q f]. \qquad (10)$$

The upper index q indicates a *quaternion* 2D signal. We can characterize each approximation function $A_j^q f(x,y)$ and the difference components $D_{j,p}^q f(x,y)$ for $p = 1, 2, 3$ via a 2D scaling function $\Phi^q(x,y)$ and its associated wavelet functions $\Psi_p^q(x,y)$ as follows:

$$A_j^q f(x,y) = \sum_{k=-\infty}^{+\infty} \sum_{l=-\infty}^{+\infty} a_{j,k,l} \Phi_{j,k,l}^q(x,y), \qquad (11)$$

$$D_{j,p}^q f(x,y) = \sum_{k=-\infty}^{+\infty} \sum_{l=-\infty}^{+\infty} d_{j,p,k,l} \Psi_{j,p,k,l}^q(x,y),$$

where

$$\Phi^q_{j,k,l}(x,y) = \frac{1}{2^j}\Phi^q\left(\frac{x-k}{2^j}, \frac{y-l}{2^j}\right), \quad (j,k,l) \in Z^3,$$

$$\Psi^q_{j,p,k,l}(x,y) = \frac{1}{2^j}\Psi^q_p\left(\frac{x-k}{2^j}, \frac{y-l}{2^j}\right) \tag{12}$$

and

$$a_{j,k,l}(x,y) = < f(x,y), \Phi^q_{j,k,l}(x,y) >, \tag{13}$$

$$d_{j,p,k,l} = < f(x,y), \Psi^q_{j,p,k,l}(x,y) > .$$

In order to carry out a separable quaternionic multiresolution analysis, we decompose the scaling function $\Phi^q(x,y)_j$ and the wavelet functions $\Psi^q_p(x,y)_j$ for each level j as follows:

$$\Phi^q(x,y)_j = \phi^{\boldsymbol{i}}(x)_j\phi^{\boldsymbol{j}}(y)_j,$$

$$\Psi^q_1(x,y)_j = \phi^{\boldsymbol{i}}(x)_j\psi^{\boldsymbol{j}}(y)_j,$$

$$\Psi^q_2(x,y)_j = \psi^{\boldsymbol{i}}(x)_j\phi^{\boldsymbol{j}}(y)_j,$$

$$\Psi^q_3(x,y)_j = \psi^{\boldsymbol{i}}(x)_j\psi^{\boldsymbol{j}}(y)_j, \tag{14}$$

where $\phi^{\boldsymbol{i}}(x)_j$ and $\psi(x)^{\boldsymbol{i}}_j$ are 1D complex filters applied along the rows and columns respectively. Note that in ϕ and ψ, we use the imaginary number $\boldsymbol{i}, \boldsymbol{j}$ of quaternions that satisfies $\boldsymbol{ji} = \boldsymbol{k}$.

By using these formulas, we can build quaternionic wavelet pyramids. Figure 4 shows the two primary levels of the pyramid (fine to coarse). According to equation (14), the approximation after the first level $A^q_1 f(x,y)$ is the output of $\Phi^q(x,y)_1$, and the differences $D^q_{1,1}f, D^q_{1,2}f, D^q_{1,3}f$ are the outputs of $\Psi^q_{1,1}(x,y)$, $\Psi^q_{1,2}(x,y)$ and $\Psi^q_{1,3}(x,y)$. The procedure continues through the j levels decimating the image at the outputs of the levels (indicated in figure 4 within the circle).

The quaternionic wavelet analysis from level $j-1$ to level j corresponds to the transformation of one quaternionic approximation to a new quaternionic approximation and three quaternionic differences, i.e.,

$$\{A^q_{j-1}\} \rightarrow \{A^q_j, D^q_{j,p}, p = 1, 2, 3\}. \tag{15}$$

Note that we do not use the idea of a mirror tree [2]. As a result, the quaternionic wavelet tree is a compact and economic processing structure which can be used for the case of n-dimensional multi-resolution analysis.

6   Results

Figure 5 shows the original image and four resulting images after convolution with components of the filter. The real part is observed in a, and i, j, k, imaginary

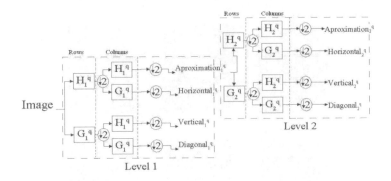

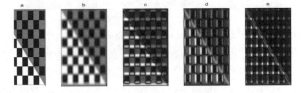

Fig. 4. Abstraction of two levels of the quaternionic wavelet pyramid

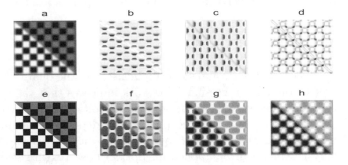

Fig. 5. Convolution of the test image with the *qup*. a) Original image. b) real-part c) i-part, d) j-part and e) k-part.

Fig. 6. The amplitude of the filtered Image *a*) and the three phases (ϕ, θ, φ), *b*), *c*), *d*) respectively. The second row shows the original image *f*) and the subtraction of the original image and the three phases (ϕ, θ, φ) of the filtered image.

parts can be appreciate in b, c, d respectively. This figure illustrates how the QAF or *qup* filter works in different directions such as vertical, horizontal and combination of both. The direct convolution with the image is sensitive to the contrast of the image. Figure 6 shows the amplitude (a) (real part) and the three phases (ϕ, θ, φ) of quaternionic phase of the filtered image. The phase information is immune to changes of the contrast. In the second row of the Figure 6 we can see a subtraction of the original image and the three phases, it shows how the phase information can be used to localize and extract more information independently of the contrast of the image.

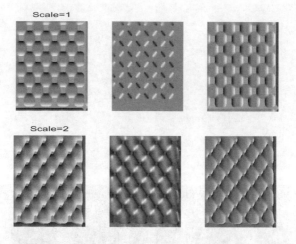

Fig. 7. (upper row) Thresholded quaternionic phases (ϕ, θ, φ) at first scale. (second row) Thresholded quaternionic phases (ϕ, θ, φ) at a second scale.

The QAF qup kernel was used as the mother wavelet in the multi-resolution pyramid. Figure 7 presents the three quaternionic phases at two scale levels of the pyramid. The lower row shows the phases after thresholding to enhance the phase structure. You can see how vertical lines and crossing points are highlighted.

7   Conclusion

This work introduces the theory and some applications of the quaternion Atomic Function Wavelet in image processing. This work indicates that the QAF (qup) can be more useful than simply up because it exploits the quaternion phase concept. The information of the three phases is independent of illumination changes. We present the use of this AF quaternionic mother wavelet for multi-resolution analysis which can be applied for optical flow, texture segmentation and image matching. The QAF wavelet filter disentangles structure symmetries of the image through the levels of an multi-resolution pyramid. A future work will include multi-resolution analysis for optical flow using real images.

References

1. Kravchenko, V.F., Perez-Meana, H.M., Ponomaryov, V.I.: Adaptive digital processing of multidimensional signals with applications. MOSCOW FIZMATLIT, MOSCOW (2009)
2. Bayro-Corrochano: Geometric Computing for Wavelet Transforms, Robot Vision, Learning, Control and Action. Springer, London (2010)
3. Bülow, T.: Hypercomplex Spectral Signal Representations for the Processing and Analysis of Images. Christian- Albert, Kiel University, Ph.D Thesis (1999)

4. Jähne, B.: Digital Image Processing. Springer, Germany (2002)
5. Kovesi, P.: Invariant measures of images features from phase information. University of Western Australia, PhD Thesis (1996)
6. Guyaev Yu, V., Kravchenko, V.F.: A New class of WA-Systems of Kravchenko-Rvachev Functions. MOSCOW Doklady Mathematics 75(2), 325–332 (2007)

A Complex Network-Based Approach for Texture Analysis

André Ricardo Backes[1],*, Dalcimar Casanova[2],**,
and Odemir Martinez Bruno[2],***

[1] Faculdade de Computação - Universidade Federal de Uberlândia
Uberlândia MG Brasil
backes@facom.ufu.br
[2] IFSC - Instituto de Física de São Carlos, São Carlos, Brasil
dalcimar@gmail.com, bruno@ifsc.usp.br

Abstract. In this paper, we propose a novel texture analysis method using the complex network theory. It was investigated how a texture image can be effectively represented, characterized and analyzed in terms of a complex network. The propose uses degree measurements in a dynamic evolution network to compose a set of feasible shape descriptors. Results show that the method is very robust and it presents a very excellent texture discrimination for all considered classes.

1 Introduction

Texture analysis is a basic issue in image processing and computer vision. It is a key problem in many application areas, such as object recognition, remote sensing, content-based image retrieval and so on. Even though there is no exact definition for the term texture, this is an attribute easily comprehended by humans and it is a wealthy source of visual informations (when considered the tri-dimensional nature of physical objects) [15].

Generally speaking, textures are complex visual patterns composed by entities, or sub-patterns, which present characteristics such bright, color, deepness, size, etc. So, texture can be considered as a group of similarities on a image [15]. Due this characteristic, the definition of a texture class must take into account not just the isolated primitives, but the relation among pixels and its neighbors [12]. Consequently, texture characterization and identification requires a methodology capable to express the context surrounding each pixel, joining local and global texture characteristics.

Numerous methods have been proposed in the literature and, several of them use implicitly the approach of joining local and global texture characteristics. These methods, in general, are based the spectral analysis of the pixels of the

---

* Is grateful to FAPESP (Proc. #2006/54367-9).
** Is grateful to FAPESP (Proc. #2008/57313-2).
*** Is grateful to FAPESP (Proc. #303746/2004-1).

I. Bloch and R.M. Cesar, Jr. (Eds.): CIARP 2010, LNCS 6419, pp. 354–361, 2010.

image (e.g., Fourier desciptors [2] and Gabor Filters [14]), statistical analysis of the pixels (e.g., co-ocorrence matrices [11]) and complexity analysis (e.g., Fractal Dimension [13]).

This paper proposes a novel approach to represent and characterize the relation among these structural elements using the Complex Networks Theory. To accomplish this task, is necessary to represent texture as a complex network, incorporating to the vertices and edges the information about image pixels and their neighbors, followed by an analysis of the topological features of the computed network. These features may be used to discriminate different classes of images. In the fact, every discrete structure such as lists, trees, networks, texts [1] and images [9] can be suitably represented as graphs. Taking this into account, various studies include investigations of the problem representation as a Complex Network, followed by an analysis of its topological characteristics and its features extraction [6,4,3,7,8].

In [4,3] the shape analysis is performed using the complex network theory. After the modeling of the shape as an complex network, simple measurements are extracted. Thoses measurements are used to classify shapes in differents classes. In [6,7] and [8], the problem of texture characterization is presented in terms of complex networks: image pixels are represented as nodes and similarities between such pixels are mapped as links between the network nodes. It is verified that several types of textures present distinct node degree distributions, suggesting complex organization of those textures. Traditional measurements of the network connectivity are then applied in order to obtain feature vectors from which the textures can be characterized and classified.

The idea of this work is similar of the cited works above, model the texture as a complex network and the posterior feature extraction. The main difference are in the manner as complex network is modeled, and in what measurements used. The works of [6,7] and [8] uses an hierarchical representation as model. We propose use direct pixels relations to model the texture and use a set of thresholds values to characterize the network. The work of [6,7] and [8] uses the degree and clustering coeficient to characterize the network. We will use only degree, due the high computational time of the clustering coeficient. In this time we can say that the idea proposed here is more similar with [4,3], but applied in texture analysis context.

2 Texture as a Pixel Network

A graph representation of the texture is built as $G = (P, E)$, where each pixel corresponds to a vertex in the graph G. In this graph, two pixels $p = (i, j) \in P$ and $p' = (i', j') \in P$ are connected when the Euclidean distance between them is no longer than a r value:

$$E = \left\{ ((i,j),(i',j')) \in P \times P | \sqrt{(i-i')^2 + (j-j')^2} \leq r \right\} \qquad (1)$$

For each non-directed edge $e \in E$ is associated a weight, which is defined by the square of the Euclidean distance between two connected vertexes, when considered the pixels intensity $v_{i,j}$ and $v_{i',j'}$:

$$d(e) = (i - i')^2 + (j - j')^2 + (v_{i,j} - v_{i',j'})^2 \ \forall e = \{(i,j), (i',j')\} \in E \quad (2)$$

This approach allows to include context information about pixel surrounding, which refers to a local texture analysis.

Once the connection between pixels depends on the parameter r, which is associated to the covering radius of an pixel in the image, the weight function $d(e)$ may assume a very large range of values. It makes necessary to normalize this weight into the interval $[0, 1]$, which is performed using the largest value possible in a connection. This value corresponds to the maximum difference of intensity between two pixels that are to a distance of r:

$$w(e) = \frac{d(e)}{255^2 + r^2} \quad (3)$$

Initially, each network vertex presents a similar number of connections, so the computed network presents a regular behavior. However, a regular network is not considered a complex network, and it does not present any relevant property. It is necessary to transform this network in a complex network that owns relevant properties. More explanation about this can be read in [4].

An interesting approach for achieving additional information about structure and dynamic of complex networks is to apply a transformation over the original network and then to compute the properties of the resulting network [10]. Figure 1 shows an example of a transformation δ applied over a network, so a set of features are computed.

There are several possibilities to perform this transformation. A straight and simple way is applying a threshold t over the original set of edges E, so as to

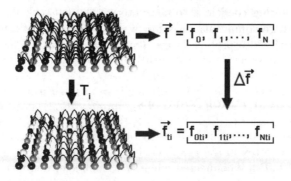

Fig. 1. Difference Δf between feature vectors f and f_{T_i} after applying a T_i transformation over the original network. This difference can be used as additional information about the proprieties of the network. Adapted from [10].

select a subset E^*, $E^* \subseteq E$, where each edge of E^* has a weight equal or smaller than t. This transformation δ_T, henceforth represented as

$$E^* = \delta_t(E) = \{e \in E | w(e) \leq t\}. \tag{4}$$

In this case, the δ_t transformation can be interpreted as a intermediate step on network dynamics. So, a richer set of measurements that describes the network dynamics involves to take into account several instances along its degradation. A feature is computed at each time instant t. Figure 2 shows four instances of an evolving network. In such a way, the evolution of a network can now be investigated in terms of a trajectory in dynamical evolution of δ transformation.

In other words, the network characterization is performed using various δ transformations, where the threshold T_i is incremented in a regular interval T_{inc}. Also can be interpreted as acquisition of several samplings of complex network throughout it life (between it creation and extinction).

2.1 Network Characterization

Several measurements can be computed through analysis of the network. One measurement particularly relevant for texture characterization is the average degree of G, $Av(G)$:

$$Av(G) = \sum_{p \in P} \frac{deg(p)}{|P|} \tag{5}$$

where $deg(p)$ is the *degree* (or *connectivity*) of a node p, i.e., the number of neighbors of p and $|P|$ denotes the cardinality (number of nodes).

Note that such measurements are particularly relevant for texture characterization because they provides a good compromise between local (i.e. the measurements are centered at each image point) and global (i.e. the measurement take into account the immediate context of the image properties around the reference point) information.

Considering $f(x, y)$ the texture under analysis and G the network built using Equations 1,2 and 3, the feature vector consists of the average degree in several δ_t transformations. This process is better understood through Figure 2. There, a texture is modeled as a complex network and different δ_{T_i} transformations are applied over the resulting network. For each threshold T_i a numeric value representing the average degree $(Av(\delta_{T_i} G))$ of the network is computed and used as a feasible texture signature. Figure 3 shows two complex networks computed from different textures using the same threshold value.

3 Evaluation

In order to evaluate the proposed method, signatures have been calculated for different configurations and they have been used in a texture analysis context. For this, an image database have been prepared selecting a set of 111 natural textures obtained from Brodatz texture album [5]. This database is broadly used

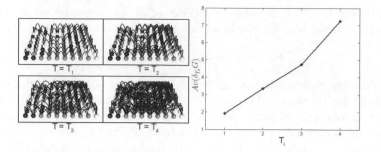

Fig. 2. Complex network characterization through dynamical evolution investigations

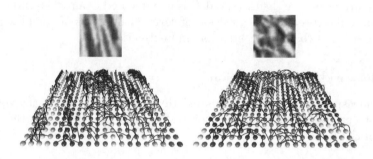

Fig. 3. Example of resulting complex network for two different texture samples

in computer vision and image processing literature as benchmark for texture analysis. Each texture image is of size 640×640 with 256 gray levels. A database constituted of 1110 image regions of 111 texture classes was constructed by subdivided each image into 10 sub-images of 200×200 size.

In addition, to corroborate properties such rotation invariance, an additional database was built by rotating of the original textures in $15°$, $30°$, $45°$, $60°$, $75°$, $90°$, $105°$, $120°$, $135°$ and $150°$ degrees.

The analysis has been carried out by applying the Linear Discriminant Analysis (LDA) in a leave-one-out cross-validation scheme.

3.1   Experiments

Experiments have been idealized to show the high potential of the method to analyze and characterize texture images, and its results have been compared with others descriptors found in the literature:

Fourier descriptors[2]: composed by the 99 coeficients of Fourier Transform, were each one corresponds to the sum of the spectrum absolute values placed to a radial distance from the center of the bi-dimensional transformation.

Co-occurrence matrices[11]: distances of 1 and 2 pixels with angles of $-45°$, $0°$, $45°$, $90°$ were used. Energy and entropy were computed from resulting matrices, totalizing a set of 16 descriptors. A non-symmetric version has been adopted.

Gabor filters[14]: we use a family of 16 filters (4 rotation and 4 scale), with frequency lower than 0.01 and superior than 0.3. Definition of the individual parameters of each filter follows mathematical model presented in [14].

4   Results and Discussion

A important characteristic in the proposed method is that it has only two parameters to be configured when it is applied in the texture recognition task: the radius r and the number of evolutions periods T. Several tests have been performed in order to evaluate the method behavior for different values of r and different T periods. Table 1 summarizes the results for 9 vectors $(F1, F2, \ldots, F9)$.

Table 1. Result for the proposed method under different parameter values. T_{ini} and T_Q are, respectively, the initial and final threshold defined by user, while T_{inc} is the increment used to go from T_{ini} to T_Q.

Set	Parameters				N° of descriptors	Images correctly classified	Success rate(%)	Maximum error rate (%) per class
	r	T_{ini}	T_{inc}	T_Q				
F1	2	0.005	0.005	0.333	66	1066	96.03	60.00
F2	3	0.005	0.005	0.333	66	1067	96.12	60.00
F3	4	0.005	0.005	0.333	66	1071	96.48	50.00
F4	5	0.005	0.005	0.333	66	1071	96.48	40.00
F5	5	0.005	0.005	0.166	33	1058	95.31	60.00
F6	5	0.166	0.005	0.333	33	1017	91.62	70.00
F7	5	0.333	0.005	0.500	34	927	83.51	100.00
F8	5	0.005	0.010	0.333	33	1054	94.95	60.00
F9	5	0.005	0.015	0.333	22	1033	93.06	80.00

We observed no significant improvement in performance for $F1$, $F2$, $F3$ and $F4$ sets, although they are using different r values. Even though a higher r value be able to model a more dense network, this does not affect straight the results.

We see that the chosen sequence of T values should have a small influence over the final results. This affirmation is corroborated by $F4$, $F8$ and $F9$ parameters set, where we notice a satisfactory classification rate, even when it is used different sampling (T values with intervals of 0.005, 0.010 e 0.015 respectively). We see too that most part of information lies on the beginning of the dynamic evolution process. This is validated by $F5$, $F6$ and $F7$ parameters set. $F5$, whose set yielded the best result among these three (95.31%), uses only the beginning of dynamic evolution process to compose its feature vector ($T \leq 0.166$). Otherwise, the $F7$ set, which uses only the final stages ($0.333 \leq T \leq 0.500$), yielded the worst result (83.51%). As expected, the $F6$ set, which uses intermediate stages ($0.166 \leq T \leq 0.333$), yielded an average result (91.62%).

For comparison, the proposed method have been compared with traditional texture analysis methods described in Section 3.1. Table 2 shows the yielded results presented by each method. The our method presents a superior success rate. Even though the number of descriptors is higher than in other methods, this presents a discrimination ability also higher when it uses only the initial

Table 2. Comparison of the proposed method with traditional texture analysis methods

Method	N° of descriptors	Images correctly classified	Success rate (%)	Maximum error rate (%) per class
Gabor Filters	16	992	89.37	100.00
Fourier	99	888	80.00	90.00
Co-occurrence	16	968	87.21	80.00
Complex Network	66	1071	96.48	40.00

Table 3. Result for the proposed method over rotated textures database

Method	N° of descriptors	Images correctly classified	Success rate (%)	Maximum error rate (%) per class
Gabor Filters	16	885	79.73	100.00
Fourier	99	966	87.02	50.00
Co-occurrence	16	751	67.66	90.00
Complex Network	66	1106	99.64	10.00

stages of dynamic evolution. This is corroborated by result archived with only 16 descriptors (e.g. $T = (0.005 \leq 0.005 \leq 0.08)$, the same number os descriptors used for Gabor filters and Haralick methods), with a success rate of 92.97%.

Due the texture model used here, using Euclidean distance, a small error is added to the distance between a pairs of rotated pixels. Considering the intensity of the pixel too, and the fact that this does not change during image rotation we have method invariant to the rotation. Table 3 shows the result from when the method is applied over rotated textures database.

5   Conclusion

In this paper, we have proposed a novel method of texture analysis using the complex network theory. It was investigated how a texture image can be effectively represented, characterized and analyzed in terms of complex network.

Although the method uses two configuration parameters, they do not have a great influence in the final results. Investigations about the influence of the radius r and the set of thresholds T in texture discrimination show that most of texture information lays in the beginning of the dynamic evolution process. However, using a large sampling of thresholds and/or higher values for r parameter also yield a excellent success rate in spite of a superior computational cost.

Results show that the method is very robust, because it presents a very excellent texture discrimination for all considered classes, it has a great capacity to work with both micro and macro texture, overcoming traditional texture methods, and is invariant a rotataion. So, it have been shown that, besides the compromise between local and global proprieties, the interplay between structural and dynamical aspects can provide precious informations about the structure under analysis. Concerning of Complex Networks theory, the sucess on discrimination of Brodats textures demonstrates the potential of the application of this approach in computer vision problems and digital imaging processing.

References

1. Antiqueira, L., Nunes, M.G.V., Oliveira, O.N., Costa, L.F.: Strong correlations between text quality and complex networks features. Physica A 373(1), 811–820 (2007)
2. Azencott, R., Wang, J.P., Younes, L.: Texture classification using windowed fourier filters. IEEE Transactions on Pattern Analysis and Machine Intelligence 19(2), 148–153 (1997)
3. Backes, A.R., Bruno, O.M.: Shape classification using complex network and multiscale fractal dimension. Pattern Recognition Letters 31, 44–51 (2010)
4. Backes, A.R., Casanova, D., Bruno, O.M.: A complex network-based approach for boundary shape analysis. Pattern Recognition 42(1), 54–67 (2009)
5. Brodatz, P.: Textures: A photographic album for artists and designers. Dover Publications, New York (1966), http://www.ux.uis.no/~tranden/brodatz.html
6. Chalumeau, T., Costa, L.F., Laligant, O., Meriaudeau, F.: Texture discrimination using hierarchical complex networks. In: Proceedings of the Second International Conference on Signal-Image Technology and Internet-Based Systems, pp. 543–550 (2006)
7. Chalumeau, T., da Costa, L.F., Laligant, O., Meriaudeau, F.: Complex networks: application for texture characterization and classification. Electronic Letters on Computer Vision and Image Analysis 7(3), 93–100 (2008)
8. Chalumeau, T., da Costa, L.F., Laligant, O., Meriaudeau, F.: Texture discrimination using hierarchical complex networks. Multimedia Systems and Applications 31(2), 95–102 (2008)
9. Costa, L.F.: Complex networks, simple vision (2004), http://arxiv.org/abs/cond-mat/0403346
10. Costa, L.F., Rodrigues, F.A., Travieso, G., Boas, P.R.V.: Characterization of complex networks: A survey of measurements. Advances in Physics 56(1), 167–242 (2007)
11. Haralick, R.M.: Statistical and structural approaches to texture. Proceedings of IEEE 67(5), 786–804 (1979)
12. Julesz, B.: Experiments in the visual perception of texture. Scientific American 232(4), 34–43 (1975)
13. Kasparis, T., Charalampidis, D., Georgiopoulos, M., Rolland, J.P.: Segmentation of textured images based on fractals and image filtering. Pattern Recognition 34(10), 1963–1973 (2001)
14. Manjunath, B.S., Ma, W.Y.: Texture features for browsing and retrieval of image data. IEEE Transactions on Pattern Analysis and Machine Intelligence 18(8), 837–842 (1996)
15. Tuceryan, M., Jain, A.K.: Texture analysis. In: Handbook of Pattern Recognition and Computer Vision, pp. 235–276 (1993)

Enhancing Gabor Wavelets Using Volumetric Fractal Dimension

Alvaro Gomez Zuniga[1] and Odemir Martinez Bruno[2]

[1] Instituto de Ciências Matemáticas e de Computação
[2] Instituto de Física de São Carlos
Universidade de São Paulo
Av. Trabalhador São Carlense 400, São Carlos, São Paulo Brasil
alvarog@icmc.usp.br
bruno@ifsc.usp.br

Abstract. Texture plays an important role on image analysis and computer vision. Local spatial variations of intensity and color indicate significant differences among several types of surfaces. One of the most widely adopted algorithms for texture analysis is the Gabor wavelets. This technique provides a multi-scale and multi-orientation representation of an image which is capable of characterizing different patterns of texture effectively. However, the texture descriptors used does not take full advantage of the richness of detail from the Gabor images generated in this process. In this paper, we propose a new method for extracting features of the Gabor wavelets space using volumetric fractal dimension. The results obtained in experimentation demonstrate that this method outperforms earlier proposed methods for Gabor space feature extraction and creates a more accurate and reliable method for texture analysis and classification.

Keywords: Volumetric fractal dimension; Texture analysis; Gabor Wavelets; Feature extraction.

1 Introduction

Texture reflects the variations of optical properties on object surfaces. Different surfaces produce distinctive texture patterns. This makes texture an important source of discriminating information for image classification [1]. Recently Gabor filters have become a widely used technique for texture analysis. These filters have desirable characteristics of localization on spatial and frequency domains being the best method to represent a signal jointly in both domains. Using this filter we can create multi-scale and multi-orientation representations of an image each with unique characteristics. The process consists on the convolution of an image with a series of filters constructed by varying its scales and orientations. Energy is then used as the descriptor of each convoluted image to form the final feature vector. However, a single measure such as energy has a limited power in seizing the richness of detail of the generated images. Recent work done on

I. Bloch and R.M. Cesar, Jr. (Eds.): CIARP 2010, LNCS 6419, pp. 362–369, 2010.

the field attempts to generate methods to extract more useful information of the Gabor space: First and second order statistic descriptors. Invariant moments that achieve resistance to rotation, translation and scaling [8] [9], [4], [11]. And more recently, the local binary pattern (LBP) operator offering the best results found in the literature [12],[13],[14].

In this paper, we introduce the use of fractal descriptors on the Gabor space as an alternative to improve the feature extraction process. This proposed method improves the results obtained by the Gabor wavelets process. This new method consists in calculating the fractal signature of each convoluted image and generating a feature vector that concatenates these signatures into a final vector.The article starts by making a quick review of Gabor filters and feature extraction from Gabor space. Next, the proposed method is presented. Finally experiments are performed with the Brodatz texture database where the method is compared with the most important feature extraction methods of the Gabor space found on the literature: first and second order statistics and local binary patterns. The article ends with the final discussions and conclusions.

2   Gabor Wavelets

In recent years the Gabor filter has become popular in image processing and analysis, particularly in texture feature extraction [3]. Besides the classical approach in texture, the filter has been used in other applications such as biometrics [23], image segmentation [8], pattern recognition and OCR [24].

The two-dimensional Gabor transform is a complex sine wave with frequency W modulated by a Gaussian function. Its form in space $g(x, y)$ and frequency domains $G(u, v)$, is given by Eqs.1 and 2:

$$g\left(x,y\right) = \left(\frac{1}{2\pi\sigma_x\sigma_y}\right)\exp\left[-\frac{1}{2}\left(\frac{x^2}{\sigma_x^2} + \frac{y^2}{\sigma_y^2}\right) + 2\pi jWx\right] \qquad (1)$$

$$G\left(u,v\right) = \exp\left\{-\frac{1}{2}\left[\frac{(u-W)^2}{\sigma_u^2} + \frac{v^2}{\sigma_v^2}\right]\right\} \qquad (2)$$

Although the Gabor transforms is older than wavelets, due to its multi-scale nature it can be used as mother wavelet. For the process is employed a filter bank constructed by varying the scale and orientations of each filter. In [3] the authors describe how to compose the bank of Gabor filters to make the Gabor wavelet with a set of parameters that assures maximum spectrum coverage with lowest redundancy. We use this approach to design the Gabor wavelet.

The Most common approach to analyze and characterize textures with Gabor is to adopt a set of filters with different scales and orientations. This characterizes the Gabor wavelets process [3], then each filter is convoluted with the image as shown in Figure 1. For each of the spaces obtained a feature is extracted. A simple way of extracting this feature is using energy as the general descriptor. The energy of each space is concatenated into a feature vector according to:

$$f = [E_{11}, E_{12}, ..., E_{21}, E_{22}, ..., E_{MN}]; \tag{3}$$

Where M and N are the number of scales and orientations respectively.

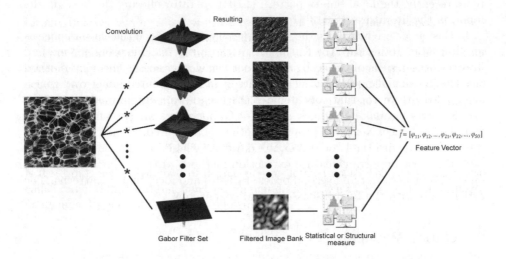

Fig. 1. General process used to obtain the Gabor signatures

3   Feature Extraction on the Gabor Space

Most of the methods found in the literature makes use of statistical descriptors. Being fairly simple to compute, they have the advantage of generating feature vectors of low dimensionality. The descriptors that obtain the best results are based on first and second order statistics: Variance, energy and percentiles [5]. Other approaches use descriptors based on the local binary pattern (LBP) operator. The LBP operator analyzes the image using a nxn window generating a binary code for each region. Then a histogram with the values obtained for each window is generated and this represents the feature vector of the image. The LBP operator has proven to be one of the most suitable texture descriptors found on the literature, and it has been successfully applied in the Gabor wavelets process [12] (LBP1),[13] (LBP2).

4   Volumetric Fractal Dimension

The fractal concept was first used by Mandelbrot in his book [18]. This concept suggests that natural objects are not formed by Euclidean geometry objects; instead, they form sub-patterns that are repeated to form more complex objects. In recent years this concept has been widely used in the field of image analysis [19], [20]. Many natural forms have fractal patterns (structures of plants, coastlines, plants). The fractal dimension of the image is taken as a measure of the irregularity of the objects. However, in order to calculate the fractal dimension

(FD) of non-fractal objects we need a method to estimate the FD in discrete finite images. One of the most accurate methods to calculate the fractal dimension of a non-fractal object is the Bouligand-Minkowski method [19]. To calculate the volumetric fractal dimension (VFD) using the Minkowski-Bouligand method on a grayscale image we must first readapt the image. For this we use the approach taken in [20]. The 3-D projection of the image is generated from a grayscale image to meet the conditions to apply the Euclidean distance transform. Each pixel of the image is transformed into a point $p = (y, x, z) \epsilon S$, where Y and X correspond to the coordinates of the pixel in the image and $z = f(x, y)$ is the intensity. Then the Minkowski-Bouligand fractal dimension of the surface S can be estimated by:

$$FD = 3 - \lim_{r->0} \frac{\log(V(r))}{\log(r)} \qquad (4)$$

$$V(r) = \{p' \epsilon R^3 \mid \exists p \epsilon S : |p - p'| \leq r\} \qquad (5)$$

This method calculates the variation of a volume $V(r)$ given by the application of exact dilations of the image $f(x, y)$ with a sphere of radius r. Small changes on the structure of the image can produce significant changes in the calculated FD. The FD and $V(r)$ are given by:

$$E = 1, \sqrt{2}, \sqrt{3}, ..., r_{max} \qquad (6)$$

$$\psi(r_{max}) = [\log V(1), \log V(\sqrt{2}), \log V(\sqrt{3}), ..., \log V(r_{max})] \qquad (7)$$

5   Experimentation and Evaluation

Image database. In experiments we used the Brodatz texture database [22]. This album has been widely used to test and compare techniques used to extract texture features. The album is composed of 111 images of artificial textures. From this album we derive an image database formed by selecting 10 random non-overlapping windows of 200 x 200 pixels size from each image in the original album. These images are coded in 8-bit depth and saved in a lossless format. The final database generated is composed of 1110 images with 111 classes and 10 images per class. Some samples are shown in Figure 2.

The classification of the samples was made using a Bayesian probability method. Specifically, the Naïve Bayes method. The 1110 samples are divided in training and testing set in a proportion of 8 to 2. This means 80% of the samples were used for training and 20% for testing with a random selection of each set ensuring that each class is represented with a consistent number of samples. This scenario is repeated 10 times in order to obtain an accurate and robust estimation of the predictions for each class. Moreover, to determinate the best combination of the Gabor parameters and the feature extractor we use a wide range of scales and orientations for all the experiments. The near ideal parameters for the Gabor filters are extracted from [3].

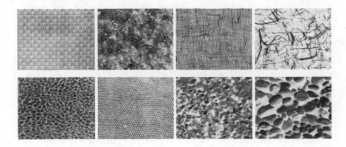

Fig. 2. Sample images from the Brodatz texture database used in experimentation

Table 1. Results for experimentation using the feature extractors explained

No of Descriptors	Average No. Of Correctly Classified Images	Average Success Rate (%)	Standard Deviation	Root Relative Squared error(%)	Reliability
1	185.26	83.45	2.78	63.08	78.92
3	191.12	86.09	1.8	52.67	86.33
7	192.67	86.79	2.09	50.48	87.24
11	200.67	90.39	2.59	40.51	90.42
16	201.11	90.59	1.99	39.38	91.79
20	201.44	90.74	2.12	41.82	92.71
22	204	**91.89**	1.65	38.8	93.62
30	200.55	90.34	1.91	44.59	91.5
38	196	88.29	2.31	48.32	89.06
46	194.67	87.69	3.03	50.28	86.33

The use of Eq. 7 generates a signature ψ composed of N descriptors where N is the number of exact dilatations possible for a radius r_{max}. In order to reduce dimensionality we used a technique to extract the most important features of the signature called Fourier descriptors. Using this technique we obtain the approximate number of descriptors necessary to obtain the best results while keeping the dimensionality of the feature vector as low as possible.

The average success rate, standard deviation (of the success rate), the root relative squared error and reliability (average a posteriori probability for samples correctly classified) are presented in the Table 1. These values are used to asses the results and accuracy of the data modeled using the proposed technique. The maximum radius of expansion used for Eq. 7 was 9 and 16. According to [20] these values obtain the best results in classification. We only present the table corresponding to the results using a radius of 16 because it was proven on [20] that these value achieves better performance and more reliable results.

Table 2. Results for experimentation with the feature extractors applied to the Gabor space

Scales x Orientations							
Gabor +	2 x 6	3 x 4	3 x 5	4 x 4	4 x 6	5 x 5	6 x 3	6 x 6
VFD	89.06	90.64	90.32	90.84	**91.89**	91.02	89.46	88.22
Energy	60.81	80.43	79.13	79.83	**81.93**	81.78	76.83	81.83
Variance	64.76	82.13	**83.73**	79.98	82.68	81.03	77.28	82.38
Percentil25	61.36	76.88	75.07	79.48	81.18	**82.73**	77.93	80.58
Percentil75	62.71	80.98	80.78	**83.03**	83.08	82.93	79.23	82.23
LBP1	86.58	87.02	88.14	**88.99**	85.54	83.03	87.39	76.53
LBP2	87.04	85.79	**88.29**	87.29	86.54	84.63	86.29	84.63

Table 1 shows that the best result is obtained with 22 descriptors of the fractal signature obtaining a mean average success of 91.89% using a radius of 16 for Eq. 7 for the proposed technique. The results obtained can be compared with the other feature extractors in Table 2 using several parameters for the Gabor Wavelets. In experimentation we determinate that the alteration of other parameters on the Gabor process produces similar variations on all the methods without any significantly improve or deprecation on the results; therefore, we only used $U_l = 0.05$, $U_h = 0.3$ as fix parameters for the Gabor Wavelets.

In our experiments energy feature achieves 81.93% of images correctly classified on 4 scales and 6 orientations in concordance with the model and results presented on [3]. For the other feature extractors results are increasingly better accordingly to the technique used obtaining close results with the LBP methods but with higher dimensionality. From the results observed it can be shown that the proposed method offers the best performance and presents a great alternative for improving the Gabor wavelets process.

6   Conclusions

This paper presents a new approach for feature extraction by applying volumetric fractal dimension instead of energy in the Gabor wavelets process. The proposed method obtains significantly better results than other methods studied on the literature. Both the accuracy and reliability of the model show its robustness and reliability. The proposed method achieved 91.89% of images correctly classified with 93.62% reliability while maintaining an acceptable dimensionality. Therefore, considering the promising results in texture analysis and classification we can determine that the volumetric fractal dimension is a suitable technique to exploit the richness of detail of the images resulting from the convolution on the Gabor wavelets process. The method can be applied in many classification tasks due to the power of effectively representing and differentiating micro and macro texture.

Acknowledgment

A. G. Z. gratefully acknowledges the financial support of FAPESP (The State of Sao Paulo Research Foundation) Proc. 2009/04362. O.M.B. acknowledges support from CNPq (306628/2007-4).

References

1. Rosenfeld, A., Lipkin, B.S.: Picture Processing and Psychopictorics. Academic Press, London (1970)
2. Daugman, J.G.: Two-dimensional spectral analysis of cortical receptive field profiles. Vision Research 20, 847–856 (1980)
3. Manjunath, B.S., Ma, W.-Y.: Texture features for browsing and retrieval of image data. IEEE PAMI, 837–842 (1996)
4. Andrysiak, T., Choras, M.: Image Retrieval Based on Hierarchical Gabor Filters. Intl J. Applied Mathematics and Computer Science 15(4), 471–480 (2005)
5. Bandzi, P., Oravec, M., Pavlovicova, J.: New Statistics for Texture Classification Based on Gabor Filters. Intl. Radioengineering J. 16(3), 133–137 (2007)
6. Clausi, D.A., Deng, H.: Fusion of Gabor filter and co-occurrence probability features for texture recognition. IEEE Transactions on Image Processing 14(7), 925–936 (2005)
7. Shahabi, F., Rahmati, M.: Comparison of gabor-based features for writer identification of farsi/arabic handwriting. In: Proc. of 10th Intl. Workshop on Frontiers in Handwriting Recognition, pp. 545–550 (2006)
8. Muneeswaran, K., Ganesan, I., Arumugam, S., Harinarayan, P.: A novel approach combining gabor wavelet and moments for texture segmentation. Intl. J. of Wavelets, Multiresolution and Information Processing 3(4), 559–572 (2005)
9. Qaiser, N., Hussain, M., Hussain, A., Qaiser, N.: Texture Recognition by Fusion of Optimized Moment Based and Gabor Energy Features. Intl. J. CSNS 8(2), 264–270 (2008)
10. Andrysiak, T., Choras, M.: Image Retrieval Based on Hierarchical Gabor Filters. Intl. J. Applied Mathematics and Computer Science 15(4), 471–480 (2005)
11. Grigorescu, S.E., Petkov, N., Kruizinga, P.: Comparison of texture Features based on Gabor Filters. IEEE Transactions on Image processing 11(10), 1160–1167 (2002)
12. Zhang, W., Shan, S., Gao, W., Chen, X., Zhang, H.: Local Gabor Binary Pattern Histogram Sequence (LGBPHS): A Novel Non-Statistical Model for Face Representation and Recognition. In: Tenth IEEE ICCV, vol. 1, pp. 786–791 (2005)
13. Lei, Z., Liao, S., He, R., Pietikäinen, M., Li, S.: Gabor volume based local binary pattern for face representation and recognition. In: 8th IEEE Intl. Conference on Automatic Face and Gesture Recognition, pp. 1–6 (2008)
14. Ojala, T., Pietikäinen, M., Mäenpää, T.: Multiresolution Gray-Scale and Rotation Invariant Texture Classification with Local Binary Patterns. IEEE Transactions on Pattern Analysis and Machine Intelligence 24(7), 971–987 (2002)
15. Casanova, D., de Mesquita Sá Jr., J.J., Bruno, O.M.: Plant leaf identification using Gabor wavelets. Intl. J. of Imaging Systems and Technology 19(3), 236–243 (2009)
16. Haralick, R.M., Shanmugam, K., Dinstein, I.: Textural Features for Image Classification. IEEE Trans. Sys. Man Cybern. 3, 610–621 (1973)
17. Qaiser, N., Hussain, M.: Optimum Window-size Computation for Moment Based Texture Segmentation. In: Proc. IEEE INMIC, pp. 25–29 (2003)

18. Mandelbrot, B.B.: The Fractal Geometry of Nature, W.H. (1982)
19. Backes, A.R., Bruno, O.M.: Fractal and Multi-Scale Fractal Dimension analysis: a comparative study of Bouligand-Minkowski method. INFOCOMP (UFLA) 7, 74–83 (2008)
20. Backes, A.R., Casanova, D., Bruno, O.M.: Plant leaf identification based on volumetric fractal dimension. IEEE PAMI 23, 1145–1160 (2009)
21. Fabbri, R., Da Costa, F.L., Torelli, J.C., Bruno, O.M.: 2D Euclidean distance transform algorithms: A comparative survey. ACM Computing Surveys (CSUR) 40(1), 1–44 (2008)
22. Brodatz, P.: Textures; a photographic album for artists and designers (1996)
23. Daugman, J.: How iris recognition works. IEEE Transactions on Circuits and Systems for Video Technology 14, 21–30 (2004)
24. Daugman, J.: Gabor wavelets and statistical pattern recognition. In: The Handbook of Brain Theory and N.N., 2nd edn., pp. 457–463. MIT, Cambridge (2002)

Comparison of Shape Descriptors for Mice Behavior Recognition

Jonathan de Andrade Silva[1], Wesley Nunes Gonçalves[1],
Bruno Brandoli Machado[1], Hemerson Pistori[2],
Albert Schiaveto de Souza[3], and Kleber Padovani de Souza[2]

[1] Computer Science Department
University of São Paulo (USP) at São Carlos, Brazil
{jandrade,brandoli}@icmc.usp.br, wnunes@ursa.ifsc.usp.br
[2] Research Group in Engineering and Computing
Dom Bosco Catholic University, Brazil
pistori@ucdb.br, kriowloo@gmail.com
http://www.gpec.ucdb.br
[3] Department of Morphophysiology
Federal University of Mato Grosso do Sul, Brazil
albertss@hotmail.com

Abstract. Shape representation provides fundamental features for many applications in computer vision and it is known to be important cues for human vision. This paper presents an experimental study on recognition of mice behavior. We investigate the performance of the four shape recognition methods, namely Chain-Code, Curvature, Fourier descriptors and Zernike moments. These methods are applied to a real database that consists of four mice behaviors. Our experiments show that Zernike moments and Fourier descriptors provide the best results. To evaluate the noise tolerance, we corrupt each contour with different levels of noise. In this scenario, Fourier descriptor shows invariance to high levels of noise.

Keywords: Computer Vision, Shape Descriptors, Mice Behavior.

1 Introduction

Shape analysis is an important field of investigation that has been a subject of intense research for decades, further reinforced in recent years by applications in content-based information retrieval, human gait recognition, and medicine. Psychological studies have suggested that shape provides fundamental information for brain processing and are known to be important cues for human vision system [1]. In images, shape is considered one of the most important visual attributes to characterize objects. Large variations in shape, as well as varying scale, rotation and noise make the representation of shape particularly challenging from a computer vision perspective.

Several methods have been proposed in the literature and most of them can be classified into two categories: contour-based methods and region-based methods.

I. Bloch and R.M. Cesar, Jr. (Eds.): CIARP 2010, LNCS 6419, pp. 370–377, 2010.

Contour-based methods explore boundary shape information. In this category, the most common methods are chain code [2], curvature [3], Fourier descriptors [4], and simple descriptors [1]. Though chain code and curvature methods demand low computational cost, they are easily influenced by noise. Otherwise, Fourier descriptor has low sensitivity to noise when low frequency Fourier coefficients are used [4]. However, Fourier descriptor does not provide local information as chain code and curvature methods.

Unlike the contour-based methods, region-based methods extract features from the whole shape region. Different moments, such as Zernike moments [5,6] and Legendre moments [7] have been demonstrated to achieve excellent performance. Zernike moments has been suggested for shape description due to its superiority over other moments functions regarding to the robustness to deformations and noise [5].

This paper provides an experimental study of shape descriptor methods applied to mice behavior recognition, an important real-world application. This application aims at helping experts to determine the drug effect used for the medicine development and answering basic ethological questions [8]. Currently, behavioral analysis is carried out by means of visual inspection, which is considered a laborious and time consuming task. In order to enhance this procedure, we study automatic procedures through applying four shape methods (chain code, curvature, Fourier, and Zernike moments) on real database of mice behaviors. This database consists of four behaviors with similar contour characteristics, presenting an interesting challenge for the recognition task. According to the experimental results, Zernike moments and Fourier descriptors achieve the best recognition performances for mice behavior recognition. Further, results show that 20 descriptors seem to be sufficient to characterize the behaviors. Moreover, results from noised images show that Fourier Descriptor provides more invariance for high levels of noise.

This paper is organized as follows. Section 2 describes the fundamentals of the shape descriptor methods. In Section 3 experimental results and discussion have been provided. Finally, Section 4 concludes the paper.

2   Shape Descriptors

In this section we give a brief overview of the methods employed in this work. Before describing the methods, it is important considering that a parametric curve $c(t) = (x(t), y(t))$ consists of points belong to the contour of binary objects.

2.1   Fourier Descriptors

Fourier is one of the most popular descriptors for shape characterization. The basic idea of this method consists in applying the Fourier transform in a parametric curve. Initially, the complex signal $u(t) = x(t) + j\,y(t)$ is obtained from the parametric curve. Then the complex signal is expanded by a complex Fourier series defined as

$$U(s) = \frac{1}{L} \int_0^L u(t)e^{-j2\pi st/L} dt \tag{1}$$

where L is the curve perimeter.

The $FD(s)$ corresponds to the Fourier descriptors defined as $FD(s) = \frac{U(s)}{U(0)}$. Some properties from these descriptors can be discussed. For example, the 0-th component of U is associated with the centroid of the original shape. Moreover, the descriptors are also invariance to geometric transformations as a consequence of the properties of the Fourier series.

A useful property exhibited by this method is that the most of the contour information is concentrated along the first coefficients, since they contain most of the energy. Following this property, a feature vector with n features obtained from the Fourier descriptor consists of the n descriptors from $FD(s)$.

2.2   Curvature

Curvature has been identified as an important clue explored by the human visual system. Since visual information is highly redundant, curvature plays an important role in compressing information, such as straight line where the curvature is null.

The curvature $k(t)$ of a parametric curve $c(t) = (x(t), y(t))$ is defined according to Equation 2.

$$k(t) = \frac{\dot{x}(t)\ddot{y}(t) - \ddot{x}(t)\dot{y}(t)}{(\dot{x}(t)^2 \dot{y}(t)^2)^{\frac{3}{2}}} \tag{2}$$

where $\dot{x}(t)$ and $\ddot{x}(t)$ are the first and second derivative of $x(t)$.

To extract useful information from $k(t)$, a strategy based on Fourier is used. Fourier series is applied on $k(t)$ and then a feature vector of dimension n is built with the n first coefficients. Since Fourier contain most of the signal's energy concentrated in the first descriptors, the strategy discussed above is useful to remove redundancy.

2.3   Zernike Moments

The Zernike moments from a binary image can be calculated in three steps: computation of radial polynomials, computation of Zernike basis functions, and projection of the image on to the basis functions. The computation of radial polynomials is defined according to Equation 3. Usually, the indexes n and m are called order and repetition.

$$R_{nm}(p) = \sum_{s=0}^{(n-|m|)/2} c(n, m, s)p^{n-2s} \tag{3}$$

where

$$c(n, m, s) = (-1)^s \frac{(n-s)!}{s!((n+|m|)/2 - s)!((n-|m|)/2 - s)!} \tag{4}$$

Using the radial polynomials, Zernike basis functions are described in Equation 5. These basis functions are defined within a unit circle and since they are orthogonal, there is no redundancy information between moments.

$$V_{nm}(p, \theta) = R_{nm}(p)exp(jm\theta), \quad |p| \leq 1 \tag{5}$$

Finally, the Zernike moments of order n and repetition m over an image $f(x, y)$ with size $N \times N$ is defined in Equation 6. The coordinates of the image must be normalized into $[0, 1]$. Thus, the magnitudes of the Zernike moments can be used as shape descriptors.

$$Z_{nm} = \frac{n+1}{\lambda_N} \sum_{x=0}^{N-1} \sum_{y=0}^{N-1} f(x, y) V_{nm}^*(x, y)$$

$$= \frac{n+1}{\lambda_N} \sum_{x=0}^{N-1} \sum_{y=0}^{N-1} f(x, y) R_{nm}(p_{xy}) exp(-jm\theta_{xy}) \tag{6}$$

where λ_N is a normalization factor related to the number of pixels in the unit circle, $p_{xy} = \frac{\sqrt{(2x-N+1)^2+(N-1-2y)^2}}{N}$, and $\theta_{xy} = tan^{-1}(\frac{N-1-2y}{2x-N+1})$.

2.4 Chain Code

The Freeman chain code is a compact way to represent the contour of an object. The method assigns an integer i, $0 \leq i \leq 7$ for each point of the contour according to its direction to a successor point. This representation is based on the connectivity definition of neighboring pixels, usually 8-connectivity. The direction of each movement is given by a vector $v_i \in \{(1, 0), (1, 1), (0, 1), (-1, 1), (-1, 0), (-1, -1), (0, -1), (1, -1)\}$. For example, consider an starting point $s_0(3, 3)$ and a successor point $s_1(3, 4)$. The path from s_0 to s_1 is represented by the code 3 ($s_0 + v_3 \rightarrow s_1$).

In the chain code method, the contour of a binary object is represented by a vector of codes. However, this strategy has two drawbacks: it depends on the starting point and it is not rotation invariant. These drawbacks can be overcome, for example, using Fourier transform. For this, the Fourier transform is applied in the vector of codes and then, the n descriptors for the chain code method is composed by the n first Fourier coefficients.

3 Experimental Results

This section presents two experiments that were conducted to evaluate shape recognition. The first experiment is devised to compare the performance of shape descriptor methods described in Section 2. In the second experiment, we analyze the influence of noise on the classification task.

In order to assess the performance of the methods using real data, experiments were performed using a database composed by images of mice. This database consists of 4 types of behavior, namely curved horizontal, self-cleaning, vertical and horizontal exploratory behaviors, each containing 50 images captured

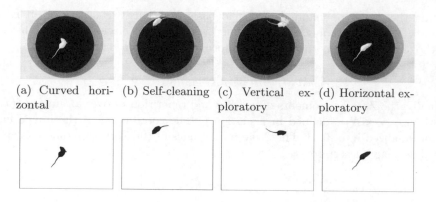

(a) Curved horizontal (b) Self-cleaning (c) Vertical exploratory (d) Horizontal exploratory

Fig. 1. Examples of the classes in the mice behavior database and its respectively segmented images

in an environment with artificial light. Each image was segmented using background subtraction technique [9,10]. The types of behavior have similar contour characteristics thus presenting an interesting challenge for classification tasks. Examples of the database can be seen in Fig. 1.

The training and the test routines were done using a 10-fold cross-validation approach. For comparisons, we selected 4 classifiers that are popular in the data mining community were used: Decision Tree - DT , K-Nearest Neighbor - KNN, Support Vector Machine - SVM, and Radial Basis Function Network - RBF. We considered the classifiers from WEKA [1] with default parameter settings.

3.1   Comparison of Methods

Fig. 2 provides a comparison of the shape descriptor methods for each classifier. The horizontal axis is the number of descriptors and the vertical axis is the Average Correct Classification Rate (ACCR). From the figures, two observations can be made: First, the ACCR did not significantly improve with more than 20 descriptors approximately, which indicates that most of the shape information concentrates on the first descriptors. Second, Zernike moments and Fourier descriptors achieved the best performance in the most of cases. Using KNN classifier, Zernike moments and Fourier descriptors achieved 89.90%($\pm$ 6.24%) and 85.93%($\pm$ 5.78%), respectively. With regard to the classifiers, KNN classifier seems to provide the highest ACCRs, followed by the decision tree classifier. On average (see Fig. 5(a)), the best result of 80.82%($\pm$ 6.98%) has been obtained by the Zernike moments with 10 descriptors.

In order to evaluate the influence of noise, each contour of the database has been corrupted with different levels of noise. Since we are interested in evaluating shape descriptors and do not evaluate algorithms for contour extract, we decided to insert noise only into the contour instead of inserting it into the image. For all the points of contour, a Gaussian noise with mean 0 and standard deviation

---

[1] Weka data mining software: http://www.cs.waikato.ac.nz/ml/weka/

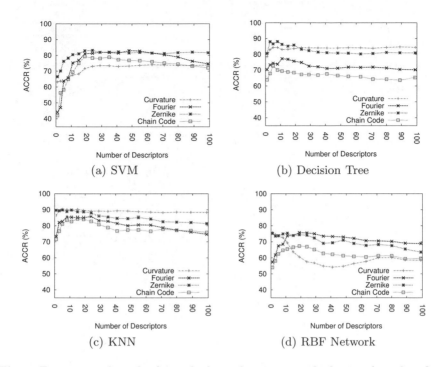

Fig. 2. Experimental results for each shape descriptor method using four classifiers

σ ranging from 0.1 to 5.0 is added to the original point, according to Equation 7. To illustrate, Fig. 3 shows examples of levels of noise.

$$x_\sigma = x + N(0, \sigma)$$
$$y_\sigma = y + N(0, \sigma) \tag{7}$$

where (x_σ, y_σ) is the noised point, (x, y) is the original point and $N(0, \sigma)$ is a random number generated from the normal distribution with mean 0 and standard deviation σ.

The results for the database with noised contour are shown in Fig. 4. The horizontal axis is the level of noise σ and the vertical axis is the ACCR. As expected, the ACCR decreases as the level of noise increases. Again, Zernike moments and

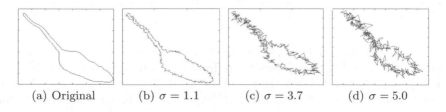

| (a) Original | (b) $\sigma = 1.1$ | (c) $\sigma = 3.7$ | (d) $\sigma = 5.0$ |

Fig. 3. Examples of level of noise

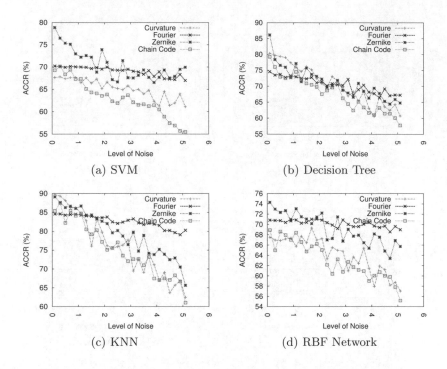

(a) SVM   (b) Decision Tree

(c) KNN   (d) RBF Network

Fig. 4. Results for the employed classifiers on the noised contours

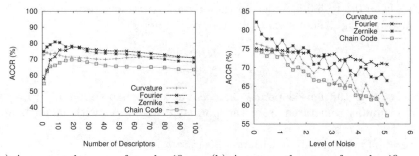

(a) Average values over four classifiers - (b) Average values over four classifiers -
original contours.   noised contours.

Fig. 5. Average values for each shape descriptor method using four classifiers for original (a) and noised contours (b)

Fourier descriptors provided the best results. From the Fig. 5(b) which plots the average from the classifiers, Fourier descriptors' ACCR decreases from 75.04%($\pm$ 6.63%) to 70.85%($\pm$ 6.34%). On the other hand, Zernike moments' ACCR decreases from 82.10%($\pm$ 6.75%) to 66.51%($\pm$ 2.31%). These results suggest that

Fourier descriptor method is more invariant to high levels of noise. Further, it is found that the KNN classifier provided the highest ACCR.

4 Conclusion and Future Works

In this paper we have presented a comparative study of shape descriptors methods. Promising results have been obtained on mice behavior images of relatively high complexity. Experimental results on this database indicate that Zernike moments and Fourier descriptors provided better performance than curvature and chain code methods. We also demonstrated how the noise levels affect shape recognition. Results for this problem suggest that Fourier descriptor method is more invariant to high levels of noise.

Regarding future work, it is proposed the analysis of other region-based methods. Moreover, further research could be focused on investigating multiscale version of the methods and the study of model selection criteria.

Acknowledgments. The authors acknowledge the Brazilian Research Agencies FINEP, CNPq, and FUNDECT for their financial support.

References

1. Luciano, Cesar, R.M.: Shape Analysis and Classification: Theory and Practice. Image Processing Series. CRC, Boca Raton (2000)
2. Salem, A.B.M., Sewisy, A.A., Elyan, U.A.: A vertex chain code approach for image recognition. Graphics, Vision and Image Processing ICGST 05 (2005)
3. Zhang, D., Lu, G.: A comparative study of curvature scale space and fourier descriptors for shape-based image retrieval. J. Visual Commun. Image Represent 14, 39–57 (2003)
4. Zhang, D., Lu, G.: Study and evaluation of different fourier methods for image retrieval. Image Vision Comput. 23, 33–49 (2005)
5. Hwang, S.K., Kim, W.Y.: A novel approach to the fast computation of zernike moments. Pattern Recognition 39, 2065–2076 (2006)
6. Chong, C.W., Raveendran, P., Mukundan, R.: Translation invariants of zernike moments. Pattern Recognition, 1765–1773 (2003)
7. Yang, G.Y., Shu, H.Z., Toumoulin, C., Han, G.N., Luo, L.M.: Efficient legendre moment computation for grey level images. Pattern Recognition 39, 74–80 (2006)
8. Morrow-Tesch, J., Dailey, J.W., JIang, H.: A video data base system for studying animal behavior. Journal of Animal Science 76, 2605–2608 (1998)
9. Gonçalves, W.N., Saueia, V.A., Machado, B.B., de Silva, J.A., de Souza, K.P., Pistori, H.: Técnicas de segmentação baseadas em subtração de fundo e modelos de cores: Um estudo comparativo. XXVIII CILAMCE (2007)
10. Pistori, H., Odakura, V.V.V.A., Monteiro, J.B.O., Gonçalves, W.N., Roel, A.R., de Silva, J.A., Machado, B.B.: Mice and larvae tracking using a particle filter with an auto-adjustable observation model. Pattern Recog. Lett. 31, 337–346 (2010)

Ridge Linking Using an Adaptive Oriented Mask Applied to Plant Root Images with Thin Structures

Talita Perciano[1,*], Roberto Hirata Jr.[1], and Lúcio André de Castro Jorge[2]

[1] Instituto de Matemática e Estatística, Universidade de São Paulo,
São Paulo, SP 05508-090, Brazil
{talitap,hirata}@ime.usp.br
[2] CNPDIA, Embrapa Instrumentação Agropecuária, São Carlos,
SP 13560-970, Brazil
lucio@cnpdia.embrapa.br

Abstract. A ridge linking algorithm and its application to plant root images is presented. The idea is an improvement of an edge linking algorithm where we explore local directional information. The experimental results show that we obtain good connections between ridge segments which tends to maintain the connectivity of structures like plant roots.

Keywords: Ridge linking, edge linking, ridge detection, image segmentation.

1 Introduction

Ridge detection, as well as edge detection, is a fundamental problem in image processing and computer vision. The detection must have a good quality in order to extract useful information. Ridge or edge detectors often provide non-contiguous ridges/edges, i.e., maps with many discontinuities and, therefore, without desired connected contours. In order to deal with this problem and to form connected ridges/edges, a linking step must be done.

Edge linking has been studied for many years being very close to ridge linking. A known algorithm is SEL (Sequential Edge Linking), proposed in 1985 by Eichel and Delp [3,4]. It is a sequential search algorithm for edge detection and linking that uses a random field and a random Markov chain to model the problem. It has been improved later by using basically the same model but adding a multiresolution idea [2]. Because of the model used, many parameters must be set to obtain acceptable results.

In [8], a two-steps algorithm was proposed. It uses distance, direction and magnitude information of edge segments to build a weighting system to link the edges. Other algorithms are based on direction, local information around ending

---

* Thanks to FAPESP, CNPq and CAPES for funding.

I. Bloch and R.M. Cesar, Jr. (Eds.): CIARP 2010, LNCS 6419, pp. 378–385, 2010.

points and function cost minimization [6,7,13]. The algorithm proposed in [13] makes some improvements to these methods related to the measurement of the edge direction and the distance used in the cost function for edge linking. The measurement of the edge direction is more precise, incorporating all possible directions between $0°$ and $360°$ degrees. The geodesic distance is used to measure the proximity between two ending points, in order to use the intensity information. We propose other improvements in this algorithm related to the edge direction and the mask used during the process. We show that the quality of the linked edges can be improved using an adaptive mask related to the local main direction around an ending point. This adaptive mask avoids unnecessary connections between ending points. Besides, it also avoids connections that are out of the global and local directional contexts of the image.

In the literature, other edge linking methods can be found using concepts of mathematical morphology and connectionist models [11,1], combining local and global measures for edge point linking [9,10]. Finally, associated with the edge linking issue, edge grouping methods can also be found [12]. However, edge grouping aims to detect salient structures and boundaries, rather than improving the edge detection by connecting short edges.

The remainder of this paper is organized as follows. In Section 2, we describe the concepts and techniques used in the proposed method. In Section 3, we show some experimental results. The conclusions in Section 4 synthesize the results of the paper and depict possible future works.

2   Methodology

The linking process of the proposed method is based on the following general steps: (1) find the ending points of the ridge/edge map, (2) select the appropriate candidate linking points for each ending point using an adaptive directional mask and (3) select the linking point using information of ridge direction and geodesic distance.

In our approach the ridges of the images are calculated combining the Canny edge detector applied directly to the original image (we do not use the gradient image) and a surround suppression proposed by [5].

This section describes the adaptive directional mask approach (the main modification over the existing methods) used by the proposed algorithm along with a review of the concepts used from the existing edge linking algorithms.

2.1   Adaptive Directional Mask

Among the existing linking approaches that use neighborhood information, the common used masks have fixed shapes and sizes given by the user. The directional local information is used only when deciding which candidate linking point should be connected with an ending point. We propose an additional strategy to explore this information to suppress some of the candidates. We use an orientation histogram to adapt a rectangular or a conical mask (shape and size chosen by the user) with the local directional context of the image.

Figure 1 illustrates this process. One particular ending point is being analyzed (red one) during the process. In Figure 1(a) a rectangular mask is represented in gray and the candidate linking points in black. Figure 1(b) presents the ridge map for the analyzed window. In order to find the local main direction, a ridge orientation histogram is calculated for this window. The orientation with the highest frequency is chosen to be the orientation of the mask. In this particular case, the diagonal orientation was chosen. Figure 1(c) presents the rotated mask and Figure 1(d) the final candidate linking points.

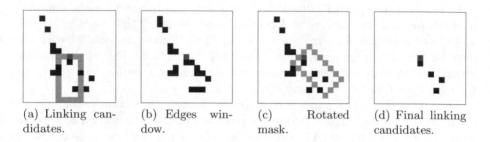

(a) Linking candidates.   (b) Edges window.   (c)   Rotated mask.   (d) Final linking candidates.

Fig. 1. Example of the mask rotation depending on local directional histogram

In a particular case that, for instance, two orientations have (almost) the same frequency in the histogram, the mask is rotated in both directions and all the candidate linking points in both cases are chosen. The orientations taken into account in the histogram depend on the edge detector used. The same orientations given by the detector will be used for the histogram.

In the following, we explain how to choose the point among the candidates to be connected to the ending point.

2.2   Ridge Direction and Geodesic Distance

After the suppression step, the remaining candidates are analyzed using the ridge/edge direction approach and geodesic distance proposed in [13].

Figure 2 illustrates the ridge/edge direction calculation. There is a portion of ridge/edge (ones), the ridge's/edge's end point P_e (gray square) and some candidates to the continuation of the ridge/edge (two isolated points at the border). For the ending point P_e all the ridge/edge points connected to it are used to fit a line l. The vector $\overrightarrow{d}_c$ represents the direction from the centroid of these points P_c (gray circle) to P_e. Between the two possible directions of l, the one closest to $\overrightarrow{d}_c$ is chosen as the ridge/edge direction of P_e, i.e., $\overrightarrow{d}_1$.

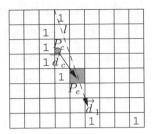

Fig. 2. Edge direction calculation by [13]

This approach has the advantage that all the orientations from $0°$ to $360°$ are possible, rather than a discrete number of orientations.

The geodesic distance also proposed by [13] is used by our algorithm. The distance, $D_g(p_i, p_j)$, between two pixels p_i and p_j of an image I is defined as the minimum path between these two pixels. Let us consider a path $P = \{p_1, p_2, \ldots, p_n\}$, where p_i and p_{i+1} are connected neighbors and $i \in \{1, 2, \ldots, n-1\}$. The length of P is

$$l(P) = \sum_{i=1}^{n-1} d_N(p_i, p_{i+1}). \tag{1}$$

Thus, particular geodesic distances can be derived depending on the neighbors connection and the distance between neighbors. In this work, pixels are eight connected and $d_N(p_i, p_{i+1}) = |I(p_i) - I(p_{i+1})|$. Using the geodesic distance, we are able to consider the information of the intensities of the pixels, rather than just their coordinates as when using the Euclidean distance.

For the evaluation of the candidate linking points, the following cost function is used:

$$H(P_e, P_c) = \frac{1}{D_g(P_e, P_c) \cdot \Theta(P_e, P_c)}, \tag{2}$$

where $D_g(P_e, P_c)$ is the geodesic distance between P_e and P_c and $\Theta(P_e, P_c)$ is the angle between $\overrightarrow{d}_1$ and the actual direction if we link directly P_e and P_c. Figure 3 illustrates the $\Theta(P_e, P_c)$ term.

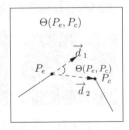

Fig. 3. $\Theta(P_e, P_c)$ term of Equation 2

The Pseudocode 1.1 resumes the proposed algorithm.

Pseudocode 1. Proposed ridge linking algorithm.

```
1    Find all the ending points in the ridge map
2    For each ending point do
3        Find the candidate linking points inside the window (
             rectangular or conical with the size chosen by the user)
4        Calculate the orientation histogram of the window and find the
             orientation with the highest frequency
5        Rotate the mask according to the orientation in the previous
             step
6        Suppress the candidate linking points outside the mask after
             rotation
7        Calculate H(Pe, Pc) for each candidate point
8        If there are any ending points
9        Find the one with the largest H(Pe, Pc) and link Pe with this
             ending point
10       End
11   End
```

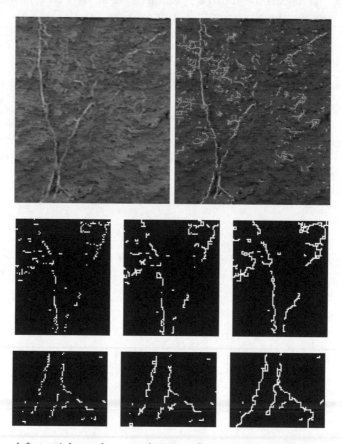

Fig. 4. From left to right and top to bottom: first row shows an original plant root image and the final linked ridge map superposed to it; second and third rows show, each one, a selected area from ridge map, linking result by [13] and linking result by our method.

3   Experiments

In this section we show some experiments using the proposed algorithm in plant root images. The original edge linking algorithm proposed by [13] was also applied to these images. However, we use the ridges instead of the edges.

First of all, in order to show the improvement related to the rotation of the mask and the directional context of the image, we present, in Figures 4 and 5, the application of our method on real images of plant roots. The first row shows the original image and the final linked ridge map superposed to it respectively. The second and third rows are organized, from left to right, as: selected area from the ridge map, linking result by [13] and linking result by our method. This kind of structure is well characterized by its directions and we can notice that our results are more connected, smoother and retain more the directional context of the structures in the image. Figure 6 presents one more example.

Besides, in order to confirm the improvements of the new algorithm, we applied it to 10 real plant root images, which are ground-truthed by an expert, and we calculated the True Positive Rate (TPR) and the False Positive Rate (FPR) in each case and for the original ridge map. The mean values are shown

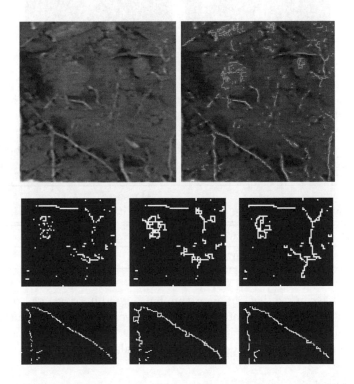

Fig. 5. From left to right and top to bottom: first row shows an original plant root image and the final linked ridge map superposed to it; second and third rows show, each one, a selected area from ridge map, linking result by [13] and linking result by our method

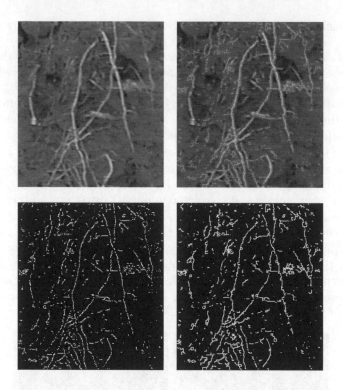

Fig. 6. From left to right and top to bottom: first row shows an original plant root image and the final linked ridge map superposed to it; second row show the ridge map and the linking result by the proposed method

Table 1. Mean values of TPR and FPR after the application of both algorithms to 10 real plant root images

| | Measures | | |
Classification rates	Ridge map	Original algorithm	Proposed algorithm
TPR	0.67	0.71	0.77
FPR	0.072	0.086	0.09

in Table 1. One can see that our algorithm has a good improvement of TPR with an acceptable low increasing of the FPR. The average number of false positives is high because of the kind of image we are using. Some improvements must be done to the ridge detector to decrease the false alarms.

4   Conclusions

We presented a new ridge linking algorithm derived from methods of edge linking already existing in the literature. Our approach aims to make a more precise decision to connect ridge segments using an adaptive directional mask. Results showed that our algorithm leads to good connections which tends to maintain the good continuation of structures like plant roots. To the best of our knowledge, there is no linking method in the literature with this characteristic. Specific applications, mainly those that deal with structures characterized by its directions, can take advantages of our technique. This approach can help in the segmentation of thin and ramified structures. We also applied this technique in common images using the edges and we obtained good results.

References

1. Basak, J., Chanda, B., Dutta Majumder, D.: On edge and line linking with connectionist models. IEEE Transactions on Systems, Man and Cybernetics 24(3), 413–428 (1994)
2. Cook, G.W., Delp, E.J.: Multiresolution sequential edge linking. In: International Conference on Image Processing, vol. 1, p. 41 (1995)
3. Eichel, P.H., Delp, E.J.: Sequential edge detection in correlated random fields. In: Proceedings of the IEEE Computer Vision and Pattern Recognition Conference, pp. 15–21 (June 1985)
4. Eichel, P.H., Delp, E.J., Koral, K., Buda, A.J.: A method for a fully automatic definition of coronary arterial edges from cineangiograms. IEEE Transactions on Medical Imaging 7(4), 313–320 (1988)
5. Grigorescu, C., Petkov, N., Westenberg, M.A.: Contour and boundary detection improved by surround suppression of texture edges. Image Vision Comput. 22(8), 609–622 (2004)
6. Hajjar, A., Chen, T.: A vlsi architecture for real-time edge linking. IEEE Transactions on Pattern Analysis and Machine Intelligence 21(1), 89–94 (1999)
7. Li, J., Randall, J., Guan, L.: Perceptual image processing for digital edge linking. In: Canadian Conference on Electrical and Computer Engineering, IEEE CCECE 2003, vol. 2, pp. 1215–1218 (May 2003)
8. Miller, F.R., Maeda, J., Kubo, H.: Template based method of edge linking using a weighted decision. In: Proceedings of the IEEE/RSJ International Conference on Intelligent Robots and Systems, IROS 1993, vol. 3, pp. 1808–1815 (July 1993)
9. Sappa, A.D.: Unsupervised contour closure algorithm for range image edge-based segmentation. IEEE Transactions on Image Processing 15(2), 377–384 (2006)
10. Sappa, A.D., Vintimilla, B.X.: Cost-based closed-contour representations. Journal of Electronic Imaging 16(2), 023009/1–023009/9 (2007)
11. Shih, F.Y., Cheng, S.: Adaptive mathematical morphology for edge linking. Inf. Sci. Inf. Comput. Sci. 167(1-4), 9–21 (2004)
12. Stahl, J.S., Wang, S.: Edge grouping combining boundary and region information. IEEE Transactions on Image Processing 16(10), 2590–2606 (2007)
13. Wang, Z., Zhang, H.: Edge linking using geodesic distance and neighborhood information. In: IEEE/ASME International Conference on Advanced Intelligent Mechatronics, AIM 2008, pp. 151–155 (July 2008)

Parameter Estimation for Ridge Detection in Images with Thin Structures

Talita Perciano[1,*], Roberto Hirata Jr.[1], and Lúcio André de Castro Jorge[2]

[1] Instituto de Matemática e Estatística, Universidade de São Paulo,
São Paulo, SP 05508-090, Brazil
{talitap,hirata}@ime.usp.br
[2] CNPDIA, Embrapa Instrumentação Agropecuária, São Carlos,
SP 13560-970, Brazil
lucio@cnpdia.embrapa.br

Abstract. This paper presents an analysis of four ridge detectors in images with thin structures: plant root images and retinal images. Two proposed detectors and two detectors from the literature are used. We estimate the optimal parameters for each detector for the two applications using a ROC curve similar approach. Simulated images of plant roots and retinal images are used. The optimal parameters are estimated and then used in real images. We conclude that the proposed detector based on mathematical morphology and the one based on the steerable filter are the best for both set of images.

Keywords: Ridge detection, parameter estimation.

1 Introduction

The segmentation of complex images is one of the hardest tasks in image processing. We consider complex images that have one or more of the following characteristics: (1) thin and elongated structures (relative to the image dimensions) eventually with ramified body, (2) subpixel structures, (3) missing borders (lack of information to fully segment the image). The objective of the study presented here is to analyze some ridge detectors and to find optimal parameters for them using a ROC curve similar approach. We used simulated images of soil profiles with plant roots generated by an existent software [15] and retinal images from the public database DRIVE (*Digital retinal images for vessel extraction* [17]).

We want to develop algorithms sensible to this kind of structures. Efficient solutions may be used in many applications: segmentation of river and road networks in SAR images [18], segmentation of trees, blood vessels [16], neurons [4] and plant roots (important application in agriculture research). We are not aware of any work in the literature which tackles the problem of segmenting plant roots, except of a procedure described in [14] (in Portuguese).

* Thanks to FAPESP, CNPq and CAPES for funding.

I. Bloch and R.M. Cesar, Jr. (Eds.): CIARP 2010, LNCS 6419, pp. 386–393, 2010.
© Springer-Verlag Berlin Heidelberg 2010

The problem of detecting ridges is well studied but we did not find any study on using information of thin structures to solve it. In [8], two methods for identification and analysis of the multiresolution behavior of ridges are described. In [10], two techniques of orientation analysis are explored for the detection of oriented structures like ridges. A new framework for automatic local control of scale levels for ridge detection is presented in [12]. In [13], the authors review some characterizations to formalize the notion of ridges and propose a new method. The detection of ridges was also used in [17] for the development of an automatic segmentation technique of vessels in retinal images. A very recent work in the literature explores methods for ridge detection [1].

This paper makes the analysis of ridge detection in images with thin structures, specifically retinal and plant root images. Four techniques are explored: a modified Canny detector, a morphological approach, the Frangi filter (see [7, 6]) and a steerable filter [11]. ROC curves are used to analyze these techniques and to find their optimal parameters. In Section 2, we describe two simple proposed ridge detectors and we briefly describe the two other detectors used from the literature. In Section 3, we explain the methodology used to estimate optimal parameters for the detectors. In Section 4, the experimental results are presented. The conclusions in Section 5 synthesize the results of the paper.

2 Ridge Detection

2.1 Proposed Detectors

The following techniques for identifying thin structures are based on the fact that: (i) the detectors are applied directly to the image, avoiding the loss of detailed information (i.e., only filters that preserve borders and ridges can be applied before the method that extracts ridges/edges); (ii) The aim is to detect the highest quantity of ridges as possible that correspond to plant roots (or vessels). The problem of false detection is not tackled in this stage of the project.

Canny Ridge Detector. The Canny edge detector [3] is one of the most known and used in image processing and computer vision because its performance is superior to other detectors in many situations, despite of being more complex [9]. This detector has four steps: (i) smooth the input image to reduce the noise; (ii) compute the gradient and the gradient angles of the image; (iii) apply non-maxima suppression to the gradient of the image; (iv) use double thresholding and connective analysis to detect and to link edges.

Canny defined an edge detector but not a ridge detector. Taking into account the two considerations made in the beginning of this section, it was necessary to modify the Canny algorithm in order to make the method detect the ridges. The first change is to remove step i), i.e., the original image is not smoothed. Another change is to use the original image instead of the gradient of the image (because ridges are the main objective) in steps ii) and iii).

Considering the image as a surface, the points of local maxima of curvature are localized in the center of the thin structures and the result of step 4 is equivalent (not equal) to a grayscale skeleton [5]. Using this variation of the algorithm, the information of the location of the ridges is not lost (Section 4).

Detection Using Mathematical Morphology. Another technique used to detect ridges from the original image is based on a composition of morphological operators. This is also a variation of top-hat algorithms found in the literature.

The mathematical morphology concepts used by the method are not presented here because the lack of space, however they can be found in [5].

Three steps are used to detect the ridges of an input image:

1. Application of the opening by reconstruction top-hat; (`mmopenrecth`)
2. Thresholding of the image resulting from the first step; (`mmthreshad`)
3. Homotopic skeleton by thinning to obtain the final result. (`mmthin`)

One important variable parameter for this detector is the threshold. It controls the level of precision when detecting the peaks in the image. The higher the threshold, the lower the number of peaks detected.

The Python script below makes the ridge detection of the an image.

```python
from morph import *

def detect_lines(image,threshold):
    # Top-hat of the openning by reconstruction
    th = mmopenrecth(image,mmsedisk(10))
    # Thresholding of the image
    bin = mmthreshad(th,threshold)
    # Thinning of the image
    m1 = mmthin(bin)
    return m1
```

2.2   The Frangi Filter

The Frangi filter is actually a Hessian-based vessel enhancement method proposed by [7]. In the literature it is assumed that the intensity profile of a vessel in the cross section can be modeled by a Gaussian function and that the intensity does not change much along vessels. In order to distinguish vessels from other structures, second order derivative features such as curvatures in Hessian-based enhancement filters are used. Vessels have small curvature along their center lines and large curvature in the sectional direction. The two principal curvatures can be acquired from the Hessian matrix (eigenvalues), λ_1 and λ_2. Frangi computes the scores $\mathcal{R}_B = |\lambda_1|/|\lambda_2|$ and $\mathcal{S} = \sqrt{\lambda_1^2 + \lambda_2^2}$ and define the response of his filter for 2D vessel as:

$$\mathcal{V}_o(s) = \begin{cases} 0 & \text{if } \lambda_2 > 0, \\ exp(-\frac{\mathcal{R}_B^2}{2\beta^2})(1 - exp(-\frac{\mathcal{S}^2}{2c^2})) \text{ , otherwise} \end{cases}$$

where parameters β and c are constants. The result of this filter is a probability map of the pixels being vessels. In order to find the medial axis of the vessels we apply a threshold followed by a thinning operator to this probability map.

2.3 Steerable Filter

The steerable filters [11] are 2D feature detectors, i.e., a class of steerable functions based on the optimization of a Canny-like model. These filters have closed-form expressions and lead to operators that have a better orientation selectivity than classical Hessian-based detectors. In order to obtain a ridge detector, high order derivates of the Gaussian are used. In the present case the 4th order is adopted. A threshold has to be applied to the final result of the image to obtain a binary image with the ridges and non-ridges map. The detailed explanation of these filters are out of the scope of this work. An implementation of these filters is available as a plugin for the famous ImageJ software.

3 Parameter Estimation

We can use various methods of ridge detection and typically these methods have some parameters that can be changed, like the ones presented in the previous section. A precision analysis using a similar idea to the ROC curves allows us to adjust the parameters associated with the methods, choosing optimal values for them. In order to make the analysis, it is necessary to have the ground-truths of the images the detector was applied to. Therefore, we used retinal images from the DRIVE database (with ground-truths made by specialists) and simulated plant root images. The ground-truths of the images are for segmentation purposes, thus we apply a thinning operator to them in order to obtain the optimal ridge maps.

For each set of images we executed a simplified version of the process described by [2]. Therefore, we were able to find the best parameters for each ridge detector. The process consists of the following steps:

1. First, the minimum and maximum values for each parameter of the detectors are chosen. The range of the parameters were found empirically, as we can find the values of the extreme cases (totally white/black images).
2. At the beginning, the intervals of each parameter are uniformly divided to generate four values for each one.
3. From the intervals with four parameters, it is possible to make some refinements:
   - For two successive values in the interval, it is generated a new value that is the half of the subinterval between these two values. So, let an initial interval for a detector be $4 \times 4 \times 4$, i.e., four values for each parameter. After the application of the refinement for the first parameter, for instance, we would have the interval $7 \times 4 \times 4$.
   The intervals are refined until the improvement of the curve is minimum.
4. Now we obtain a curve that is similar to a ROC curve. The detectors are applied for each possible parameter set obtained from the refinements resulted from the above step.
5. Finally, the median of the curves of all the images is calculated (ten images in this case).

In the end of the process, a curve for each detector is obtained. From these curves it is possible to find the optimal parameters for each one. The chosen parameters are those that lead to the highest True Positive Rate (TPR) value with acceptable values of false positives. It is important to notice that the proposed ridge detectors do not achieve totally white images (the case that all pixels would be classified as roots/vessels). However, as the Frangi filter and the steerable filter results are based on thresholding a probability map, it is clear that, in some cases the results will tend to totally white images. In such cases, we choose as the best parameter those that lead to the highest TPR with the value of False Positive Rate (FPR) related to the TPR values obtained for the other two detectors.

4   Experimental Results

The process above was applied to ten simulated root images and to ten retinal images. The median ROC curves for each set of images and for each detector are presented in Figure 1.

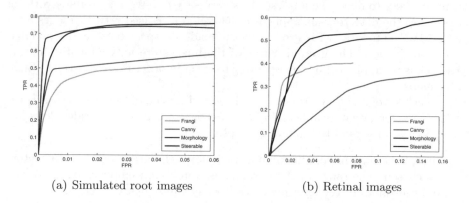

(a) Simulated root images   (b) Retinal images

Fig. 1. Median ROC curves for each application and each detector

After the previous analysis, the optimal parameters are obtained for the simulated root images and for the retinal images which are presented in Table 1.

Figures 2 and 3 present the results of the detectors for a simulated root image and a retinal image, respectively, using the optimal parameters.

The optimal parameters obtained for the simulated root images were also used experimentally for the real root images. We did not have the ground-truths of the real images of plant roots and that is why we used the parameters of the synthetic images. Figure 4 presents the results for one of the images.

Table 2 shows the summary results for each ridge detector analyzed in this paper. The set of images from where the TPR and the FPR were obtained is

Table 1. Optimal parameters for both applications and each filter

Detectors	Plant root Images			Retinal Images		
Canny	$T_L = 0.33$	$T_H = 1$	$\sigma = 1.2292$	$T_L = 0.1666$	$T_H = 1$	$\sigma = 9.375$
Morphology	$Ts = 26.3541$			$Ts = 1.0436$		
Frangi	$\beta = 11$	$T = 1 \times 10^{-5}$		$\beta = 3$	$T = 1 \times 10^{-6}$	
Steerable	$T = 51$			$T = 14$		

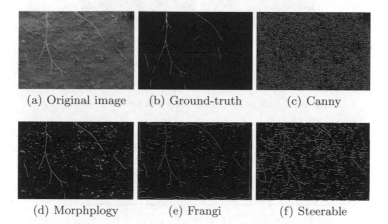

(a) Original image   (b) Ground-truth   (c) Canny

(d) Morphplogy   (e) Frangi   (f) Steerable

Fig. 2. Results applied to a simulated plant root image using optimal parameters

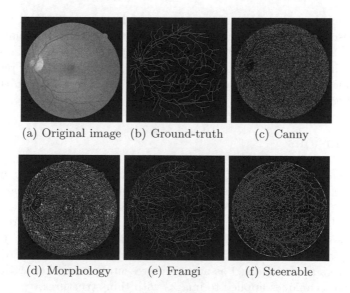

(a) Original image   (b) Ground-truth   (c) Canny

(d) Morphology   (e) Frangi   (f) Steerable

Fig. 3. Detectors results applied to a retinal image using optimal parameters

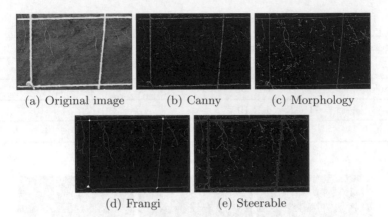

(a) Original image   (b) Canny   (c) Morphology

(d) Frangi   (e) Steerable

Fig. 4. Detectors results applied to a real root image

Table 2. Values for TPR and FPR for all detectors

Detectors	Plant root images		Retinal images	
	TPR	FPR	TPR	FPR
Canny	0.58	0.24	0.44	0.19
Morphology	0.74	0.049	0.51	0.16
Frangi filter	0.47	0.025	0.46	0.09
Steerable filter	0.76	0.052	0.58	0.14

different from the one used to obtain the optimal parameters. We can conclude that the best detectors for both set of images are the one based on mathematical morphology and the one based on the steerable filter. Despite of the simplicity of the morphology detector proposed, it obtained very comparable results with the steerable detector. These results can be also visually noticed in the images shown in Figure 2.

5   Conclusions

This work presented a study of ridge detectors in plant root images and retinal images using ROC curves aiming to obtain optimal parameters for each detector and for each application. The optimal parameters are estimated and applied to real images. The comparison among the detectors, using visual and quantitative results, shows that the best ridge detectors are the one based on mathematical morphology and the steerable filter. This study is part of a larger project where ridge detectors are being used as a basic representation for the development of segmenation techniques applied to images with thin structures.

References

1. Berlemont, S., Olivo Marin, J.C.: Combining local filtering and multiscale analysis for edge, ridge, and curvilinear objects detection. IEEE Transactions on Image Processing 19(1), 74–84 (2010)
2. Bowyer, K., Kranenburg, C., Dougherty, S.: Edge detector evaluation using empirical roc curves. Comput. Vis. Image Underst. 84(1), 77–103 (2001)
3. Canny, J.: A computational approach to edge detection. IEEE Trans. Pattern Anal. Mach. Intell. 8(6), 679–698 (1986)
4. Dima, A., Scholz, M., Obermayer, K.: Automatic segmentation and skeletonization of neurons from confocal microscopy images based on the 3-d wavelet transform. IEEE Transactions on Image Processing 11(4), 790–801 (2002)
5. Dougherty, E.R., Lotufo, R.A.: Hands-on Morphological Image Processing. SPIE Publications, Bellingham (2003)
6. Frangi, A.F.: Three-dimensional Model-based Analysis of Vascular and Cardiac Images. Ph.D. thesis, Utrecht University, The Netherlands (2001)
7. Frangi, A.F., Niessen, W.J., Vincken, K.L., Viergever, M.A.: Multiscale vessel enhancement filtering, p. 130+ (1998),
   http://www.springerlink.com/content/84rpbx096y455vtv
8. Gauch, J.M., Pizer, S.M.: Multiresolution analysis of ridges and valleys in greyscale images. IEEE Trans. Pattern Anal. Mach. Intell. 15(6), 635–646 (1993)
9. Gonzalez, R.C., Woods, R.E.: Digital Image Processing, 3rd edn. Prentice-Hall, Englewood Cliffs (2008)
10. Hou, J., Bamberger, R.: Orientation selective operators for ridge, valley, edge, and line detection in imagery. In: IEEE International Conference on Acoustics, Speech, and Signal Processing, vol. 2, pp. 25–28 (1994)
11. Jacob, M., Unser, M.: Design of steerable filters for feature detection using cannylike criteria. IEEE Transactions on Pattern Analysis and Machine Intelligence 26, 1007–1019 (2004)
12. Lindeberg, T.: Edge detection and ridge detection with automatic scale selection. International Journal of Computer Vision 30, 465–470 (1996)
13. Lopez, A.M., Lumbreras, F., Serrat, J., Villanueva, J.J.: Evaluation of methods for ridge and valley detection. IEEE Transactions on Pattern Analysis and Machine Intelligence 21(4), 327–335 (1999)
14. Neto, L.M., Vaz, C.M.P., Crestana, S.: Instrumentação avançada em ciência do solo, 1st edn. EMBRAPA (2007)
15. Perciano, T., Hirata, R., Cesar, R.M.: An image simulator of soil profiles with plant roots for image segmentation. In: Pedrini, H., ao Marques de Carvalho, J., Lewiner, T. (eds.) Workshops of Sibgrapi 2009 - Posters, SBC, Rio de Janeiro, RJ (2009), http://www.matmidia.mat.puc-rio.br/Sibgrapi2009
16. Soares, J.V.B., Leandro, J.J.G., Cesar Jr., R.M., Jelinek, H.F., Cree, M.J.: Retinal vessel segmentation using the 2-D Gabor wavelet and supervised classification. IEEE Transactions on Medical Imaging 25, 1214–1222 (2006)
17. Staal, J., Abramoff, M., Niemeijer, M., Viergever, M., van Ginneken, B.: Ridgebased vessel segmentation in color images of the retina. IEEE Transactions on Medical Imaging 23(4), 501–509 (2004)
18. Tupin, F., Houshmand, B., Dactu, M.: Road detection in dense urban areas using SAR imagery anf the usefulness of multiple views. IEEE Trans. Geosci. Remote Sensing 40(11), 2405–2414 (2002)

Experimental Comparison of Orthogonal Moments as Feature Extraction Methods for Character Recognition

Miguel A. Duval, Sandro Vega-Pons, and Eduardo Garea

Advanced Technology Application Center (CENATAV), Havana, Cuba
{mduval,svega,egarea}@cenatav.co.cu

Abstract. The selection of a good feature extraction technique is very important in any classification problem. Moments, especially orthogonal moments, seem to be a powerful option in the case of digital image compression, description and recognition. Nowadays, there is a considerable amount of orthogonal moments reported in the literature, each one with some advantages and drawbacks. In this paper, we carry out an experimental comparison of several orthogonal moments for the character recognition problem. Firstly, we compare orthogonal moments with other kinds of feature extraction methods and after that, we compare the different orthogonal moments taking into account different evaluation parameters. Experiments were made by using printed and handwritten digit datasets and the well-known measures: precision, recall and accuracy were used to validate the results. This experimental study corroborates the good performance of orthogonal moments. Besides, more specific results obtained in different kinds of experimentations allow coming to conclusions that could be very useful for the community of image recognition practitioners.

Keywords: Orthogonal moments, Feature extraction, Character recognition.

1 Introduction

Classifier effectiveness depends, in a great way, on the feature collection used to describe the involved objects. This way, the selection of a suitable feature extraction method is very important for any particular classification problem. In the case of digital images, feature extraction methods are responsible for describing the images by extracting their main attributes for a classification process. It is desirable that features extracted from images be:

- Robust: They should be low sensitive to noise, bad illumination and other adverse factors that may be present in the original image.
- Discriminative: They should have the ability to distinguish images of different classes.
- Invariant: They should be invariant to some properties like translation, rotation and scale.

A large number of feature extraction methods are reported in the literature. They can be divided in two categories. The first one, called geometric features, includes

I. Bloch and R.M. Cesar, Jr. (Eds.): CIARP 2010, LNCS 6419, pp. 394–401, 2010.

moments, histograms, and direction features, while the second one, called structural features, includes Fourier descriptors, line element and topological features [1]. Some of the most popular feature extraction methods reported in the literature are the standard and elliptic Fourier descriptors [1]. They, together with curvature approximation [2], are used to describe figure shapes.

In this paper, we center our attention on the study of moments, particularly the orthogonal moments. Moments have been used as pattern features in numerous applications for 2D image recognition. It is well known their ability to extract global characteristics from the images like: shape area, center of mass, moment of inertia, and so on. Recently, new orthogonal moments such as Krawtchouk [3], dual Hahn [4] and Racah [5] have been introduced. Nowadays, there is a considerable amount of orthogonal moments reported in the literature. Each one of them presents some intrinsic properties that could be desirable or not for a particular problem. In this paper, we make an experimental comparison of the existing orthogonal moments for the character recognition problem. Firstly, we compare orthogonal moments with other kinds of feature extraction methods. After that, we carry out a comparative study of the state-of-the-art orthogonal moments taking into account different comparison parameters.

The rest of this paper is organized as follow: A group of most used orthogonal moments are described in Section 2. Experimental results are showed and discussed in Section 3. Finally the conclusions of the research are reported in Section 4.

2   Orthogonal Moments

Moments can be defined as scalar quantities used to characterize a function and to capture its significant features. We can define a moment in a general way as

$$M_{pq} = \iint_D P_{pq}(x,y)f(x,y)dxdy \tag{1}$$

where p, q are non-negative integers and $p + q$ is called the moment order. $f(x,y)$ is the image intensity function, and $\{P_{00}(x,y), P_{01}(x,y), ..., P_{ij}(x,y)\}$ are polynomial basis functions defined on D.

Depending on the used polynomial basis function various systems of moments can be formed. By far, the most popular type of moments is the geometric, which uses as polynomial basis the standard power basis $\{x^i y^j\}$. Based on geometric moments, Hu [6] introduced a group of seven moment invariants that have also been used as features because of their rotation, scaling and translation invariance.

However, the basis set employed in geometric moments is not orthogonal. Therefore, they are not optimal with respect to the information redundancy and it is very difficult to recover an image from them [1]. In order to overcome this problem, Teague [7] suggested the use of orthogonal moments that are defined in terms of continuous orthogonal polynomials. This is the case of Legendre [1] and Zernike [8]. Another advantage of orthogonal moments is that they commonly have a low computational complexity because, we can evaluate them by using recurrent relations [9]. Hence, if the polynomial basis is orthogonal and satisfies the following condition of orthogonality:

$$\iint_\Omega P_{pq}(x,y) \cdot P_{mn}(x,y)dxdy = 0 \tag{2}$$

for any indexes $p \neq m$ and $q \neq n$, we can say that we are in the presence of ortho-gonal moments where Ω is the orthogonality area.

Two important cases of orthogonal polynomial bases that can be used for con-structing moments are the following. The first one consists in taking the direct prod-uct of two systems of orthogonal polynomials in one variable. Let $\{P_p(x)\}$ and $\{Q_q(y)\}$ be the orthogonal polynomial bases defined on the sets Ω_1 and Ω_2 respec-tively, with $\Omega = \Omega_1 \times \Omega_2$. Then,

$$P_{pq}(x,y) = P_p(x)Q_q(y) \tag{3}$$

is the orthogonal polynomial of degree $p + q$ defined on Ω. The second case, also called radial orthogonal functions, uses a unit disc, $\{(x,y): x^2 + y^2 \leq 1\}$, as orthogo-nality area. Its general form is the following:

$$P_{pq}(x,y) = R_{pq}(\rho)e^{jq\theta} \tag{4}$$

where $\rho = x^2 + y^2$, $\theta = arctan(y/x)$, and $R_{pq}(\rho)$ is a polynomial in ρ. One advantage of this form is that it is invariant with respect to rotation of axes. An exam-ple of radial orthogonal functions used for moments construction are Zernike [8], pseudo-Zernike [9] and Generalized pseudo-Zernike [10].

Besides, continuous and discrete functions can be used as polynomial bases. The use of continuous functions like Legendre [1], Gegenbauer [9], and the Zernike fami-ly, requires the transformation of the image coordinates space and an approximation of the integrals, causing some numerical errors. This problem can be avoided by using discrete orthogonal polynomials as basis functions, which eliminates the need for numerical approximation. They also exactly satisfy the orthogonal property in the discrete domain of image coordinate space [5]. Example of discrete moments are Tchebichef [11], Krawtchouk [3], Hahn [12], dual Hahn [4] and Racah [5].

3   Experimental Results

In this study, we made three kinds of experiments. Each one involves the training of a Support Vector Machine (SVM) [13] with a group of digit images. The SVM was configured to employ a lineal kernel and the parameters were optimally selected by using cross-validation. A second group of digit images were used to predict their labels using SVM, once it was trained.

Two data sets of digit images were used. The first one is composed by 3700 printed digit images taken from Cuban license plates images. And the second one is com-posed by 3200 handwritten digit images scanned from envelopes by the U.S. Postal Service [14]. Each data set was divided in two groups, one for training and the other for testing. In both data sets the image size is 30 × 30 pixels. In the case of handwrit-ten data set, different handwritten styles were taken into consideration influencing the character figure form, size, thickness and orientation. While the printed data set was

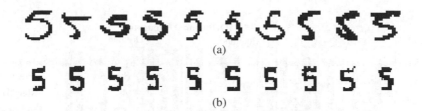

Fig. 1. Sample set of handwritten (a) and printed (b) digits images used in the experiments

constituted by images with different complexity degree, caused by segmentation and binarization errors. In addition, the used font makes different classes like {5, 6, 8, 9} share some common strokes, making more difficult their classification.

The criteria used for measuring the results are the classification precision (P), recall (R) and accuracy (A).

$$P = \frac{tp}{tp+fp} \qquad R = \frac{tp}{tp+fn} \qquad A = \frac{tp+tn}{tp+tn+fp+fn} \qquad (5)$$

were tp stands for true positive, fp false positive, tn true negative and fn false negative.

In the next three sections, we present the experiment that we made in this study.

3.1 Comparison of Feature Extraction Methods

In this experiment we compare a group of nine orthogonal moments against other feature extraction methods such as geometric moments, Hu invariants, curvature approximation (CA), standard (SFD) and elliptic (EFD) Fourier descriptors.

As it can be seen from Figs. 2 and 3, that orthogonal moment perform better for classification tasks that other feature extraction method like Fourier descriptors, curvature approximation and geometric moments. Most of them perceive precision results over the 0.90 in the case of handwritten digit recognition, and 0.95 for printed digit recognition. Notice that in this case, all discrete orthogonal moments show very good results, except Hahn moments. In the case of continuous moments, Zernike and pseudo Zernike do not bring good results.

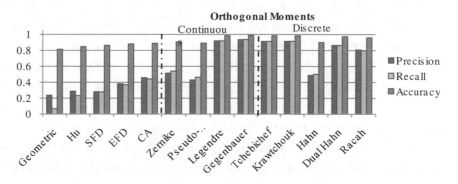

Fig. 2. Comparative analysis of feature extraction methods for handwritten digits classification

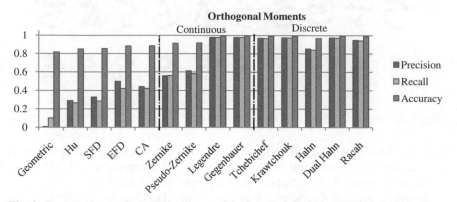

Fig. 3. Comparative analysis of feature extraction methods for printed digits classification

3.2 Discriminating Capability of Orthogonal Moments

This experiment measures the discriminating ability of orthogonal moments. They were used as feature extraction methods to solve 5 classification problems, each one with different number of classes. Digits that can be easily misclassified were grouped in the problems with fewer classes. Finally, the class groupings are: {2,7}, {5,6,8,9}, {2,5,6,7,8,9}, {0,3,2,5,6,7,8,9}, {0,1,2,3,4,5,6,7,8,9}. The maximum moment order used was 10.

In Table 1 and Table 2 the results of the experiments are summarized. It can be seen that in the case of handwritten digits classification, Gegenbauer moments perform better in problems with more than 5 classes, while Racah, dual Hahn and Tchebichef moments, do it in the problems with no more than 5 classes.

On the other hand, in the case of printed digits classification, dual Hahn moments obtained the best result for all the problems. However, it is worth mentioning the

Table 1. Comparison of the discriminating ability for handwritten character recognition

Orthogonal Moment	2 Classes			4 Classes			6 Classes			8 Classes			10 Classes		
	P	R	A	P	R	A	P	R	A	P	R	A	P	R	A
Continues Zernike	0.72	0.72	0.72	0.65	0.60	0.80	0.53	0.53	0.84	0.54	0.54	0.89	0.51	0.54	0.91
P. Zernike	0.73	0.73	0.72	0.59	0.59	0.80	0.44	0.45	0.81	0.46	0.45	0.86	0.43	0.46	0.89
Legendre	0.98	0.98	0.98	0.94	0.94	0.97	0.93	0.93	**0.98**	0.92	0.92	**0.98**	0.92	0.92	0.98
Gegenbauer	0.98	0.98	0.98	0.97	0.97	**0.99**	**0.95**	**0.95**	**0.98**	**0.94**	**0.94**	**0.98**	**0.93**	**0.94**	**0.99**
Discrete Tchebichef	0.98	0.98	0.98	**0.95**	0.94	0.97	0.93	0.93	**0.98**	0.92	0.92	**0.98**	0.91	0.91	0.98
Krawtchouk	0.98	0.98	0.98	0.94	0.94	0.97	0.93	0.93	**0.98**	0.91	0.91	**0.98**	0.91	0.91	0.98
Hahn	0.94	0.93	0.94	0.60	0.48	0.74	0.56	0.52	0.84	0.45	0.41	0.86	0.49	0.50	0.90
Dual Hahn	0.98	0.98	0.98	**0.95**	**0.95**	0.98	0.90	0.90	0.97	0.87	0.87	0.97	0.86	0.86	0.97
Racah	**0.99**	**0.99**	**0.99**	0.94	0.94	0.97	0.87	0.87	0.96	0.72	0.73	0.93	0.81	0.80	0.96

Table 2. Comparison of the discriminating ability for printed character recognition

Orthogonal Moment	2 Classes			4 Classes			6 Classes			8 Classes			10 Classes		
	P	R	A	P	R	A	P	R	A	P	R	A	P	R	A
Continues Zernike	0.92	0.91	0.92	0.66	0.63	0.81	0.58	0.56	0.85	0.62	0.58	0.89	0.56	0.56	0.91
P. Zernike	0.94	0.94	0.94	0.60	0.60	0.79	0.61	0.61	0.87	0.63	0.57	0.89	0.61	0.58	0.92
Legendre	0.98	0.98	0.98	0.97	0.97	0.98	0.97	0.97	0.99	0.97	0.97	**0.99**	**0.98**	**0.98**	**1.00**
Gegenbauer	0.98	0.98	0.98	0.97	0.98	**0.99**	0.97	0.97	0.99	0.97	0.97	**0.99**	**0.98**	**0.98**	**1.00**
Discrete Tchebichef	0.96	0.96	0.96	0.96	0.97	0.98	0.96	0.96	0.99	0.97	0.97	**0.99**	0.97	0.97	0.99
Krawtchouk	**0.99**	**0.99**	**0.99**	**0.99**	**0.99**	**0.99**	0.98	0.98	0.99	0.97	0.97	**0.99**	0.98	0.97	0.99
Hahn	0.97	0.96	0.96	0.91	0.90	0.95	0.92	0.91	0.97	0.80	0.78	0.94	0.86	0.84	0.97
Dual Hahn	**0.99**	0.98	**0.99**	**0.99**	**0.99**	**0.99**	**0.99**	**0.99**	1.00	0.98	0.98	**0.99**	0.98	0.97	0.99
Racah	0.96	0.95	0.96	0.97	0.97	0.98	0.96	0.96	0.99	0.96	0.95	**0.99**	0.95	0.94	0.99

good results of the Krawtchouk moment in the classification problems with a small number of classes, as well as the Legendre and Gegenbauer moments for the ten classes problem.

3.3 Effect of Moment Order in Classification Results

The goal of this experiment is to determine the effect of the moments order in the classification results. Handwritten and printed digit images were classified using different orders for the orthogonal moments involved in the experiment. Fig. 4 and 5 shows the results.

From the graphic we can see that high moments order can affect the precision in a drastic way for Tchebichef, dual Hahn and Racah moments in both cases, handwritten and printed digit recognition. It can be caused because of the numerical instability produced by the high moment order. Other moments like Legendre and Zernike can

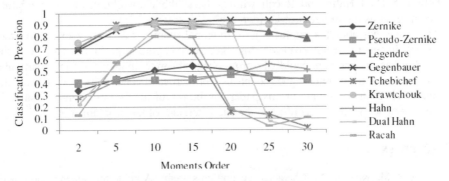

Fig. 4. Classification of handwritten digits using different moments orders

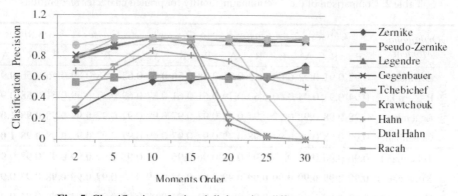

Fig. 5. Classification of printed digits using different moments orders

be affected in a minor way by the increase of the order for the handwritten recognition and the Hahn for the printed digit recognition.

The remaining moments increase the precision as the moment order is increased.

4   Conclusion

In this paper, we carried out an experimental comparison of the accuracy of several orthogonal moments as feature extraction methods in character recognition problems. Experimental results showed that orthogonal moments perform better than other more conventional feature extraction techniques such as: geometric moments, Hu invariants and Fourier descriptors, for character images classification The continuous moments Legendre and Gegenbauer have proven to describe very well image features for a classification task, especially in problems with more than 5 classes. However, discrete orthogonal moments like Krawtchouk and Dual Hahn describe better the images in classification problems with no more than 5 classes.

On the other hand, numerical instability, caused by high moment orders, affects drastically the image feature representation of some discrete orthogonal moments like Tchebichef, Dual Hahn and Racah while others like Krawtchouk and Gegenbauer perform better as the moment order increases.

This study corroborates the fact that orthogonal moments as feature extraction methods are, in general, a powerful tool for character recognition problems. However, the optimal orthogonal moment could vary from one problem to another due to the particular characteristics of the problems and the intrinsic properties of each moment. This way, the comparative results presented in this paper can be useful for the selection of a suitable feature extraction method according to the characteristics of the problem at hand.

References

1. Cheriet, M., Kharma, N.: Character recognition systems: A guide for students and practitiones. Wiley Interscience, Hoboken (2007)
2. Downton, A., Impedovo, S.: Progress in Handwriting Recognition. World Scientific, Singapore (1997)

3. Yap, P.: Image Analysis by Krawtchouk Moments. IEEE Transaction on Image Processing 12(11), 1367–1377 (2003)
4. Zhu, H., Shu, H.: Image analysis by discrete orthogonal dual Hahn moments. Pattern Recognition Letters 28, 1688–1704 (2007)
5. Zhu, H., Shu, H.: Image analysis by discrete orthogonal Racah moments. Signal Processing 87, 687–708 (2007)
6. Hu, M.: Visual pattern recognition by moment invariants. IRE Trans. Info. Theory, IT 8, 179–187 (1962)
7. Teague, M.R.: Image analysis via the general theory of moments. J. Opt. Soc. Am. 70, 920–930 (1980)
8. Khotanzad, A., Hong, Y.: Invariant image recognition by Zernike moments. IEEE Transactions on Pattern Analysis and Machine Intelligence 9(1), 489–490 (1990)
9. Flusser, J.: Moments and moments invariants for pattern recognition. Wiley Interscience, Hoboken (2009)
10. Xia, T., Zhu, H.: Image description with generalized pseudo-Zernike moments. Journal of the Optical Society of America 24(1), 50–59 (2007)
11. Mukundan, R.: Image analysis by Tchebichef moments. IEEE Image Analysis by Tchebichef Moments 10(9), 1357–1364 (2001)
12. Zhou, J., Shu, H.: Image analysis by discrete orthogonal Hahn moments. In: Kamel, M.S., Campilho, A.C. (eds.) ICIAR 2005. LNCS, vol. 3656, pp. 524–531. Springer, Heidelberg (2005)
13. Vapnik, V.: The Nature of Statistical Learning Theory. Springer, New York (1995)
14. LeCun, Y., et al.: Handwritten Digit Recognition: Applications of Neural Net Chips and Automatic Learning. IEEE Communication, 41–46 (1989)

Improving Face Segmentation in Thermograms Using Image Signatures

Sílvio Filipe and Luís A. Alexandre

Department of Computer Science
IT - Instituto de Telecomunicações
SOCIA - Soft Computing and Image Analysis Group
University of Beira Interior, 6200-Covilhã, Portugal
{m2213,lfbaa}@ubi.pt

Abstract. The aim of this paper is to present a method for the automatic segmentation of face images captured in Long Wavelength Infrared (LWIR), allowing for a large range of face rotations and expressions. The motivation behind this effort is to enable better performance of face recognition methods in the thermal Infrared (IR) images. The proposed method consists on the modelling of background and face pixels by two normal distributions each, followed by a post-processing step of face dilation for closing holes and delimitation based on vertical and horizontal images signatures. Our experiments were performed on images of the University of Notre Dame (UND) and Florida State University (FSU) databases. The obtained results improve on previous existing methods from 2.8% to more than 25% depending on the method and database.

Keywords: Face Segmentation, Human Skin Segmentation, Image segmentation, Infrared Thermal.

1 Introduction

A large amount of research has been conducted in the field of face recognition, mainly in the visible spectrum. These systems have problems dealing with light variations [6]. Some of the proposed solutions use 3D facial recognition [1] and combine face recognition in both visible and IR spectrum [7].

The growing interest in robust methods (for example, for security applications) has driven the development of facial recognition exclusively in the infrared. Recognition in the LWIR is not affected by light variations.

A crucial step in the process of face recognition is the face segmentation. This is more demanding than simple face detection since it pinpoints not only the face's locations, but also must describe its shape. A robust segmentation system can improve recognition rates regardless of the recognition method.

In contrast with the visible wavelength, where numerous methods have been proposed to accomplish this task (based on color, geometry, etc.), in the LWIR there is a lack of proposals to improve the current status.

I. Bloch and R.M. Cesar, Jr. (Eds.): CIARP 2010, LNCS 6419, pp. 402–409, 2010.

In the next sections we present a short description of two available face segmentation methods (section 2) and present our face segmentation method (section 3). In Section 4, we present the datasets used and experimental results, including a small discussion. We end the paper in section 5 with the conclusions.

2   Overview of Face Segmentation in Thermal Infrared ImagES

Face segmentation, given that it is a preprocessing step for all recognition methods, will lead to their failure if it is not correctly performed. This is not a subject much discussed by the authors of recognition methods in the infrared. Some of the proposed approaches are based only on the creation of an elliptical mask that will be put over the image of the face [5], but these approaches will work only on frontal and centered faces.

Siu-Yeung Cho et al. in [3] present a method for face segmentation in IR images based on the Sobel Edge detector and morphological operations. After the Sobel Edge detector, the largest contour is considered to be the one best describing the face. They apply the morphological operations to the area contained in this outline to connect open contours and remove small areas. Figures 2(e) and 2(f) show the segmented images in figures 2(a) and 2(b) using this method.

I. Pavlidis et al. in [8] describe a method for face segmentation using a Bayesian Approach. This method is based on the combination of two Normal Distributions per class, which are estimated using the Expectation-Maximization (EM) algorithm. This algorithm uses pixels from the skin (s) and background (b) for training. These are obtained from the training set images by selecting subregions that contain only pixels from each of these types. With this, the EM returns 4 means (μ), 4 variances (σ^2) and 4 weights (ω).

In the segmentation stage, for each pixel they have a prior distribution ($\pi^{(t)}(\theta)$) where t is the iteration) to whether that pixel is skin ($\pi^{(t)}(s)$) or background ($\pi^{(t)}(b) = 1 - \pi^{(t)}(s)$). θ is the parameter of interest, which takes two possible values (s and b) with some initial (prior) probability ($\pi^{(1)}(s) = \frac{1}{2} = \pi^{(1)}(b)$).

The input pixel value x_t has a conditional distribution $f(x_t|\theta)$ and if the particular pixel is skin we have:

$$f(x_t|s) = \sum_{i=1}^{2} \omega_{s_i} \mathcal{N}(\mu_{s_i}, \sigma_{s_i}^2) \tag{1}$$

where $\mathcal{N}(\mu_{s_i}, \sigma_{s_i}^2)$ is the Normal Distribution with mean μ_{s_i} and variance $\sigma_{s_i}^2$.

The prior distribution ($\pi^{(t)}(\theta)$) combined with the likelihood ($f(x_t|\theta)$) provides (via the Bayes theorem) the posterior distribution ($p^{(t)}(\theta|x_t)$), where, for the skin pixels, according to the Bayes theorem, we have:

$$p^{(t)}(s|x_t) = \frac{\pi^{(t)}(s)f(x_t|s)}{\pi^{(t)}(s)f(x_t|s) + \pi^{(t)}(b)f(x_t|b)} \tag{2}$$

The posterior distribution is also used to obtain the prior distribution for the next iteration:

$$\pi^{(t+1)}(\theta) = \begin{cases} \pi^{(t+1)}(s) = p^{(t)}(s|x_t), & \text{when } \theta = s \\ \pi^{(t+1)}(b) = 1 - \pi^{(t+1)}(s), & \text{when } \theta = b \end{cases} \tag{3}$$

Figures 2(g) and 2(h) show the segmented images in figures 2(a) and 2(b) using this method.

3   Proposed Method

We evaluated the methods of [3] and [8] and realized that it was possible to improve their results. Our proposal is based on the method of [8]: after analyzing the results of this method (shown in figure 1(b)) we concluded that its main problem is the removal clothing because since the body warms it, clothes have temperatures similar to the skin.

To remove the effect of the clothing, we examined the vertical and horizontal pixel signatures (see figure 1(d) and 1(g)). The vertical and horizontal signatures are the sum of the pixels values along the columns, for the vertical signature, and columns, for the horizontal signature. After this we fill small areas (shown in figure 1(c)) using a dilation with a 4×4 filter. This enables the removal of incorrectly classified pixels using a proportion of the maximum values in the two signatures (see figure 1(e)). This proportion is 20%, i.e., all signatures that have values below 20% of the maximum value are considered as background. This value was obtained searching for the best performance in the training sets of the databases.

After this, we calculate the possible location of the center of the face with new signatures (horizontal in figure 1(f) and vertical in 1(h)) in figure 1(e). The center point is given by the maximum values of the signatures (when more than one maximum value exist in the horizontal or vertical signatures the average of these maximums is used). This possible center location of the face (marked with a cross in figure 1(e)) will be used for the search for the largest contour (see figure 1(j)). Before we look for the largest contour, we apply an erosion followed by dilation with a filter of 3×3 and 2×2, respectively. This is used to remove some links between areas. For contour extraction we use the Canny edge detector. To enhance the contours extracted by the Canny method used a dilation with a 3×3 filter (see figure 1(i)). Only boundaries that have the center point inside are accepted, producing the end result of figure 1(k).

A possible drawback of this method occurs when the calculated center position of the face is not correct. This may cause the largest contour to be only partially over the actual face.

Figures 2(i) and 2(j) show the segmented images in figures 2(a) and 2(b) using our method.

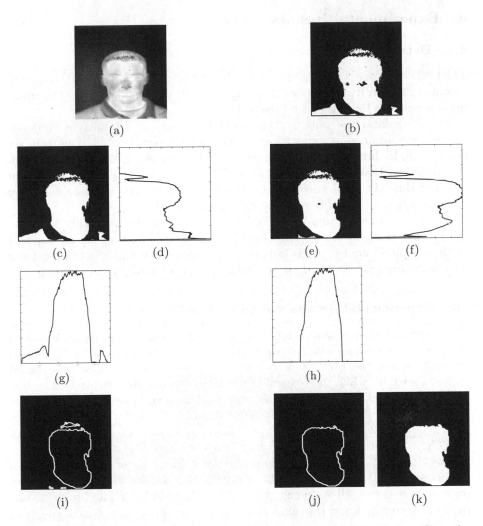

Fig. 1. Thermal face segmentation process. Figure 1(a) is the original image, from the training set of the UND database. Figure 1(b) is the original image (figure 1(a)) segmented by the method [8]. Figure 1(c) is the image (figure 1(b)) after filling small areas. Figure 1(d) is the horizontal signature of figure 1(c). Figure 1(e) is the result of the analysis of horizontal and vertical signatures of figure 1(c). Figure 1(f) is the horizontal signature of figure 1(e). Figure 1(g) is the vertical signature of figure 1(c). Figure 1(h) is the vertical signature of figure 1(e). Figure 1(i) is the result of enhancement (using a dilation with a 3×3 filter) of the contours extracted from the figure 1(e) by the Canny edge detector. Figure 1(j) is the largest contour of the figure 1(i). Figure 1(k) is the result of the face segmentation in the original image (figure 1(a)) using our method, after filling the area inside the contour of the figure 1(j).

4   Experimental Results

4.1   Datasets

The UND database is presented in [4,2]. The "Collection C" of the UND database contains 2293 LWIR frontal face IR images from 81 different subjects. The training set contains 159 images and the test set 163.

The FSU database contains 234 frontal IR images of 10 different subjects, which were obtained at varying angles and facial expressions [9]. The train set contains 40 IR images (four per subject) and the test set 194. The images from this database have color representation. The color channels (Red (R), Green (G) and Blue (B)) and grayscale conversion were processed separately, ie., the algorithm process R, G, B and grayscale independently.

All test set images from both databases were segmented manually to create the ground truth for test sets. Method [3] does not need a training set and method [8] and ours use pixels from manually segmented regions of the training set images avoiding the need for accurate segmentation of the training set.

4.2   Experimental Results and Discussion

The requested task is quite simple: for each input image (see figure 2(a) and 2(b)) a corresponding binary output (shown in figure 2(c) and 2(d)) should be built, where the pixels that belong to the face and are noise-free should appear as white, while the remaining pixels are represented in black. The test set of the databases were used to measure pixel-by-pixel agreement between the binary maps produced by each of the algorithm $O = O_1, ..., O_n$ (images in figures 2(e), 2(f), 2(g), 2(h), 2(i) and 2(j)) presented earlier and the ground-truth data $C = C_1, ..., C_n$, manually built *apriori* (shown in figure 2(c) and 2(d)).

The classification error rate (E^1) of the algorithm is given by the proportion of correspondent disagreeing pixels (through the logical exclusive-or operator, see equation 4) over all the image, where $O(c', r')$ and $C(c', r')$ are, respectively, pixels of the output and true class images.

$$E^1 = \frac{1}{c \times r} \sum_{c'} \sum_{r'} O(c', r') \otimes C(c', r') \qquad (4)$$

The second error measure aims to compensate the disproportion between the *apriori* probabilities of "face" and "non-face" pixels in the images. The type-I and type-II error rate (E^2) of the images is given by the average between the False Positive Rate (FPR) and False Negative Rate (FNR).

$$E^2 = 0.5 \times FNR + 0.5 \times FPR \qquad (5)$$

The results of segmentation for the described methods are presented in table 1. For the UND database, we can observe that error rates obtained with our method improved upon the results of the other two methods. The same was not the case for the FSU database. In this, the FPR increased, but the final

(a) Images from the UND database.

(b) Images in grayscale from the FSU database.

(c) Manually segmented images of figure 2(a).

(d) Manually segmented images of figure 2(b).

(e) Images of figure 2(a) segmented by the method [3].

(f) Images of figure 2(b) segmented by the method [3].

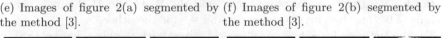

(g) Images of figure 2(a) segmented by the method [8].

(h) Images of figure 2(b) segmented by the method [8].

(i) Images of figure 2(a) segmented by our method.

(j) Images of figure 2(b) segmented by our method.

Fig. 2. Input images for the two databases, manually segmented images and the segmented images by the three methods

two errors (E^1 and E^2) decreased due to the FNR decrease significant. In this database the FPR's increased because when the subject wears glasses and we dilate the images from the method described in [8] we include part of the glasses as face pixels and they do not belong to the face. For the FSU images (shown in figure 2(b)), most of the noise comes from the hair since that the face fills almost entirely the image unlike what happens in the UND database, where there is a large area not covered by the face (see figure 2(a)).

Table 1. Segmentation methods results in the test sets from the UND and FSU databases. The FSU $Fusion^1$ is the fusion between the results of segmentation for the R, G and B channels using the majority vote between them. The FSU $Fusion^2$ is the fusion of the results of grayscale and the R, G and B channels using a weight of 0.3 for the grayscale channel and $\frac{0.7}{3}$ for the other.

	Siu-Yeung Cho et al.[3]				I. Pavlidis et al.[8]				Ours			
	FNR	FPR	E^1	E^2	FNR	FPR	E^1	E^2	FNR	FPR	E^1	E^2
UND	0.369	0.354	0.356	0.362	0.166	0.080	0.093	0.123	0.145	0.050	**0.065**	**0.097**
FSU Gray	0.502	0.048	0.308	0.275	0.200	0.174	0.189	0.187	0.044	0.206	**0.114**	**0.125**
FSU R	0.533	0.046	0.325	0.290	0.206	0.169	0.190	0.187	0.058	0.186	**0.112**	**0.122**
FSU G	0.502	0.047	0.307	0.275	0.171	0.184	0.171	0.178	0.044	0.206	**0.114**	**0.125**
FSU B	0.366	0.085	0.246	0.226	0.170	0.186	0.177	0.178	0.033	0.242	**0.123**	**0.138**
FSU $Fusion^1$	0.494	0.048	0.303	0.271	0.171	0.184	0.177	0.178	0.045	0.206	**0.114**	**0.125**
FSU $Fusion^2$	0.482	0.049	0.296	0.265	0.171	0.184	0.177	0.178	0.045	0.206	**0.114**	**0.125**

The database FSU was analyzed for each channel independently and two fusions ($Fusion^1$ and $Fusion^2$) were made to verify what would be the best approach for the segmentation.

The FSU $Fusion^1$ is the fusion between the results of segmentation for the R, G and B channels using the majority vote between them. The FSU $Fusion^2$ is the fusion of the results of grayscale and the R, G and B channels using a weight of 0.3 for the grayscale channel and $\frac{0.7}{3}$ for the other.

For the method [3] the best result was obtained with the blue channel (FSU B) for both errors E^1 and E^2. For the method [8] the smallest error E^1 is obtained with the green (FSU G) and the smallest error E^2 appears in the green (FSU G) and blue (FSU B) channels and for the FSU $Fusion^1$ and FSU $Fusion^2$.

Our method has the best result in the red channel (FSU R) for both errors E^1 and E^2. With this, we can say the best result of each method in this database depends on the type of images and that fusions does not always improve the results.

The improvements brought by our approach in relation to method [8] are the removal of clothing and the inclusion of larger number of pixels of the face. Removal of clothing is quite visible in the difference between the images resulting from [8] (figure 2(g)) and our method (figure 2(i)). In these examples it is possible to see that almost all the clothes were removed in the images of the UND database. The inclusion of the pixels of the face is most visible in the FSU database as can be seen in the images of figures 2(h) and 2(j), the first being the result of [8] and ours is the second. With this we minimize the FNRs, causing us to obtain more pixels for face recognition tasks.

5   Conclusion

In this paper we proposed a face segmentation method for LWIR images. The method creates two Gaussian distributions for each type of pixel (face and background) and post-processes the obtained images by closing small holes using morphological operators (decreasing FNRs) and removing the effect of clothes through the analysis of vertical and horizontal image signatures.

The experimental results show that our proposal improves accuracy from 2.8% to over 25% depending on the dataset and the method against which we are comparing.

We are currently searching for new features that may improve segmentation performance.

Acknowledgments

We acknowledge the financial support given by "FCT - Fundação para a Ciência e Tecnologia" and "FEDER" in the scope of the PTDC/EIA/69106/2006 research project "BIOREC: Non-Cooperative Biometric Recognition".

We wish to thank Professor Cho Siu-Yeung David, Assistant Professor in the School of Computer Engineering at Nanyang Technological University (NTU) for the source code of his method[3].

References

1. Bowyer, K., Chang, K., Flynn, P.: A survey of approaches to three-dimensional face recognition. In: 17th International Conference on Pattern Recognition (ICPR 2004), pp. 358–361 (2004)
2. Chen, X., Flynn, P., Bowyer, K.: IR and visible light face recognition. Computer Vision and Image Understanding 99, 332–358 (2005)
3. Cho, S., Wang, L., Ong, W.: Thermal imprint feature analysis for face recognition. In: IEEE International Symposium on Industrial Electronics (ISlE), pp. 1875–1880
4. Flynn, P., Bowyer, K., Phillips, P.: Assessment of Time Dependency in Face Recognition: An Initial Study. In: Kittler, J., Nixon, M.S. (eds.) AVBPA 2003. LNCS, vol. 2688, pp. 44–51. Springer, Heidelberg (2003)
5. Gyaourova, A., Bebis, G., Pavlidis, I.: Fusion of infrared and visible images for face recognition. In: Pajdla, T., Matas, J. (eds.) ECCV 2004, Part IV. LNCS, vol. 3024, pp. 456–468. Springer, Heidelberg (2004)
6. Jain, A., Flynn, P., Ross, A.: Handbook of Biometrics. Springer, New York (2007)
7. Kong, S., Heo, J., Abidi, B., Paik, J., Abidi, M.: Recent advances in visual and infrared face recognition - a review. Computer Vision and Image Understanding (1), 103–135
8. Pavlidis, I., Tsiamyrtzis, P., Manohar, C., Buddharaju, P.: Biometrics: Face recognition in thermal infrared. ch. 29, pp. 1–15. CRC Press, Boca Raton (2006)
9. Srivastava, A., Liu, X.: Statistical hypothesis pruning for identifying faces from infrared images. Image and Vision Computing, 651–661

On Combining Local DCT with Preprocessing Sequence for Face Recognition under Varying Lighting Conditions

Heydi Méndez-Vázquez[1], Josef Kittler[2],
Chi-Ho Chan[2], and Edel García-Reyes[1]

[1] Advanced Technologies Application Center,
7th Avenue #21812 b/ 218 and 222, Siboney, Playa, P.C. 12200, Havana, Cuba
{hmendez,egarcia}@cenatav.co.cu
[2] Center for Vision, Speech and Signal Processing,
University of Surrey. Guildford, Surrey, GU2 7XH, UK
{J.Kittler,Chiho.Chan}@surrey.ac.uk

Abstract. Face recognition under varying lighting conditions remains an unsolved problem. In this work, a new photometric normalisation method based on local Discrete Cosine Transform in the logarithmic domain is proposed. The method is experimentally evaluated and compared with other algorithms, achieving a very good performance with a total error rate very similar to that produced by the preprocessing sequence, which is the best performing state of the art photometric normalisation algorithm. An in-depth analysis of both methods revealed notable differences in their behaviour. This diversity is exploited in a multiple classifier fusion framework to achieve further performance improvement.

1 Introduction

In different face recognition studies it has been shown that variation in lighting is one of the major limiting factors of face recognition system performance [1]. To cope with the problem of face recognition under illumination variation, several methods have been proposed [2]. Among them, preprocessing methods, better known as photometric normalisation, are very popular since they are very efficient and generally do not require a complex training process [3].

Most of the existing preprocessing methods have been compared with each other, and the main conclusion that can be drawn is that the better they deal with the illumination problem, the less stable behaviour they exhibit on images obtained in normal lighting conditions [3,4,5]. Better approaches are still needed in order to best balance the advantages of preprocessing for illumination degraded images and the loss of performance on normally illuminated images.

Under the Lambertian model for representing face images, i.e. $I(x,y) = R(x,y)L(x,y)$, a number of preprocessing methods make the assumption that the luminance, L, changes slowly over the scene and is therefore a low frequency phenomenon, whereas reflectance R, which characterises skin texture, contributes

I. Bloch and R.M. Cesar, Jr. (Eds.): CIARP 2010, LNCS 6419, pp. 410–417, 2010.
© Springer-Verlag Berlin Heidelberg 2010

a higher frequency content. The luminance is a byproduct of the incident light and the surface orientation, which will be a low frequency function for a surface with slowly varying surface normal. However the face contains morphological features such as eyes, nose and mouth, which inject high frequency components to the luminance function and contribute information which should be preserved to aid face discrimination. Similarly, the reflectance term contains low and high frequency information. Although in the locality of facial features, the albedo changes rapidly, introducing high frequency signal to the reflectance function, the skin texture is basically homogeneous, changing very slowly over the face surface, so the dominant skin characteristic is of low frequency. This analysis suggests that both the luminance and reflectance components of a face image contain low and high frequencies. It is then difficult to separate the luminance effect from reflectance purely on the basis of frequency content. However, in general, high frequency components are associated with discriminatory information while illumination variations lie in the low frequency part of the spectrum. Variations in illumination can be compensated by estimating and removing the low frequency information, but the filter and the cut-off frequency have to be chosen carefully, so that the discriminatory information content is not compromised.

In this work, a new photometric normalisation method based on the local Discrete Cosine Transform (DCT), is presented. A photometrically normalised face image is obtained by subtracting a compensation term from the original image in the logarithmic domain. The compensation term is estimated by smoothing the image constructed using low-frequency coefficients extracted from the local DCT of the original image in the logarithmic domain. The proposed method is tested on the XM2VTS face database and compared with state of the art photometric normalisation methods. Our method and the *preprocessing sequence* (PS) [5] exhibit a similar performance as measured in terms of total error rates, and both are superior to other photometric normalisation methods. An in-depth analysis of the two methods revealed differences in their performance on individual images, suggesting that the methods provide complementary information. Drawing on their diversity, we propose to use them jointly to improve the results for face recognition under varying lighting conditions, while at the same time ensuring that good results are obtained for normally illuminated images. Significant improvements in performance are experimentally demonstrated.

This paper is organized as follows. In Section 2 the proposed (LDCT) preprocessing method is presented. In Section 3 the method is evaluated and compared with some of the state of the art photometric normalisation methods. Section 4 presents a novel face verification scheme which combines the outputs of face verification experts employing the LDCT and the PS preprocessing methods, and reports on the experimental results. Finally, Section 5 concludes the paper.

2   Illumination Compensation Using DCT in Log Domain

The use of DCT to compensate for illumination variations was first presented in [6]. The authors used low-frequency DCT coefficients of an image in the logarithm domain as an approximation of the illumination compensation term, setting them to zero and reconstructing a normalised image in that way. This method outperformed many of the existing methods dealing with illumination variations when comparing on the Yale B face database. Recently, two extensions of that method were presented in [7] and [8], aiming at more computational efficiency. None of them improve the results obtained by [6] on the Yale B face database.

In [9] a method using DCT in a local way was presented, based on the idea that local approaches are better to deal with illumination problems than the global ones [10]. Dividing the face image into rectangular regions and setting to zero low-frequency DCT coefficients of each region, a better performance was achieved. Uniform Local Binary Pattern (LBP) histograms [11] are computed for each region and used for classification. Note that the same region division is used for the preprocessing with the DCT and for the classification step using the LBP, so in this case, the photometric normalisation is tightly coupled with the image structure used for feature extraction and classification.

Unfortunately, the number of methods where the congruency between preprocessing and feature extraction exists naturally is severely limited. Thus, the objective of our work is to develop a new photometric normalisation method based on local DCT, retaining the local sensitivity without introducing any blocky artefact. Such a method can be used with any feature descriptor or classifier regardless of image partitioning.

2.1   The New Photometric Normalisation Method

The proposed method, as the previous techniques, aims at subtracting a compensation term from the original image in the logarithm domain in order to suppress illumination variations. Here, the low-frequencies DCT coefficients of the image blocks in the logarithm domain are used to estimate the compensation term instead of setting them to zero, avoiding the blockiness effect.

Once the face image is transformed to log intensity domain, it is divided into rectangular blocks and the DCT is computed over them. Using only the low-frequency coefficients of each block, a low pass version of the log image can be reconstructed by applying the inverse DCT, which can be used as an approximation of the compensation term.

In a DCT block, the top left coefficients, selected in a zig-zag scan manner correspond to the low frequency information. However, the $C(0,0)$ coefficient, usually called DC coefficient, conveys the mean intensity value of the block, as can be seen in eq. (1), where $M \times N$ is the size of the block and $i(x,y)$ the intensity value of each pixel:

$$C(0,0) = \frac{1}{\sqrt{M}\sqrt{N}} \cdot \sum_{x=0}^{M-1} \sum_{y=0}^{N-1} i(x,y), \tag{1}$$

The DC values of the different blocks of an image not only track to the incident illumination but also contain information relating to the surface normals in the vicinity of the structural facial features and they can not be just removed. It is

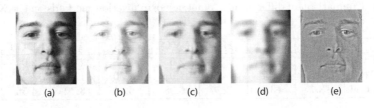

Fig. 1. Effect of each one of the steps of the proposed preprocessing method: (a) original image, (b) logarithm transformation, (c) illumination compensation image with block effect, (d) smoothed compensation image and (e) resulting image after subtraction.

necessary to modify the DC coefficients that will be used for each block in the reconstruction, in a way that they represent only the changes in the incident illumination. Accordingly, a constant value, representing a "good" DC value, is subtracted from each DC coefficient, obtaining as result a representation of the information injected by the variation in the lighting.

The reconstructed low pass image still exhibits a block effect produced by the image subdivision. In order to reduce this effect, we apply a low pass smoothing filter to the reconstructed image before subtracting it from the original image in the logarithmic domain.

The proposed procedure can be summarized in the following steps: 1) to apply the logarithmic transformation to the original face image, 2) to reconstruct the low pass version of the log image using the low-frequency DCT coefficients and replacing the local DC one by its original computed value minus a constant reference value, 3) to smooth the resulting image and 4) to subtract the smoothed compensation term from the original image in the logarithmic domain. The effect of each step is evident in Figure 1, showing at the end the photometrically normalised image obtained with the proposed method.

3   Experimental Evaluation

The XM2VTS database with the Lausanne protocol [12] was used to evaluate the performance of the proposed method. The database contains 2360 images of 295 subjects under controlled illumination conditions, divided into a Training set composed of images of 200 subjects as clients, an Evaluation set (Eval) with images of the same subjects as clients and of 25 additional subjects as imposters, and a Test set with 70 subjects as imposters. There is an additional "Dark" set which contains images from every subject under non frontal lighting. The Equal Error Rate (EER), which is the point where the False Rejection Rate (FRR) is equal to the False Acceptance Rate (FAR), is obtained for the images in the Eval set and the value obtained by the classification method at this point is used as a threshold for the decision of acceptance or rejection in the Test and Dark sets. The Total Error Rate (TER), the sum of FRR and FAR, is used to evaluate the performance of the verification systems on the database.

Table 1. Comparison of different photometric normalisation methods on the XM2VTS database using MLBP+LDA in terms of TER (%)

	OI	HE	HF	TVQI	AS	PS	LDCT
Eval	1.90	2.10	2.35	2.65	2.08	2.00	2.00
Test	1.16	1.17	1.35	1.98	1.50	1.56	1.32
Dark	13.7	13.5	12.7	6.98	6.15	3.72	4.55

The recent extension of the popular LBP method, which is based on a multi-scale representation with linear discriminant analysis (MLBP+LDA) [13] was used to represent and classify the face images preprocessed with the proposed LDCT method. Table 1 shows the TER obtained for each subset of the database and compares it with the results obtained with the original images (OI) using the same database and classification method. It is compared also with state of the art photometric normalisation methods including the well known *histogram equalization* (HE), *homomorphic filtering* (HF) [4] and *anisotropic smoothing* (AS) [14], and newer approaches like the *total variation quotient image* (TVQI) [15] and the *processing sequence* (PS) [5][1].

It can be appreciated that the proposed method achieved a very good performance for the Dark set, the one containing images affected by illumination variations. The performance is very close to that obtained with the PS method, which shows the best results. On the other hand on the Test set, where the images do not present large illumination variations, PS shows a slightly worse performance than LDCT. Comparing PS and the proposed method, the most important difference between them is in the frequency information that is retained and suppressed in the main step of each algorithm. Both methods work differently but the total error rates achieved by them on the XM2VTS database are very similar. It is then pertinent to check whether the specific misclassifications committed by each method were correlated.

In [16], a statistical test, known as z statistics, to determine whether of two classifiers deliver different outputs is described. The z statistics is defined as:

$$z = \frac{|n_{01} - n_{10}| - 1}{\sqrt{n_{10} + n_{01}}} \tag{2}$$

where n_{01} represents the number of samples misclassified using PS but not using LDCT and n_{10} the number misclassified by LDCT but not by PS.

If $|z| > 1.96$ it can be said that the two methods do not have the same error (with a 0.05 probability of incorrect decision).

In Table 2, we show the z statistic value computed for the sets of the XM2VTS database. In all cases the statistical test is higher than 1.96, which means that the two methods misclassify images in a different way. A deeper analysis of the coincidences in misclassification, reported in Table 3, shows that less than one half of the incorrectly classified images are jointly misclassified by both methods.

---

[1] The method in [9] was not tested here because of its incongruence with the block structure of the multi-scale approach, however using the original LBP as it is proposed, a TER of 58% is obtained for the Dark set.

Table 2. The z statistics computed in each set of the XM2VTS

	Eval	Test	Dark
$|z|$	8.19	15.26	8.15

Table 3. Proportion of coincident misclassification for PS and LDCT methods

	Eval	Test	Dark
PS	35.80%	36.28%	35.55%
LDCT	45.39%	46.92%	26.72%

These results show clearly that the methodological differences between the two methods inject diversity into the outputs generated by the face recognition method. This diversity can be exploited to improve the recognition performance by multiple expert fusion, as discussed in the next section.

4   Classifier Fusion

It is well known that multiple classifier fusion is an effective method to improve the performance of pattern recognition systems. Classifier diversity can be achieved in many different ways. In our approach the face recognition system, including its method of representation and matching, is the same for all (the two) component systems. The diversity is achieved by using different face image preprocessing techniques to perform photometric normalisation.

We opted for a simple fusion by a fixed rule, sum. The sum fusion rule is known to be effective and also robust to noise [17]. The use of a simple fusion rule avoids the problems of generalisation to data sets affected by drift caused by various phenomena, such as illumination changes.

Thus, let us denote the score delivered by the face system for an input image, photometrically normalised by LDCT, as S_{LDCT} and that delivered for the same input with the PS preprocessing as S_{PS}. The fused score is then given as

$$S = S_{LDCT} + S_{PS} \tag{3}$$

The merit of this simple fusion method can be gleaned from Table 4. Using the proposed photometric normalisation and classifier fusion scheme, a significant improvement in performance was achieved for all data sets, regardless of whether the images were affected by illumination variations or not.

Table 5 compares our proposal with the reported results of some state-of-art systems tested in the XM2VTS database. The performance of 2.87% TER on the Dark set is very close to the best ever error rate reported on the Dark set, in the ICB 2006 competition [19]. However the winning performance in the ICB 2006 competition was achieved by training the face recognition system on

Table 4. Fusion results

	Eval	Test	Dark
PS	2.00	1.56	3.72
LDCT	2.00	1.32	4.55
PS+LDCT	1.79	1.17	2.87

Table 5. TER (%) of face recognition methods in the XM2VTS database

	Eval	Test	Dark
LBP_ LDA [18]	-	9.12	18.22
LBP_ HMM [18]	-	2.74	19.22
AS_ LDA [19]	6.50	9.76	25.24
AS_ HMM [19]	10.50	8.38	24.00
ICB06-Best^2 [19]	1.63	0.96	-
ICB06-Best^3 [19]	2.35	-	2.02
PS+LDCT	1.79	1.17	2.87

poorly illuminated face images, that causes a drop in the performance on well illuminated images (Eval). In our approach the improvement is achieved entirely through photometric normalisation. This is of practical significance as in real scenarios it would be impossible to collect representative data for all illumination conditions and a solution that involves no training is preferable.

5 Conclusions

In this work, a new face image photometric normalisation method based on the local DCT in the logarithmic domain has been proposed. The photometric normalisation process proposed in conjunction with the MLBP+LDA classification method was tested on the XM2VTS face database, achieving a very good performance when compared to other preprocessing algorithms. The total error rate obtained was very similar to that produced by the PS method, the winning algorithm, on the subset of images affected by illumination variations in the database. Despite the similarities in the average error rates of PS and LDCT, an in-depth analysis of the two preprocessing methods revealed notable differences in their behaviour. This diversity motivated a new recognition framework based on score level fusion, which achieved a very good performance on all data sets of the XM2VTS database, regardless of whether the images were affected by illumination variations or not. The proposal was compared with the state of the art systems tested on the XM2VTS database, and found to be comparable with the best ever method reported on the Dark set of the database, which requires training on poorly illuminated images and degrades on good quality images. The practical advantage of our approach which is applicable without the need for any data collection and training is extremely valuable.

References

1. Phillips, J., Scruggs, T., O'toole, A., Flynn, P., Bowyer, K., Schott, C., Sharpe, M.: FRVT 2006 and ICE 2006 Large scale results. Technical report, National Institute of Standards and Technology (March 2007)

---

[2] Trained and tested on well illuminated images.

[3] Trained and tested on variable illuminated images.

2. Zou, X., Kittler, J., Messer, K.: Illumination invariant face recognition: A survey. In: BTAS 2007 (September 2007)
3. Du, B., Shan, S., Qing, L., Gao, W.: Empirical comparisons of several preprocessing methods for illumination insensitive face recognition. In: ICASSP 2005, vol. 2, pp. 981–984 (2005)
4. Short, J., Kittler, J., Messer, K.: A comparison of photometric normalisation algorithms for face verification. In: AFGR 2004, pp. 254–259 (2004)
5. Tan, X., Triggs, B.: Enhanced local texture feature sets for face recognition under difficult lighting conditions. In: Zhou, S.K., Zhao, W., Tang, X., Gong, S. (eds.) AMFG 2007. LNCS, vol. 4778, pp. 168–182. Springer, Heidelberg (2007)
6. Chen, W., Er, M., Wu, S.: Illumination compensation and normalization for robust face recognition using discrete cosine transform in logarithm domain. IEEE Trans. on Systems, Man and Cybernetics 36(2), 458–466 (2006)
7. Abbas, A., Khalil, M., AbdelHay, S., Fahmy, H.: Illumination invariant face recognition in logarithm discrete cosine transform domain. In: ICIP, pp. 4157–4160 (2009)
8. Liau, H., Isa, D.: New illumination compensation method for face recognition. Int. J. of Computer and Network Security 2(3), 5–12 (2010)
9. Mendez-Vazquez, H., Garcia-Reyes, E., Condes-Molleda, Y.: A new combination of local appearance based methods for face recognition under varying lighting conditions. In: Ruiz-Shulcloper, J., Kropatsch, W.G. (eds.) CIARP 2008. LNCS, vol. 5197, pp. 535–542. Springer, Heidelberg (2008)
10. Villegas, M., Paredes, R.: Comparison of illumination normalization methods for face recognition. In: Third COST 275 Workshop-Biometric on the Internet, pp. 27–30 (2005)
11. Ahonen, T., Hadid, A., Pietikäinen, M.: Face recognition with local binary patterns. In: Pajdla, T., Matas, J(G.) (eds.) ECCV 2004. LNCS, vol. 3021, pp. 469–481. Springer, Heidelberg (2004)
12. Messer, K., Matas, J., Kittler, J., Jonsson, K.: Xm2vtsdb: The extended m2vts database. In: Second International Conference on Audio and Video-based Biometric Person Authentication, pp. 72–77 (1999)
13. Chan, C., Kittler, J., Messer, K.: Multi-scale local binary pattern histograms for face recognition. In: Lee, S.-W., Li, S.Z. (eds.) ICB 2007. LNCS, vol. 4642, pp. 809–818. Springer, Heidelberg (2007)
14. Gross, R., Brajovic, V.: An image preprocessing algorithm for illumination invariant face recognition. In: Kittler, J., Nixon, M.S. (eds.) AVBPA 2003. LNCS, vol. 2688, pp. 10–18. Springer, Heidelberg (2003)
15. Chen, T., Yin, W., Zhou, X., Comaniciu, D., Huang, T.: Illumination normalization for face recognition and uneven background correction using total variation based image models. In: CVPR 2005, vol. 2, pp. 532–539 (2005)
16. Webb, A.R.: 8.3. In: Statistical Pattern Recognition, 2nd edn., pp. 266–271. John Wiley and Sons Ltd., Chichester (2002)
17. Kittler, J., Hatef, M., Duin, R., Matas, J.: On combining classifiers. IEEE TPAMI 20, 226–239 (1998)
18. Heusch, G., Rodriguez, Y., Marcel, S.: Local binary patterns as an image preprocessing for face authentication. In: FGR 2006: Proceedings of the 7th International Conference on Automatic Face and Gesture Recognition, pp. 9–14 (2006)
19. Messer, K., Kittler, J., Short, J., Heusch, G., Cardinaux, F., Marcel, S., Rodriguez, Y., Shan, S., Su, Y., Gaod, W., Chen, X.: Performance characterisation of face recognition algorithms and their sensitivity to severe illumination changes. In: Zhang, D., Jain, A.K. (eds.) ICB 2006. LNCS, vol. 3832, pp. 1–11. Springer, Heidelberg (2006)

On Improving Dissimilarity-Based Classifications Using a Statistical Similarity Measure*

Sang-Woon Kim[1] and Robert P.W. Duin[2]

[1] Dept. of Computer Science and Engineering, Myongji University,
Yongin, 449-728 South Korea
kimsw@mju.ac.kr
[2] Faculty of Electrical Engineering, Mathematics and Computer Science,
Delft University of Technology, The Netherlands
r.p.w.duin@tudelft.nl

Abstract. The aim of this paper is to present a dissimilarity measure strategy by which a new philosophy for pattern classification pertaining to dissimilarity-based classifications (DBCs) can be efficiently implemented. In DBCs, classifiers are not based on the feature measurements of individual patterns, but rather on a suitable dissimilarity measure among the patterns. In image classification tasks, such as face recognition, one of the most intractable problems is the distortion and lack of information caused by the differences in illumination and insufficient data. To overcome the above problem, in this paper, we study a new way of measuring the dissimilarity distance between two images of an object using a statistical similarity metric, which is measured based on intra-class statistics of data and does not suffer from the insufficient number of the data. Our experimental results, obtained with well-known benchmark databases, demonstrate that when the dimensionality of the dissimilarity representation has been appropriately chosen, DBCs can be improved in terms of classification accuracies.

1 Introduction

Dissimilarity-based classifications (DBCs) [11] are a way of defining classifiers among the classes; and the process is not based on the feature measurements of individual patterns, but rather on a suitable dissimilarity measure among the individual patterns. The characteristic of the dissimilarity approach is that it offers a different way to include expert knowledge on the objects. The three major questions we encountered when designing DBCs are summarized as follows: (1) How can prototype subsets be selected (or created) from the training samples? (2) How can the dissimilarities between samples be measured? (3) How can a classifier in the dissimilarity space be designed?

Several strategies have been used to explore these questions. First, various methods have been proposed in the literature [11], [12] as a means of selecting a representation subset of data that is both compact and capable of representing the entire data set. In

---

* We acknowledge financial support from the FET programme within the EU FP7, under the SIMBAD project (contract 213250). This work was generously supported by the National Research Foundation of Korea funded by the Korean Government (NRF-2010-0015829).

I. Bloch and R.M. Cesar, Jr. (Eds.): CIARP 2010, LNCS 6419, pp. 418–425, 2010.

these methods, however, it is difficult to find the optimal number of prototypes and, furthermore, selecting prototype stage may potentially lose some useful information for discrimination. To avoid these problems, Bunke and his colleagues [12] and Kim and Gao [8] prefer not to directly select the representative prototypes from the training samples; rather, they use a dimension reduction scheme after computing the dissimilarity matrix with the *entire* training samples.

With regard to the second question, investigations have focused on measuring the appropriate dissimilarity by using various L_p norms, modified Hausdorff norms [7], and traditional measures, such as those used in template matching and correlation-based analysis [1], [11]. On the final question, the learning paradigms, Pekalska and Duin [11] reported the use of many traditional decision classifiers, including the k-NN rule and the linear/quadratic normal-density-based classifiers. Recently, in [4], they tried to refine the dissimilarity matrix by employing a pseudo-Euclidean embedding algorithm [3]. In addition, optimizing DBCs through combining dissimilarity matrices generated with different measures has been investigated in the literature [9], [15].

On the other hand, when designing a specific classification system, sometimes we suffer from the difficulty of collecting sufficient data for each object. In face recognition, for example, there are many kinds of variations based on such factors as pose (direction), expression, and illumination [1], [6]. However, as mentioned above, collecting sufficient facial data is difficult. To solve this problem, Lee and Park [10] proposed a measuring scheme to extract more robust and essential information of data distributions in biometric problems and applied it to developing a similarity measure. The information obtained with the scheme does not depend on the distribution of each class for each object, but depends on all the data. From this point of view, they claimed to get a more reliable similarity measure.

The major task of this study is to deal with how the dissimilarity measure can be effectively computed. However, when a limited number of object samples are available or the representational capability is insufficient to cover the possible variations of data, it is difficult to improve the performance of DBCs in the dissimilarity space. To overcome this limitation and thereby improve the classification performance of DBCs, in this paper, we study a new way of enriching the representational capability of dissimilarity measures. In particular, this goal can be achieved by using a statistical similarity measure based on intra-class statistics of data [10].

The main contribution of this paper is to demonstrate that the classification performance of DBCs can be improved by employing a similarity measure based on the intra-class statistics of all the training samples. Here, the measuring system has been used to accommodate some useful information for discrimination and to avoid the difficulty of collecting sufficient training data. The remainder of the paper is organized as follows: In Section 2, after providing a brief introduction to DBCs, we present an explanation of the statistical similarity measure and an improved DBC. In Section 3, we present the experimental results obtained with real-life benchmark data sets. In Section 4, we present our concluding remarks.

2   Related Work

Dissimilarity Representation: A dissimilarity representation of a set of samples, $T = \{x_i\}_{i=1}^n \in \mathbb{R}^{n \times d}$, is based on pair-wise comparisons, and is expressed, for example, as an $n \times m$ dissimilarity matrix, $D_{T,Y}[\cdot, \cdot]$, where $Y = \{y_j\}_{j=1}^m \in \mathbb{R}^{m \times d}$, a prototype set, is extracted from T, and the subscripts of D represent the set of elements, on which the dissimilarities are evaluated. Thus, each entry, $D_{T,Y}[i, j]$, corresponds to the dissimilarity between the pairs of objects, $\langle x_i, y_j \rangle$, where $x_i \in T$ and $y_j \in Y$. Consequently, an object, x_i, is represented as a column vector as follows:

$$[d(x_i, y_1), d(x_i, y_2), \cdots, d(x_i, y_m)]^T, 1 \le i \le n. \tag{1}$$

Here, the dissimilarity matrix, $D_{T,Y}[\cdot, \cdot]$, is defined as a *dissimilarity space*, on which the d-dimensional object, x, given in the feature space, is represented as an m-dimensional vector, $\delta(x, Y)$, where if $x = x_i$, $\delta(x_i, Y)$ is the i-th row of $D_{T,Y}[\cdot, \cdot]$. In this paper, the column vector, $\delta(x, Y)$, is simply denoted by $\delta_Y(x)$, where the latter is an m-dimensional vector, while x is d-dimensional.

On the basis of what we have briefly discussed, we assert that the state-of-the-art strategy for DBCs involves the following steps:

1. Select the representation subset, Y, from the training set, T, by using one of the selection methods described in the literature.

2. Using Eq. (1), compute the dissimilarity matrix, $D_{T,Y}[\cdot, \cdot]$, in which each dissimilarity is computed on the basis of the measures described in the literature.

3. For a testing sample, x, compute a dissimilarity column vector, $\delta_Y(x)$, by using the same measure used in Step 2.

4. Achieve the classification by invoking a classifier built in the dissimilarity space and operating it on the dissimilarity vector $\delta_Y(x)$.

Here, we can see that the performance of DBCs relies heavily on how well the dissimilarity space, which is determined by the dissimilarity matrix, is constructed. To improve the performance, we need to ensure that the matrix is well designed.

A Statistical Similarity Measure [10]: To define a new similarity measure based on the statistics of data, let us represent the data as a random variable, $x_i = (x_{i1}, x_{i2}, \cdots, x_{id})^T$. The data set, T, can be decomposed into subsets, T_k, as follows: $T = \bigcup_{k=1}^c T_k, T_i = \{x_1, \cdots, x_{n_i}\}$, with $n = \sum_{i=1}^c n_i, T_i \cap T_j = \phi, \forall i \ne j$.

First, we introduce a random variable, z_i, which is defined by using a pair of data, $\langle x_k, x_l \rangle$, where $x_k, x_l \in T_i$, from the same class ω_i. We then try to estimate a multivariate Gaussian distribution, $p_i(z)$, instead of $p_i(x)$, $i = 1, \cdots, c$, and use it to define the similarity measure. Let us define the random variable, z_i, as follows:

$$z_i = x_k - x_l, \forall x_k, x_l \in T_i, (k \ne l). \tag{2}$$

This is given under the assumption that the difference between each pair of samples from the same class originates from some additive Gaussian noises [10].

To define a distance measuring system, we first construct a representation set, $S = \{z_i\}_{i=1}^m$, from the training set, $T = \{x_j\}_{j=1}^n$, as follows: (1) For every class

ω_i, compute $S_i = \{z_i\}_{i=1}^{m_i} \in \mathbb{R}^{m_i \times d}$, $m_i = n_i(n_i - 1)$, using Eq. (2). (2) Return $S = S_1 \cup S_2 \cup \cdots \cup S_c \in \mathbb{R}^{m \times d}$, where $m = \sum_{i=1}^{c} m_i$, as the final representation set.

After obtaining the representation set S, we estimate intra-class statistics of the set, such as mean values and standard deviations, as follows:

$$\mu_i = \frac{1}{m} \sum_{j=1}^{m} z_{ji}, \ (1 \le i \le d), \tag{3}$$

$$\sigma_i = \left(\frac{1}{m} \sum_{j=1}^{m} (z_{ji} - \mu_i)^2 \right)^{1/2}, \ (1 \le i \le d). \tag{4}$$

Using these statistics, we define a similarity measure between two points, x_i and y_j, as follows:

$$s(x_i, y_j) = \sum_{k=1}^{d} \left(\frac{x_{ik} - y_{jk} - \mu_k}{\sigma_k} \right)^2, \ \forall x_i, y_j \in T. \tag{5}$$

Here, since the cardinality of S, m_i, is much larger than that of each T_i, n_i, the intra-class statistics computed are more accurate and more robust against some additive Gaussian noises. Consequently, the similarity measure obtained with these statistics is also robust against the noises and works well with the insufficient data.

Optimized Dissimilarity-Based Classification: As mentioned earlier, there are a few ways by which the classification efficiency of DBCs can be improved. To overcome the limitation caused by the variations in illumination and the insufficient number of data, in this paper, we used the similarity function of Eq. (5). The proposed approach, which is referred to as an optimized DBC (ODBC), is summarized in the following:

1. Select the whole training set, T, as the representation subset Y.
2. After constructing S from T, compute the intra-class statistics, μ and σ, of S using Eqs. (3) and (4), respectively.
3. Using Eq. (1), compute the dissimilarity matrix $D_{T,Y}[\cdot, \cdot]$, in which each individual dissimilarity is computed using the similarity function of Eq. (5), rather than using one of the Euclidean measures.
4. This step is the same as Step 3 in the conventional DBC.
5. This step is the same as Step 4 in the conventional DBC.

The time complexities of the above algorithm, ODBC, can be analyzed as follows: As in the case of DBC, almost all the processing CPU-time of ODBC is consumed in computing the dissimilarity matrices. So, the difference in magnitude between the computational complexities of DBC and ODBC depends on the computational costs associated with the dissimilarity matrix. More specifically, in DBC, Step 2 of computing the $n \times n$ dissimilarity matrix requires $O(dn^2)$ time. On the other hand, the computation of that of ODBC needs $O(dn^2 + cn^2)$ time[1] in executing Steps 2 and 3. Here, n, d, and c are the numbers of total samples, dimensions, and classes, respectively.

---

[1] For large data sets, to reduce the CPU-time of ODBC, a sample reduction technique can be considered.

3   Experimental Results

Experimental Data: The proposed method has been tested and compared with the conventional ones. This was done by performing experiments on well-known face databases, namely, AT&T [13], Yale [6], and CMU-PIE [14], and other multivariate data sets cited from UCI Machine Learning Repository [2].

AT&T database consists of ten different images of 40 distinct objects, for a total of 400 images. The size of each image is 112×92 pixels, for a total dimensionality of 10304 pixels. Yale database contains 165 gray scale images of 15 individuals. The size of each image is 178×236 pixels, for a total dimensionality of 42008 pixels. To obtain a different data set, a partial image, which is 64×78 pixels in size and contains only facial components without background, was extracted from each of the Yale images. This database is referred to as "Yale2" in the following sections. CMU-PIE database involves 41368 images of 68 people. To reduce the computational complexity of this experiment and, furthermore, to investigate the run-time characteristics of the method, a number of subsets, such as 175 (= 25 people $\times$ 7 pictures), 350 (=25 people $\times$ 14 pictures), and 525 (=25 people $\times$ 21 pictures) images, were selected from the database and down-sampled into 92×80 pixels, for a total dimensionality of 7360 pixels.

Experimental Method: In this experiment, first, data sets are randomly split into training sets and test sets in the ratio of 75 : 25. Then, the training and testing procedures are repeated 15 times and the results obtained are averaged. To evaluate the classification accuracies of DBCs and ODBCs, different classifiers, such as k-nearest neighbor classifiers and support vector machines [5], are employed and implemented with PRTools[2], and will be denoted as *knnc* and *libsvm*, respectively, in subsequent sections.

Experimental Results: First, the experimental results obtained with *knnc* and *libsvm* trained in DBCs and ODBCs for the face databases, namely, AT&T, Yale (Yale2), and CMU-PIE, were probed into. Here, we first reduced the dimensionality of the image vectors by performing a principal component analysis (PCA). Then, we constructed the dissimilarity matrix, D, with respect to *all* the training samples. Fig. 1 shows a comparison of the error rates of *knnc* and *libsvm* trained in DBCs and ODBCs for the four databases, where x and y axes are those of the reduced dimensions (which are obtained with a PCA) and the estimated error rates, respectively.

The observations obtained from the figure are the followings: First, it should be pointed out that the difference in the estimated error rates between DBCs and ODBCs increases as the dimension of the subspaces increases. This is clearly shown in the error rates represented with two lines marked with $\diamond$ and $\times$, or $\circ$ and $+$, respectively, in the pictures. This comparison shows that the classification accuracy of ODBCs is higher than that of DBCs when the dimensionality of the subspace is appropriately chosen (refer to Fig. 1 (b), (c), and (d)). Next, for the experiment of CMU-PIE, the two error rates of ODBCs, obtained with the two subsets of 175 (= 25×7) and 350 (= 25×14) images, respectively, are almost the same, while those of DBCs are different; the error rates of the latter subset are lower than that of the former. However, for the experiment of AT&T, in which all of the facial images have a uniform background, the classification

---

[2] PRTools is a Matlab toolbox for pattern recognition(refer to http://prtools.org/).

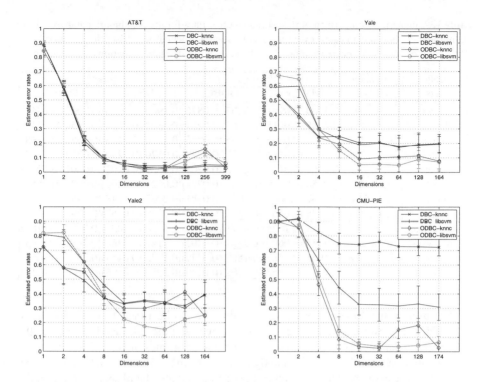

Fig. 1. A comparison of the estimated error rates of DBCs and ODBCs: (a) top left, (b) top right, (c) bottom left, and (d) bottom right; (a) - (d) are obtained with AT&T, Yale, Yale2, and CMU-PIE 175 (25 people × 7 pictures) databases, respectively. Here, the error rates are evaluated with *knnc* and *libsvm* trained in the subspaces of different dimensions. (The error rates of CMU-PIE 350(25 × 14) and 525(25 × 21) subsets are omitted here in the interest of compactness.)

accuracies have not increased with the proposed method (refer to Fig. 1 (a)). From these considerations, the reader should observe that DBCs can be improved by employing the statistical similarity measure and the resultant DBCs, i.e., ODBCs, do not suffer from the insufficient number of data.

In addition, the scaling of the features by σ_k may work in two directions. It works well for features that contribute to class differences by their separateness, but that have a small variability and that thereby have a too small contribution to the dissimilarities if there is no scaling. In case of bad features with a small variability, however, the noise of these features is emphasized. This happens for the peaking points in Fig. 1 (a) and (d) as the smallest eigenvectors are most emphasized.

To further investigate the advantage of using the proposed method, and, especially, to find out which kinds of significant data set are more suitable for the scheme, we repeated the experiment with the UCI benchmark databases. Table 1 shows a numerical comparison of the averaged error rates and their standard deviations for the benchmark databases. Here, the estimated error rates that increase and/or decrease more than the sum of the standard deviations are underlined.

Table 1. A numerical comparison of the estimated error rates for the benchmark databases. Here, the numbers in brackets in each row represent the standard deviations. Also, the estimated error rates that increase and/or decrease more than the sum of the standard deviations are underlined.

data sets	parameters (c, d, n)	*knnc*		*libsvm*	
		DBCs	ODBCs	DBCs	ODBCs
apect	2, 44, 80	0.3400 (0.0761)	0.3367 (0.0876)	0.1900 (0.0660)	0.2067 (0.0842)
chromo	24, 30, 1143	0.4285 (0.0215)	0.4662 (0.0254)	0.3860 (0.0341)	0.4754 (0.0244)
cmc	3, 9, 1473	0.5241 (0.0225)	0.5755 (0.0256)	0.4816 (0.0173)	0.4652 (0.0148)
dermatology	6, 34, 366	0.2418 (0.0381)	0.0681 (0.0228)	0.0520 (0.0240)	0.0476 (0.0237)
diabetes	2, 8, 768	0.2161 (0.0413)	0.0542 (0.0201)	0.0623 (0.0293)	0.0505 (0.0238)
ecoli	3, 7, 272	0.0756 (0.0279)	0.0796 (0.0274)	0.0527 (0.0202)	0.0925 (0.0556)
glass	4, 9, 214	0.3167 (0.0645)	0.3033 (0.0421)	0.2967 (0.0647)	0.3450 (0.0649)
heart	2, 13, 297	0.4396 (0.0402)	0.2360 (0.0442)	0.3270 (0.0567)	0.1793 (0.0308)
lung-cancer	3, 56, 32	0.5429 (0.1724)	0.4571 (0.1344)	0.5238 (0.1034)	0.5238 (0.1285)
malaysia	20, 8, 291	0.4757 (0.0606)	0.2531 (0.0402)	0.7141 (0.0466)	0.2802 (0.0543)
sonar	2, 60, 208	0.1961 (0.0385)	0.1882 (0.0479)	0.1725 (0.0414)	0.2575 (0.0662)
wine	3, 13, 178	0.2837 (0.0458)	0.0202 (0.0149)	0.2558 (0.0596)	0.0186 (0.0219)

We observed the same characteristics in Table 1 as in Fig. 1 (see the underlined numbers). This improvement can be seen by observing how the estimated error rates (%) change. For example, for the last data set, wine, the error rates of *knnc* (and *libsvm*) designed with DBC and ODBC significantly decrease from 28.37% to 2.02% (and 25.58% to 1.86%), respectively. The same characteristics could also be observed in the underlined data sets. However, for the other data sets, the error rates of the both of DBCs and ODBCs are *almost* the same; the increase and/or decrease of the error rates is not significant. Additionally, what can be observed in the table for the feature based data sets can for a large deal be explained by scaling differences between the features. Malaysia and diabetes are typically data sets with entirely different features that are not scaled properly. The sonar data set consists of spectra. By scaling the tails of the spectra are emphasized.

4   Conclusions

In our efforts to improve the classification performance of DBCs, we used a statistical measuring technique based on intra-class statistics of data. To achieve this improvement of DBCs, we first computed the intra-class statistics, such as the mean and the standard deviation, of the training data set. Using these statistics, we then constructed the dissimilarity matrices, where the dissimilarity was measured with the similarity function. This measuring technique has been employed to solve the problems caused by the differences in illumination and the insufficient number of data. The proposed method was tested on four face databases and some UCI data sets, and the results were compared with those of a Euclidean method. Our experimental results demonstrate that the classification accuracies of DBCs were improved significantly when the dimensionality of the dissimilarity representation has been appropriately chosen. Although we have shown that DBCs can be improved by employing the statistical measuring scheme, many tasks remain open. One of them is to improve the classification efficiency by combining the optimized DBCs in the dissimilarity space. Also, it is not yet clear that which kinds of significant data sets are more suitable for the scheme. Therefore, the problem of theoretically investigating the measuring method developed for the proposed DBCs remains to be done. Future research will address these concerns.

References

1. Adini, Y., Moses, Y., Ullman, S.: Face recognition: the problem of compensating for changes in illumination direction. IEEE Trans. Pattern Anal. and Machine Intell. 19(7), 721–732 (1997)
2. Asuncion, A., Newman, D.J.: UCI Machine Learning Repository. University of California, School of Information and Computer Science, Irvine, CA (2007), Can also be downloaded as of http://www.ics.uci.edu/~mlearn/MLRepository.html (February 2010)
3. Borg, I., Groenen, P.: Morden Mutlidimensional Scaling: Theory and Applications. Springer, New York (1997)
4. Duin, R.P.W., Pekalska, E., Harol, A., Lee, W.-J., Bunke, H.: On Euclidean corrections for non-Euclidean dissimilarities. In: da Vitoria Lobo, N., Kasparis, T., Roli, F., Kwok, J.T., Georgiopoulos, M., Anagnostopoulos, G.C., Loog, M. (eds.) SS+SSPR 2008. LNCS, vol. 5342, pp. 664–673. Springer, Heidelberg (2008)
5. Fan, R.-E., Chen, P.-H., Lin, C.-J.: Working set selection using the second order information for training SVM. Journal of Machine Learning Research 6, 1889–1918 (2005)
6. Georghiades, A.S., Belhumeur, P.N., Kriegman, D.J.: From few to many: Illumination cone models for face recognition under variable lighting and pose. IEEE Trans. Pattern Anal. and Machine Intell. 23(6), 643–660 (2001)
7. Hu, Y., Wang, Z.: A similarity measure based on Hausdorff distance for human face recognition. In: Proceedings of 18th International Conference on Pattern Recognition (ICPR 2006), Hong Kong, vol. 3, pp. 1131–1134 (2006)
8. Kim, S.-W., Gao, J.: On using dimensionality reduction schemes to optimize dissimilarity-based classifiers. In: Ruiz-Shulcloper, J., Kropatsch, W.G. (eds.) CIARP 2008. LNCS, vol. 5197, pp. 309–316. Springer, Heidelberg (2008)
9. Kim, S.-W., Duin, R.P.W.: On optimizing dissimilarity-based classifier using multi-level fusion strategies. Journal of The Institute of Electronics Engineers of Korea 45-CI(5), 15–24 (2008) (in Korean); A preliminary version of this paper was presented at Kobti, Z., Wu, D. (eds.): Canadian AI 2007. LNCS (LNAI), vol. 4509, pp. 110–121. Springer, Heidelberg (2007)
10. Lee, K., Park, H.: A new similarity measure based on intraclass statistics for biometric systems. ETRI Journal 25(5), 401–406 (2003)
11. Pekalska, E., Duin, R.P.W.: The Dissimilarity Representation for Pattern Recognition: Foundations and Applications. World Scientific Publishing, Singapore (2005)
12. Riesen, K., Kilchherr, V., Bunke, H.: Reducing the dimensionality of vector space embeddings of graphs. In: Perner, P. (ed.) MLDM 2007. LNCS (LNAI), vol. 4571, pp. 563–573. Springer, Heidelberg (2007)
13. Samaria, F., Harter, A.: Parameterisation of a stochastic model for human face identification. In: Proceedings of 2nd IEEE Workshop on Applications of Computer Vision, Sarasota FL, pp. 215–220 (1994)
14. Sim, T., Baker, S., Bsat, M.: The CMU pose, illumination, and expression(PIE) database of human faces, Technical report CMU-RI-TR-01-02, Robotics Institute, Carnegie Mellon University, Pittsburgh, PA (2001)
15. Woznica, A., Kalousis, A., Hilario, M.: Learning to combine distances for complex representations. In: Proceedings of the 24th International Conference on Machine Learning, Corvallis OR, pp. 1031–1038 (2007)

A Rotation Invariant Face Recognition Method Based on Complex Network

Wesley Nunes Gonçalves, Jonathan de Andrade Silva,
and Odemir Martinez Bruno

Instituto de Física de São Carlos
University of São Paulo
Av. do Trabalhador Sãocarlense, 400, São Carlos, São Paulo, Brazil
wnunes@ursa.ifsc.usp.br, jsilva@icmc.usp.br, bruno@ifsc.usp.br

Abstract. Face recognition is an important field that has received a lot of attention from computer vision community, with diverse set of applications in industry and science. This paper introduces a novel graph based method for face recognition which is rotation invariant. The main idea of the approach is to model the face image into a graph and use complex network methodology to extract a feature vector. We present the novel methodology and the experiments comparing it with four important and state of art algorithms. The results demonstrated that the proposed method has more positive results than the previous ones.

Keywords: Face Recognition, Complex Network, Graph.

1 Introduction

Face recognition is a field of investigation that has been become popular in the science and also in the industry. It has gained increasing attention in the community due to the successful applications in various areas, specially in the security industry. Although face recognition is not the most accurate biometric method, it is the most non invasive technology. This characteristic makes it suitable for many special secure applications, such as crowd supervision in airports.

In the literature, there are two main approaches to facial feature extraction: analytic and holistic approaches. The former extracts information based on structural face regions (e.g. eyes, mouth and nose), which contain important information for human identification. The latter considers the whole face image in the identification process. Holistic approach has some advantages to the analytic approach, such as: (i) it uses information of texture and shape which contribute to face recognition and (ii) it does not require pre-segmentation methods. For both approaches, most of the methods are not rotation invariant. This causes inaccuracy in real applications as it is very common for people to incline their head. In this work, we considered the second approach and propose a novel methodology based on complex network which are rotation invariant.

Complex network is a relatively recent field of research that combines graph analysis and statistical physics. Complex network research is close to graph research. In fact, the distinction between them is the approach. On one hand,

I. Bloch and R.M. Cesar, Jr. (Eds.): CIARP 2010, LNCS 6419, pp. 426–433, 2010.

graphs are quite traditional in computer science and mathematics. On the other hand, complex networks emerge from physics and use a statistical approach to perform the analysis. Complex networks have been popularized with works of Watts and Strogatz [1] and Barabasi [2], and have been applied in different fields of science, such as physics, biology, economy among others. Despite the successful applications, there are few applications in computer vision and pattern recognition. Some applications, such as texture classification [3] and pixel clustering [4], can be found in the literature.

This paper introduces a novel method for face recognition which is based on the complex network theory. Using the holistic approach, a face image is transformed into multi-scale graphs and then, they are analyzed using the complex network theory. In the analysis, measurements are extracted in order to compose a feature vector that characterizes the face image. To assess the quality of the proposed method, we conducted two experiments. The first experiment was performed using face images from a public database, while the second experiment test the proposed method by classifying rotate face images. For comparisons, we selected four popular face recognition methods belonging to holistic approach.

The paper is organized as follows. Section 2 and 3 briefly review the complex networks and their measurements, respectively. In Section 4, the proposed method is described in detail for face recognition applications. The experiments performed and the results are presented in Section 5. Finally, the conclusions and improvement of the method are discussed in Section 6.

2   Complex Networks

Complex network is a recent area which joins graph theory and statistical physics analysis. The complex networks are represented by graphs consisting of a set of vertices connected by edges. The graph is described by $G(V, E)$, where $V = \{v_1, v_2, ..., v_n\}$ is the set of vertices and $E = \{e_1, e_2, ..., e_M\}$ is the set of edges.

The complex networks were classified according to their properties into three main models: random networks, small-world and scale-free. Random networks, proposed by Erdós e Rényi [5], are considered the simplest model. In this model, the edges are added at random. Watts and Strogatz, who studied random networks in applications, concluded that networks have highly connected vertices with closed paths of length three. Therefore, a complex network that has no edges added completely at random, called small-world network, was proposed [1]. Barabási and Albert proposed a scale invariant network namely scale-free network [2]. In this model, the distribution of connectivity of vertices follows a scale-free distribution given by $P(k) \sim k^{-\gamma}$, with $\gamma = 3$ and $n \to \infty$ [2].

2.1   Measures

Once a system is modeled by a complex network, measures can be extracted in order to analysis and characterize the network topology. A survey where the reader can find a good discussion about different measurements is available in

[6]. In this work, a network is used to model a face image and then, measures are extracted for the pattern recognition proposal. The sections below describe measures related to connectivity and hierarchy, both presenting a good performance in the topology characterization [7,6].

Connectivity. Complex networks present as main characteristic a set of vertices and edges that forms particular topographic properties. These properties can be measured by the number of connections among vertices [7]. For weighted networks, the vertex degree kw_i is obtained by $kw_i = \sum_{j=1}^{N} w_{ij}$, where w_{ij} is the weight of the connection between vertex i and j. Although simple, the vertex grade performs well in characterizing the networks, as it provides information about the topology and distribution of the connectivity throughout the network.

Hierarchical Degree. Hierarchy performs an important role in the complex network approach. The hierarchical level can be defined as a graph dilatation $\delta(g)$, resulting in a sub graph containing the vertices from g and the vertices directly connected to g. The graph dilation can be iterative. The d-dilatation process, which means that, a graph g is dilated d times, is shown below:

$$\delta_d(g) = \underbrace{\delta(\delta(...(g)...))}_{d} \tag{1}$$

The d-ring of a subgraph g is defined as $R_d(g)$ and it is composed by the vertices and edges according to:

$$R_d(g) = V(\delta_d(g)) - V(\delta_{d-1}(g)) \tag{2}$$

where $V(.)$ is the set of vertices and $-$ is the subtraction operation between sets.

The hierarchical degree k_i^d can be defined by the number of edges that connect the rings $R_d(i)$ and $R_{d-1}(i)$ to the vertex i. The weighed hierarchical degree kw_i^d is calculated similarly by summing the weights.

3   Face Recognition Using Complex Networks

The proposed method can be split into two stages: network modeling and feature extraction. To model an image as a network $G = (V, E)$, each pixel is mapped to a vertex of the set V. Two vertices i and j, related to the pixels p_i and p_j, are connected if the distance between the pixels is less than a given radius r. The connection weight is defined by the pixel intensity difference (see Equation 3).

$$w_{ij} = \begin{cases} |I(p_i) - I(p_j))|, & \text{if } dist(p_i, p_j) \leq r \\ 0, & \text{otherwise} \end{cases} \tag{3}$$

where w_{ij} is the edge weight, $I(x)$ is the pixel intensity of the pixel x, $dist$ is the Euclidean distance and r is the radius of neighborhood.

The next step is to transform the graph into a complex network, with a rich structure and topology. In this work, the authors demonstrated that a simple regular graph similar to the one obtained until now can be transformed into a small world complex network. The transform, defined as $\psi(t, G)$, consists of the selection of edges according to their weights and a threshold t, which can vary from $0 \leq t \leq max(W)$ (see Equation 4). Figure 1 illustrates the transform $\psi(t, G)$.

$$
w_{ij} = \begin{cases} w_{ij}, & \text{if } w_{ij} \leq t \\ 0, & \text{otherwise} \end{cases} \tag{4}
$$

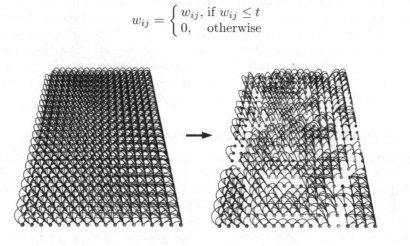

Fig. 1. Transformation ψ in a complex network

The transform $\psi(t, G)$ can be considered as a multi-scale network analysis. For each value of t the original network is transformed into a t scaled network. Thus, the t scaled network presents different properties and reveals the structure and topology related to its scale. For small values of t, the network provides information of image details, presenting better small sets of pixels or regions and as t increases, it presents better global information. For high values of t, the network can provide the image edges. The proposal of our method is to combine measures from some values of t achieving a multi-scale analysis.

3.1 Feature Vector Extraction

The face characterization is performed by extracting measures from networks $G_t = \psi(t, G)$ varying the thresholding t. The values are between the interval $t_0 \leq t \leq t_f$ and incremented by a constant t_{inc}. The metrics discussed in Section 2.1 are calculated for each vertex of G_t. Then, a vector $\boldsymbol{f}_t$ is carried out by calculating the mean, variance and kurtosis from each metric. If n metrics are used, the feature vector f_t for a given scale t is a $3n$ vector (mean variance and kurtosis for each metric). Equation 5 shows how to calculate $\boldsymbol{f}_t$, where i is related to each metric. The final feature vector f for a given face is the concatenation of the individual feature vectors f_t at different scales, according to Equation 6.

$$
\begin{aligned}
m_i &= [mean(G_t) \; variance(G_t) \; kurtosis(G_t)] \\
\boldsymbol{f}_t &= [m_0 \; \ldots \; m_i \; \ldots \; m_n]
\end{aligned} \tag{5}
$$

$$\boldsymbol{f} = [f_{t_0} \; f_{(t_0+t_{inc})} \; \cdots \; f_{t_f}] \tag{6}$$

4 Face Recognition Experiments

In order to validate the proposed method, a set of experiments was carried out using a well-known public face database - ORL database [8]. This database has 10 images of 40 subjects, with changes in illumination, facial details and expressions. Two experiments were conducted: parameter analysis and comparison with other methods. For both experiments, 10-folds cross-validation was carried out using K-neighbor nearest [9], with $k = 1$. A simple statistical classifier was chosen in order to show evidence of the feature role in pattern recognition.

4.1 Analysis of the Method Parameters

This subsection presents a study of the proposed method parameters and its consequences on the pattern recognition performance. The parameters considered are: (i) the radius influence for the transformation which converts the image to the network, (ii) the thresholds used for the multi-scale transform, (iii) the measures considered to compose the feature vector. The objective of this analysis is to present the method behavior and determine the best set of parameters.

The main parameters of the method are the neighbor radius r and the initial threshold t_0. Both parameters are related to the network structure and changes in them can directly influence the face recognition performance. The parameter analysis starts choosing a range for r and t_0 where the method achieves its optimum performance. For this, we evaluated various combinations of these parameters and the method achieved the best performance for $r \approx \sqrt{73}$ and $t_0 \approx 10$. These values can be combined with the other parameters to find the optimal parameter set of the method.

Figure 2 presents an analysis of all the parameters. In Figure 2(a) the plot ratio r versus classification rates is shown. Notice that the classification rate achieves its maximum 98% for $r = \sqrt{73}$. Figure 2(b) shows a plot of t_0 versus classification rates. The maximum classification rate is achieved for $t_0 = 10$. For low values of t_0, such as those less than 5, the network can be highly disturbed by noise. On the other hand, for high values of t_0, the network cannot present the face details and lose important face information. Figures 2(c) and 2(d) present respectively t_{inc} versus classification rates and l_f versus classification rates. To compute the plots $t_f = t_0 + x * t_{inc}$ was used, where x is the number of times of t_{inc}. This function makes t_{inc} and t_f correlated values. In the first analysis, $x = 7$ (see Figure 2(d)) was used. The plot shows that the best results are achieved for high values of t_{inc}. It is expected as, for high values of t_{inc} the method can explore a better range of scales for the multi-scale analysis. In Figure 2(d), the plot shows the classification rates versus the number of thresholds, given by x which determines t_f. Notice that the curve achieves its maximum when $x = 7$ and it maintains stabilized. Using these four plots, we can determine the best chosen parameters, which are $r = \sqrt{73}$, $t_0 = 10$, $t_{inc} = 10$ and $t_f = t_0 + 7 * t_{inc}$.

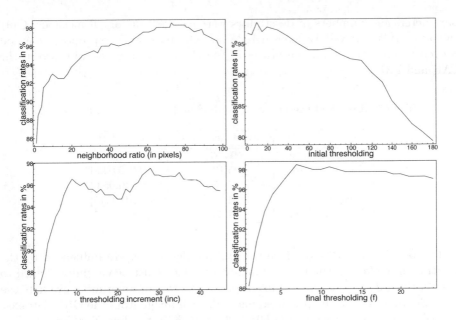

Fig. 2. (a) Comparison results for different radius, (b) Threshold t_0 X Correct percent, (c) Threshold t_{inc} X Correct percent and (d) Threshold t_f X Correct percent

The feature vector consists of metrics extracted from the transformed networks. Three measurements were evaluated: the degree, two level hierarchical degree and three level hierarchical degree. Table 1 compares performance of the three combined feature vector (Full) to each individual metric in terms of classification rate, the false acceptance rate (FAR) and false rejection rate (FRR). The best individual metric was the degree which achieved a correct percentage of 94.75%. The combined feature vector (full) has the best correct percentage and the smallest FRR and FAR, which suggests that the individual metric extracts different information from the networks.

Table 1. Comparison results for measures and the three combined feature vector (Full)

	Correct Percentage	FAR	FRR
Full	98.5%	0.00045	0.015
Degree	94.75%	0.00145	0.053
Hier. D. 2	93.75%	0.00178	0.063
Hier. D. 3	91.5%	0.00233	0.085

4.2 Comparing with Other Methods

The results of the proposed method are compared to the results of the eigenfaces [10], fisherfaces [11], laplacianfaces [12] and neighborhood preserving embedding - NPE [13] in Table 2. It is important to notice that various combinations of parameters and numbers of descriptors were carried out for all methods. Only the best result achieved was considered in the comparison. The proposed method proved to be better than the others in the classification rates and also in the FAR and FRR.

Table 2. Results of the proposed method and state of the art methods

	Correct Percentage	FAR	FRR
Proposed Method	98.5%	0.0005	0.015
FisherFaces	95.73%	0.0011	0.042
NPE	94.75%	0.0014	0.053
EigenFaces	94.55%	0.0014	0.0545
LaplacianFaces	94.25%	0.0014	0.0575

The performance of most face recognition algorithms are influenced by the position of the face in the image. Usually, the faces must be carefully aligned to extract the features relative to a fixed coordinate system. In order to evaluate the rotation invariance of the proposed method, each image from the ORL database was rotated in four directions ($-60°, -30°, 30°, 60°$), totaling 2000 images.

The proposed method results in the increased database are compared with other methods in Table 3. In this experiment, the cross-validation strategy with 2-folds was performed to increase the amount of images in the test step (50% of the images are used to test the model in the 2-folds cross-validation). The proposed method had more positive results than the others in the classification rates and also in the FAR and FRR. The method achieved a correct percentage of 93.65% compared to only 58.45% achieved by the Fisherfaces.

Table 3. Results of the methods in the increased ORL database

	Correct Percentage	FAR	FRR
Proposed Method	93.65%	0.0019	0.064
FisherFaces	58.45%	0.0168	0.415
LaplacianFaces	54.45%	0.0202	0.456
EigenFaces	42.75%	0.0197	0.573
NPE	41.8%	0.0171	0.582

5   Conclusion

This paper presented a novel approach to face recognition based on the complex network theory. In the proposed method, the face image is mapped onto a regular graph and then it is transformed into a small-world network. Using the complex network theory, various features are extracted, providing a feature vector that can identify faces.

The method was compared with popular and the state-of-art methods. The proposed method proved to be better than the others in the classification rates and also in the FAR and FRR measures. Moreover, according to the nature of the graphs, the proposed method is rotation invariant, which differs from most of the holistic face recognition methods. As part of the future work, we plan to focus on evaluating the proposed method in large scale face image data sets.

Acknowledgements. The authors acknowledges support from CNPq.

References

1. Watts, D.J., Strogatz, S.H.: Collective dynamics of 'small-world' networks. Nature 393(6684), 440–442 (1998)
2. Barabasi, A.L., Albert, R.: Emergence of scaling in random networks. Science 286(5439), 509–512 (1999)
3. Backes, A.R., Casanova, D., Bruno, O.M.: A complex network-based approach for boundary shape analysis. Pattern Recognition 42(1), 54–67 (2009)
4. Silva, T.C., Zhao, L.: Pixel clustering by using complex network community detection technique. In: ISDA, pp. 925–932. IEEE Computer Society, Los Alamitos (2007)
5. Erdős, P., Rényi, A.: On random graphs. I. Publ. Math. Debrecen 6, 290–297 (1959)
6. Costa, L.F., Rodrigues, F.A., Travieso, G., Boas, P.R.V.: Characterization of complex networks: A survey of measurements. Advances In Physics 56, 167–242 (2007)
7. Boccaletti, S., Latora, V., Moreno, Y., Chavez, M., Hwang, D.U.: Complex networks: Structure and dynamics. Physics Reports 424(4-5), 175–308 (2006)
8. Samaria, F.S., Harter, A.C.: Parameterisation of a stochastic model for human face identification. In: IEEE Workshop on Appl. of Computer Vision, pp. 138–142 (1994)
9. Mitchell, T.M.: Machine Learning. McGraw-Hill, New York (1997)
10. Belhumeur, P.N., Jo, a.P.H., Kriegman, D.J.: Eigenfaces vs. fisherfaces: Recognition using class specific linear projection. IEEE PAMI 19(7), 711–720 (1997)
11. Zuo, W., Wang, K., Zhang, D., Zhang, H.: Combination of two novel lda-based methods for face recognition. Neurocomputing 70(4-6), 735–742 (2007)
12. He, X., Yan, S., Hu, Y., Niyogi, P., Zhang, H.J.: Face recognition using laplacianfaces. IEEE Trans. Pattern Anal. Mach. Intell. 27(3), 328–340 (2005)
13. He, X., Cai, D., Yan, S., Zhang, H.J.: Neighborhood preserving embedding. In: IEEE International Conference on Computer Vision, vol. 2, pp. 1208–1213 (2005)

Illumination Invariant Face Image Representation Using Quaternions

Dayron Rizo-Rodríguez, Heydi Méndez-Vázquez, and Edel García-Reyes

Advanced Technologies Application Center. 7th Avenue #21812
b/ 218 and 222, Siboney, Playa, P.C. 12200, Havana, Cuba
{drizo,hmendez,egarcia}@cenatav.co.cu

Abstract. Variations in illumination is a well-known affecting factor of face recognition system performance. Feature extraction is one of the principal steps on a face recognition framework, where it is possible to alleviate the illumination effects on face images. The aim of this work is to study the illumination invariant properties of a hypercomplex image representation. A quaternion description from the image is built using second order derivatives decomposition. This representation is transformed to quaternion frequency domain in order to analyze its illumination invariant and discriminative properties, which are compared against the ones of the complex frequency domain representation obtained by using first order derivative decomposition. The hypercomplex quaternion representation was found to be more discriminative than the complex one, when comparing on face recognition with images under varying lighting conditions.

1 Introduction

Illumination invariant features are desirable in face recognition systems due to the degradation of the performance when face images are affected by lighting variations. Despite the work of Chen et al. [1], which states that no discriminative illumination invariant exists, different illumination invariant face image descriptors have been proposed. Their demonstration is based on the construction of an arbitrary object, which is able to generate the two images at hand under two different lighting sources, in a way that there is no guarantee that such images correspond to the same object or to different objects (the real and the generated one). However, when working on face image domain, faces are always detected first, which guarantees that the object which invalidates the discriminative invariant function, will no belong to the specific domain.

Some of the illumination invariant descriptors proposed for face recognition are based on statistical tools such as Principal Component Analysis and Linear Discriminant Analysis [2]. Others, transform the image to frequency domain, where illumination variations are supposed to be mainly in the low frequency spectrum, and aim at removing this frequency components while emphasizing high frequencies using them for comparison in that domain [3–5]. Another group of methods obtains features derived from face surface, like borders and texture

I. Bloch and R.M. Cesar, Jr. (Eds.): CIARP 2010, LNCS 6419, pp. 434–441, 2010.
© Springer-Verlag Berlin Heidelberg 2010

descriptors [6, 7], taking into account morphological characteristics of the face. Among these groups of methods, the ones which work on frequency domain have shown better performance when dealing with illumination problems [8].

An image representation in the frequency domain can be described using complex components. In [9], an initial complex description $g(x, y)$ is obtained using as components the gradient of the image I in x and y directions, i.e.:

$$g(x, y) = \nabla_x I(x, y) + \nabla_y I(x, y)\mathbf{j} \tag{1}$$

The aim of the authors is to transform the initial representation in Eq.1 to frequency domain applying Discrete Fourier Transform (DFT) and, working from cartesian and polar coordinates representation, to explore the illumination invariant properties of these four descriptions individually. The real part of cartesian coordinates yielded the best performance among them.

Hypercomplex numbers algebra has been recently used to solve pattern recognition problems. An attempt to include the quaternion representation on face recognition approaches is proposed in [10]. The authors used a two-level wavelet decomposition to obtain the image description and designed a quaternion correlation filter. They achieved very good results on CMU-PIE Database [11], but there is not any justification about quaternion usage and it seems a little empirical. Precisely, the motivation of our work is to understand and explain the reason for the inclusion of these hypercomplex numbers on face recognition frameworks.

Since it is possible to encapsulate until four bands of information in the quaternion representation, in this paper we proposed the construction of a quaternion representation using second order derivatives of the image decomposition. The proposed image representation is based on the idea in [9] but trying to obtain a more illumination invariant representation, presuming that with a wider decomposition of the image information, the lighting effects might be less perceptible. The obtained image descriptor is transformed to quaternion frequency domain and its representation in both cartesian and polar coordinates are used to compare their illumination invariant and discriminative properties among them and against those presented in [9]. Results on face image verification and identification experiments on XM2VTS and Extended Yale B databases, show that the quaternion outperforms the complex representation.

The paper is organized as follows. In Section 2, the quaternion theory and its uses in image domain is reviewed. In Section 3, face image decomposition using second order derivatives to construct the quaternion frequency domain representation is presented. The experimental results are drawn in Section 4. Finally, Section 5 gives the conclusions of the paper.

2   Quaternion Theory

Quaternion algebra was originally introduced by Hamilton in 1843 [12]. A quaternion is composed by a real part and an imaginary part consisting of three orthogonal components.

The cartesian representation of quaternion numbers would be as follows.

$$q = a + b\mathbf{i} + c\mathbf{j} + d\mathbf{k} \tag{2}$$

where a, b, c, d are real and $\mathbf{i}$, $\mathbf{j}$, $\mathbf{k}$ are imaginary operators.

Any quaternion may be represented in the classic polar form [13]:

$$q = |q|e^{\mu\theta} \tag{3}$$

where θ is a real angle, as the generalization of the complex exponential $e^{i\theta} = cos\theta + isin\theta$ by replacing i by any unit pure quaternion μ.

In [13] it is shown that every quaternion admits the following polar form:

$$q = Ae^{Bj} \tag{4}$$

where $A = a + bi$ and $B = c + di$ are complex, and is remarked its analogy to the Cayley-Dickson form of a quaternion $q = (w + x\mathbf{i}) + (y + z\mathbf{i})\mathbf{j} = w + x\mathbf{i} + y\mathbf{j} + z\mathbf{k}$, also based on two complex numbers.

2.1   Image Applications

Quaternions have been used in color image processing, aiming at taking into account the true nature of vector signals [14]. According to [15], the opportunity to encode the image color information using algebraical representations provides the theoretical tools of the algebra to work with less dimensional data.

In [15], quaternion space is used to define frequency filters in color images. The author also reported the use of the frequency information of the quaternion spectrum on color image watermarking and to compute color image correlation. Color image edge detection was developed applying quaternion algebra in [16].

On the other hand, Bayro in [17] shows the improvement of two-level images when representation and processing are carried out in geometric algebra. The author states that quaternions are useful to reveal the properties of an n-dimensional representation of 2D signals and that they allow to disentangle the symmetries of 2D signals. A quaternion Gabor filter is designed based on this idea. The important conclusion that quaternions constitute a wide open area for the design and implementation of filters and estimators for the analysis of signals in the quaternion frequency domain, is presented.

3   Image Quaternion Representation in the Frequency Domain

To obtain image quaternion representation in the frequency domain, the first step is to decompose the image in four bands of information in order to use them for constructing the initial quaternion description.

We will use the second order derivatives of the face image to form the initial quaternion number, in the following way:

$$q(x, y) = \nabla^2_{xx}I(x, y) + \nabla^2_{xy}I(x, y)\mathbf{i} + \nabla^2_{yx}I(x, y)\mathbf{j} + \nabla^2_{yy}I(x, y)\mathbf{k} \tag{5}$$

where ∇^2_{xx}, ∇^2_{xy}, ∇^2_{yx} and ∇^2_{yy} are second order derivatives of the image. In Figure 1 a) this decomposition from a face image is depicted. This representation allows us to encode more information about image in order to find an image description in the frequency domain with better illumination invariant attributes.

Once we have the initial quaternion description, Quaternion Discrete Fourier Transform (QDFT) [14], is used to transform it to the frequency domain. The QDFT is defined as:

$$Q(p,s) = \sum_{m=0}^{M-1} \sum_{n=0}^{N-1} e^{-\mu 2\pi((pm/M)+(sn/M))} q(m,n) \qquad (6)$$

where μ is any unit pure quaternion and q is the initial quaternion number obtained in Eq. (5).

After obtaining a quaternion frequency domain representation of a face image using Eq. (6), it is possible to express it in polar coordinates by Eq. (4). We have then 8 descriptions of the image in order to analyze their illumination invariant properties and to determine the one less affected by illumination variations.

In Figure 1 (b) both cartesian and polar quaternion frequency domain components are shown. They are obtained using an initial quaternion description with the second order derivatives of the face image shown in (a).

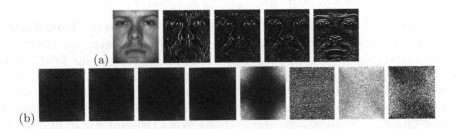

Fig. 1. Representation of (a) a face image with its second order derivatives, and (b) the quaternion frequency domain components obtained using them

4   Experimental Evaluation

Each quaternion frequency component is analyzed in order to determine the most illumination invariant one when used as face features and is compared with the ones obtained using the complex representation in [9]. The most invariant components that were selected, are used as face image descriptor for verification and identification experiments. Since we are less concerned with the classification step and more with the feature extraction, a simple normalized correlation is used as a similarity measure in all cases with a nearest neighbourhood classifier in the case of identification.

To analyze the different quaternion components the experimental setup described in [9] is used. The intra-class variations are analyzed comparing images in XM2VTS [18] database. Images corresponding to the same subject with different illumination conditions are compared among them in two experiments: in the first one (1), frontal illuminated images are compared, while in the second one (2), non frontal illuminated images are used. Table 1 shows the mean correlations obtained when comparing face images using the different components for both, the quaternion and the complex representations.

Table 1. Mean correlations obtained with quaternion and complex components

	Complex [9]				Quaternion							
	Real	Im	Mg	Ph	Real	Im1	Im2	Im3	Polar1	Polar2	Polar3	Polar4
1)	**0.83**	0.57	0.69	0.12	0.50	0.44	0.46	0.58	**0.85**	0.19	0.25	0.25
2)	**0.90**	0.75	0.72	0.13	0.56	0.50	0.51	0.61	**0.86**	0.29	0.34	0.40

It can be appreciated that Polar1 exhibits the best illumination invariant properties among quaternion components, although when comparing with the complex representation, the Real component shows a little better performance. However, this is not enough for a face recognition task, it is necessary to evaluate the discriminative properties of both descriptions in face verification and identification experiments.

4.1 Verification Experiment

The XM2VTS database with the Lausanne protocol [18], specifically the Configuration I, is used to verify the performance of the proposed quaternion representation in face verification setup. The XM2VTS database contains 2360 images of 295 subjects, captured in 4 different sessions. The database is divided into a Training, an evaluation (Eval) and a Test sets, each of them composed of face images under controlled illumination conditions used as clients and others as imposters. There is an additional set (Dark) which contains non frontal illuminated images from the same subjects which are also used as client and impostor comparisons.

The Equal Error Rate (EER) is the point at which the False Rejection Rate (FRR) is equal to the False Acceptance Rate (FAR). The value obtained by the classification method at this point in the Eval set is used as a threshold for the decision of acceptance or rejection in the Test and Dark sets. On the other hand, the Total Error Rate (TER) is the sum of FRR and FAR and is used to measure the performance of the verification system.

The TER obtained in each set of the database using the proposed quaternion and the complex representations is shown in Table 2. The Table also shows the results when the original face images are compared.

It can be concluded from the table, that quaternion discriminative properties are very similar to the ones of original images when they are not affected by

Table 2. Obtained Results (TER) in Verification Experiment

	Eval	Test	Dark
Original	0.2324	0.1982	0.9022
Complex	1.0034	1.0007	1.0470
Quaternion	0.3367	0.2924	0.5148

illumination variations (Eval and Test sets). However, the Polar1 component of quaternion is the most discriminative feature when they are affected by illumination variations (Dark set). As can be appreciated, although the Real component of complex representation seemed to be more illumination invariant, the quaternion description is significantly more discriminative for face verification.

4.2   Identification Experiment

The Extended Yale B [19] database was used for face identification experiments. It contains images of 28 subjects seen under 64 different illumination conditions, in which the angle between the light source direction and the camera axis was changed each time, in a way that the larger the angle, the more unfavorable the lighting conditions are. Images with frontal angles were used as gallery and the others, were divided into 5 subsets according to the angle in the following way: S1 contains 225 images with angles between 0 - 12^0, S2 is composed by 456 images with 13^0 - 25^0 angles, S3 have 525 images with angles between 26^0 - 50^0, 456 images with angles between 51^0 - 70^0 are in S4 and S5 contains 562 images with angles between 71^0 - 130^0.

Table 3. Recognition Rates (%) obtained in Identification Experiment

	S1	S2	S3	S4	S5
Original	100.0	96.93	46.10	11.40	3.91
Complex	100.0	95.39	37.14	11.40	3.02
Quaternion	100.0	100.0	93.14	38.60	6.05

The recognition rates obtained using the three different representations in each subset are presented in Table 3. Also in Figure 2 the cumulative match score vs. rank curve illustrates the performance of the three representations in S5, the most difficult one.

It can be appreciated from the Table 3 and Figure 2 that the quaternion representation outperforms both, the original and the complex representations in all subsets of the database, being more significant in those cases where the images have greater angles of variations in illumination. This also confirms the more discriminative properties of Polar1 component of quaternion representation.

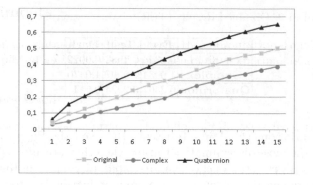

Fig. 2. S5 Cumulative Score vs. Rank Curve

5   Conclusions and Future Works

In this work, a quaternion representation starting from second order derivatives of face images is proposed. This representation is based on quaternion algebra properties, which encodes image information in a vectorial way. Using this representation eight quaternion components were obtained. Among them, Polar1 component proved to be the most illumination invariant one.

Although Polar1 component probed to be a feature with enough illumination invariant properties, these were a bit lower than the Real component of complex representation. Discriminative properties of both descriptions were analyzed on face recognition tasks. Results on face images verification and identification experiments confirmed that this quaternion representation is better than original images and complex representations, when dealing with images under varying lighting conditions. This shows the importance of the combination of illumination invariant and discriminative properties on face recognition frameworks.

Analyzing our work, it is possible to consider the quaternion representation as a wide area of research to develop new approaches in quaternion frequency domain. Taking into account that in complex frequency domain many face recognition methods with good performances have been developed, it can be presumed that turning to a higher dimension space as quaternions, the performance will increase. This higher dimension representation does not imply a dimensionality problem due to its algebraical properties.

As future work, it is necessary to evaluate the proposed quaternion representation with a more sophisticated similarity measure, instead of using the simple normalized correlation, which should improve the obtained results.

References

1. Chen, H., Belhumeur, P., Jacobs, D.: In search of illumination invariants. In: IEEE International Conference on Computer Vision and Pattern Recognition (2000)
2. Belhumeur, P., Pentland, J., Kriegman, D.: Eigenfaces vs. fisherfaces: Recognition using class specific linear projection. IEEE Trans. Pattern Anal. Machine Intell. 19, 711–720 (1997)

3. Hafed, Z.M., Levine, M.D.: Face recognition using the discrete cosine transform. Int. J. Comput. Vision 43(3), 167–188 (2001)
4. Savvides, M., Vijaya Kumar, B., Khosla, P.: Corefaces-robust shift invariant pca based correlation filter for illumination tolerant face recognition. In: Proc. IEEE CVPR 2004 (2004)
5. Qing, L., Shan, S., Chen, X., Gao, W.: Face recognition under varying lighting based on the probabilistic model of gabor phase. IEEE Computer Society, Los Alamitos (2006)
6. Pujol, A.: Contributions to Shape and Texture Face Similarity Measurement. PhD thesis, Universitat Autónoma de Barcelona (2001)
7. Ahonen, T., Hadid, A., Pietikäinen, M.: Face recognition with local binary patterns. In: Pajdla, T., Matas, J(G.) (eds.) ECCV 2004. LNCS, vol. 3021, pp. 469–481. Springer, Heidelberg (2004)
8. Vijayakumar, B., Savvides, K., Venkataramani, K., Xie, C.: Spatial frequency domain image processing for biometric recognition. In: IEEE International Conference on Image Processing, pp. 53–56 (2002)
9. Garea, E., Kittler, J., Messer, K., Mendez, H.: An illumination insensitive representation for face verification in the frequency domain. In: ICPR 2006, pp. 215–218. IEEE Computer Society, Los Alamitos (2006)
10. Chunyan, X., Savvides, M., Vijayakumar, B.: Quaternion correlation filters for face recognition in wavelet domain. In: Proc. IEEE Int. Conf. on Acoustics, Speech, and Signal Processing (2005)
11. Sim, T., Baker, S., Bsat, M.: The cmu pose, illumination, and expression (pie) database of human faces. Technical report (2007)
12. Hamilton, W.: 24. In: Elements of Quaternions. Longmans, Green (1866)
13. Sangwine, S., Le Bihan, N.: Quaternion polar representation with a complex modulus and complex argument inspired by the cayley-dickson form. In: Proc. IEEE Int. Conf. on Acoustics, Speech, and Signal Processing (2005)
14. Moxey, C., Sangwine, S., Ell, T.: Hypercomplex correlation techniques for vector images. IEEE Transaction on Signal Processing 51, 1941–1953 (2003)
15. Denis, P.: Quaternions et Algèbres Géométriques, de nouveaux outils pour les images numériques couleur. PhD thesis, Université de Poitiers (2006)
16. Mahecha, V.: Aplicación de los números hipercomplejos o cuaterniones en imágenes de color. Ingeniería y desarrollo (023), 72–83 (2008)
17. Bayro, E.: 6. In: Geometric Computing for Perception Action Systems, pp. 115–136. Springer, New York (2001)
18. Messer, K., Matas, J., Kittler, J., Jonsson, K.: Xm2vtsdb: The extended m2vts database. In: Second International Conference on Audio and Video-based Biometric Person Authentication, pp. 72–77 (1999)
19. Lee, K.C., Ho, J., Kriegman, D.J.: Acquiring linear subspaces for face recognition under variable lighting. IEEE Transactions on Pattern Analysis and Machine Intelligence 27(5), 684–698 (2005)

A Contrario Detection of False Matches in Iris Recognition

Marcelo Mottalli, Mariano Tepper, and Marta Mejail

Departamento de Computación, Universidad de Buenos Aires, Argentina

Abstract. The pattern of the human iris contains rich information which provides one of the most accurate methods for recognition of individuals. Identification through iris recognition is achieved by matching a biometric template generated from the texture of the iris against an existing database of templates. This relies on the assumption that the probability of two different iris generating similar templates is very low. This assumption opens a question: how can one be sure that two iris templates are similar because they were generated from the same iris and not because of some other random factor?

In this paper we introduce a novel technique for iris matching based on the *a contrario* framework, where two iris templates are decided to belong to the same iris according to the unlikelyness of the similarity between them. This method provides an intuitive detection thresholding technique, based on the probability of occurence of the distance between two templates. We perform tests on different iris databases captured in heterogeneous environments and we show that the proposed identification method is more robust than the standard method based on the Hamming distance.

1 Introduction

The human iris is regarded as one of the richest biometric features. It is an external and visible part of the eye and contains enough information for the identification of a person with very low error rates. This fact allows to build an automatic system for identification of individuals via iris recognition.

The fundamentals of iris recognition were proposed by Daugman [4]. Starting from a picture of the human eye with enough quality, the picture is segmented to locate the iris and isolate it from the rest of the image. Once the iris is isolated, a *biometric template* is generated from its texture and the recognition takes place by comparing this template against a set of templates previously stored in a database.

The identification itself is done by global thresholding on the distance between two iris templates, for an appropriate distance function (usually the Hamming distance). Both templates are assumed to be generated by the same iris if and only if the distance between them is lower than a given threshold. This distance-based identification step provides good results, but three issues remain open:

I. Bloch and R.M. Cesar, Jr. (Eds.): CIARP 2010, LNCS 6419, pp. 442–449, 2010.
© Springer-Verlag Berlin Heidelberg 2010

1. Which value for the decision threshold provides an acceptable level of identification errors while not producing many rejections?
2. Once this threshold is defined, how can we be certain that two templates that are considered similar were obtained from the same iris and not by chance (for example, if both templates were generated from two low-quality images of different iris)?
3. Does a change in the database affect the identification results? For example, after a new iris template is added to the database or if the capture conditions change, is the same threshold still suitable?

One of the central problems in any automated recognition system is to have a tool to make a sound judgement about the accuracy of its output, however, the vast majority of related works concentrate on other parts of the recognition process. For example, for iris recognition, most works focus on segmentation or template generation algorithms, while template matching is often overlooked and is done by simple template distance thresholding [2].

In this work we analyse and improve iris template matching. For this, we propose a novel method based on an *a contrario* [3] detection of meaningful matches between templates (sections 2 and 3) and we analyse its performance (section 4).

2   The *A Contrario* Framework

The *a contrario* framework [3] provides a way to address the aforementioned issues. The framework is based on the Helmholtz principle that, in this case, states that a match between two iris templates is *meaningful* when it is not likely to occur in a context where noise overwhelms the information. In other words, *we detect by modeling what we do not want to detect.*

Formally, assume we have one query iris template Q and an iris template database $T = \{T_i : 1 \leq i \leq N\}$ composed of N templates. Given an appropriate distance function, the distances between Q and each T_i, $d(Q, T_i)$ can be seen as observations of a random variable D that follows some unknown random process.

Under these assumptions, we can perform an hypothesis test for each pair (Q, T_i), where we have two hypothesis:

- $\mathcal{H}_0$ *(null hypothesis):* $d(Q, T_i)$ *is observed by chance,* i.e. because the database is large.
- $\mathcal{H}_1$ *(alternate hypothesis):* $d(Q, T_i)$ *is observed because of some causality,* i.e. because both templates were generated from the same iris.

On one hand, $P(D \mid \mathcal{H}_0)$ (the probability distribution of the distances between iris templates) can be modeled with relative ease, even if the model is not perfectly realistic. On the other hand, it is not possible to model $P(D \mid \mathcal{H}_1)$ (the probability distribution of the distance when two templates belong to the same iris) because we assume no other information than the observed templates. Hence, the full hypothesis test cannot be done: we cannot control false negatives.

However, controlling false positives, or *false alarms*, under $\mathcal{H}_0$ is enough to decide whether a given iris template matches another template in the database. In other words, two templates are considered as belonging to the same iris *a contrario* if the distance between them has a very low probability of occurring by chance.

We formally state the *a contrario* hypothesis as:

> $\mathcal{H}_0$: $d(Q, T_i)$ are observations of the random variable D that follows some stochastic process.

3   Iris Template Matching

Now, given a pair of iris templates (Q, T_i) and the distance between them $\delta_i = d(Q, T_i)$ we want to know what is the probability of occurence of their distance under $\mathcal{H}_0$, i. e. the probability of false alarms $p_i = P(D \leq \delta_i \mid \mathcal{H}_0)$. If it is small enough, we can claim that Q and T_i are not similar just by chance [3].

Since we do not make any assumptions on the distribution of D, the probability p_i cannot be calculated directly. However, p_i can be estimated empirically over the database as the cumulative histogram of the distances between Q and each T_j, $1 \leq j \leq N$.

The expected *number of false alarms* (NFA) between Q and T_i under $\mathcal{H}_0$ on a database of size N is defined as:

$$\text{NFA}(Q, T_i) = N \cdot P(D \leq \delta_i \mid \mathcal{H}_0) \tag{1}$$

If $\text{NFA}(Q, T_i) \leq \varepsilon$ for a given ε, then the pair (Q, T_i) is said to be an *ε-meaningful match*.

We claim that Q and T_i are not similar just by chance if the match (Q, T_i) is ε-meaningful, i. e. they must be generated by the same iris. This provides a simple rule to decide whether a single pair of templates (Q, T_i) belongs to the same individual or not. Moreover, the expected number of ε-meaningful matches in a set of random matches can be proven to be smaller than ε [3]. Thus the threshold ε has a clear and intuitive meaning: it represents a bound on expected number of false matches (or *false alarms*) we're willing to accept when a template is compared against another template stored in a database if those two templates are considered to be generated by the same iris.

Basing the decision on the NFA we obtain a robust method, since the threshold ε is taken on the probability of false alarms instead of the distances themselves. Also, the same threshold ε is suitable for different database configurations because the probabilities are computed with respect to the entire database.

This provides us with a straightforward way of comparing the query template Q against a template T_i in the database: if $\text{NFA}(Q, T_i) \leq \varepsilon$, that is, if (Q, T_i) is an ε-meaningful match, it is assumed that Q and T_i are not similar just by chance, and it is assumed that they were generated by the same iris.

3.1   Partitioning the Iris Template

Estimating $P(D \leq \delta_i \mid \mathcal{H}_0)$ using the cumulative histogram of the distancies between Q and every T_j poses a problem: since any bin of the histogram is at least $1/N$ (one occurence over the database), this necessarily means that $P(D \leq \delta_i \mid \mathcal{H}_0) \geq 1/N$. Then:

$$\text{NFA}(Q, T_i) = N \cdot P(D \leq \delta_i \mid \mathcal{H}_0) \geq N \cdot \frac{1}{N} = 1 \qquad (2)$$

That is, we would never be able to achieve a NFA lower than 1. Since having in average more than one false alarm for every query is not desirable, this is not an acceptable bound.

Following [9], we solve this problem by *partitioning* the iris template into C independent and non-overlapping parts, not necessarily of the same size. We refer to the k-th partition of the template T using the notation $T^{(k)}$, where $1 \leq k \leq C$.

Under these assumptions, given the query template Q and a template T_i in the database, we redefine

$$\delta_i = \max_{1 \leq k \leq C} \delta_i^{(k)}, \quad \text{where} \quad \delta_i^{(k)} = d(Q^{(k)}, T_i^{(k)}) \qquad (3)$$

and $d(\cdot, \cdot)$ is a properly chosen distance.

As before, we formulate the *a contrario* hypothesis:

$\mathcal{H}_0$: δ_i *and* $\delta_i^{(k)}$ *are observations of identically distributed variables* D *and* $D^{(k)}$, *respectively, that follow some stochastic process.*

Then, the probability of false alarms is:

$$P(D \leq \delta_i \mid \mathcal{H}_0) = P\left(\max_{1 \leq k \leq C} D^{(k)} \leq \delta_i \ \middle| \ \mathcal{H}_0 \right)$$
$$= \prod_{k=1}^{C} P\left(D^{(k)} \leq \delta_i \mid \mathcal{H}_0 \right) \qquad (4)$$

and the NFA is:

$$\text{NFA}(Q, T_i) = N \cdot \prod_{k=1}^{C} P\left(D^{(k)} \leq \delta_i \mid \mathcal{H}_0 \right) \qquad (5)$$

Now, since we have C different histograms to compute the NFA, it turns out that $\text{NFA}(Q, T_i) \geq N \cdot \left(\frac{1}{N} \right)^C = \frac{1}{N^{C-1}}$ That is, we can achieve lower values for the NFA by partitioning the iris template into $C > 1$ independent parts.

It is important to note that, while most bits in the iris template present local spatial correlation [6], it is expected that this correlation will only be observable in one of the parts and it will not spread through all the parts, thus we can still claim that all the parts are independent between themselves.

3.2   Other Considerations

In addition to partitioning the template, two other issues need to be addressed when matching the templates: the noise mask and rotation invariance.

The noise mask marks, for each template, which bits should not be matched. This can happen for example when those bits were calculated in regions obscured by eyelids or eyelayes, or affected by external illumination. When performing the *a contrario* matching, the masks will also need to be partitioned the same way as the templates. Since the distances between the parts are usually normalized by the number of available bits, equation 5 still holds.

Regarding rotation invariance, the most common solution is shifting the iris template on its x axis in both directions and keeping the lowest distance. The same method is used to calculate the distance between parts: one of the templates is rotated, partitioned, and the minimum distance is selected for each part.

4   Performance Evaluation

We tested the proposed matching method using the publicly available Bath iris database [1] composed of 1000 images of 25 persons, with 40 iris images per person (20 for each eye). Iris templates are generated using Daugman's algorithm introduced in [4]: first, the iris images are segmented using an algorithm based on flexible contours [8]. Then, the iris texture is isolated from the image and normalized using the *ruber sheet* model. The texture is then filtered using a set of 2D Gabor filters, and resulting texture is then quantized to create a 2D binary iris template of 256×8 bits. Additionally, a *noise mask* is also associated to the template. This mask marks the bits of the template that were influenced by noise (eyelashes, eyelids and light reflections) and should not be considered on the matching stage.

As mentioned in section 3.1, the iris template must be partitioned to achieve a lower number of false alarms. The best results were achieved when the template is partitioned in four equal parts in the angular direction, exploiting the fact that the iris texture presents more variation in the angular direction than on the radial direction [5]. Thus, an iris template T is partitioned in four parts $T^{(k)}$, $k = 1 \ldots 4$.

Recognition is performed as follows: given a query template Q and an iris template database $\mathcal{T} = \{T_i : 1 \leq i \leq N\}$, the distance $\delta_i^{(k)}$ between the k-th partition of Q and the k-th partition of T_i is calculated using the normalized Hamming distance. As mentioned before, one of the templates is shifted in the radial direction to compensate for rotations in the eye, and the minimum distance for each independent partition is used.

Then, a histogram of the values of $\delta_i^{(k)}$ is computed for each partition k, giving a total of four different histograms, as seen in Fig. 1. Once the histograms are obtained, the NFA betwen Q and each T_i is computed using Eq. 5.

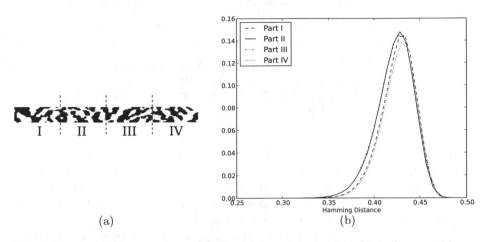

(a)   (b)

Fig. 1. Partioning the templates. (a) The iris template is splitted into four partitions. (b) Four histograms obtained while comparing each partition of a given iris template against an entire database of partitioned templates (one for each partition).

4.1 Results

Following this approach we calculate the NFA between every pair of templates stored in the database using a leave-one-out cross-validation approach. We calculate the False Match Rate (FMR) for different values of ε and the corresponding False Nonmatch Rate (FNMR), where a pair of templates (Q, T_i) is considered a match if $\mathrm{NFA}(Q, T_i) \leq \varepsilon$.

The Table 1 shows the FMR and FNMR for different values of ε. It can be observed that the FMR is bounded by ε. This was expected for the reasons mentioned in section 3, and it implies that by setting the value of ε beforehand we can effectively control the number of false matches of the system.

Table 1. FMR and FNMR for different values of ε

ε	FMR	FNMR
10^{-4}	0	9.07×10^{-2}
10^{-3}	1.34×10^{-6}	2.34×10^{-2}
10^{-2}	5.49×10^{-5}	5.55×10^{-3}
10^{-1}	2.24×10^{-3}	1.49×10^{-3}

Additionally, the performance of the system is analysed and compared in Table 2 by using the Equal Error Rate (EER) and the decidability d', which is a dimentionless measure of the distance between the distributions of the inter-class and intra-class comparisons. It is also compared against recent results obtained by Hollingsworth et al [7].

Table 2. Performance results using different methods

Method	EER	d'
Hamming distance	9.7×10^{-3}	3.49
Hollingsworth et al [7]	6.99×10^{-3}	6.06
NFA matching	1.5×10^{-3}	7.72

It can be observed that the EER has decreased and at the same time the decidability has been more than doubled with respect to using the Hamming distance alone. This means that the separation of the distribution between intra-class and inter-class comparisons is greatly increased using the NFA rather than the Hamming distance, as can be seen on Fig. 2.

It should be noted that the *a contrario* method only allows us to set a limit on the number of false matches, and it has no control over the false nonmatches. However, the results indicate that this method has considerably better performance than using the Hamming distance alone.

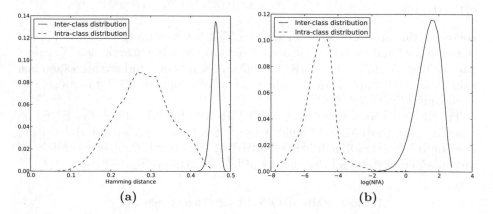

Fig. 2. Comparison of inter-class and intra-class distances (a) using the Hamming distance and (b) using the NFA (the NFA is plotted in logarithmic scale for visualization purposes). A greater separation between classes can be seen using the NFA.

5   Conclusions

The novel contribution in this work is to apply the *a contrario* detection framework for template based iris recognition. The *a contrario* matching has the important advantage of not requiring to compute by hand an "optimum" threshold. It is possible to directly define the acceptable number of false matches for the system with *no* a priori information on the database.

The proposed method proved to give results consistent with the theory presented in section 2. The number of false matches observed in the tests were consistent with the expected number of false alarms defined beforehand with the parameter ε.

Since the *a contrario* method does not make assumptions about the method used for encoding the iris texture or for measuring the distance between templates, it can be adapted for different scenarios. This is an important feature, since most works deal with increasing the separation between the classes by improving the segmentation or codification algorithms. We show that it is possible to achieve this just by changing the matching algorithm, which is often overlooked in the bibliography.

Also, since the NFA is calculated against all the templates in the database, it is a robust measure that is not affected by changes in the capture conditions. For example, if the database is composed by templates generated from blurry or low quality images, then a query template generated in similar conditions will be more likely to be rejected by our method.

References

1. Smart sensors iris database, `http://www.irisbase.com/`
2. Bowyer, K., Hollingsworth, H., Flynn, P.: Image understanding for iris biometrics: A survey. Computer Vision and Image Understanding 110, 281–307 (2007)
3. Cao, F., Lisani, J.L., Morel, J.M., Musé, P., Sur, F.: A Theory of Shape Identification, vol. 1948. Springer, Heidelberg (2008)
4. Daugman, J.: High confidence visual recognition of persons by a test of statistical independence. IEEE Transactions on Pattern Analysis and Machine Intelligence 15(11), 1148–1161 (1993)
5. Gentile, J.E., Ratha, N., Connell, J.: Slic: Short-length iris codes. In: IEEE 3rd International Conference on Biometrics: Theory, Applications, and Systems, BTAS 2009, pp. 1–5 (September 2009)
6. Hollingsworth, K., Bowyer, K., Flynn, P.: The best bits in an iris code. IEEE Transactions on Pattern Analysis and Machine Intelligence 31, 1–10 (2009)
7. Hollingsworth, K., Peters, T., Bowyer, K., Flynn, P.: Iris recognition using signal-level fusion of frames from video. IEEE Transactions on Information Forensics and Security 4(4), 837–848 (2009)
8. Mottalli, M., Mejail, M., Jacobo-Berlles, J.: Flexible image segmentation and quality assessment for real-time iris recognition. In: 16th IEEE International Conference on Image Processing (ICIP), pp. 1941–1944 (November 2009)
9. Proena, H., Alexandre, L.: Toward non-cooperative iris recognition: A classification approach using multiple signatures. IEEE Transactions on Pattern Analysis and Machine Intelligence 29(4), 607–612 (2007)

A Functional Density-Based Nonparametric Approach for Statistical Calibration

Noslen Hernández[1], Rolando J. Biscay[2,3],
Nathalie Villa-Vialaneix[4,5], and Isneri Talavera[1]

[1] Advanced Technology Application Centre, CENATAV - Cuba
[2] Institute of Mathematics, Physics and Cybernetics - Cuba
[3] Departamento de Estadística de la Universisad de Valparaíso, CIMFAV - Chile
[4] Institut de Mathématiques de Toulouse, Université de Toulouse - France
[5] IUT de Perpignan, Département STID, Carcassonne - France

Abstract. In this paper a new nonparametric functional method is introduced for predicting a scalar random variable Y from a functional random variable X. The resulting prediction has the form of a weighted average of the training data set, where the weights are determined by the conditional probability density of X given Y, which is assumed to be Gaussian. In this way such a conditional probability density is incorporated as a key information into the estimator. Contrary to some previous approaches, no assumption about the dimensionality of $\mathbb{E}(X|Y = y)$ is required. The new proposal is computationally simple and easy to implement. Its performance is shown through its application to both simulated and real data.

1 Introduction

The fast development of instrumental analysis equipment and modern measurement devices provides huge amounts of data as high-resolution digitized functions. As a consequence, Functional Data Analysis (FDA) has become a growing research field. In the FDA setting, each individual is treated as a single entity described by a continuous real-valued function rather than by a finite-dimensional vector: functional data (FD) are then supposed to have values in an infinite dimensional space, often particularized as a Hilbert space.

An extensive review of the methods developed for FD can be found in the monograph of Ramsay and Silverman [1]. In the case of functional regression, where one intends to estimate a random scalar variable Y from a functional variable X taking values in a functional space $\mathcal{X}$, earlier works were focused on linear methods such as the functional linear model with scalar response [2–8] or the functional Partial Least Squares [9]. More recently, the problem has also been addressed nonparametrically with smoothing kernel estimates [10], multilayer perceptrons [11], and support vector regression [12, 13]. Another point of view between these two approaches is to use a semi-parametric approach, such as the SIR (Sliced Inverse Regression [14]) that has been extended to functional data (FIR) in [15–17]. In this approach, the functional regression problem is addressed

I. Bloch and R.M. Cesar, Jr. (Eds.): CIARP 2010, LNCS 6419, pp. 450–457, 2010.
© Springer-Verlag Berlin Heidelberg 2010

through the opposite regression problem i.e., the estimation of $\mathbb{E}(X|Y = y)$, by assuming that this quantity belongs to a finite dimensional subspace of $\mathcal{X}$.

In this paper, a new functional regression method to estimate $\gamma(X) = \mathbb{E}(Y|X)$ is introduced that also relies on regarding the inverse regression model $X = F(Y) + e$. Its main practical motivation arises from calibration problems in Chemometrics, specifically in spectroscopy, where some chemical variable Y (e.g., concentration) needs to be predicted from a digitized function X (e.g., an spectrum). In this setting, said "inverse" model represents the physical data generation process in which the output spectrum X is determined by the input chemical concentration Y, and e is a functional random perturbation mainly due to the measurement procedure. The specific form of the conditional density of X given Y, which is assumed to be Gaussian, is incorporated as a key information into the estimator. This regression estimate, will be refereed to as functional Density-Based Nonparametric Regression (DBNR). Unlike the FIR approach, few assumptions are required: in particular, γ does not need to be a function of a finite number of projections nor X has to follow an elliptical distribution (or any other given distribution). DBNR is computationally very easy to use.

This paper is organized as follows. Section 2 presents the functional Density-Based Nonparametric Regression method. Sections 3 and 4 illustrate the use of this approach in simulated and real data. Conclusions are given in Section 5.

2 Functional Density-Based Nonparametric Regression

2.1 Definition of DBNR in a General Setting

Let (X, Y) be a pair of random variables taking values in $\mathcal{X} \times \mathbb{R}$ where $(\mathcal{X}, \langle ., . \rangle)$ is a Hilbert space. Suppose also that n i.i.d. realizations of (X, Y) are given, denoted by $(x_i, y_i)_{i=1,\ldots,n}$. The goal is to build, from $(x_i, y_i)_i$, a way to predict a new value for Y from a given (observed) value of X. This problem is usually addressed by the estimation of the regression function $\gamma(x) = \mathbb{E}(Y|X = x)$.

The functional density-based nonparametric regression implicitly supposes that the inverse model makes sense; this inverse model is:

$$X = F(Y) + \epsilon \tag{1}$$

where ϵ is a random process (perturbation or noise) with zero mean, independent of Y, and $y \to F(y)$ is a function from $\mathbb{R}$ into $\mathcal{X}$. As was stated in Section 1, this is a common background for calibration problems, amongs others.

Additionally, the following assumptions are made: first, it exists a probability measure P_0 on $\mathcal{X}$ (not depending on y) such that the conditional probability measure of X given $Y = y$, say $P(\cdot/y)$, has a density $f(\cdot/y)$ with respect to P_0:

$$P(A/y) = \int_A f(x/y) P_0(dx)$$

for any measurable set A in $\mathcal{X}$. Furthermore, it is assumed that Y is a continuous random variable, i.e., that its distribution has a density $f_Y(y)$ (with respect to the Lebesgue measure on $\mathbb{R}$).

Under these assumptions, the regression function is:

$$\gamma(x) = \frac{\int_{\mathbb{R}} f(x/y) f_Y(y) y\, dy}{f_X(x)}, \quad \text{where} \quad f_X(x) = \int_{\mathbb{R}} f(x/y) f_Y(y)\, dy.$$

Hence, given an estimate $\widehat{f}(x/y)$ of $f(x/y)$, the following estimate of $\gamma(x)$ can be constructed from the previous equation:

$$\widehat{\gamma}(x) = \frac{\sum_{i=1}^{n} \widehat{f}(x/y_i) y_i}{\widehat{f}_X(x)}, \quad \text{where} \quad \widehat{f}_X(x) = \sum_{i=1}^{n} \widehat{f}(x/y_i). \tag{2}$$

2.2   Specification in the Gaussian Case

The general estimation scheme given in Equation (2) will be here specified for the case in which $P(\cdot/y)$ is a Gaussian measure on $\mathcal{X} = \mathcal{L}_2[0,1]$ for each $y \in \mathbb{R}$. $P(\cdot/y)$ is then supposed to have a mean function $\mu(\cdot/y) \in \mathcal{X}$ (which is then equal to $F(y)(\cdot)$ according to Equation (1)) and a covariance operator r (not depending on y), which is a Hilbert-Schmidt operator on the space $\mathcal{X}$. Then, there exists an eigenvalue decomposition of r, $(\varphi_j, \lambda_j)_{j \geq 1}$ such that $(\lambda_j)_j$ is a decreasing series of positive real numbers, $(\varphi_j)_j$ take values in $\mathcal{X}$ and $r = \sum_j \lambda_j \varphi_j \otimes \varphi_j$ where $\varphi_j \otimes \varphi_j(h) = \langle \varphi_j, h \rangle \varphi_j$ for any $h \in \mathcal{X}$.

Denote by P_0 the Gaussian measure on $\mathcal{X}$ with zero mean and covariance operator r. Assume the following usual regularity condition holds: for each $y \in \mathbb{R}$,

$$\sum_{j=1}^{\infty} \frac{\mu_j^2(y)}{\lambda_j} < \infty, \quad \text{with} \quad \mu_j(y) = \langle \mu(\cdot/y), \varphi_j \rangle.$$

Then, $P(\cdot/y)$ and P_0 are equivalent Gaussian measures, and the density $f(\cdot/y)$ has the explicit form:

$$f(x/y) = \exp\left\{ \sum_{j=1}^{\infty} \frac{\mu_j(y)}{\lambda_j} \left(x_j - \frac{\mu_j(y)}{2} \right) \right\},$$

where $x_j = \langle x, \varphi_j \rangle$ for all $j \geq 1$. This leads to the following estimation scheme for $f(x/y)$:

1. Obtain an estimate $\widehat{\mu}(\cdot/y)$ of $t \to \mu(t/y)$ for all $y \in \mathbb{R}$. This may be carried out trough any standard nonparametric regression from $\mathbb{R}$ to $\mathbb{R}$, based on the learning set $(y_i, x_i(t))_{i=1,\ldots,n}$; e.g., a smoothing kernel method.
2. Obtain estimates $(\widehat{\varphi}_j, \widehat{\lambda}_j)_j$ of the eigenfunctions and eigenvalues $(\varphi_j, \lambda_j)_j$ of the covariance r on the basis of the empirical covariance of the residuals $x_i - \widehat{\mu}(\cdot/y_i)$, $i = 1,\ldots,n$. Only the first p eigenvalues and eigenfunctions are estimated, where $p = p(n)$ is a given integer, smaller than n.
3. Estimate $f(x/y)$ by

$$\widehat{f}(x/y) = \exp\left\{ \sum_{j=1}^{p} \frac{\widehat{\mu}_j(y)}{\widehat{\lambda}_j} \left(\widehat{x}_j - \frac{\widehat{\mu}_j(y)}{2} \right) \right\} \tag{3}$$

where $\widehat{\mu}_j(y) = \langle \widehat{\mu}(\cdot/y), \widehat{\varphi}_j \rangle$ and $\widehat{x}_j = \langle x, \widehat{\varphi}_j \rangle$.

Finally, substituting (3) into (2) leads to an estimate $\widehat{\gamma}(x)$ of $\gamma(x)$. Under some technical assumptions the consistency of the DBNR method can be proved: $\lim_{n\to\infty} \widehat{\gamma}(x) =^{\mathbb{P}} \gamma(x)$.

3   A Simulation Study

The feasibility and the performance of the introduced nonparametric functional regression method are first explored through a simulation study. For comparison, results obtained by the functional Nadaraya-Watson kernel (NWK) estimator [10] are also shown.

3.1   Data Generation

The data were simulated in the following way: values for the real random variable, Y, were drawn from a uniform distribution in the interval $[0, 10]$. Then, X was generated by 4 different models or settings:

M1 $X = Ye_1 + 2Ye_2 + 3Ye_5 + 4Ye_{10} + \epsilon$
M2 $X = (\exp(Y)/\exp(10))e_1 + (Y^2/100)e_2 + (Y^3/1000)e_5 + \log(Y+1)e_{10} + \epsilon$
M3 $X = \sin(Y)e_1 + \log(Y+1)e_5 + \epsilon$
M4 $X = \alpha \exp\left(\frac{Y}{10}e_1\right) + \epsilon$

where $(e_i)_{i\geq 1}$ is the trigonometric basis of $\mathcal{X} = \mathcal{L}^2([0,1])$ (i.e., $e_{2k-1} = \sqrt{2}\cos(2\pi kt)$, and $e_{2k} = \sqrt{2}\sin(2\pi kt)$), and ϵ a Gaussian process independent of Y with zero mean and covariance operator $\Gamma_e = \sum_{j\geq 1} \frac{1}{j} e_j \otimes e_j$. More precisely, ϵ was simulated by using a truncation of Γ_e, $\Gamma_e(s,t) \simeq \sum_{j=1}^{q} \frac{1}{j} e_j(t)e_j(s)$ with $q = 500$.

A sample of size $n_L = 300$ was simulated for training and a sample of size $n_T = 200$ for testing. Figure 1 gives examples of X obtained for model **M3** for three different values of y and of the underlying (non noisy) function, $F(y)(\cdot)$. In this example, the simulated data have a high level of noise so that the regression estimation is a rather hard statistical task.

3.2   Simulation Results

To apply the DBNR method, the discretized functions X were approximated by a continuous function using a functional basis expansion. Specifically, the data were approximated using 128 B-spline basis functions of order 4, as it is shown in Figure 1. The conditional mean $\mu(\cdot/y)$ was estimated by a kernel smoothing in which the bandwidth parameter h was selected by 10-fold cross-validation minimizing the mean squared error (MSE) criterion. A similar procedure was used to select the parameter p (number of eigenvalues and eigenfunctions used in (3)).

Finally, DBNR performance was compared with those obtained by the functional NWK estimate with two kinds of metrics for the kernel: the usual $\mathcal{L}^2$-norm and the PCA based semi-metric norm (see [10] for further details about these

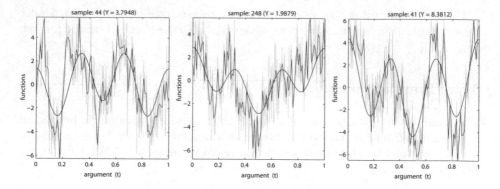

Fig. 1. True function, $F(y)(\cdot)$ (smooth continuous line), simulated data, X, (gray rough line) and approximation of X using B-splines (rough black line) in **M3** for three different values of y

Table 1. RMSE for all the methods and all generating models

Model	DBNR	NWK (PCA)	NWK ($\mathcal{L}^2$)
M1	0.08	0.10	0.09
M2	1.47	1.60	1.77
M3	1.79	1.79	2.00
M4	0.94	2.16	1.91

methods). The resulting root mean squared errors (RMSE) are presented in Table 1. The results show that DBNR is a good alternative to common NWK methods. Indeed, DBNR outperforms NWK methods in all the the cases considered in this simulation study that includes both linear (**M1**) and nonlinear (**M2 − M4**) models.

Figures 2 and 3 show how the method performs for each step of the estimation scheme (described in Section 2.2) for the model **M3**. In particular, Figure 2 gives the result of the first step by displaying the true value and the estimate of $F(y)(\cdot)$ for various values of y (top) and the true value and the estimate of $F(\cdot)(t)$ for various values of t (bottom). The results are very satisfactory given the fact that the data have a high level of noise (which is stressed on in the bottom of the figure): a minor estimation problem appears at the boundaries of $F(\cdot)(t)$, which is a known drawback of the kernel smoothing method. Also, those estimates are smoother than the estimates of $F(y)(\cdot)$: this can be explained by the fact that the kernel estimator is used regarding y and not regarding t, but this aspect can be improved in the future.

Figure 3 shows the results of the steps 2-3 of the estimation scheme: the estimated eigendecomposition of r is compared to the true one and finally, the predicted value for Y are compared to the true ones, both on training and test sets. The estimation of the eigendecomposition is, once again very satisfactory given the high level of noise, and the comparison between training and test sets show that the method does not overfit the data.

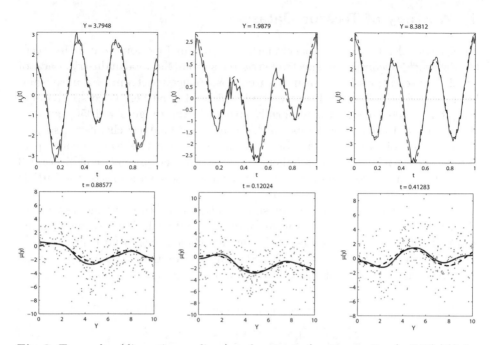

Fig. 2. True value (discontinuous lines) and estimate (continuous lines) of $F(y)(\cdot)$ for various values of y (top) and true value and estimate of $F(\cdot)(t)$ for various values of t (bottom) in model **M3**. The dots (bottom) are the simulated data, $X(t)$.

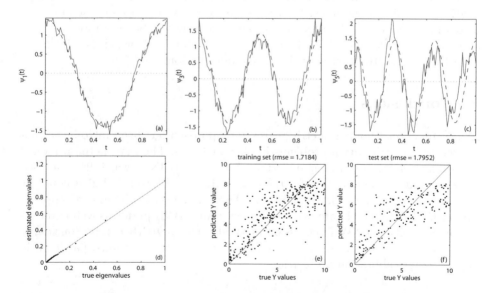

Fig. 3. Model **M3**: (a-c)True (dashed line) and estimated eigenfunctions (continuous line), (d) true and estimated eigenvalues and (d-e) predicted vs. true Y values for training and test sets.

4   A Study of Tecator Dataset

DBNR was also tested on a benchmark data set for functional data: the Tecator dataset[1]. It consists of spectrometric data from the food industry. Each of the 215 observations is the near infrared absorbance spectrum of a meat sample recorded on a Tecator Infratec Food and Feed Analyzer. Each spectrum is sampled at 100 wavelengths uniformly spaced in the range 850–1050 nm. The composition of each meat sample is determined by analytic chemistry, so percentages of moisture, fat and protein are associated in this way to each spectrum. This problem is more challenging than the one presented in Section 3 where the data were generated to fulfill exactly the conditions of the DBNR model.

The whole data set was randomly split 100 times into training and test sets of almost the same size. The splits were randomly built such that also the training and test set were equally represented over the whole range of fat content.

Table 2 reports the mean of the MSE (and its standard deviation) over the 100 divisions both for DBNR and NWK methods.

Table 2. Prediction results on Tecator dataset

Model	DBNR	NWK (PCA)	NWK ($\mathcal{L}^2$)
MSE	1.91 (0.41)	9.1 (2.1)	8.9 (2.1)

Results obtained on Tecator by DBNR are the best in the sense of minimum MSE among all the methods. In [10] results based on the use of a semi-metric involving the second order derivatives (which is known to be useful for this data set) were also reported. A MSE of 3.5 was also obtained, which is still larger than the use of DBNR without derivative information.

5   Conclusions

A new functional nonparametric regression approach has been introduced motivated by the calibration problems in chemometrics. The new method, named functional density-based nonparametric regression (DBNR) was fully described under a Gaussian assumption for the distribution of X given Y but it could be extended to other kinds of distributions. The simulation study and the application of DBNR to a real data set have shown that DBNR performs well and outperforms functional NWK regression methods. Thus, DBNR can be considered a promising alternative to existing functional regression methods, particularly appealing for calibration problems.

---

[1] Data are available on statlib at
http://lib.stat.cmu.edu/datasets/tecator; see [18].

References

1. Ramsay, J., Silverman, B.: Functional Data Analysis, 2nd edn. Springer, New York (2005)
2. Ramsay, J., Dalzell, C.: Some tools for functional data analysis. Journal of the Royal Statistical Society, Series B 53, 539–572 (1991)
3. Hastie, T., Mallows, C.: A discussion of a statistical view of some chemometrics regression tools by I. E. Frank and J. H. Friedman. Technometrics 35, 140–143 (1993)
4. Marx, B.D., Eilers, P.H.: Generalized linear regression on sampled signals and curves: a p-spline approach. Technometrics 41, 1–13 (1999)
5. Cardot, H., Ferraty, F., Sarda, P.: Functional linear model. Statistics and Probability Letter 45, 11–22 (1999)
6. Cardot, H., Ferraty, F., Sarda, P.: Spline estimators for the functional linear model. Statistica Sinica 13, 571–591 (2003)
7. Cardot, H., Crambes, C., Kneip, A., Sarda, P.: Smoothing spline estimators in functional linear regression with errors in variables. Comput. Statist. Data Anal. 51, 4832–4848 (2007)
8. Crambes, C., Kneip, A., Sarda, P.: Smoothing splines estimators for functional linear regression. The Annals of Statistics (2008)
9. Preda, C., Saporta, G.: PLS regression on stochastic processes. Comput. Statist. Data Anal. 48, 149–158 (2005)
10. Ferraty, F., Vieu, P.: Nonparametric Functional Data Analysis: Theory and Practice. Springer Series in Statistics. Springer, New York (2006)
11. Rossi, F., Conan-Guez, B.: Functional multi-layer perceptron: a nonlinear tool for functional data anlysis. Neural Networks 18(1), 45–60 (2005)
12. Preda, C.: Regression models for functional data by reproducing kernel Hilbert space methods. J. Stat. Plan. Infer. 137, 829–840 (2007)
13. Hernández, N., Biscay, R.J., Talavera, I.: Support vector regression methods for functional data. In: Rueda, L., Mery, D., Kittler, J. (eds.) CIARP 2007. LNCS, vol. 4756, pp. 564–573. Springer, Heidelberg (2007)
14. Li, K.: Sliced inverse regression for dimension reduction. J. Am. Stat. Assoc. 86, 316–327 (1991)
15. Dauxois, J., Ferré, L., Yao, A.: Un modèle semi-paramétrique pour variable aléatoire hilbertienne. C.R. Acad. Sci. Paris 327(I), 6947–6952 (2001)
16. Ferré, L., Yao, A.: Functional sliced inverse regression analysis. Statistics 37, 475–488 (2003)
17. Ferré, L., Villa, N.: Multi-layer perceptron with functional inputs: an inverse regression approach. Scandinavian Journal of Statistics 33, 807–823 (2006)
18. Thodberg, H.: A review of bayesian neural network with an application to near infrared spectroscopy. IEEE Transaction on Neural Networks 7(1), 56–72 (1996)

Feature Extraction Using Circular Statistics Applied to Volcano Monitoring

César San-Martin[1,4], Carlos Melgarejo[1,2], Claudio Gallegos [1,2], Gustavo Soto[3],
Millaray Curilem[4], and Gustavo Fuentealba[5]

[1] Information Processing Laboratory, Department of Electrical Engineering,
Universidad de La Frontera. Casilla 54-D Temuco, Chile
csmarti@ufro.cl
[2] Observatorio Volcanológico de los Andes del Sur Dinamarca 691, Temuco, Chile
cmelgarejo@sernageomin.cl, cgallegos@sernageomin.cl
[3] Center for Mathematical Model, Universidad de Chile Casilla 412-3, Santiago, Chile
gsoto@dim.uchile.cl
[4] Department of Electrical Engineering, Universidad de La Frontera. Casilla 54-D
Temuco, Chile
millaray@ufro.cl
[5] Department of Physics, Universidad de La Frontera. Casilla 54-D Temuco, Chile
gustavo@ufro.cl

Abstract. In this work, the applicability of the circular statistics to feature extraction on seismic signals is presented. The seismic signals are captured from Llaima Volcano, located in Southern Andes Volcanic Zone at 38°40'S 71°40'W. Typically, the seismic signals can be divided in long-period, tremor, and volcano-tectonic earthquakes. The seismic signals are time-segmented using a rectangular window of 1 minute of duration. In each segment, the instantaneous phase is calculated using the Hilbert Transform, and then, one feature is obtained. Thus, the principal hypothesis of this work is that the instantaneous phase can be assumed as a circular random variable in $[0, 2\pi)$ interval. A second feature is obtained using the wavelet transform due to the fact that seismic signals present high energy located in low frequency. Then, in the range 1.55 and 3.11 Hz the wavelet coefficients were obtained and their mean energy is calculated as the second feature. Real seismic data represented using this two features are classified using a linear discriminant with a 92.5% of correct recognition rate.

Keywords: seismic classifications, feature extraction, circular statistic, wavelet transform.

1 Introduction

An adequate study of the activity of an active volcano requires the use of indirect methods for evaluating information related to the dynamics of magma [1]. The scientific literature has shown that volcanic activity can generate a wide range of seismic signals [2]. The study of the waveforms of these signals differentiate the

I. Bloch and R.M. Cesar, Jr. (Eds.): CIARP 2010, LNCS 6419, pp. 458–466, 2010.
© Springer-Verlag Berlin Heidelberg 2010

various types of source mechanisms of earthquakes [3]. Until the late twentieth century, most studies were restricted to the spectral analysis and its variation over time. Today, new processing techniques are being incorporated into the analysis, in an attempt to automate the identification of the most important patterns of seismic signals. The main structure used to classify them considers a preprocessing stage and a classification stage.

The first one depurates the signals and performs its spectrum, amplitude (energy) and waveform feature extraction [4]. [5] proposed a linear predictive coding to extract spectral features and a parameterizations of the signal to extract information about the waveform. In [6] autocorrelation functions obtained by the FFT represent the spectral content and the short-term average to long-term average ratio (LTA/STA) relationship is used to distinguish between peaks and signals of long duration, often with similar spectral content. Some studies incorporate many frequency, amplitude and waveform features and use genetic algorithms to search a representative feature subset that improves the classifier performance [7,4]. Other methods are the wavelet transform [8,9], cross correlation methods [10] and hidden Markov models [11].

As seismic signals are inherently nonlinear and nonstationary [12] techniques such as artificial neural networks (ANN) [13] are being incorporated to perform classification. In many works, ANNs have outperformed traditional methods of analysis. ANN were used to predict the evolution of the seismicity of the Vesuvius, Campi Flegrei, Etna and Hawaii volcanoes [14] or to discriminate between local earthquakes and other Mt Vesuvius volcanic signals [5] and also for classifying transient signals representative of the Montserrat Volcano [6]. Some studies show that support vector machines (SVM) [15] have performed better than ANN [16]. [17] used spectral characteristics of four types of tremor of the Etna volcano and conducted a comparative study in which the SVM outperformed the ANN. [18] obtained the same result to classify three different seismic events of the Stromboli volcano.

It should be noted in the previous studies that the methods of analysis are difficult to generalize and every work is specialized in a certain type of patterns related to specific volcanoes. In this paper, we consider the Llaima Volcano, located in Southern Andes Volcanic Zone at 38°40'S 71°40'W, at Chile. In particular, the applicability of circular statistics as feature extraction is studied. This kind of signal processing technique has received little attention in the literature maybe due to the representability of the original signal by the instantaneous phase, estimated by the use of Hilbert transform. Here, a feature vectors based on circular summary statistics taken from the instantaneous phase of the seismic signals, and the mean energy of the wavelet coefficients are used to distinguish among different seismic event. In this work, we address discrimination among long period events (LP) and volcano tectonic (VT) earthquakes from three components of Llaima volcano.

This paper has been organized as follow. In section 2 the Llaima volcano description is introduced. In section 3, mathematical concepts and their application

Fig. 1. Llaima volcano located in the South of Chile

to seismic signal are presented. In section 4, feature extraction proposed method applied to real data is shown. Finally, the conclusion and future work are presented in section 5.

2   Volcano Monitoring

Llaima volcano is located in Southern Andes Volcanic Zone at 38°40'S 71°40'W. It is located 82 km northeast of Temuco and 663 km southeast of Santiago de Chile. Llaima volcano is one of the largest and more active volcanoes in Southamerica. Llaima volcano is a stratovolcano, a steep sloped cone composed of alternating layer of solidified ash, hardened lava and rocks ejected by previous eruptions. It has frequent eruptions but fortunately moderate explosive eruptions with occasional lava flows. One of the most recent eruption occurred in January 1, 2008, producing a column of smoke skyward, released a plume of sulfur dioxide and forcing the evacuation of dozens of tourists from volcano's base. On July 1, 2008, another eruption forced the evacuation of hundreds of people from nearby villages. An eruption occurred on April 5, 2009, with pyroclastic flows, ash and lava seen on the slopes.

The goal of volcano monitoring is allowing to know what is happening in the volcano. This implies the study of the past activity and keep a close watch on any current eruptions. The data are obtained from stations near the volcano that register seismic information, deformation and other events in real time. The data are collected and sent to the Southern Andes Volcano Observatory (OVDAS) located in Temuco, where the specialists analyze the information. OVDAS depends on the Servicio Nacional de Geología y Minería (SERNAGEOMIN), the public statement in charge to carry out the actions based on the results of volcano information analysis.

2.1   Seismic Signals

Volcanic activity generates seismic events whose name and nature are common to all of them. However each volcano has its own seismic activity, that is, the characteristics of the events are particular. In this paper, we address discrimination among long period events (LP) and volcano tectonic (VT) earthquakes from three components of Llaima volcano. The data used have been collected using a three-component wide-band seismic sensor located in south-western of the Llaima volcano (Lave station), around 7.4 km from the vent. The seismometric used is the Oyogeospace SEIS-Monitor. The Lave station operates in continuous registration mode with 16 bit at 50 sample per second. All the events have been classified by an expert of OVDAS.

VT event is an earthquake originated in the center of a volcano. The VT event is associated to the fracture of solid of the volcano or the conduits of fluid ascent. The temporal signal present high amplitude with exponential decay with a lower time duration than LP event. In frequency domain, the VT signals presents a component higher that 8 Hz initially, but the most important range corresponds to the 6 - 8 Hz. In Llaima volcano they are very important because they are present in volcanic eruptions principally. Due to this, the amount of VT events is lower than LP, and in our database we have only 85 samples of VT events. The principal disadvantage in VT detection is the low possibility of being identified due to the presence of other events or noise.

LP events are very important to be detected because the type of LP allows identifying particular families of seismic signals which allow to know more precisely what is happening inside the volcano structure. The principal characteristic of an LP event is the high energy located in low frequency, typically below 3 Hz. From this characteristic intuitively it is possible to obtain this feature using a bandpass filter in order to estimate the energy in this frequency range.

In order to identify LP and VT events we built a pattern with two features based on circular statistic and wavelet transform applied to the seismic signal. In the next section we show in detail the procedure to obtain each feature.

3   Mathematical Background

In this section we briefly review the statistics moments of circularly distributed signals, wavelet transform and their applications to real seismic data.

3.1   The Analytic Signal

In order to obtain the analytic signal from sampled real data, the Hilbert transform [19] is used. The analytic signal represent all real-valuated signals as complex signals, which turn out to have especially attractive properties for signal processing. Let $x(t)$ be a signal in the time domain t. The analytic signal $x_a(t)$ is given by:

$$x_a(t) = x(t) + j\mathcal{H}\{x\}(t), \tag{1}$$

where $\mathcal{H}\{x\}(t)$ is the Hilbert transform of $x(t)$ given by [20]:

$$\mathcal{H}\{x\}(t) = \text{p.v.} \int_{-\infty}^{\infty} \frac{x(\tau)}{t - \tau} \, d\tau, \tag{2}$$

where $\mathcal{H}$ is the Hilbert transform operator. Because of the pole at $t = \tau$, the Cauchy principal value p.v. of the integral is used. The analytic signal of (1) can be expressed in the form:

$$x_a(t) = \psi(t) \exp(j\theta(t)), \tag{3}$$

where $\psi(t) = |x_a(t)|$ is the amplitude envelope and $\theta(t) = \arg(x_a(t))$, the instantaneous phase of the signal $x(t)$, with $\theta(t) \in [0, 2\pi)$. Thus, from this analytic signal, it is possible to define in a unique way the concepts of instantaneous amplitude and instantaneous phase.

3.2   Circular Statistics

The key assumption of this work is representing the seismic signals by features extracted from their random circular variables.

Circular statistics is similar to linear statistics [21], but in this case, sample trigonometric moments of a random circular variable are estimated from a well-known probability density function. Let $\Theta = \{\theta_n\}$ be a set of instantaneous phase values, where $n = 1, ..., N$, then the pth-order sample trigonometric moment is given by:

$$\mu_p = \frac{1}{N} \sum_{n=1}^{N} \exp(jp\theta_n). \tag{4}$$

As with linear statistics, measures of spread and symmetry, i.e., variance and skewness, can be defined in terms of sample trigonometric moments. Then, the sample circular variance of the data set Θ is defined as:

$$\sigma^2 = 1 - |\mu_1|, \tag{5}$$

The sample circular skewness is defined as:

$$\gamma = \frac{|\mu_2| \sin(\arg(\mu_2) - 2\arg(\mu_1))}{(\sigma^2)^{\frac{3}{2}}}, \tag{6}$$

where $\arg(\mu_p)$ denotes the angle of the (complex valued) p^{th}-order sample trigonometric moment ($p = 1, 2$), and σ^2 is as defined in (5). Circular kurtosis, a measure

of peakedness in the circular density, can also be defined with sample trigonometric moments as follows:

$$\kappa = \frac{|\mu_2|\cos(\arg(\mu_2) - 2\arg(\mu_1)) - |\mu_1|^4}{(\sigma^2)^2}. \tag{7}$$

A comprehensive description of trigonometric moments and other statistics for
circular data can be found in [22].

3.3   Wavelet Transform

Briefly, the discrete WT can reconstruct any signal $x(t)$ by the formula:

$$x(t) = \sum_m \sum_n <x, \psi_{m,n}> \psi_{m,n}(t), \tag{8}$$

where $\psi_{m,n}(t) = a^{-m/2}\psi(a^{-m}t - nb)$ is the wavelet function and a and b are
the scale and shift parameters respectively. The wavelet coefficients are given by
$<x, \psi_{m,n}>$ and the multi resolution decomposition is obtained when $a = 2$ and
$b = 1$. In this case we have an orthogonal decomposition. Two sequences exist
that satisfies:

$$h_n = <\phi_{0,0}, \phi_{-1,n}>, \phi(t) = 2^{1/2}\sum_n h_n\phi(2t - n), \tag{9}$$

$$g_n = <\psi_{0,0}, \phi_{-1,n}>, \phi(t) = 2^{1/2}\sum_n g_n\phi(2t - n) \tag{10}$$

where h_n and g_n are the low and high pass filters with 0.25 cutoff frequency when
1 is the sampling rate. Then, the approximation an detail wavelet coefficients
for the level k with sampling rate of 2^{-k} are respectively:

$$A_k^{[x(t)]}(t) = \sum_n 2^{-k} <x(t), \psi(2^{-k}t - n)> \psi(2^{-k}t - n), \tag{11}$$

$$D_k^{[x(t)]}(t) = \sum_n 2^{-k} <x(t), \psi(2^{-k}t - n)> \phi(2^{-k}t - n), \tag{12}$$

that can be calculated using (9) and (10). In our case, the wavelet filter used
corresponds to the Daubechies with 10 taps, the sampling rate is 50 samples per
second, and the detail for k = 4 corresponds to the frequency range of interest,
i.e., between 1.55 and 3.11 Hz. Calculating the power of this coefficient, the mean
energy in this band is obtained in the form:

$$E = \int (D_4^{[x(t)]}(t))^2 dt. \tag{13}$$

By the use of multi resolution analysis [23] is possible to obtain a band pass
component and then, obtain the energy over the wavelet coefficient in the corresponding level.

4   Results

Real seismic data was captured from Llaima volcano between May 2009 and June 2009 and used to test the performance of the proposed method. A database with 2509 samples has been built, containing 404 samples of LP events, 85 of VT events in one component and 404 no-event signals. A sample corresponds to data interval of 1 minute of registered data non-continuous between intervals captured from the vertical, north-south, and east-west components denoted as Z, N-S, and E-W, respectively. The data has been labeled by expert from OVDAS. In this database, only LP and VT events are presented.

For each segment a pattern $\mathbf{x}$ is built using equation (4) and (13) forming the pattern $\mathbf{x} = (u_1, E)$. Then, the database contains the 404 values $\mathbf{x}_1, ..., \mathbf{x}_{404}$ for LP, 404 for no-events and 85 for VT events. In this case, only the Z component is considered. In Fig. 2 we illustrate the scatter plot for all data set for LP, VT and no-event patterns. Clearly, the VT events present a separation from LP events and no-events signals considering only the first circular moment. As a preliminary approach to the classification problem and based on the distribution of the classes shown in Fig. 2, a linear classifier was designed. Its performance reached 100% for VT identification and more than 90% for LP identification. More sophisticated classifiers will be evaluated during the research ongoing.

The discrimination between LP and no-events is given only by wavelet energy. But it is possible to include the first circular moment in order to improve the performance of the classifier. Table 1 presents the results using only wavelet energy and the incorporation of the first circular moment in three components.

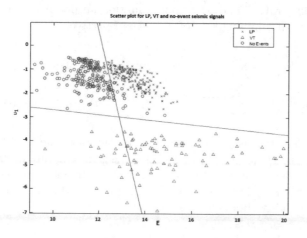

Fig. 2. Scatter plot for LP, VT and no-events patterns using wavelet energy and circular statistic

Table 1. The correct classification rate for LP and no-events identification

Component	% CC with $\mathbf{x} = E$	% CC with $\mathbf{x} = (u_1, E)$
Z	87.95	94.05
N-S	94.14	93.56
E-W	78.79	90.01

5   Conclusions and Future Work

In this paper we applied the circular statistic as a feature extraction technique to the seismic signal of the Llaima volcano. This implies that the instantaneous phase of seismic signal can be considered as circular random variable in the $[0, 2\pi)$ range. The first circular moment allows discriminating clearly the VT events from others with a high performance. For the case of LP events, a combination between energy located between 1.55 and 3.11 Hz is improved when the first circular moment is added. In fact, the correct identification increase from 86.96% to 92.54%. Future work include more extensive tests with a larger database, the evaluation of this feature extraction process to on line operation and to evaluate other classifier using neural networks among others.

Acknowledgments

The authors gratefully acknowledge to OVDAS Sernageomin for supplied the seismic data of Llaima Volcano, Temuco, CHILE.

References

1. Shick, R.: Volcanic Tremor- Source Mechanism And Correlation With Eruptive Activity. Natural Hazard, 125–144 (1988)
2. Minakami, T.: Seismology of Volcanoes in Japan. Physical Volcanology. Developments In Solid Earth Geophysics 6 (1982)
3. Chouet, B.: Volcano Seismology As An Approach To Eruption Forecasting. Submitted To Nature, Draft Of (1993)
4. Orlic, N., Loncaric, S.: Earthquake-explosion discrimination using genetic algorithm-based boosting approach. Computers and Geosciences 36(2), 179–185 (2010)
5. Scarpetta, S., Giudicepietro, F., Ezin, E.C., Petrosino, S., Del Pezzo, E., Martín, M., Marinaro, M.: Automatic Classification of Seismic Signals at Mt Vesuvius Volcano, Italy, using Neural Networks. Bulletin of the Seismological Society of America 95(1), 185–196 (2005)
6. Langer, H., Falsaperla, S., Powell, T., Thompson, G.: Automatic classification and a-posteriori analysis of seismic event identification at Soufrière Hills volcano, Monserrat. Journal of Volcanology and Geothermal Research 153, 1–10 (2006)
7. Curilem, G.M.S., Vergara, J., Fuentealba, G., Acuña, G., Chacón, M.: Classification of Seismic Signals at Villarrica Volcano (Chile) using Neural Networks and Genetic Algorithms. Journal of Volcanology and Geothermal Research 180(1), 1–8 (2009)

8. Gendron, P., Nandram, B.: An empirical Bayes estimator of seismic events using wavelet packet bases. Journal of Agricultural, Biological, and Environmental Statistics 6(3), 379–402 (2001)

9. Erlebacher, G., Yuen, D.A.: A wavelet toolkit for visualization and analysis of large data sets. Earthquake Research, Pure Appl. Geophys. 161, 2215–2229 (2004)

10. Lesage, P., Glangeaud, F., Mars, J.: Applications of autoregressive models and time-frequency analysis to the study of volcanic tremor and long-period events. Journal of Volcanology and Geothermal Research 114, 391–417 (2002)

11. Ibanez, J.M., Benitez, C., Gutierrez, L.A., Cortés, G., García-Yeguas, A., Alguacil, G.: The classification of seismo-volcanic signals using Hidden Markov Models as applied to the Stromboli and Etna volcanoes. Journal of Volcanology and Geothermal 187(3-4), 218–226 (2009)

12. Dowla, F.U.: Neural networks in seismic discrimination. In: Husebye, E.S., Dainty, A.M. (eds.) NATO ASI (Advanced Science Institutes). Series E, vol. 303, pp. 777–789. Kluwer, Dordrecht (1995)

13. Bishop, C.: Neural Networks for Pattern Recognition. Oxford University Press, Inc., New York (1995)

14. Luongo, G., Marandola, C., Mazzarella, A.: Neural forecasting of seismicity and ground displacements in different volcanic areas. Journal of Volcanology and Geothermal Research 130, 133–146 (2004)

15. Vapnik, V.: The Nature of Statistical Learning Theory. Springer, New York (1995)

16. Cherkassky, V., Krasnopolsky, V., Solomatine, D.P., Valdes, J.: Computational intelligence in earth sciences and environmental applications: Issues and challenges. Neural Networks 19(2), 113–121 (2006)

17. Langer, H., Falsaperla, S., Masotti, M., Campanini, R., Spampinato, S., Messina, A.: Synopsis of supervised and unsupervised pattern classification techniques applied to volcanic tremor data at Mt Etna. Italy Geophysical Journal International 178(2), 1132–1144 (2009)

18. Giacco, F., Esposito, A.M., Scarpetta, S., Giudicepietro, F., Marinaro, M.: Support Vector Machines and MLP for automatic classification of seismic signals at Stromboli volcano. In: Proceeding of the 2009 conference on Neural Nets WIRN 2009: Proceedings of the 19th Italian Workshop on Neural Nets. Frontiers in Artificial Intelligence and Applications, vol. 204, pp. 116–123 (2009)

19. Nunes, J.-C., Naït-Ali, A.: Hilbert transform-based ECG modeling. Biomedical Engineering 39, 133–137 (2005)

20. Cohen, L.: Time-frequency analysis. Prentice-Hall, Englewood Cliffs (1995)

21. Fisher, N.I.: Statistical Analysis of Circular Data. Cambridge University Press, Cambridge (1995)

22. Jammalamadaka, S.R., SenGupta, A.: Topics in circular statistics. World Scientific Publishing, Singapore (2001)

23. Mallat, S.: A wavelet tour of signal processing, 2nd edn. Academic Press, London (1999)

Improving the Accuracy of the Optimum-Path Forest Supervised Classifier for Large Datasets

César Castelo-Fernández[1,*], Pedro J. de Rezende[1,**],
Alexandre X. Falcão[1,***], and João Paulo Papa[2,†]

[1] Institute of Computing, State University of Campinas - UNICAMP,
Campinas, Brazil,
ccastelo@liv.ic.unicamp.br,{rezende,afalcao}@ic.unicamp.br
[2] Department of Computing, São Paulo State University - UNESP,
Baurú, Brazil,
papa@fc.unesp.br

Abstract. In this work, a new approach for supervised pattern recognition is presented which improves the learning algorithm of the Optimum-Path Forest classifier (OPF), centered on detection and elimination of outliers in the training set. Identification of outliers is based on a penalty computed for each sample in the training set from the corresponding number of imputable false positive and false negative classification of samples. This approach enhances the accuracy of OPF while still gaining in classification time, at the expense of a slight increase in training time.

Keywords: Optimum-Path Forest Classifier, Outlier Detection, Supervised Classification, Learning Algorithm.

1 Introduction

Pattern recognition aims at the capacity of classifying a pattern based in its inherent characteristics, represented as a feature vector (i.e., a point in a higher dimensional space) [5]. Usually, this task is divided into two phases, namely, training and classification. During the training phase the classifier learns the distribution of the data in the feature space through a subset of the dataset, inferring rules which then allow for predicting the correct classes of unknown

* Supported by Capes – Coordenação de Aperfeiçoamento de Pessoal de Nível Superior – Grant # 01-P-04388/2010.
** Partially supported by CNPq – Conselho Nacional de Desenvolvimento Científico e Tecnológico – Grants # 472504/2007-0, 483177/2009-1 and FAPESP – Fundação de Amparo à Pesquisa do Estado de São Paulo – Grant #07/52015-0 and a Grant from FAEPEX/UNICAMP.
*** Partially supported by CNPq Grants # 481556/2009-5 (ARPIS), 302617/2007-8 and FAPESP Grant #2007/52015-0.
† Partially supported by CNPq Grant # 481556/2009-5 (ARPIS) and FAPESP Grant # 2009/16206-1.

I. Bloch and R.M. Cesar, Jr. (Eds.): CIARP 2010, LNCS 6419, pp. 467–475, 2010.
© Springer-Verlag Berlin Heidelberg 2010

data. Several methods also include a learning phase, based on two labeled sets with training and evaluating samples, which are usually selected at random, with the goal of improving the performance of the classifier. This phase employs the evaluating set as a pseudo-test of the quality of the training set and for its improvement.

Support Vector Machines (SVM) [9], a largely used classification method, is formulated as an optimization problem that seeks to determine the hyperplane which best splits the data. Also, given non-separable data, a prior mapping to a higher dimensional space is required, assuming that the mapped data becomes separable. SVM's main deficiency is that, depending on the size of the training set, too much computational time is needed before convergence to a solution occurs. This lack of efficiency for large datasets can render SVM infeasible in these cases. Furthermore, the assumption of class-separability in higher-dimensional space may not always hold [4].

The Optimum-Path Forest classifier (OPF) [8] is a graph-based technique which models classification problems as optimum-path searches in graphs derived from an adjacency relation between samples in a given feature space (a complete relation in the case of this paper). Class representatives (prototypes) are chosen among the training samples and used to classify the remaining samples based on lengths of paths on the graph. This method has as an advantage a very low computational training cost, since it does not have to optimize parameters. Furthermore, it can deal with non-separable data since its formulation is based on multiple prototypes that represent the various classes.

As showed in [8], OPF can attain an accuracy as high as SVM's, while keeping the training time much lower. Those results show that OPF is the best choice for several classification problems, mainly in the case of large datasets. However, a disadvantage of the original learning algorithm proposed in [8], is that it does not attempt to eliminate outliers in the training set which may cause classification errors.

The main contribution of the present work is the development of a learning algorithm for the OPF classifier focused on the detection and elimination of outliers from the training set. This paper describes the OPF classifier in Section 2, introduces the new method in Section 3, shows the experiments in Section 4 and Section 5 brings together the conclusions.

2   Optimum-Path Forest Classifier

For the sake of completion, the OPF classifier will be briefly described. For more details, see [8].

Let Z_1, Z_2 and Z_3 be the disjoint training, evaluating and testing sets, randomly chosen from a dataset Z, such that $Z = Z_1 \cup Z_2 \cup Z_3$. Let $\lambda(s)$ be a function which maps each sample $s \in Z$ to its correct class $i, i = 1, \ldots, c$. Let $\vec{v}(s)$ denote the feature vector of sample s, computed by some feature extractor v and $d(s,t)$ denote the distance between s and t (e.g. euclidean distance).

A specially chosen subset $S \subset Z_1$, whose elements are called *prototypes*, contains the samples responsible for classifying each $t \in Z \setminus S$. This classification is accomplished by determining, for each t, which $s \in S$ is the most closely (strongly) connected to t and setting the class of t to be that of s.

The strategy of the OPF classifier is to first obtain an optimum discrete partition of the feature space of Z_1, so that it becomes possible to classify every $t \in Z_2 \cup Z_3$ based on that partition, in an incremental way.

Let (Z_1, A) be the complete graph which represents the training set, where to each sample $s \in Z_1$ corresponds a node and such that to each edge $\langle s, t \rangle$ is assigned a cost equal to $d(s, t)$. Let $f(\pi_t^{s_1})$ be a function which evaluates the cost of the path $\pi_t^{s_1} = \langle s_1 = t_1, t_2, \ldots, t_n = t \rangle$, starting at some $s_1 \in S$ and ending at $t \in Z_1$. A path π_t^s is considered optimum if, for any other path $\pi_t^{s'}$, $f(\pi_t^s) \leq f(\pi_t^{s'})$. The union of optimum-paths for all $t \in Z_1$ forms a forest (an acyclic graph).

The optimum path forest is computed using the Image Foresting Transform algorithm [6] by basically solving the following optimization problem:

$$C(t) = \min_{\forall s \in S} \{ f_{max}(\pi_t^s) \} \tag{2.1}$$

which gives an optimum path-cost $C(t)$ for each $t \in Z_1$ of an optimum path, denoted π_t^* for short, which starts at some $s \in S$. The function $f_{max}(\pi_t^s)$ computes the maximum edge cost along the path π_t^s.

Algorithm 1 shows the general procedure to compute the Optimum-Path Forest [8].

Algorithm 1. – OPF-Algorithm

INPUT: Training set Z_1, λ-labeled prototypes $S \subset Z_1$.
OUTPUT: Optimum-Path Forest P (predecessor map), path-cost map C and label map L and a list Z_1' of the training nodes ordered by their path-cost.
AUXILIARY: Priority queue Q and cost variable cst.

1. **For each** $s \in Z_1 \backslash S$ **do** $C(s) \leftarrow +\infty$.
2. **For each** $s \in S$ **do**
3. $\quad$ $C(s) \leftarrow 0$, $P(s) \leftarrow nil$
4. $\quad$ $L(s) \leftarrow \lambda(s)$, insert s into Q.
5. **While** Q is not empty **do**
6. $\quad$ Remove from Q a sample s with minimum $C(s)$ and insert s in Z_1'.
7. $\quad$ **For each** $t \in Z_1$ such that $C(t) > C(s)$ **do**
8. $\quad\quad$ Compute $cst \leftarrow \max\{C(s), d(s, t)\}$.
9. $\quad\quad$ **If** $cst < C(t)$ **then**
10. $\quad\quad\quad$ **If** $C(t) \neq +\infty$ **then** remove t from Q.
11. $\quad\quad\quad$ $P(t) \leftarrow s$, $L(t) \leftarrow L(s)$ and $C(t) \leftarrow cst$.
12. $\quad\quad\quad$ Insert t in Q.

The training process (i.e., finding the set S of prototypes) consists of computing a Minimum Spanning Tree (MST) on Z_1 and, for each edge $\{s, t\}$ of the MST, if $\lambda(s) \neq \lambda(t)$ then s and t are marked as prototypes.

In the classification phase, for every sample $t \in Z_3$ all possible paths from each $s \in Z_1$ to t are computed and the optimum one, π_t^*, is chosen. This path can easily be identified by incrementally evaluating the optimum cost $C(t)$ as follows:

$$C(t) = \min_{\forall s \in Z_1'} \{\max\{C(s), d(s,t)\}\}. \tag{2.2}$$

The (first) role of Z_1' is to speed up the evaluation of Equation 2.2 which can halt when $\max\{C(s), d(s,t)\} < C(p)$, for a node p whose position in Z_1' succeeds the position of s [7].

The learning phase consists of performing, after the training process, the classification of each sample in Z_2 through the method just described and, subsequently, swapping each incorrectly classified sample from Z_2 for a randomly chosen sample from $Z_1 \setminus S$.

3   Optimum-Path Forest Classifier with Outliers Detection: OPF-OD

Outliers in the training set might be identified through two kinds of errors: when a sample is attributed an incorrect label (false positive - FP) and, when a classifying sample does not identify a sample of its own class (false negative - FN). Samples that cause such errors negatively impact the accuracy in the classification phase unless they are detected during the learning phase (through incorrect classifications) and properly dealt with, as will be described later.

Additionally, it becomes necessary to compute the number of correct classifications (true positives - TP) and of correct rejections (true negatives - TN) to be contrasted with the false positives and false negatives in order to deduce the usefulness of a sample in the training set.

To understand this bookkeeping, let $s \in Z_1'$ be the sample in Equation 2.2 which classifies a sample $t \in Z_2$.

- The false positive counter for s, FP_s, is incremented if $L(t) \neq \lambda(t)$, otherwise, the true positive counter for s, TP_s, is incremented.

Now, proceeding upwards (i.e., as $C(\cdot)$ decreases) on Z_1', let p_1 and p_2 be the first samples found such that $L(p_1) = \lambda(t)$ and $L(p_2) \neq \lambda(t)$.

- The false negative counter for p_1, FN_{p_1}, and the true negative counter for p_2, TN_{p_2}, are incremented.

After computing FP, TP, FN and TN for all samples in Z_1, a penalty pen_s is calculated for each $s \in Z_1$ so that a sample s can be considered an outlier whenever $pen_s > \varepsilon$, for some threshold $0 < \varepsilon < 1$.

Let

$$E_{s+} = \frac{\mathrm{FP}_s}{\mathrm{TP}_s} \qquad E_{s-} = \frac{\mathrm{FN}_s}{\mathrm{TN}_s},$$

where E_{s+} and E_{s-} are defined as *acceptance* and *rejection rates* for s, which are then normalized in ξ_{s+} and ξ_{s-}, respectively, by their maximum possible values.

Define pen_s as follows:

$$pen_s = \mu \cdot (\xi_{s_+}) + (1 - \mu) \cdot (\xi_{s_-}) \qquad (3.3)$$

where $0 \leq \mu \leq 1$, and hence, $0 \leq pen_s \leq 1$.

In other words, this penalty corresponds to the convex combination of the normalized acceptance and rejection rates, weighted by a parameter μ which allows for a user-controlled balance between FP and FN, that can be application dependent.

Once the penalties are computed for all samples in Z_1, any sample s identified as an outlier (i.e., $pen_s > \varepsilon$) is swapped for a random sample from Z_2. However, care is taken to prevent s from being swapped back into Z_1, if it happens to be misclassified in Z_2 during the learning phase (see Section 2). This will guarantee that previously identified outliers are immovable from Z_2 so as not to negatively impact the accuracy of the classification of Z_3.

Algorithm 2 explains the proposed approach.

Algorithm 2. – OPF-LEARNING-WITH-OUTLIERS-DETECTION

INPUT: λ-labeled training and evaluating sets Z_1 and Z_2, number T of iterations, and threshold ε.
OUTPUT: Instance of the OPF-OD classifier with best accuracy over Z_2.
AUXILIARY: List LM of misclassified samples and Acc.

1. **For each** *iteration* $i \leftarrow 1, 2, \ldots, T$ **do**
2.   *Compute S from Z_1.*
3. $(P, C, L, Z_1') \leftarrow$ *Algorithm-1(Z_1, S).*
4.   **For each** *sample* $t \in Z_2$ **do** ▷▷▷ classify all samples in Z_2
5.   *Use the classifier computed in Line 3 to classify t with label L(t).*
6.   **If** $\lambda(t) \neq L(t)$ **then** $LM \leftarrow LM \cup t$. ▷▷▷ save missclassified samples
7.   *Update FP, TP, FN, TN for the corresponding samples (Section 3).*
8.   **For each** *sample* $s \in Z_1$ **do** ▷▷▷ compute all penalties
9.   *Compute pen_s using Equation 3.3*
10.   **If** $pen_s > \varepsilon$ **then** *Swap s for a sample from Z_2.*
11.   *Compute accuracy Acc and save the actual instance of the classifier if*
12.   *its accuracy is maximum so far.*
13. $k \leftarrow |Z_1'|$.
14.   **While** $LM \neq \emptyset$ *and* $k > 0$ **do** ▷▷▷ swap missclassified samples
15.   *Choose a random sample t from LM, $LM \leftarrow LM \backslash t$*
16.   **While** $Z_1'[k]$ *is a prototype and* $k > 0$ **do** $k \leftarrow k - 1$.
17.   **If** $k > 0$ **then** *Swap t for sample $Z_1'[k]$.*
18. $k \leftarrow k - 1$
19. **Return** *instance of the classifier with highest accuracy.*

The samples to be swapped from Z_1 in Line 10 are not randomly chosen as in [8], but in decreasing order of path-cost using Z_1', because samples with higher path-cost have less probability of correctly classifying samples from Z_2. Therefore, this gives a third important role for the ordered list Z_1'.

4   Experiments

In this section, the datasets used in the tests, the computational environment, the classifiers employed and the overall approach of the experiments are described.

4.1   Datasets Used

To validate the proposed approach, the following datasets from the UC Irvine Repository [3] were used:

- The "Adult" dataset, with about 45000 samples, 14 attributes and 2 classes.
- The "King-Rook vs. King" dataset (krk), with about 30000 samples, 6 attributes and 18 different classes.
- The "Gamma telescope" dataset, with about 20000 samples, 11 attributes and 2 possible classes.

Also, the "Mpeg 7" dataset [1] was used, which consists of about 1400 samples, 70 classes and whose features were extracted using a shape descriptor called Bean Angle Statistics (BAS) [2]. The distance between feature vectors was measured using euclidean distance and optimal correspondence subsequence (OCS) which is more appropriate for the BAS descriptor.

The classifiers used were the OPF with the traditional learning algorithm and the proposed OPF-OD method which refines OPF.

The accuracy measure used to evaluate the classifiers is computed as follows [8]:

$$e_{i,1} = \frac{\text{FP}(i)}{|Z_3| - |Z_3(i)|} \quad e_{i,2} = \frac{\text{FN}(i)}{|Z_3(i)|}, i = 1, \ldots c$$

$$E(i) = e_{i,1} + e_{i,2} \quad Acc = 1 - \frac{\sum_{i=1}^{c} E(i)}{2c}$$

where $\text{FP}(i)$ and $\text{FN}(i)$ are the number of false positives and false negatives for class i and $Z_3(i)$ is the number of samples from class i which belong to Z_3.

4.2   Sizes of Z_1 and Z_2

Due to the fact that OPF-OD is based on a learning phase, the evaluating set Z_2 must be significantly larger that the training set Z_1 to allow for the computation of meaningful penalties for each sample in Z_1. To ensure a good trade-off between accuracy and learning time, the most beneficial ratio $|Z_2|/|Z_1|$ was experimentally determined to be 5.

4.3   Results

In this section, comparisons between OPF and OPF-OD are presented. All the experiments reported here were run on an Intel™ Xeon™ 4-core 2.50 GHz processor, with 8 GB of RAM, under Linux but *without* multi-thread execution.

Firstly, the Adult dataset was used to test 10 different sizes for the training set Z_1 averaged over 10 executions for each size. Figure 1 presents the accuracy obtained, showing the average value and the standard deviation for each size. Note that in *all* cases, OPF-OD obtained higher accuracy than standard OPF.

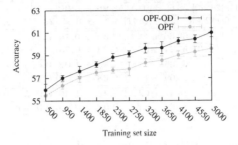

Fig. 1. Accuracy for OPF and OPF-OD calculated over the classification of Z_3 using different sizes for Z_1. Average of ten runs and standard deviation are shown. Here $|Z_2|/|Z_1| = 5$.

Considering the extra time required for the learning phase, the training time for OPF-OD was, as expected, higher than for OPF, as shown in Figure 2.(a) for the Adult dataset.

However, swapping out the outliers from Z_1 leads to some gain, time-wise, in the classification phase, as it can be seen in Figure 2.(b). This is due to the faster convergence of the optimization process that searches, for each sample in Z_3, for its closest sample from Z_1, as per Equation 2.2, since fewer samples have to be tested when outliers are no longer present.

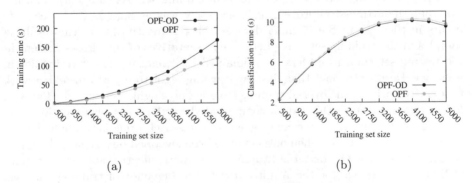

(a)   (b)

Fig. 2. (a) Training time, and (b) Classification time in seconds for OPF and OPF-OD using different sizes for Z_1. Average of ten runs is shown. Here $|Z_2|/|Z_1| = 5$.

Finally, Table 1 shows the accuracy and time results for the other datasets. Two different sizes for Z_1 (depending on the dataset) were considered. The accuracy of OPF-OD for these datasets was higher than OPF's, while OPF-OD's performance was slightly worse in the training phase and better in the classification phase.

Table 1. Accuracy (mean ± standard deviation), Training time (mean) and Classification time (mean) in seconds for several datasets. Best values are in bold.

Datasets	$|Z_1|$	$|Z_2|$	$|Z_3|$	Accuracy		Training time		Classification time	
				OPF	OPF-OD	OPF	OPF-OD	OPF	OPF-OD
krk	280	1400	26320	58.66 ± 0.64	**58.90 ± 0.90**	**0.155**	0.328	0.468	**0.460**
krk	2800	14000	11200	**69.24 ± 0.47**	67.68 ± 0.54	**26.773**	29.367	1.976	**1.915**
gamma	190	950	17860	63.66 ± 1.24	**67.36 ± 0.74**	**0.115**	0.190	0.261	**0.228**
gamma	1900	9500	7600	67.24 ± 0.72	**70.74 ± 0.75**	**11.589**	15.997	1.109	**0.982**
mpeg7	70	350	980	68.09 ± 1.76	**71.53 ± 1.02**	**0.039**	0.105	0.0194	**0.0192**
mpeg7	140	700	560	78.09 ± 1.49	**79.68 ± 1.49**	**0.145**	0.348	0.0223	**0.0221**
mpeg7-OCS	70	350	980	75.57 ± 0.82	**78.40 ± 1.65**	**0.013**	0.039	**0.0007**	0.0008
mpeg7-OCS	140	700	560	89.93 ± 0.66	**90.92 ± 0.65**	**0.022**	0.065	**0.0010**	0.0011

Note that the accuracy grows higher for all datasets as the training set becomes larger. For instance, with a training set of 140 samples for the mpeg7-OCS dataset, the accuracy was 11 percentage points higher than with half as many samples. Furthermore, it is critical to highlight that accuracy depends on other factors such as the distance function, as was the case of the mpeg7 dataset computed with euclidean distance vs. OCS distance.

5   Conclusions

In this work, a novel learning algorithm was presented that improves the time performance and accuracy of the supervised Optimum Path Forest classifier. This algorithm is essentially based on an ingenious method of detecting outliers in the training set and their subsequent swapping for new random samples from the evaluating set leading to a refined training set. As substantiation, notice that the attained improvement in accuracy was as high as 3.7 percentage points in the case of the Gamma dataset. This is mostly due to the resulting samples in the training set being better representatives of the classes present in the testing set than if outliers had remained in it, causing negative impact in accuracy. Despite the fact that the new learning algorithm performs extra work to identify outliers, the overall training time is only slightly increased. However, for most applications, this is well compensated by the lower classification time which results from the faster convergence of the search process through the elements of the training set when outliers have been swapped out. Hence, the forest computed by OPF-OD over the training set is more effective and efficient than OPF's. For instance, for the Adult dataset, the behavior of training time vs. classification time is illustrated in Figures 2.(a) and 2.(b).

References

1. MPEG-7: The generic multimedia content description standard, part 1. IEEE MultiMedia 9, 78–87 (2002)
2. Arica, N., Vural, F.T.Y.: BAS: a perceptual shape descriptor based on the beam angle statistics. Pattern Recognition Letters 24(9-10), 1627–1639 (2003)

3. Asuncion, A., Newman, D.J.: UCI machine learning repository (2007)
4. Boser, B.E., Guyon, I.M., Vapnik, V.N.: A training algorithm for optimal margin classifiers. In: Proceedings of the 5th Workshop on Computational Learning Theory, pp. 144–152. ACM Press, New York (1992)
5. Duda, R.O., Hart, P.E., Stork, D.G.: Pattern Classification, 2nd edn. Wiley-Interscience, Hoboken (2000)
6. Falcão, A.X., Stolfi, J., Lotufo, R.A.: The image foresting transform: Theory, algorithms, and applications. IEEE Transactions on Pattern Analysis and Machine Intelligence 26(1), 19–29 (2004)
7. Papa, J.P., Cappabianco, F.A.M., Falcão, A.X.: Optimizing optimum-path forest classification for huge datasets. In: Proceedings of The 20th International Conference on Pattern Recognition (to appear, 2010)
8. Papa, J.P., Falcão, A.X., Suzuki, C.T.N.: Supervised pattern classification based on optimum-path forest. International Journal of Imaging Systems and Technology 19, 120–131 (2009)
9. Vapnik, V.N.: An overview of statistical learning theory. IEEE Transactions on Neural Networks 10(5), 988–999 (1999)

Assessment of a Modified Version of the EM Algorithm for Remote Sensing Data Classification

Thales Sehn Korting, Luciano Vieira Dutra,
Guaraci José Erthal, and Leila Maria Garcia Fonseca

Image Processing Division
National Institute for Space Research – INPE
São José dos Campos – SP, Brazil
{tkorting,dutra,gaia,leila}@dpi.inpe.br

Abstract. This work aims to present an assessment of a modified version of the standard EM clustering algorithm for remote sensing data classification. As observing clusters with very similar mean vectors but differing only on the covariance structure is not natural for remote sensing objects, a modification was proposed to avoid keeping clusters whose centres are too close. Another modification were also proposed to improve the EM initialization by providing results of the well known K-means algorithm as seed points and to provide rules for decreasing the number of modes once a certain a priori cluster probability is very low. Experiments for classifying Quickbird high resolution images of an urban region were accomplished. It was observed that this modified EM algorithm presented the best agreement with a reference map ploted on the scene when compared with standard K-means and SOM results.

1 Introduction

Many supervised and unsupervised parametric classification methods usually follow a unimodal assumption for class conditional feature distribution. In general, this assumption is not suitable for remote sensing data, particularly for those of very high spatial resolution. One way to improve classification results is describing the class conditional distribution as a mixture of distributions.

The finite mixture model (FMM) is a useful tool for multimodal density estimation. Given the observed data X, an FMM $p(\mathbf{x}; \Theta)$ where $\mathbf{x} \in X$ can be defined as

$$p(\mathbf{x}; \Theta) = \sum_{j=1}^{M} p(\mathbf{x}|C_j; \theta_j) P_j \qquad (1)$$

where M is the number of components, P_j is the jth mixing proportion, $p(\mathbf{x}|C_j)$ the corresponding component density and Θ denotes the parameter vector of the density. If the jth underlying density is the multivariate gaussian

I. Bloch and R.M. Cesar, Jr. (Eds.): CIARP 2010, LNCS 6419, pp. 476–483, 2010.

$p(\mathbf{x}|C_j) = \left(|2\pi\Sigma_j|\exp((\mathbf{x}-\mu_j)^T\Sigma_j^{-1}(\mathbf{x}-\mu_j))\right)^{-1/2}$, with mean vector μ_j and covariance matrix Σ_j, the model is refered to as the gaussian mixture model (GMM).

One way to estimate mixture models is to assume that data points have a "membership" to the unimodal components of data distributions and such membership is unknown. The objective is to estimate suitable parameters for the model, where the connection to the data points is represented as their membership in the individual model distributions.

In statistical pattern recognition, mixture models allow a formal approach to unsupervised learning [5]. A standard method to estimate FMM from observed data is the *Expectation-Maximization* (EM) algorithm, firstly proposed by [3].

Given a complete set $Z = (X, Y)$ where X is the observed data (the incomplete data) and Y the unobserved data, the joint probability density of Z is given as $p(X, Y; \Theta)$. The ML estimate of Θ is obtained by maximizing the incomplete-data log-likelihood function

$$L(\Theta; X) = \log p(X; \Theta) = \log \int p(X, Y; \Theta) dY \qquad (2)$$

The incomplete data log-likelihood function is maximized through EM algorithm by iteratively maximizing the expectation of the complete data log-likelihood function given by

$$L_c(\Theta; Z) = \log p(X, Y; \Theta) \qquad (3)$$

At $(t+1)$th iteration the E-step of the algoritm computes the expected complete data log-likelihood as follows:

$$Q(\Theta|\Theta(0)) = E[L_c(\Theta; Z)|X; \Theta(t)] \qquad (4)$$

and the M-step calculates Θ by maximizing $Q(\Theta|\Theta(t))$.

EM is an iterative procedure which under mild conditions converges to a (local) maximum of $L(\Theta; X)$ depending on the initial solution $\Theta(0)$.

In other words, EM is a general method of estimating the features of a given data set, when the data are incomplete or have missing values [1]. Finite mixture models are able to represent arbitrarily complex probability density functions [4]. This fact makes EM proper for representing complex likelihood functions. This algorithm has been used in several areas, such as image reconstruction, signal processing, and machine learning [9], [11].

Being an iterative procedure, EM presents high computational cost. This article presents a variation of the algorithm EM to improve the classification results, particularly for remote sensing applications. It is done first taking in account particularities of optical remote sensing data distribution, and providing the first set of parameters from K-means algorithm and by performing clustering validation techniques.

The paper is organized as follows. Section 2 describes the basic EM approach and its application to mixture models. In Section 3 we show our main contribution describing the improved EM. Section 4 presents some experimental results for applying the proposed method to urban remote sensing images as well as a discussion about the classification method performance. Finally, Section 5 presents the conclusion.

2   The Standard EM for GMM

We assume that the algorithm will estimate M class distributions $C_j, j = 1, \ldots M$. For each of the N input vectors $\mathbf{x}_k \in X, k = 1, \ldots N$, the algorithm calculates the probability $P(C_j|\mathbf{x}_k)$ [12]. The highest probability will point to the vector's class.

To apply EM for remote sensing imagery analysis we have created the input vectors with one vector per pixel. The vector contains the pixel values for each spectral channel in the image. An image with l bands produces a $l - D$ attribute space.

The EM algorithm works iteratively by applying two steps: the E-step (*Expectation*) and the M-step (*Maximization*). Formally, $\hat{\Theta}(t) = \{\mu_j(t), \Sigma_j(t), P_j(t)\}$, $j = 1, \ldots M$ stands for successive parameter estimates. In the standard EM, $\hat{\Theta}(0)$ is randomly defined, and EM approximates $\hat{\Theta}(t)$ to the real data distribution when $t \to \infty$.

2.1   E-Step

This step calculates the conditional expectation of the complete *a posteriori* probability function. Each cluster probability, given a certain attribute-vector, is estimated as following:

$$P(C_j|\mathbf{x}) = \frac{|\Sigma_j(t)|^{-\frac{1}{2}} e^{\eta_j(t)} P_j(t)}{\sum_{k=1}^{M} |\Sigma_k(t)|^{-\frac{1}{2}} e^{\eta_k(t)} P_k(t)} \tag{5}$$

where

$$\eta_i(t) = -\frac{1}{2}(\mathbf{x} - \mu_i(t))^T \Sigma_i^{-1}(t)(\mathbf{x} - \mu_i(t))$$

2.2   M-Step

This step updates the parameter estimation $\hat{\Theta}(t)$. Given the cluster probabilities, the mean and covariance values for each cluster are estimated as

$$\mu_j(t+1) = \frac{\sum_{k=1}^{N} P(C_j|\mathbf{x}_k)\mathbf{x}_k}{\sum_{k=1}^{N} P(C_j|\mathbf{x}_k)} \tag{6}$$

$$\Sigma_j(t+1) = \frac{\sum_{k=1}^{N} P(C_j|\mathbf{x}_k)(\mathbf{x}_k - \mu_j(t))(\mathbf{x}_k - \mu_j(t))^T}{\sum_{k=1}^{N} P(C_j|\mathbf{x}_k)} \tag{7}$$

The overall probability for each cluster is also calculated in this step as:

$$P_j(t+1) = \frac{1}{N} \sum_{k=1}^{N} P(C_j|\mathbf{x}_k) \tag{8}$$

2.3   Convergence

Both steps, E and M, are performed until convergence, according to

$$\| \, \mathbf{\Sigma}(t+1) - \mathbf{\Sigma}(t) \, \|_F < \varsigma \tag{9}$$

where $\| \, . \, \|_F$ stands for the Frobenius norm, the square root of the sum of the absolute squares of its elements [12], and ς is a threshold for convergence. The second stop criteria is given by

$$\| \, \mu(t+1) - \mu(t) \, \| < \varepsilon \tag{10}$$

where $\| \, . \, \|$ is the Euclidean distance between vectors, and ε is second a convergence threshold. When both equations are true, the algorithm reaches convergence and Equation 5 is applied to classify the image.

3   Modifications to the Standard EM Algorithm

In this section we explain our main contributions to the EM algorithm. Figure 1 illustrates our method, which is composed by three main modules. The first one describes the data initialization, followed by the probabilities estimation, and finished by the data classification. The "Initialization" and "Probabilities estimation" modules were adjusted to carry out the improvements in the results.

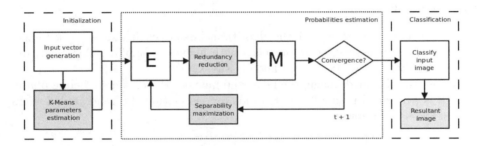

Fig. 1. The improved EM diagram

3.1   Initialization

The instance set $\mathbf{x}$ is built with the pixels of each image spectral channel. [6] used agglomerative hierarqical clustering based on the classification likelihood to estimate the initial parameters for EM. Besides this approach, [10] have also suggested the parameter estimation from K-means. This work employs K-means algorithm for producing the first set of unknown parameters Θ, *i.e.* when $t = 0$. It is important to point out that K-means defines its initial parameters randomly, and provides to our algorithm the clusters means. Therefore, in the beginning the set of covariance matrix is created with identity matrices. By applying this to the EM approach, we reduce the number of iterations, thus reducing computational time.

3.2   Probabilities Estimation

This module performs the iterative procedure for probabilities estimation. We suggest to remove redundant clusters and to maximize the separability between them to correct the number of clusters.

The approach performs cluster exclusion when some cluster presents low probability, according the equation 8. In Figure 1, such operation is defined by the "Redundancy reduction" module. Through a threshold η, the cluster exclusion is defined as:

$$\text{if } P_i(t) < \eta \text{ then exclude cluster } C_i \tag{11}$$

As observing clusters with very similar mean vectors but differing only on the covariance structure is not natural for remote sensing objects, another modification was proposed to avoid keeping clusters whose centres are too close. If a cluster center is approaching another cluster center, one of them has its parameters randomly changed. We define a module called "Separability maximization", as the following equation:

$$\text{if } \|\mu_i(t) - \mu_j(t)\| < \zeta \text{ then } \mu_j(t) = \vartheta \text{ and } \Sigma_j(t) = I \tag{12}$$

where ζ is a threshold, ϑ is a random vector, and I is the identity matrix.

3.3   Classification

After convergence is acchieved, the algorithm classifies each pixel k in the image. The vector $\mathbf{x}_k$ is associated to one class with higher probability. The algorithm finds $P(C_j|\mathbf{x}_k) > P(C_i|\mathbf{x}_k), j \neq i$ and classify $\mathbf{x}_k$ as C_j.

Given the classified image, the next step includes the clusters labeling phase, which is performed manually, and stands for associating the generated clusters to the classes of interest.

4   Results

Figure 2a shows a color composition (R3G2B1) image acquired in January 2004 by the Quickbird satellite, and covers and urban area of São José dos Campos – Brazil. By visual inspection, we can identify four main classes, namely *Shadow, Vegetation, Ground,* and *Roofs.* To analyze the results and compare the obtained agreement with reference regions, we also classified using well known unsupervised methods K-means and Self-Organizing Maps (SOM) [8].

The initial number of clusters was set to 15, a number that was big enough to consider all possibilities of class definitions in the test image. For EM and K-means we set $k = 15$, and for SOM, we created a map with 3×5 neurons. As the algorithm initializations are random we performed 10 classifications, using the same image for each algorithm, trying to avoid sub-optimal solutions. Considering all tests, the minimum detected number of Gaussians, considered as elements of the mixture, was 9. After classification, we manually assigned the clusters to one of the four reference classes.

We obtained an agreement coefficient with a reference classification map and the best results for each clustering procedure. The best classification results are shown in Figure 2, and the obtained agreement matrices are displayed on Table 1. The overall agreement with reference regions for EM was 70.58% of correct matches, whereas K-means obtained 68.12% and SOM obtained 65%. Kappa indices for every algorithm were $\kappa = 0.557$ for EM, $\kappa = 0.483$ for K-means and $\kappa = 0.474$ for SOM.

EM algorithm presents some drawbacks. Being a local method, it is sensitive to the initialization because the mixture model likelihood function is not unimodal [5]. This was the main reason for using K-means as first set of parameters. For certain mixture types, it may converge to the parameter space boundary, leading to meaningless estimates. It would be expected to get better results for EM

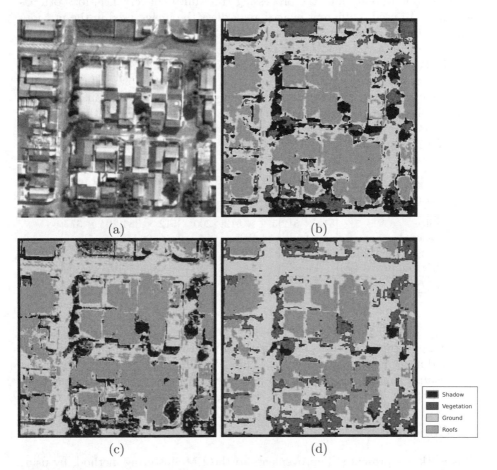

Fig. 2. a) Color composition R3G2B1 of QuickBird scene from São José dos Campos – Brazil. b) Improved EM result, c) K-means result, and d) SOM result.

Table 1. Agreement Matrices. The reference data are displayed in the rows.

EM	■	■	□	▣
■	52	6	0	3
▣	20	79	13	1
□	32	47	245	52
▣	11	22	101	363

K-means	■	■	□	▣
■	36	14	0	7
▣	17	38	12	22
□	16	26	223	108
▣	7	20	78	402

SOM	■	■	□	▣
■	16	40	4	1
▣	3	71	22	0
□	1	49	278	19
▣	5	45	161	285

than for K-means, since it provides the first set of parameters, and improved EM adjust them in a better way, including also the estimation of covariance matrices.

Therefore, to test the better performance of our method we performed several tests using the original EM and the modified EM approach. The experimental tests took into account the processing time until convergence, for both approaches. We used 5 different images, regardless the image used in the previous experiment, with different parameters. Table 2 shows the results considering the image size, number of classes, and computational time until convergence.

Calculating the average values for time speed up, showed at the line $\frac{\Delta t_1}{\Delta t_2}$ of the table, we reach the value 3.35, *i.e.* our improved approach is around $3\times$ faster than the original one. However, even becoming faster than the original approach, EM is still more expensive in terms of processing time than the other methods. It performs calculations of inverse matrix and determinant at each iteration for the whole set of data.

Table 2. Comparison between original and improved approaches

	Image1	Image2	Image3	Image4	Image5
Size	512×512	512×512	200^2	512×384	264×377
# of classes	4	4	5	6	5
Δt_1 original EM	467s	467s	103s	402s	202s
Δt_2 improved EM	140s	148s	29s	105s	70s
$\frac{\Delta t_1}{\Delta t_2}$	3.33	3.15	3.55	3.82	2.88

Images classified by pixel-based methods (non region-based) generally present a noisy appearance because of some isolated pixels that are misclassified [7]. As observed in the agreement matrix, the class *Roofs* presented the worst classification results. This was due to the fact that such class varies a lot and some parts of the roofs are very similar to roads, leading to misclassifications.

5   Conclusion

This work has presented improvements to the EM clustering method, by using K-means results as input, and some changes in the "Probabilities estimation" module.

Afterall, one of the main conclusions drawn from the experiments is that mixture models seems to be the best way to characterize the distributions for high resolution images, since the minimum number of detected modes was 9 for a 4 class problem, considering all tested methods. When compared with standard clustering approaches like K-means and SOM, the modified EM algorithm presented the best agreement with the reference map. This fact suggests that the proposed EM algorithm can be adopted as a standard choice for this task. Future works include a complete assessment of our method comparing it with other algorithms such as the original implementation of EM, hierarchical clustering, and fuzzy approaches.

Wrong initial parameters might result in meaningless classification, therefore initial estimation from K-means increased the resultant agreement. We have implemented the algorithm using TerraLib library [2], which is available for free download at http://www.terralib.org/.

References

1. Bilmes, J.: A Gentle Tutorial of the EM Algorithm and its Application to Parameter Estimation for Gaussian Mixture and Hidden Markov Models. TR-97-021, International Computer Science Institute (1998)
2. Câmara, G., et al.: TerraLib: An Open Source GIS Library for Large-scale Environmental and Socio-economic Applications. Open Source Approaches in Spatial Data Handling, 247–270 (2008)
3. Dempster, A., Laird, N., Rubin, D.: Maximum likelihood estimation from incomplete data via the EM algorithm. Journal of the Royal Statistical Society 39 (1977)
4. Figueiredo: Lecture Notes on the EM Algorithm. Tech. rep., Institute of Telecommunication (May 19, 2004)
5. Figueiredo, M., Jain, A.: Unsupervised learning of finite mixture models. IEEE Transactions on Pattern Analysis and Machine Intelligence 24(3), 381–396 (2002)
6. Fraley, C.: How Many Clusters? Which Clustering Method? Answers Via Model-Based Cluster Analysis. The Computer Journal 41(8), 578–588 (1998)
7. Guo, L., Moore, J.: Post-classification Processing For Thematic Mapping Based On Remotely Sensed Image Data. In: Geoscience and Remote Sensing Symposium. IGARSS, vol. 4 (1991)
8. Kohonen, T.: Self-Organizing Maps. Springer, Heidelberg (2001)
9. McLachlan, G., Krishnan, T.: The EM Algorithm and Extensions, 1st edn. Wiley Interscience, Hoboken (1997)
10. McLachlan, G., Peel, G., Basford, K., Adams, P.: The EMMIX software for the fitting of mixtures of normal and t-components. Journal of Statistical Software 4 (1999)
11. Moon, T.: The expectation-maximization algorithm. IEEE Signal Processing Magazine 13(6), 47–60 (1996)
12. Theodoridis, S., Koutroumbas, K.: Pattern Recognition. Academic Press, London (2003)

A Sequential Minimal Optimization Algorithm for the All-Distances Support Vector Machine[*]

Diego Candel[1], Ricardo Ñanculef[1], Carlos Concha[1], and Héctor Allende[1,2]

[1] Universidad Técnica Federico Santa María,
Departamento de Informática, CP 110-V Valparaíso, Chile
{dcontard,jnancu,cconcha,hallende}@inf.utfsm.cl
[2] Universidad Adolfo Ibáñez, Facultad de Ingeniería y Ciencia, Santiago, Chile
hallende@uai.cl

Abstract. The All-Distances SVM is a single-objective light extension of the binary μ-SVM for multi-category classification that is competitive against multi-objective SVMs, such as *One-against-the-Rest* SVMs and *One-against-One* SVMs. Although the model takes into account considerably less constraints than previous formulations, it lacks of an efficient training algorithm, making its use with medium and large problems impracticable. In this paper, a *Sequential Minimal Optimization*-like algorithm is proposed to train the All-Distances SVM, making large problems abordable. Experimental results with public benchmark data are presented to show the performance of the AD-SVM trained with this algorithm against other single-objective multi-category SVMs.

Keywords: Kernel Machines, Multi-category Classification, Support Vector Machines, Sequential Minimal Optimization.

1 Introduction

Support Vector Machines [20] (SVMs) are currently well known methods for pattern recognition and other data analysis, with strong theoretical properties and practical results when applied to real-world problems. Originally formulated to deal with linearly separable binary classification problems, they can also deal with noisy data and non-linearly separable cases using a regularization and a kernel method extension respectively.

Although the training of these machines can be assumed as finding the solution to a quadratic optimization problem with linear restrictions, traditional approaches are impractical due to the dense nature of the Hessian Matrix involved in the problem definition. To deal with this, chunking and decomposition algorithms have been proposed through time, being the Sequential Minimal Optimization (SMO) [18,14,10] one of the most popular methods employed for this purpose.

---

[*] This work was supported in part by Research Grant FB0821 "Centro Científico Tecnológico de Valparaíso" UTFSM and by DGIP-UTFSM Grant.

I. Bloch and R.M. Cesar, Jr. (Eds.): CIARP 2010, LNCS 6419, pp. 484–491, 2010.

In a multi-category context, the use of these training algorithms is straight forward when several binary SVMs are used in combination (a multi-objective approach), as with the *One-against-the-Rest* scheme [20] and the *One-versus-One* scheme [15]. The same is not true when the classifier is a single machine extending a binary SVM to classify more than two classes (a mono-objective approach), since the objective function of the machine has changed and the underlying components in which the solvers relay on are not the same (like the Karush-Kuhn-Tucker conditions used by the SMO algorithm). In these cases, a suitable training algorithm needs to be designed to address the single-objective formulation of this new kind of machines. This is the case of the method of Weston and Watkins [21], the framework of Crammer and Singer [8,7] and the All-Distances SVM (AD-SVM) [17], among others. Here we focus on AD-SVMs, a method recently proposed to formulate the multi-category problem using a reduced number of constraints.

An efficient solver for the AD-SVMs does not currently exist, and only general-purpose solvers like the one proposed in [6] have been employed until now, making possible the use of this machine only for small problems (no more than 500 training examples). The use of general-purpose solvers gets impractical as the problem size grows, since training time and memory requirements scale above a quadratic rate, due to the dense Hessian Matrix issue mentioned above. Therefore a solver specifically designed for the AD-SVM is needed.

In this paper, a specific algorithm to train the AD-SVM is proposed. Its design, derivation and components are based in the SMO algorithm for binary SVMs. The SMO was chosen as base for this new solver as it is a fast and well-known algorithm commonly used in SVM training. The performance of the new solver is compared against other multi-category mono-objective machine (described in [7]) both in terms of accuracy and training time efficiency.

The rest of the paper is organized as follow: An overview of binary SVMs and the AD-SVM is given in section 2; The components and the general structure of the new training algorithm for the AD-SVM are described in section 3; Finally, experiments and conclusions are provided in section 4.

2   Background

Given a set of examples $S = \{\mathbf{x}_i : i \in I\} \subset \mathcal{X} \subset \mathbb{R}^n$ of two classess, $\mathcal{C}_-$ and $\mathcal{C}_+$, the binary classification problem asks to learn a decision function $f(\mathbf{x})$: $\mathcal{X} \to \{-1, +1\}$ to distinguish patterns of one class from the other class. SVMs accomplish this by modeling the boundary between $\mathcal{C}_-$ and $\mathcal{C}_+$ as the hyperplane $H = \{x : \mathbf{w}^T \mathbf{x} + b = 0\}$ whose parameters $\mathbf{w}$ and b are determined by minimizing a risk functional [20]. To deal with non linearly separable data, SVMs use non-linear kernel functions $\mathbf{K}(\mathbf{x}_i, \mathbf{x}_j)$ instead of the linear inner products $\mathbf{x}i^T\mathbf{x}_j$ and have different ways to treat noisy data through the use of slag variables, being the C-SVM and the ν-SVM [19] two of the most popular approaches.

The All-Distances SVM (AD-SVM) [17] can be considered the natural extension of the μ-SVM [9] to multiple-classes. The extension consists in minimizing the sum of all pairwise distances among the different K convex hulls (each generated for one class). Its dual form can be stated as follows:

$$D(\mathbf{u}) : \mathbf{minimize}_{\{\mathbf{u}\}} \frac{1}{4} \sum_{i \in I} \sum_{j \in I} u_i \overline{k}_{ij} u_j \tag{1}$$

$$\text{subject to} \quad \sum_{i \in I_r} u_i = 1, \ r \in \{1, \cdots, K\} \ \wedge \ 0 \leq u_i \leq \mu, \ \forall i \in I, \tag{2}$$

where $\overline{k}_{ij} = \alpha_{ij} k_{ij}$, $k_{ij} = \mathbf{K}(\mathbf{x}_i, \mathbf{x}_j)$, I is the set of all indexes and I_r is the subset of indexes belonging only to class $\mathcal{C}_r$. Values α_{ij} involved in the definition of $\overline{k}_{ij}$ are defined as:

$$\alpha_{ij} = \mathbf{y}_i \cdot \mathbf{y}'_j = \begin{cases} K - 1, \text{ if } i \in I_r \wedge j \in I_r \\ -1, \text{ in any other case,} \end{cases} \tag{3}$$

$$\text{where } \mathbf{y}_i = [y_{i1}, y_{i2}, \dots, y_{iK}], \quad y_{is} = \begin{cases} K - 1, \text{ if } s = r, \text{ where } i \in I_r \\ -1, \text{ in any other case.} \end{cases} \tag{4}$$

Note that the labels are not scalar values but K-dimensional vectors, equivalent to those proposed in the formulation of other multi-category classifier [16]. Note also that, when $K = 2$, the possible values of α_{ij} are the same that those calculated with the scalar y_i labels used within the binary SVM [9]. The formulation lead to one hyperplane $\mathbf{w}_r$, one offset b_r and one ρ_r for every class $r \in \{1, \cdots, K\}$:

$$\mathbf{w}_r = \frac{1}{K} \sum_{i \in I} \alpha_{ir} u_i \mathbf{x}_i, \ b_r = \frac{-1}{K^2} \sum_{i \in I} \sum_{j \in I} u_i \alpha_{ir} k_{ij} u_j, \tag{5}$$

$$\rho_r = \frac{1}{K^2} \sum_{i \in I} \sum_{j \in I} u_i \alpha_{ir} k_{ij} \alpha_{jr} u_j, \text{ where } \alpha_{ir} = \begin{cases} K - 1, \text{ if } i \in I_r \\ -1, \text{ in any other case.} \end{cases} \tag{6}$$

As with the α_{ij} values, for $K = 2$, $\mathbf{w}_1 = \mathbf{w}_2 = \mathbf{w}$, $\rho_1 = \rho_2 = \rho$ and $b_2 = -b_1 = b$, that is the hyperplanes model the half-spaces induced by the binary SVM hyperplane. With this elements, the decision funtion $f(\cdot)$ used to classify new examples is given by

$$f(\mathbf{x}) = \arg \max_r \left(\frac{1}{K} \sum_{i \in I} \alpha_{ir} u_i \mathbf{K}(\mathbf{x}_i, \mathbf{x}) + b_r - \rho_r \right). \tag{7}$$

which again coincides with the binary SVM decision function for $K = 2$ [9].

3   SMO Algorithm for the AD-SVM

The SMO scheme to train binary SVMs works iterating through a sequence of steps until convergence is reached. At every step, only two variables are selected for optimization and the others are temporary frozen. An algorithm of this kind requires of the following principal components: an (usually) analytic **optimization step** to calculate new values for two Lagrange multipliers; a **selection strategy** (heuristic or not) to choose these two Lagrange multipliers, so that the convergence to the optimum is as fast as possible in every step; a **stopping criteria** to efficiently determine when the optimal (or a near optimal) solution has been achieved; an **update system** that efficiently updates the values involved in the selection and optimization of two Lagrange multipliers, every time that the vector of Lagrange multipliers is changed; and an algorithm that utilizes all of the later components to achieve the optimal or near optimal solution of the SVM problem. Here, extensions of each of these components are given to define a functional SMO solver to train the AD-SVM. We start by defining the subsets I_r^0, I_r^1 and I_r^2

$$I_r^0 = \{i : i \in I_r,\ 0 < u_i < \mu\}\,,\ I_r^1 = \{i : i \in I_r,\ u_i = 0\}\,,\ I_r^2 = \{i : i \in I_r,\ u_i = \mu\}\,,$$

and the quantities β_r^{up} and β_r^{low}

$$\beta_r^{\mathrm{up}} = \min\left\{F_i\ ,\ i \in I_r^{\mathrm{up}} := I_r^0 \cup I_r^1\right\},\ \beta_r^{\mathrm{low}} = \max\left\{F_i\ ,\ i \in I_r^{\mathrm{low}} := I_r^0 \cup I_r^2\right\}$$

$$\text{where } F_i = \sum_{j \in I} u_j \overline{\mathbf{k}}_{ij}.$$

These elements will be useful for the definition of the SMO components.

3.1 Stopping Criteria

At any given moment of the training, it is useful and necesary to know if optimality has been reached. As demonstrated in [13] for the binary case and futher extended in [3] for multi-category instances, when $\beta_r^{\mathrm{low}} - \beta_r^{\mathrm{up}} \leq 0$ for all $r \in \{1, \ldots, K\}$ classes, the algorithm has reached its optimum. Since it is not always possible to achieve optimality due to the limits of computer arithmetics and other numerical issues, a tolerance $\tau > 0$ is conveniently defined by the user. If well defined, the use of this tolerance also allows a faster convergency of the algorithm at expenses of a low precision loss. With this in mind, a τ-tolerance optimum is achieved when $\beta_r^{\mathrm{low}} - \beta_r^{\mathrm{up}} \leq 2\tau$.

3.2 Selection Strategy

If the algorithm has not achieved optimality, it means that at least one pair of indexes $\{i,\ j\}$ in a class r is violating optimality, i.e. $F_j - F_i > 2\tau$, with $i \in I_r^{\mathrm{up}}$ and $j \in I_r^{\mathrm{low}}$. Most of the time, there will be several of these violating pairs, and choosing the most violating one at each step will lead to a faster convergence.

Here, we implement an extension for the AD-SVM of the heuristic proposed in [10] that uses second order information: For the index $i = \arg\min_t \{F_t\ ,\ t \in I_r^{\mathrm{up}}\}$ of every class r, find index j such that

$$j = \arg\max_t \left\{ \frac{b_{it}^2}{a_{it}}\ ,\ t \in I_r^{\mathrm{low}} \wedge F_t > F_i \right\} \tag{8}$$

$$\text{where } a_{it} = \overline{\mathbf{k}}_{ii} - 2\overline{\mathbf{k}}_{it} + \overline{\mathbf{k}}_{tt},\ b_{it} = F_t - F_i \tag{9}$$

Select the pair of indexes $\{i, j\}$ among all K classes such that the factor b_{it}^2/a_{it} is maximal. Note that a similar strategy can be followed with $i = \arg\max_t \{F_t, \ t \in I_r^{\text{low}}\}$.

If the kernel function is not positive definite, there will be cases in which a_{it} will adopt problematic values ($a_{it} \leq 0$). It has been shown in [5] for binary SVMs that in these cases the value of a_{it} can be set to a very small positive value $0 < \varepsilon \ll 1$, redefining the problem as convex and thus it can be solved in the same way as when $a_{it} > 0$. In the experiments that have been carried for the AD-SVM, this strategy has worked in the same way as expected for the binary case.

3.3   Optimization Step

As it is shown in [3], when two Lagrange multipliers u_i, u_j exist whose indexes are a violating pair, new values can be analytically calculated in order to achieve optimality for the problem when all other variables are left constant. Here, we start by calculating the new Lagrange multiplier for j, as $u_j^{\text{new}} = u_j - \frac{b_{ij}}{a_{ij}}$. Note that, since a_{ij} and b_{ij} were already calculated for selecting the pair $\{i, j\}$ in (8), they do not need to be recomputed here. Also note that u_j^{new} needs to be clipped to satisfy its boundary constraints, that is

$$u_j^{\text{new,clipped}} = \begin{cases} \text{L}, & \text{if } u_j^{\text{new}} \leq \text{L} \\ u_j^{\text{new}}, & \text{if } \text{L} < u_j^{\text{new}} < \text{H} \\ \text{H}, & \text{if } u_j^{\text{new}} \geq \text{H} \end{cases} \tag{10}$$

$$\text{where } L = \max\{0, (\gamma - \mu)\}, \ \ H = \min\{\gamma, \mu\}, \ \ \gamma = u_i + u_j \tag{11}$$

Now u_i^{new} can be computed as $u_i^{\text{new}} = \gamma - u_j^{\text{new}}$. Since u_i^{new} also needs to fulfill boundary constraints, it must be clipped as u_j^{new} was. After this step, the new Lagrange multipliers $u_i^{\text{new,clipped}}$ and $u_j^{\text{new,clipped}}$ are returned to the main algorithm.

3.4 F_t's Update

As with traditional SMO algorithms, F_t's values can be updated efficiently after new values of a pair of Lagrange multipliers are calculated:

$$F_t^{\text{new}} = F_t + \left(u_i^{\text{new,clipped}} - u_i\right) \cdot \overline{\mathbf{k}}_{it} + \left(u_j^{\text{new,clipped}} - u_j\right) \cdot \overline{\mathbf{k}}_{jt} \tag{12}$$

3.5   Algorithm Structure

The components of the SMO procedure just defined are organized in algorithm 1.1.

Algorithm 1.1 is a very general implementation of the SMO algorithm. In practice, the SMO implemented for the experiments of this contribution [2] follows a scheme similar to those proposed in [18] or [14], where each iteration in the training process works first by using only the I_r^0 set of each class, and then, in a second stage, optimality is checked with all remaining indexes. Also, a LRR cache strategy is used to store $\mathbf{k}_{ij}$ products.

Algorithm 1.1. SMO Algorithm for the AD-SVM

1: Initialize u satisfying constraints stated in 2.
2: Calculate F_t, $\forall t \in I$.
3: Find β_r^{low} and β_r^{up} for each class.
4: **while** $\beta_r^{\text{low}} - \beta_r^{\text{up}} > 2\tau$ for at least one $r \in \{1, \ldots, K\}$, **do**
5:     For every class r, select $i = \arg\min_t \{F_t \,,\, t \in I_r^{\text{up}}\}$.
6:     For the selected $i \in I_r$, select $j = \arg\max_t \left\{ \frac{b_{it}^2}{a_{it}} \,,\, t \in I_r^{\text{low}} \wedge F_t > F_i \right\}$.
7:     Select the pair of Lagrange multipliers $\{u_i, u_j\}$ with maximal $\frac{b_{ij}^2}{a_{ij}}$ among all the classes.
8:     Calculate $\left\{ u_i^{\text{new,clipped}}, u_j^{\text{new,clipped}} \right\}$.
9:     Update F_t, $\forall t$.
10:     Find new β_r^{low} and new β_r^{up} for each class.
11: **end while**

4   Experiments and Conclusions

Experiments were conducted to measure and compare the classification accuracy and training runtime of the AD-SVM trained with the proposed SMO algorithm against the Multi-Category SVM proposed in [7] (MC-SVM). In order to obtain a platform and implementation independent comparison, the *number of kernel calls*[1] was used instead of the execution time to measure runtime complexity. Also, no *cooling* of the tolerance[2] was used in any of the algorithms.

A RBF Kernel $\mathbf{K}(\mathbf{x}_j, \mathbf{x}_j) = e^{\left(-\|\mathbf{x}_i - \mathbf{x}_j\|^2 / \sigma^2\right)}$ was used in all the experiments, with parameter σ. To find optimal values for μ and σ, a grid search was performed using k-fold cross-validation, with $k = 10$ folds for relatively small datasets (Glass, Vowel, Satimage, Shuttle small, Letter small, MNIST small) and $k = 5$ folds for relatively large datasets (USPS, Letter, Shuttle).

The values tested for hyper-parameters correspond as usual to a regular logarithmic grid in base 2: for σ it was $\{2^{-4/2}, 2^{-3/2}, \ldots, 2^{9/2}, 2^{10/2}\}$ and for μ, $\left\{1, 2^{-(1\cdot\log_2(m_s)/14)}, \ldots, 2^{-(13\cdot\log_2(m_s)/14)}, 2^{-(14\cdot\log_2(m_s)/14)}\right\}$, where $m_s = \min\left(\overline{\overline{I_1}}, \overline{\overline{I_2}}, \ldots, \overline{\overline{I_K}}\right)$ is the size of the smaller class in the training sets of the cross-validation folds. The values for μ obey to the observation that values lower than $2^{-(14\cdot\log_2(m_s)/14)} = 1/m_s$ lead to an infeasible optimization problem, while values greater than 1 do not change the feasible space. In the case of the MC-SVM, a parameter B must be set instead of μ. The same values for σ were tested, with $B \in \{2^{-2}, 2^{-1}, \ldots, 2^{11}, 2^{12}\}$.

---

[1] The *number of kernel calls* counts every time a $\mathbf{k}_{ij}$ product is used in the algorithm, either being calculated in the moment or retrieved from the cache.

[2] The *cooling* of the tolerance is the iterative refinement of the numerical tolerance until a desired precision is obtained.

The usps [11], Glass, Vowel, Satimage, Shuttle and Letter datasets [1] were used in their normalized and publicly available versions [4] (this reference also provides datasets descriptions). The training datasets for Shuttle small, Letter small and MNIST small are all subsets of 5000 examples randomly selected from the original datasets. Unlike the others, the Glass dataset does not have a separated test set. In this case, 5-fold cross-validation with the whole dataset was used to evaluate test performance. Results obtained with the values of hyper-parameters selected in the cross-validation procedure are listed in table 1.

Table 1. Experiment Results

Datasets	Machine	σ	$B \& \mu$	Test Acc. %	Kernel Calls
Glass	MC-SVM	0.707	0.5	72.89	2.96×10^6
$m_s = 8$	AD-SVM	2.828	0.125	**80.61**	$\mathbf{1.97 \times 10^5}$
Vowel	MC-SVM	0.25	0.25	**50.87**	$\mathbf{7.43 \times 10^5}$
$m_s = 43$	AD-SVM	2	0.068	44.81	2.97×10^6
Satimage	MC-SVM	2	0.5	**91.40**	2.60×10^9
$m_s = 374$	AD-SVM	2.828	0.034	88.30	$\mathbf{4.49 \times 10^7}$
Shuttle small	MC-SVM	2	0.25	**99.79**	3.46×10^8
$m_s = 5$	AD-SVM	4	0.224	99.71	$\mathbf{2.85 \times 10^7}$
Letter small	MC-SVM	2.828	0.25	**63.73**	7.02×10^{10}
$m_s = 1$	AD-SVM	2.828	1	60.82	$\mathbf{1.19 \times 10^8}$
MNIST small	MC-SVM	16	1	**99.04**	5.05×10^8
$m_s = 407$	AD-SVM	32	0.032	93.55	$\mathbf{8.14 \times 10^7}$
USPS	MC-SVM	5.657	0.5	**95.37**	5.48×10^9
$m_s = 433$	AD-SVM	32	0.272	93.21	$\mathbf{1.22 \times 10^8}$
Letter	MC-SVM	2.828	0.25	**71.31**	1.24×10^{12}
$m_s = 1$	AD-SVM	2	1	65.66	$\mathbf{8.43 \times 10^8}$
Shuttle	MC-SVM	0.707	0.25	**99.90**	2.26×10^9
$m_s = 5$	AD-SVM	4	0.447	99.89	$\mathbf{5.15 \times 10^8}$

As it can be noted, in most cases the number of kernel calls is bigger for the MC-SVM than the AD-SVM, with a difference in order of magnitude of at least 1. In the classification performance, the situation changes, exhibiting the MC-SVM a better classification accuracy most of the time. This is expected, since the AD-SVM is a light extension of the μ-SVM with a number of constraints significatively lower than MC-SVM. Nevertheless, note that the difference is not larger than 6%.

Further work can be done to improve the time performance of the algorithm applying for example *tolerance cooling* or *dinamic shrinking* techniques [12]. The theoretical analysis of the algorithm can be also expanded concerning the algorithm: We believe that the convergence proof for the binary SMO presented in [13] can be extended to this multi-category SMO. The same can be said about the redefinition of the term a_{ij} explained at the end of subsection 3.1 to handle semi-definite or indefinite kernels.

References

1. Blake, C., Merz, C.: UCI repository of machine learning databases (1998), http://mlr.cs.umass.edu/ml/index.html
2. Candel, D.: Source code of the smo algorithm for the ad-svm, http://git.inf.utfsm.cl/?p=dcontard.git;a=summary
3. Candel, D.: Algoritmo tipo SMO para la AD-SVM aplicado a Clasificación Multi-categoría. Master's thesis, Universidad Técnica Federico Santa María, Valparaíso, Chile (2010), http://www.alumnos.inf.utfsm.cl/~dcontard/tesis.pdf
4. Chang, C.C., Lin, C.J.: Libsvm data: Classification, multi-class (2001), http://www.csie.ntu.edu.tw/~cjlin/libsvmtools/datasets/multiclass.html
5. Chen, P.H., Fan, R.E., Lin, C.J.: A study on SMO-type decomposition methods for support vector machines. IEEE transactions on neural networks / a publication of the IEEE Neural Networks Council 17(4), 893–908 (2006)
6. Coleman, T.F., Li, Y.: A reflective newton method for minimizing a quadratic function subject to bounds on some of the variables. SIAM J. on Optimization 6(4), 1040–1058 (1996)
7. Crammer, K., Singer, Y.: On the algorithmic implementation of multiclass kernel-based vector machines. Journal of Machine Learning Research (2), 265–292 (2001)
8. Crammer, K., Singer, Y.: On the learnability and design of output codes for multiclass problems. Machine Learning 47(2-3), 201–233 (2002)
9. Crisp, D., Burges, C.: A Geometric Interpretation of ν-SVM Classifiers. In: Advances in Neural Information, vol. (12), pp. 244–250. MIT, Cambridge (2000)
10. Fan, R.e., Chen, P.h., Lin, C.j.: Working Set Selection Using Second Order Information for Training Support Vector Machines. Journal of Machine Learning Research 6, 1889–1918 (2005)
11. Hull, J.J.: A database for handwritten text recognition research. IEEE Trans. Pattern Anal. Mach. Intell. 16(5), 550–554 (1994)
12. Joachims, T.: Making large-scale support vector machine learning practical (1998)
13. Keerthi, S., Gilbert, E.: Convergence of a Generalized SMO Algorithm for SVM Classifier Design. Machine Learning 46(1), 351–360 (2002)
14. Keerthi, S., Shevade, S., Murthy, K., Bhattacharyya, C.: Improvements to Platt's SMO Algorithm for SVM Classifier Design. Neural Computation 13(3), 637–649 (2001)
15. Kressel, U.: Pairwise classification and support vector machines. In: Advances in kernel methods: support vector learning, pp. 255–268. MIT Press, Cambridge (1999)
16. Lee, Y., Li, Y., Wahba, G.: Multicategory support vector machines: Theory and application to the classification of microarray data and satellite radiance data. Journal of the American Statistical Association 99(465), 67–81 (2004)
17. Ñanculef, R., Concha, C., Allende, H., Candel, D., Moraga, C.: Ad-svms: A light extension of svms for multicategory classification. International Journal of Hybrid Intelligent Systems 6(2), 69–79 (2009)
18. Platt, J.C.: Fast training of support vector machines using sequential minimal optimization, pp. 185–208 (1999)
19. Scholkopf, B., Smola, A., Williamson, R., Bartlett, P.: New support vector algorithms. Neural computation 12(5), 1207–1245 (2000)
20. Vapnik, V.N.: The nature of statistical learning theory. Springer, Heidelberg (1995)
21. Weston, J., Watkins, C.: Support vector machines for multiclass pattern recognition. In: Proceedings of the Seventh ESSAN, pp. 219–224 (1999)

Aerosol Optical Thickness Retrieval from Satellite Observation Using Support Vector Regression

Thi Nhat Thanh Nguyen[1,2], Simone Mantovani[2,3], Piero Campalani[1,2], Mario Cavicchi[2], and Maurizio Bottoni[3]

[1] University of Ferrara, Via Saragat 1, 44122, Ferrara, Italy
[2] MEEO S.r.l, Via Saragat 9, 44122, Ferrara, Italy
[3] SISTEMA GmbH, Währingerstrasse 61, A-1090, Vienna, Austria
{thanhntn,mantovani}@meeo.it, cmppri@unife.it,
cavicchi@meeo.it, bottoni@sistema.at

Abstract. Processing of data recorded by the MODIS sensors on board the Terra and Aqua satellites has provided AOT maps that in some cases show low correlations with ground-based data recorded by the AERONET. Application of SVR techniques to MODIS data is a promising, though yet poorly explored, method of enhancing the correlations between satellite data and ground measurements. The article explains how satellite data recorded over three years on central Europe are correlated in space and time with ground based data and then shows results of the application of the SVR technique which somewhat improves previously computed correlations. Hints about future work in testing different SVR variants and methodologies are inferred from the analysis of the results thus far obtained.

Keywords: MODIS, Aerosol Optical Thickness, Earth Observation, Remote Sensing, Support Vector Regression.

1 Introduction

Remote Sensing allows measuring physical properties of distant objects often on dangerous or inaccessible areas where ground-based measurements are unfeasible. Using devices installed on board aircrafts or satellites, Remote Sensing applied to the Earth Observation makes it possible to monitor the Earth-Atmosphere system through the analysis of the interaction of radiation with matter. The signal received from the sensors is the sum of several contributions due to scattering, absorption, reflection and emission processes. Image processing techniques and specific algorithms allow extracting (direct measurement) or estimating (indirect measurement) the environmental parameters and their characteristics. Active and passive sensors with spectral capabilities ranging from visible to thermal infrared wavelengths are used for a large variety of applications for Earth Observation: Agriculture, Atmosphere, Forestry, Geology, Land Cover and Land Use, Ocean and Coastal monitoring.

Aerosol Optical Thickness (AOT) is representative of the amount of particulates presented in a vertical column of the Earth's atmosphere. AOT is largely used in air

I. Bloch and R.M. Cesar, Jr. (Eds.): CIARP 2010, LNCS 6419, pp. 492–499, 2010.

pollution monitoring applications because Particulate Matter (PM) concentration, one of the major pollutants that affect air quality, can be derived from it. Based on developments of observation technology, nowadays aerosol concentration can be predicted by elaboration of data recorded by satellite-based sensors, airborne instruments or ground-based measurements. Satellites provide monitoring at global scale, but with low temporal frequency and moderated retrieval accuracy. Conversely, ground-based measurements have higher precision and temporal frequency, but limits in spatial coverage.

MODerate resolution Imaging Spectrometer (MODIS) is onboard two polar orbiting satellites Terra and Aqua, launched in 1999 and 2002, respectively and operated by the National Aeronautic and Space Administration (NASA). The methodology for deriving AOT information from MODIS data consists of two main algorithms separated for land and ocean [1][2]. Validation of MODIS aerosol retrieval has shown that these algorithms perform on ocean better than on land [3]. In theory, this limitation occurs over bright surfaces and cloud-contaminated scenes as a result of the reflectance variability of clouds and different land surfaces. These factors strongly affect the Dense Dark Vegetation (DDV) approach used to estimate AOT on dark areas which usually correspond to pixels of vegetation and bare soil. This limitation was also shown in [4] in which AOT maps were validated over different land surfaces to point out the impact of the land cover types.

Data mining approach has recently been investigated to improve quality of aerosol monitoring. The application types ranged from classification, forecasting to estimation of aerosol content and properties from different sensors. Aerosol was distinguished from cloud in CALIPSO data by using Support Vector Machine (SVM) [5]. A series of data mining techniques was applied to analyze aerosol into chemical components and then processed their streams to understand aerosol dynamics in [6]. Besides, many studies emphasized on processing time-serial data to give prediction of air pollutants by using improved BP neural network [7], SVM [8], ensemble of SVM [9], or SVM and wavelet decomposition [10]. In aerosol estimation field, various applications of Neural Network (NN) were also considered [11][12].

Following this trend, in order to improve the traditional MODIS aerosol retrieval, many works proposed the application of data mining techniques on data collected by different instruments. Firstly, integrations of ground-based measurements AERONET (AErosol RObotic NETwork) and satellite data (MISR and MODIS [13], MODIS [14]) were made. Then, NNs techniques were applied on merged data to derive aerosol content and properties. This method proved efficiency in dealing with data uncertainties and in improving estimation accuracy which became comparable with that of results obtained at ground level. The same approach was mentioned in [15] to correct the bias of MODIS Aerosol Optical Depth (AOD) over different land covers by using both NNs and Support Vector Regression (SVR). In this work, SVR presented more advantages in performance than NNs.

In this paper we propose a driven-data approach that applies SVR, firstly introduced by Vapnik [16], on MODIS and AERONET data for AOT retrievals. This proposal is motivated by the better performance of SVR with respect to NNs in finding a global solution instead of a local one, and in coping with huge and high dimensional satellite data. Some similarities can be found in the work done by Vucetic et al. [14] in which NNs were applied on AERONET and MODIS (Collection 004) data covering the U.S. continental area, recorded between 2002 and 2004. In our approach, we investigated using different prediction methods applied to a different data set: (i) the area of interest covered Europe instead of U.S. continental area and (ii) the improved MODIS Collection 005 products [1] were collected from 2006 to 2008. Moreover, AOT for each MODIS pixel sized 10 km is predicted instead of AOT for a box of 30x30 km^2. This approach is more appropriate for air pollution monitoring over urban areas where the assumption of aerosol stableness in an area of 50x50 km^2 [17] is less appropriate and higher spatial resolution is desirable.

The data fusion methodology and some details of SVR application are presented in section 2. Numerical experiments and their results are discussed in section 3. Finally, conclusions are given in section 4, together with hints about future works.

2 Methodology

The methodology applied for AOT retrievals based on SVR technique consists of three main steps: (i) collecting and processing satellite-based data (MODIS) and ground-based sensor measurements (AERONET) over Europe for a period of three years, (ii) integrating and combining data from two sources having different temporal and spatial resolutions, and (iii) applying SVR technique in form of "instance SVR" and "aggregate SVR" [18] for aerosol estimation.

2.1 Data Sets

AERONET is a global system of ground-based remote sensing aerosol network established by NASA and PHOTONS (Univ. of Lille 1, CNES, and CNRS-INSU) [19]. It uses CIMEL Electronique 318A spectral radiometers, sun and sky scanning sun photometers, to provide AOT retrievals in various wavelengths: 0.340, 0.380, 0.440, 0.500, 0.675, 0.870, 0.940, and 1.020 μm, in intervals of 15 minutes. Because of high accuracy, AERONET data are often used to validate satellite AOT retrievals.

AERONET data level 2.0, cloud-screened and quality-assured, of 105 sites distributed in Europe, in 2006, 2007, and 2008, were collected. AOT at 0.500 μm, the closest to MODIS AOT at 0.550 μm, was used to create SVR aerosol retrievals.

MODIS provides Level 1B Calibrated Geolocation Data Set, presenting a spectrum region from 0.415 to 14.235 μm, separated into 36 bands at 1 km, 500 m, and 250 m resolutions at nadir. Original MODIS data are pre-elaborated by a software package, the most recent version of which is known as "Collection 005" described in detail in [1]. One of the most important products of the MODIS Atmosphere algorithms applied in Collection 005 is the retrieval of aerosol MOD04. It is based on data from Terra platform and supports the monitoring of the ambient aerosol optical thickness over oceans globally and over the continents. MOD04 products consist of AOT maps at seven wavelengths over ocean (0.470, 0.550, 0.670, 0.870, 1.240, 1.630, and 2.130 μm) and three wavelengths over land (0.470, 0.550, and 0.670 μm). All maps have the same spatial resolution of 10x10 km^2. Geometry information such as solar zenith angle, solar azimuth angle, sensor zenith angle, sensor azimuth angle, and scattering angle are also provided in this product.

We collected MODIS data in corresponding period of the retrieved AERONET data. Reflectance of seven bands, geometry information, and aerosol concentration are considered at 10x10 km^2 spatial resolution.

2.2 AERONET-MODIS Combination

AERONET and MODIS data are products of separate sensors, which causes problems of temporal and spatial resolution differences. Data combination aims at obtaining data collocated in space and synchronized in time. MODIS data are considered if their distances from AERONET sites are within a radius of 30 km, while the contemporaneous measurements of AERONET instruments are selected and averaged within a temporal window of 60 minutes around the satellite overpasses.

AERONET-MODIS combinations are separated into two sets: *instance data set* and *aggregate data set*. The first one consists of 66,225 samples, each of which is a combination of measurements on a single MODIS pixel with an averaged AERONET AOT value satisfying collocation and synchronization conditions. One sample is presented as a vector including AERONET AOT at 0.500 μm, MODIS geometric data (solar zenith angle, solar azimuth angle, sensor zenith angle, sensor azimuth angle, scattering angle) and seven MODIS reflectances (0.646, 0.855, 0.466, 0.553, 1.243, 1.632, and 2.119 μm). The aggregate data set contains 5,289 samples that are combinations of an AERONET AOT, averaged MODIS geometric data and averaged MODIS reflectances calculated on all cloud-free pixels around this AERONET site. These vectors are stored in the same format as ones in the instance data set.

2.3 Support Vector Regression

SVR was applied to instance data set and aggregate data set in order to create different data models for AOT retrievals, called *instance SVR* and *aggregate SVR* respectively. SVR with epsilon loss function and Radial Basic Function (RBF) kernel provided by LIBSVM [20] was used. The accuracy was measured on three year data cross-validation in which we repeated selections of two year data for training and one year data for testing. Root Mean Square (RMS) error and correlation coefficient (CORR) were calculated from SVR AOT prediction and AERONET AOT data. SVR regularizations were searched in appropriate range with exponentially growing sequences. For each case, cross-validation was applied on a training data set and the best accuracy was picked. At the end of searching process, the chosen regularizations minimized mean square error in the training phase.

Both instance and aggregate SVR were used to bring out data models for AOT prediction at pixels of 10x10 km^2. We made experiments on them to investigate their accuracy and consuming time. Besides, SVRs were applied separately on different land cover types in order to investigate the effect of surface reflectance on aerosol retrievals. Concerning the land cover analysis, a spectral rule-based software system, called SOIL MAPPER [21], were used to distinguish surface types. This software uses reflectances in eight wavelengths (0.66, 0.87, 0.47, 0.55, 1.64, 2.13, 11.03, and 12.02 μm) to identify 57 different classes, out of which 40 refer to different land types. In our experiments a compact classification mode with 12 land cover classes was used. Cloud, snow, and unclassified pixels were discarded, whereas the nine remaining classes (see Table 4) were utilized to evaluate the SVR prediction model on a land cover basis. A land cover class for each pixel sized 10x10 km^2 was determined as result of application of the classification system on reflectances averaged from all cloudy-free pixels of 1x1 km^2 available in this area.

3 Experimental Results

Our experiments focused on assessing accuracy of the SVRs' AOT in comparison with AERONET AOT. We applied and considered results obtained by aggregate SVR, instance SVR, and MODIS aerosol algorithm at different conditions: by year, by season, and by surface type.

The accuracies of both instance and aggregate SVR estimators are slightly better than those of the MODIS algorithm, as summarized in Table 1. Based on RMS error and correlation coefficient between predicted AOT and AERONET AOT measurements, averaged in 3 year data, instance SVR achieves the highest accuracy, then aggregate SVR follows and finally the MODIS algorithm is. This order is justified by the increase of RMS errors (0.077, 0.084, and 0.090, respectively) and the decrease of correlation coefficients (0.835, 0.812, and 0.807, respectively). The MODIS and SVRs AOT data in 2008 seem to have low quality as shown by the lowest correlation with AERONET AOT. However, instance SVR, in this case, still outperforms (CORR=0.802) the aggregate SVR (CORR=0.758) and MODIS algorithm (CORR=0.764).

Table 1. MODIS algorithm, Aggregate SVR, and Instance SVR accuracy by year

Year	Obs.	MODIS		Aggregate SVR		Instance SVR	
		RMS	CORR	RMS	CORR	RMS	CORR
2006	21,555	0.095	0.831	0.087	0.847	0.086	0.850
2007	24,251	0.087	0.827	0.081	0.831	0.074	0.853
2008	20,455	0.087	0.764	0.084	0.758	0.072	0.802
Total	**66,225**	**0.090**	**0.807**	**0.084**	**0.812**	**0.077**	**0.835**

Table 2 shows in detail the consuming time of aggregate SVR and instance SVR for the above experiment. Executions are tested on a computer with Intel (R) Core(TM)2 CPU 6400 @2.13 GHz, 2Gb RAM and Ubuntu 8.10 platform. Instance SVR spends about 240 seconds to predict 66,255 data, while aggregate SVR uses much smaller amount of time, 26 seconds. This difference is mainly due to the number of aggregate data set used for training in aggregate SVR less than instance data set used in instance SVR (132,522 data compared to 10,778), which induces data models with different sizes. The performance time will be meaningful for further SVR applications that aim at increasing spatial resolution of aerosol retrievals. In fact, with 10x10 km^2 spatial resolution, each MODIS image consists of 135x203 pixels. Increasing spatial resolution up to 1x1 km^2, more than 2 million pixels in an image would need to be processed. Also, the slow performance of instance SVRs hints at the need for further investigations of data selection and application of pruning techniques in the training phase.

Table 2. Aggregate SVR vs. Instance SVR in consuming time performance

Year	Obs.	Aggregate SVR		Instance SVR	
		Training Data	Time (s)	Training Data	Time (s)
2006	21,555	3,549	7.4563	44,706	66.59
2007	24,251	3,378	8.9790	42,010	106.69
2008	20,455	3,851	9.4843	45,806	70.94
Total	**66,225**	**10,778**	**25.9196**	**132,522**	**244.22**

We carried out the same further experiments on data sets separated by seasons and surface types to consider effects of meteorological conditions and surface reflectance on aerosol retrieval. Data in pairs of years were used for training SVRs, while data on the remaining year were classified by seasons and surface classes for testing purposes.

In autumn period (Oct.-Dec.), aerosol retrieval has the lowest accuracy obtained in all algorithms. As shown in Table 3, instance SVR has the most competitive accuracies that are better than those of MODIS algorithm in spring (Apr.-Jun.), summer (Jul.-Sep.) and autumn (Oct.-Dec.) and slightly worse in winter (Jan.-Mar.). The aggregate SVR presents its weakness for AOT estimation in winter (CORR=0.799). The RMS errors of all retrieval algorithms, which are higher in spring and summer, reflect the fact that larger AOT values are observed during these periods [2].

Table 3. MODIS algorithm, Aggregate SVR, and Instance SVR accuracy by season

Season	Obs.	MODIS		Aggregated SVR		Instance SVR	
		RMS	CORR	RMS	CORR	RMS	CORR
Jan. - Mar.	9,014	0.074	0.828	0.073	0.799	0.066	0.819
Apr. - Jun.	21,885	0.094	0.824	0.088	0.814	0.082	0.837
Jul. - Sep.	24,465	0.096	0.791	0.089	0.798	0.081	0.825
Oct. - Dec.	10,452	0.079	0.728	0.073	0.733	0.071	0.742

MODIS used two algorithms for land and ocean because of different physical interactions between aerosol and matters. Among all surface types listed in Table 4, only the water class refers to water pixels while remaining surfaces present the land pixels. MODIS ocean algorithm gained high accuracy (RMS=0.067, CORR=0.822), but it can be further improved by instance SVR (RMS=0.062, CORR=0.850). Out of land surface types, four classes Peat Bog, Evergreen Forest, Agricultural Areas and/or Artificial non Agricultural, Areas Scrub/Herbaceous Vegetation have a small number of samples, so their results should not be considered. In all remaining cases, instance SVR is more accurate than the MODIS algorithm. The biggest improvement can be observed at Artificial Surfaces and/or Open Spaces with little or no Vegetation surface, which is consistent with results of previous studies that showed the poor performance of the MODIS algorithm on bright surfaces [4].

Aggregate SVR has the worst accuracy on water pixels. It can be explained as result of the small contribution of water pixels on averaged data used for training aggregate SVR model, that didn't occur with instance SVR. This phenomenon influences pixels belonging to other surface types except Deciduous Forest and/or Agriculture Area class that has a large data set and therefore can be represented well by averaged values.

Table 4. MODIS algorithm, Aggregate SVR, and Instance SVR accuracy by surface

Classes	Obs.	MODIS		Aggregate SVR		Instance SVR	
		RMS	CORR	RMS	CORR	RMS	CORR
Water	2,981	0.067	**0.822**	0.071	**0.799**	0.062	**0.850**
Peat Bogs	91	0.112	**0.622**	0.151	**0.527**	0.129	**0.550**
Deciduous Forest	2,734	0.086	**0.692**	0.072	**0.681**	0.065	**0.700**
Evergreen Forest	19	0.054	**0.489**	0.065	**0.584**	0.053	**0.714**
Deciduous Forest and/or Agricultural Area	34,316	0.080	**0.824**	0.075	**0.824**	0.702	**0.833**
Agricultural Areas and/or Artificial non Agricultural Areas	25	0.103	**0.895**	0.086	**0.926**	0.080	**0.950**
Scrub/Herbaceous Vegetation and/or Agricultural Areas	5,302	0.082	**0.825**	0.083	**0.806**	0.075	**0.829**
Artificial Surfaces and/or Open Spaces with little or no Vegetation	5,961	0.096	**0.746**	0.085	**0.769**	0.078	**0.808**
Scrub/Herbaceous Vegetation	134	0.060	**0.892**	0.075	**0.871**	0.066	**0.882**

4 Conclusion and Future Works

In this paper an application of SVR technique on MODIS and AERONET data to predict AOT information has been presented. Satellite and ground-based data covering the European areas from 2006 to 2008 were considered. Then, SVRs were applied on instance data set and aggregate data set to make different non-linear regressions for aerosol retrievals. The experiment results show that SVR approach is competitive to MODIS algorithm and, especially, can improve prediction accuracy over areas having no or little vegetation. Out of two SVR models, instance SVR outperforms the aggregate SVR, but more improvements should be investigated to deal with training data overload and time execution.

In future, we will investigate the instance SVR more deeply in order to overcome the mentioned disadvantages. Also, this approach will be applied to estimate AOT at 1x1 km^2 spatial resolution, which is suitable for local-scale monitoring applications.

References

1. Remer, L.A., Tanré, D., Kaufman, Y.J.: Algorithm for Remote Sensing of Tropospheric Acrosol From MODIS: Collection 5. MODIS ATBD (2004)
2. Kaufman, Y.J., Tanre, D.: Algorithm for Remote Sensing of Tropospheric Aerosol from MODIS. In: MODIS ATBD (1997)
3. Abdou, W.A., Diner, D.J., Martonchik, J.V., Bruegge, C.J., Kahn, R.A., Gaitley, B.J., Crean, K.A.: Comparison of coincident Multiangle Imaging Spectroradiometer and Moderate Resolution Imaging Spectroradiometer aerosol optical depths over land and ocean scenes containing Aerosol Robotic Network sites. Journal of Geophysical research 110(D10S07), 11967–11976 (2005)
4. Nguyen, T.N.T., Mantovani, S., Bottoni, M.: Estimation of Aerosol and Air Quality Fields with PM MAPPER – An Optical Multispectral Data Processing Package. In: ISPRS Commission VII Symposium, Vienna, Austria (2010)

5. Ma, Y., Gong, W., Zhu, Z., Zhang, L., Li, P.: Cloud Amount and Aerosol Characteristic Research in the Atmosphere over Hubei Province, China, pp. III-631–III-634. IEEE/IGARSS (2009)

6. Ramakrishnan, R., Schauer, J.J., Chen, L., Huang, Z., Shafer, M.M., Gross, D.S., Musicant, D.R.: The EDAM project: Mining atmospheric aerosol datasets: Research Articles. International Journal of Intelligent Systems 20(7), 759–787 (2005)

7. Chen, Q., Shao, Y.: The Application of Improved BP Neural Network Algorithm in Urban Air Quality Prediction: Evidence from China. In: 2008 IEEE Pacific-Asia Workshop on Computational Intelligence and Industrial Application, pp. 160–163 (2008)

8. Lu, W., Wang, W., Leung, A.Y.T., Lo, S.M., Yuen, R.K.K., Xu, Z., Fan, H.: Air Pollutant Parameter Forecasting Using Support Vector Machine. In: Proceedings of the 2002 International Joint Conference on Neural Network, pp. 630–635 (2002)

9. Siwek, K., Osowski, S., Garanty, K., Sowinski, M.: Ensemble of Neural Predictors for Forecasting the Atmospheric Pollution. In: Proceedings of IEEE International Joint Conference on Neural Network, pp. 643–648 (2008)

10. Osowski, S., Garanty, K.: Wavelets and Support Vector Machine for Forecasting the Meteorological Pollution. In: Proceedings of the 7th Nordic Signal Processing Symposium 2006, pp. 158–161 (2006)

11. Okada, Y., Mukai, S., Sano, I.: Neural Network Approach for Aerosol Retrieval. IEEE/IGARSS 4, 1716–1718 (2001)

12. Han, B., Vucetic, S., Braverman, A., Obradovic, Z.: A statistical complement to deterministic algorithms for the retrieval of aerosol optical thickness from radiance data. Engineering Applications of Artificial Intelligence 19, 787–795 (2006)

13. Xu, Q., Obradovic, Z., Han, B., Li, Y., Braverman, A., Vucetic, S.: Improving Aerosol Retrieval Accuracy by Integrating AERONET, MISR and MODIS Data. In: 8th Intenational Conference on Information Fusion, Philadelphia, PA (2005)

14. Vucetic, S., Han, B., Mi, W., Li, Z., Obradovic, Z.: A Data-Mining Approach for the Validation of Aerosol Retrievals. IEEE Geoscience and Remote Sensing Letter 5(1), 113–117 (2008)

15. Lary, D.J., Remer, L.A., MacNeill, D., Roscoe, B., Paradise, S.: Machine Learning Bias Correction of MODIS Aerosol Optical Depth. IEEE Geoscience and Remote Sensing Letters 6(4), 694–698 (2009)

16. Vapnik, V.N.: The nature of statistical learning theory. Springer, New York (1995)

17. Ichoku, C., Chu, D.A., Mattoo, S., Kaufman, Y.J., Remer, L.A., Tanre, D.T., Slutsker, I., Holben, B.N.: A spatio-temporal approach for global validation and analysis of MODIS aerosol products. Geophysical Research Letter 29(12), 1–4 (2002)

18. Wang, Z., Radosavljevic, V., Han, B., Obradovic, Z., Vucetic, S.: Aerosol Optical Depth Prediction from Satellite Observations by Multiple Instance Regression. In: SIAM Conference on Data Mining, Atlanta, GA (2008)

19. AERONET - AErosol Robotic Network, http://aeronet.gsfc.nasa.gov/

20. LIBSVM: A Library for Support Vector Machines, http://www.csie.ntu.edu.tw/~cjlin/libsvm/

21. MEEO: Meteorological Environmental Earth Observation, http://www.meeo.it/

An Overproduce-and-Choose Strategy to Create Classifier Ensembles with Tuned SVM Parameters Applied to Real-World Fault Diagnosis

Estefhan Dazzi Wandekokem, Flávio M. Varejão, and Thomas W. Rauber

Department of Computer Science, Federal University of Espírito Santo. Vitória, ES, Brazil

Abstract. We present a supervised learning classification method for model-free fault detection and diagnosis, aiming to improve the maintenance quality of motor pumps installed on oil rigs. We investigate our generic fault diagnosis method on 2000 examples of real-world vibrational signals obtained from operational faulty industrial machines. The diagnostic system detects each considered fault in an input pattern using an ensemble of classifiers, which is composed of accurate classifiers that differ on their predictions as much as possible. The ensemble is built by first using complementary feature selection techniques to produce a set of candidate classifiers, and finally selecting an optimized subset of them to compose the ensemble. We propose a novel ensemble creation method based on feature selection. We work with Support Vector Machine (SVM) classifiers. As the performance of a SVM strictly depends on its hyperparameters, we also study whether and how varying the SVM hyperparameters might increase the ensemble accuracy. Our experiments show the usefulness of appropriately tuning the SVM hyperparameters in order to increase the ensemble diversity and accuracy.

Keywords: Fault diagnosis, feature selection, feature extraction, classifier ensemble, Support Vector Machine, multi-label classification.

1 Introduction

The detection and diagnosis of faults in industrial machines is advantageos for economical and security reasons. The objective is to repair damaged components during planned maintanence, which minimizes machinery standstill besides providing more secure operations.

Two principal approaches to create a fault predictor exist: model-based techniques and model-free techniques. The model-based line of research relies on an analytical model of the studied process, involving time dependent differential equations [1]. However in real-world processes the availability of an analytical model is often unrealistic or inaccurate due to the complexity of the process. In this case model-free techniques are an alternative method [2].

I. Bloch and R.M. Cesar, Jr. (Eds.): CIARP 2010, LNCS 6419, pp. 500–508, 2010.
© Springer-Verlag Berlin Heidelberg 2010

We present a model-free method based on the *supervised learning* [3] classification paradigm as the primal mechanism to automatically generate the fault classifiers. This presents as advantage the requirement of a minimum of a priori knowledge about the plant, as the fault predictor is automatically defined based on training data. We work with 2000 examples of vibrational signals obtained from operational faulty motor pumps, acquired from 25 oil platforms off the Brazilian coast during five years. Human experts provided a label for every fault present in each acquired example.

We focus on the horizontal motor pump with extended coupling between the electric motor and the pump. Accelerometers are placed at strategic positions along the main directions to capture specific vibrations of the main shaft. To extract features, we apply well known signal processing techniques like Fourier transform, envelope analysis based on the Hilbert transform [9] and median filtering. So the features correspond to the vibrational energy in a predetermined frequency band. The cardinality of an extracted feature vector G is 95. Several faults can simultaneously occur in a motor pump, which increases the diagnosis complexity. We build a predictor for detecting six fault categories in an input pattern: rolling element bearing failures; pump blade unbalance; hydrodynamic fault; shaft misalignment; mechanical looseness; and structural looseness.

The novelty of this paper is two-fold. First, we present a generic model-free diagnosis procedure for diagnosing faults using features extracted from the machine signals. Each fault is predicted by a distinct ensemble [7] of support vector machine (SVM) [4] classifiers. We propose a novel ensemble creation method well suited to fault diagnosis as suggested by our experiments. Second, we work with data from real-world operating industrial machines instead of using data from a controlled laboratory environment which is almost always found in the literature. That is highly desirable, as laboratory hardware cannot realistically represent intricate real-world fault occurrences.

The remainder of this paper is organized as follows. Our model-free approach to fault diagnosis based on feature extraction, feature selection and ensemble classification is explained in section 2. Section 3 outlines the proposed ensemble creation method for dealing with real-world fault diagnosis. In section 4 we show the experimental results achieved by the studied faults predictors using the acquired database. Finally, section 5 draws conclusions and points out to future research.

2   Model-Free Approach to Fault Diagnosis

We formulate the fault diagnosis problem as a multi-label classification task in which several labels (fault classes) may be simultaneously assigned to an example. Each fault category is represented by a binary predictor, diagnosing the presence or absence of that individual fault in an input pattern. Therefore the problem at hand is the one of creating accurate binary predictors.

We work with the *support vector machine* [4] (SVM) classifier which is currently considered one of the most powerful machine learning approaches for solving binary classification problems. We use a widely adopted SVM model, namely a Radial Basis Function kernel and the C-SVM classification architecture [3]. So we work with two hyperparameters, namely the regularization parameter C which controls the model complexity and the kernel parameter γ which controls the nonlinear mapping of the features. As the performance of a SVM strictly depends on its hyperparameters, we use an effective method to tune them, namely grid search combined with cross-validation on each candidate parameter vector.

To increase the accuracy achieved by an individual classifier, the research in *classifier ensembles* [7] indicates that a better generalization power is achieved when the class of an input pattern is predicted by a set of very accurate classifiers that collectively disagree on their predictions as much as possible. The traditional approach to create an ensemble is to vary the training data set used by the classifiers (see [5] for a reference on SVM ensembles). However such an approach usually is not well suited to SVMs, as a small variation on the training data set tends to cause a small variation on the SVM decision function. On the other hand, varying the SVM parameters does decisively change the SVM decision function [10]. This is useful for ensemble creation because the divergence among the SVMs in an ensemble increases, and so does its accuracy [8].

Another useful approach for ensemble creation is to vary the feature set of the classifiers (see [11] for a reference on fault diagnosis). But at the present time the role of SVM parameters in feature-based ensembles of SVM classifiers has not been investigated yet. In this work we propose a novel ensemble creation method based on feature selection, and study whether and how varying also the SVM hyperparameters might increase the ensemble accuracy.

3   Feature-Based Classifier Ensembles

In this work we propose a novel method for creating an ensemble. This method presents as advantages simplicity and a relatively low computational cost. Besides, it is well suited to fault diagnosis as it is based on feature selection, an approach that allows the crucial features to be detected and prioritized.

3.1   Feature Selection

Feature selection [6] is the process of choosing an optimized subset of features for classification from a larger set. In this work we employ the wrapper approach in which the learning algorithm itself is used to access the saliency of the candidate feature sets. So the selection criterion J used to estimate the performance of a candidate feature set X_k is the Area Under the ROC Curve (AUC) achieved by a classifier which uses X_k (estimated by cross-validation).

As an exhaustive search is not feasible in general we work with suboptimal search strategies. We work with two complementary hill-climbing searches. The *Sequential Forward Selection* (SFS) search method starts with an empty set of currently selected features, and at each step one feature is definitely included in it. Consider that k features have already been selected and included in the feature set X_k. To include one more feature in X_k, each non-selected feature

ξ_j must be tested individually together with the already selected features and ranked according to the criterion J, so that the feature ξ_h which provided the highest criterion J is selected and included in X_k. The *Sequential Backward Selection* (SBS) search method operates in a similar way as SFS, but SFS includes features, while SBS removes features. SBS starts with every feature already included within the set of selected features X_k. At each step, one feature is definitely removed from the set, namely the one that provided the highest criterion J with its individual exclusion from X_k.

3.2 Best Selected Feature Subsets Ensemble Creation

The proposed ensemble creation method, which we call *Best Selected Feature Subsets* (BSFS), is based on a two-stage *overproduce-and-choose* [7] strategy. It operates by initially using complementary hill-climbing feature selection methods to build a large set $\mathcal{L}$ of classifiers that are candidates to constitute the ensemble, and further using a hill-climbing search to select just a reduced, optimized subset of classifiers $\mathscr{E}$ from $\mathcal{L}$.

To combine the individual predictions of the classifiers in an ensemble into a single decision we use an effective, simple method, namely averaging the classification scores given to an input pattern by the classifiers in that ensemble.

The classifier overproduction stage. To create the set $\mathcal{L}$ of candidate classifiers to compose the ensemble, we first build a set of feature sets Ξ composed of several promising feature sets. Each of these feature sets uses features from the global pool G of available features. We perform m distinct sequential feature selection searches, $\{\mathcal{S}_1, \ldots, \mathcal{S}_i, \ldots, \mathcal{S}_m\}$, so that the feature sets in Ξ are determined by taking each produced feature set $X_k^{\mathcal{S}_i}$ which uses a number k of features selected by a search $\mathcal{S}_i$, for every combination of k and i with $k = 1, 2, \ldots, |G|$ and $i = 1, 2, \ldots, m$. To obtain the feature sets, if the search $\mathcal{S}_i$ operates in a forward way (for instance SFS), we require $\mathcal{S}_i$ to select a total of $|G - 1|$ features. On the other hand if the search $\mathcal{S}_i$ operates in a backward way (for instance SBS), we require $\mathcal{S}_i$ to select a total of 1 feature.

Then the set of candidate classifiers $\mathcal{L}$ is defined by building, for each feature set $X_k^{\mathcal{S}_i}$ in the set Ξ, a classifier c_j that uses this feature set, and we also automatically tune the hyperparameters of this classifier c_j aiming to increase its accuracy. So $\mathcal{L}$ is composed of every produced c_j.

The classifier selection stage. After building the set of candidate classifiers $\mathcal{L}$, we use a method to select an optimized set of n_c classifiers to compose the final ensemble $\mathscr{E}$, selecting from $\mathcal{L}$. For performing this ensemble classifier selection $\mathrm{ECS}(\mathcal{L}, n_c)$ we employ the Sequential Forward Selection (SFS) search. We define the criterion J of a particular candidate subset of classifiers to compose the ensemble (a subset of $\mathcal{L}$) as the AUC on training data achieved by this candidate ensemble. The score that a candidate ensemble gives to a training pattern $\mathbf{x}$ can be obtained by averaging the scores given to $\mathbf{x}$ by the classifiers in that ensemble (the scores of the training data are estimated by cross-validation).

As we use the SFS search to select the classifiers in the ensemble, the first selected classifier c_l to compose the ensemble is the one with the highest individual cross-validation AUC. Following, each next selected classifier is the non-selected one which enables the highest criterion J with its individual inclusion in the current ensemble. When n_c classifiers are selected, the inclusion process stops, so the ensemble $\mathcal{E}$ is finally built.

4   Experimental Results

To access the effectiveness of the studied classification approaches, we performed a stratified 5×2 cross-validation [7]. So in the experiments we performed five replications of a 2-fold cross-validation. In each replication, the complete database of 2000 examples was randomly partitioned, in a stratified manner, into two sets each one with approximately 1000 examples (the stratification process preserves the distribution of the six fault categories between both sets). Then in each replication each considered classification model for creating the predictor of a fault was trained on a set and tested on the remaining one; so after the five replications we averaged the ten distinct test accuracies it achieved.

4.1   Studied Classification Approaches

For each of the six considered faults, we studied four different classification models for creating the predictor of that fault. Our objective is to evaluate the efficiency of feature-based SVM ensembles besides studying an approach for varying the hyperparameters of the SVM classifiers in an ensemble.

For the studied classification models based on the proposed BSFS ensemble creation method, to build the set $\mathcal{L}$ of candidate classifiers we ran four distinct feature selection experiments $\{\mathcal{S}_1, \ldots, \mathcal{S}_4\}$, which were: the SFS search using the SVM hyperparameters values ($C = 8.0, \gamma = 0.5$) for building SVMs to estimate the selection criterion (that was the AUC estimated by 10-fold cross-validation); SFS using ($C = 2.0, \gamma = 8.0$); SBS using ($C = 8.0, \gamma = 0.5$); and SBS using ($C = 2.0, \gamma = 8.0$). Then for each produced feature subset $X_k^{\mathcal{S}_i}$ (obtained by using, for each $\mathcal{S}_i$, each number of selected features from $k = 1$ to $k = 95$) we built a SVM classifier to compose $\mathcal{L}$. In order to select a subset $\mathcal{E}$ of classifier from $\mathcal{L}$ to compose the ensemble, we set the desired ensemble size as $n_c = 10$ as we observed a tendency of an AUC decrease using a larger set.

The SVM classification model. We studied the effectiveness of a single SVM which used as feature set the complete global pool of features G. We used the grid-search parameter optimization method to tune its hyperparameters. We refer to this classification model as SVM.

The BSFS-n classification model. In this experiment we aim to get an insight into the effectiveness of the proposed ensemble creation method to generate a feature-based ensemble, without varying the SVM hyperparameters of the classifiers. So after performing the four feature selection experiments, we built every SVM in the set of candidate classifiers $\mathcal{L}$ using the hyperparameters values $C = 8.0$, $\gamma = 0.5$ (which usually provided accurate SVMs). So the selected SVMs in the final ensemble $\mathcal{E}$ also used $C = 8.0$, $\gamma = 0.5$. We refer to this classification model as BSFS-n.

The BSFS-t classification model. We studied the usefulness of directly tuning the SVM hyperparameters of the classifiers in an SVM ensemble, aiming to increse the individual accuracy of each of those SVMs. So we used the grid search method to tune the hyperparameters of each SVM in an ensemble initially defined by BSFS-n. We refer to this classification model as BSFS-t.

The BSFS-o classification model. Finally we evaluated an ensemble in which we used grid search method to tune the hyperparameters of every SVM in the set of candidate classifiers $\mathcal{L}$. It is expected that the subsequent selection process actively searches for a set of diverse SVMs which differ on their feature set and also on their SVM hyperparameters, therefore composing a more diverse and accurate ensemble. We refer to this classification model as BSFS-o.

4.2   Misalignment Predictor Overproduced SVMs

We present some graphs related to the construction of the misalignment predictor, for the first pair of train-test data of the 5×2 cross-validation process. Figures 1 and 2 present, respectively to the BSFS-o and BSFS-n classification models, the test data AUC achieved by each produced SVM in the set $\mathcal{L}$. It can be seen that the AUC value individually achieved by the SVMs presented much more variation among them for the BSFS-o model (in figure 1) than for the BSFS-n model (in figure 2), as even for similar feature sets (with a similar

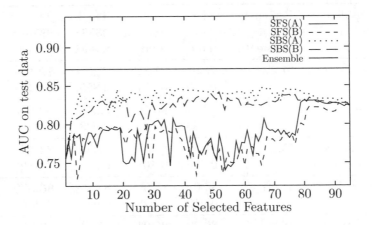

Fig. 1. AUC on test data achieved by the SVMs in the set $\mathcal{L}$ of candidate classifiers, for the BSFS-o classification model. For comparison we also show as a horizontal line the test data AUC achieved by the final ensemble.

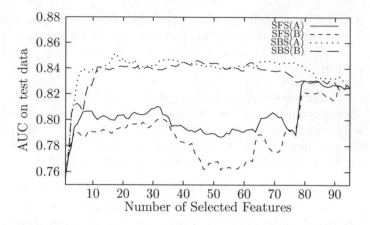

Fig. 2. AUC on test data achieved by the SVMs in the set $\mathcal{L}$ of candidate classifiers, for the BSFS-n classification model

number of features) the AUC value considerably changed. This suggests that BSFS-o is able to produce more diverse SVMs than BSFS-n due to the different hyperparameters values that are used.

4.3   5 × 2 Cross-Validation Estimation Results

Table 1 presents, for each considered fault, the percentage of negative class (non-faulty) data, and also the accuracy and AUC estimated on test data by the

Table 1. Class distribution and 5x2 test data accuracy, AUC

Considered fault classifier	Percentage of negative class data	The SVM model	The BSFS-n model	The BSFS-t model	The BSFS-o model
Misalignment	57.4%	75.9%	77.8%	77.5%	**79.3%**
		0.829	0.851	0.855	**0.872**
Bearing	64.3%	83.4%	86.5%	86.7%	**88.0%**
		0.909	0.932	0.933	**0.945**
Unbalance	75.1%	81.5%	82.4%	82.6%	**83.1%**
		0.836	0.861	0.867	**0.882**
Hydrodynamic	57.6%	84.0%	85.9%	85.8%	**86.5%**
		0.912	0.928	0.929	**0.936**
Structural looseness	78.8%	86.7%	86.9%	87.2%	**87.8%**
		0.873	0.877	0.881	**0.919**
Mechanical looseness	89.0%	92.9%	93.0%	93.1%	**93.5%**
		0.878	0.880	0.889	**0.901**

5×2 cross-validation estimation process, individually achieved by each considered classification model for creating the predictor of that fault.

5   Conclusions and Future Work

In this paper we presented a data-driven supervised learning classification method for performing real-world fault diagnosis. We proposed a novel approach for creating ensembles of SVM classifiers based on the variation of the feature sets and also the SVM hyperparameters.

We focused on the role of SVM parameters in feature-based SVM ensembles. Our experiments show that tuning the hyperparameters of each candidate SVM to compose the ensemble, aiming to increase its individual accuracy, enables the creation of a more accurate ensemble, as an optimized subset of SVMs might be selected to finally constitute the ensemble. In this case the ensemble is composed of accurate SVMs which are as divergent as possible due different feature sets and also SVM hyperparameters. In opposition to that, our experiments show that the ensemble accuracy gain is lower if that process of hyperparameters tuning is only performed in an already defined ensemble. This suggests that, to create a more accurate ensemble, the divergence among the produced classifiers should be taken into account during the process of varying the SVM hyperparameters.

We intend to acquire more real-world data, from different machines and also from more sources than just vibrational signals, which increases the classification accuracy as the features are extracted from complementary information sources. Thus we plan to develop a multiparametric diagnostic system, which uses vibration signals complemented with electrical signals such as current and power.

Acknowledgments

This work was supported by COPES-Petrobrás.

References

1. Angelo, C.H.D., Bossio, G.R., Giaccone, S.J., Valla, M.I., Solsona, J.A., Garcia, G.O.: Online model-based stator-fault detection and identification in induction motors. IEEE Transactions on Industrial Electronics 56 (November 2009)
2. Bellini, A., Filippetti, F., Tassoni, C., Capolino, G.A.: Advances in diagnostic techniques for induction machines. IEEE Transactions on Industrial Electronics 55 (December 2008)
3. Bishop, C.M.: Pattern Recognition and Machine Learning. Springer, Berlin (2007)
4. Cortes, C., Vapnik, V.: Support-vector network. Machine Learning 20, 273–297 (1995)
5. Evgeniou, T., Pontil, M., Elisseeff, A.: Leave-one-out error, stability, and generalization of voting combinations of classifiers. Machine Learning (2002)
6. Guyon, I., Elisseeff, A.: An introduction to variable and feature selection. J. Mach. Learn. Res. 3, 1157–1182 (2003)

7. Kuncheva, L.I.: Combining Pattern Classifiers: Methods and Algorithms. Springer, Heidelberg (2004)
8. Li, X., Wang, L., Sung, E.: Adaboost with svm-based component classifiers. Engineering Applications of Artificial Intelligence 21 (2008)
9. Mendel, E., Mariano, L.Z., Drago, I., Loureiro, S., Rauber, T.W., Varejao, F.M.: Automatic bearing fault pattern recognition using vibration signal analysis. In: Proc. of the IEEE International Symposium on Industrial Electronics (ISIE 2008) (2008)
10. Valentini, G., Dietterich, T.G.: Bias-variance analysis of support vector machines for the development of svm-based ensemble methods. The Journal of Machine Learning Research 5 (January 2004)
11. Zio, E., Baraldi, P., Gola, G.: Feature-based classifier ensembles for diagnosing multiple faults in rotating machinery. Applied Soft Computing 8, 1365–1380 (2008)

Multi-Objective Semi-Supervised Feature Selection and Model Selection Based on Pearson's Correlation Coefficient

Frederico Coelho[1], Antonio Padua Braga[1], and Michel Verleysen[2]

[1] Universidade Federal de Minas Gerais,
Belo Horizonte, MG, Brazil
{fredgfc,apbraga}@ufmg.br
www.ufmg.br
[2] Universite Catholique de Louvain,
Louvain-la-Neuve, Belgium
michel.verleysen@uclouvain.be
www.uclouvain.be

Abstract. This paper presents a Semi-Supervised Feature Selection Method based on a univariate relevance measure applied to a multiobjective approach of the problem. Along the process of decision of the optimal solution within Pareto-optimal set, atempting to maximize the relevance indexes of each feature, it is possible to determine a minimum set of relevant features and, at the same time, to determine the optimal model of the neural network.

Keywords: Semi-supervised, feature selection, Pearson, Relief.

1 Introduction

In recent years, especially in the fields of bioinformatics and web-based information retrieval, the problem of Semi-Supervised Learning [6] (SSL) has gained increased interest. Broadly speaking, the problem involves the construction of classifiers with very limited labeling information and large amount of unlabeled data. Particularly in these areas, new samples are easily generated but model induction from input-output data is faced with scarce data due to the high cost for labeling. Due to the availability of a large amount of untagged input data, the question that arises is whether to use or not such a huge amount of information in model induction.

The general problem is characterized by the induction of a model from the labeled dataset $D_L = \{\mathbf{x}_i, y_i\}_{i=1}^{N_L}$ considering also the structural information contained in the unlabeled set $D_U = \{\mathbf{x}_i\}_{i=1}^{N_U}$ [1]. The approaches for such a problem usually involve jointly solving the supervised problem defined by D_L and the unsupervised one defined by D_U [1,4].

---

[1] N_L and N_U are, respectively, the sizes of the labeled and unlabeled datasets, x_i is the ith observation and y_i is the class label of ith observation.

I. Bloch and R.M. Cesar, Jr. (Eds.): CIARP 2010, LNCS 6419, pp. 509–516, 2010.

Feature selection in such a framework is also faced with the same problem of dealing with small input-output samples under the availability of large amounts of untagged data, so the problem should also be handled in both fronts. Clearly, unsupervised feature selection methods [12,7] could be applied to the whole dataset $D_L \cup D_U$, but disregarding the labels $y_i \in D_L$ could represent loss of (available) information. Therefore, Semi-Supervised Feature Selection (SSFS) is also faced with the problem of selecting features by considering both datasets D_L and D_U [24,21,3]. In addition, the Supervised Learning (SL) problem characterized by D_L, involves the many issues related to supervised learning, such as minimizing both the empirical and the structural risks of the model [22]. Feature selection with embedded [3] or wrapped [14] models should also take into consideration such general issues in order to guarantee reliability in the search for representative models.

In this paper, we present a new SSFS method that allows both the selection of a classifier from a set of neural networks candidate solutions generated by a multi-objective (MOBJ) learning method [17] and the selection of relevant features for such a model. The Pareto-set solutions of the MOBJ method are obtained according to the general statistical learning principles [22], by minimizing both the empirical and the structural risks, represented by the sum of squared errors $\sum e^2$ and the norm of the neural network weight vectors $||\mathbf{w}||$ [17]. Once the Pareto-Optimal solutions are generated in a supervised manner, by considering only D_L, they also yield labels for D_U, since each Pareto-Optimal classifier is valid in the whole input domain. Therefore, for each Pareto-set solution S_k, there is a labeling $D_U^k \{\mathbf{x}_i \, \hat{y}_i^k\}_{i=1}^{N_U}$ for D_U. The aim of the feature selection method is to find the optimal solution S_* that maximizes the separability of $D_L \cup D_U^k$; the features with the highest relevance indexes (RI) are then selected.

The method can be regarded both as Semi-Supervised Learning (SSL) and as SSFS, since labeled and unlabeled data are used for both model and feature selection. The final classifier selected is the one that maximizes the RI of both the labeled and unlabeled data and the features selected are those that yield the highest RI.

In this paper, the general idea of the method is presented and the obtained results are very consistent as discussed at the end. The general organization of the paper is as follows. Section 2 deals with the Semi-supervised Learning and Feature Selection; Section 3 aboard the Multi-objective learning and section 3.1 presents the proposed method. After that the results are shown and a discussion and conclusions take place.

2   Semi-Supervised Learning

In supervised learning the methods need labeled data for training, however, labeling can be difficult, expensive and time consuming. The reason for that lies in the frequent requirement of specific human experience efforts to label patterns. In contrast, unlabeled data can be easy to obtain. In order to handle both types of information, there are many SSL methods in the literature, however, most algorithms are based on a pre-established assumption about the unlabeled data, such as data set contiguity or low density in the margin region [6, Introduction] [2,9]. The assumption usually imposes a strong bias in the kind of solutions that may be achieved by the algorithm, although it is an important principle to compensate the missing labeling information.

Recent works in the field can be mentioned like the one in [23] where labeled and unlabeled data are integrated using the clustering structure of unlabeled data as well as the smoothness structure of the estimated class priors. In [15] the authors combined transductive inference with the *Multi-relational data mining* (MRDM) classification. Other interesting work is presented in [20], where authors applied transductive learning to K-Nearest Neighbors (KNN). A long list of references in the area can be found in [13].

The algorithm described in this paper is based on the separability assumption between classes. The decision making procedure is based on a relevance index for features that estimates separability. A restricted set of Pareto-Optimal [5] solutions is obtained from the labeled data and a decision making procedure is accomplished in order to select the one that maximizes the relevance index over labeled and unlabeled data.

2.1 Semi-Supervised Feature Selection

Semi-supervised feature selection is based on the same principles of SSL. The goal is, therefore, to select features in the framework of a very small number of labeled data and a large number of unlabeled samples. It is clear, however, that feature selection does not depend uniquely on labeled data, since redundancy elimination methods can be applied to the whole dataset regardless of any existing labels [16]. Nevertheless, in order to estimate a relevance index for features, a quantitative measure of how an individual feature or a group of features discriminates the likelihood of classes, should be considered. Fischer Linear Discriminant [8] and Relief [11] are examples of such Supervised Feature Selection approaches. In the absence of labels, one may search for some structural information in the data in order to accomplish Unsupervised Feature Selection [12,16]. The use of information coming from both sources is the goal of Semi-Supervised Feature Selection (SSFS), which has been the subject of many recent publications [24,21,3].

3 Multi-Objective Learning

It is well known that learning algorithms that are based only on error minimization do not guarantee good generalization performance models. In addition to the training set error, some other network-related parameters should be adapted in the learning phase in order to control generalization performance. The need for more than a single objective function paves the way for treating the supervised learning problem with multi-objective optimization (MOBJ) techniques [19].

Usual approaches explicitly consider the two objectives of minimizing the sum of squares error and the norm of the weight vectors. The learning task is carried on by minimizing both objectives simultaneously, using vector optimization methods. This leads to a set of solutions that is called the Pareto-optimal set [5], from which the best network for modeling the data is selected. Finding the Pareto-optimal set can be interpreted as a way for reducing the search space to a one-dimensional set of candidate solutions, from which the best one is to be chosen. This one-dimensional set exactly follows a trade-off direction between flexibility and rigidity, which means that it can be used for reaching a suitable compromise solution [19].

The decision-making strategy from the Pareto-set is clearly described by a third objective function, such as validation error or separation margin, that also needs to be optimized. The choice of the decision-making objective function defines the kind of solution that one aims to obtain. The strategy described in this paper aims at selecting the solution that maximizes the separability of classes, measured by the Pearson's Correlation Coefficient [18], as will be described in the next section.

3.1 Multi-Objective Semi-Supervised Feature Selection (MOBJ-SSFS)

In general, the MOBJ learning problem can be defined according to the Equation 2

$$w^* = arg\min \frac{1}{n} \sum_{k=1}^{n} \left(d_k - y\left(w, x_k\right) \right)^2 \tag{1}$$

$$Subject\ to\ :\ \|w\| \leq \lambda_i$$

where w and w^* are respectively the weight and the optimal weight vectors, n is the number of observations, d_k is the expected class label of observation k, y_k is the class label found by the neural network and λ_i is the norm constraint value.

Basically, what we do is the following:

- train a Multi-Layer Perceptron with the labeled set D_L, using the ellipsoid method [25] to solve the MOBJ problem described above, for different values of λ_i. This procedure will generate a Pareto-optimal set of solutions, each one representing a different classifier;
- for each different classifier:
  - Label D_U;
  - Calculate Pearson's RI for all features of set $D_L \cup D_U$;
- Select the best solution according to one of two strategies discussed ahead

For each solution in the Pareto-set a ranking of features is obtained. The interpretation of the feature ranking information is accomplished in such a way that the solution that yields a better class separation according to Pearson's correlation coefficient is selected.

We would like to select the solution that maximizes RI, however, there is no guarantee that there is a single solution that jointly maximizes RI for all features, so the solution selected is the one that maximizes the majority of features (Strategy 1). In addition to selecting a solution from the Pareto-set, this strategy also comes-up with a ranking of features, that is obtained considering $D_L \cup D_U$ and classifier's performance resulted from MOBJ learning. SSFS can now be accomplished by taking into consideration the resulting ranking of features. An alternative strategy is to select the solution that maximizes the most relevant features among all the Pareto-set solutions (Strategy 2).

4   Results and Discussions

A Multi-Layer-Perceptron (MLP) Neural Network (NN) was trained with the MOBJ algorithm described in the previous sections for the Wisconsin Breast Cancer data from the UCI repository. The data set has 683 samples (patients) with 9 features each one. In order to observe the approach for different proportions of labeled and unlabeled data, the model was trained 30 times for different values of $(\rho = N_L/N_U)$, as can be seen in Figures 1 and 2. The results are presented for the two selection strategies (Strategies 1 and 2) described in the previous paragraph. A benchmark result is also presented in the two graphs for comparison purposes. It is always the lowest curve in the graph (smaller error) and was obtained by selecting each solution from the prior knowledge of the correct labels of all patterns.

Figure 2 shows the absolute classification errors for different features sets. The set composed by features 2,3 and 6 ($S_1 = \{F_2, F_3, F_6\}$) was selected by the MOBJ-SSFS method. The set $S_2 = \{F_1, F_4, F_5, F_6, F_8\}$ was selected by FS-redundancy method [16] and set $S_3 = \{F_1, F_3, F_6, F_8\}$ was selected by RELIEF [10].

The proposed method has an interesting property: while it performs feature selection it also yields Pareto-set selection, i.e. one can use this method also as a decision-making strategy in a MOBJ learning. As expected, the larger the labeled set size the smaller the classification error. The classification errors of networks trained with features selected by recurrence in the highest Person's index positions, and trained networks chosen by Maximum Pearson criteria, are close and have similar performance for different values of ρ. In other words, training the MLP with feature set $S_1 = \{F_2, F_3, F_6\}$ leads to results very close to the benchmark, regardless of the proportion between labeled and unlabeled data. It's also interesting to notice that the average final classification errors with the reduced data set S_1 has lower variance than the obtained with Strategy 1.

Relief RI [10] was also calculated for each possible combination of features subsets in order to identify which are the features that in presence of other combinations of features are always well ranked. The results are very consistent with MOBJ-SSFS. Subset S_1 is well ranked, i.e. even in the presence of one or more features they receive the highest relief's indexes. Depending on Relief's parameter k other subset of features stands (S_3), and it's considered in our

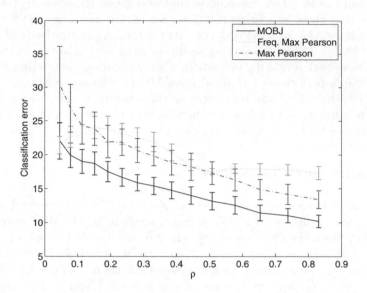

Fig. 1. The solid curve shows the real absolute classification error for the entire data set (samples and features) after training MLP with each amount of N_L defined by ρ. The dash dot one shows the error obtained by solution whose majority of features reaches max Pearson's index. The dot curve shows the error after training MLP using only features 6,2 and 3 that mostly has the three higher indexes in each solution of Pareto.

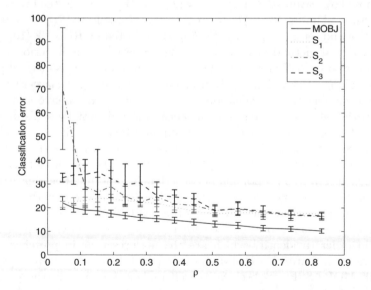

Fig. 2. Set's comparison

results. However, the subset S_1 of features perform better. Features 2,3 and 6 in S_1 are respectively *uniformity of cell size, uniformity of cell shape* and *Bare nuclei*. Features 1 and 8 are *Clump Thickness* and *Normal Nucleoli*.

The method proposed here should not be regarded as a wrapper nor embedded method since it does not use directly the classification results to select model parameters. A MLP was used, although other possible approaches like Support Vector Machines can be applied. The same holds for the rank *metric* used. Here we applied the *Pearson's correlation coefficient* because of its simplicity and because it is simpler to manipulate as an univariate method, but other metrics like *Relief* or *Fischer score* can also be applied.

5   Conclusions

The general concepts of a new SSFS method was presented. The results indicated that the selected features are consistent leading to coherent results for model selection. One interesting issue is that even for small values of ρ, the method was capable to select the feature subset S_1 leading to good classification results and with good stability, when compared to other subsets and even when compared with the results considering all features together. Finally, the ability of choosing one solution from MOBJ Pareto-set, when performing feature selection, is an interesting characteristic of the presented method, since it integrates model selection and feature selection under the frameworks of semi-supervised learning and statistical learning theory.

References

1. Niyogi, P., Belkin, M.: Semi-supervised learning on riemannian manifolds. Machine Learning 56, 209–239 (2004)
2. Coelho, F., de Braga, A.P., Natowicz, R., Rouzier, R.: Semi-supervised model applied to the prediction of the response to preoperative chemotherapy for breast cancer. In: Soft Computing - A Fusion of Foundations, Methodologies and Applications (July 2010)
3. Le Cun, Y., Denker, J.S., Solla, S.A.: Optimal brain damage. In: Advances in Neural Information Processing Systems, pp. 598–605. Morgan Kaufmann, San Francisco (1990)
4. Cover, T., Hart, P.: Nearest neighbor pattern classification. IEEE Transactions on Information Theory 13(1), 21–27 (1967)
5. Chankong, V., Haimes, Y.Y.: Multiobjective Decision Making Theory and Methodology. Elsevier Science, New York (1983)
6. Chapelle, O., Schölkopf, B., Zien, A. (eds.): Semi-Supervised Learning. MIT Press, Cambridge (2006)
7. Dy, J.G., Brodley, C.E.: Feature selection for unsupervised learning. J. Mach. Learn. Res. 5, 845–889 (2004)
8. Fisher, R.A.: The use of multiple measurements in taxonomic problems. Annals Eugen. 7, 179–188 (1936)

9. Kasabov, N., Pang, S.: Transductive support vector machines and applications in bioinformatics for promoter recognition. In: Proc. of International Conference on Neural Network & Signal Processing, Nangjing. IEEE Press, Los Alamitos (2004)

10. Kira, K., Rendell, L.A.: The feature selection problem: Traditional methods and a new algorithm. In: AAAI, Cambridge, MA, USA, pp. 129–134. AAAI Press and MIT Press (1992)

11. Kira, K., Rendell, L.A.: A practical approach to feature selection. In: ML 1992: Proc. of the Ninth International Workshop on Machine Learning, pp. 249–256. Morgan Kaufmann Publishers Inc., San Francisco (1992)

12. Kruskal, J., Wish, M.: Multidimensional Scaling. Sage Publications, Thousand Oaks (1978)

13. Liang, F., Mukherjee, S., West, M.: The use of unlabeled data in predictive modeling. Statistical Science 22, 189 (2007)

14. Lawler, E.L., Wood, D.E.: Branch-and-bound methods: A survey. Operations Research 14(4), 699–719 (1966)

15. Malerba, D., Ceci, M., Appice, A.: A relational approach to probabilistic classification in a transductive setting. Eng. Appl. Artif. Intell. 22(1), 109–116 (2009)

16. Mitra, P., Murthy, C.A., Pal, S.K.: Unsupervised feature selection using feature similarity. IEEE Trans. Pattern Anal. Mach. Intell. 24(3), 301–312 (2002)

17. Parma, G.G., Menezes, B.R., Braga, A.P., Costa, M.A.: Sliding mode neural network control of an induction motor drive. Int. Jour. of Adap. Cont. and Sig. Proc. 17(6), 501–508 (2003)

18. Press, W.H., Teukolsky, S.A., Vetterling, W.T.: Numerical recipes in C (2nd ed.): the art of scientific computing. Cambridge University Press, New York (1992)

19. Takahashi, R.H.C., Teixeira, R.A., Braga, A.P., Saldanha, R.R.: Improving generalization of MLPs with multi-objective optimization. Neurocomputing 35(1-4), 189–194 (2000)

20. Wu, J., Yu, L., Meng, W., Shu, L.: Kernel-based transductive learning with nearest neighbors. In: Li, Q., Feng, L., Pei, J., Wang, S.X., Zhou, X., Zhu, Q.-M. (eds.) APWeb/WAIM 2009. LNCS(LNAI), vol. 5446, pp. 345–356. Springer, Heidelberg (2009)

21. Tenenbaum, J.B., de Silva, V., Langford, J.C.: A Global Geometric Framework for Nonlinear Dimensionality Reduction. Science 290(5500), 2319–2323 (2000)

22. Vapnik, V.N.: The nature of statistical learning theory. Springer, New York (1995)

23. Wang, J., Shen, X., Pan, W.: On efficient large margin semisupervised learning: Method and theory. J. Mach. Learn. Res. 10, 719–742 (2009)

24. Zhang, D., Zhou, Z.-h., Chen, S.: Semi-Supervised Dimensionality Reduction. In: SIAM Conference on Data Mining (SDM), pp. 629–634 (2007)

25. Bland, R.G., Goldfarb, D., Todd, M.J.: The Ellipsoid Method: A Survey. Operations Research 29(6), 1039–1091 (1980)

Introducing ROC Curves as Error Measure Functions: A New Approach to Train ANN-Based Biomedical Data Classifiers

Raúl Ramos-Pollán[1], Miguel Ángel Guevara-López[2], and Eugénio Oliveira[3]

[1] CETA-CIEMAT Centro Extremeño de Tecnologías Avanzadas,
Calle Sola 1, 10200 Trujillo, Spain,
raul.ramos@ciemat.es
[2] INEGI Instituto de Engenharia, Mecanica e Gestão Industrial, Universidade do Porto,
Campus da FEUP, Rua Roberto Frias 400, 4200-465 Porto, Portugal
mguevaral@inegi.up.pt
[3] LIACC-DEI-Faculdade de Engenharia, Universidade do Porto, Rua Roberto Frias s/n,
4200-465 Porto, Portugal
eco@fe.up.pt

Abstract. This paper explores the usage of the area (Az) under the Receiver Operating Characteristic (ROC) curve as error measure to guide the training process to build machine learning ANN-based classifiers for biomedical data analysis. Error measures (like root mean square error, RMS) are used to guide training algorithms measuring how far solutions are from the ideal classification, whereas it is well known that optimal classification rates do not necessarily yield to optimal Az's. Our hypothesis is that Az error measures can guide existing training algorithms to obtain better Az's than other error measures. This was tested after training 280 different configurations of ANN-based classifiers, with simulated annealing, using five biomedical binary datasets from the UCI machine learning repository with different test/train data splits. Each ANN configuration was trained both using the Az and RMS based error measures. In average Az was improved in 7.98% in testing data (9.32% for training data) when using 70% of the datasets elements for training. Further analysis reveals interesting patterns (Az improvement is greater when Az are lower). These results encourage us to further explore the usage of Az based error measures in training methods for classifiers in a more generalized manner.

Keywords: ROC Curves, Artificial Neural Networks, Machine learning Classifiers, Biomedical Data.

1 Introduction

After preliminary data preparation, pattern recognition systems consist of two major stages: (1) feature extraction and selection and (2) classification. This means that a set of features is extracted from the pattern to be recognized and then classified into one of the possible classes. To achieve high recognition accuracy, the feature extractor is

I. Bloch and R.M. Cesar, Jr. (Eds.): CIARP 2010, LNCS 6419, pp. 517–524, 2010.
© Springer-Verlag Berlin Heidelberg 2010

required to discover salient characteristics suited for classification and the classifier is required to set class boundaries accurately in the feature space. Progress made in sensor technology and data management allows researchers to gather datasets of ever increasing sizes [1].

The integration of biomedical information has become an essential task for health care, biology and biotechnology professionals and researchers. Integration is therefore much more than a plain collection of digital biomedical data. Homogenization of data description and storage, followed by normalization across the various experimental conditions would be a prerequisite to enable procedures of knowledge extraction [2].

The area under a ROC curve (or Az [3]) is a decisive factor used in many applications to measure classifier quality (performance). However, it is known that optimal classification rates do not necessarily yield to optimal Az's [4] and a few attempts have tried to use Az in optimization problems [5-6]. This paper explores the usage of the ROC Az as error measure to guide the training process to build machine learning ANN-based classifiers for biomedical data analysis. Our hypothesis is that by doing this, we will obtain better Az's than those obtained through other error measures.

This paper is structured as follows. Section 2 establishes the theoretical background of this work. Section 3 describes the technological framework used to experimentally validate our hypothesis on a Grid infrastructure. Section 4 describes the experiments performed and Section 5 discusses the results obtained. Section 6 draws some conclusions and outlines future work.

2   ROC Az Based Error Measures

2.1   ANNs Trained with Simulated Annealing

Simulated annealing was first proposed in [9] and it is inspired by the physical process of annealing to find good values of functions depending on many parameters. In short, the algorithm includes a parameter, simulating temperature starting at a given value, which is lowered gradually at known steps. For each temperature, the function parameters are randomized and the range of possible values that they can take is proportional to the temperature, so that at lower temperatures that range is smaller. At each temperature step the process is repeated a predetermined number of times and the set of parameters giving the best function value are retained and passed on to the following cycle iteration.

We use the simulated annealing approach to train ANNs as described and implemented in [7] which the weights of an ANN population are randomized iteratively and, at each step, the ANN with the minimum root mean square (RMS) error is retained. Notice that, in this case, the error used by the algorithms is the RMS of the whole training set, as opposed to other algorithms such as backpropagation, where it is the individual RMS error of each element of the training set with respect to the output neurons the one that is used.

More formally, for binary classifiers, we use the following definitions:

Table 1. Definitions

$\mathcal{X} \subset \mathbb{R}^p$	Domain of input vectors (with p features)
$\mathcal{Y} = \{-1, 1\}$	The two classes into which input vectors are classified
$(x_i, y_i)\ x_i \in \mathcal{X}, y_i \in \mathcal{Y}$	Input vector with its associated class (for supervised training)
$S = \{(x_1, y_1), \ldots, (x_n, y_n)\}$	Training set (for supervised training)
$\|S\| = n$	Size of training set
$\mathcal{F} = \{f : \mathcal{X} \to \mathcal{Y}\ \}$	Set of functions representing binary classifiers
$h \in \mathcal{F}$	A binary classifier
$h(x_i) \in \mathcal{Y}$	Output of binary classifier h when applied to input vector x_i, $h(x_i)$ typically applies some threshold notion to $h_{score}(x_i)$ to obtain the final class assigned to x_i
$h_{score}(x_i) \in \mathbb{R}$	Score assigned by binary classifier h to input vector x_i,
$\mathcal{E}(S, h)$	A global error measure of classifier h when applied to training set S
$e(x_i, h)$	An individual error measure of classifier h when applied to input vector x_i
$Az(S, h)$	Area under the ROC curve of training set S when classified with classifier h

In particular, an RMS error measure is typically defined as follows:

$$\mathcal{E}_{RMS}(S, h) = \frac{\sum e_{RMS}(x_i, h)}{\|S\|} \tag{1}$$

where $e_{RMS}(x_i, h)$ represents some distance measure between $h_{score}(x_i)$ and y_i, possibly using the output values of the output neurons in case of ANN based classifiers. Algorithms such as backpropagation in ANN based classifiers use the individual values $e_{RMS}(x_i, h)$ iterating through each element of the training set to incrementally correct the ANN weights, whereas simulated annealing uses only the global $\mathcal{E}_{RMS}(S, h)$ value to select the best classifier at each cycle of each cooling step.

2.2 ROC Az Error with Simulated Annealing

We now use ROC Az to define a global error measure as follows:

$$\mathcal{E}_{ROC}(S, h) = 1 - Az(S, h) \tag{2}$$

and use this definition, instead of (1), as error measure in the simulated annealing based ANN training process described above. $\mathcal{E}_{ROC}$ is implemented in the *ffsaroc* engine included in **Biomedtk** (see Section 3) whereas $\mathcal{E}_{RMS}$ is used in the *ffsa* engine.

Note that when using RMS there is a direct relation between the individual error measures of the elements of the training set (e_{RMS}) and the global error ($\mathcal{E}_{RMS}$) which is given by equation (1) and this is why it can be used by backpropagation-like training algorithms, whereas there is no such direct relation in $\mathcal{E}_{ROC}$ since $Az(S, h)$ is a global measure of a classified set. It is the fact that simulated annealing does not use individual error measures for each element of the training set that allows us to replace $\mathcal{E}_{RMS}$ by $\mathcal{E}_{ROC}$ in a straight forward manner.

3 The Biomedtk Framework

The Biomedical Data Analysis Toolkit (**Biomedtk**) is a Java software tool developed by the authors that exploits existing libraries for data analysis with methods and metrics commonly used in the biomedical field. In addition, it provides the means to massively search, explore and combine different configurations of data classifiers provided by the underlying libraries to build robust data analysis tools. With this, it is possible manipulate datasets, train Artificial Neural Networks (ANN) based binary and multiclass classifiers with many different configurations, search for best ensemble classifiers, generate different types of ROC curve analysis, etc.

An ANN-based configuration specifies a certain network structure (number of layers and neurons per layer), a training algorithm to use (such as backpropagation or simulated annealing) and algorithm dependant train parameters (such as learning rate, start/end temperatures, etc.). **Biomedtk** allows defining explorations of ANN configurations (see Section 4) and sending them for massive training to a Grid computing infrastructure. Currently, **biomedtk** supports training engines from the Encog [7] and Weka [8] toolkits, as listed in table 2.

Table 2. Biomedtk supported training engines

Engine name	Description
ffbp	Feedforward with backpropagation-based training.
ffga	Feedforward with genetic algorithm-based training.
ffsa	Feedforward with simulated annealing-based training.
ffsaroc	ffsa with WEKA ROC based error evaluation.
Rb	Radial basis.
som	Self-organizing feature map.

It also includes the *ffsaroc* which is a modification of the *ffsa* engine including the ROC Az based error evaluation described in Section 3. **Biomedtk** uses the Mann-Whitney statistic to calculate ROC Az as implemented in Weka[8].

4 Experimental Setup

A set of experiments was set up in order to test whether the error measure proposed in Section 2 effectively improves the Az of the trained ANN classifiers. The tests were carried out using the binary biomedical UCI datasets [10] listed in table 3.

Table 3. UCI Datasets used in the experiments

Dataset	Description	# elements
Haber	Survival of patients with breast cancer surgery	306
Liver	Liver disorders from excessive alcohol consumption	345
Mmass	Benign/malign mammographic masses	961
Pimadiab	Diabetes diagnoses for Pima Indian populations	768
Spectf	Data on cardiac Single Proton Emission Computed Tomography (SPECT) images	267

For each UCI dataset we generated two dataset splits, one using 50% of the dataset for training and 50% for testing, and one using 70% for training and 30% for testing. A **Biomedtk** exploration was defined for each dataset split with ANN configurations having one to three hidden layers and different classifier parameters. Each dataset split and configuration was then trained with both the *ffsa* and the *ffsaroc* engines. This is an extract of the exploration definition file for the two *haber* dataset splits:

```
explore.neurons.input     = 3
explore.neurons.output    = 2
explore.neurons.layer.01  = 8:18
explore.neurons.layer.02  = 8:18
explore.neurons.layer.03  = 3:8
explore.trainingsets      = haber-30:haber-50
explore.trainengines      = ffsa:ffsaroc
explore.stop.epochs       = 200
explore.stop.error        = 0.0001
explore.starttemp         = 10:20
explore.ffsa.endtemp      = 2
explore.ffsa.cycles       = 100
```

This exploration includes ANNs with one, two or three hidden layers, where the first and second hidden layers may have 8 or 18 neurons, with a start temperature of 10 or 20, etc. For each dataset, this exploration generates 112 ANN configurations, 56 using the *ffsa* engine and 56 using the *ffsaroc* engine. In total, for all datasets, 560 ANN configurations were trained on a gLite [11] Grid infrastructure using **Biomedtk** and consuming about 140 CPU hours.

Finally, to check whether each *ffsa* configuration is improved by using *ffsaroc* instead, we compared each ANN configuration trained with the *ffsa* engine with the same configuration (same number of hidden layers, neurons and parameters) but trained with the *ffsaroc* engine. We name such pair a *classifier pair*. Therefore 56 classifier pairs are made for each dataset, 28 for the 50/50 test/train data split and 28 for the 30/70 split.

5   Results and Discussion

Table 4 below summarizes the average improvement obtained by *ffsaroc* over *ffsa* classifier pairs for each data set both for training and testing data. Results are also shown for the 30/70 and 50/50 test/train split for each dataset.

Table 4. FFSAROC improvement of FFSA per training set

Dataset	test Az increase avg	std dev	train Az increase avg	std dev	avg test Az ffsaroc	ffsa
haber-30	7.92%	5.58	6.90%	1.53	0.691	0.642
haber-50	2.33%	3.94	8.25%	2.13	0.729	0.713
liver-30	3.91%	3.81	4.50%	1.94	0.698	0.672
liver-50	0.98%	2.46	7.60%	2.99	0.725	0.718
mmass-30	3.24%	5.43	6.83%	3.27	0.807	0.782
mmass-50	-0.59%	4.94	7.46%	2.78	0.786	0.790
pimadiab-30	5.44%	4.42	7.91%	3.88	0.704	0.669
pimadiab-50	1.45%	6.69	11.83%	5.35	0.691	0.684
spectf-30	19.38%	20.57	20.45%	8.43	0.830	0.712
spectf-50	8.34%	17.35	25.85%	16.40	0.757	0.711
total 30% test sets	7.98%	11.77	9.32%	7.27	0.746	0.695
total 50% test sets	2.50%	9.37	12.20%	10.62	0.738	0.723
total all datasets	**5.24%**	**10.98**	**10.76%**	**9.21**	**0.742**	**0.709**

Table 5 shows the same classifier pairs grouped by *ffsa testAz* value ranges.

Table 5. FFSAROC improvement over FFSA per FFSA Test Az range

FFSA Test Az range	Number of Classifier Pairs	test Az increase avg	std dev	train Az increase avg	std dev
(0.00, 0.60]	8	51.16%	17.31	43.81%	20.36
(0.60, 0.65]	30	12.94%	7.12	10.73%	6.13
(0.65, 0.70]	82	5.17%	6.77	9.10%	7.01
(0.70, 0.75]	81	2.26%	5.39	9.39%	5.34
(0.75, 0.80]	67	1.28%	5.90	9.80%	6.79
(0.85, 1.00]	12	-1.96%	5.65	14.76%	6.60
total all ranges	**280**	**5.24%**	**10.98**	**10.76%**	**9.21**

As it can be seen in the tables above there is in general a significant average improvement in Az both for train and test parts of the datasets. Note that the improvement percentages shown are the average of the compared classifier pairs (between *ffsaroc* and *ffsa* trained classifiers with the same network structure and training parameters), which is different from the average *testAz* of **all** *ffsaroc* and *ffsa* classifiers in each training set shown in the last two columns of table 4.

Improvement is constantly better when splitting datasets in 30/70 test/train data than when splitting in 50/50. Even if the 30/70 datasets have better average *testAz* than 50/50 (such as in the *mmass*, *pimadiab* and *spectf* datasets). Improvement is also constantly better in the train parts of the dataset than in the test parts and, in any case, its standard deviation is always high. This seems to indicate that the method presented in this paper may be hard for classifiers to generalize and does not behave homogeneously for all classifiers. From table 5, it can be clearly seen that for test data, improvement is better when the *testAz* for the *ffsa* classified dataset is worse. Finally, the following plots show the ROC curves of the classifier pairs for which the best improvement was obtained (*ffsaroc* over *ffsa*) for the *haber* and *spectf* datasets both for the 30/70 and 50/50 data splits

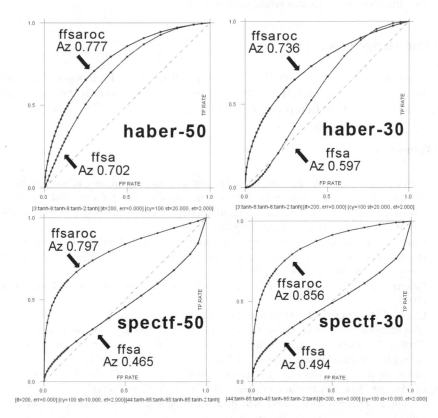

Fig. 1. Most improved classifiers for *spectf* and *haber*, 30% and 50% test data splits

To simplify visual comparison, these plots use the bi-normal distribution method as provided by JLABROC [12] which is also supported by **Biomedtk**. Also, each plot shows the ANN layers structure (neurons per layer and activation function) and the training parameters for the simulated annealing processes (start temperature, end temperature and number of cycles)

6 Conclusions

The experimental results obtained here confirm that the usage of a ROC Az based error function to guide a simulated annealing algorithm for training ANNs improves the ROC Az of the obtained classifiers with respect to an RMS error function. In addition, **Biometk** demonstrated to be a robust framework to massively explore large amounts of configurations of data classifiers exploiting computing power harnessed by Grid infrastructures.

Future work is focused on (1) better understanding of the behavior of the proposed method to better explain deviations observed in the experiments and (2) on applying the method in a generalized manner to machine learning classifiers and validate them in real computer-aided detection/diagnosis systems.

Acknowledgements

Prof. Guevara acknowledges POPH - QREN-Typology 4.2 – Promotion of scientific employment funded by the ESF and MCTES, Portugal. Prof. Ramos-Pollán acknowledges the support of the European Regional Development Fund.

References

1. Kostka, P., Tkacz, E.J.: Feature extraction and selection algorithms in biomedical data classifiers based on time-frequency and principle component analysis. In: Proc. 11th Mediterranean Conference on Medical and Biomedical Engineering and Computing 2007, vol. 16, pp. 70–73. Springer, Heidelberg (2007)
2. Drakos, J., Karakantza, M., Zoumbos, N., Lakoumentas, J., Nikiforidis, G., Sakellaropoulos, G.: A perspective for biomedical data integration: Design of databases for flow cytometry. BMC Bioinformatics 9(1), 99 (2008)
3. Fawcett, T.: An introduction to ROC analysis. Pattern Recognition Letters 27(8), 861–874 (2006)
4. Castro, C.L., Braga, A.P.: Optimization of the Area under the ROC Curve. In: Proc. of 10th Brazilian Symposium on Neural Networks, SBRN 2008, pp. 141–146 (2008)
5. Cortes, C., Mohri, M.: AUC optimization vs. error rate minimization. In: Advances in Neural Information Processing Systems. MIT Press, Cambridge (2003)
6. Rakotomamonjy, A.: Optimizing Area under ROC Curve with SVMs. In: Proc. Workshop of ROC Analysis in Artificial Intelligence, pp. 71–80. ROCAI (2004)
7. Heaton, J.: Programming Neural Networks with Encog 2 in Java. Heaton Research, Inc. (2010)
8. Hall, M., Frank, E., Holmes, G., Pfahringer, B., Reutemann, P.: Witten, I.H.: The WEKA Data Mining Software: An Update. SIGKDD Explorations 11(1) (2009)
9. Kirkpatrick, S., Gelatt Jr., C.D., Vecchi, M.P.: Optimization by Simulated Annealing. Science 220(4598), 671–680 (1983)
10. Asuncion, A., Newman, D.J.: UCI Machine Learning Repository. University of California, School of Information and Computer Science, Irvine, CA (2007), http://www.ics.uci.edu/~mlearn/MLRepository.html
11. EGEE: The gLite middleware, vol. 2010 (2009)
12. John Eng, M.D.: ROC analysis: web-based calculator for ROC curves, vol. 2010. Johns Hopkins University, Baltimore (2006)

Partition Selection Approach for Hierarchical Clustering Based on Clustering Ensemble

Sandro Vega-Pons and José Ruiz-Shulcloper

Advanced Technologies Application Center (CENATAV), Havana, Cuba

Abstract. Hierarchical clustering algorithms are widely used in many fields of investigation. They provide a hierarchy of partitions of the same dataset. However, in many practical problems, the selection of a *representative* level (partition) in the hierarchy is needed. The classical approach to do so is by using a cluster validity index to select the *best* partition according to the criterion imposed by this index. In this paper, we present a new approach based on the clustering ensemble philosophy. The *representative* level is defined here as the consensus partition in the hierarchy. In the consensus computation process, we take into account the similarity between partitions and information from the evaluation of partitions with different cluster validity indexes. An experimental comparison on several datasets shows the superiority of the proposed approach with respect to the classical approach.

Keywords: Hierarchical clustering, partition selection, clustering ensemble, cluster validity index.

1 Introduction

Clustering algorithms can be divided into *Partitional* and *Hierarchical* [1]. Partitional clustering algorithms create a partition of the data by grouping the objects in clusters according to their (dis)similarity values. On the other hand, hierarchical clustering algorithms build a hierarchy of nested partitions of a dataset. This hierarchy is usually associated to a *dendrogram*, which can be cut at different levels to obtain the different partitions in the hierarchy (see Fig. 1).

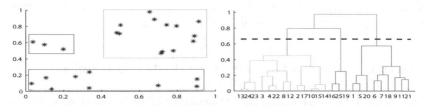

Fig. 1. A dataset of 25 2D points and the dendrogram produced by the Average-Link algorithm. The broken line cutting the dendrogram (right) produces a partition of the objects with 3 clusters (left).

I. Bloch and R.M. Cesar, Jr. (Eds.): CIARP 2010, LNCS 6419, pp. 525–532, 2010.

Hierarchy of partitions can offer more information about the structure of the objects in the dataset. With a hierarchy, the group of objects can be seen at different levels; from the bottom level where each object forms an independent cluster (singleton clusters) to the top level with only 1 cluster containing all the objects. However, working with the entire hierarchy is commonly very complex. Thus, in many practical problems, the selection of a *representative* partition of the hierarchy is needed.

In the traditional approach, the *representative* partition is obtained by using cluster validity indexes (CVI). Every partition in the hierarchy is evaluated by a CVI (used as *stopping rule*) and the partition with better results is selected. Many CVIs have been used with this purpose, e.g., in [2] 30 CVIs are presented and experimentally evaluated. Nowadays, classical CVIs like *Calinski-Harabasz* (CH) index, *Hartigan* (HA) index and the *Dunn* index [3] together with the *Highest-Lifetime*(HL) index [4] are some of the most used. However, new indexes still appear every year in the literature, e.g., the COP index [5].

The main drawback of the CVI (stopping rule) based approach to determine the *representative* level in a hierarchy is that there is no CVI capable of working *correctly* for all datasets and for all clustering algorithms. In other words, every CVI implicitly or explicitly evaluates a partition, according to a particular property given by the mathematical definition of the index. These properties are usually related to *compactness*, *separability* or *connectivity* among clusters. If the property measured by the index is *consistent* with the used clustering algorithm and the particular dataset, the index could contribute with valuable information, but if this is not the case, the results could be very different from the expected ones. Due to this limitation of CVIs, Everitt *et al.* [6] said that it is advisable not to depend on a single CVI for selecting the *representative* partition, but to synthesize the results of several indexes.

In this paper, we propose a new approach for the selection of the *representative* partition in a hierarchy based on the clustering ensemble philosophy. We call it *Partition Selection based on Cluster Ensemble* (PSCE) approach. With PSCE, we define the *representative* partition in a hierarchy taking into account the evaluation of several CVIs, as well as the similarity measures between partitions in the hierarchy. This way, we select as a result the partition in the hierarchy that better represents the common characteristics in the hierarchy.

In Section 2, the proposed approach is formally presented. In Section 3, experimental results by using different datasets and hierarchical clustering algorithms, as well as the comparison with the classical approach are shown. Finally, in Section 4, we present the conclusions of this research.

2 Partition Selection Based on Cluster Ensemble

Clustering ensemble methods combine partitions of the same dataset in a final consensus clustering. Formally, we denote $X = \{x_1, x_2, \ldots, x_n\}$ the original set of objects, where each x_i is a tuple of some α−dimensional feature space $\mathbb{G}^\alpha$ for all $i = 1, \ldots, n$. $\mathbb{P} = \{P_1, P_2, \ldots, P_m\}$ is a clustering ensemble, where each

$P_j = \{C_1^j, C_2^j, \ldots, C_{d_j}^j\}$ is a partition of the set of objects X with d_j clusters, for all $j = 1, \ldots, m$. We also denote $\mathbb{P}_X$ the set of all possible partitions of X and the consensus partition is represented by P^*. The consensus partition P^* is usually defined through the *median partition* problem:

$$P^* = \arg\max_{P \in \mathbb{P}_X} \sum_{i=1}^{m} \Gamma(P, P_i) \tag{1}$$

where Γ is a similarity measure between partitions.

Our approach to determine the *representative* partition in a hierarchy is based on the philosophy of clustering ensembles. When a hierarchical clustering algorithm is applied to the set of objects X, a hierarchy of partitions is obtained. A hierarchy $\mathbb{H} = \{P_1, P_2, \ldots, P_m\}$ is a set of nested partitions of X, where $P_i \preceq P_j, \forall i < j$. $\preceq$ is the partial order relationship *nested in*, and $P \preceq P'$ if and only if, for all cluster $C' \in P'$ there are clusters $C_{i_1}, C_{i_2}, \ldots, C_{i_v} \in P$ such that $C' = \bigcup_{j=1}^{v} C_{i_j}$. It is easy to see that $\mathbb{H} \subset \mathbb{P}_X$. Thus, we define the *representative level in the hierarchy* as the partition that better summarizes the information in the hierarchy $\mathbb{H}$ taking into account two parameters. First, the evaluation of several CVIs to all partitions in the hierarchy. Second, the similarity values between each pair of partitions in the hierarchy. Formally, the *representative* partition $\hat{P}$ in the hierarchy $\mathbb{H}$ is defined as:

$$\hat{P} = \arg\max_{P \in \mathbb{H}} \sum_{i=1}^{m} (\mathcal{E}(P_i) \cdot \Gamma(P, P_i)) \tag{2}$$

where $\mathcal{E}(P_i)$ is an evaluation of each partition $P_i \in \mathbb{H}$ and Γ a similarity measure between partitions. This evaluation can be used to give more importance to partitions that hold some desired properties. Notice that unlike the original median partition problem (1), our *best* partition $\hat{P}$ is one of the partitions in the clustering ensemble as it is shown in (2) ($\hat{P} \in \mathbb{H}$). Thus, this problem is easier than the original median partition problem, since the search space here ($\mathbb{H}$) is much more smaller than the search space ($\mathbb{P}_X$) in (1).

Among the different clustering ensemble methods, we based our approach on the *Weighted Partition Consensus via Kernels* (WPCK) [7] method. This method satisfies the following properties that are convenient for the partition selection problem:

- It is possible to compute a weight value for each partition, taking into account the evaluation of several cluster validity indexes. The weight value ω_i assigned to P_i can be used as the value $\mathcal{E}(P_i)$ in equation (2).
- It is very easy to restrict the search to partitions in $\mathbb{H}$. In fact, this is an intermediate step of WPCK. In WPCK, firstly, the *best* partition in the cluster ensemble is computed and this solution is improved afterwards by searching in the whole search space $\mathbb{P}_X$.
- The algorithm is theoretically well grounded and has a low computational cost, $\mathcal{O}(n \cdot m \cdot rMax)^1$.

---

[1] n is the number of objects, m the number of partitions and $rMax$ is a maximum number of iteration for the algorithm.

Therefore, the steps of the proposed algorithm to find the *representative* partition in the hierarchy (PSCE) are the following:

Subhierarchy selection

We extract from the hierarchy $\mathbb{H}$ a subset of partitions. Every partition in the hierarchy has a different number of clusters. Consequently, we will select a subset of partitions that has a number of clusters in a *reasonable* range. This range is a parameter of the algorithm, e.g., $[2, 10]$, $[2, 30]$, $[2, \sqrt{n}]$ could be used. We denote $\mathbb{H}_{[q,t]}$ the *subhierarchy* of $\mathbb{H}$, where P_q is the top level, P_t is the bottom level, and every partition $P_s \in \mathbb{H}$ with s clusters belongs to $\mathbb{H}_{[q,t]}$ if and only if $p \leq s \leq t$. For simplicity, we denote $v = t - q + 1$ the number of partitions in $\mathbb{H}_{[q,t]}$. The complete hierarchy $\mathbb{H}$ could be used, i.e., selecting the range $[1, n]$ ($v = n$). However, smaller ranges are recommended in order to decrease the computational cost.

Evaluation of each partition

We obtain the evaluation value of each partition through the application of several cluster validity indexes. Firstly, a set of internal CVIs $\mathbb{I} = \{I_1, I_2, \ldots, I_r\}$ is defined. We use this set of indexes to evaluate the behavior of each partition with respect to a set of different properties, where each index evaluates a particular property. These properties can be related with one or more of the following concepts: *compactness*, *separability*, *connectivity*, *symmetry*, etc. The property measured by each index is given by its mathematical expression. Formally, we define a *hierarchy index* as a function $I : \mathbb{H}_{[q,t]} \rightarrow [0, 1]$, where $I(P)$ is the evaluation of the partition P by the index I. It is assumed that the highest values represent better fulfilment of the index. Traditional internal CVIs such as CH, HA and HL can be easily transformed to satisfy the *hierarchy index* definition. This way, the evaluation of each partition $\mathcal{E}(P_i)$ in (2) is computed by:

$$\mathcal{E}(P_i) = \frac{1}{r} \cdot \sum_{j=1}^{r} (1 - |I_j(P_i) - M_j|) \tag{3}$$

where $M_j = \max_{P_i \in \mathbb{H}_{[q,t]}} I_j(P_i)$. Thus, $\mathcal{E}(P_i)$ is computed as a measure of how close to the maximum value, the evaluation of each index in $\mathbb{I}$ in the partition P_i is. As we obtain a weight value for each partition, for simplicity, we denote $\omega_i = \mathcal{E}(P_i)$.

Similarity measure between partitions

Besides the evaluation measure $\mathcal{E}$, we need a similarity measure Γ between partitions in order to solve the problem (2). We use the similarity measure $\hat{k}$ ($\Gamma = \hat{k}$) between partitions proposed in [7], which is formally defined as $\hat{k} : \mathbb{P}_X \times \mathbb{P}_X \rightarrow [0, 1]$ such that:

$$\hat{k}(P_i, P_j) = \frac{k(P_i, P_j)}{\sqrt{k(P_i, P_i) \cdot k(P_j, P_j)}}, \quad \text{where} \quad k(P_i, P_j) = \sum_{S \subseteq X} \delta_S^{P_i} \delta_S^{P_j} \tag{4}$$

$$\text{and} \quad \delta_S^{P_a} = \begin{cases} \frac{|S|}{|C|}, & \text{if } \exists C \in P_a, S \subseteq C; \\ 0, & \text{otherwise.} \end{cases}$$

This similarity measure is a positive semi-definite kernel [7].

In this method, the general problem (2) can be transformed by using the results of the above steps in the following way:

$$\hat{P} = \arg \max_{P \in \mathbb{H}_{[q,t]}} \sum_{i=1}^{v} \left(\omega_i \cdot \hat{k}(P, P_i) \right) \tag{5}$$

Obtaining the *representative* partition

As $\hat{k}$ is a kernel function, there is a mapping from $\mathbb{P}_X$ into a Hilbert space $\mathcal{H}$, $\phi : \mathbb{P}_X \to \mathcal{H}$, such that $\hat{k}(P_i, P_j) = \langle \phi(P_i), \phi(P_j) \rangle_{\mathcal{H}}$. A similar problem to (5) (*kernel consensus problem*) is presented in [7], the only difference is that the search space is $\mathbb{P}_X$ instead of $\mathbb{H}_{[q,t]}$. The kernel property of $\hat{k}$ allows mapping the *kernel consensus problem* in an equivalent problem in $\mathcal{H}$ that can be easily solved. Let ψ be the solution in the Hilbert space $\mathcal{H}$, in order to solve the *kernel consensus problem* would be necessary to find P^* such that $\psi = \phi(P^*)$, i.e., finding the pre-image of the solution [8]. However, in our case, we are solving problem (5) where the search space is $\mathbb{H}_{[q,t]}$. Thus, we need to find the partition $P \in \mathbb{H}_{[q,t]}$ such that $\phi(P)$ is closest to ψ. Formally, the *representative* partition is defined as:

$$\hat{P} = \arg \min_{P \in \mathbb{H}_{[q,t]}} \|\phi(P) - \psi\|_{\mathcal{H}}^2$$

where

$$\|\phi(P) - \psi\|_{\mathcal{H}}^2 = \tilde{k}(P, P) - 2 \sum_{i=1}^{v} \omega_i \tilde{k}(P, P_i) + \sum_{i=1}^{v} \sum_{j=1}^{v} \omega_i \omega_j \tilde{k}(P_i, P_j) \tag{6}$$

Therefore, we can find the *representative* partition by computing the distance of each partition in the hierarchy $\mathbb{H}_{[q,t]}$ to the theoretical solution ψ using equation (6), and selecting the partition closer to ψ.

2.1   Computational Complexity Analysis

The computation of all weight values for all partitions is $\mathcal{O}(v \cdot r \cdot f(\mathbb{I}))$, where v is the number of partitions in $\mathbb{H}_{[q,t]}$, r is the number of *hierarchy indexes* and $f(\mathbb{I})$ is the computational cost of the most computationally expensive *hierarchy index*. In practice, r is a small number, hence, we can consider $\mathcal{O}(v \cdot f(\mathbb{I}))$ the computational complexity of the weight assigning mechanism. Given the weight values, it is needed to compute equation (6) for each partition in $\mathbb{H}_{[q,t]}$. The last term in equation (6) does not depend on the particular partition analyzed and can be computed only one time in $\mathcal{O}(v^2 \cdot n)$, where n is the number of objects. This is because the computational complexity of the similarity measure $\hat{k}$ is $\mathcal{O}(n)$ (see [7]). Once this last value is obtained, equation (6) can be solved in $\mathcal{O}(v \cdot n)$ for one partition, and for the v partitions in $\mathbb{H}_{[q,t]}$ can be computed in $\mathcal{O}(v^2 \cdot n)$. Thus, the complete computation of equation (6) for all partitions in $\mathbb{H}_{[q,t]}$ is $\mathcal{O}(v^2 \cdot n)$. Finally, the global computational complexity of the selection of the *representative* partition is $\mathcal{O}(v \cdot f(\mathbb{I})) + \mathcal{O}(v^2 \cdot n)$. With a proper selection of the *hierarchical indexes* $\mathbb{I}$ and the subhierarchy $\mathbb{H}_{[q,t]}$, this computational cost will be lower than $O(n^2)$, which is the common complexity of the hierarchical clustering algorithms. However, in the worst case (v close to n) the algorithm complexity becomes $\mathcal{O}(n^3)$, thereby the importance of a proper selection of the subhierarchy and the hierarchy indexes.

3   Experimental Results

We used 8 datasets in our experiments (see Table 1), 5 from the UCI Machine Learning Repository [9] and the other 3 are 2D synthetical datasets. For all these datasets the ideal data partition (*ground-truth*) is available. Therefore, in the experiments, we compared the obtained results with the *ground-truth* of each dataset. We used the Normalized Mutual Information (NMI) [10] measure to evaluate the algorithm results. This is a very used similarity measure between partitions that evaluates the resulting partition by measuring the information shared between the result and the *ground-truth*.

Table 1. Overview of datasets

Name	Inst-per-classes	2D synthetic datasets		
Cassini	120-60-120			
Half-Rings	100-100			
Smiley	33-33-50-84			
Wine	59-41-78			
Opt-Digits	10-11-11-11-12-5-8-12-9-11			
Iris	50-50-50			
Glass	70-76-17-13-9-29			
Ionosphere	126-225	Cassini	Half-Rings	Smiley

In each experiment, hierarchies are obtained by using 3 well-known hierarchical clustering algorithms: *Single-Link* (SL), *Complete-Link* (CL) and *Average-Link* (AL) [1]. For each dataset, we compare the results obtained by the proposed *Partition Selection based on Cluster Ensemble* (PSCE) approach and the stopping rule approach with the following indexes: *Highest-Lifetime*(HL), *Calinski-Harabasz* (CH) and *Hartigan* (HA). In Table 2, they are denoted SR-HL, SR-CH and SR-HA respectively. We also present for each algorithm the *Nearest to Ground-Truth* (NGT) value, which is computed by evaluating all the partitions in the hierarchy with respect to the *ground-truth* using the NMI measure and taking the highest value. Notice that NGT values depend on the quality of the hierarchies. Besides, the results of SR-HL, SR-CH, SR-HA and PSCE are upper bounded by the NGT value of each hierarchy. In all cases, we used the subhierarchy $\mathbb{H}_{[2,35]}$ composed by the partitions with s clusters, with $2 \leq s \leq 35$. For all generated hierarchy, the NGT value was obtained in a partition of the subhierarchy $\mathbb{H}_{[2,35]}$. Hence, the range $[2, 35]$ is appropriated for these experiments and allows decreasing the computational cost of the algorithms.

We used 5 *hierarchy indexes* in the evaluation of partitions step of our approach: Variance, Connectivity, HL, CH and HA. The first two are very simple indexes [7].

Table 2. Comparison of SR-HL, SR-CH, SR-HA and PSCE methods for the selection of the representative partition in a hierarchy. The hierarchies were generated by the application of the SL, CL, and AL hierarchical clustering algorithms on the 8 datasets. The results were evaluated by using the NMI measure. In each case, the best results are highlighted. The NGT value is also presented for each hierarchy. Each cell in the most right column (AVE) is the average value of its entire row.

Alg	Method	Cassini	Half-R	Smiley	Wine	Opt-D	Iris	Glass	Ionosp	AVE
SL	SR-HL	**0.941**	**0.720**	0.846	**0.102**	0.706	**0.733**	**0.154**	**0.076**	0.534
	SR-CH	**0.941**	0.488	**0.863**	0.092	0.250	**0.733**	**0.154**	0.008	0.441
	SR-HA	**0.941**	0.488	**0.863**	0.092	0.250	0.545	**0.154**	**0.076**	0.426
	PSCE	**0.941**	**0.720**	0.853	**0.102**	**0.798**	0.720	**0.154**	**0.076**	**0.545**
	NGT	0.970	0.961	1.0	0.502	0.801	0.733	0.394	0.129	0.686
CL	SR-HL	0.657	0.197	0.712	**0.790**	0.789	**0.756**	0.446	0.143	0.561
	SR-CH	0.551	0.353	0.291	0.665	0.250	**0.756**	0.442	0.037	0.418
	SR-HA	0.522	0.353	0.646	0.709	0.723	**0.756**	0.442	0.037	0.523
	PSCE	**0.743**	**0.393**	**0.820**	0.709	**0.805**	**0.756**	**0.516**	**0.160**	**0.612**
	NGT	0.792	0.442	0.865	0.798	0.825	0.756	0.590	0.193	0.657
AL	SR-HL	**0.779**	0.066	**0.766**	0.693	0.730	0.643	0.452	0.082	0.526
	SR-CH	**0.779**	0.347	0.685	**0.775**	0.250	**0.685**	0.452	0.082	0.506
	SR-HA	0.513	0.347	0.623	**0.775**	0.712	0.643	0.452	0.082	0.518
	PSCE	**0.779**	**0.433**	0.728	**0.775**	**0.814**	0.661	**0.454**	**0.083**	**0.590**
	NGT	0.792	0.474	0.883	0.775	0.843	0.783	0.501	0.169	0.652

Variance is a way of measuring the compactness of the clusters in a partition. Connectivity evaluates the degree of connectedness of clusters in a partition, by measuring how many neighbors of each object belong to the same cluster as the object. The other 3 indexes are the same used independently in the stopping rule approach. However, in this case, all of them were normalized to the range $[0, 1]$. We do not report the results of Variance and Connectivity used as stopping rules because the results were very bad. The simplicity of these indexes does not allow them to play as a stopping rule with a certain degree of accuracy. However, in the PSCE approach they can be very useful, since each index evaluates the partitions from a different perspective and all these points of view are combined to obtain the final result.

In Table 2, the experimental results are summarized. From the last column of this table it can be seen that PSCE has the best average performance in all cases. In the Single-Link (SL) hierarchies, SR-HL and PSCE work very similar. However, in the Complete-Link (CL), and Average-Link (AL) hierarchies, the PSCE approach clearly outperforms the other techniques. The results in this table corroborate the capability of the PSCE approach to work well in different circumstances, i.e., different clustering algorithms and different datasets.

From Table 2 it can also be seen that the *Nearest to Ground-Truth* NGT value is almost never reached. This fact ratifies that a single index cannot work correctly for all datasets in the case of the stopping rule approach. Besides, this means that a better and more complete set of hierarchy indexes could be used in order to improve even more the results of the PSCE approach.

4   Conclusions

In this paper, we have presented a new approach for the selection of a representative partition in a hierarchy, based on the philosophy of clustering ensembles. In this approach, the evaluation of the partitions in the hierarchy by using different cluster validity indexes is considered in order to obtain the final result. Hence, different criteria about the quality of the partitions in the hierarchy are combined to compute the representative level. Besides, the similarity values between partitions are also taken into account in this process. Consequently, the representative partition is theoretically well defined as a weighted consensus among the partitions in the hierarchy. The main drawback of the traditional (stopping rule) approach is that if the characteristics of the used index are not in correspondence with the dataset and with the algorithm applied to generate the hierarchy, the results will not be satisfactory. The proposed approach is more robust to the change of datasets and clustering algorithms, due to the consensus definition of the representative partition and the possibility of combining the information from different cluster validity indexes. Experimental results, obtained by using different clustering algorithms and different datasets, corroborate this last assertion. On the other hand, the proposed approach is computationally more expensive than the traditional approach. However, a proper selection of the subhierarchy and hierarchy indexes used by the algorithm could decrease the computational complexity to be comparable with the classical approach.

Recently, the idea of searching for the representative partition of a hierarchy, not only in the explicit levels of the hierarchy, but in an extended partition set was proposed [5]. As future work, we will generalize our current approach to this extended partition set, where better results could be found.

References

[1] Jain, A.K., Murty, M., Flynn, P.: Data clustering: A review. ACM Computing Surveys (CSUR) 31(3), 264–323 (1999)

[2] Milligan, G.W., Cooper, M.C.: An examination of procedures for determing the number of clusters in a data set. Psychometrika 50(2), 159–179 (1985)

[3] Xu, R., Wunsch, D.C.: Clustering. IEEE Press Series on Computational Intelligence. John Wiley & Sons, Chichester (2009)

[4] Fred, A.L.N., Jain, A.K.: Combining multiple clustering using evidence accumulation. IEEE Trans. on Pat. Analysis and Mach. Intelligence 27, 835–850 (2005)

[5] Gurrutxaga, I., Albisua, I., Arbelaitz, O., Martín, J., Muguerza, J., Pérez, J., Perona, I.: Sep/cop: An efficient method to find the best partition in hierarchical clustering based on a new cluster validity index. Pattern Recognition 43(10), 3364–3373 (2010)

[6] Everitt, B., Landau, S., Leese, M.: Cluster analysis, 4th edn. Arnold, London (2001)

[7] Vega-Pons, S., Correa-Morris, J., Ruiz-Shulcloper, J.: Weighted partition consensus via kernels. Pattern Recognition 43(8), 2712–2724 (2010)

[8] Bakir, G., Weston, J., Scholkopf, B.: Learning to find pre-images. In: Thrun, S., Saul, L. (eds.) Advances in Neural Information Processing Systems (NIPS 2003), vol. 16, pp. 449–456. MIT Press, Cambridge (2004)

[9] Frank, A., Asuncion, A.: UCI machine learning repository. University of California, Irvine (2010), http://archive.ics.uci.edu/ml

[10] Strehl, A., Ghosh, J.: Cluster ensembles: a knowledge reuse framework for combining multiple partitions. J. Mach. Learn. Res. 3, 583–617 (2002)

The Imbalanced Problem in Morphological Galaxy Classification

Jorge de la Calleja[1], Gladis Huerta[1], Olac Fuentes[2], Antonio Benitez[1],
Eduardo López Domínguez[1], and Ma. Auxilio Medina[1]

[1] Ingeniería en Informática, Universidad Politécnica de Puebla,
Puebla, 72640, México
{jdelacalleja,ghuerta,abenitez,elopez,mmedina}@uppuebla.edu.mx
[2] Computer Science Department, University of Texas at El Paso,
Texas, 79968, U.S.A.
ofuentes@utep.edu

Abstract. In this paper we present an experimental study of the performance of six machine learning algorithms applied to morphological galaxy classification. We also address the learning approach from imbalanced data sets, inherent to many real-world applications, such as astronomical data analysis problems. We used two over-sampling techniques: SMOTE and Resampling, and we vary the amount of generated instances for classification. Our experimental results show that the learning method Random Forest with Resampling obtain the best results for three, five and seven galaxy types, with a F-measure about .99 for all cases.

Keywords: machine learning, imbalanced data sets, galaxies.

1   Introduction

Imbalanced class problems are often encountered in many real world applications. The problem occurs when the number of instances in one class heavily outnumbers the instances in the other class. With imbalanced data sets we will have biased classifiers that obtain high predictive accuracy over the majority class, but poor predictive accuracy over the minority class which is generally the class of interest. Some examples of domains that present an imbalanced class are: text classification, detection of fraudulent telephone calls, disease detection, astronomical object classification, and many others.

A short time ago, there has been a great deal of interest from astronomers in applying machine learning techniques in order to solve astronomical problems such as classification of galaxies, classification of stars, classification of binary stars, galaxy/star discrimination, astronomical object classification in spectral images, among others. Although they have used a wide variety of learning algorithms, these approaches have not addressed the class imbalance inherent to this kind of problems.

I. Bloch and R.M. Cesar, Jr. (Eds.): CIARP 2010, LNCS 6419, pp. 533–540, 2010.

We present an experimental study of the performance of six machine learning algorithms applied to morphological galaxy classification considering the imbalanced data set problem. Classification of galaxy images is one of the most important challenges for astronomers because it provides significant clues about the origin and evolution of the Universe. The paper is organized as follows: Section 2 describes related work to deal with imbalanced data sets and a brief introduction of galaxy classification. In Section 3 we describe the methods used for doing the experiments. In Section 4 we show experimental results and finally in Section 5 conclusions and future work are presented.

2   Related Work

2.1   Imbalanced Data Sets

The class imbalance problem has received much attention from the machine learning community. This problem has been addressed in two main approaches: internal and external approaches. The first approach consists of modifying or creating new learning methods, while in the second approach, sampling techniques are used in order to build a more balanced data set. We now present some works proposed to deal with imbalanced data sets.

Kubat and Matwin [8] presented a heuristic under-sampling method to balance the data set in order to eliminate noisy, borderline, and redundant training examples of the majority class, keeping the original population of the minority class. Chawla et al. [3], devised a method called Synthetic Minority Over-sampling Technique (SMOTE). This technique creates new synthetic examples from the minority class. SMOTEBoost is an approach introduced by Chawla et al. [4] that combines SMOTE with the boosting ensemble. Han et al. presented two new minority over-sampling methods: borderline-SMOTE1 and borderline-SMOTE2, in which only the minority examples near the borderline are oversampled. Hongyu and Herna [7] introduced a method that combines boosting and data generation (DataBoost-IM), that achieved comparable and slightly better predictions, when using G-mean and F-measures metrics. Liu et al. [9] proposed an ensemble of SVMs with an integrated sampling technique, which combines both over-sampling and under-sampling. Wang and Japkowicz [15] proposed the boosting-SVMs with Asymmetric Cost algorithm, and they obtained very good results for the majority class as well as the minority class.

2.2   Automated Galaxy Classification

Increasing astronomical data is becoming available in quantities vastly too large to analyze by traditional methods. Therefore, automated and robust tools are required for any kind of analysis, such as morphological classification of galaxies.

Recently, there has been a great deal of interest from astronomers in applying machine learning techniques to solve astronomical problems, such as morphological galaxy classification. The morphology of galaxies is generally an important issue in the large scale study of the Universe. Galaxy classification is the first step towards a greater understanding of the origin an formation process of galaxies, and the evolution process of the Universe. The easiest way to classify galaxies is by their shape, and Edwin Hubble devised a basic scheme for classify them into three main types: Spirals, Ellipticals and Irregulars.

Automated classification of galaxies has been tackled using several machine learning techniques [1,5,11,12,13,16,17] such as neural networks, decision trees, ensembles of classifiers, instance-based methods, self organized maps, random forest, just to name a few. Nevertheless, they have not have not addressed the class imbalance inherent to this problem.

3   The Methods

In this section we briefly describe the learning methods we used for the experiments. For a deeper introduction of the algorithms we recommend the reader review the references.

3.1   Naive Bayes Classifier

The Naive Bayes classifier [10] is a probabilistic algorithm based on the assumption that the attribute values are conditionally independent given the target values. The Naive Bayes classifier applies to learning tasks where each instance x can be described as a tuple of attribute values $a_1, a_2, \ldots a_n$ and the target function $f(x)$ can take on any value from a finite set V. When a new instance x is presented, the Naive Bayes classifier assigns to it the most probable target value by applying the rule:

$$f(x) = argmax_{v_j \epsilon V} P(v_j) \Pi_i P(a_i \mid v_j) \qquad (1)$$

The learning task of the Naive Bayes is to build a hypothesis by estimating the different $P(v_i)$ and $P(a_i \mid v_j)$ terms based on their frequencies over the training data.

3.2   C4.5

C4.5 [10] operates by recursively splitting a training set based on feature values to produce a tree such that each example can end up in only one leaf. An initial feature is chosen as the root of the tree, and the examples are split among branches based on the feature value for each example. If the values are continuous, then each branch takes a certain range of values. Then a new feature is chosen, and the process is repeated for the remaining examples. Then the tree is converted to an equivalent rule set, which is pruned.

3.3   Radial Basis Function Networks

A radial basis function network (RBFNet) [10] is a variant of artificial neural networks. RBFNets are embedded in a two layer neural network, where each hidden unit implements a radial activated function. The output units implement a weighted sum of hidden unit outputs. Due to their nonlinear approximation properties, RBFNets are able to model complex tasks.

3.4   Random Forest

Random forest [2] is an ensemble of unpruned classification trees, induced from bootstrap samples of the training data, using random feature selection in the tree induction process. Prediction is made by aggregating the predictions of the ensemble. Random forest generally yields better performance than single tree classifiers such as C4.5.

3.5   Support Vector Machines

Support Vector Machines (SVMs) [14] are based on the Structural Risk Minimization principle from computational learning theory. This principle provides a formal mechanism to select a hypothesis from a hypothesis space for learning from finite training data sets. The aim of SVMs is to compute the hyperplane that best separates a set of training examples. Two cases are analyzed: the linear separable case and the non-linear separable case. In the first case we are looking for the optimal hyperplane in the set of hyper-planes separating the given training examples. The optimal hyperplane maximizes the sum of the distances to the closest positive and negative training examples (considering only two classes). The second case is solved by mapping training examples to a high-dimensional feature space using kernel functions. In this space the decision boundary is linear and we can apply the first case. There are several kernels such as polynomial, radial basis functions, neural networks, Fourier series, and splines, among others; that are chosen depending on the application.

3.6   SMOTE

The Synthetic Minority Over-sampling TEchnique [3] is an over-sampling method to deal with imbalanced data sets. This technique operates in the feature space rather than the data space. The minority class is over-sampled by taking each minority class sample and introducing synthetic examples along the line segments joining any/all of the k minority class nearest neighbors. Depending upon the amount of over-sampling required, neighbors from the k nearest neighbors are randomly chosen.

4   Experimental Results

The experiments were done using a data set of 310 galaxy images to classify three types of galaxies (E, S, Irr), and 293 for five (E, S0, Sa+Sb, Sc+Sd, Irr) and seven classes (E, S0, Sa, Sb, Sc, Sd, Irr). The minority class was represented by the Irregular galaxies, about 3.5% for three types and 3.7% for five and seven types.

We used 13 features to perform the classification task, which were obtained in an automated manner using principal component analysis (details can be found in [5]).

We used the Naive Bayes classifier, a RBF Network (a normalized Gaussian radial basis function network), SMO (Support Vector Machines), J48 (a particular C4.5 implementation), J48graft (J48 with pruning) and Random Forest that are implemented in Weka[1]. For SVMs we use a linear kernel, with 1.0 for the complexity constant and 0.0010 for rescale kernel. In the case of RBF we use logistic regression applied to k-means clusters as basis functions, with 2 clusters, a minimum standard deviation of 0.1, until convergence is reached. We also used the SMOTE and Resampling methods for over-sampling, testing different amounts for generating new instances: 100%, 200% and 500%.

In learning imbalanced data sets, accuracy is often not a good measure of performance, because a classifier that labels everything with the majority class can still achieve very high accuracy. We use metrics such as precision, recall, and F-measure to evaluate the performance of the learning algorithms. These metrics have been widely used for comparison and can be defined as:

$$Recall = TP/(TP + FN) \qquad (2)$$

$$Precision = TP/(TP + FP) \qquad (3)$$

$$F - measure = 2 \times Recall \times Precision/(Recall + Precision) \qquad (4)$$

where TP and TN denote the number of positive and negative examples that are classified correctly, while FN and FP denote the number of misclassified positive and negative examples, respectively.

Tables 1, 2 and 3 show the results for three, five and seven classes, respectively. This results were obtained by averaging ten runs of 10-fold cross-validation for each learning method. Analyzing the tree-class case, we can observe that Random Forest obtained the best results for SMOTE-100%, SMOTE-500%, Resampling-100%, Resampling-200% and Resampling-500%. We can also note that J48, J48graft and RBFNet obtained very good results for SMOTE as well as for Resampling.

For the five-class case, when we use SMOTE, RBFNet obtained the best results for 100% and 200%, while Random Forest obtained the best precision, recall and F-measure using 500%. For the case of Resampling, Random Forest again obtained the best results with over .77 for 100%, over .91 for 200% and over .99 for 500%.

Finally, for the seven-class case, RBFNet obtained the best results in eight of the nine results for SMOTE. However, Random Forest again obtained the best results for Resampling, with about .75, .91 and .99, for 100%, 200% and 500%, respectively.

---

[1] Weka is a collection of machine learning algorithms for data mining tasks. http://www.cs.waikato.ac.nz/ml/weka/

Table 1. Results for 3 types of galaxies

	SMOTE								
	100%			200%			500%		
	Prec	Rec	F-m	Prec	Rec	F-m	Prec	Rec	F-m
Naive Bayes	0.8678	0.8189	0.8333	0.8493	0.7995	0.8154	0.8001	0.7616	0.7719
J48	0.8310	0.8358	0.8323	0.8137	0.8166	0.8145	0.7890	0.7937	0.7908
J48graft	0.8384	0.8519	0.8421	0.8218	0.8364	0.8272	0.7890	0.7937	0.7908
RBFNet	0.8632	0.8834	0.8632	0.8464	0.8645	0.8485	0.8076	0.8191	0.8090
Random Forest	0.8825	0.8919	0.8615	0.8462	0.8622	0.8303	0.8684	0.8706	0.8559
SMO	0.7660	0.8750	0.8170	0.7160	0.8460	0.7760	0.5930	0.7700	0.6700
	Resampling								
	100%			200%			500%		
	Prec	Rec	F-m	Prec	Rec	F-m	Prec	Rec	F-m
Naive Bayes	0.8879	0.8777	0.8790	0.8927	0.8589	0.8691	0.9885	0.9882	0.9881
J48	0.9336	0.9345	0.9330	0.9724	0.9715	0.9716	0.9945	0.9944	0.9944
J48graft	0.9468	0.9468	0.9440	0.9820	0.9820	0.9818	0.9953	0.9952	0.9952
RBFNet	0.9272	0.9280	0.9257	0.9320	0.9296	0.9275	0.9186	0.9271	0.9189
Random Forest	0.9689	0.9682	0.9659	0.9888	0.9888	0.9885	0.9997	0.9997	0.9997
SMO	0.7980	0.8940	0.8430	0.7840	0.8850	0.8320	0.8180	0.9050	0.8590

Table 2. Results for 5 types of galaxies

	SMOTE								
	100%			200%			500%		
	Prec	Rec	F-m	Prec	Rec	F-m	Prec	Rec	F-m
Naive Bayes	0.4481	0.4588	0.4420	0.4248	0.4334	0.4171	0.4565	0.4570	0.4449
J48	0.4034	0.4207	0.4045	0.3947	0.4144	0.3996	0.4188	0.4354	0.4233
J48graft	0.4080	0.4280	0.4107	0.3954	0.4159	0.4008	0.4197	0.4382	0.4244
RBFNet	0.4667	0.4914	0.4686	0.4586	0.4813	0.4599	0.4808	0.4949	0.4788
Random Forest	0.4719	0.4684	0.4590	0.4537	0.4507	0.4439	0.5236	0.5208	0.5181
SMO	0.2772	0.4574	0.2997	0.2731	0.4414	0.2824	0.3597	0.4178	0.2892
	Resampling								
	100%			200%			500%		
	Prec	Rec	F-m	Prec	Rec	F-m	Prec	Rec	F-m
Naive Bayes	0.4659	0.4453	0.4466	0.5115	0.4875	0.4892	0.4804	0.4875	0.4656
J48	0.7163	0.7149	0.7143	0.8699	0.8692	0.8694	0.9729	0.9726	0.9724
J48graft	0.7146	0.7133	0.7123	0.8666	0.8662	0.8660	0.9729	0.9727	0.9725
RBFNet	0.6005	0.6005	0.5954	0.5991	0.6020	0.5902	0.5828	0.5924	0.5652
Random Forest	0.7786	0.7744	0.7744	0.9132	0.9123	0.9122	0.9941	0.9939	0.9939
SMO	0.3913	0.4990	0.4352	0.4142	0.5196	0.4263	0.3853	0.4705	0.3380

Table 3. Results for 7 types of galaxies

	SMOTE								
	100%			200%			500%		
	Prec	*Rec*	*F*-m	*Prec*	*Rec*	*F*-m	*Prec*	*Rec*	*F*-m
Naive Bayes	0.3407	0.3760	0.3446	0.3525	0.3829	0.3544	0.3503	0.3831	0.3550
J48	0.3369	0.3455	0.3393	0.3424	0.3478	0.3429	0.3598	0.3642	0.3611
J48graft	0.3395	0.3505	0.3422	0.3413	0.3508	0.3434	0.3623	0.3693	0.3652
RBFNet	0.3739	0.4300	0.3846	0.3769	0.4254	0.3880	0.4231	0.4632	0.4335
Random Forest	0.3496	0.3943	0.3641	0.3800	0.4093	0.3860	0.4198	0.4548	0.4326
SMO	0.1950	0.4420	0.2710	0.1850	0.4300	0.2590	0.1635	0.3966	0.2287
	Resampling								
	100%			200%			500%		
	Prec	*Rec*	*F*-m	*Prec*	*Rec*	*F*-m	*Prec*	*Rec*	*F*-m
Naive Bayes	0.4141	0.3977	0.3875	0.5571	0.5592	0.5386	0.4804	0.4875	0.4656
J48	0.6715	0.6708	0.6686	0.8272	0.8247	0.8248	0.9729	0.9726	0.9724
J48graft	0.6657	0.6634	0.6617	0.8285	0.8263	0.8262	0.9729	0.9727	0.9725
RBFNet	0.5564	0.5569	0.5474	0.5590	0.5700	0.5433	0.5828	0.5924	0.5652
Random Forest	0.7582	0.7540	0.7488	0.9166	0.9148	0.9145	0.9941	0.9939	0.9939
SMO	0.2631	0.3936	0.2522	0.1950	0.4415	0.2707	0.3853	0.4705	0.3380

5   Conclusions

We have presented an experimental study of the performance of six machine learning algorithms applied to galaxy classification, addressing the imbalanced class inherent to this astronomical problem. From the results we can say that Random Forest was the best classifier for most of the cases, nevertheless, RBFNets and J48 obtained very good results. In addition, we can mention that the Resampling technique obtained better results than SMOTE in almost all cases for all the classifiers.

Future work includes addressing the class imbalanced problem in other domains such as text classification, astronomical classification in wide-field images, biological structures, where the imbalanced problem is very common.

Acknowledgements

First author wants to thank PROMEP for supporting this research work under grant UPPUE-PTC-023.

References

1. Bazell, D., Aha, D.: Ensembles of classifiers for morphological galaxy classificacion. The Astrophysical Journal 548, 219–233 (2001)
2. Breiman, L.: Random Forests. Machine Learning 45(1), 5–32 (2001)
3. Chawla, N., Bowyer, K., Hall, L., Kegelmeyer, W.P.: SMOTE: synthetic minority oversampling technique. Journal of Artificial Intelligence Research 16, 321–357 (2002)

4. Chawla, N., Lazarevic, A., Hall, L., Bowyer, K.: SMOTEBoost: Improving Prediction of the Minority Class in Boosting. In: Lavrač, N., Gamberger, D., Todorovski, L., Blockeel, H. (eds.) PKDD 2003. LNCS (LNAI), vol. 2838, pp. 107–119. Springer, Heidelberg (2003)

5. De la Calleja, J., Fuentes, O.: Machine learning and image analysis for morphological galaxy classification. Montly Notices of the Royal Astronomical Society 349, 87–93 (2004)

6. Han, H., Wang, W., Mao, B.: Borderline-smote: A new over-sampling method in imbalanced data sets learning. In: Huang, D.-S., Zhang, X.-P., Huang, G.-B. (eds.) ICIC 2005. LNCS, vol. 3644, pp. 878–887. Springer, Heidelberg (2005)

7. Hongyu, G., Herna, L.V.: Learning from imbalanced data sets with boosting and data generation: The databoost-IM approach. SIGKDD Explor. Newsl. 6(1), 30–39 (2004)

8. Kubat, M., Matwin, S.: Addressing the curse of imbalanced training sets: One-sided selection. In: Proceedings of the Fourteenth International Conference on Machine Learning, pp. 179–186 (1997)

9. Liu, Y., An, A., Huang, X.: Boosting predicion accuracy on imbalanced datasets with svm ensembles. In: Ng, W.-K., Kitsuregawa, M., Li, J., Chang, K. (eds.) PAKDD 2006. LNCS (LNAI), vol. 3918, pp. 107–118. Springer, Heidelberg (2006)

10. Mitchell, T.: Machine Learning. McGraw Hill, New York (1997)

11. Mohamed, M.A., Atta, M.M.: Classification of galaxies using transformed domain features. Internartional Journal of Computer Science and Network Security 10(2), 86–91 (2010)

12. Naim, A., Lahav, O., Sodre Jr., L., Storrie-Lombardi, M.: Automated morphological classification of apm galaxies by supervised artificial neural networks. Monthly Notices of the Royal Astronomical Society 275, 567 (1995)

13. Philip, N., Wadadekar, Y., Kembhavi, A., Joseph, K.: A difference boosting neural network for automated star-galaxy classification. Astronomy and Astrophysics 385, 1119–1126 (2002)

14. Vapnik, V.: The nature of statistical learning theory. Springer, New York (1995)

15. Wang, B., Japkowicz, N.: Boosting support vector machines for imbalanced data sets. In: An, A., Matwin, S., Raś, Z.W., Ślęzak, D. (eds.) Foundations of Intelligent Systems. LNCS (LNAI), vol. 4994, pp. 38–47. Springer, Heidelberg (2008)

16. Yagi, M., Nakamura, Y., Doi, M., Shimasaku, K., Okamura, S.: Morphological classification of nearby galaxies based on asymmetry and luminosity concentration. Monthly Notices of the Royal Astronomical Society 368(1), 211–220 (2006)

17. Zhang, Y., Zhao, Y.: Automated clustering algorithms for classification of astronomical objects. The Astrophysical Journal 422, 1113–1121 (2004)

Exploiting Contextual Information for Image Re-ranking

Daniel Carlos Guimarães Pedronette and Ricardo da S. Torres

RECOD Lab - Institute of Computing - University of Campinas
CEP 13083-970, Campinas/SP - Brazil

Abstract. This paper presents a novel re-ranking approach based on *contextual information* used to improve the effectiveness of Content-Based Image Retrieval (CBIR) tasks. In our approach, image processing techniques are applied to ranked lists defined by CBIR descriptors. Conducted experiments involving shape, color, and texture descriptors demonstrate the effectiveness of our method.

1 Introduction

Technological improvements in image acquisition and the decreasing cost of storage devices have enabled the dissemination of large image collections. In this scenario, there is the need of methods for indexing and retrieving these data. One of the most common approaches to support image searches relies on the use of Content-Based Image Retrieval (CBIR) systems.

Basically, given a query image, a CBIR system aims at retrieving the most similar images in a collection by taking into account image visual properties (such as, shape, color, and texture). Collection images are ranked in decreasing order of similarity, according to a given *image descriptor*. However, in general, these approaches perform only pairwise image analysis and compute similarity (or distance) measures considering only pair of images, ignoring the rich information encoded in the relations among several images.

Some post-processing methods have been proposed for improving effectiveness of information retrieval tasks [5,18,17,9]. Efforts were put on post-processing the similarity scores by analyzing the relations among all documents in a given collection. The influence among shape similarities is analized in [18], using Markov chains to perform a diffusion process on a graph formed by a set of shapes, where the influences of other shapes are propagated. An unsupervised clustering algorithm is used in [5], aiming to capture the manifold structure of the image relations by defining a neighborhood for each data point in terms of a mutual k-nearest neighbor graph. A graph transduction learning approach is introduced in [17]. The algorithm computes the shape similarity of a pair of shapes in the context of other shapes. In [9], a distance optimization algorithm has been proposed. The objective is to cluster shapes by taking into account the similariy among ranked lists. Distances between shapes are updated based on created clusters aiming at improving the retrieval effectiveness.

I. Bloch and R.M. Cesar, Jr. (Eds.): CIARP 2010, LNCS 6419, pp. 541–548, 2010.

Recently, *contextual information* have also been considered for improving the effectiveness of image retrieval [4,10,12]. The objective of these methods is somehow mimic the human behavior on judging the similarity among objects by considering specific *contexts*. More specifically, the notion of *context* can refer to updating image similarity measures by taking into account information encoded on the ranked lists defined by a CBIR system [12].

In this paper we present a new post-processing method that re-ranks images by taking into account *contextual information*. We propose a novel approach for retrieving contextual information, by creating a *gray scale image* representation of distance matrices computed by CBIR descriptors. The gray scale image is constructed for k-nearest neighbor of a query and analyzed using image processing techniques. The use of image processing techniques for *contextual information* representation and processing is the main novelty of our work. We believe that our strategy opens a new are of investigation related to the used of image processing approaches for image re-ranking in CBIR systems.

We evaluated the proposed method on shape, color, and texture descriptors. Experimental results demonstrate that the proposed method can be used in several CBIR tasks and yields better results in terms of effectiveness performance than various post-processing algorithms recently proposed in the literature.

2   A Re-ranking Method Based on Contextual Information

2.1   Contextual Information Representation

Let $\mathcal{C}=\{img_1, img_2, \ldots, img_N\}$ be an image collection and let $\mathcal{D}$ be an image descriptor that deinfes a distance function $\rho : \mathcal{C} \times \mathcal{C} \to \mathbb{R}$, where $\mathbb{R}$ denotes real numbers. Consider $\rho(X, Y) \geq 0$ for all (X, Y) and $\rho(X, Y) = 0$ if $X = Y$. The distance $\rho(img_i, img_j)$ among all images $img_i, img_j \in \mathcal{C}$ can be computed to obtain an $N \times N$ distance matrix A.

Our goal is to represent the distance matrix A as a gray scale image (named *context image* $\hat{I}$) and analyse this image for extracting *contextual information*. For this representation we consider two reference images $img_i, img_j \in \mathcal{C}$.

Let the *context image* $\hat{I}$ be a gray scale image defined by the pair (D_I, f), where D_I is a finite set of pixels (points in $\mathbb{N}^2$, defined by a pair (x, y)) and $f : D_I \to \mathbb{R}$ is a function that assigns to each pixel $p \in D_I$ a real number. We define the values of f function in terms of the distance function ρ (encoded into matrix A) and reference images $img_i, img_j \in \mathcal{C}$.

Let $R_i = \{img_{i_1}, img_{i_2}, \ldots, img_{i_N}\}$ be the ranked list defined by matrix A considering the reference image img_i as query image; and $R_j = \{img_{j_1}, img_{j_2}, \ldots, img_{j_N}\}$ the ranked list of reference image img_j. On this way, the axis of *context image* $\hat{I}$ are ordered according to the order defined by ranked lists R_i and R_j. Let $img_{i_x} \in R_i$ be an image at x postion of ranked list R_i and $img_{j_y} \subset R_j$ an image at y position of the ranked list R_j, the value of $f(x, y)$ (function that defines the gray scale of pixel $p(x, y)$) is defined as follows: $f(x, y) = \bar{\rho}(img_{i_x}, img_{j_y})$, where $\bar{\rho}$ is defined by the distance function ρ normalized in the interval [0,255].

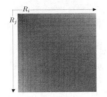

Fig. 1. Similar reference images   **Fig. 2.** Dissimilar reference images

Fig. 3. Representation for similar images   **Fig. 4.** Representation for dissimilar images

An example considering similar reference images (from MPEG-7 database) is illustrated in Figure 1. The respective gray scale image representing matrix A is illustrated in Figure 3. An analogous example for dissimilar images is illustrated in figures 2 and 4.

Our goal is to exploit useful *context information* provided by these images. Low distance values (similar images) are associated with dark pixels in the image, while high values (non-similar images) refers to non-black pixels. Considering two similar images as reference images, the begining of two ranked lists should have similar images as well. This behavior creates a *dark region* in top left corner of context image (as we can observe in Figure 3). The region represents a neighborhood of similar images with low distances.

We aim to characterize *contextual information* by analyzing this region using image processing techniques. These information will be used by the re-ranking method presented in next section.

2.2   Exploiting Contextual Information for Image Re-ranking

Given an image $img_i \in \mathcal{C}$, we aim to process *contextual information* of img_i by constructing *context images* for the *k-nearest neighbors* of img_i (based on distance matrix A). We use an affinity matrix W to store the results of *contextual information*. Let N be the size of collection $\mathcal{C}$, the affinity matrix W is a $N \times N$ matrix where $W[k, l]$ represents the similarity between k and l.

We apply image processing techniques to process the *context image* of each *k-nearest neighbor* of img_i and then update the affinity matrix W. The same process is performed for all $img_i \in \mathcal{C}$. Since all images of $\mathcal{C}$ are processed, the affinity matrix W is used as input for computing a new distance martix A_{t+1} (where t indicates the current iteration). These steps are repeated along several iterations. Finally, after a number T of iterations a re-ranking is performed based on final distance matrix A_T. Algorithm 1 outlines the re-ranking method.

The affinity matrix W is initialized with value 1 for all positions in step 4. *Context images* are created in step 7, as explained in Section 2.1, considering

---

Algorithm 1. Contextual Re-Ranking Algorithm

Require: Original distance matrix A
Ensure: Processed distance matrix A_T
1: $t \leftarrow 0$
2: $A_t \leftarrow A$
3: **while** $t < T$ **do**
4:     $initializeAffinityMatrix(W, 1)$
5:     **for all** $img_i \in C$ **do**
6:         **for all** $img_j \in KNN(img_i)$ **do**
7:             $grayImg \leftarrow createGrayScaleImage(img_i, img_j, A_t, L)$
8:             $grayImg' \leftarrow processGrayScaleImage(grayImg, L)$
9:             $W \leftarrow incrementaAffinityMatrix(grayImg', W, j)$
10:         **end for**
11:     **end for**
12:     $A_{t+1} \leftarrow computeDistanceMatrix(W)$
13:     $t = t + 1$
14: **end while**
15: $performReRanking(A_T)$

---

img_i (image being processed) and img_j (current neighbor of img_i) as reference images. Parameter L refers to the size of the square in top left corner of *context image* that will be analyzed.

Image processing techniques are applied to *context images* in step 8. Our goal is to identify dense regions of dark pixels (low distance values). We use a limiarization for obtaining a binary image and discriminating dark pixels. In the following, we apply a median filter for determining regions of dense black pixels. The threshold l used for limiarization is computed based on average and maximum distance values contained in $L \times L$ square in top left corner of *context image*: $l = \frac{avg(\rho(img_i, img_j))}{max(\rho(img_i, img_j))}$ with $i, j < L$. Figure 5 illustrates an example of limiarized image and Figure 6 shows the limiarized image after applying the median filter.

Step 9 updates the affinity matrix W based on *context images*. For updating, only black pixels (and their positions) are considered. The idea consists of giving more relevance to pixels next to the origin $(0,0)$, e.g., pixels that represent the beginning of ranked lists. The importance of neighbors should also be considered: neighbors at first k positions should be considered more relevant when updating W.

Fig. 5. Example of limiarized image

Fig. 6. Example of filtered image

Fig. 7. Computing updates of matrix W

Let $img_i \in C$ be the current image being processed. Let img_j be the k (such that $k < K$) neighbor of img_i. Let img_i and img_j be reference images and let $\hat{I}(D_I, f)$ be the *context image* after limiarization and applying median filter. Let L be the size of top left corner square that should be processed and let $p(x, y) \in D_I$ be a black pixel ($f(x, y) = 0$), such that $x, y < L$. Let $H = \sqrt{2 \times L^2}$ be the maximum distance of a pixel $p(x, y)$ to origin $(0, 0)$, as illustrated in Figure 7. Let $W[img_{i_x}, img_{i_y}]$ represent the similarity between images img_{i_x} and img_{i_y}. Then, for each black pixel $p(x, y)$ the matrix W is updated as follows:

$$W[img_{i_x}, img_{i_y}] = W[img_{i_x}, img_{i_y}] + [(K - k) \times (H/\sqrt{x^2 + y^2})] \quad (1)$$

Note that low values of k, x, y (the begining of ranked lists) leads to high increments of W. Smaller increments occur when k has high values and $x, y = L$. In this case, the term $H/\sqrt{x^2 + y^2}$ is equal to 1.

At the end of an iteration (when all images have been processed), W presents high values for similar images. But there may be positions of W that did not receive any increments (e.g., dissimilar images), and have the initial value 1. The new distance matrix A_{t+1} (step 12 of Algorithm 1) is computed as follows:

$$A_{t+1}[x, y] = \begin{cases} 1 + \bar{A}_t[x, y] & \text{if W[x,y]} = 1 \\ 2 \times (1/W[x, y]) & \text{if W[x,y]} > 1 \end{cases} \quad (2)$$

where $\bar{A}_t$ is the distance matrix A_t normalized in the interval $[0,1]$. When $W[x, y] = 1$, e.g., $W[x, y]$ was not updated by equation 1, we use the old distance matrix A_t for determining values of A_{t+1}. Otherwise (when $W[x, y] > 1$), values of new distance matrix A_{t+1} is equal to inverse of affinity matrix W. Since the smaller increment for W is 1 (and therefore $W[x, y] = 2$), the largest value of a new distance in A_{t+1} is 0.5. Therefore we normalize distance values in the interval $[0,1]$ by multiplying by 2. A_{t+1} will have values in the interval $[0,2]$: (*i*) in the interval $[0,1]$ when $W[x, y] > 1$, and (*ii*) in the interval $[1,2]$ when $W[x, y] = 1$. A last operation is performed on new distance matrix A_{t+1} for ensure the simetry in terms of distances between images ($\rho(x, y) = \rho(y, x)$): $A_{t+1}[x, y] = A_{t+1}[y, x] = min(A_{t+1}[x, y], A_{t+1}[y, x])$.

At the end of T iterations, a new computed distance matrix A_T is obtained. Finally, a re-ranking is performed based on values of A_T (step 15 of Algorithm 1).

3   Experimental Evaluation

3.1   Impact of Parameters

The execution of Algorithm 1 considers three parameters: (*i*) K - number of neighbors used as reference images; (*ii*) L - size of top left square of context image to be analyzed; and (*ii*) T - number of iterations that the algorithm is executed.

To evaluate the influence of different parameter settings on the retrieval scores and for determining the best parameters values we conducted a set of experiments. We use MPEG-7 database with the so-called bullseye score, which counts all matching objects within the 40 most similar candidates. Since each class consists of 20 objects, the retrieved score is normalized with the highest possible number of hits. For distance computation, we used the CFD [9] shape descriptor.

Retrieval scores are computed ranging parameters K in the interval [1,10] and L in the interval [1,60] (with increments of 5) for each iteration. For each iteration, the best retrieval score was determined.

We observed that best retrieval scores increased along iterations and parameters converged for values $K = 4$ and $L = 25$. The best retrieval score was reached in iteration 4: 94.55%. Note that these parameters may change for database with different sizes.

3.2   Experimental Results

In this section, we present a set of conducted experiments for demonstrating the applicability and effectiveness of our method. We analyzed our method with respect its use fo re-ranking images considering shape, color, and texture descriptors. We also compared our method to state-of-the-art post-processing methods.

Table 1 presents results (bullseye score - Recall@40) for shape descriptors on MPEG-7 database. We can observe a significative gains from +5.09% to +11.99%.

Table 1. Contextual Re-Ranking for Shape Descriptors on MPEG-7 *(Recall@40)*

Shape Descriptor	Score [%]	Contextual Re-Ranking	Gain
SS [11]	43.99%	49.08%	+11.57%
BAS [1]	75.20%	80.35%	+6.85%
IDSC+DP [7]	85.40%	89.75%	+5.09%
CFD [9]	84.43%	94.55%	+11.99%

In addition to shape descriptors, we conducted experiments with color and texture descriptors. For texture descriptor, we used the Brodatz [2] dataset, a popular dataset for texture descriptors evaluation. For color descriptor, we used a soccer data set proposed in [16] and composed by images from 7 soccer teams, containing 40 images per class. For Brodatz dataset, we used the same parameter of MPEG-7 (determined in previous section). Since the soccer dataset have a very different size, we used $K = 1$, $L - 50$, and $T = 2$. Table 2 presents results for 10 image descriptors in 3 different datasets. The measure adopted is *Mean Average Precision (MAP)*. We can observe that the proposed re-ranking method presented positive precision gains for all descriptors, ranging from +0.87% to +14.75%.

Finally, we also evaluated our method in comparison to other state-of-the-art post-processing methods. We use MPEG-7 database with the called bullseye score. Table 3 presents results of our contextual re-ranking method and four post-processing methods. We also present the retrieval scores for IDSC+DP [7] and CFD [9] shape descriptors, that has been used as input for these methods. Note

Table 2. Contextual Re-Ranking Evaluation on Content-Based Image Retrieval Tasks

Descriptor	Type	Dataset	Score [%] (MAP)	Contextual Re-Ranking	Gain
SS [11]	Shape	MPEG-7	37.67%	43.23%	+14.75%
BAS [1]	Shape	MPEG-7	71.52%	75.88%	+6.09%
IDSC+DP [7]	Shape	MPEG-7	81.70%	85.65%	+4.83%
CFD [9]	Shape	MPEG-7	80.71%	91.28%	+13.09%
GCH [14]	Color	Soccer Dataset	32.24%	32.52%	+0.87%
ACC [3]	Color	Soccer Dataset	37.23%	39.05%	+4.89%
BIC [13]	Color	Soccer Dataset	39.26%	41.81%	+6.50%
LBP [8]	Texture	Brodatz	48.40%	49.59%	+2.46%
CCOM [6]	Texture	Brodatz	57.57%	63.48%	+10.27%
LAS [15]	Texture	Brodatz	75.15%	78.39%	+4.31%

Table 3. Post-processing methods comparison on MPEG-7 database *(Recall@40)*

Algorithm	Descriptor	Score [%]	Gain
CFD [9]	-	84.43%	-
IDSC+DP [7]	-	85.40%	-
Graph Transduction [17]	IDSC+DP	91.00%	+6.56%
Distance Optmization [9]	CFD	92.56%	+9.63%
Constrained Diffusion Process [18]	IDSC+DP	93.32%	+9.27%
Mutual kNN Graph [5]	IDSC+DP	93.40%	+9.37%
Contextual Re-Ranking	**CFD**	**94.55%**	**+11.99%**

that our **contextual re-ranking** method (last line) has the best effectiveness performace when compared to all other post-processing methods.

4   Conclusions

In this work, we presented a new re-ranking method based on contextual information. The main idea consists in creating gray scale image representations of distance matrix and performs a re-ranking based on information extracted from these images. We conducted a large set of experiments and experimental results demonstrated the applicability of our method to several image retrieval tasks based on shape, color and texture descriptors. The proposed method achieves very high effectiveness performance when compared with state-of-the-art post-processing methods on the well-known MPEG-7 dataset. Future work focuses on using other image processing techniques, as dynamic limiarization and filtering.

Acknowledgment

Authors thank CAPES, FAPESP and CNPq for financial support. Authors also thanks DGA/UNICAMP for its support in this work.

References

1. Arica, N., Vural, F.T.Y.: Bas: a perceptual shape descriptor based on the beam angle statistics. Pattern Recogn. Lett. 24(9-10), 1627–1639 (2003)
2. Brodatz, P.: Textures: A Photographic Album for Artists and Designers. Dover, New York (1966)
3. Huang, J., Kumar, S.R., Mitra, M., Zhu, W.J., Zabih, R.: Image indexing using color correlograms. In: CVPR 1997, p. 762 (1997)
4. Jégou, H., Harzallah, H., Schmid, C.: A contextual dissimilarity measure for accurate and efficient image search. In: CVPR, pp. 1–8 (2007)
5. Peter, K.: Donoser Michael, B.H.: Beyond pairwise shape similarity analysis. In: Asian Conference on Computer Vision (ACCV), pp. 655–666 (2009)
6. Kovalev, V., Volmer, S.: Color co-occurence descriptors for querying-by-example. In: MMM 1998, p. 32 (1998)
7. Ling, H., Jacobs, D.W.: Shape classification using the inner-distance. PAMI 29(2), 286–299 (2007)
8. Ojala, T., Pietikäinen, M., Mäenpää, T.: Multiresolution gray-scale and rotation invariant texture classification with local binary patterns. PAMI 24(7), 971–987 (2002)
9. Pedronette, D.C.G., da Torres, R.S.: Shape retrieval using contour features and distance optmization. In: VISAPP. vol. 1, pp. 197 – 202 (2010)
10. Perronnin, F., Liu, Y., Renders, J.M.: A family of contextual measures of similarity between distributions with application to image retrieval. In: CVPR, pp. 2358–2365 (2009)
11. da, S., Torres, R., Falcao, A.X.: Contour Salience Descriptors for Effective Image Retrieval and Analysis. Image and Vision Computing 25(1), 3–13 (2007)
12. Schwander, O., Nielsen, F.: Reranking with contextual dissimilarity measures from representational bregmanl k-means. In: VISAPP, vol. 1, pp. 118–122 (2010)
13. Stehling, R.O., Nascimento, M.A., Falcao, A.X.: A compact and efficient image retrieval approach based on border/interior pixel classification. In: CIKM 2002, pp. 102–109 (2002)
14. Swain, M.J., Ballard, D.H.: Color indexing. IJCV 7(1), 11–32 (1991)
15. Tao, B., Dickinson, B.W.: Texture recognition and image retrieval using gradient indexing. JVCIR 11(3), 327–342 (2000)
16. van de Weijer, J., Schmid, C.: Coloring local feature extraction. In: Leonardis, A., Bischof, H., Pinz, A. (eds.) ECCV 2006, Part II. LNCS, vol. 3952, pp. 334–348. Springer, Heidelberg (2006)
17. Yang, X., Bai, X., Latecki, L.J., Tu, Z.: Improving shape retrieval by learning graph transduction. In: Forsyth, D., Torr, P., Zisserman, A. (eds.) ECCV 2008, Part IV. LNCS, vol. 5305, pp. 788 801. Springer, Heidelberg (2008)
18. Yang, X., Koknar-Tezel, S., Latecki, L.J.: Locally constrained diffusion process on locally densified distance spaces with applications to shape retrieval. In: CVPR, pp. 357–364 (2009)

Assessing the Role of Spatial Relations for the Object Recognition Task

Annette Morales-González and Edel García-Reyes

Advanced Technologies Application Center. 7a # 21812 b/ 218 and 222,
Rpto. Siboney, Playa, P.C. 12200, La Habana, Cuba
{amorales,egarcia}@cenatav.co.cu

Abstract. It has been proved that spatial relations among objects and object's parts play a fundamental role in the human perception and understanding of images, thus becoming very relevant in the computational fields of object recognition and content-based image retrieval. In this work we propose a spatial descriptor to represent topological and orientation/directional relationships, which are obtained by means of combinatorial pyramids. A combination of visual and spatial features is performed to improve the object recognition task. We ran an experiment to evaluate the expressiveness of this representation and it has shown promising results. It was performed on the benchmark ETH-80 Image Set database and we compare our approach with a state-of-the-art method recently published.

Keywords: object recognition, spatial relations, topological relations.

1 Introduction

Spatial relations between objects of a scene have received much attention in the field of image analysis and retrieval, due to the fact that they can reveal important properties of the scene being analyzed. Moreover, it has been stated that structural relations among image components are fundamental in the human process of similarity comparison.

In general, spatial relations can be classified into three major categories [1]: (1) Topological relations, which remain invariant under transformations such as translation, scaling and rotating. (2) Direction (orientation) relations, which specify the absolute or relative spatial locations of objects. (3) Metric relations, which deals with sizes of objects or the distance between them.

Within this context, there are many works related to region-based representation of images that do not use the spatial information between regions, or they do it poorly. Also, there are methods that only use direction relations [2][3], only topological relations [4][5], and others that combine them together [6][7][8]. Most of these representations consider that each object is ideally identified or deals with their bounding box to compute the spatial relations descriptors. Yet, this does not match the case in a segmented image where objects are often arbitrarily over-segmented, or the cases when bounding boxes overlap.

I. Bloch and R.M. Cesar, Jr. (Eds.): CIARP 2010, LNCS 6419, pp. 549–556, 2010.
© Springer-Verlag Berlin Heidelberg 2010

One explicit representation of spatial relations among regions is the region adjacency graph (RAG)[9]. However, the unique notion of adjacency is too poor to describe complex spatial organization of the different parts of an object, and does not provide enough information to differentiate an adjacency relationship from a contains or inside one[9].

Irregular graph pyramids [10] can overcome these drawbacks by using dual graphs to determine important edges in the pyramid construction. In this case, each level will be an extended RAG, where parallel edges and self-loops encode important relations between two regions (relevant parallel edges represent several common boundaries and self-loops represent a *contains* relation).

In this work we use the combinatorial pyramid framework [11] to obtain a hierarchy of partitions from an image and to determine the spatial relations between the regions found at each level. We propose a new representation to compute a spatial relations descriptor, taking into account topological and orientation relations. A similarity measure for this descriptor is proposed and a graph matching algorithm is used to identify similar images from a database. The spatial description of regions relationships is combined with visual descriptions of them to make more robust the recognition task.

Section 2 of this paper explains the visual representation used for describing the images and the similarity measures selected for comparison. In Section 3 we present our novel spatial descriptor and a way for computing the similarity using this representation. Finally Section 4 provides the results of an experiment to evaluate the proposed representation.

2   Visual Description of Images

Graph pyramids and combinatorial pyramids are built from bottom (each vertex is a pixel in the image) to top (each vertex is a group of pixels forming a region), and all levels in between form partitions of the image at different scales. To build a new level, a series of topology-preserving edge contractions are performed from the previous level, following some criteria [10]. The criteria for combining pixels into regions may vary.

In the present case, we are using only the color value in RGB color space of the image pixels. The difference between the color value of pixels is computed, and if it falls beneath a threshold, these pixels are merged into a region, which will survive to the next level and its color value will be the average of the pixels that were combined. That is why, one of the features selected for similarity purposes is the average color of each region.

For texture representation we chose the locally binary patterns (LBP) histogram of regions [12]. The LBP operator codes a local window pattern from a texture patch, and its histogram is often treated as texture feature in classification problems. Among the advantages of LBP are its invariance to any monotonic change in gray level and its computational simplicity.

The structure of the combinatorial pyramid is perfect for computing statistical features, such as histograms. The computation of each region's histogram can be performed during the construction of the pyramid very easily, updating each level from the data of the level below. Given an image obtained by computing the LBPs from the original image, it is possible to update each region's histogram at each level by using the following equation:

$$H(R)_j = \sum_{i=1}^{n} H(i)_{j-1} \tag{1}$$

Where n is the number of regions merged into the current region R, and j is the level of the pyramid.

2.1 Computing Visual Similarity

Once defined the visual features to be used, one important step is to select the similarity measures for them. Since our main contribution is not in the aspects of visual similarity, we chose two well-known similarity measures for our features.

For computing visual similarity between two pairs of regions regarding color value, we will compute the Euclidean distance in RGB space. Since this distance will yield a dissimilarity value, we will turn it into a similarity value S_C.

The LBP histograms of each region of the pyramid are normalized, since the different sizes of regions produce uneven histograms. For the LBP histogram similarity we use the Bhattacharyya distance, which is then transformed into a similarity measure S_H.

For combining these similarity values, we add two weights, ω_C and ω_H, in order to give different importance to the features and to have a final value of visual similarity between two regions:

$$S_V = \omega_C * S_C + \omega_H * S_H, \qquad \text{where } S_V \in [0, 1] \tag{2}$$

3 Our Proposed Spatial Descriptor

There have been several models proposed for representing spatial relations among regions. For topological relations, the 4IM and 9IM [13] are well known. In these models, and for the case of 2D images, eight topological relations are described: *disjoint, contains, inside, equal, meet, covers, covered by* and *overlap*. The main drawback of these models is their inability to represent complex topological relations (i.e. when two regions have more than one boundary in common).

For the case of 2D images, eight relations are unnecessary since some of them will never be present (i.e the *overlap* relation). In 2D images, we certainly can have occlusion (two objects overlapped), but at the time of segmentation we will be unable to establish a difference between this and a simple adjacency relation, since we will have only a boundary in common. We selected from these eight relations, three of them that will be representative for 2D images. These relations can be seen in Figure 1.

We consider that orientation relations between regions can also provide important information, this is why we choose to create a spatial descriptor that

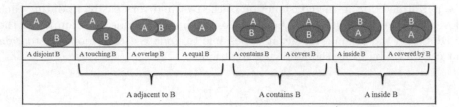

Fig. 1. Topological relations between 2D regions and the selection for 2D images

would take both types of relations into account. For this matter we decided to use the relations *left of, right of, top of, bottom of, horizontally aligned* and *vertically aligned,* somehow similar to the order relations proposed in [8]. These relations will be computed based on the spatial disposition of the centroids for every pair of regions.

3.1   The Spatial Descriptor

Our spatial description proposal consists of a binary vector that will encode both topological and orientation relations. The vector will have 9 elements, each representing one basic spatial relation, as shown in Figure 2. For every position, we put a 1 if the two regions share that spatial relation and 0 otherwise. These basic relations are split into three categories: (1) Topological relations - *adjacent, contains* and *inside,* (2) Alignment relations - *horizontally aligned* and *vertically aligned,* (3) Orientation relations - *left of, right of, top of* and *bottom of.*

H	**L**	**R**	**V**	**T**	**B**	**A**	**C**	**I**

H – Horizontally aligned	V – Vertically aligned	A – Adjacent
L – Left of	T – Top of	C – Contains
R – Right of	B – Bottom of	I - Inside

Fig. 2. Spatial descriptor combining topological and orientation relations

We also store for every pair of related regions the number of common boundary segments, which will be a descriptor of the adjacency between them.

For computational purposes, each value of the descriptor will be stored as bits. This leads us to a 9 bit (2 bytes with 7 unused bits) representation, which is very simple, compact and easy to use.

3.2   The Spatial Relationship Similarity

In order to compute the similarity between two spatial relations, we need to find out how many basic relations they share, this is why we chose a similarity measure that can be used with binary vectors. We are proposing to use the Sokal-Michener measure [14] since it treats positive and negative matches equally. Let X and Y be binary vectors of the same length d and let x_i denote the ith value which is either 0 or 1. The Sokal-Michener measure can be computed as:

$$S_{SD} = \frac{xy + \overline{xy}}{d} \tag{3}$$

The term xy denotes the positive matches (i.e. the number of 1 bits that matched between X and Y) and the term $\overline{xy}$ denotes the negative matches (i.e. the number of 0 bits that matched between X and Y).

We believe that, when computing the spatial similarity between two pairs of regions, all the basic relations should not contribute in the same way in the final result. We consider that topological relations are more relevant than the others, since they are invariant to transformations such as scaling, translating and rotation. Therefore, they must have a bigger weight in the decision of whether two spatial relations are similar or not. In the same way, we consider the alignment relations to be more important than the orientation relations. For this reason we decided to use three weights ω_T, ω_A and ω_O for topological, alignment and orientation relations respectively, following the criteria $\omega_T > \omega_A > \omega_O$. These weights will be applied to every element's match/mismatch in the computation of the Sokal-Michener measure, using the weight corresponding to the basic spatial relation represented by the element in each case.

4   Experiments

For validating this representation, we chose to implement a graph matching algorithm since this makes possible to compute similarity between images. In the present case, we're not interested in finding the similarity between two images, but to find similarities between the objects of each image, so we are talking about a subgraph matching problem.

4.1   Matching Strategy

We are using a greedy algorithm to find matchings between structures but, in order to avoid the high complexity of this kind of algorithm, we used the visual similarity measure and the spatial similarity measure proposed previously to discriminate nodes and edges that are too different to be taken into account.

In a nutshell, the algorithm takes an input graph that must be compared to an irregular pyramid of graphs. For each graph (level) in the pyramid we find all the similar structures to the input graph. We take every node in the input graph and compare it to each node in a level of the pyramid, and if they are visually similar, according to equation 2, then we try to expand the structure by testing the node's edges using the weighted S_{SD} measure in equation 3. If they are spatially similar, we repeat the process for every node they connect. This matching strategy is based on the algorithm proposed in [15], please refer to this work for further details in its implementation. We compute the final similarity between the structures as a combination of the average of spatial similarities of the matched edges and the average of visual similarities of the matched nodes.

4.2   Experiment Description and Results

We carry out the experiments using the ETH-80 Image Set database [16] which contains 80 objects from 8 categories (*apples, cars, cows, cups, dogs, horses, pears* and *tomatoes*). Each object is represented by 41 different views yielding a total of 3280 images (See Figure 3).

Fig. 3. Example images from the ETH-80 Image Set database

For this experiment we used 6 categories. For each category we took 4 objects and for each object we took 10 different views, leaving a total of 240 images in the database. From the remaining images we took 60 per category (15 views per object) to be used as the examples to be classified. The main goal was to recognize similar objects in the database, then we found the nearest neighbor of each example image among the images in the database. We consider a positive match if the nearest neighbor of the example image belongs to its category.

The combinatorial pyramids for the images of this database have an average of 16 levels. The base level contains 16385 nodes and 33020 edges, while the uppermost level usually has 2 nodes and 1 edge. The level selected for representing the example images has between 40 and 50 nodes, and about 130 edges.

For selecting the sub-graph that will represent the image for the matching process, we draw a square box having the same center of the image, and we get all the regions (nodes) that this box touches at a given level of the pyramid. A global view of the structure matching process can be seen in Figure 4.

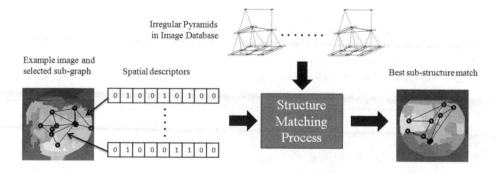

Fig. 4. Sub-structure matching process

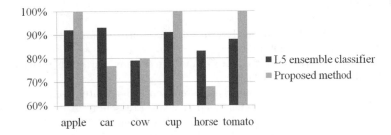

Fig. 5. Recognition accuracy for the L5 ensemble classifier and the proposed method

We compared our results with those obtained in [17]. They proposed a collaborative ensemble learning model where they construct four types of ensemble classifiers (L2 , L3 , L4 and L5) by integrating two, three, four and five base learners respectively. We compared our method with the L5 ensemble classifier, which showed the best results. The comparison result regarding the recognition accuracy for each category can be seen in Figure 5.

According to these results, our algorithm outperforms the recognition of *apples, cups, tomatoes* and *cows* having a 100% of recognition accuracy for the first three of them. The categories of *cars* and *horses* did not show improvements in the recognition accuracy compared to the L5 ensemble classifier. We believe that this may be due to the form of selecting the initial graph for comparing, since the square box used to select the regions of the graph may incorporate several background regions in the case of horses and cars, due to their elongated shape.

The overall recognition accuracy for the L5 ensemble classifier is of 87.6%, while our method yields 87.5%. It is important to notice that, although we achieved a very similar global accuracy to the one obtain with the L5 ensemble classifier, the visual description that we used is much simpler, thus showing the relevance of the spatial relations.

5   Conclusions

In this work we have proposed a new approach for describing spatial relations between regions of images based on the partitions provided by combinatorial pyramids and we proposed a spatial similarity measure to test the similarity between this kind of features. We performed an experiment that proved that the object recognition accuracy can be improved by taking into account the spatial distribution of object's parts, even when the visual description of the image regions is very simple. In future works we plan to study the selection of the sub-graph in the example images, and to find optimal levels for comparison in the irregular pyramids in order to increase the performance of the method.

References

1. Guting, R.H., Iv, P.I., Hagen, F.: An introduction to spatial database systems. VLDB Journal 3, 357–399 (1994)
2. Skiadopoulos, S., Koubarakis, M.: Composing cardinal direction relations. Artif. Intell. 152(2), 143–171 (2004)
3. Punitha, P., Guru, D.S.: An effective and efficient exact match retrieval scheme for symbolic image database systems based on spatial reasoning: A logarithmic search time approach. IEEE Trans. on Knowl. and Data Eng. 18(10), 1368–1381 (2006)
4. Hsieh, J.-W., Grimson, W.E.L.: Spatial template extraction for image retrieval by region matching. IEEE Transactions on Image Processing 12(11), 1404–1415 (2003)
5. Lin, P.L., Tan, W.H.: An efficient method for the retrieval of objects by topological relations in spatial database systems. Inf. Process. Manage. 39(4), 543–559 (2003)
6. Hodé, Y., Deruyver, A.: Qualitative spatial relationships for image interpretation by using semantic graph. In: Escolano, F., Vento, M. (eds.) GbRPR. LNCS, vol. 4538, pp. 240–250. Springer, Heidelberg (2007)
7. Tsapatsoulis, N., Petridis, S.: Classifying images from athletics based on spatial relations. In: International Workshop on Semantic Media Adaptation and Personalization, pp. 92–97 (2007)
8. Hernández-Gracidas, C., Sucar, L.E.: Markov random fields and spatial information to improve automatic image annotation. In: Mery, D., Rueda, L. (eds.) PSIVT 2007. LNCS, vol. 4872, pp. 879–892. Springer, Heidelberg (2007)
9. Brun, L., Kropatsch, W.: Contains and inside relationships within combinatorial pyramids. Pattern Recogn. 39(4), 515–526 (2006)
10. Brun, L., Kropatsch, W.: Introduction to combinatorial pyramids, pp. 108–128 (2001)
11. Illetschko, T., Ion, A., Haxhimusa, Y., Kropatsch, W.G.: Effective programming of combinatorial maps using coma - a c++ framework for combinatorial maps. Technical Report PRIP-TR-106, PRIP, TU Wien (2006)
12. Pietikainen, M., Ojala, T., Harwood, D.: A comparative study of texture measures with classification based on featured distribution. Pattern Recognition 29(1), 51–59 (1996)
13. Egenhofer, M.J., Sharma, J., Mark, D.M.: A critical comparison of the 4-intersection and 9-intersection models for spatial relations: Formal analysis. Autocarto 11, 1–11 (1993)
14. Sokal, R.R., Michener, C.: A statistical method for evaluating systematic relationships. University of Kansas Science Bulletin 38, 1409–1438 (1958)
15. Iglesias-Ham, M., Bazán-Pereira, Y., García-Reyes, E.B.: A multiple substructure matching algorithm for fingerprint verification. In: Rueda, L., Mery, D., Kittler, J. (eds.) CIARP 2007. LNCS, vol. 4756, pp. 172 181. Springer, Heidelberg (2007)
16. Leibe, B., Schiele, B.: Analyzing appearance and contour based methods for object categorization. In: IEEE Conference on Computer Vision and Pattern Recognition (CVPR 2003), pp. 409–415 (2003)
17. Nomiya, H., Uehara, K.: Data Mining and Knowledge Discovery in Real Life Applications. IN-TECH, ch. 9, pp. 157–166 (2009)

Automatic Representation of Semantic Abstraction of Geographical Data by Means of Classification

Rainer Larin Fonseca and Eduardo Garea Llano

Advanced Technologies Application Centre, 7ma # 21812, Siboney,
Playa, Havana - 12200, Cuba
{rlarin,egarea}cenatav.co.cu

Abstract. Providing Geographical Information Systems (GIS) with the mechanisms for processing geographical data based on their semantic abstraction is a task that at present is carried out in a number of research given their scope of applications. Tackling this issue may help to solve many problems of geographical data like its heterogeneity, since the SIG could process geographical data focusing on their meaning and not on their syntax and/or structure, thus reducing the Man-Machine semantic gap. An important aspect for achieving these objectives is the establishment of an automatic way of correspondence between geographical data and their conceptualization in a Domain Ontology. In this work, we propose a new type of Ontology, a Data-Representation Ontology. We also propose a new method for the automatic generation of the Data-Representation Ontology from geographical data and his interrelationships with the Domain Ontology. For this we use pattern classification techniques and a dissimilarity measure. The experiments showed that once the Data-Representation Ontology was generated, the classifier using dissimilarities could correctly classify all the data.

Keywords: Ontology, Classification, Semantic, Geographical data.

1 Introduction

For some years, scientists have been working with the aim of having a uniform access to geographical data. One of the principal problems of geographical data [1] is the heterogeneity in them. This implies that it becomes very difficult to work with this data in a uniform way, mainly by compatibility problems between them.

The problem of getting a uniform access to heterogeneous data is known as integration of geographical data. Efforts in this direction are focused mainly on these two types of integration:

- *Syntactic-Structural Integration:* It proposes the existence of a technical interconnection between data that may be in different reference systems or in different formats.
- *Semantic Integration:* It proposes the integration of heterogeneous data based on their meaning and not based on what they are, ensuring a mutual understanding over a context defined between different systems including human beings who may interact with them.

I. Bloch and R.M. Cesar, Jr. (Eds.): CIARP 2010, LNCS 6419, pp. 557–568, 2010.

In the literature there are recent papers [2-7] that deal with the issue of semantic integration of geographical data. In them, the use of Ontologies as the knowledge representation mechanism for the integration process is proposed, precisely because Ontologies are based on both Object-Oriented (OO) and Relationship-Entity (RE) paradigms. These paradigms are essential to phenomena modeling in geographical scope.

One of the major problems for geodata processing from the semantic point of view is precisely the way in which they will be conceptualized. Firstly, one must have knowledge about the nature of data based on conceptual domain that it is wished to model. On the other hand we have the geographical data complexity and finally the conceptualization way of these data; this means the way to represent the structure semantic abstraction of data and their interrelationships with the Domain Ontology. In this paper we focus on the task of representing geographical data based on their semantic abstraction supported by a Domain Ontology that models their nature with a higher level of abstraction.

This paper continues with a brief section where some key concepts for the understanding are defined. After that, the types of Ontologies existing in the literature are presented followed by the proposal of a new type of Ontology and its structural description. Then, the principal steps for establishing the correspondence between the semantic abstraction of geographical data and the Domain Ontology is described using a classification technique based on a distance. Paper continues with experiments and its results and fallow by the conclusions.

2 Definitions

- *Geographical Datum:* The geographical dictionary ESDIG[8] defines Geographical Datum as *"Object or Entity resulting from an abstraction of the real geographical space. (...), its definitive characteristic is a spatial reference in two or three dimensions"*. It also states that in some cases the following terms are considered synonymous with geographical datum: geospatial datum, geographical object and others that correspond with these definitions. These synonyms will be used throughout this paper indistinctly.
- *Class:* Class could be defined as *"A set of similar objects"* [9] e.g.: Objects that share common features, taking this into our context we could say that a Class is defined as a concept that could contain other sub-concepts and represents the semantic nature of geographical objects that have common features on a set.
- *Semantic Abstraction:* We understand by semantic abstraction the process that implies a reduction of the main components of the information from a phenomenon so as to preserve its most important features aiming at extrapolating this phenomenon to a semantic space in which it is defined according to their meaning.

3 Ontologies

There are forms of semantic representation and in general they are limited or focused to a specific semantic domain such as shown in [10-11]. Ontologies are the most widely used since they provide formal specifications of the logical models in which the data is based. Ontologies have appeared to provide a common vocabulary in a knowledge domain and to specify, at different formalism levels, the meaning of terms and their relationships. Therefore Ontologies provide a shared and accepted understanding of the knowledge of a domain, which can be communicated among human beings, between heterogeneous systems and between human beings and systems. One of the most popular and quoted definitions of ontology is the one proposed by Gruber and later extended by Studer "*An ontology is an explicit specification of a shared conceptualization*"[12-13], which shows that they have been developed for interchange and use of knowledge efficiently.

Guarino in [14] defines several levels of generality that give rise to different types of ontologies, see Fig. 1:

- *Top-Level Ontologies:* Contains reusable generic terms in different domains.
- *Domain Ontologies and Task Ontologies:* Contain terms that are specific in a particular domain (e.g.: Soils or Geology) or specific task (e.g.: Selling). These terms are usually defined as specializations of existing concepts in Top-Levels Ontologies.
- *Application Ontologies:* Contain all necessary terms to model a particular application. They are often specializations of Domain Ontologies or Task Ontologies.

Fig. 1. Graphic representation of kinds of Ontologies proposed by Guarino

4   Data-Representation Ontology (DRO)

To face the semantic integration problems of heterogeneous geographical data it is then necessary to extrapolate this data into a common space independent of type and/or format in which they have been stored based on their semantic abstraction. The Ontologies mentioned above are designed to to capture the semantics from the different geographical domains but in a broad manner. These Ontologies only express the different concepts and their relationships up to a specific abstraction level, since it does not take into account the semantic embed in the geographical data integrated in GIS. As result of this, the characteristic of these data and the relationships between them (see Fig.3-A) are not used, therefore valuable information may be lost. Furthermore, these Ontologies are neither capable of discovering new and more specialized concepts that could be embedded in the data, see Fig.3 –C. These new concepts may be obtained from the data processing, e.g. a process of data clustering. It contributes to a major granularity in the Ontology and therefore the new abstraction levels. Both the information embedded in the data and the new abstraction levels contributes to better accuracies in the results after its use in many tasks like information retrieval and/or data analysis for the decision making.

To tackle these issues we consider it necessary to define a new type of Ontology that covers this semantic emptiness above the geographical data integrated in GIS. To this end we propose the definition of a new type of Ontology, "*Data-Representation Ontology (DRO)*" it will represent the features that describe the nature of data and the existing relationships between them.

It would be formally defined as:

- *Data Representation Ontology:* Contains the necessary definitions for the representation of features and relationships that model and give meaning to objects belonging to a domain from a semantic point of view.

Based on the scheme proposed by Guarino[14] , see Fig.1, we have included the Data Representation Ontology (DRO) in the lowest level of generality since the DRO represents the major degree of specialization with respect to the other Ontologies, see Fig. 2:

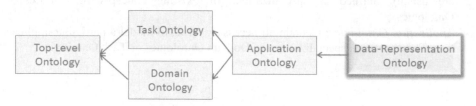

Fig. 2. Graphic representation of kinds of Ontologies, including DRO

The DRO is essentially a dynamic ontology since its structure; terms and relationships are always going to depend on the data the user is working with. The use of DRO allows the integration of heterogeneous data, see Fig.3 and it also provides a greater semantic enrichment from the complement generated between DRO and the Ontology employed by the user (e.g.: Domain Ontology (DO)). This complement is addressed in both directions, from DO to DRO and from DRO to DO, see Fig. 3. This is explained by the fact that on the one hand the DO will have exact information of the data being worked with allowing a major level of specialization and therefore a major granularity; and on the other hand the DRO will contain more levels of abstraction from the semantic point of view, which is provided by DO. Here a process of synergy is shown in which the results obtained through the use of the two ontologies (DRO and DO) are better than the sum of the results obtained by each of them separately.

The user could change (add, delete or modify) his working data, this implies the restructuring of Ontology (generation of new terms and relationships), here we would like to distinguish that the Domain Ontology does not change, retaining its original structure; only the DRO undergoes the changes. These changes occur below the interconnection layer, see Fig. 3.

4.1 Structure of the DRO

As mentioned above, the DRO is the projection in the semantic space of geographical data, see Fig. 3, in which all the represented geographical data is described in the same structure and consequently a uniform access to it is possible, taking a step forward in the process of integration of heterogeneous data.

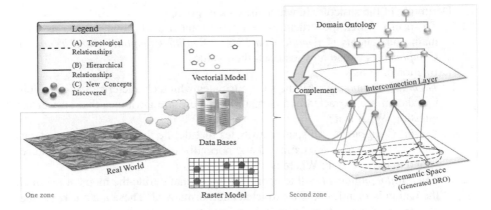

Fig. 3. Graphic representation of the different models in which the geographical data can be stored (one zone) and the projection in the semantic space of geographical data and the complement between the DRO and the DO (second zone). The Legend shows in (A) the representation of the relationships between geographic objects (e.g. topological relationships), in (B) the hierarchical relations are shown (e.g. sub_class or super_class) and (C) shows the new concepts that may be obtained from the data processing e.g. a process of data clustering.

In this paper, an architecture for the DRO construction is proposed. The basic unit of this architecture is constituted by Data-Representation Nodes (DRN) and edges that interconnect these DRN. Each DRN represents the semantic abstraction of a single datum and the edges representing the existing relationships between data, e.g.: topological relationships see Fig. 4. The structure of these DRN is based on the representation of thematic features, spatial features and temporal features of geographical data, by means of three substructures (*Thematic Component, Spatial Component and Temporal Component*) in semantic space.

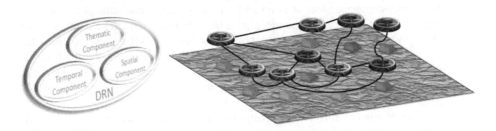

Fig. 4. Graphic representation of Data-Representation Node

4.2 Principals Steps for Automatic Generation of DRO

The DRO is generated from the data information the user is working with. In this section the main steps of the algorithm for automatic generation of the DRO are shown, these are:

1. Definition of the structure in which the data is stored:
   1.1. To specify which the structures of a geographical datum that refer to its three main components (*Thematic Component, Spatial Component, and Temporal Component*) are and how to access their values.
2. Extraction of values:
   2.1. *Thematic Component:* All thematic attributes which characterize the geographical datum are extracted and normalized. These are attributes that answer the question: What is it?
   2.2. *Spatial Component:* All spatial attributes that define location in space and cartographic projection are extracted and normalized. These are attributes that respond to the question: Where is it?
   2.3. *Temporal Component:* All temporal attributes that define the moment in which the datum is manifested are extracted and normalized. These are attributes that respond to the question: When? Also from these components the changes occurred in time with respect to both the thematic component and spatial component are extracted, e.g.: the changing values of its properties or its position in space.
3. Extraction of Relations:
   3.1. To extract all existing relations in the geographical datum with respect to other data, e.g.: Topological relationships.

The way to carry out these steps depends mainly on the formats and standards of the data. Each kind of formats and standards has its own characteristics that can modify the way in which the steps for automatic generation of DRO are carried out.

5 Semantic Abstraction of Geographical Data

As mentioned above the semantic abstraction of data refers to the operation by which certain properties of a geographical phenomenon are isolated for their processing from a semantic point of view. In this sense, geographical data can be represented in different semantic spaces, since it is possible to do several observations of the same phenomenon from different viewpoints, e.g.: a biologist can see a lake as a fish habitat while a hydrologist can see it as a body of water. Fonseca in [7] defines this phenomenon as roles. Therefore, in our context, the role played by the data will be determined by the ontology that defines its application domain, e.g. the lake object seen previously could play the role of fish habitat or body of water depending on the domain ontology used.

To increase levels of semantics abstraction of data it is necessary to link it with the domain ontology, i.e. to establish a correspondence with the concept it belongs to in the Domain Ontology. In such a way the data acquires more expressiveness and this turns out to be vital for the processing of data from an abstract point of view. To achieve this we propose the following steps:

1. For the Domain Ontology (DO):
   1.1. To extract the features present in each concept of type leaf[1] with the aim of identifying all the features that are to be processed. The concepts in the

---

[1] *Concept of type Leaf:* A concept does not contain sub concepts and allows being instantiated.

Domain Ontology represent the samples and the classes that will be used in the classification process.

1.2. To build a vector of occurrences and absences of the features present in classes taking into account the features extracted in step (1.1).

2. For the Data-Representation Nodes (DRN):

2.1. To extract the features present in each Data Representation Nodes.

2.2. To build vector occurrences and absences from the features present in the DRN, taking into account the features extracted in step (1.1).

3. To classify the DRN with respect to the classes present in the Domain Ontology using the classification process that is presented in the next section.

Since these vectors represent the occurrence or absence of features it is very convenient to represent these vectors with binary values. These values are usually encoded with one or zero denoting whether the property exists or not in the datum or the sample of the class. With these steps we automatically provide higher levels of semantic abstraction and definition of the role the data is playing according to the Domain Ontology being used.

5.1 Classification of Data Representation Nodes (DRN)

There are several techniques for data classification; between these techniques we can find those that use distances. The k-NN [15] is an example of a classifier based on distances that can even work with dissimilarities that do not meet metric properties such as symmetry or the triangle inequality. In essence, when it comes to classifying new data, the method calculates the distances to all the classes, then sorts the distances and assigns to the new data the label of the class that had the smallest distance to it; this means that the smaller distance between the data and the class, the bigger will be the correspondence.

As we only have one sample per class, where the sample "i" and the class "i" are precisely represented by the concept "i" in the Domain Ontology, then the K-NN classifier with K=1 (1-NN) is used. It is precisely for this reason that the 1-NN classifier is proposed. It is suitable furthermore to establish a threshold for classification, in order to avoid the risk of assigning a class with a low probability of being the correct one. In this way it is ensured that classification is made offering a certain guarantee, therefore a datum will not be classified in a class if it is not likely to belong to this class. To this end the 1-NN with reject is used, this variant of 1-NN classification excludes those data for which the threshold was not reached.

On the other hand, for computing the distances between objects there are a several measures that differ essentially in the type of data for which they have been designed. These measures are grouped into two main groups: Similarity Measures and Dissimilarity Measures.

- *Similarity Measures:* Measures that make more emphasis on the nearness between objects, where smaller values indicate that the elements are more different.

- *Dissimilarity Measures:* Measures that make more emphasis on the remoteness between objects, where smaller values indicate that the elements are more similar.

In our case, to classify a new DRN "n" is equivalent to finding the class whose distance is minimal with respect to "n", therefore the use of a dissimilarity measure to calculate the resemblance between DRN and classes is proposed. This dissimilarity measure is explained in details in the next section.

5.2 Dissimilarity Measure

In general, there is not a dissimilarity measure for all kinds of data, this must be chosen or adapted depending on the kind of data of the problem at hand. In the case of DRN classification we can take into account the present features in the *Thematic Component* since it represents the most adequate point of contact, at semantic level, between DRN and its conceptualization in the Domain Ontology.

As explained above, for the classification, the DRN and classes will be represented by vectors that will contain the occurrence or not of common characteristics between them, thus simplifying the problem in the sense of working with binary data. Among the measures to calculate dissimilarities between binary data, it was chosen the Simple Matching Distance [16] due to the nature of binary vectors with which we are working. As its name suggests this dissimilarity is a distance. It uses the coefficient shown in equation (1) and the distance is defined as shown in expression (2):

$$S_{(T,K)} = \frac{a+d}{a+b+c+d} \qquad (1) \qquad D_{(T,K)} = 1 - S_{(T,K)} \qquad (2)$$

Where:
- T: Classi.
- K: DRNp.
- S(T,K): Simple Matching Coefficient between Classi and DRNp.
- D(T,K): Simple Matching Distance between Classi and DRNp.

- a: Number of properties where T and K have an occurrence.
- b and c: Number of properties where T and K have different values.
- d: Number of properties where T and K have an absence.

This measure should be used in data in which the existence of occurrences and absences of the same features have a significant contribution in the classification. From the other distance measures for binary data it could also be used the Jaccard´s distance, but this measure only considers the common features for both individuals, which means that important information could be discarded in the classification process. Therefore the type of measure to be used must be selected depending on the nature of data.

The classification of geographical data based furthermore on its semantic abstraction tends to be more robust than the classification based only on spatial and geometrics features, since e.g., different data as Soil and Geology can be represented in the same form from the spatial and geometrical point of view and visually they are similar objects but from the semantic point of view they are different.

6 Experimental Results

In order to be able to represent automatically the semantic abstraction of geographical data a case study to illustrate the above methods is shown in this section. For this case study, Soil and Geological data layers were taken from the stored database in Spatial Data Infrastructure of the Republic of Cuba (IDERC)[17] (Geology.shp and Soil.shp). These data were stored in ESRI Shapefile format. This is a geospatial vector data format developed by ESRI company[18] and lately it has become de facto standard format for the exchange of geographical data. For each geographic object stored in the shapefile layers the information stored in both files * .dbf and * .shp were extracted for the creation of the Thematic and Spatial component in the NRD. The Temporal component has not been taken into account since these data lacks temporal characteristics. The ESRI Shapefile lacks the capability for the topologic information storage, therefore the relations between these objects has been defined based on 9-Intersections model [19] and the topological relationships proposed in the paper of JDARE'10 event[20].

To determine the semantic abstraction of data in the classification process we used a Land Cover Ontology, where apart from other concepts we can cite Soil and Geology concepts. Soil data and Geology data have been chosen to illustrate this study case, precisely because these data are similar from a geospatial representation point of view but not from a semantic point of view. Samples of classes, as noted above, are represented by each concept in the Domain Ontology, e.g. the Soil concept in the Land Cover Ontology itself represents the class of Soil and the sample of the Soil class. These samples for Soil and Geology classes contain the following features:

- *Soil Class:* ID, NAME, GROUP, TYPE, TEXTURE, EROSION, ACIDITY and SALINITY.
- *Geology Class:* ID, CODE, NAME, DESCRIPTION, AGE, TEXTURE and HARDNESS.

These classes contain some common characteristics, since they are likely to happen. The vector extracted per class contains the occurrences or absences of the common features that have been taken into account and it has constructed the following array of features per class, see Table.1:

Table 1. Vectors of occurrences and absences of common features per classes

Features / Classes	id	code	name	description	age	Texture	...	salinity
Geology	1	1	1	1	1	1	...	0
Soil	1	0	1	0	0	1	...	1

All the used data in the classification contains a subset of all these features. Each row of Table 3 represents a data layer that belongs to Geological or Soil classes; see Table.3 and Fig. 5, in which these features were collected. Therefore, a good classification of the layer represents a good classification of the objects therein. Table 2 shows the number of geographical objects both Geological and Soil layers.

The classification accuracy using 1-NN classifier of Distools toolbox[21] and using the structures "dataset" of PRTools [22] was 100% for all layers analyzed. Fig.7 shows the vectors of dissimilarity of each data layer regarding Geology and Soil classes, which shows that the layers belonging to the same class are grouped.

Table 2. Number of geographic objects both Geological and Soil layers

Geology Layer		Soil Layer	
Layer Name	Number of objects	Layer Name	Number of objects
geoLayer_1	928	sueLayer_1	307
geoLayer_2	1145	sueLayer_2	385
geoLayer_3	712	sueLayer_3	524
geoLayer_4	1098	sueLayer_4	233
geoLayer_5	977	sueLayer_5	189

Fig. 5. Graphic representation of data layers of Geology (A) and soil (B)

Table 3. Vectors of occurrences and absences of common features per Layers

Classes \ Features	id	code	name	description	age	Texture	...	salinity
geoDat_1	1	0	1	0	1	1	...	0
...	...	...	...	...	...	...	...	...
geoDat_5	0	1	1	1	1	1	...	0
sueDat_1	1	0	1	0	0	0	...	1
...	...	...	...	...	...	...	...	...
sueDat_5	1	0	0	0	0	1	...	1

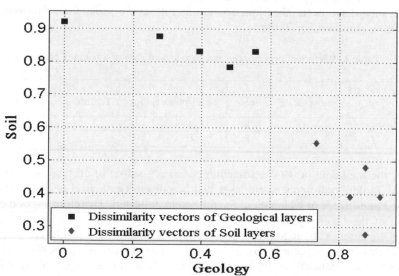

Fig. 6. Graphic representation of dissimilarity vectors of each layer respecting to Geology and Soil classes

This case study demonstrates the feasibility of automatically representing the semantic abstraction of geographical data, which means a step forward in the integration and processing of geographic data from a semantic point of view.

7 Conclusions

The work with geographical data from a semantic point of view and with the use of Ontologies as a way to represent knowledge, allows new and better ways of analyzing and exploiting these data. These ways undoubtedly improve existing tasks in the conventional Geographical Information Systems such as information retrieval and decision making. Nowadays it is necessary to create new mechanisms to represent automatically the semantic abstraction of geographical data given the great volume and heterogeneity that they present. The Ontologies that have been proposed in the literature cannot represent the characteristics and relationships that may exist in the geographical data integrated on GIS. We consider that the use of the information extracted from these data can improve the conventional task like the analysis task and/or information retrieval. For that reason in this paper a new type of Ontology has been proposed (*Data-Representation Ontology (DRO)*), which is automatically generated from the user data using the algorithms also proposed in this paper. The DRO represents the semantic abstraction of user data providing a bigger degree of specialization in the results and therefore a bigger granularity from interrelationship between the DRO and DO. Furthermore we have proposed a method to provide with more abstraction levels in the geographical data across the use of Domain Ontology based on classification techniques based on distances using a dissimilarity measure, something which is currently being done by hand.

References

1. Leung, Y.: Knowledge Discovery in Spatial Data. Springer, Heidelberg (2010)
2. Visser, U.: Intelligent Information Integration for the Semantic Web. LNCS. Springer, Heidelberg (2004)
3. Kavouras, M., Kokla, M., Tomai, E.: Comparing categories among geographic ontologies. In: Computers & Geosciences, Special Issue, Geospatial Research in Europe: AGILE 2003 (2003)
4. Schwering, A., Raubal, M.: Spatial relations for semantic similarity measurement. In: Akoka, J., Liddle, S.W., Song, I.-Y., Bertolotto, M., Comyn-Wattiau, I., van den Heuvel, W.-J., Kolp, M., Trujillo, J., Kop, C., Mayr, H.C. (eds.) ER Workshops 2005. LNCS, vol. 3770, pp. 259–269. Springer, Heidelberg (2005)
5. Hakimpour, F.: Using Ontologies to Resolve Semantic Heterogeneity for Integrating Spatial Database Schemata. PhD thesis Zurich University (2003)
6. Hess, G.N., Iochpe, C.: Ontology-driven resolution of semantic heterogeneities in gdb conceptual schemas. In: Proceedings of the GEOINFO 2004: VI Brazilian Symposium on GeoInformatics (2004)
7. Fonseca, F.T.: Ontology-Driven Geographic Information Systems, The University of Maine (2001)

8. ESDIG. Diccionario del Espacio Digital Geografico ESDIG (2010), http://infoteca.semarnat.gob.mx/website/diccionario/ diccionario_d.html (cited 2010 Enero)
9. Pekalska, E., Duin, R.P.W.: The dissimilarity representation for pattern recognition. Foundations and Applications 64 (2005)
10. Lehmann, F.: Semantic networks. Computers Math. Applic. 23, 1–50 (1992)
11. Minsky, M.: A framework for representing knowledge. In: Winston, P.H. (ed.) The Psychology of Computer Vision. McGraw-Hill, New York (1975)
12. Gruber, T.: Ontolingua: A mechanism to support portable ontologies. Stanford University, Stanford (1992)
13. Studer, S., Benjamins, R., Fensel, D.: Knowledge Engineering: Principles and Methods. Data and Knowledge Engineering (1998)
14. Guarino, N.: Formal Ontology and Information Systems. In: Proceedings of FOIS 1998. National Research Council, LADSEB–CNR (1998)
15. Fix, E., Hodges, J.L.: Discriminatory analysis, nonparametric discrimination: Consistency properties. Technical Report 4, USAF School of Aviation Medicine, Randolph Field, Texas (1951)
16. Backhaus, K., et al.: Multivariate analysis methods. In: An application-oriented introduction. Springer, Berlin (2000)
17. IDERC: Infraestructura de Datos Espaciales de la República de Cuba (2010), http://www.iderc.co.cu/ (cited 2010 Marzo)
18. ESRI: ESRI Home Page (2010), http://www.esri.com/ (cited 2010 Enero)
19. Egenhhofer, M.J.: A model for detailed binary topological relationships. Geomatica 47(3&4) (1993)
20. Larin-Fonseca, R., Garea-Llano, E.: Topological Relations as Rule for Automatic Generation of Geospatial Application Ontology. In: Proceedings of VII Jornadas para el Desarrollo de Grandes Aplicaciones de Red (2010) (in press)
21. Duin, R.P.W., et al.: DisTools A Matlab Toolbox for Pattern Recognition Delft Pattern Recognition Research, Faculty EWI - ICT, Delft University of Technology, The Netherlands (2009), http://prtools.org
22. Duin, R.P.W., et al.: PRTools4 A Matlab Toolbox for Pattern Recognition Version 4.1.5. Delft Pattern Recognition Research, Faculty EWI - ICT, Delft University of Technology, The Netherlands (2009), http://prtools.org

Author Index

Printing: Mercedes-Druck, Berlin
Binding: Stein+Lehmann, Berlin